Second Edition

Java™
Foundations

Introduction to
Program Design & Data Structures

Second Edition

Java™
Foundations

Introduction to
Program Design & Data Structures

John Lewis

Virginia Tech

Peter DePasquale

The College of New Jersey

Joseph Chase

Radford University

Addison-Wesley

Boston   Columbus   Indianapolis   New York   San Francisco
Upper Saddle River   Amsterdam   Cape Town   Dubai   London   Madrid
Milan   Munich   Paris   Montreal   Toronto   Delhi   Mexico City
Sao Paulo   Sydney   Hong Kong   Seoul   Singapore   Taipei   Tokyo

Editor-in-Chief:	Michael Hirsch
Editorial Assistant:	Stephanie Sellinger
Director of Marketing:	Margaret Whaples
Marketing Coordinator:	Kathryn Ferranti
Managing Editor:	Jeffrey Holcomb
Production Project Manager:	Heather McNally
Senior Manufacturing Buyer:	Carol Melville
Media Manufacturing Buyer:	Ginny Michaud
Art Director:	Linda Knowles
Cover Designer:	Susan Paradise
Cover Art:	Marc Romanelli/Getty Images
Media Project Manager:	Katelyn Boller
Full-Service Project Management:	Rose Kernan, Nesbitt Graphics, Inc.
Composition:	Nesbitt Graphics, Inc.

Credits and acknowledgments borrowed from other sources and reproduced, with permission, in this textbook appear on appropriate page within text.

Microsoft® and Windows® are registered trademarks of the Microsoft Corporation in the U.S.A. and other countries. Screen shots and icons reprinted with permission from the Microsoft Corporation. This book is not sponsored or endorsed by or affiliated with the Microsoft Corporation.

The programs and applications presented in this book have been included for their instructional value. They have been tested with care, but are not guaranteed for any particular purpose. The publisher does not offer any warranties or representations, nor does it accept any liabilities with respect to the programs or applications.

Many of the designations by manufacturers and sellers to distinguish their products are claimed as trademarks. Where those designations appear in this book, and the publisher was aware of a trademark claim, the designations have been printed in initial caps or all caps.

Library of Congress Cataloging-in-Publication Data
Lewis, John, 1963-
  Java foundations : introduction to program design & data structures / John Lewis, Peter J. DePasquale, Joseph Chase. -- 2nd ed.
      p. cm.
  ISBN 0-13-212881-0
  1. Java (Computer program language) I. DePasquale, Peter J. (Peter Joseph) II. Chase, Joseph, 1964- III. Title.
  QA76.73.J38L48845 2010
  005.13'3--dc22

                                                        2009051134

10 9 8 7 6 5 4 3 2 1–EB–14 13 12 11 10

Addison-Wesley
is an imprint of

ISBN-10:   0-13-212881-0
ISBN-13: 978-0-13-212881-0

To my wife, Sharon, for everything.
– John

To my wife, Lisa, and our twins: Lily and Adam.
– Pete

To my loving wife, Melissa, for her support and encouragement.
– Joe

Preface

Welcome to *Java Foundations*. This book is designed to serve as the primary resource for a two- or three-term introductory course sequence, ranging from the most basic programming concepts to the design and implementation of complex data structures. This unified approach makes the important introductory sequence more cohesive and accessible for students.

We've borrowed the best elements from the industry-leading text *Java Software Solutions* for the introductory material, reworked to complement the design and vision of the overall text. For example, instead of having graphics sections spread throughout many chapters, the coverage of graphical user interfaces is accomplished in a well-organized chapter of its own.

In the later chapters, the exploration of collections and data structures is modeled somewhat after the coverage in *Java Software Structures*, but has been thoroughly retooled to flow cleanly from the introductory material. The result is a comprehensive, cohesive, and seamless exploration of programming concepts.

New in the Second Edition

We appreciate the feedback we've received about this book and are pleased that it served so well as an introductory text. The following modifications have been made to improve the presentation of particular topics and the overall flow:

- A stack is now used as the initial example of a collection so that the concept of a collection is more clearly established.

- The discussion of Generics has been expanded and clarified.

- The coverage of the Quick Sort and Merge Sort algorithms has been expanded.

- The coverage of Analysis of Algorithms has been separated into its own chapter and expanded.

- Material on Testing and Debugging has been incorporated into more appropriate locations of the text.

- The coverage of Search Trees and Heaps have been divided into separate chapters.

- Two new chapters covering Hashing and Databases have been added.
- End-of-chapter exercises and projects have been updated to reflect changes in the book.

Regarding Objects

Phrases like *objects-first*, *objects-early*, and *objects-late* continue to be bandied about by computing educators, despite the fact that the nuances of the pedagogy of the introductory sequence cannot be summed up so easily. We'll take this opportunity to discuss our approach.

First, this book is **purely object-oriented**, presented in a gradual, natural manner. Concepts that overlap with procedural programming, such as methods and their invocation, are discussed in terms of an object-oriented approach. Thus, no example is ever made up of a single class with multiple methods. In fact, in our examples the class that contains the `main` method never contains another.

We **use objects** right from the start, and discuss everything in object-oriented terms at all times. An overview of object-oriented concepts is given in Chapter 1, then reinforced and fleshed out throughout the book. Classes from the Java standard class library are introduced immediately, and objects from these classes are instantiated and used for the various services they provide. In the first four chapters, students explore and write programs made up of a single class with a single `main` method—but these programs actively *use* predefined classes and objects from the standard library in addition to exploring fundamental programming concepts such as expressions and conditionals.

We **never introduce third-party classes** simply as fodder to create examples. That approach can confuse students by blurring the distinction between classes that are part of the standard library (and thus always available) and "extras" thrown in by textbook authors as a convenience. Every non-library class used in an example is fully explored in this book. There's no "magic" behind the scenes.

The debate continues: should coverage of control structures come before the details of writing classes, or vice versa? The truth is there are advantages either way, and a knowledgeable instructor can capitalize on either approach. If class composition comes first, it exposes the underlying essence of objects earlier and demystifies their use. However, without the ability to use basic control structures, the examples at that point are often uninteresting and unrealistic. This book **explores control structures before writing classes**. Chapter 4 uses small, single-method examples to examine the details of conditionals and loops, providing a strong foundation for the multiclass examples in Chapter 5.

Chapter Breakdown

Chapter 1 (Introduction) introduces the Java programming language and the basics of program development. It contains an introduction to object-oriented development, including an overview of concepts and terminology. This chapter contains broad introductory material that can be covered while students become familiar with their development environment.

Chapter 2 (Data and Expressions) explores some of the basic types of data used in a Java program and the use of expressions to perform calculations. It discusses the conversion of data from one type to another, and how to read input interactively from the user with the help of the `Scanner` class.

Chapter 3 (Using Classes and Objects) explores the use of predefined classes and the objects that can be created from them. Classes and objects are used to manipulate character strings, produce random numbers, perform complex calculations, and format output. Packages, enumerated types, and wrapper classes are also discussed.

Chapter 4 (Conditionals and Loops) covers the use of boolean expressions to make decisions. All related statements for conditionals and loops are discussed, including the enhanced version of the `for` loop. The `Scanner` class is revisited for iterative input parsing and reading text files.

Chapter 5 (Writing Classes) explores the basic issues related to writing classes and methods. Topics include instance data, visibility, scope, method parameters, and return types. Constructors, method design, static data, and method overloading are covered as well. Testing and debugging are now covered in this chapter as well.

Chapter 6 (Graphical User Interfaces) is a thorough exploration of Java GUI processing, focusing on components, events, and listeners. Many types of components and events are discussed using numerous GUI examples. Additionally, layout mangers, containment hierarchies, borders, tooltips, and mnemonics are introduced.

Chapter 7 (Arrays) contains extensive coverage of arrays and array processing. Topics include bounds checking, initializer lists, command-line arguments, variable-length parameter lists, and multidimensional arrays.

Chapter 8 (Inheritance) covers class derivations and associated concepts such as class hierarchies, overriding, and visibility. Strong emphasis is put on the proper use of inheritance and its role in software design.

Chapter 9 (Polymorphism) explores the concept of binding and how it relates to polymorphism. Then we examine how polymorphic references can be accomplished using either inheritance or interfaces. Design issues related to polymorphism are examined as well.

Chapter 10 (**Exceptions**) covers exception handling and the effects of uncaught exceptions. The `try-catch` statement is examined, as well as a discussion of exception propagation. The chapter also explores the use of exceptions when dealing with input and output, and examines an example that writes a text file.

Chapter 11 (**Recursion**) covers the concept, implementation, and proper use of recursion. Several examples are used to elaborate on the discussion, including a maze traversal and the classic Towers of Hanoi problem.

Chapter 12 (**Analysis of Algorithms**) discusses the techniques for analyzing the complexity of algorithms, including recursive algorithms. Big Oh notation is introduced.

Chapter 13 (**Searching and Sorting**) explores the linear and binary searching algorithms, as well as five sorting algorithms. The sorts include both quadratic and O(N log N) algorithms. The efficiency of these algorithms is examined.

Chapter 14 (**Stacks**) introduces the concept of a collection and establishes the importance of separating the interface from the implementation. Stacks are used as the initial example of a collection, and both dynamic and fixed implementations of a stack are explored. Generic types are introduced in this chapter, detailing their use in supporting the collection classes.

Chapter 15 (**Queues**) introduces FIFO queues and discusses options for their implementation. As with stacks, a queue is explored first conceptually, then as tools to help us solve problems, and finally by examining their underlying data structures. Both array-based and dynamic link implementations are discussed.

Chapter 16 (**Trees**) introduces the terms and concepts behind trees. Various implementation strategies are discussed, and a recursive, linked approach is examined in detail. An example of a binary decision tree is explored as well.

Chapter 17 (**Binary Search Trees**) covers the concept of search trees and a linked implementation for a classic binary search tree. Tree rotation algorithms are also discussed.

Chapter 18 (**Heaps and Priority Queues**) discusses the concept of a heap and its relationship to trees. A full linked implementation of a heap is explored. Priority queues are used as an example of a collection in its own right, and the natural relationship between heaps and priority queues are explored.

Chapter 19 (**Graphs**) discusses both directed and undirected graphs. Additionally, weighted graphs are explored, and the differences between breadth-first and depth-first graph traversals are covered. Minimal spanning trees are introduced, and implementation strategies are discussed.

Chapter 20 (**Hashing**) covers the concept of creating a hash table to facilitate storage and retrieval of objects. Various classes that relate to hashing from the Java API are explored.

Chapter 21 (Databases) explores the concept of databases and their management, and discusses the basics of SQL queries. It then explores the techniques for establishing a connection between a Java program and a database, and the API used to interact with it.

Student CD

The CD included with each textbook contains:

- Source code for all of the programs in the text.
- The Java Software Development Kit (SDK).
- Various Java development environments, including NetBeans™, Eclipse™, DrJava, jGRASP™, and TextPad®.

Instructor Resources

The following supplements are available to qualified instructors only. Visit the Pearson Education Instructor Resource Center (www.pearsonhighered.com/irc) or send email to computing@aw.com for information on how to access these resources.

- Presentation Slides—lecture-ready presentations for each chapter in Microsoft PowerPoint® format.
- Solutions—full solutions to the exercises and programming projects.
- Test Bank with powerful test generator software—includes a wealth of free-response, multiple-choice, and true/false questions.

Acknowledgments

Educators and students from around the world have provided feedback on previous work that has allowed us to mold this book into a fresh, valuable resource. Your comments and questions are always welcome.

The talent and commitment of the team at Addison-Wesley continues to amaze us. We greatly appreciate the insight of Michael Hirsch, our editor, and the hard work of his assistant, Stephanie Sellinger. Rose Kernan at Nesbitt Graphics was a great help throughout the production process. We thank all of these people for ensuring that this book meets the highest quality standards.

We'd like to acknowledge the collective input from hundreds of professors and students around the world in the development of the material upon which this book is based. There are too many of you to individually name, but your influence on *Java Software Solutions* and *Java Software Structures* is evident in *Java Foundations*.

Special thanks go to Ruth Dannenfelser, Cory Samaha, and Zach Zappala at the College of New Jersey for their help with solutions to the database projects. And our continued thanks go to Jason Snyder at Virginia Tech for his assistance testing code and many other contributions.

Groups like the ACM Special Interest Group on Computer Science Education (SIGCSE), the Consortium for Computing Sciences in Colleges (CCSC), and the Computer Science Teachers Association (CSTA) are phenomenal resources. Their conferences and online activities provide opportunities for educators from all levels and all types of schools to share ideas and materials. If you are a computing educator and are not involved with these groups, you're missing out.

Finally, we thank our families for their support and patience during the busy process of writing.

Contents

Chapter 20 Hashing   689

Second Edition

Java™ Foundations

Introduction to Program Design & Data Structures

Introduction

1

CHAPTER OBJECTIVES

- Introduce the Java programming language.
- Describe the steps involved in program compilation and execution.
- Explore the issues related to problem solving in general.
- Discuss the activities involved in the software development process.
- Present an overview of object-oriented principles.

This book is about writing well-designed software. We begin by examining a very basic Java program and using it to explore some initial programming concepts. We then lay the groundwork for software development on a larger scale, exploring the foundations of problem solving, the activities involved in software development, and the principles of object-oriented programming.

1.1 The Java Programming Language

A computer is made up of hardware and software. The *hardware* components of a computer system are the physical, tangible pieces that support the computing effort. They include chips, boxes, wires, keyboards, speakers, disks, cables, printers, and so on. The hardware is essentially useless without instructions to tell it what to do. A *program* is a series of instructions that the hardware executes one after another. Programs are sometimes called *applications. Software* consists of programs and the data those programs use. Software is the intangible counterpart to the physical hardware components. Together, they form a tool that we can use to solve problems.

> **KEY CONCEPT**
>
> A computer system consists of hardware and software that work in concert to help us solve problems.

A program is written in a particular *programming language* that uses specific words and symbols to express the problem solution. A programming language defines a set of rules that determines exactly how a programmer can combine the words and symbols of the language into *programming statements*, which are the instructions that are carried out when the program is executed.

Since the inception of computers, many programming languages have been created. We use the Java language in this book to demonstrate various programming concepts and techniques. Although our main goal is to learn these underlying software development concepts, an important side effect will be to become proficient in the development of Java programs.

Java is a relatively new programming language compared to many others. It was developed in the early 1990s by James Gosling at Sun Microsystems. Java was introduced to the public in 1995 and has gained tremendous popularity since.

Java has undergone various changes since its creation. The most recent Java technology is generally referred to as the *Java 2 Platform*, which is organized into three major groups:

- Java 2 Platform, Standard Edition (J2SE)
- Java 2 Platform, Enterprise Edition (J2EE)
- Java 2 Platform, Micro Edition (J2ME)

This book focuses on the Standard Edition, which, as the name implies, is the mainstream version of the language and associated tools. Furthermore, this book is based on the most recent version of the Standard Edition, which is J2SE 6.0.

Some parts of early Java technologies have been *deprecated*, which means they are considered old-fashioned and should not be used. When it is important, we point out deprecated elements and discuss their preferred alternatives.

Java is an *object-oriented programming language*. Objects are the fundamental elements that make up a program. The principles of object-oriented software development are the cornerstone of this book. We explore object-oriented programming concepts later in this chapter and throughout the rest of the book.

> **KEY CONCEPT**
> This book focuses on the principles of object-oriented programming.

The Java language is accompanied by a library of extra software that we can use when developing programs. This software, referred to as the Java *standard class library*, provides the ability to create graphics, communicate over networks, and interact with databases, among many other features. The standard library that supports Java programming is huge and quite versatile. Although we won't be able to cover all aspects of the library, we will explore many of them.

Java is used in commercial environments all over the world. It is one of the fastest growing programming technologies of all time. So not only is it a good language in which to learn programming concepts, it is also a practical language that will serve you well in the future.

A Java Program

Let's look at a simple but complete Java program. The program in Listing 1.1 prints two sentences to the screen. This particular program prints a quote by Abraham Lincoln. The output is shown below the program listing.

All Java applications have a similar basic structure. Despite its small size and simple purpose, this program contains several important features. Let's carefully dissect it and examine its pieces.

The first few lines of the program are *comments*, which start with the // symbols and continue to the end of the line. Comments don't affect what the program does but are included to make the program easier to understand by humans. Programmers can and should include comments as needed throughout a program to clearly identify the purpose of the program and describe any special processing. Any written comments or documents, including a user's guide and technical references, are called *documentation*. Comments included in a program are called *inline documentation*.

> **KEY CONCEPT**
> Comments do not affect a program's processing; instead, they serve to facilitate human comprehension.

The rest of the program is a *class definition*. This class is called `Lincoln`, though we could have named it just about anything we wished. The class definition runs from the first opening brace ({) to the final closing brace (}) on the last line of the program. All Java programs are defined using class definitions.

Inside the class definition are some more comments describing the purpose of the `main` method, which is defined directly below the comments. A *method* is a group of programming statements that is given a name. In this case, the name of the method is `main` and it contains only two programming statements. Like a class definition, a method is also delimited by braces.

LISTING 1.1

```java
//********************************************************************
//  Lincoln.java        Java Foundations
//
//  Demonstrates the basic structure of a Java application.
//********************************************************************

public class Lincoln
{
    //-----------------------------------------------------------------
    //  Prints a presidential quote.
    //-----------------------------------------------------------------
    public static void main (String[] args)
    {
        System.out.println ("A quote by Abraham Lincoln:");

        System.out.println ("Whatever you are, be a good one.");
    }
}
```

OUTPUT

```
A quote by Abraham Lincoln:
Whatever you are, be a good one.
```

All Java applications have a `main` method, which is where processing begins. Each programming statement in the `main` method is executed, one at a time in order, until the end of the method is reached. Then the program ends, or *terminates*. The `main` method definition in a Java program is always preceded by the words `public`, `static`, and `void`, which we examine later in the text. The use of `String` and `args` does not come into play in this particular program. We describe these later also.

The two lines of code in the `main` method invoke another method called `println` (pronounced print line). We *invoke*, or *call*, a method when we want it to execute. The `println` method prints the specified characters to the screen. The characters to be printed are represented as a *character string*, enclosed in double quote characters (`"`). When the program is executed, it calls the `println` method to print the first statement, calls it again to print the second statement, and then, because that is the last line in the `main` method, the program terminates.

The code executed when the `println` method is invoked is not defined in this program. The `println` method is part of the `System.out` object, which is part of the Java standard class library. It's not technically part of the Java language, but is always available for use in any Java program. We explore the `println` method in more detail in Chapter 2.

Comments

Let's examine comments in more detail. Comments are the only language feature that allows programmers to compose and communicate their thoughts independent of the code. Comments should provide insight into the programmer's original intent. A program is often used for many years, and often many modifications are made to it over time. The original programmer often will not remember the details of a particular program when, at some point in the future, modifications are required. Furthermore, the original programmer is not always available to make the changes; thus, someone completely unfamiliar with the program will need to understand it. Good documentation is therefore essential.

As far as the Java programming language is concerned, the content of comments can be any text whatsoever. Comments are ignored by the computer; they do not affect how the program executes.

The comments in the `Lincoln` program represent one of two types of comments allowed in Java. The comments in `Lincoln` take the following form:

```
// This is a comment.
```

This type of comment begins with a double slash (`//`) and continues to the end of the line. You cannot have any characters between the two slashes. The computer ignores any text after the double slash to the end of the line. A comment can follow code on the same line to document that particular line, as in the following example:

```
System.out.println ("Monthly Report"); // always use this title
```

The second form a Java comment may have is the following:

```
/* This is another comment. */
```

This comment type does not use the end of a line to indicate the end of the comment. Anything between the initiating slash-asterisk (`/*`) and the terminating asterisk-slash (`*/`) is part of the comment, including the invisible *newline* character that represents the end of a line. Therefore, this type of comment can extend over multiple lines. No space can be between the slash and the asterisk.

If there is a second asterisk following the `/*` at the beginning of a comment, the content of the comment can be used to automatically generate external documentation about your program by using a tool called *javadoc*. More information about javadoc is given in Appendix I.

The two basic comment types can be used to create various documentation styles, such as:

```
// This is a comment on a single line.


//- - - - - - - - - - - - - - - - - - - - - - - - - - - - -
// Some comments such as those above methods or classes
// deserve to be blocked off to focus special attention
// on a particular aspect of your code. Note that each of
// these lines is technically a separate comment.
//- - - - - - - - - - - - - - - - - - - - - - - - - - - - -


/*
   This is one comment
   that spans several lines.
*/
```

> **KEY CONCEPT**
>
> Inline documentation should provide insight into your code. It should not be ambiguous or belabor the obvious.

Programmers often concentrate so much on writing code that they focus too little on documentation. You should develop good commenting practices and follow them habitually. Comments should be well written, often in complete sentences. They should not belabor the obvious but should provide appropriate insight into the intent of the code. The following examples are *not* good comments:

```
System.out.println ("hello");   // prints hello
System.out.println ("test");    // change this later
```

The first comment paraphrases the obvious purpose of the line and does not add any value to the statement. It is better to have no comment than a useless one. The second comment is ambiguous. What should be changed later? When is later? Why should it be changed?

Identifiers and Reserved Words

The various words used when writing programs are called *identifiers*. The identifiers in the `Lincoln` program are `class`, `Lincoln`, `public`, `static`, `void`, `main`, `String`, `args`, `System`, `out`, and `println`. These fall into three categories:

- words that we make up when writing a program (`Lincoln` and `args`)
- words that another programmer chose (`String`, `System`, `out`, `println`, and `main`)
- words that are reserved for special purposes in the language (`class`, `public`, `static`, and `void`)

While writing the program, we simply chose to name the class `Lincoln`, but we could have used one of many other possibilities. For example, we could have called it `Quote`, or `Abe`, or `GoodOne`. The identifier `args` (which is short for arguments) is

abstract	default	goto*	package	this
assert	do	if	private	throw
boolean	double	implements	protected	throws
break	else	import	public	transient
byte	enum	instanceof	return	true
case	extends	int	short	try
catch	false	interface	static	void
char	final	long	strictfp	volatile
class	finally	native	super	while
const*	float	new	switch	
continue	for	null	synchronized	

FIGURE 1.1 Java reserved words

often used in the way we use it in `Lincoln`, but we could have used just about any other identifier in its place.

The identifiers `String`, `System`, `out`, and `println` were chosen by other programmers. These words are not part of the Java language. They are part of the Java standard library of predefined code, a set of classes and methods that someone has already written for us. The authors of that code chose the identifiers in that code—we're just making use of them.

Reserved words are identifiers that have a special meaning in a programming language and can only be used in predefined ways. A reserved word cannot be used for any other purpose, such as naming a class or method. In the `Lincoln` program, the reserved words used are `class`, `public`, `static`, and `void`. Figure 1.1 lists all of the Java reserved words in alphabetical order. The words marked with an asterisk are reserved for possible future use in later versions of the language but currently have no meaning in Java.

An identifier that we make up for use in a program can be composed of any combination of letters, digits, the underscore character (_), and the dollar sign ($), but it cannot begin with a digit. Identifiers may be of any length. Therefore, `total`, `label7`, `nextStockItem`, `NUM_BOXES`, and `$amount` are all valid identifiers, but `4th_word` and `coin#value` are not valid.

Both uppercase and lowercase letters can be used in an identifier, and the difference is important. Java is *case sensitive*, which means that two identifier names that differ only in the case of their letters are considered to be different identifiers. Therefore, `total`, `Total`, `ToTaL`, and `TOTAL` are all different identifiers. As you can imagine, it is not a good idea to use multiple identifiers that differ only in their case, because they can be easily confused.

> **KEY CONCEPT**
> Java is case sensitive. The uppercase and lowercase versions of a letter are distinct.

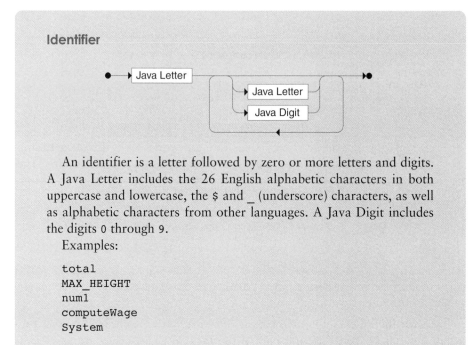

Identifier

An identifier is a letter followed by zero or more letters and digits. A Java Letter includes the 26 English alphabetic characters in both uppercase and lowercase, the $ and _ (underscore) characters, as well as alphabetic characters from other languages. A Java Digit includes the digits 0 through 9.

Examples:

```
total
MAX_HEIGHT
num1
computeWage
System
```

Although the Java language doesn't require it, using a consistent case format for each kind of identifier makes your identifiers easier to understand. There are various Java conventions regarding identifiers that should be followed, though technically they don't have to be. For example, we use *title case* (uppercase for the first letter of each word) for class names. Throughout the text, we describe the preferred case style for each type of identifier when it is first encountered.

While an identifier can be of any length, you should choose your names carefully. They should be descriptive but not verbose. You should avoid meaningless names such as a or x. An exception to this rule can be made if the short name is actually descriptive, such as using x and y to represent (*x, y*) coordinates on a two-dimensional grid. Likewise, you should not use unnecessarily long names, such as the identifier theCurrentItemBeingProcessed. The name currentItem would serve just as well. As you might imagine, the use of identifiers that are verbose is a much less prevalent problem than the use of names that are not descriptive.

> **KEY CONCEPT**
>
> Identifier names should be descriptive and readable.

You should always strive to make your programs as readable as possible. Therefore, you should always be careful when abbreviating words. You might think curStVal is a good name to represent the current stock value, but another person trying to understand the code may have trouble figuring out what you meant. It might not even be clear to you two months after writing it.

A *name* in Java is a series of identifiers separated by the dot (period) character. The name `System.out` is the way we designate the object through which we invoked the `println` method. Names appear quite regularly in Java programs.

White Space

All Java programs use *white space* to separate the words and symbols used in a program. White space consists of blanks, tabs, and newline characters. The phrase white space refers to the fact that, on a white sheet of paper with black printing, the space between the words and symbols is white. The way a programmer uses white space is important because it can be used to emphasize parts of the code and can make a program easier to read.

Except when it's used to separate words, the computer ignores white space. It does not affect the execution of a program. This fact gives programmers a great deal of flexibility in how they format a program. The lines of a program should be divided in logical places and certain lines should be indented and aligned so that the program's underlying structure is clear.

> **KEY CONCEPT**
> Appropriate use of white space makes a program easier to read and understand.

Because white space is ignored, we can write a program in many different ways. For example, taking white space to one extreme, we could put as many words as possible on each line. The code in Listing 1.2, the `Lincoln2` program, is formatted quite differently from `Lincoln` but prints the same message.

LISTING 1.2

```java
//************************************************************************
//   Lincoln2.java          Java Foundations
//
//   Demonstrates a poorly formatted, though valid, program.
//************************************************************************

public class Lincoln2{public static void main(String[]args){
System.out.println("A quote by Abraham Lincoln:");
System.out.println("Whatever you are, be a good one.");}}
```

OUTPUT

```
A quote by Abraham Lincoln:
Whatever you are, be a good one.
```

LISTING 1.3

```java
//************************************************************
//  Lincoln3.java        Java Foundations
//
//  Demonstrates another valid program that is poorly formatted.
//************************************************************

        public         class
      Lincoln3
   {
                    public
   static
         void
  main
         (
String
             []
     args                           )
   {
   System.out.println            (
"A quote by Abraham Lincoln:"            )
   ;            System.out.println
                 (
       "Whatever you are, be a good one."
       )
   ;
}
            }
```

OUTPUT

```
A quote by Abraham Lincoln:
Whatever you are, be a good one.
```

Taking white space to the other extreme, we could write almost every word and symbol on a different line with varying amounts of spaces, such as Lincoln3, shown in Listing 1.3.

All three versions of Lincoln are technically valid and will execute in the same way, but they are radically different from a reader's point of view. Both of the latter examples show poor style and make the program difficult to understand. You may be asked to adhere to particular guidelines when you write your programs. A software

> **KEY CONCEPT**
>
> You should adhere to a set of guidelines that establishes the way you format and document your programs.

development company often has a programming style policy that it requires its programmers to follow. In any case, you should adopt and consistently use a set of style guidelines that increases the readability of your code.

1.2 Program Development

The process of getting a program running involves various activities. The program has to be written in the appropriate programming language, such as Java. That program has to be translated into a form that the computer can execute. Errors can occur at various stages of this process and must be fixed. Various software tools can be used to help with all parts of the development process as well. Let's explore these issues in more detail.

Programming Language Levels

Suppose a particular person is giving travel directions to a friend. That person might explain those directions in any one of several languages, such as English, Russian, or Italian. The directions are the same no matter which language is used to explain them, but the manner in which the directions are expressed is different. The friend must be able to understand the language being used in order to follow the directions.

Similarly, a problem can be solved by writing a program in one of many programming languages, such as Java, Ada, C, C++, C#, Pascal, and Smalltalk. The purpose of the program is essentially the same no matter which language is used, but the particular statements used to express the instructions, and the overall organization of those instructions, vary with each language. A computer must be able to understand the instructions in order to carry them out.

Programming languages can be categorized into the following four groups. These groups basically reflect the historical development of computer languages.

- machine language
- assembly language
- high-level languages
- fourth-generation languages

In order for a program to run on a computer, it must be expressed in that computer's *machine language*. Each type of CPU has its own language. For that reason, we can't run a program specifically written for a Sun Workstation, with its Sparc processor, on a Dell PC, with its Intel processor.

Each machine language instruction can accomplish only a simple task. For example, a single machine language instruction might copy a value into a register or compare a value to zero. It might take four separate machine language instructions to add two numbers together and to store the result. However, a computer can do millions of these instructions in a second, and therefore many simple commands can be executed quickly to accomplish complex tasks.

Machine language code is expressed as a series of binary digits and is extremely difficult for humans to read and write. Originally, programs were entered into the computer by using switches or some similarly tedious method. Early programmers found these techniques to be time consuming and error prone.

These problems gave rise to the use of *assembly language*, which replaced binary digits with *mnemonics*, short English-like words that represent commands or data. It is much easier for programmers to deal with words than with binary digits. However, an assembly language program cannot be executed directly on a computer. It must first be translated into machine language.

Generally, each assembly language instruction corresponds to an equivalent machine language instruction. Therefore, similar to machine language, each assembly language instruction accomplishes only a simple operation. Although assembly language is an improvement over machine code from a programmer's perspective, it is still tedious to use. Both assembly language and machine language are considered *low-level languages*.

Today, most programmers use a *high-level language* to write software. A high-level language is expressed in English-like phrases, and thus is easier for programmers to

read and write. A single high-level language programming statement can accomplish the equivalent of many—perhaps hundreds—of machine language instructions. The term *high-level* refers to the fact that the programming statements are expressed in a way that is far removed from the machine language that is ultimately executed. Java is a high-level language, as are Ada, C++, Smalltalk, and many others.

Figure 1.2 shows equivalent expressions in a high-level language, assembly language, and machine language. The expressions add two numbers together. The assembly language and machine language in this example are specific to a Sparc processor.

The high-level language expression in Figure 1.2 is readable and intuitive for programmers. It is similar to an algebraic expression. The equivalent assembly language code is somewhat readable, but it is more verbose and less intuitive. The machine language is basically unreadable and much longer. In fact, only a small portion of the binary machine code to add two numbers together is shown in Figure 1.2. The complete machine language code for this particular expression is over 400 bits long.

A high-level language insulates programmers from needing to know the underlying machine language for the processor on which they are working. But

High-Level Language	Assembly Language	Machine Language
<a + b>	ld [%fp-20], %o0	. . .
	ld [%fp-24], %o1	1101 0000 0000 0111
	add %o0, %o1, %o0	1011 1111 1110 1000
		1101 0010 0000 0111
		1011 1111 1110 1000
		1001 0000 0000 0000
		. . .

FIGURE 1.2 A high-level expression and its assembly language and machine language equivalent

high-level language code must be translated into machine language in order to be executed.

Some programming languages are considered to operate at an even higher level than high-level languages. They might include special facilities for automatic report generation or interaction with a database. These languages are called *fourth-generation languages*, or simply 4GLs, because they followed the first three generations of computer programming: machine, assembly, and high-level.

Editors, Compilers, and Interpreters

Several special-purpose programs are needed to help with the process of developing new programs. They are sometimes called *software tools* because they are used to build programs. Examples of basic software tools include an editor, a compiler, and an interpreter.

Initially, you use an *editor* as you type a program into a computer and store it in a file. There are many different editors with many different features. You should become familiar with the editor you will use regularly because it can dramatically affect the speed at which you enter and modify your programs.

Figure 1.3 on the next page shows a very basic view of the program development process. After editing and saving your program, you attempt to translate it from high-level code into a form that can be executed. That translation may result in errors, in which case you return to the editor to make changes to the code to fix the problems. Once the translation occurs successfully, you can execute the program and evaluate the results. If the results are not what you want, or if you want to enhance your existing program, you again return to the editor to make changes.

The translation of source code into (ultimately) machine language for a particular type of CPU can occur in a variety of ways. A *compiler* is a program that

FIGURE 1.3 Editing and running a program

translates code in one language to equivalent code in another language. The original code is called *source code*, and the language into which it is translated is called the *target language*. For many traditional compilers, the source code is translated directly into a particular machine language. In that case, the translation process occurs once (for a given version of the program), and the resulting executable program can be run whenever needed.

An *interpreter* is similar to a compiler but has an important difference. An interpreter interweaves the translation and execution activities. A small part of the source code, such as one statement, is translated and executed. Then another statement is translated and executed, and so on. One advantage of this technique is that it eliminates the need for a separate compilation phase. However, the program generally runs more slowly because the translation process occurs during each execution.

The process generally used to translate and execute Java programs combines the use of a compiler and an interpreter. This process is pictured in Figure 1.4.

> **KEY CONCEPT**
>
> A Java compiler translates Java source code into Java bytecode, a low-level, architecture-neutral representation of the program.

The Java compiler translates Java source code into Java *bytecode*, which is a representation of the program in a low-level form similar to machine language code. The Java interpreter reads Java bytecode and executes it on a specific machine. Another compiler could translate the bytecode into a particular machine language for efficient execution on that machine.

The difference between Java bytecode and true machine language code is that Java bytecode is not tied to any particular processor type. This approach has the distinct advantage of making Java *architecture neutral*, and therefore easily portable from one machine type to another. The only restriction is that there must be a Java interpreter or a bytecode compiler for each processor type on which the Java bytecode is to be executed.

Since the compilation process translates the high-level Java source code into a low-level representation, the interpretation process is more efficient than interpreting high-level code directly. Executing a program by interpreting its bytecode is still slower than executing machine code directly, but it is fast enough for most applications. Note that for efficiency, Java bytecode could be compiled into machine code.

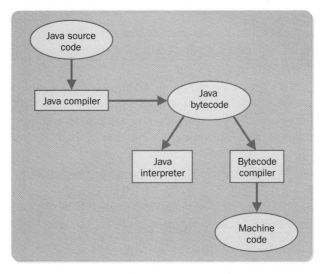

FIGURE 1.4 The Java translation and execution process

Development Environments

A software *development environment* is the set of tools used to create, test, and modify a program. Some development environments are available for free while others, which may have advanced features, must be purchased. Some environments are referred to as *integrated development environments* (IDEs) because they integrate various tools into one software program.

Any development environment will contain certain key tools, such as a Java compiler and interpreter. Some will include a *debugger*, which helps you find errors in a program. Other tools that may be included are documentation generators, archiving tools, and tools that help you visualize your program structure.

Sun Microsystems, the creator of the Java programming language, provides the Java *Software Development Kit* (SDK), which is sometimes referred to simply as the *Java Development Kit* (JDK). The SDK can be downloaded free of charge for various hardware platforms from Sun's Java Web site, java.sun.com, and is also included on the CD that accompanies this book.

The SDK tools are not an integrated environment. The commands for compilation and interpretation are executed on the command line. That is, the SDK does not have a *graphical user interface* (GUI), with windows, menus, buttons, etc. It also does not include an editor, although any editor that can save a document as simple text can be used.

Sun also has a Java IDE called NetBeans (www.netbeans.org) that incorporates the development tools of the SDK into one convenient GUI-based program. IBM promotes a similar IDE called Eclipse (www.eclipse.org). Both NetBeans and Eclipse are *open source* projects, meaning that they are developed by a wide collection of programmers and are available for free.

A research group at Auburn University has developed jGRASP, a free Java IDE that is included on the CD that accompanies this book. It can also be downloaded from www.jgrasp.org. In addition to fundamental development tools, jGRASP contains tools that graphically display program elements.

Various other Java development environments are available, and several are provided on this book's CD. The choice of which development environment to use is important. The more you know about the capabilities of your environment, the more productive you can be during program development.

Syntax and Semantics

Each programming language has its own unique *syntax*. The syntax rules of a language dictate exactly how the vocabulary elements of the language can be combined to form statements. These rules must be followed in order to create a program. We've already discussed several Java syntax rules. For instance, the fact that an identifier cannot begin with a digit is a syntax rule. The fact that braces are used to begin and end classes and methods is also a syntax rule. Appendix J formally defines the basic syntax rules for the Java programming language, and specific rules are highlighted throughout the text.

During compilation, all syntax rules are checked. If a program is not syntactically correct, the compiler will issue error messages and will not produce bytecode. Java has a similar syntax to the programming languages C and C++, and therefore the look and feel of the code is familiar to people with a background in those languages.

The *semantics* of a statement in a programming language define what will happen when that statement is executed. Programming languages are generally unambiguous, which means the semantics of a program are well defined. That is, there is one and only one interpretation for each statement. On the other hand, the *natural languages* that humans use to communicate, such as English and Italian, are full of ambiguities. A sentence can often have two or more different meanings. For example, consider the following sentence:

Time flies like an arrow.

The average human is likely to interpret this sentence as a general observation: that time moves quickly in the same way that an arrow moves quickly. However, if we interpret the word *time* as a verb (as in "run the 50-yard dash and I'll time you") and the word *flies* as a noun (the plural of fly), the interpretation changes completely. We know that arrows don't time things, so we wouldn't normally interpret the sentence that way, but it is a valid interpretation of the words in the sentence. A computer would have a difficult time trying to determine which meaning is intended. Moreover, this sentence could describe the preferences of an unusual insect known as a "time fly," which might be found near an archery range. After all, fruit flies like a banana.

> **KEY CONCEPT**
> Syntax rules dictate the form of a program. Semantics dictate the meaning of the program statements.

The point is that one specific English sentence can have multiple valid meanings. A computer language cannot allow such ambiguities to exist. If a programming language instruction could have two different meanings, a computer would not be able to determine which one should be carried out.

Errors

Several different kinds of problems can occur in software, particularly during program development. The term *computer error* is often misused and varies in meaning depending on the situation. From a user's point of view, anything that goes awry when interacting with a machine can be called a computer error. For example, suppose you charged a $23 item to your credit card, but when you received the bill, the item was listed at $230. After you have the problem fixed, the credit card company apologizes for the "computer error." Did the computer arbitrarily add a zero to the end of the number, or did it perhaps multiply the value by 10? Of course not. A computer follows the commands we give it and operates on the data we provide. If our programs are wrong or our data inaccurate, then we cannot expect the results to be correct. A common phrase used to describe this situation is "garbage in, garbage out."

> **KEY CONCEPT**
> The programmer is responsible for the accuracy and reliability of a program.

You will encounter three kinds of errors as you develop programs:

- compile-time error
- run-time error
- logical error

The compiler checks to make sure you are using the correct syntax. If you have any statements that do not conform to the syntactic rules of the language, the compiler will produce a *syntax error*. The compiler also tries to find other problems, such as the use of incompatible types of data. The syntax might be technically correct, but you may be attempting to do something that the language doesn't semantically allow. Any error identified by the compiler is called a *compile-time error*. If a compile-time error occurs, an executable version of the program is not created.

> **KEY CONCEPT**
> A Java program must be syntactically correct or the compiler will not produce bytecode.

The second kind of problem occurs during program execution. It is called a *run-time error* and causes the program to terminate abnormally. For example, if we attempt to divide by zero, the program will "crash" and halt execution at that point. Because the requested operation is undefined, the system simply abandons its attempt to continue processing your program. The best programs are *robust*; that is, they avoid as many run-time errors as possible. For example, the program code could guard against the possibility of dividing by zero and handle the situation appropriately if it arises. In Java, many run-time problems are called *exceptions* that can be caught and dealt with accordingly.

The third kind of software problem is a *logical error*. In this case, the software compiles and executes without complaint, but it produces incorrect results. For example, a logical error occurs when a value is calculated incorrectly or when a graphical button does not appear in the correct place. A programmer must test the program thoroughly, comparing the expected results to those that actually occur. When defects are found, they must be traced back to the source of the problem in the code and corrected. The process of finding and correcting defects in a program is called *debugging*. Logical errors can manifest themselves in many ways, and the actual root cause might be difficult to discover.

1.3 Problem Solving

Creating software involves much more than just writing code. The mechanics of editing and running a program are necessary steps, but the heart of software development is *problem solving*. We write a program to solve a particular problem.

In general, problem solving consists of multiple steps:

1. Understanding the problem.
2. Designing a solution.
3. Considering alternatives to the solution and refining the solution.
4. Implementing the solution.
5. Testing the solution and fixing any problems that exist.

Although this approach applies to any kind of problem solving, it works particularly well when developing software. These steps aren't purely linear. That is, some of the activities will overlap others. But at some point, all of these steps should be carefully addressed.

The first step, understanding the problem, may sound obvious, but a lack of attention to this step has been the cause of many misguided software development efforts. If we attempt to solve a problem we don't completely understand, we often end up solving the wrong problem or at least going off on improper tangents.

Each problem has a *problem domain*, the real-world issues that are key to our solution. For example, if we are going to write a program to score a bowling match, then the problem domain includes the rules of bowling. To develop a good solution, we must thoroughly understand the problem domain.

The key to designing a problem solution is breaking it down into manageable pieces. A solution to any problem can rarely be expressed as one big task. Instead, it is a series of small cooperating tasks that interact to perform a larger task. When developing software, we don't write one big program. We design separate pieces that are responsible for certain parts of the solution, and then we integrate them with the other parts.

> **KEY CONCEPT**
>
> Problem solving involves breaking a solution down into manageable pieces.

Our first inclination toward a solution may not be the best one. We must always consider alternatives and refine the solution as necessary. The earlier we consider alternatives, the easier it is to modify our approach.

Implementing the solution is the act of taking the design and putting it in a usable form. When developing a software solution to a problem, the implementation stage is the process of actually writing the program. Too often programming is thought of as writing code. But in most cases, the act of designing the program should be far more interesting and creative than the process of implementing the design in a particular programming language.

At many points in the development process, we should test our solution to find any errors that exist so that we can fix them. Testing cannot guarantee that there aren't still problems yet to be discovered, but it can raise our confidence that we have a viable solution.

Throughout this text we explore techniques that allow us to design and implement elegant programs. Although we will often get immersed in these details, we should never forget that our primary goal is to solve problems.

1.4 Software Development Activities

Given that the goal of software development is to solve problems, it shouldn't surprise you that the activities involved in the software development process mirror the general problem solving steps we discussed in the previous section. In particular, any proper software development effort consists of four basic *development activities*:

- Establishing the requirements.
- Creating a design.
- Implementing the design.
- Testing.

It would be nice if these activities, in this order, defined a step-by-step approach for developing software. However, although they may seem to be sequential, they are almost never completely linear in reality. They overlap and interact. Let's discuss each development activity briefly.

Software requirements specify *what* a program must accomplish. They indicate the tasks that a program should perform, not how it performs them. Often, requirements are expressed in a document called a *functional specification*.

Requirements are a clear expression of the problem to be solved. Until we truly know what problem we are trying to solve, we can't actually solve it.

In a classroom setting, students are generally provided the software requirements in the form of the problem assignment. However, even when they are provided, such requirements need to be discussed and clarified. In professional development, the person or group who wants a software product developed (the *client*) will often provide an initial set of requirements. However, these initial requirements are often incomplete, ambiguous, and perhaps even contradictory. The software developer must work with the client to refine the requirements until all key decisions about what the system will do have been addressed.

Requirements often address user interface issues such as output format, screen layouts, and graphical interface components. Essentially, the requirements establish the characteristics that make the program useful for the end user. They may also apply constraints to your program, such as how fast a task must be performed.

A *software design* indicates *how* a program will accomplish its requirements. The design specifies the classes and objects needed in a program and defines how they interact. It also specifies the relationships among the classes. Low-level design issues deal with how individual methods accomplish their tasks.

A civil engineer would never consider building a bridge without designing it first. The design of software is no less essential. Many problems that occur in software are directly attributable to a lack of good design effort. It has been shown time and again that the effort spent on the design of a program is well worth it, saving both time and money in the long run.

> **KEY CONCEPT**
> The effort put into design is both crucial and cost-effective.

During software design, alternatives need to be considered and explored. Often, the first attempt at a design is not the best solution. Fortunately, changes are relatively easy to make during the design stage.

Implementation is the process of writing the source code that will solve the problem. More precisely, implementation is the act of translating the design into a particular programming language. Too many programmers focus on implementation exclusively when actually it should be the least creative of all development activities. The important decisions should be made when establishing the requirements and creating the design.

Testing is the act of ensuring that a program will solve the intended problem given all of the constraints under which it must perform. Testing includes running a program multiple times with various inputs and carefully scrutinizing the results. But it means far more than that. Testing in one form or another should be a part of every stage of development. The accuracy of the requirements, for instance, should be tested by reviewing them with the client. We revisit the issues related to testing in Chapter 11.

1.5 Object-Oriented Programming

As we stated earlier in this chapter, Java is an object-oriented language. As the name implies, an *object* is a fundamental entity in a Java program. This book is focused on the idea of developing software by defining objects that interact with each other.

The principles of object-oriented software development have been around for many years, essentially as long as high-level programming languages have been used. The programming language Simula, developed in the 1960s, had many characteristics that define the modern object-oriented approach to software development. In the 1980s and 1990s, object-oriented programming became wildly popular, due in large part to the development of programming languages like C++ and Java. It is now the dominant approach used in commercial software development.

One of the most attractive characteristics of the object-oriented approach is the fact that objects can be used quite effectively to represent real-world entities. We can use a software object to represent an employee in a company, for instance. We'd create one object per employee, each with behaviors and characteristics that we need to represent. In this way, object-oriented programming allows us to map our programs to the real situations that the programs represent. That is, the object-oriented approach makes it easier to solve problems, which is the point of writing a program in the first place.

Let's explore the specific characteristics of the object-oriented approach that help us solve those problems.

Object-Oriented Software Principles

Object-oriented programming ultimately requires a solid understanding of the following terms:

- object
- attribute
- method

- class

- encapsulation

- inheritance

- polymorphism

In addition to these terms, there are many associated concepts that allow us to tailor our solutions in innumerable ways. This book is designed to help you evolve your understanding of these concepts gradually and naturally. This section provides an overview of these ideas at a high level to establish some terminology and provide the big picture.

We mentioned earlier that an *object* is a fundamental element in a program. A software object often represents a real object in our problem domain, such as a bank account. Every object has a *state* and a set of *behaviors*. By "state" we mean state of being—fundamental characteristics that currently define the object. For example, part of a bank account's state is its current balance. The behaviors of an object are the activities associated with the object. Behaviors associated with a bank account probably include the ability to make deposits and withdrawals.

In addition to objects, a Java program also manages primitive data. *Primitive data* includes fundamental values such as numbers and characters. Objects usually represent more interesting or complex entities.

An object's *attributes* are the values it stores internally, which may be represented as primitive data or as other objects. For example, a bank account object may store a floating point number (a primitive value) that represents the balance of the account. It may contain other attributes, such as the name of the account owner. Collectively, the values of an object's attributes define its current state.

> **KEY CONCEPT**
>
> Each object has a state, defined by its attributes, and a set of behaviors, defined by its methods.

As mentioned earlier in this chapter, a *method* is a group of programming statements that is given a name. When a method is invoked, its statements are executed. A set of methods is associated with an object. The methods of an object define its potential behaviors. To define the ability to make a deposit into a bank account, we define a method containing programming statements that will update the account balance accordingly.

An object is defined by a *class*. A class is the model or blueprint from which an object is created. Consider the blueprint created by an architect when designing a house. The blueprint defines the important characteristics of the house—its walls, windows, doors, electrical outlets, and so on. Once the blueprint is created, several houses can be built using it, as depicted in Figure 1.5.

In one sense, the houses built from the blueprint are different. They are in different locations, have different addresses, contain different furniture, and are inhabited by different people. Yet in many ways they are the "same" house. The

FIGURE 1.5 A house blueprint and three houses created from it

layout of the rooms and other crucial characteristics are the same in each. To create a different house, we would need a different blueprint.

A class is a blueprint of an object. It establishes the kind of data an object of that type will hold and defines the methods that represent the behavior of such objects. However, a class is not an object any more than a blueprint is a house. In general, a class contains no space to store data. Each object has space for its own data, which is why each object can have its own state.

Once a class has been defined, multiple objects can be created from that class. For example, once we define a class to represent the concept of a bank account, we can create multiple objects that represent specific, individual bank accounts. Each bank account object would keep track of its own balance.

> **KEY CONCEPT**
>
> A class is a blueprint of an object. Multiple objects can be created from one class definition.

An object should be *encapsulated*, which means it protects and manages its own information. That is, an object should be self-governing. The only changes made to the state of the object should be accomplished by that object's methods. We should design an object so that other objects cannot "reach in" and change its state.

Classes can be created from other classes by using *inheritance*. That is, the definition of one class can be based on another class that already exists. Inheritance is a form of *software reuse*, capitalizing on the similarities between various kinds of classes that we may want to create. One class can be used to derive several new classes. Derived classes can then be used to derive even more classes. This creates a hierarchy of classes, where the attributes and methods defined in one class are inherited by its children, which in turn pass them on to their children, and so on. For example, we might create a hierarchy of classes that represent various types of accounts. Common characteristics are defined in high-level classes, and specific differences are defined in derived classes.

Polymorphism is the idea that we can refer to multiple types of related objects over time in consistent ways. It gives us the ability to design powerful and elegant solutions to problems that deal with multiple objects.

Some of the core object-oriented concepts are depicted in Figure 1.6. We don't expect you to understand these ideas fully at this point. Most of this book is designed to flesh out these ideas. This overview is intended only to set the stage.

FIGURE 1.6 Various aspects of object-oriented software

Summary of Key Concepts

- A computer system consists of hardware and software that work in concert to help us solve problems.
- This book focuses on the principles of object-oriented programming.
- Comments do not affect a program's processing; instead, they serve to facilitate human comprehension.
- Inline documentation should provide insight into your code. It should not be ambiguous or belabor the obvious.
- Java is case sensitive. The uppercase and lowercase versions of a letter are distinct.
- Identifier names should be descriptive and readable.
- Appropriate use of white space makes a program easier to read and understand.
- You should adhere to a set of guidelines that establishes the way you format and document your programs.
- All programs must be translated to a particular CPU's machine language in order to be executed.
- High-level languages allow a programmer to ignore the underlying details of machine language.
- A Java compiler translates Java source code into Java bytecode, a low-level, architecture-neutral representation of the program.
- Many different development environments exist to help you create and modify Java programs.
- Syntax rules dictate the form of a program. Semantics dictate the meaning of the program statements.
- The programmer is responsible for the accuracy and reliability of a program.
- A Java program must be syntactically correct or the compiler will not produce bytecode.
- Problem solving involves breaking a solution down into manageable pieces.
- The effort put into design is both crucial and cost-effective.
- Each object has a state, defined by its attributes, and a set of behaviors, defined by its methods.
- A class is a blueprint of an object. Multiple objects can be created from one class definition.

Self-Review Questions

SR 1.1   What is hardware? What is software?

SR 1.2   What is the relationship between a high-level language and machine language?

SR 1.3   What is Java bytecode?

SR 1.4   What is white space? How does it affect program execution? How does it affect program readability?

SR 1.5   Which of the following are not valid Java identifiers? Why?

a. `RESULT`

b. `result`

c. `12345`

d. `x12345y`

e. `black&white`

f. `answer_7`

SR 1.6   What do we mean by the syntax and semantics of a programming language?

SR 1.7   Name the four basic activities that are involved in a software development process.

SR 1.8   What are the primary concepts that support object-oriented programming?

Exercises

EX 1.1   Give examples of the two types of Java comments and explain the differences between them.

EX 1.2   Which of the following are not valid Java identifiers? Why?

a. `Factorial`

b. `anExtremelyLongIdentifierIfYouAskMe`

c. `2ndLevel`

d. `level2`

e. `MAX_SIZE`

f. `highest$`

g. `hook&ladder`

EX 1.3   Why are the following valid Java identifiers not considered good identifiers?

a. `q`

b. `totVal`

c. `theNextValueInTheList`

EX 1.4   Java is case sensitive. What does that mean?

EX 1.5   What do we mean when we say that the English language is ambiguous? Give two examples of English ambiguity (other than the example used in this chapter) and explain the ambiguity. Why is ambiguity a problem for programming languages?

EX 1.6   Categorize each of the following situations as a compile-time error, run-time error, or logical error:

a. multiplying two numbers when you meant to add them

b. dividing by zero

c. forgetting a semicolon at the end of a programming statement

d. spelling a word wrong in the output

e. producing inaccurate results

f. typing a { when you should have typed (

Programming Projects

PP 1.1   Enter, compile, and run the following application:

```java
public class Test
{
    public static void main (String[] args)
    {
        System.out.println ("An Emergency Broadcast");
    }
}
```

PP 1.2   Introduce the following errors, one at a time, to the program from the programming project 1.1. Record any error messages that the compiler produces. Fix the previous error each time before you introduce a new one. If no error messages are produced, explain why. Try to predict what will happen before you make each change.

a. change `Test` to `test`

b. change `Emergency` to `emergency`

c. remove the first quotation mark in the string

d. remove the la st quotation mark in the string

e. change `main` to `man`

f. change `println` to `bogus`

g. remove the semicolon at the end of the `println` statement

h. remove the last brace in the program

PP 1.3   Write an application that prints, on separate lines, your name, your birthday, your hobbies, your favorite book, and your favorite movie. Label each piece of information in the output.

PP 1.4   Write an application that prints the phrase `Knowledge is Power`:

a. on one line

b. on three lines, one word per line, with the words centered relative to each other

c. inside a box made up of the characters = and |

PP 1.5   Write an application that prints a list of four or five Web sites that you enjoy. Print both the site name and the URL.

PP 1.6   Write an application that prints the first few verses of a song (your choice). Label the chorus.

PP 1.7   Write an application that prints the following diamond shape. Don't print any unneeded characters. (That is, don't make any character string longer than it has to be.)

```
    *
   ***
  *****
 *******
*********
 *******
  *****
   ***
    *
```

PP 1.8   Write an application that displays your initials in large block letters. Make each large letter out of the corresponding regular character. For example:

```
JJJJJJJJJJJJJJJ     AAAAAAAAA       LLLL
JJJJJJJJJJJJJJJ     AAAAAAAAAA      LLLL
          JJJJ      AAA      AAA    LLLL
          JJJJ      AAA      AAA    LLLL
          JJJJ      AAAAAAAAAA      LLLL
J         JJJJ      AAAAAAAAAA      LLLL
JJ        JJJJ      AAA      AAA    LLLL
   JJJJJJJJJJ       AAA      AAA    LLLLLLLLLLLLL
     JJJJJJJ        AAA      AAA    LLLLLLLLLLLLL
```

Answers to Self-Review Questions

SR 1.1   The hardware of a computer system consists of its physical components such as a circuit board, monitor, and keyboard. Software is the programs that are executed by the hardware and the data that those programs use. Hardware is tangible, whereas software is intangible.

SR 1.2   High-level languages allow a programmer to express a series of program instructions in English-like terms that are relatively easy to read and use. However, in order to execute, a program must be expressed in a particular computer's machine language, which consists of a series of bits that is basically unreadable by humans. A high-level language program must be translated into machine language before it can be run.

SR 1.3   Java bytecode is a low-level representation of a Java source code program. The Java compiler translates the source code into bytecode, which can then be executed using the Java interpreter. The bytecode might be transported across the Web before being executed by a Java interpreter that is part of a Web browser.

SR 1.4   *White space* is a term that refers to the spaces, tabs, and newline characters that separate words and symbols in a program. The compiler ignores extra white space; therefore, it doesn't affect execution. However, it is crucial to use white space appropriately to make a program readable to humans.

SR 1.5   All of the identifiers shown are valid except `12345` (since an identifier cannot begin with a digit) and `black&white` (since an identifier cannot contain the character `&`). The identifiers `RESULT` and
`result` are both valid, but should not be used together in a program because they differ only by case. The underscore character
(as in `answer_7`) is a valid part of an identifier.

SR 1.6   Syntax rules define how the symbols and words of a programming language can be put together. The semantics of a programming language instruction determine what will happen when that
instruction is executed.

SR 1.7   The four basic activities in software development are requirements analysis (deciding what the program should do), design
(deciding how to do it), implementation (writing the solution in
source code), and testing (validating the implementation).

SR 1.8   The primary elements that support object-oriented programming
are objects, classes, encapsulation, and inheritance. An object is
defined by a class, which contains methods that define the operations on those objects (the services that they perform). Objects are
encapsulated such that they store and manage their own data.
Inheritance is a reuse technique in which one class can be derived
from another.

Data and Expressions

2

CHAPTER OBJECTIVES

- Discuss the use of character strings, concatenation, and escape sequences.

- Explore the declaration and use of variables.

- Describe the Java primitive data types.

- Discuss the syntax and processing of expressions.

- Define the types of data conversions and the mechanisms for accomplishing them.

- Introduce the Scanner class to create interactive programs.

This chapter explores some of the basic types of data used in a Java program and the use of expressions to perform calculations. It discusses the conversion of data from one type to another, and how to read input interactively from the user running a program.

2.1 Character Strings

In Chapter 1 we discussed the basic structure of a Java program, including the use of comments, identifiers, and white space, using the `Lincoln` program as an example. Chapter 1 also included an overview of the various concepts involved in object-oriented programming, such as objects, classes, and methods. Take a moment to review these ideas if necessary.

A character string is an object in Java, defined by the class `String`. Because strings are so fundamental to computer programming, Java provides the ability to use a *string literal*, delimited by double quotation characters, as we've seen in previous examples. We explore the `String` class and its methods in more detail in Chapter 3. For now, let's explore the use of string literals further.

The following are all examples of valid string literals:

```
"The quick brown fox jumped over the lazy dog."
"2201 Birch Leaf Lane, Blacksburg, VA 24060"
"x"
""
```

A string literal can contain any valid characters, including numeric digits, punctuation, and other special characters. The last example in the list above contains no characters at all.

The `print` and `println` Methods

In the `Lincoln` program in Chapter 1, we invoked the `println` method as follows:

```
System.out.println ("Whatever you are, be a good one.");
```

This statement demonstrates the use of objects. The `System.out` object represents an output device or file, which by default is the monitor screen. To be more precise, the object's name is `out` and it is stored in the `System` class. We explore that relationship in more detail at the appropriate point in the text.

The `println` method is a service that the `System.out` object performs for us. Whenever we request it, the object will print a character string to the screen. We can say that we send the `println` message to the `System.out` object to request that some text be printed.

Each piece of data that we send to a method is called a *parameter*. In this case, the `println` method takes only one parameter: the string of characters to be printed.

The `System.out` object also provides another service we can use: the `print` method. The difference between `print` and `println` is small but important. The println method prints the information sent to it, then moves to the beginning of the next line. The print method is similar to println, but does not advance to the next line when completed.

The program shown in Listing 2.1 is called Countdown, and it invokes both the print and println methods.

Carefully compare the output of the Countdown program, shown at the bottom of the program listing, to the program code. Note that the word Liftoff is printed on the same line as the first few words, even though it is printed using the println method. Remember that the println method moves to the beginning of the next line *after* the information passed to it is printed.

> **KEY CONCEPT**
>
> The print and println methods represent two services provided by the System.out object.

LISTING 2.1

```java
//********************************************************************
//  Countdown.java       Java Foundations
//
//  Demonstrates the difference between print and println.
//********************************************************************

public class Countdown
{
    //-----------------------------------------------------------------
    //  Prints two lines of output representing a rocket countdown.
    //-----------------------------------------------------------------
    public static void main (String[] args)
    {
        System.out.print ("Three...");
        System.out.print ("Two...");
        System.out.print ("One...");
        System.out.print ("Zero...");

        System.out.println ("Liftoff!"); // appears on first output line

        System.out.println ("Houston, we have a problem.");
    }
}
```

OUTPUT

```
Three... Two... One... Zero... Liftoff!
Houston, we have a problem.
```

String Concatenation

A string literal cannot span multiple lines in a program. The following program statement is improper syntax and would produce an error when attempting to compile:

```
// The following statement will not compile
System.out.println ("The only stupid question is
the one that's not asked.");
```

When we want to print a string that is too long to fit on one line in a program, we can rely on *string concatenation* to append one string to the end of another. The string concatenation operator is the plus sign (+). The following expression concatenates one character string to another, producing one long string:

```
"The only stupid question is " + "the one that's not asked."
```

The program called `Facts` shown in Listing 2.2 contains several `println` statements. The first one prints a sentence that is somewhat long and will not fit on one line of the program. Since a character literal cannot span two lines in a program, we split the string into two and use string concatenation to append them. Therefore, the string concatenation operation in the first `println` statement results in one large string that is passed to the method to be printed.

Note that we don't have to pass any information to the `println` method, as shown in the second line of the `Facts` program. This call does not print any visible characters, but it does move to the next line of output. So in this case calling `println` with no parameters has the effect of printing a blank line.

The last three calls to `println` in the `Facts` program demonstrate another interesting thing about string concatenation: Strings can be concatenated with numbers. Note that the numbers in those lines are not enclosed in double quotes and are therefore not character strings. In these cases, the number is automatically converted to a string, and then the two strings are concatenated.

Because we are printing particular values, we simply could have included the numeric value as part of the string literal, such as:

```
"Speed of ketchup: 40 km per year"
```

Digits are characters and can be included in strings as needed. We separate them in the `Facts` program to demonstrate the ability to concatenate a string and a number. This technique will be useful in upcoming examples.

As you might think, the + operator is also used for arithmetic addition. Therefore, what the + operator does depends on the types of data on which it

LISTING 2.2

```java
//********************************************************************
//  Facts.java        Java Foundations
//
//  Demonstrates the use of the string concatenation operator and the
//  automatic conversion of an integer to a string.
//********************************************************************

public class Facts
{
   //-----------------------------------------------------------------
   //  Prints various facts.
   //-----------------------------------------------------------------
   public static void main (String[] args)
   {
      //  Strings can be concatenated into one long string
      System.out.println ("We present the following facts for your "
                       + "extracurricular edification:");

      System.out.println ();

      //  A string can contain numeric digits
      System.out.println ("Letters in the Hawaiian alphabet: 12");

      //  A numeric value can be concatenated to a string
      System.out.println ("Dialing code for Antarctica: " + 672);

      System.out.println ("Year in which Leonardo da Vinci invented "
                       + "the parachute: " + 1515);

      System.out.println ("Speed of ketchup: " + 40 + " km per year");
   }
}
```

OUTPUT

```
We present the following facts for your extracurricular edification:

Letters in the Hawaiian alphabet: 12
Dialing code for Antarctica: 672
Year in which Leonardo da Vinci invented the parachute: 1515
Speed of ketchup: 40 km per year
```

operates. If either or both of the operands of the + operator are
strings, then string concatenation is performed.

The Addition program shown in Listing 2.3 demonstrates the
distinction between string concatenation and arithmetic addition.
The Addition program uses the + operator four times. In the first
call to println, both + operations perform string concatenation, because the operators are executed left to right. The first operator concatenates the
string with the first number (24), creating a larger string. Then that string is concatenated with the second number (45), creating an even larger string, which gets
printed.

In the second call to println, we use parentheses to group the + operation
with the two numeric operands. This forces that operation to happen first.
Because both operands are numbers, the numbers are added in the arithmetic

LISTING 2.3

```java
//********************************************************************
//  Addition.java        Java Foundations
//
//  Demonstrates the difference between the addition and string
//  concatenation operators.
//********************************************************************

public class Addition
{
    //-----------------------------------------------------------------
    //  Concatenates and adds two numbers and prints the results.
    //-----------------------------------------------------------------
    public static void main (String[] args)
    {
        System.out.println ("24 and 45 concatenated: " + 24 + 45);

        System.out.println ("24 and 45 added: " + (24 + 45));
    }
}
```

OUTPUT

```
24 and 45 concatenated: 2445
24 and 45 added: 69
```

sense, producing the result 69. That number is then concatenated with the string, producing a larger string that gets printed.

We revisit this type of situation later in this chapter when we formalize the precedence rules that define the order in which operators get evaluated.

Escape Sequences

Because the double quotation character (") is used in the Java language to indicate the beginning and end of a string, we must use a special technique to print the quotation character. If we simply put it in a string (""""), the compiler gets confused because it thinks the second quotation character is the end of the string and doesn't know what to do with the third one. This results in a compile-time error.

To overcome this problem, Java defines several *escape sequences* to represent special characters. An escape sequence begins with the backslash character (\), which indicates that the character or characters that follow should be interpreted in a special way. Figure 2.1 lists the Java escape sequences.

> **KEY CONCEPT**
>
> An escape sequence can be used to represent a character that would otherwise cause compilation problems.

The program in Listing 2.4 on the next page, called `Roses`, prints some text resembling a poem. It uses only one `println` statement to do so, despite the fact that the poem is several lines long. Note the escape sequences used throughout the string. The \n escape sequence forces the output to a new line, and the \t escape sequence represents a tab character. (Note that you may see a different amount of indentation when you run this program—tab stops depend on the system settings.) The \" escape sequence ensures that the quote character is treated as part of the string, not the termination of it, which enables it to be printed as part of the output.

Escape Sequence	Meaning
\b	backspace
\t	tab
\n	newline
\r	carriage return
\"	double quote
\'	single quote
\\	backslash

FIGURE 2.1 Java escape sequences

LISTING 2.4

```java
//********************************************************************
//  Roses.java        Java Foundations
//
//  Demonstrates the use of escape sequences.
//********************************************************************

public class Roses
{
   //-----------------------------------------------------------------
   //  Prints a poem (of sorts) on multiple lines.
   //-----------------------------------------------------------------
   public static void main (String[] args)
   {
      System.out.println ("Roses are red,\n\tViolets are blue,\n" +
         "Sugar is sweet,\n\tBut I have \"commitment issues\",\n\t" +
         "So I'd rather just be friends\n\tAt this point in our " +
         "relationship.");
   }
}
```

OUTPUT

```
Roses are red,
        Violets are blue,
Sugar is sweet,
        But I have "commitment issues",
        So I'd rather just be friends
        At this point in our relationship.
```

2.2 Variables and Assignment

Most of the information we manage in a program is represented by variables. Let's examine how we declare and use them in a program.

Variables

A *variable* is a name for a location in memory used to hold a data value. A variable declaration instructs the compiler to reserve a portion of main memory

Local Variable Declaration

Variable Declarator

A variable declaration consists of a Type followed by a list of variables. Each variable can be initialized in the declaration to the value of the specified Expression. If the `final` modifier precedes the declaration, the identifiers are declared as named constants whose values cannot be changed once set.

Examples:

```
int total;
double num1, num2 = 4.356, num3;
char letter = 'A', digit = '7';
final int MAX = 45;
```

space large enough to hold a particular type of value and indicates the name by which we refer to that location.

Consider the program `PianoKeys`, shown in Listing 2.5 on the next page. The first line of the `main` method is the declaration of a variable named `keys` that holds an integer (`int`) value. The declaration also gives `keys` an initial value of 88. If an initial value is not specified for a variable, the value is undefined. Most Java compilers give errors or warnings if you attempt to use a variable before you've explicitly given it a value.

> **KEY CONCEPT**
>
> A variable is a name for a memory location used to hold a value of a particular data type.

The `keys` variable, with its value, could be pictured as follows:

keys   88

In the `PianoKeys` program, two pieces of information are used in the call to the `println` method. The first is a string, and the second is the variable `keys`. When a variable is referenced, the value currently stored in it is used. Therefore, when the call to `println` is executed, the value of `keys`, which is 88, is obtained.

LISTING 2.5

```
//********************************************************************
//   PianoKeys.java         Java Foundations
//
//   Demonstrates the declaration, initialization, and use of an
//   integer variable.
//********************************************************************

public class PianoKeys
{
   //-----------------------------------------------------------------
   //   Prints the number of keys on a piano.
   //-----------------------------------------------------------------
   public static void main (String[] args)
   {
      int keys = 88;

      System.out.println ("A piano has " + keys + " keys.");
   }
}
```

OUTPUT

```
A piano has 88 keys.
```

Because that value is an integer, it is automatically converted to a string and concatenated with the initial string. The concatenated string is passed to println and printed.

A variable declaration can have multiple variables of the same type declared on one line. Each variable on the line can be declared with or without an initializing value. For example:

```
int count, minimum = 0, result;
```

The Assignment Statement

Let's examine a program that changes the value of a variable. Listing 2.6 shows a program called Geometry. This program first declares an integer variable called sides and initializes it to 7. It then prints out the current value of sides.

LISTING 2.6

```java
//********************************************************************
//  Geometry.java        Java Foundations
//
//  Demonstrates the use of an assignment statement to change the
//  value stored in a variable.
//********************************************************************

public class Geometry
{
    //-----------------------------------------------------------------
    //  Prints the number of sides of several geometric shapes.
    //-----------------------------------------------------------------
    public static void main (String[] args)
    {
        int sides = 7;  // declaration with initialization
        System.out.println ("A heptagon has " + sides + " sides.");

        sides = 10;  // assignment statement
        System.out.println ("A decagon has " + sides + " sides.");

        sides = 12;
        System.out.println ("A dodecagon has " + sides + " sides.");
    }
}
```

OUTPUT

```
A heptagon has 7 sides.
A decagon has 10 sides.
A dodecagon has 12 sides.
```

The next line in `main` changes the value stored in the variable `sides`:

```java
sides = 10;
```

This is called an *assignment statement* because it assigns a value to a variable. When executed, the expression on the right-hand side of the assignment operator (=) is evaluated, and the result is stored in the memory location indicated by the variable on the left-hand side. In this example, the expression is simply a number, 10. We discuss expressions that are more involved than this in the next section.

> **KEY CONCEPT**
> Accessing data leaves it intact in memory, but an assignment statement overwrites the old data.

Basic Assignment

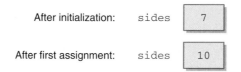

The basic assignment statement uses the assignment operator (=) to store the result of the Expression into the specified Identifier, usually a variable.

Examples:

```
total = 57;
count = count + 1;
value = (min / 2) * lastValue;
```

A variable can store only one value of its declared type. A new value overwrites the old one. In this case, when the value 10 is assigned to sides, the original value 7 is overwritten and lost forever, as follows:

After initialization:	sides	7
After first assignment:	sides	10

When a reference is made to a variable, such as when it is printed, the value of the variable is not changed. This is the nature of computer memory: Accessing (reading) data leaves the values in memory intact, but writing data replaces the old data with the new.

The Java language is *strongly typed*, meaning that we are not allowed to assign a value to a variable that is inconsistent with its declared type. Trying to combine incompatible types will generate an error when you attempt to compile the program. Therefore, the expression on the right-hand side of an assignment statement must evaluate to a value compatible with the type of the variable on the left-hand side.

> **KEY CONCEPT**
> We cannot assign a value of one type to a variable of an incompatible type.

Constants

Sometimes we use data that is constant throughout a program. For instance, we might write a program that deals with a theater that can hold no more than 427 people. It is often helpful to give a constant value a name, such as `MAX_OCCUPANCY`, instead of using a literal value, such as `427`, throughout the code. The purpose and meaning of literal values such as `427` is often confusing to someone reading the code. By giving the value a name, you help explain its role in the program.

Constants are identifiers and are similar to variables except that they hold a particular value for the duration of their existence. Constants are, to use the English meaning of the words, not variable. Their value doesn't change.

In Java, if you precede a declaration with the reserved word `final`, the identifier is made a constant. By convention, uppercase letters are used when naming constants to distinguish them from regular variables, and individual words are separated using the underscore character. For example, the constant describing the maximum occupancy of a theater could be declared as follows:

```
final int MAX_OCCUPANCY = 427;
```

The compiler will produce an error message if you attempt to change the value of a constant once it has been given its initial value. This is another good reason to use constants. Constants prevent inadvertent coding errors because the only valid place to change their value is in the initial assignment.

There is a third good reason to use constants. If a constant is used throughout a program and its value needs to be modified, then you have to change it in only one place. For example, if the capacity of the theater changes (because of a renovation) from 427 to 535, then you have to change only one declaration, and all uses of `MAX_OCCUPANCY` automatically reflect the change. If the literal `427` had been used throughout the code, each use would have to be found and changed. If you were to miss any uses of the literal value, problems would surely arise.

2.3 Primitive Data Types

There are eight *primitive data types* in Java: four subsets of integers, two subsets of floating point numbers, a character data type, and a boolean data type. Everything else is represented using objects. Let's examine these eight primitive data types in some detail.

Integers and Floating Points

Java has two basic kinds of numeric values: integers, which have no fractional part, and floating points, which do. There are four integer data types (`byte`,

Type	Storage	Min Value	Max Value
byte	8 bits	−128	127
short	16 bits	−32,768	32,767
int	32 bits	−2,147,483,648	2,147,483,647
long	64 bits	−9,223,372,036,854,775,808	9,223,372,036,854,775,807
float	32 bits	Approximately −3.4E+38 with 7 significant digits	Approximately 3.4E+38 with 7 significant digits
double	64 bits	Approximately −1.7E+308 with 15 significant digits	Approximately 1.7E+308 with 15 significant digits

FIGURE 2.2 The Java numeric primitive types

> **KEY CONCEPT**
>
> Java has two kinds of numeric values: integer and floating point. There are four integer data types and two floating point data types.

short, int, and long) and two floating point data types (float and double). All of the numeric types differ by the amount of memory space used to store a value of that type, which determines the range of values that can be represented. The size of each data type is the same for all hardware platforms. All numeric types are *signed*, meaning that both positive and negative values can be stored in them. Figure 2.2 summarizes the numeric primitive types.

A *bit*, or binary digit, can be either a 1 or a 0. Because each bit can represent two different states, a string of N bits can be used to represent 2^N different values. Appendix B describes number systems and these kinds of relationships in more detail.

When designing programs, we sometimes need to be careful about picking variables of appropriate size so that memory space is not wasted. This occurs in situations where memory space is particularly restricted, such as a program that runs on a personal data assistant (PDA). In such cases, we can choose a variable's data type accordingly. For example, if the value of a particular variable will not vary outside of a range of 1 to 1000, then a two-byte integer (short) is large enough to accommodate it. On the other hand, when it's not clear what the range of a particular variable will be, we should provide a reasonable, even generous, amount of space. In most situations memory space is not a serious restriction, and we can usually afford generous assumptions.

Note that even though a float value supports very large (and very small) numbers, it only has seven significant digits. Therefore, if it is important to accurately maintain a value such as 50341.2077, we need to use a double.

As we've already discussed, a *literal* is an explicit data value used in a program. The various numbers used in programs such as Facts and Addition and

PianoKeys are all *integer literals*. Java assumes all integer literals are of type int, unless an L or l is appended to the end of the value to indicate that it should be considered a literal of type long, such as 45L.

Likewise, Java assumes that all *floating point literals* are of type double. If we need to treat a floating point literal as a float, we append an F or f to the end of the value, as in 2.718F or 123.45f. Numeric literals of type double can be followed by a D or d if desired.

The following are examples of numeric variable declarations in Java:

```
int answer = 42;
byte smallNumber1, smallNumber2;
long countedStars = 86827263927L;
float ratio = 0.2363F;
double delta = 453.523311903;
```

Characters

Characters are another fundamental type of data used and managed on a computer. Individual characters can be treated as separate data items, and, as we've seen in several examples, they can be combined to form character strings.

A *character literal* is expressed in a Java program with single quotes, such as 'b' or 'J' or ';'. You will recall that *string literals* are delineated using double quotation marks, and that the String type is not a primitive data type in Java, it is a class name. We discuss the String class in detail in the next chapter.

Note the difference between a digit as a character (or part of a string) and a digit as a number (or part of a larger number). The number 602 is a numeric

Decimal Integer Literal

An integer literal is composed of a series of digits followed by an optional suffix to indicate that it should be considered a long integer. Negation of a literal is considered a separate operation.

Examples:

5
2594
4920328L

value that can be used in an arithmetic calculation. But in the string "602 Greenbriar Court" the 6, 0, and 2 are characters, just like the rest of the characters that make up the string.

The characters we can manage are defined by a *character set*, which is simply a list of characters in a particular order. Each programming language supports a particular character set that defines the valid values for a character variable in that language. Several character sets have been proposed, but only a few have been used regularly over the years. The *ASCII character set* is a popular choice. ASCII stands for the American Standard Code for Information Interchange. The basic ASCII set uses 7 bits per character, providing room to support 128 different characters, including:

- uppercase letters, such as 'A', 'B', and 'C'
- lowercase letters, such as 'a', 'b', and 'c'
- punctuation, such as the period ('.'), semicolon (';'), and comma (',')
- the digits '0' through '9'
- the space character, ' '
- special symbols, such as the ampersand ('&'), vertical bar ('|'), and backslash ('\')
- control characters, such as the carriage return, null, and end-of-text marks

The *control characters* are sometimes called nonprinting or invisible characters because they do not have a specific symbol that represents them. Yet they are as valid as any other character and can be stored and used in the same ways. Many control characters have special meaning to certain software applications.

As computing became a worldwide endeavor, users demanded a more flexible character set containing other language alphabets. ASCII was extended to use 8 bits per character, and the number of characters in the set doubled to 256. The extended ASCII contains many accented and diacritical characters used in languages other than English.

However, even with 256 characters, the ASCII character set cannot represent the world's alphabets, especially given the various Asian alphabets and their many thousands of ideograms. Therefore, the developers of the Java programming language chose the *Unicode character set*, which uses 16 bits per character, supporting 65,536 unique characters. The characters and symbols from many languages are included in the Unicode definition. ASCII is a subset of the Unicode character set. Appendix C discusses the Unicode character set in more detail.

KEY CONCEPT

Java uses the 16-bit Unicode character set to represent character data.

A character set assigns a particular number to each character, so by definition the characters are in a particular order. This is referred to as lexicographic order. In the ASCII and Unicode ordering, the digit characters `'0'` through `'9'` are continuous (no other characters intervene) and in order. Similarly, the lowercase alphabetic characters `'a'` through `'z'` are continuous and in order, as are the uppercase alphabetic characters `'A'` through `'Z'`. These characteristics make it relatively easy to sort data, such as a list of names, in alphabetical order. Sorting is discussed in Chapter 13.

In Java, the data type `char` represents a single character. The following are some examples of character variable declarations in Java:

```java
char topGrade = 'A';
char symbol1, symbol2, symbol3;
char terminator = ';', separator = ' ';
```

Booleans

A boolean value, defined in Java using the reserved word `boolean`, has only two valid values: `true` and `false`. A boolean variable is usually used to indicate whether a particular condition is true, but it can also be used to represent any situation that has two states, such as a light bulb being on or off. The term boolean is named in honor of English mathematician George Boole, who developed a form of algebra (Boolean algebra) in which variables take on only one of two values.

A boolean value cannot be converted to any other data type, nor can any other data type be converted to a boolean value. The words `true` and `false` are reserved in Java as *boolean literals* and cannot be used outside of this context.

The following are some examples of boolean variable declarations in Java:

```java
boolean flag = true;
boolean tooHigh, tooSmall, tooRough;
boolean done = false;
```

2.4 Expressions

An *expression* is a combination of one or more operators and operands that usually performs a calculation. The value calculated does not have to be a number, but often is. The operands used in the operations might be literals, constants, variables, or other sources of data. The manner in which expressions are evaluated and used is fundamental to programming. For now we will focus on arithmetic expressions that use numeric operands and produce numeric results.

> **KEY CONCEPT**
>
> Expressions are combinations of operators and operands used to perform a calculation.

Arithmetic Operators

The usual arithmetic operations are defined for both integer and floating point numeric types, including addition (+), subtraction (−), multiplication (*), and division (/). Java also has another arithmetic operation: The remainder operator (%) returns the remainder after dividing the second operand into the first. The remainder operator is sometimes called the modulus operator. The sign of the result of a remainder operation is the sign of the numerator. This table shows some examples:

Operation	Result
17 % 4	1
−20 % 3	−2
10 % −5	0
3 % 8	3

As you might expect, if either or both operands to any numeric operator are floating point values, the result is a floating point value. However, the division operator (/) produces results that are less intuitive, depending on the types of the operands. If both operands are integers, the / operator performs *integer division*, meaning that any fractional part of the result is discarded. If one or the other or both operands are floating point values, the / operator performs *floating point division*, and the fractional part of the result is kept. For example, the result of 10/4 is 2, but the results of 10.0/4 and 10/4.0 and 10.0/4.0 are all 2.5.

> **KEY CONCEPT**
>
> The type of result produced by arithmetic division depends on the types of the operands.

A *unary operator* has only one operand, while a *binary operator* has two. The + and − arithmetic operators can be either unary or binary. The binary versions accomplish addition and subtraction, and the unary versions represent positive and negative numbers. For example, −1 is an example of using the unary negation operator to make the value negative. The unary + operator is rarely used.

Java does not have a built-in operator for raising a value to an exponent. However, the Math class provides methods that perform exponentiation and many other mathematical functions. The Math class is discussed in Chapter 3.

Operator Precedence

Operators can be combined to create more complex expressions. For example, consider the following assignment statement:

```
result = 14 + 8 / 2;
```

The entire right-hand side of the assignment is evaluated, and then the result is stored in the variable. But what is the result? If the addition is performed first, the result is 11; if the division operation is performed first, the result is 18. The order of operator evaluation makes a big difference. In this case, the division is performed before the addition, yielding a result of 18.

Note that in this and subsequent examples, we use literal values rather than variables to simplify the expression. The order of operator evaluation is the same if the operands are variables or any other source of data.

All expressions are evaluated according to an *operator precedence hierarchy* that establishes the rules that govern the order in which operations are evaluated. The arithmetic operators generally follow the same rules you learned in algebra. Multiplication, division, and the remainder operator all have equal precedence and are performed before (have higher precedence than) addition and subtraction. Addition and subtraction have equal precedence.

> **KEY CONCEPT**
> Java follows a well-defined set of precedence rules that governs the order in which operators will be evaluated in an expression.

Any arithmetic operators at the same level of precedence are performed left to right. Therefore we say the arithmetic operators have a *left-to-right association*.

Precedence, however, can be forced in an expression by using parentheses. For instance, if we really wanted the addition to be performed first in the previous example, we could write the expression as follows:

```
result = (14 + 8) / 2;
```

Any expression in parentheses is evaluated first. In complicated expressions, it is good practice to use parentheses even when it is not strictly necessary, to make it clear how the expression is evaluated.

Parentheses can be nested, and the innermost nested expressions are evaluated first. Consider the following expression:

```
result = 3 * ((18 − 4) / 2);
```

In this example, the result is 21. First, the subtraction is performed, forced by the inner parentheses. Then, even though multiplication and division are at the same level of precedence and usually would be evaluated left to right, the division is performed first because of the outer parentheses. Finally, the multiplication is performed.

After the arithmetic operations are complete, the computed result is stored in the variable on the left-hand side of the assignment operator (=). In other words, the assignment operator has a lower precedence than any of the arithmetic operators.

The evaluation of a particular expression can be shown using an *expression tree*, such as the one in Figure 2.3. The operators are executed from the bottom up, creating values that are used in the rest of the expression. Therefore, the operations

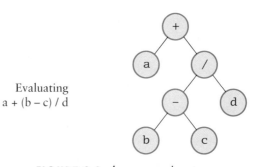

Evaluating
a + (b − c) / d

FIGURE 2.3   An expression tree

lower in the tree have a higher precedence than those above, or they are forced to be executed earlier using parentheses.

The parentheses used in expressions are actually operators themselves. Parentheses have a higher precedence than almost any other operator. Figure 2.4 shows a precedence table with the relationships between the arithmetic operators, parentheses, and the assignment operator. Appendix D includes a full precedence table showing all Java operators.

For an expression to be syntactically correct, the number of left parentheses must match the number of right parentheses and they must be properly nested. The following examples are *not* valid expressions:

```
result = ((19 + 8) % 3) − 4);   // not valid
result = (19 (+ 8 %) 3 − 4);    // not valid
```

Precedence Level	Operator	Operation	Associates
1	+	unary plus	R to L
	−	unary minus	
2	*	multiplication	L to R
	/	division	
	%	remainder	
3	+	addition	L to R
	−	subtraction	
	+	string concatenation	
4	=	assignment	R to L

FIGURE 2.4 Precedence among some of the Java operators

Keep in mind that when a variable is referenced in an expression, its current value is used to perform the calculation. In the following assignment statement, the current value of the variable count is added to the current value of the variable total, and the result is stored in the variable sum:

```
sum = count + total;
```

The original value contained in sum before this assignment is overwritten by the calculated value. The values stored in count and total are not changed.

The same variable can appear on both the left-hand side and the right-hand side of an assignment statement. Suppose the current value of a variable called count is 15 when the following assignment statement is executed:

```
count = count + 1;
```

Because the right-hand expression is evaluated first, the original value of count is obtained and the value 1 is added to it, producing the result 16. That result is then stored in the variable count, overwriting the original value of 15 with the new value of 16. Therefore, this assignment statement *increments*, or adds one to, the variable count.

Let's look at another example of expression processing. The program in Listing 2.7 on the next page, called TempConverter, converts a particular Celsius temperature value to its equivalent Fahrenheit value using an expression that computes the following formula:

$$\text{Fahrenheit} = \frac{9}{5}\text{ Celsius} + 32$$

Note that in the TempConverter program, the operands to the division operation are floating point literals to ensure that the fractional part of the number is kept. The precedence rules dictate that the multiplication happens before the addition in the final conversion computation.

The TempConverter program is not very useful because it converts only one data value that we included in the program as a constant (24 degrees Celsius). Every time the program is run it produces the same result. A far more useful version of the program would obtain the value to be converted from the user each time the program is executed. Interactive programs that read user input are discussed later in this chapter.

Increment and Decrement Operators

There are two other useful arithmetic operators. The *increment operator* (++) adds 1 to any integer or floating point value. The two plus signs that make up the operator cannot be separated by white space. The *decrement operator* (--) is similar

---

LISTING   2.7

```java
//********************************************************************
//  TempConverter.java       Java Foundations
//
//  Demonstrates the use of primitive data types and arithmetic
//  expressions.
//********************************************************************

public class TempConverter
{
   //-----------------------------------------------------------------
   //  Computes the Fahrenheit equivalent of a specific Celsius
   //  value using the formula F = (9/5)C + 32.
   //-----------------------------------------------------------------
   public static void main (String[] args)
   {
      final int BASE = 32;
      final double CONVERSION_FACTOR = 9.0 / 5.0;

      double fahrenheitTemp;
      int celsiusTemp = 24;   // value to convert

      fahrenheitTemp = celsiusTemp * CONVERSION_FACTOR + BASE;

      System.out.println ("Celsius Temperature: " + celsiusTemp);
      System.out.println ("Fahrenheit Equivalent: " + fahrenheitTemp);
   }
}
```

OUTPUT

```
Celsius Temperature: 24
Fahrenheit Equivalent: 75.2
```

except that it subtracts 1 from the value. They are both unary operators because they operate on only one operand. The following statement causes the value of count to be incremented:

```
count++;
```

The result is stored back into the variable count. Therefore it is functionally equivalent to the following statement, which we discussed in the previous section:

```
count = count + 1;
```

The increment and decrement operators can be applied after the variable (such as count++ or count--), creating what is called the *postfix form* of the operator. They can also be applied before the variable (such as ++count or --count), in what is called the *prefix form*. When used alone in a statement, the prefix and postfix forms are functionally equivalent. That is, it doesn't matter if you write

```
count++;
```

or

```
++count;
```

However, when such a form is written as a statement by itself, it is usually written in its postfix form.

When the increment or decrement operator is used in a larger expression, it can yield different results depending on the form used. For example, if the variable count currently contains the value 15, the following statement assigns the value 15 to total and the value 16 to count:

```
total = count++;
```

However, if count contains 15, the following statement assigns the value 16 to both total and count:

```
total = ++count;
```

The value of count is incremented in both situations, but the value used in the larger expression depends on whether a prefix or postfix form of the increment operator is used.

Because of the subtle differences between the prefix and postfix forms of the increment and decrement operators, they should be used with care. As always, favor the side of readability.

Assignment Operators

As a convenience, several *assignment operators* have been defined in Java that combine a basic operation with assignment. For example, the += operator can be used as follows:

```
total += 5;
```

This performs the same operation as the following statement:

```
total = total + 5;
```

The right-hand side of the assignment operator can be a full expression. The expression on the right-hand side of the operator is evaluated, then that result is added to the current value of the variable on the left-hand side, and that value is stored in the variable. Therefore, the following statement:

```
total += (sum - 12) / count;
```

is equivalent to:

```
total = total + ((sum - 12) / count);
```

Many similar assignment operators are defined in Java, including those that perform subtraction (-=), multiplication (*=), division (/=), and remainder (%=). The entire set of Java operators is discussed in Appendix D.

All of the assignment operators evaluate the entire expression on the right-hand side first, then use the result as the right operand of the other operation. Therefore, the following statement:

```
result *= count1 + count2;
```

is equivalent to:

```
result = result * (count1 + count2);
```

Likewise, the following statement:

```
result %= (highest - 40) / 2;
```

is equivalent to:

```
result = result % ((highest - 40) / 2);
```

Some assignment operators perform particular functions depending on the types of the operands, just as their corresponding regular operators do. For example, if the operands to the += operator are strings, then the assignment operator performs string concatenation.

2.5 Data Conversion

Because Java is a strongly typed language, each data value is associated with a particular type. It is sometimes helpful or necessary to convert a data value of one type to another type, but we must be careful that we don't lose important information in the process. For example, suppose a short variable that holds the number 1000 is converted to a byte value. Because a byte does not have enough bits to represent the value 1000, some bits would be lost in the conversion, and the number represented in the byte would not keep its original value.

A conversion between one primitive type and another falls into one of two categories: widening conversions and narrowing conversions. *Widening conversions*

From	To
byte	short, int, long, float, or double
short	int, long, float, or double
char	int, long, float, or double
int	long, float, or double
long	float or double
float	double

FIGURE 2.5 Java widening conversions

are the safest because they usually do not lose information. They are called widening conversions because they go from one data type to another type that uses an equal or greater amount of space to store the value. Figure 2.5 lists the Java widening conversions.

For example, it is safe to convert from a byte to a short because a byte is stored in 8 bits and a short is stored in 16 bits. There is no loss of information. All widening conversions that go from an integer type to another integer type, or from a floating point type to another floating point type, preserve the numeric value exactly.

Although widening conversions do not lose any information about the magnitude of a value, the widening conversions that result in a floating point value can lose precision. When converting from an int or a long to a float, or from a long to a double, some of the least significant digits may be lost. In this case, the resulting floating point value will be a rounded version of the integer value, following the rounding techniques defined in the IEEE 754 floating point standard.

Narrowing conversions are more likely to lose information than widening conversions are. They often go from one type to a type that uses less space to store a value, and therefore some of the information may be compromised. Narrowing conversions can lose both numeric magnitude and precision. Therefore, in general, they should be avoided. Figure 2.6 on the next page lists the Java narrowing conversions.

> **KEY CONCEPT**
> Narrowing conversions should be avoided because they can lose information.

An exception to the space-shrinking situation in narrowing conversions is when we convert a byte (8 bits) or short (16 bits) to a char (16 bits). These are still considered narrowing conversions because the sign bit is incorporated into the new character value. Since a character value is unsigned, a negative integer will be converted into a character that has no particular relationship to the numeric value of the original integer.

Note that boolean values are not mentioned in either widening or narrowing conversions. A boolean value cannot be converted to any other primitive type and vice versa.

From	To
byte	char
short	byte or char
char	byte or short
int	byte, short, or char
long	byte, short, char, or int
float	byte, short, char, int, or long
double	byte, short, char, int, long, or float

FIGURE 2.6 Java narrowing conversions

Conversion Techniques

In Java, conversions can occur in three ways:

- assignment conversion
- promotion
- casting

Assignment conversion occurs when a value of one type is assigned to a variable of another type during which the value is converted to the new type. Only widening conversions can be accomplished through assignment. For example, if `money` is a `float` variable and `dollars` is an `int` variable, then the following assignment statement automatically converts the value in `dollars` to a `float`:

```
money = dollars;
```

Therefore, if `dollars` contains the value 25, after the assignment, money contains the value 25.0. However, if we attempt to assign `money` to `dollars`, the compiler will issue an error message alerting us to the fact that we are attempting a narrowing conversion that could lose information. If we really want to do this assignment, we have to make the conversion explicit by using a cast.

Conversion via *promotion* occurs automatically when certain operators need to modify their operands in order to perform the operation. For example, when a floating point value called `sum` is divided by an integer value called `count`, the value of `count` is promoted to a floating point value automatically, before the division takes place, producing a floating point result:

```
result = sum / count;
```

A similar conversion is taking place when a number is concatenated with a string. The number is first converted (promoted) to a string, then the two strings are concatenated.

Casting is the most general form of conversion in Java. If a conversion can be accomplished at all in a Java program, it can be accomplished using a cast. A cast is a Java operator that is specified by a type name in parentheses. It is placed in front of the value to be converted. For example, to convert money to an integer value, we could put a cast in front of it:

```
dollars = (int) money;
```

The cast returns the value in money, truncating any fractional part. If money contained the value 84.69, then after the assignment, dollars would contain the value 84. Note, however, that the cast does not change the value in money. After the assignment operation is complete, money still contains the value 84.69.

Casts are helpful in many situations where we need to treat a value temporarily as another type. For example, if we want to divide the integer value total by the integer value count and get a floating point result, we could do it as follows:

```
result = (float) total / count;
```

First, the cast operator returns a floating point version of the value in total. This operation does not change the value in total. Then, count is treated as a floating point value via arithmetic promotion. Now the division operator will perform floating point division and produce the intended result. If the cast had not been included, the operation would have performed integer division and truncated the answer before assigning it to result. Also note that because the cast operator has a higher precedence than the division operator, the cast operates on the value of total, not on the result of the division.

2.6 Reading Input Data

It is often useful to design a program to read data from the user interactively during execution. That way, new results can be computed each time the program is run, depending on the data that is entered.

The Scanner Class

The Scanner class, which is part of the standard Java class library, provides convenient methods for reading input values of various

> **KEY CONCEPT**
> The Scanner class provides methods for reading input of various types from various sources.

types. The input could come from various sources, including data typed interactively by the user or data stored in a file. The Scanner class can also be used to parse a character string into separate pieces. Figure 2.7 lists some of the methods provided by the Scanner class.

```
Scanner (InputStream source)
Scanner (File source)
Scanner (String source)
        Constructors: sets up the new scanner to scan values from the specified source.


String next()
        Returns the next input token as a character string.


String nextLine()
        Returns all input remaining on the current line as a character string.


boolean nextBoolean()
byte nextByte()
double nextDouble()
float nextFloat()
int nextInt()
long nextLong()
short nextShort()
        Returns the next input token as the indicated type. Throws
        InputMismatchException if the next token is inconsistent with the type.


boolean hasNext()
        Returns true if the scanner has another token in its input.


Scanner useDelimiter (String pattern)
Scanner useDelimiter (Pattern pattern)
        Sets the scanner's delimiting pattern.


Pattern delimiter()
        Returns the pattern the scanner is currently using to match delimiters.


String findInLine (String pattern)
String findInLine (Pattern pattern)
        Attempts to find the next occurrence of the specified pattern, ignoring delimiters.
```

FIGURE 2.7 Some methods of the Scanner class

We must first create a `Scanner` object in order to invoke its methods. Objects in Java are created using the new operator. The following declaration creates a `Scanner` object that reads input from the keyboard:

```
Scanner scan = new Scanner(System.in);
```

This declaration creates a variable called `scan` that represents a `Scanner` object. The object itself is created by the new operator and a call to a special method called a *constructor* to set up the object. The `Scanner` constructor accepts a parameter that indicates the source of the input. The `System.in` object represents the *standard input stream*, which by default is the keyboard. Creating objects using the new operator is discussed further in the next chapter.

Unless specified otherwise, a `Scanner` object assumes that whitespace characters (space characters, tabs, and new lines) are used to separate the elements of the input, called *tokens*, from each other. These characters are called the input *delimiters*. The set of delimiters can be changed if the input tokens are separated by characters other than white space.

The `next` method of the `Scanner` class reads the next input token as a string and returns it. Therefore, if the input consisted of a series of words separated by spaces, each call to `next` would return the next word. The `nextLine` method reads all of the input until the end of the line is found, and returns it as one string.

The program `Echo`, shown in Listing 2.8 on the next page, simply reads a line of text typed by the user, stores it in a variable that holds a character string, then echoes it back to the screen. User input is shown in red in the output section below the listing.

The `import` declaration above the definition of the `Echo` class tells the program that we will be using the `Scanner` class in this program. The `Scanner` class is part of the `java.util` class library. The use of the `import` declaration is discussed further in Chapter 3.

Various `Scanner` methods such as `nextInt` and `nextDouble` are provided to read data of particular types. The `GasMileage` program, shown in Listing 2.9 on page 61, reads the number of miles traveled as an integer, and the number of gallons of fuel consumed as a double, then computes the gas mileage.

As you can see by the output of the `GasMileage` program, the calculation produces a floating point result that is accurate to several decimal places. In the next chapter we discuss classes that help us format our output in various ways, including rounding a floating point value to a particular number of decimal places.

A `Scanner` object processes the input one token at a time, based on the methods used to read the data and the delimiters used to separate the input values.

LISTING 2.8

```java
//********************************************************************
//  Echo.java        Java Foundations
//
//  Demonstrates the use of the nextLine method of the Scanner class
//  to read a string from the user.
//********************************************************************

import java.util.Scanner;

public class Echo
{
   //-----------------------------------------------------------------
   //  Reads a character string from the user and prints it.
   //-----------------------------------------------------------------
   public static void main (String[] args)
   {
      String message;
      Scanner scan = new Scanner (System.in);

      System.out.println ("Enter a line of text:");

      message = scan.nextLine();

      System.out.println ("You entered: \"" + message + "\"");
   }
}
```

OUTPUT

```
Enter a line of text:
Set your laser printer on stun!
You entered: "Set your laser printer on stun!"
```

Therefore, multiple values can be put on the same line of input or can be separated over multiple lines, as appropriate for the situation.

In Chapter 5 we use the Scanner class to read input from a data file and modify the delimiters it uses to parse the data. Appendix H explores how to use the Scanner class to analyze its input using patterns called *regular expressions*.

LISTING 2.9

```java
//********************************************************************
//  GasMileage.java        Java Foundations
//
//  Demonstrates the use of the Scanner class to read numeric data.
//********************************************************************

import java.util.Scanner;

public class GasMileage
{
    //----------------------------------------------------------------
    //  Calculates fuel efficiency based on values entered by the
    //  user.
    //----------------------------------------------------------------
    public static void main (String[] args)
    {
        int miles;
        double gallons, mpg;

        Scanner scan = new Scanner (System.in);

        System.out.print ("Enter the number of miles: ");
        miles = scan.nextInt();

        System.out.print ("Enter the gallons of fuel used: ");
        gallons = scan.nextDouble();

        mpg = miles / gallons;

        System.out.println ("Miles Per Gallon: " + mpg);
    }
}
```

OUTPUT

```
Enter the number of miles: 369
Enter the gallons of fuel used: 12.4
Miles Per Gallon: 29.758064516129032
```

Summary of Key Concepts

- The `print` and `println` methods represent two services provided by the `System.out` object.

- In Java, the + operator is used both for addition and for string concatenation.

- An escape sequence can be used to represent a character that would otherwise cause compilation problems.

- A variable is a name for a memory location used to hold a value of a particular data type.

- Accessing data leaves it intact in memory, but an assignment statement overwrites the old data.

- We cannot assign a value of one type to a variable of an incompatible type.

- Constants hold a particular value for the duration of their existence.

- Java has two kinds of numeric values: integer and floating point. There are four integer data types and two floating point data types.

- Java uses the 16-bit Unicode character set to represent character data.

- Expressions are combinations of operators and operands used to perform a calculation.

- The type of result produced by arithmetic division depends on the types of the operands.

- Java follows a well-defined set of precedence rules that governs the order in which operators will be evaluated in an expression.

- Narrowing conversions should be avoided because they can lose information.

- The `Scanner` class provides methods for reading input of various types from various sources.

Self-Review Questions

SR 2.1   What is primitive data? How are primitive data types different from objects?

SR 2.2   What is a string literal?

SR 2.3   What is the difference between the `print` and `println` methods?

SR 2.4   What is a parameter?

SR 2.5   What is an escape sequence? Give some examples.

SR 2.6   What is a variable declaration?

SR 2.7   How many values can be stored in an integer variable at one time?

SR 2.8   What are the four integer data types in Java? How are they different?

SR 2.9   What is a character set?

SR 2.10   What is operator precedence?

SR 2.11   What is the result of 19%5 when evaluated in a Java expression? Explain.

SR 2.12   What is the result of 13/4 when evaluated in a Java expression? Explain.

SR 2.13   If an integer variable `diameter` currently holds the value 5, what is its value after the following statement is executed? Explain.

```
diameter = diameter * 4;
```

SR 2.14   If an integer variable `weight` currently holds the value 100, what is its value after the following statement is executed? Explain.

```
weight -= 17;
```

SR 2.15   Why are widening conversions safer than narrowing conversions?

Exercises

EX 2.1   Explain the following programming statement in terms of objects and the services they provide:

```
System.out.println ("I gotta be me!");
```

EX 2.2   What output is produced by the following code fragment? Explain.

```
System.out.print ("Here we go!");
System.out.println ("12345");
System.out.print ("Test this if you are not sure.");
System.out.print ("Another.");
System.out.println ();
System.out.println ("All done.");
```

EX 2.3   What is wrong with the following program statement? How can it be fixed?

```
System.out.println ("To be or not to be, that is the
question.");
```

EX 2.4   What output is produced by the following statement? Explain.

```
System.out.println ("50 plus 25 is " + 50 + 25);
```

EX 2.5   What output is produced by the following statement? Explain.

```
System.out.println ("He thrusts his fists\n\tagainst" +
" the post\nand still insists\n\the sees the \"ghost\"");
```

EX 2.6   What value is contained in the integer variable `size` after the following statements are executed?

```
size = 18;
size = size + 12;
size = size * 2;
size = size / 4;
```

EX 2.7   What value is contained in the floating point variable `depth` after the following statements are executed?

```
depth = 2.4;
depth = 20 — depth * 4;
depth = depth / 5;
```

EX 2.8   What value is contained in the integer variable `length` after the following statements are executed?

```
length = 5;
length *= 2;
length *= length;
length /= 100;
```

EX 2.9   Write four different program statements that increment the value of an integer variable `total`.

EX 2.10   Given the following declarations, what result is stored in each of
the listed assignment statements?

```
int iResult, num1 = 25, num2 = 40, num3 = 17, num4 = 5;
double fResult, val1 = 17.0, val2 = 12.78;
```

a. iResult = num1 / num4;

b. fResult = num1 / num4;

c. iResult = num3 / num4;

d. fResult = num3 / num4;

e. fResult = val1 / num4;

f. fResult = val1 / val2;

g. iResult = num1 / num2;

h. fResult = (double) num1 / num2;

i. fResult = num1 / (double) num2;

j. fResult = (double) (num1 / num2);

k. iResult = (int) (val1 / num4);

l. fResult = (int) (val1 / num4);

m. fResult = (int) ((double) num1 / num2);

n. iResult = num3 % num4;

o. iResult = num2 % num3;

p. iResult = num3 % num2;

q. iResult = num2 % num4;

EX 2.11   For each of the following expressions, indicate the order in which the operators will be evaluated by writing a number beneath each operator.

a. a – b – c – d

b. a – b + c – d

c. a + b / c / d

d. a + b / c * d

e. a / b * c * d

f. a % b / c * d

g. a % b % c % d

h. a – (b – c) – d

i. (a – (b – c)) – d

j. a – ((b – c) – d)

k. a % (b % c) * d * e

l. a + (b – c) * d – e

m. (a + b) * c + d * e

n. (a + b) * (c / d) % e

Programming Projects

PP 2.1   Create a revised version of the Lincoln application from Chapter 1 such that quotes appear around the quotation.

PP 2.2   Write an application that reads three integers and prints their average.

PP 2.3   Write an application that reads two floating point numbers and prints their sum, difference, and product.

PP 2.4   Create a version of the TempConverter application to convert from Fahrenheit to Celsius. Read the Fahrenheit temperature from the user.

PP 2.5   Write an application that converts miles to kilometers. (One mile equals 1.60935 kilometers.) Read the miles value from the user as a floating point value.

PP 2.6   Write an application that reads values representing a time duration in hours, minutes, and seconds, and then prints the equivalent total number of seconds. (For example, 1 hour, 28 minutes,
and 42 seconds is equivalent to 5322 seconds.)

PP 2.7   Create a version of the previous project that reverses the computation. That is, read a value representing a number of seconds,
then print the equivalent amount of time as a combination of
hours, minutes, and seconds. (For example, 9999 seconds is
equivalent to 2 hours, 46 minutes, and 39 seconds.)

PP 2.8   Write an application that determines the value of the coins in a jar
and prints the total in dollars and cents. Read integer values that
represent the number of quarters, dimes, nickels, and pennies.

PP 2.9   Write an application that prompts for and reads a `double` value
representing a monetary amount. Then determine the fewest
number of each bill and coin needed to represent that amount,
starting with the highest (assume that a ten-dollar bill is the maximum size needed). For example, if the value entered is 47.63
(forty-seven dollars and sixty-three cents), then the program
should print the equivalent amount as:

```
4 ten dollar bills
1 five dollar bills
2 one dollar bills
2 quarters
1 dimes
0 nickles
3 pennies
```

PP 2.10   Write an application that prompts for and reads an integer representing the length of a square's side, then prints the square's
perimeter and area.

PP 2.11   Write an application that prompts for and reads the numerator
and denominator of a fraction as integers, then prints the decimal
equivalent of the fraction.

Answers to Self-Review Questions

SR 2.1   Primitive data are basic values such as numbers or characters.
Objects are more complex entities that usually contain primitive
data that help define them.

SR 2.2 A string literal is a sequence of characters delimited by double quotes.

SR 2.3 Both the `print` and `println` methods of the `System.out` object write a string of characters to the monitor screen. The difference is that, after printing the characters, the `println` method performs a carriage return so that whatever is printed next appears on the next line. The `print` method allows subsequent output to appear on the same line.

SR 2.4 A parameter is data that is passed into a method when it is invoked. The method usually uses that data to accomplish the ser vice that it provides. For example, the parameter to the `println` method indicates what characters should be printed.

SR 2.5 An escape sequence is a series of characters that begins with the backslash (\) and that implies the following characters should be treated in some special way. Examples: \n represents the newline character, \t represents the tab character, and \" represents the quotation character (as opposed to using it to terminate a string).

SR 2.6 A variable declaration establishes the name of a variable and the type of data that it can contain. A declaration may also have an optional initialization, which gives the variable an initial value.

SR 2.7 An integer variable can store only one value at a time. When a new value is assigned to it, the old one is overwritten and lost.

SR 2.8 The four integer data types in Java are `byte`, `short`, `int`, and `long`. They differ in how much memory space is allocated for each and therefore how large a number they can hold.

SR 2.9 A character set is a list of characters in a particular order. A character set defines the valid characters that a particular type of computer or programming language will support. Java uses the Unicode character set.

SR 2.10 Operator precedence is the set of rules that dictates the order in which operators are evaluated in an expression.

SR 2.11 The result of 19%5 in a Java expression is 4. The remainder operator % returns the remainder after dividing the second operand into the first. Five goes into 19 three times, with 4 left over.

SR 2.12 The result of 13/4 in a Java expression is 3 (not 3.25). The result is an integer because both operands are integers. Therefore the / operator performs integer division, and the fractional part of the result is truncated.

SR 2.13   After executing the statement, `diameter` holds the value 20. First the current value of `diameter` (5) is multiplied by 4, and then the result is stored back in `diameter`.

SR 2.14   After executing the statement, `weight` holds the value 83. The assignment operator `-=` modifies `weight` by first subtracting 17 from the current value (100), then storing the result back into `weight`.

SR 2.15   A widening conversion tends to go from a small data value, in terms of the amount of space used to store it, to a larger one. A narrowing conversion does the opposite. Information is more likely to be lost in a narrowing conversion, which is why narrowing conversions are considered to be less safe than widening ones.

Using Classes and Objects

3

CHAPTER OBJECTIVES

- Discuss the creation of objects and the use of object reference variables.

- Explore the services provided by the `String` class.

- Describe how the Java standard class library is organized into packages.

- Explore the services provided by the `Random` and `Math` classes.

- Discuss ways to format output using the `NumberFormat` and `DecimalFormat` classes.

- Introduce enumerated types.

- Discuss wrapper classes and the concept of autoboxing.

This chapter further explores the use of predefined classes and the objects we can create from them. Using classes and objects for the services they provide is a fundamental part of object-oriented software, and sets the stage for writing classes of our own. In this chapter, we use classes and objects to manipulate character strings, produce random numbers, perform complex calculations, and format output. This chapter also introduces the concept of an enumerated type, which is a special kind of class in Java, and discusses the concept of a wrapper class.

3.1 Creating Objects

At the end of Chapter 1 we presented an overview of object-oriented concepts, including the basic relationship between classes and objects. Then in Chapter 2, in addition to discussing primitive data, we provided some examples of using objects for the services they provide. This chapter explores these ideas further.

In previous examples, we've used the `println` method many times. As we mentioned in Chapter 2, the `println` method is a service provided by the `System.out` object, which represents the standard output stream. To be more precise, the identifier `out` is an object variable that is stored in the `System` class. It has been predefined and set up for us as part of the Java standard class library. We can simply use it.

In Chapter 2 we also used the `Scanner` class, which represents an object that allows us to read input from the keyboard or a file. We created a `Scanner` object using the `new` operator. Once the object was created, we were able to use it for the various services it provides. That is, we were able to invoke its methods.

Let's carefully examine the idea of creating an object. In Java, a variable name represents either a primitive value or an object. Like variables that hold primitive types, a variable that refers to an object must be declared. The class used to define an object can be thought of as the type of an object. The declarations of object variables have a similar structure to the declarations of primitive variables.

Consider the following two declarations:

```
int num;
String name;
```

The first declaration creates a variable that holds an integer value, as we've seen many times before. The second declaration creates a `String` variable that holds a *reference* to a `String` object. An object variable doesn't hold the object itself, it holds the address of an object.

Initially, the two variables declared above don't contain any data. We say they are *uninitialized*, which can be depicted as follows:

As we pointed out in Chapter 2, it is always important to make sure a variable is initialized before using it. For an object variable, that means we must make sure it refers to a valid object prior to using it. In most situations the compiler will issue an error if you attempt to use a variable before initializing it.

An object reference variable can also be set to `null`, which is a reserved word in Java. A null reference specifically indicates that a variable does not refer to an object.

Note that, although we've declared a `String` reference variable, no `String` object actually exists yet. The act of creating an object using the new operator is called *instantiation*. An object is said to be an *instance* of a particular class. To instantiate an object, we can use the new operator, which returns the address of the new object. The following two assignment statements give values to the two variables declared above:

```
num = 42;
name = new String("James Gosling");
```

After the new operator creates the object, a *constructor* is invoked to help set it up initially. A constructor is a special method that has the same name as the class. In this example, the parameter to the constructor is a string literal that specifies the characters that the string object will hold. After these assignments are executed, the variables can be depicted as:

Since an object reference variable holds the address of the object, it can be thought of as a *pointer* to the location in memory where the object is held. We could show the numeric address, but the actual address value is irrelevant—what's important is that the variable refers to a particular object.

After an object has been instantiated, we use the *dot operator* to access its methods. We've used the dot operator many times already, such as in calls to `System.out.println`. The dot operator is appended directly after the object reference, followed by the method being invoked. For example, to invoke the `length` method defined in the `String` class, we can use the dot operator on the name reference variable:

```
count = name.length()
```

The `length` method does not take any parameters, but the parentheses are still necessary to indicate that a method is being invoked. Some methods produce a value that is *returned* when the method completes. The purpose of the `length` method of the `String` class is to determine and return the length of the string (the number of characters it contains). In this example, the returned value is assigned to the variable `count`. For the string `"James Gosling"`, the `length` method returns 13, which includes the space between the first and last names. Some methods do not return a value. Other `String` methods are discussed in the next section.

The act of declaring the object reference variable and creating the object itself can be combined into one step by initializing the variable in the declaration, just as we do with primitive types:

```
String title = new String("Java Software Solutions");
```

Even though they are not primitive types, character strings are so fundamental and so often used that Java defines string literals delimited by double quotation marks, as we've seen in various examples. This is a shortcut notation. Whenever a string literal appears, a `String` object is created automatically. Therefore the following declaration is valid:

```
String city = "London";
```

That is, for `String` objects, the explicit use of the `new` operator and the call to the constructor can be eliminated. In most cases, we will use this simplified syntax.

Aliases

Because an object reference variable stores an address, a programmer must be careful when managing objects. First, let's review the effect of assignment on primitive values. Suppose we have two integer variables, `num1`, initialized to 5, and `num2`, initialized to 12:

num1   5

num2   12

In the following assignment statement, a copy of the value that is stored in `num1` is stored in `num2`:

```
num2 = num1;
```

The original value of 12 in num2 is overwritten by the value 5. The variables num1 and num2 still refer to different locations in memory, and both of those locations now contain the value 5:

num1   5

num2   5

Now consider the following object declarations:

```
String name1 = "Ada, Countess of Lovelace";
String name2 = "Grace Murray Hopper";
```

Initially, the references name1 and name2 refer to two different String objects:

Now suppose the following assignment statement is executed, copying the value in name1 into name2:

```
name2 = name1;
```

This assignment works the same as the integer assignment—a copy of the value of name1 is stored in name2. But remember, object variables hold the address of an object, and it is the address that gets copied. Originally, the two references referred to different objects. After the assignment, both name1 and name2 contain the same address and therefore refer to the same object:

The name1 and name2 reference variables are now *aliases* of each other because they are two different variables that refer to the same object. All references to the object originally referenced by name2 are now gone; that object cannot be used again in the program.

One important implication of aliases is that when we use one reference to change an object, it is also changed for the other reference because there is really only one object. Aliases can produce undesirable effects unless they are managed carefully.

All interaction with an object occurs through a reference variable, so we can use an object only if we have a reference to it. When all references to an object are lost (perhaps by reassignment), that object can no longer contribute to the program. The program can no longer invoke its methods or use its variables. At this point the object is called *garbage* because it serves no useful purpose.

Java performs automatic *garbage collection*. When the last reference to an object is lost, the object becomes a candidate for garbage collection. Occasionally, behind the scenes, the Java environment executes a method that "collects" all the objects marked for garbage collection and returns their memory to the system for future use. The programmer does not have to worry about explicitly reclaiming memory that has become garbage.

3.2 The `String` Class

Let's examine the `String` class in more detail. Figure 3.1 lists some of the more useful methods of the `String` class.

Once a `String` object is created, its value cannot be lengthened or shortened, nor can any of its characters change. Thus we say that a `String` object is *immutable*. However, several methods in the `String` class return new `String` objects that are the result of modifying the original string's value.

Note that some of the `String` methods, such as `charAt`, refer to the *index* of a particular character. An index specifies a particular position, and therefore a particular character, in a string. The index of the first character in a string is zero, the index of the next character is one, and so on. Therefore, in the string `"Hello"`, the index of the character `'H'` is zero and the character at index four is `'o'`.

Several `String` methods are exercised in the program shown in Listing 3.1 on page 78. As you examine the `StringMutation` program, keep in mind that this is not a single `String` object that changes its data; this program creates five separate `String` objects using various methods of the `String` class. Originally, the `phrase` object is set up:

```
String (String str)
    Constructor: creates a new string object with the same characters as str.

char charAt (int index)
    Returns the character at the specified index.

int compareTo (String str)
    Returns an integer indicating if this string is lexically before (a negative return
    value), equal to (a zero return value), or lexically after (a positive return value),
    the string str.

String concat (String str)
    Returns a new string consisting of this string concatenated with str.

boolean equals (String str)
    Returns true if this string contains the same characters as str (including
    case) and false otherwise.

boolean equalsIgnoreCase (String str)
    Returns true if this string contains the same characters as str (without
    regard to case) and false otherwise.

int length ()
    Returns the number of characters in this string.

String replace (char oldChar, char newChar)
    Returns a new string that is identical with this string except that every
    occurrence of oldChar is replaced by newChar.

String substring (int offset, int endIndex)
    Returns a new string that is a subset of this string starting at index offset
    and extending through endIndex-1.

String toLowerCase ()
    Returns a new string identical to this string except all uppercase letters are
    converted to their lowercase equivalent.

String toUpperCase ()
    Returns a new string identical to this string except all lowercase letters are
    converted to their uppercase equivalent.
```

FIGURE 3.1 Some methods of the String class

After printing the original phrase and its length, the concat method is executed to create a new String object referenced by the variable mutation1:

mutation1 [ ] ──────▶ "Change is inevitable, except from vending machines."

LISTING 3.1

```java
//********************************************************************
//  StringMutation.java        Java Foundations
//
//  Demonstrates the use of the String class and its methods.
//********************************************************************

public class StringMutation
{
   //-----------------------------------------------------------------
   //  Prints a string and various mutations of it.
   //-----------------------------------------------------------------
   public static void main (String[] args)
   {
      String phrase = "Change is inevitable";
      String mutation1, mutation2, mutation3, mutation4;

      System.out.println ("Original string: \"" + phrase + "\"");
      System.out.println ("Length of string: " + phrase.length());

      mutation1 = phrase.concat (", except from vending machines.");
      mutation2 = mutation1.toUpperCase();
      mutation3 = mutation2.replace ('E', 'X');
      mutation4 = mutation3.substring (3, 30);

      // Print each mutated string
      System.out.println ("Mutation #1: " + mutation1);
      System.out.println ("Mutation #2: " + mutation2);
      System.out.println ("Mutation #3: " + mutation3);
      System.out.println ("Mutation #4: " + mutation4);

      System.out.println ("Mutated length: " + mutation4.length());
   }
}
```

OUTPUT

```
Original string: "Change is inevitable"
Length of string: 20
Mutation #1: Change is inevitable, except from vending machines.
Mutation #2: CHANGE IS INEVITABLE, EXCEPT FROM VENDING MACHINES.
Mutation #3: CHANGX IS INXVITABLX, XXCXPT FROM VXNDING MACHINXS.
Mutation #4: NGX IS INXVITABLX, XXCXPT F
Mutated length: 27
```

Then the toUpperCase method is executed on the mutation1 object, and the resulting string is stored in mutation2:

mutation2 → "CHANGE IS INEVITABLE, EXCEPT FROM VENDING MACHINES."

Notice that the length and concat methods are executed on the phrase object, but the toUpperCase method is executed on the mutation1 object. Any method of the String class can be executed on any String object, but for any given invocation, the method is executed on a particular object. The results of executing toUpperCase on mutation1 would be very different than the results of executing toUpperCase on phrase. Remember, each object has its own state, which often affects the results of method calls.

> **KEY CONCEPT**
> Methods are often executed on a particular object, and that object's state usually affects the results.

Finally, the String object variables mutation3 and mutation4 are initialized by the calls to mutation2.replace and mutation3.substring, respectively:

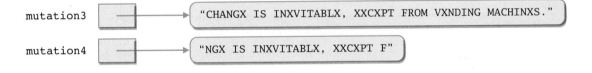

mutation3 → "CHANGX IS INXVITABLX, XXCXPT FROM VXNDING MACHINXS."

mutation4 → "NGX IS INXVITABLX, XXCXPT F"

3.3 Packages

We mentioned earlier that the Java language is supported by a standard class library that we can make use of as needed. Let's examine that idea further.

A *class library* is a set of classes that supports the development of programs. A compiler or development environment often comes with a class library. Class libraries can also be obtained separately through third-party vendors. The classes in a class library contain methods that are often valuable to a programmer because of the special functionality they offer. In fact, programmers often become dependent on the methods in a class library and begin to think of them as part of the language. However, technically, they are not in the language itself.

> **KEY CONCEPT**
> A class library provides useful support when developing programs.

The String class, for instance, is not an inherent part of the Java language. It is part of the Java standard class library that can be found in any Java development environment. The classes that make up the library were created by employees at Sun Microsystems, the people who created the Java language.

The class library is made up of several clusters of related classes, which are sometimes called Java APIs, or *application programming interfaces*. For example, we may refer to the Java Database API when we're talking about the set of classes that helps us write programs that interact with a database. Another example of an API is the Java Swing API, which refers to a set of classes that defines special graphical components used in a graphical user interface. Sometimes the entire standard library is referred to generically as the Java API.

> **KEY CONCEPT**
> The Java standard class library is organized into packages.

The classes of the Java standard class library are also grouped into *packages*. Each class is part of a particular package. The `String` class, for example, is part of the `java.lang` package. The `System` class is part of the java.lang package as well. We mentioned in Chapter 2 that the `Scanner` class is part of the `java.util` package.

The package organization is more fundamental and language-based than the API organization. Though there is a general correspondence between package and API names, the groups of classes that make up a given API might cross packages. In this book, we primarily refer to classes in terms of their package organization.

Figure 3.2 describes some of the packages that are part of the Java standard class library. These packages are available on any platform that supports Java software development. Some of these packages support highly specific programming techniques and will not come into play in the development of basic programs.

Various classes of the Java standard class library are discussed throughout this book.

The `import` Declaration

The classes of the `java.lang` package are automatically available for use when writing a Java program. To use classes from any other package, however, we must either *fully qualify* the reference or use an *import declaration*. Let's consider these two options.

When you want to use a class from a class library in a program, you could use its fully qualified name, including the package name, every time it is referenced. For example, every time you want to refer to the `Scanner` class that is defined in the `java.util` package, you could write `java.util.Scanner`. However, completely specifying the package and class name every time it is needed quickly becomes tiring. Java provides the `import` declaration to simplify these references.

The `import` declaration specifies the packages and classes that will be used in a program so that the fully qualified name is not necessary with each reference. Recall that the example programs that use the `Scanner` class in Chapter 2 include an `import` declaration like this one:

```
import java.util.Scanner;
```

Package	Provides support to
`java.applet`	Create programs (applets) that are easily transported across the Web.
`java.awt`	Draw graphics and create graphical user interfaces; AWT stands for Abstract Windowing Toolkit.
`java.beans`	Define software components that can be easily combined into applications.
`java.io`	Perform a wide variety of input and output functions.
`java.lang`	General support; it is automatically imported into all Java programs.
`java.math`	Perform calculations with arbitrarily high precision.
`java.net`	Communicate across a network.
`java.rmi`	Create programs that can be distributed across multiple computers; RMI stands for Remote Method Invocation.
`java.security`	Enforce security restrictions.
`java.sql`	Interact with databases; SQL stands for Structured Query Language.
`java.text`	Format text for output.
`java.util`	General utilities.
`javax.swing`	Create graphical user interfaces with components that extend the AWT capabilities.
`javax.xml.parsers`	Process XML documents; XML stands for eXtensible Markup Language.

FIGURE 3.2 Some packages in the Java standard class library

This declaration asserts that the `Scanner` class of the `java.util` package may be used in the program. Once this `import` declaration is made, it is sufficient to use the simple name `Scanner` when referring to that class in the program.

If two classes from two different packages have the same name, `import` declarations will not suffice because the compiler won't be able to figure out which class is being referenced in the flow of the code. When such situations arise, which is rare, the fully qualified names should be used in the code.

Another form of the `import` declaration uses an asterisk (*) to indicate that any class inside the package might be used in the program. Therefore, the following declaration allows all classes in the `java.util` package to be referenced in the program without qualifying each reference:

```
import java.util.*;
```

If only one class of a particular package will be used in a program, it is usually better to name the class specifically in the `import` declaration because it provides more specific information to anyone reading the code. However, if two or more will be used, the * notation is usually fine.

The classes of the `java.lang` package are automatically imported because they are fundamental and can be thought of as basic extensions to the language. Therefore, any class in the `java.lang` package, such as `System` and `String`, can be used without an explicit `import` declaration. It's as if all program files automatically contain the following declaration:

> **KEY CONCEPT**
>
> All classes of the `java.lang` package are automatically imported for every program.

```
import java.lang.*;
```

3.4 The Random Class

The need for random numbers occurs frequently when writing software. Games often use random numbers to simulate the roll of a die or the shuffle of a deck of cards. A flight simulator may use random numbers to determine how often a simulated flight has engine trouble. A program designed to help high school students prepare for the SATs may use random numbers to choose the next question to ask.

The `Random` class, which is part of the `java.util` package, represents a *pseudorandom number generator*. A random number generator picks a number at random out of a range of values. Program code that serves this role is technically pseudorandom, because a program has no means to actually pick a number randomly. A pseudorandom number generator performs a series of complicated calculations, based on an initial *seed value*, and produces a number. Though they are technically not random (because they are calculated), the values produced by a pseudorandom number generator usually appear random, at least random enough for most situations.

> **KEY CONCEPT**
>
> A pseudorandom number generator performs a complex calculation to create the illusion of randomness.

Figure 3.3 lists some of the methods of the `Random` class. The `nextInt` method can be called with no parameters, or we can pass it a single integer value. If no parameter is passed in, the `nextInt` method generates a random number across the entire range of `int` values, including negative numbers. Usually, though, we need a random number within a more specific range. For instance, to simulate the roll of a die, we might want a random number in the range of 1 to 6. The `nextInt` method returns a value that's in the range from 0 to one less than its parameter. For example, if we pass 100 as a parameter to `nextInt`, we'll get a return value that is greater than or equal to 0 and less than or equal to 99.

Note that the value that we pass to the `nextInt` method is also the number of possible values we can get in return. We can shift the range as needed by adding

Random ()
    Constructor: creates a new pseudorandom number generator.

float nextFloat ()
    Returns a random number between 0.0 (inclusive) and 1.0 (exclusive).

int nextInt ()
    Returns a random number that ranges over all possible int values (positive
    and negative).

int nextInt (int num)
    Returns a random number in the range 0 to num−1.

FIGURE 3.3   Some methods of the Random class

or subtracting the proper amount. To get a random number in the range of 1 to 6, we can call nextInt(6) to get a value from 0 to 5, and then add 1.

The nextFloat method of the Random class returns a float value that is greater than or equal to 0.0 and less than 1.0. If desired, we can use multiplication to scale the result, cast it into an int value to truncate the fractional part, and then shift the range as we do with integers.

The program shown in Listing 3.2 produces several random numbers in various ranges.

LISTING 3.2

```
//********************************************************************
//   RandomNumbers.java        Java Foundations
//
//   Demonstrates the creation of pseudo-random numbers using the
//   Random class.
//********************************************************************

import java.util.Random;

public class RandomNumbers
{
    //-----------------------------------------------------------------
    //   Generates random numbers in various ranges.
    //-----------------------------------------------------------------
```

LISTING 3.2   *continued*

```java
public static void main (String[] args)
{
   Random generator = new Random();
   int num1;
   float num2;

   num1 = generator.nextInt();
   System.out.println ("A random integer: " + num1);

   num1 = generator.nextInt(10);
   System.out.println ("From 0 to 9: " + num1);

   num1 = generator.nextInt(10) + 1;
   System.out.println ("From 1 to 10: " + num1);

   num1 = generator.nextInt(15) + 20;
   System.out.println ("From 20 to 34: " + num1);

   num1 = generator.nextInt(20) - 10;
   System.out.println ("From -10 to 9: " + num1);

   num2 = generator.nextFloat();
   System.out.println ("A random float (between 0-1): " + num2);

   num2 = generator.nextFloat() * 6;   // 0.0 to 5.999999
   num1 = (int)num2 + 1;
   System.out.println ("From 1 to 6: " + num1);
}
}
```

OUTPUT

```
A random integer: 243057344
From 0 to 9: 9
From 1 to 10: 2
From 20 to 34: 33
From -10 to 9: -4
A random float (between 0-1): 0.58384484
From 1 to 6: 3
```

3.5 The Math Class

The Math class provides a large number of basic mathematical functions that are often helpful in making calculations. The Math class is defined in the java.lang package of the Java standard class library. Figure 3.4 lists several of its methods.

```
static int abs (int num)
    Returns the absolute value of num.

static double acos (double num)

static double asin (double num)

static double atan (double num)
    Returns the arc cosine, arc sine, or arc tangent of num.

static double cos (double angle)

static double sin (double angle)

static double tan (double angle)
    Returns the angle cosine, sine, or tangent of angle, which is measured in
    radians.

static double ceil (double num)
    Returns the ceiling of num, which is the smallest whole number greater than or
    equal to num.

static double exp (double power)
    Returns the value e raised to the specified power.

static double floor (double num)
    Returns the floor of num, which is the largest whole number less than or equal
    to num.

static double pow (double num, double power)
    Returns the value num raised to the specified power.

static double random ()
    Returns a random number between 0.0 (inclusive) and 1.0 (exclusive).

static double sqrt (double num)
    Returns the square root of num, which must be positive.
```

FIGURE 3.4 Some methods of the Math class

All the methods in the `Math` class are *static methods* (also called *class methods*), which means they can be invoked through the name of the class in which they are defined, without having to instantiate an object of the class first. Static methods are discussed further in Chapter 5.

The methods of the `Math` class return values, which can be used in expressions as needed. For example, the following statement computes the absolute value of the number stored in `total`, adds it to the value of `count` raised to the fourth power, and stores the result in the variable `value`:

```
value = Math.abs(total) + Math.pow(count, 4);
```

Note that you can pass an integer value to a method that accepts a `double` parameter. This is a form of assignment conversion, which was discussed in Chapter 2.

It's also interesting to note that the `Math` class contains a method called `random` that returns a random floating point value in the range 0.0 to 1.0. Therefore, this method could be used as an alternative to creating a `Random` object and calling its methods, as described in the previous section. However, the `Math` class does not have a method that returns an integer, or lets you specify the range of the result, as `Random` does.

The `Quadratic` program, shown in Listing 3.3, uses the `Math` class to compute the roots of a quadratic equation. Recall that a quadratic equation has the following general form:

$$ax^2 + bx + c$$

LISTING 3.3

```java
//********************************************************************
//   Quadratic.java      Java Foundations
//
//   Demonstrates the use of the Math class to perform a calculation
//   based on user input.
//********************************************************************

import java.util.Scanner;

public class Quadratic
{
    //-----------------------------------------------------------------
    //   Determines the roots of a quadratic equation.
    //-----------------------------------------------------------------
    public static void main (String[] args)
```

LISTING 3.3   *continued*

```
    {
        int a, b, c; // ax^2 + bx + c
        double discriminant, root1, root2;

        Scanner scan = new Scanner (System.in);

        System.out.print ("Enter the coefficient of x squared: ");
        a = scan.nextInt();

        System.out.print ("Enter the coefficient of x: ");
        b = scan.nextInt();

        System.out.print ("Enter the constant: ");
        c = scan.nextInt();

        // Use the quadratic formula to compute the roots.
        // Assumes a positive discriminant.

        discriminant = Math.pow(b, 2) - (4 * a * c);
        root1 = ((-1 * b) + Math.sqrt(discriminant)) / (2 * a);
        root2 = ((-1 * b) - Math.sqrt(discriminant)) / (2 * a);

        System.out.println ("Root #1: " + root1);
        System.out.println ("Root #2: " + root2);
    }
}
```

OUTPUT

```
Enter the coefficient of x squared: 3
Enter the coefficient of x: 8
Enter the constant: 4
Root #1: -0.6666666666666666
Root #2: -2.0
```

The `Quadratic` program reads values that represent the coefficients in a quadratic equation (a, b, and c), and then evaluates the quadratic formula to determine the roots of the equation. The quadratic formula is:

$$\text{roots} = \frac{-b \pm \sqrt{b^2 - 4ac}}{2a}$$

Note that this program assumes that the discriminant (the value under the square root) is positive. If it's not, the result will not be a valid number, which

Java represents as NAN, which stands for Not A Number. In Chapter 5 we discuss how such situations can be avoided.

3.6 Formatting Output

The NumberFormat class and the DecimalFormat class are used to format information so that it looks appropriate when printed or displayed. They are both part of the Java standard class library and are defined in the java.text package.

The NumberFormat Class

The NumberFormat class provides generic formatting capabilities for numbers. You don't instantiate a NumberFormat object by using the new operator. Instead, you request an object from one of its static methods that you invoke through the class name itself. Figure 3.5 lists some of the methods of the NumberFormat class.

Two of the methods in the NumberFormat class, getCurrencyInstance and getPercentInstance, return an object that is used to format numbers. The getCurrencyInstance method returns a formatter for monetary values, and the getPercentInstance method returns an object that formats a percentage. The format method is invoked through a formatter object and returns a String that contains the number formatted in the appropriate manner.

The Purchase program shown in Listing 3.4 uses both types of formatters. It reads in a sales transaction and computes the final price, including tax.

The getCurrencyInstance and getPercentInstance methods are called *factory methods*, because they produce and return an instance of an object set up in a particular manner. So, essentially, a NumberFormat factory method uses the new operator to create a NumberFormat object, then sets up the object to format values in a particular way and returns it so that it can be used.

```
String format (double number)
   Returns a string containing the specified number formatted according to this
   object's pattern.

static NumberFormat getCurrencyInstance()
   Returns a NumberFormat object that represents a currency format for the
   current locale.

static NumberFormat getPercentInstance()
   Returns a NumberFormat object that represents a percentage format for the
   current locale.
```

FIGURE 3.5 Some methods of the NumberFormat class

LISTING 3.4

```java
//********************************************************************
//   Purchase.java        Java Foundations
//
//   Demonstrates the use of the NumberFormat class to format output.
//********************************************************************

import java.util.Scanner;
import java.text.NumberFormat;

public class Purchase
{
   //-----------------------------------------------------------------
   //  Calculates the final price of a purchased item using values
   //  entered by the user.
   //-----------------------------------------------------------------
   public static void main (String[] args)
   {
      final double TAX_RATE = 0.06; // 6% sales tax

      int quantity;
      double subtotal, tax, totalCost, unitPrice;

      Scanner scan = new Scanner (System.in);

      NumberFormat fmt1 = NumberFormat.getCurrencyInstance();
      NumberFormat fmt2 = NumberFormat.getPercentInstance();

      System.out.print ("Enter the quantity: ");
      quantity = scan.nextInt();

      System.out.print ("Enter the unit price: ");
      unitPrice = scan.nextDouble();

      subtotal = quantity * unitPrice;
      tax = subtotal * TAX_RATE;
      totalCost = subtotal + tax;

      // Print output with appropriate formatting
      System.out.println ("Subtotal: " + fmt1.format(subtotal));
      System.out.println ("Tax: " + fmt1.format(tax) + " at "
                          + fmt2.format(TAX_RATE));
      System.out.println ("Total: " + fmt1.format(totalCost));
   }
}
```

LISTING 3.4   *continued*

OUTPUT

```
Enter the quantity: 6
Enter the unit price: 1.69
Subtotal: $10.14
Tax: $0.61 at 6%
Total: $10.75
```

The `DecimalFormat` Class

Unlike the `NumberFormat` class, the `DecimalFormat` class is instantiated in the traditional way using the `new` operator. Its constructor takes a `String` parameter that represents the pattern that will guide the formatting process. We can then use the `format` method to format a particular value. At a later point, if we want to change the pattern that the formatter object uses, we can invoke the `applyPattern` method. Figure 3.6 describes these methods.

The pattern defined by the string that is passed to the `DecimalFormat` constructor can get fairly elaborate. Various symbols are used to represent particular formatting guidelines. The pattern defined by the string `"0.###"`, for example, indicates that at least one digit should be printed to the left of the decimal point and should be a zero if the integer portion of the value is zero. It also indicates that the fractional portion of the value should be rounded to three digits.

This pattern is used in the `CircleStats` program, shown in Listing 3.5, which reads the radius of a circle from the user and computes the circle's area

```
DecimalFormat (String pattern)
    Constructor:  creates a new DecimalFormat object with the specified pattern.

void applyPattern (String pattern)
    Applies the specified pattern to this DecimalFormat object.

String format (double number)
    Returns a string containing the specified number formatted according to the
    current pattern.
```

FIGURE 3.6 Some methods of the `DecimalFormat` class

LISTING 3.5

```java
//********************************************************************
//  CircleStats.java       Java Foundations
//
//  Demonstrates the formatting of decimal values using the
//  DecimalFormat class.
//********************************************************************

import java.util.Scanner;
import java.text.DecimalFormat;

public class CircleStats
{
    //-----------------------------------------------------------------
    //  Calculates the area and circumference of a circle given its
    //  radius.
    //-----------------------------------------------------------------
    public static void main (String[] args)
    {
        int radius;
        double area, circumference;

        Scanner scan = new Scanner (System.in);

        System.out.print ("Enter the circle's radius: ");
        radius = scan.nextInt();

        area = Math.PI * Math.pow(radius, 2);
        circumference = 2 * Math.PI * radius;

        // Round the output to three decimal places
        DecimalFormat fmt = new DecimalFormat ("0.###");

        System.out.println ("The circle's area: " + fmt.format(area));
        System.out.println ("The circle's circumference: "
                            + fmt.format(circumference));
    }
}
```

OUTPUT

```
Enter the circle's radius: 5
The circle's area: 78.54
The circle's circumference: 31.416
```

and circumference. Trailing zeros, such as in the circle's area of 78.540, are not printed using this pattern.

The `printf` Method

In addition to `print` and `println`, the `System` class has another output method called `printf`, which allows the user to print a formatted string containing data values. The first parameter to the method represents the format string, and the remaining parameters specify the values that are inserted into the format string.

For example, the following line of code prints an ID number and a name:

```
System.out.printf ("ID: %5d\tName: %s", id, name);
```

The first parameter specifies the format of the output and includes literal characters that label the output values as well as escape characters such as `\t`. The pattern `%5d` indicates that the corresponding numeric value (`id`) should be printed in a field of five characters. The pattern `%s` matches the string parameter `name`. The values of `id` and `name` are inserted into the string, producing a result such as:

```
ID: 24036 Name: Larry Flagelhopper
```

The `printf` method was added to Java to mirror a similar function used in programs written in the C programming language. This makes it easier for a programmer to translate (or *migrate*) an existing C program into Java.

Older software that still has value is called a *legacy system*. Maintaining a legacy system is often a costly effort because, among other things, it is based on older technologies. But in many cases, maintaining a legacy system is still more cost-effective than migrating it to new technology, such as writing it in a newer language. Adding the `printf` method is an attempt to make such migrations easier, and therefore less costly, by providing the same kind of output statement that C programmers have come to rely on.

> **KEY CONCEPT**
>
> The `printf` method was added to Java to support the migration of legacy systems.

However, using the `printf` method is not a particularly clean object-oriented solution to the problem of formatting output, so we avoid its use in this book.

3.7 Enumerated Types

Java provides the ability to define an *enumerated type*, which can then be used as the type of a variable when it is declared. An enumerated type establishes all possible values of a variable of that type by listing, or enumerating, them. The values are identifiers, and can be anything desired.

For example, the following declaration defines an enumerated type called `Season` whose possible values are `winter`, `spring`, `summer`, and `fall`:

```
enum Season {winter, spring, summer, fall}
```

There is no limit to the number of values that you can list for an enumerated type. Once the type is defined, a variable can be declared of that type:

```
Season time;
```

> **KEY CONCEPT**
> Enumerated types are type-safe, ensuring that invalid values will not be used.

The variable `time` is now restricted in the values it can take on. It can hold one of the four `Season` values, but nothing else. Java enumerated types are considered to be *type-safe*, meaning that any attempt to use a value other than one of the enumerated values will result in a compile-time error.

The values are accessed through the name of the type. For example:

```
time = Season.spring;
```

Enumerated types can be quite helpful in situations in which you have a relatively small number of distinct values that a variable can assume. For example, suppose we wanted to represent the various letter grades a student could earn. We might declare the following enumerated type:

```
enum Grade {A, B, C, D, F}
```

Any initialized variable that holds a `Grade` is guaranteed to have one of those valid grades. That's better than using a simple character or `String` variable to represent the grade, which could take on any value.

Suppose we also wanted to represent plus and minus grades, such as A– and B+. We couldn't use A– or B+ as values, because they are not valid identifiers (the characters `'–'` and `'+'` cannot be part of an identifier in Java). However, the same values could be represented using the identifiers `Aminus`, `Bplus`, etc.

Internally, each value in an enumerated type is stored as an integer, which is referred to as its *ordinal value*. The first value in an enumerated type has an ordinal value of 0, the second one has an ordinal value of 1, the third one 2, and so on. The ordinal values are used internally only. You cannot assign a numeric value to an enumerated type, even if it corresponds to a valid ordinal value.

An enumerated type is a special kind of class, and the variables of an enumerated type are object variables. As such, there are a few methods associated with all enumerated types. The `ordinal` method returns the numeric value associated with a particular enumerated type value. The `name` method returns the name of the value, which is the same as the identifier that defines the value.

Listing 3.6 on the next page shows a program called `IceCream` that declares an enumerated type and exercises some of its methods. Because enumerated types are special types of classes, they are not defined within a method. They can be defined

LISTING   3.6

```java
//********************************************************************
//  IceCream.java         Java Foundations
//
//  Demonstrates the use of enumerated types.
//********************************************************************

public class IceCream
{
  enum Flavor {vanilla, chocolate, strawberry, fudgeRipple, coffee,
               rockyRoad, mintChocolateChip, cookieDough}

  //-----------------------------------------------------------------
  //  Creates and uses variables of the Flavor type.
  //-----------------------------------------------------------------
  public static void main (String[] args)
  {
    Flavor cone1, cone2, cone3;

    cone1 = Flavor.rockyRoad;
    cone2 = Flavor.chocolate;

    System.out.println ("cone1 value: " + cone1);
    System.out.println ("cone1 ordinal: " + cone1.ordinal());
    System.out.println ("cone1 name: " + cone1.name());

    System.out.println ();
    System.out.println ("cone2 value: " + cone2);
    System.out.println ("cone2 ordinal: " + cone2.ordinal());
    System.out.println ("cone2 name: " + cone2.name());

    cone3 = cone1;

    System.out.println ();
    System.out.println ("cone3 value: " + cone3);
    System.out.println ("cone3 ordinal: " + cone3.ordinal());
    System.out.println ("cone3 name: " + cone3.name());
  }
}
```

LISTING 3.6   *continued*

OUTPUT

```
cone1 value: rockyRoad
cone1 ordinal: 5
cone1 name: rockyRoad

cone2 value: chocolate
cone2 ordinal: 1
cone2 name: chocolate

cone3 value: rockyRoad
cone3 ordinal: 5
cone3 name: rockyRoad
```

either at the class level (within the class but outside a method), as in this example, or at the outermost level.

3.8 Wrapper Classes

As we've discussed previously, Java represents data by using primitive types (such as `int`, `double`, `char`, and `boolean`) in addition to classes and objects. Having two categories of data to manage (primitive values and object references) can present a challenge in some circumstances. There are times when you may want to treat primitive data as if they were objects. In these cases we need to "wrap" a primitive value into an object.

A *wrapper class* represents a particular primitive type. For instance, the `Integer` class represents a simple integer value. An object created from the `Integer` class stores a single `int` value. The constructors of the wrapper classes accept the primitive value to store. For example:

```
Integer ageObj = new Integer(40);
```

Once this declaration and instantiation are performed, the `ageObj` object effectively represents the integer 40 as an object. It can be used wherever an object is needed in a program rather than a primitive type.

> **KEY CONCEPT**
> A wrapper class allows a primitive value to be managed as an object.

For each primitive type in Java there exists a corresponding wrapper class in the Java class library. All wrapper classes are defined in the `java.lang` package. Figure 3.7 on the next page shows the wrapper class that corresponds to each primitive type.

Primitive Type	Wrapper Class
byte	Byte
short	Short
int	Integer
long	Long
float	Float
double	Double
char	Character
boolean	Boolean
void	Void

FIGURE 3.7 Wrapper classes in the `java.lang` package

Note that there is even a wrapper class that represents the type void. However, unlike the other wrapper classes, the Void class cannot be instantiated. It simply represents the concept of a void reference.

Wrapper classes also provide various methods related to the management of the associated primitive type. For example, the Integer class contains methods that return the int value stored in the object and that convert the stored value to other primitive types. Figure 3.8 lists some of the methods found in the Integer class. The other wrapper classes have similar methods.

```
Integer (int value)
    Constructor: creates a new Integer object storing the specified value.

byte byteValue ()
double doubleValue ()
float floatValue ()
int intValue ()
long longValue ()
    Return the value of this Integer as the corresponding primitive type.

static int parseInt (String str)
    Returns the int corresponding to the value stored in the specified string.

static String toBinaryString (int num)
static String tohexString (int num)
static String toOctalString (int num)
    Returns a string representation of the specified integer value in the
    corresponding base.
```

FIGURE 3.8 Some methods of the Integer class

Note that the wrapper classes also contain static methods that can be invoked independent of any instantiated object. For example, the `Integer` class contains a static method called `parseInt` that converts an integer that is stored in a `String` to its corresponding `int` value. If the `String` object `str` holds the string `"987"`, the following line of code converts the string into the integer value `987` and stores that value in the `int` variable num:

```
num = Integer.parseInt(str);
```

The Java wrapper classes often contain static constants that are helpful as well. For example, the `Integer` class contains two constants, `MIN_VALUE` and `MAX_VALUE`, that hold the smallest and largest `int` values, respectively. The other wrapper classes contain similar constants for their types.

Autoboxing

Autoboxing is the automatic conversion between a primitive value and a corresponding wrapper object. For example, in the following code, an `int` value is assigned to an `Integer` object reference variable:

```
Integer obj1;
int num1 = 69;
obj1 = num1;  // automatically creates an Integer object
```

The reverse conversion, called *unboxing*, also occurs automatically when needed. For example:

```
Integer obj2 = new Integer(69);
int num2;
num2 = obj2;  // automatically extracts the int value
```

Assignments between primitive types and object types are generally incompatible. The ability to autobox occurs only between primitive types and corresponding wrapper classes. In any other case, attempting to assign a primitive value to an object reference variable, or vice versa, will cause a compile-time error.

> **KEY CONCEPT**
>
> Autoboxing provides automatic conversions between primitive values and corresponding wrapper objects.

Summary of Key Concepts

- The `new` operator returns a reference to a newly created object.
- Multiple reference variables can refer to the same object.
- Methods are often executed on a particular object, and that object's state usually affects the results.
- A class library provides useful support when developing programs.
- The Java standard class library is organized into packages.
- All classes of the `java.lang` package are automatically imported for every program.
- A pseudorandom number generator performs a complex calculation to create the illusion of randomness.
- All methods of the `Math` class are static, meaning they are invoked through the class name.
- The `printf` method was added to Java to support the migration of legacy systems.
- Enumerated types are type-safe, ensuring that invalid values will not be used.
- A wrapper class allows a primitive value to be managed as an object.
- Autoboxing provides automatic conversions between primitive values and corresponding wrapper objects.

Self-Review Questions

SR 3.1   What does the `new` operator accomplish?

SR 3.2   What is a null reference?

SR 3.3   What is an alias? How does it relate to garbage collection?

SR 3.4   Write a declaration for a `String` variable called `author` and initialize it to the string `"Fred Brooks"`. Draw a graphic representation of the variable and its value.

SR 3.5   Write a statement that prints the value of a `String` object called `title` in all uppercase letters.

SR 3.6   Write a declaration for a `String` variable called `front` and initialize it to the first 10 characters of another `String` object called `description`.

SR 3.7   What is a Java package?

SR 3.8   What does the `java.net` package contain? The `java.swing` package?

SR 3.9   What package contains the `Scanner` class? The `String` class? The `Random` class? The `Math` class?

SR 3.10   What does an `import` declaration accomplish?

SR 3.11   Why doesn't the `String` class have to be specifically imported into our programs?

SR 3.12   Given a `Random` object called `rand`, what does the call `rand.nextInt()` return?

SR 3.13   Given a `Random` object called `rand`, what does the call `rand.nextInt(20)` return?

SR 3.14   What is a class method (also called a static method)?

SR 3.15   Write a statement that prints the sine of an angle measuring 1.23 radians.

SR 3.16   Write a declaration for a `double` variable called `result` and initialize it to 5 raised to the power 2.5.

SR 3.17   What are the steps to output a floating point value as a percentage using Java's formatting classes?

SR 3.18   Write the declaration of an enumerated type that represents movie ratings.

SR 3.19   How can we represent a primitive value as an object?

Exercises

EX 3.1   Write a statement that prints the number of characters in a `String` object called `overview`.

EX 3.2   Write a statement that prints the eighth character of a `String` object called `introduction`.

EX 3.3   Write a declaration for a `String` variable called `change` and initialize it to the characters stored in another `String` object called `original` with all `'e'` characters changed to `'j'`.

EX 3.4   What output is produced by the following code fragment?

```
String m1, m2, m3;
m1 = "Quest for the Holy Grail";
m2 = m1.toLowerCase();
m3 = m1 + " " + m2;
System.out.println (m3.replace('h', 'z'));
```

EX 3.5   What is the effect of the following `import` declaration?

```
import java.awt.*;
```

EX 3.6   Assuming that a `Random` object has been created called `generator`, what is the range of the result of each of the following expressions?

a. `generator.nextInt(20)`

b. `generator.nextInt(8) + 1`

c. `generator.nextInt(45) + 10`

d. `generator.nextInt(100) − 50`

EX 3.7   Write code to declare and instantiate an object of the `Random` class (call the object reference variable `rand`). Then write a list of expressions using the `nextInt` method that generates random numbers in the following specified ranges, including the end points. Use the version of the `nextInt` method that accepts a single integer parameter.

a. 0 to 10

b. 0 to 500

c. 1 to 10

d. 1 to 500

e. 25 to 50

f. −10 to 15

EX 3.8   Write an assignment statement that computes the square root of the sum of `num1` and `num2` and assigns the result to `num3`.

EX 3.9   Write a single statement that computes and prints the absolute value of `total`.

EX 3.10   Write code statements to create a `DecimalFormat` object that will round a formatted value to four decimal places. Then write a statement that uses that object to print the value of the result, properly formatted.

EX 3.11   Write code statements that prompt for and read a `double` value from the user, and then print the result of raising that value to the fourth power. Output the results to three decimal places.

EX 3.12   Write a declaration for an enumerated type that represents the days of the week.

Programming Projects

PP 3.1   Write an application that prompts for and reads the user's first and last name (separately). Then print a string composed of the first letter of the user's first name, followed by the first five characters of the user's last name, followed by a random number in the range 10 to 99. Assume that the last name is at least five letters long. Similar algorithms are sometimes used to generate usernames for new computer accounts.

PP 3.2   Write an application that prints the sum of cubes. Prompt for and read two integer values and print the sum of each value raised to the third power.

PP 3.3   Write an application that creates and prints a random phone number of the form XXX-XXX-XXXX. Include the dashes in the output. Do not let the first three digits contain an 8 or 9 (but don't be more restrictive than that), and make sure that the second set of three digits is not greater than 742. *Hint:* Think through the easiest way to construct the phone number. Each digit does not have to be determined separately.

PP 3.4   Write an application that reads the (x,y) coordinates for two points. Compute the distance between the two points using the following formula:

$$\text{Distance} = \sqrt{(x_2 - x_1)^2 + (y_2 - y_1)^2}$$

PP 3.5   Write an application that reads the radius of a sphere and prints its volume and surface area. Use the following formulas, in which r represents the sphere's radius. Print the output to four decimal places.

$$\text{Volume} = \frac{4}{3}\pi r^3$$

$$\text{Surface area} = 4\pi r^2$$

PP 3.6   Write an application that reads the lengths of the sides of a triangle from the user. Compute the area of the triangle using Heron's formula (below), in which s represents half of the perimeter of the triangle, and a, b, and c represent the lengths of the three sides. Print the area to three decimal places.

$$\text{Area} = \sqrt{s(s - a)(s - b)(s - c)}$$

myCodeMate

Answers to Self-Review Questions

SR 3.1   The new operator creates a new instance (an object) of the specified class. The constructor of the class is then invoked to help set
up the newly created object.

SR 3.2   A null reference is a reference that does not refer to any object.
The reserved word null can be used to check for null references
to avoid following them.

SR 3.3   Two references are aliases of each other if they refer to the same
object. Changing the state of the object through one reference
changes it for the other because there is actually only one object.
An object is marked for garbage collection only when there are
no valid references to it.

SR 3.4   The following declaration creates a String variable called
author and initializes it:

```
String author = new String ("Fred Brooks");
```

For strings, this declaration could have been abbreviated as follows:

```
String author = "Fred Brooks";
```

This object reference variable and its value can be depicted as
follows:

SR 3.5   The following statement prints the value of a String object in all
uppercase letters:

```
System.out.println (title.toUpperCase());
```

SR 3.6   The following declaration creates a String object and sets it equal
to the first 10 characters of the String called description:

```
String front = description.substring(0, 10);
```

SR 3.7   A Java package is a collection of related classes. The Java standard class library is a group of packages that supports common
programming tasks.

SR 3.8   Each package contains a set of classes that supports particular programming activities. The classes in the `java.net` package support network communication, and the classes in the `javax.swing` class support the development of graphical user interfaces.

SR 3.9   The `Scanner` class and the `Random` class are part of the `java.util` package. The `String` and `Math` classes are part of the `java.lang` package.

SR 3.10   An `import` declaration establishes the fact that a program uses a particular class, specifying the package that the class is a part of. This allows the programmer to use the class name (such as `Random`) without having to fully qualify the reference (such as `java.util.Random`) every time.

SR 3.11   The `String` class is part of the `java.lang` package, which is automatically imported into any Java program. Therefore, no separate `import` declaration is needed.

SR 3.12   A call to the `nextInt` method of a `Random` object returns a random integer in the range of all possible `int` values, both positive and negative.

SR 3.13   Passing a positive integer parameter x to the `nextInt` method of a `Random` object returns a random number in the range of 0 to $x-1$. So a call to `nextInt(20)` will return a random number in the range 0 to 19, inclusive.

SR 3.14   A class (or static) method can be invoked through the name of the class that contains it, such as `Math.abs`. If a method is not static, it can be executed only through an instance (an object) of the class.

SR 3.15   The following statement prints the sine of 1.23 radians:

```
System.out.println (Math.sin(1.23));
```

SR 3.16   The following declaration creates a `double` variable and initializes it to 5 raised to the power 2.5:

```
double result = Math.pow(5, 2.5);
```

SR 3.17   To output a floating point value as a percentage, you first obtain a formatter object using a call to the static method `getPercentInstance` of the `NumberFormat` class. Then you pass the value to be formatted to the `format` method of the formatter object, which returns a properly formatted string. For example:

```
NumberFormat fmt = NumberFormat.getPercentageInstance();
System.out.println (fmt.format(value));
```

SR 3.18   The following is a declaration of an enumerated type for movie ratings:

```
enum Ratings {G, PG, PG13, R, NC17}
```

SR 3.19   A wrapper class is defined in the Java standard class library for each primitive type. In situations where objects are called for, an object created from a wrapper class may suffice.

Conditionals and Loops

CHAPTER OBJECTIVES

- Discuss the flow of control through a method.

- Explore boolean expressions that can be used to make decisions.

- Perform basic decision making using `if` and `switch` statements.

- Discuss issues pertaining to the comparison of certain types of data.

- Execute statements repetitively using `while`, `do`, and `for` loops.

- Discuss the concept of an iterator object and use one to read a text file.

All programming languages have statements that allow you to make decisions to determine what to do next. Some of those statements allow you to repeat a certain activity multiple times. This chapter discusses several such statements, as well as exploring some issues related to comparing data and objects. We begin with a discussion of boolean expressions, which form the basis of any decision.

4.1 Boolean Expressions

The order in which statements are executed in a running program is called the *flow of control*. Unless otherwise specified, the basic execution of a program proceeds in a linear fashion. That is, a running program starts at the first programming statement and moves down one statement at a time until the program is complete. A Java application begins executing with the first line of the main method and proceeds step by step until it gets to the end of the main method.

Invoking a method alters the flow of control. When a method is called, the flow of control jumps to the code defined for that method and it begins executing. When the method completes, control returns to the place in the calling method where the invocation was made and processing continues from there. Methods and their invocation are discussed further in the next chapter.

> **KEY CONCEPT**
>
> Conditionals and loops allow us to control the flow of execution through a method.

Within a given method, we can alter the flow of control through the code by using certain types of programming statements. Statements that control the flow of execution through a method fall into two categories: conditionals and loops.

A *conditional statement* is sometimes called a *selection statement* because it allows us to choose which statement will be executed next. The conditional statements in Java are the if statement, the if-else statement, and the switch statement. These statements allow us to decide which statement to execute next.

Each decision is based on a *boolean expression*, also called a *condition*, which is an expression that evaluates to either true or false. The result of the expression determines which statement is executed next.

The following is an example of an if statement:

```
if (count > 20)
    System.out.println ("Count exceeded");
```

> **KEY CONCEPT**
>
> An if statement allows a program to choose whether to execute a particular statement.

The condition in this statement is count > 20. That expression evaluates to a boolean (true or false) result. Either the value stored in count is greater than 20 or it's not. If it is, the println statement is executed. If it's not, the println statement is skipped and processing continues with whatever code follows it. The if statement and other conditionals are explored in detail in this chapter.

The need to make decisions like this comes up all the time in programming situations. For example, the cost of life insurance might be dependent on whether the insured person is a smoker. If the person smokes, we calculate the cost using a particular formula; if not, we calculate it using another. The role of a conditional statement is to evaluate a boolean condition (whether the person smokes) and then to execute the proper calculation accordingly.

A *loop*, or *repetition statement*, allows us to execute a programming statement over and over again. Like a conditional, a loop is based on a boolean expression that determines how many times the statement is executed.

For example, suppose we wanted to calculate the grade point average of every student in a class. The calculation is the same for each student; it is just performed on different data. We would set up a loop that repeats the calculation for each student until there are no more students to process.

Java has three types of loop statements: the `while` statement, the `do` statement, and the `for` statement. Each type of loop statement has unique characteristics that distinguish it from the others.

All conditionals and loops are based on boolean expressions, which use equality operators, relational operators, and logical operators to make decisions. Before we discuss the details of conditional and loop statements, let's explore these operators.

Equality and Relational Operators

The `==` and `!=` operators are called *equality operators*. They test whether two values are equal or not equal, respectively. Note that the equality operator consists of two equal signs side by side and should not be mistaken for the assignment operator that uses only one equal sign.

The following `if` statement prints a sentence only if the variables `total` and `sum` contain the same value:

```
if (total == sum)
    System.out.println ("total equals sum");
```

Likewise, the following `if` statement prints a sentence only if the variables `total` and `sum` do not contain the same value:

```
if (total != sum)
    System.out.println ("total does NOT equal sum");
```

Java also has several *relational operators* that let us decide the relative ordering between two values. Earlier in this section we used the greater than operator (`>`) to decide if one value was greater than another. We can ask such questions using various operators, depending on the relationship. These include less than (`<`), greater than or equal to (`>=`), and less than or equal to (`<=`). Figure 4.1 lists the Java equality and relational operators.

The equality and relational operators have lower precedence than the arithmetic operators. Therefore, arithmetic operations are evaluated first, followed by equality and relational operations. As always, parentheses can be used to explicitly specify the order of evaluation.

Operator	Meaning
==	equal to
!=	not equal to
<	less than
<=	less than or equal to
>	greater than
>=	greater than or equal to

FIGURE 4.1 Java equality and relational operators

We'll see more examples of relational operators as we examine conditional and loop statements throughout this chapter.

Logical Operators

In addition to the equality and relational operators, Java has three *logical operators* that produce boolean results. They also take boolean operands. Figure 4.2 lists and describes the logical operators.

The ! operator is used to perform the *logical NOT* operation, which is also called the *logical complement*. The ! operator is unary, taking only one boolean operand. The logical complement of a boolean value yields its opposite value. That is, if a `boolean` variable called `found` has the value false, then `!found` is true. Likewise, if `found` is true, then `!found` is false. Note, the logical NOT operation does not change the value stored in `found`—it creates an expression that returns a boolean result.

A logical operation can be described by a *truth table* that lists all possible combinations of values for the variables involved in an expression. Because the logical NOT operator is unary, there are only two possible values for its one operand, true or false. Figure 4.3 shows a truth table that describes the ! operator.

Operator	Description	Example	Result
!	logical NOT	! a	true if a is false and false if a is true
&&	logical AND	a && b	true if a and b are both true and false otherwise
||	logical OR	a || b	true if a or b or both are true and false otherwise

FIGURE 4.2 Java logical operators

a	!a
false	true
true	false

FIGURE 4.3 Truth table describing the logical NOT operator

The `&&` operator performs a *logical AND* operation. The result of an `&&` operation is true if both operands are true, but false otherwise. Compare that to the result of the *logical OR* operator (`||`), which is true if one or the other or both operands are true, but false otherwise.

The AND and OR operators are both binary operators since each uses two operands. Therefore there are four possible combinations to consider: both operands are true, both are false, one is true and the other false, and vice versa. Figure 4.4 depicts a truth table that shows both the `&&` and `||` operators.

The logical NOT has the highest precedence of the three logical operators, followed by logical AND, then logical OR.

The logical operators allow us to create complex expressions when making decisions. Consider the following `if` statement:

```
if (!done && (count > MAX))
    System.out.println ("Completed.");
```

Under what conditions would the `println` statement be executed? The value of the boolean variable `done` is either true or false, and the NOT operator reverses that value. The value of `count` is either greater than `MAX` or it isn't. The truth table in Figure 4.5 breaks down all of the possibilities.

An important characteristic of the `&&` and `||` operators is that they are "short-circuited" in Java. That is, if their left operand is sufficient to decide the boolean result of the operation, the right operand is not

> **KEY CONCEPT**
>
> Logical operators can be used to construct sophisticated conditions.

a	b	a && b	a || b
false	false	false	false
false	true	false	true
true	false	false	true
true	true	true	true

FIGURE 4.4 Truth table describing the logical AND and OR operators

done	count > MAX	!done	!done && (count > MAX)
false	false	true	false
false	true	true	true
true	false	false	false
true	true	false	false

FIGURE 4.5 A truth table for a specific condition

evaluated. This situation can occur with both operators, but for different reasons. If the left operand of the `&&` operator is false, then the result of the operation will be false no matter what the value of the right operand is. Likewise, if the left operand of the `||` operator is true, then the result of the operation is true no matter what the value of the right operand is.

Sometimes you can capitalize on the fact that an operator is short-circuited. For example, the condition in the following `if` statement will not attempt to divide by zero if the left operand is false. If `count` has the value zero, the left side of the `&&` operation is false; therefore the whole expression is false and the right side is not evaluated.

```
if (count != 0 && total/count > MAX)
    System.out.println ("Testing.");
```

You should consider carefully whether or not to rely on these kinds of subtle programming language characteristics. Not all programming languages short-circuit these operations, and such code would produce a divide-by-zero error in those languages. As we have stressed before, you should err on the side of readability. You should always strive to make the logic of your program extremely clear to anyone reading your code.

4.2 The `if` Statement

We've used a basic `if` statement in earlier examples in this chapter. Let's now explore it in detail.

An *if statement* consists of the reserved word `if` followed by a boolean expression, followed by a statement. The condition is enclosed in parentheses and must evaluate to true or false. If the condition is true, the statement is executed and then processing continues with any statement that follows. If the condition is false, the statement controlled by the condition is skipped and processing continues immediately with any statement that follows. Figure 4.6 shows this processing.

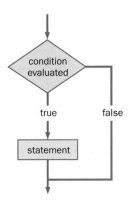

FIGURE 4.6 The logic of an if statement

Consider the following example of an if statement:

```
if (total > amount)
    total = total + (amount + 1);
```

In this example, if the value in total is greater than the value in amount, the assignment statement is executed; otherwise the assignment statement is skipped.

Note that the assignment statement in this example is indented under the header line of the if statement. This communicates to a human reader that the assignment statement is part of the if statement; it implies that the if statement governs whether the assignment statement will be executed. This indentation is extremely important for human readability, although it is ignored by the compiler.

The example in Listing 4.1 reads the age of the user and then makes a decision as to whether to print a particular sentence based on the age that is entered.

The Age program echoes the age value that is entered in all cases. If the age is less than the value of the constant MINOR, the statement about youth is printed. If the age is equal to or greater than the value of MINOR, the println statement is skipped. In either case, the final sentence about age being a state of mind is printed.

Let's look at a few more examples of basic if statements. The following if statement causes the variable size to be set to zero if its current value is greater than or equal to the value in the constant MAX:

```
if (size >= MAX)
    size = 0;
```

The condition of the following if statement first adds three values together, then compares the result to the value stored in numBooks:

```
if (numBooks < stackCount + inventoryCount + duplicateCount)
    reorder = true;
```

LISTING 4.1

```java
//********************************************************************
//  Age.java          Java Foundations
//
//  Demonstrates the use of an if statement.
//********************************************************************

import java.util.Scanner;

public class Age
{
    //-----------------------------------------------------------------
    //  Reads the user's age and prints comments accordingly.
    //-----------------------------------------------------------------
    public static void main (String[] args)
    {
        final int MINOR = 21;

        Scanner scan = new Scanner (System.in);

        System.out.print ("Enter your age: ");
        int age = scan.nextInt();

        System.out.println ("You entered: " + age);

        if (age < MINOR)
            System.out.println ("Youth is a wonderful thing. Enjoy.");

        System.out.println ("Age is a state of mind.");
    }
}
```

OUTPUT

```
Enter your age: 43
You entered: 43
Age is a state of mind.
```

If numBooks is less than the other three values combined, the boolean variable reorder is set to true. The addition operations are performed before the less than operator because the arithmetic operators have a higher precedence than the relational operators.

Assuming the variable `generator` refers to an object of the `Random` class, the following `if` statement examines the value returned from a call to `nextInt` to determine a random winner:

```
if (generator.nextInt(CHANCE) == 0)
    System.out.println ("You are a randomly selected winner!");
```

The odds of this code picking a winner are based on the value of the `CHANCE` constant. That is, if `CHANCE` contains `20`, the odds of winning are 1 in 20. The fact that the condition is looking for a return value of `0` is arbitrary; any value between `0` and `CHANCE-1` would have worked.

The `if-else` Statement

Sometimes we want to do one thing if a condition is true and another thing if that condition is false. We can add an *else clause* to an `if` statement, making it an *if-else* statement, to handle this kind of situation. The following is an example of an if-else statement:

```
if (height <= MAX)
    adjustment = 0;
else
    adjustment = MAX - height;
```

If Statement

An `if` statement tests the boolean Expression and, if true, executes the first Statement. The optional `else` clause identifies the Statement that should be executed if the Expression is false.

Examples:

```
if (total < 7)
    System.out.println ("Total is less than 7.");

if (firstCh != 'a')
    count++;
else
    count = count / 2;
```

If the condition is true, the first assignment statement is executed; if the condition is false, the second assignment statement is executed. Only one or the other will be executed, because a boolean condition evaluates to either true or false. Note that proper indentation is used again to communicate that the statements are part of the governing if statement.

The Wages program shown in Listing 4.2 uses an if-else statement to compute the proper payment amount for an employee.

LISTING 4.2

```java
//********************************************************************
//  Wages.java          Java Foundations
//
//  Demonstrates the use of an if-else statement.
//********************************************************************

import java.text.NumberFormat;
import java.util.Scanner;

public class Wages
{
   //-----------------------------------------------------------------
   //  Reads the number of hours worked and calculates wages.
   //-----------------------------------------------------------------
   public static void main (String[] args)
   {
      final double RATE = 8.25;  // regular pay rate
      final int STANDARD = 40;   // standard hours in a work week

      Scanner scan = new Scanner (System.in);

      double pay = 0.0;

      System.out.print ("Enter the number of hours worked: ");
      int hours = scan.nextInt();

      System.out.println ();

      // Pay overtime at "time and a half"
      if (hours > STANDARD)
         pay = STANDARD * RATE + (hours-STANDARD) * (RATE * 1.5);
      else
         pay = hours * RATE;
```

LISTING 4.2 *continued*

```
        NumberFormat fmt = NumberFormat.getCurrencyInstance();
        System.out.println ("Gross earnings: " + fmt.format(pay));
    }
}
```

OUTPUT

```
Enter the number of hours worked: 46

Gross earnings: $404.25
```

In the Wages program, if an employee works over 40 hours in a week, the payment amount takes into account the overtime hours. An if-else statement is used to determine whether the number of hours entered by the user is greater than 40. If it is, the overtime hours are paid at a rate one and a half times the normal rate. If there are no overtime hours, the total payment is based simply on the number of hours worked and the standard rate.

Let's look at another example of an if-else statement:

```
if (roster.getSize() == FULL)
    roster.expand();
else
    roster.addName (name);
```

This example makes use of an object called roster. Even without knowing what roster represents, or from what class it was created, we can see that it has at least three methods: getSize, expand, and addName. The condition of the if statement calls getSize and compares the result to the constant FULL. If the condition is true, the expand method is invoked (apparently to expand the size of the roster). If the roster is not yet full, the variable name is passed as a parameter to the addName method.

Using Block Statements

We may want to do more than one thing as the result of evaluating a boolean condition. In Java, we can replace any single statement with a *block statement*. A block statement is a collection of statements enclosed in braces. We've used these braces many times in previous examples to delimit method and class definitions.

The program called Guessing, shown in Listing 4.3, uses an if-else statement in which the statement of the else clause is a block statement.

LISTING 4.3

```java
//********************************************************************
//  Guessing.java         Java Foundations
//
//  Demonstrates the use of a block statement in an if-else.
//********************************************************************

import java.util.*;

public class Guessing
{
   //-----------------------------------------------------------------
   //  Plays a simple guessing game with the user.
   //-----------------------------------------------------------------
   public static void main (String[] args)
   {
      final int MAX = 10;
      int answer, guess;

      Scanner scan = new Scanner (System.in);
      Random generator = new Random();

      answer = generator.nextInt(MAX) + 1;

      System.out.print ("I'm thinking of a number between 1 and "
                        + MAX + ". Guess what it is: ");

      guess = scan.nextInt();

      if (guess == answer)
         System.out.println ("You got it! Good guessing!");
      else
      {
         System.out.println ("That is not correct, sorry.");
         System.out.println ("The number was " + answer);
      }
   }
}
```

OUTPUT

```
I'm thinking of a number between 1 and 10. Guess what it is: 4
That is not correct, sorry.
The number was 8
```

If the guess entered by the user equals the randomly chosen answer, an appropriate acknowledgement is printed. However, if the answer is incorrect, two sentences are printed, one that states that the guess is wrong and one that prints the actual answer. A programming project at the end of this chapter expands the basic idea in this example into the Hi-Lo game.

Note that if the block braces were not used, the sentence stating that the answer is incorrect would be printed if the answer was wrong, but the sentence revealing the correct answer would be printed in all cases. That is, only the first statement would be considered part of the else clause.

Remember that indentation means nothing except to the human reader. Statements that are not blocked properly can lead to the programmer making improper assumptions about how the code will execute. For example, the following code is misleading:

```
if (depth > 36.238)
    delta = 100;
else
    System.out.println ("WARNING: Delta is being reset to ZERO");
    delta = 0;  // not part of the else clause!
```

The indentation (not to mention the logic of the code) implies that the variable delta is reset only when depth is less than 36.238. However, without using a block, the assignment statement that resets delta to zero is not governed by the if-else statement at all. It is executed in either case, which is clearly not what is intended.

A block statement can be used anywhere a single statement is called for in Java syntax. For example, the if portion of an if-else statement could be a block, or the else portion could be a block (as we saw in the Guessing program), or both parts could be block statements. For example:

```
if (boxes != warehouse.getCount())
{
    System.out.println ("Inventory and warehouse do NOT match.");
    System.out.println ("Beginning inventory process again!");
    boxes = 0;
}
else
{
    System.out.println ("Inventory and warehouse MATCH.");
    warehouse.ship();
}
```

In this if-else statement, the value of boxes is compared to a value obtained by calling the getCount method of the warehouse object (whatever that is). If they do not match exactly, two println statements and an assignment statement are executed. If they do match, a different message is printed and the `ship` method of `warehouse` is invoked.

The Conditional Operator

The Java *conditional operator* is similar to an `if-else` statement in some ways. It is a *ternary operator* because it requires three operands. The symbol for the conditional operator is usually written `?:`, but it is not like other operators in that the two symbols that make it up are always separated. The following is an example of an expression that contains the conditional operator:

```
(total > MAX) ? total + 1 : total * 2;
```

Preceding the `?` is a boolean condition. Following the `?` are two expressions separated by the `:` symbol. The entire conditional expression returns the value of the first expression if the condition is true, and returns the value of the second expression if the condition is false.

Keep in mind that this is an expression that returns a value, and usually we want to do something with that value, such as assign it to a variable:

```
total = (total > MAX) ? total + 1 : total * 2;
```

In many ways, the `?:` operator serves like an abbreviated `if-else` statement. The previous statement is functionally equivalent to, but sometimes more convenient than, the following:

```
if (total > MAX)
    total = total + 1;
else
    total = total * 2;
```

Now consider the following declaration:

```
int larger = (num1 > num2) ? num1 : num2;
```

If `num1` is greater than `num2`, the value of `num1` is returned and used to initialize the variable `larger`. If not, the value of `num2` is returned and used to initialize `larger`. Similarly, the following statement prints the smaller of the two values:

```
System.out.print ("Smaller: " + ((num1 < num2) ? num1 : num2));
```

As we've seen, the conditional operator is occasionally helpful. However, it is not a replacement for an `if-else` statement because the operands to the `?:` operator are expressions, not necessarily full statements. And even when the conditional operator is a viable alternative, you should use it carefully because it may be less readable than an `if-else` statement.

Nested `if` Statements

The statement executed as the result of an `if` statement could be another `if` statement. This situation is called a *nested if*. It allows us to make another decision after determining the results of a previous decision. The program in Listing 4.4, called `MinOfThree`, uses nested `if` statements to determine the smallest of three integer values entered by the user.

Carefully trace the logic of the `MinOfThree` program, using various input sets with the minimum value in all three positions, to see how it determines the lowest value.

An important situation arises with nested `if` statements. It may seem that an `else` clause after a nested `if` could apply to either `if` statement. For example:

```
if (code == 'R')
    if (height <= 20)
        System.out.println ("Situation Normal");
    else
        System.out.println ("Bravo!");
```

Is the `else` clause matched to the inner `if` statement or the outer `if` statement? The indentation in this example implies that it is part of the inner `if` statement, and that is correct. An `else` clause is always matched to the closest unmatched `if` that preceded it. However, if we're not careful, we can easily mismatch it in our mind and misalign the indentation. This is another reason why accurate, consistent indentation is crucial.

> **KEY CONCEPT**
>
> In a nested `if` statement, an `else` clause is matched to the closest unmatched `if`.

Braces can be used to specify the `if` statement to which an `else` clause belongs. For example, if the previous example should have been structured so that the string `"Bravo!"` is printed if `code` is not equal to `'R'`, we could force that relationship (and properly indent) as follows:

```
if (code == 'R')
{
    if (height <= 20)
        System.out.println ("Situation Normal");
}
else
    System.out.println ("Bravo!");
```

By using the block statement in the first `if` statement, we establish that the `else` clause belongs to it.

LISTING 4.4

```java
//********************************************************************
//  MinOfThree.java       Java Foundations
//
//  Demonstrates the use of nested if statements.
//********************************************************************

import java.util.Scanner;

public class MinOfThree
{
    //-----------------------------------------------------------------
    //  Reads three integers from the user and determines the smallest
    //  value.
    //-----------------------------------------------------------------
    public static void main (String[] args)
    {
        int num1, num2, num3, min = 0;

        Scanner scan = new Scanner (System.in);

        System.out.println ("Enter three integers: ");
        num1 = scan.nextInt();
        num2 = scan.nextInt();
        num3 = scan.nextInt();

        if (num1 < num2)
            if (num1 < num3)
                min = num1;
            else
                min = num3;
        else
            if (num2 < num3)
                min = num2;
            else
                min = num3;

        System.out.println ("Minimum value: " + min);
    }
}
```

OUTPUT

```
Enter three integers:
43   26   69
Minimum value: 26
```

4.3 Comparing Data

When comparing data using boolean expressions, it's important to understand some nuances that arise depending on the type of data being examined. Let's look at a few key situations.

Comparing Floats

An interesting situation occurs when comparing floating point data. Two floating point values are equal, according to the == operator, only if all the binary digits of their underlying representations match. If the compared values are the results of computation, it may be unlikely that they are exactly equal even if they are close enough for the specific situation. Therefore, you should rarely use the equality operator (==) when comparing floating point values.

A better way to check for floating point equality is to compute the absolute value of the difference between the two values and compare the result to some tolerance level. For example, we may choose a tolerance level of 0.00001. If the two floating point values are so close that their difference is less than the tolerance, then we are willing to consider them equal. Comparing two floating point values, f1 and f2, could be accomplished as follows:

```java
if (Math.abs(f1 - f2) < TOLERANCE)
    System.out.println ("Essentially equal.");
```

The value of the constant TOLERANCE should be appropriate for the situation.

Comparing Characters

We know what it means when we say that one number is less than another, but what does it mean to say one character is less than another? As we discussed in Chapter 2, characters in Java are based on the Unicode character set, which defines an ordering of all possible characters that can be used. Because the character 'a' comes before the character 'b' in the character set, we can say that 'a' is less than 'b'.

> **KEY CONCEPT**
>
> The relative order of characters in Java is defined by the Unicode character set.

We can use the equality and relational operators on character data. For example, if two character variables ch1 and ch2 hold two characters, we might determine their relative ordering in the Unicode character set with an if statement as follows:

```java
if (ch1 > ch2)
    System.out.println (ch1 + " is greater than " + ch2);
else
    System.out.println (ch1 + " is NOT greater than " + ch2);
```

The Unicode character set is structured so that all lowercase alphabetic characters ('a' through 'z') are contiguous and in alphabetical order. The same is true of uppercase alphabetic characters ('A' through 'Z') and characters that represent digits ('0' through '9'). The digits precede the uppercase alphabetic characters, which precede the lowercase alphabetic characters. Before, after, and in between these groups are other characters. See the chart in Appendix C for details.

Comparing Objects

The Unicode relationships among characters make it easy to sort characters and strings of characters. If you have a list of names, for instance, you can put them in alphabetical order based on the inherent relationships among characters in the character set.

However, you should not use the equality or relational operators to compare String objects. The String class contains a method called equals that returns a boolean value that is true if the two strings being compared contain exactly the same characters, and is false otherwise. For example:

```
if (name1.equals(name2))
    System.out.println ("The names are the same.");
else
    System.out.println ("The names are not the same.");
```

> **KEY CONCEPT**
>
> The compareTo method can be used to determine the relative order of strings.

Assuming that name1 and name2 are String objects, this condition determines whether the characters they contain are an exact match. Because both objects were created from the String class, they both respond to the equals message. Therefore the condition could have been written as name2.equals(name1) and the same result would occur.

It is valid to test the condition (name1 == name2), but that actually tests to see whether both reference variables refer to the same String object. For any object, the == operator tests whether both reference variables are aliases of each other (whether they contain the same address). That's different than testing to see whether two different String objects contain the same characters.

An interesting issue related to string comparisons is the fact that Java creates a unique object for string literals only when needed. Keep in mind that a string literal (such as "Howdy") is a convenience, and is actually a shorthand technique for creating a String object. If the string literal "Hi" is used multiple times in a method, Java creates only one String object to represent it. Therefore, in the following code, the conditions of both if statements are true:

```
String str = "software";
if (str == "software")
    System.out.println ("References are the same");
```

```
if (str.equals("software"))
    System.out.println ("Characters are the same");
```

The first time the string literal `"software"` is used, a `String` object is created to represent it, and the reference variable `str` is set to its address. Each subsequent time the literal is used, the original object is referenced.

To determine the relative ordering of two strings, use the `compareTo` method of the `String` class. The `compareTo` method is more versatile than the `equals` method. Instead of returning a `boolean` value, the `compareTo` method returns an integer. The return value is negative if the `String` object through which the method is invoked precedes (is less than) the string that is passed in as a parameter. The return value is zero if the two strings contain the same characters. The return value is positive if the `String` object through which the method is invoked follows (is greater than) the string that is passed in as a parameter. For example:

```
int result = name1.compareTo(name2);
if (result < 0)
    System.out.println (name1 + " comes before " + name2);
else
    if (result == 0)
        System.out.println ("The names are equal.");
    else
        System.out.println (name1 + " follows " + name2);
```

Keep in mind that comparing characters and strings is based on the Unicode character set (see Appendix C). This is called a *lexicographic ordering*. If all alphabetic characters are in the same case (upper or lower), the lexicographic ordering will be alphabetic ordering as well. However, when comparing two strings, such as `"able"` and `"Baker"`, the `compareTo` method will conclude that `"Baker"` comes first because all of the uppercase letters come before all of the lowercase letters in the Unicode character set. If a string is the prefix of a longer string, it is considered to precede the longer string. For example, when comparing two strings such as `"horse"` and `"horsefly"`, the `compareTo` method will conclude that `"horse"` comes first.

4.4 The switch Statement

Another conditional statement in Java is called the *switch statement*, which causes the executing program to follow one of several paths based on a single value. We also discuss the *break statement* in this section because it is usually used with a `switch` statement.

The `switch` statement evaluates an expression to determine a value and then matches that value with one of several possible *cases*. Each case has statements associated with it. After evaluating the expression, control jumps to the statement associated with the first case that matches the value. Consider the following example:

```
switch (idChar)
{
   case 'A':
      aCount = aCount + 1;
      break;
   case 'B':
      bCount = bCount + 1;
      break;
   case 'C':
      cCount = cCount + 1;
      break;
   default:
      System.out.println ("Error in Identification Character.");
}
```

First, the expression is evaluated. In this example, the expression is a simple `char` variable. Execution then transfers to the first statement identified by the case value that matches the result of the expression. Therefore, if `idChar` contains an `'A'`, the variable `aCount` is incremented. If it contains a `'B'`, the case for `'A'` is skipped and processing continues where `bCount` is incremented.

If no case value matches that of the expression, execution continues with the optional *default case*, indicated by the reserved word `default`. If no default case exists, no statements in the `switch` statement are executed and processing continues with the statement after the `switch` statement. It is often a good idea to include a default case, even if you don't expect it to be executed.

When a `break` statement is encountered, processing jumps to the statement following the `switch` statement. A `break` statement is usually used to break out of each case of a `switch` statement. Without a `break` statement, processing continues into the next case of the `switch`. Therefore if the `break` statement at the end of the `'A'` case in the previous example were not there, both the `aCount` and `bCount` variables would be incremented when `idChar` contains an `'A'`. Usually we want to perform only one case, so a `break` statement is almost always used. Occasionally, though, the "pass through" feature comes in handy.

The expression evaluated at the beginning of a `switch` statement must be of type `char`, `byte`, `short`, or `int`. In particular, it cannot be a `boolean`, a floating point value, or a `String`. Furthermore, the value of each case must be a constant; it cannot be a variable or other expression.

Switch Statement

The switch statement evaluates the initial Expression and matches its value with one of the cases. Processing continues with the Statement corresponding to that case. The optional default case will be executed if no other case matches.

Example:

```
switch (numValues)
{
    case 0:
        System.out.println ("No values were entered.");
        break;
    case 1:
        System.out.println ("One value was entered.");
        break;
    case 2:
        System.out.println ("Two values were entered.");
        break;
    default:
        System.out.println ("Too many values were entered.");
}
```

Note that the implicit boolean condition of a switch statement is based on equality. The expression at the beginning of the statement is compared to each case value to determine which one it equals. A switch statement cannot be used to determine other relational operations (such as less than), unless some preliminary processing is done. For example, the GradeReport program in Listing 4.5 prints a comment based on a numeric grade that is entered by the user.

In GradeReport, the category of the grade is determined by dividing the grade by 10 using integer division, resulting in an integer value between 0 and 10 (assuming a valid grade is entered). This result is used as the expression of the switch, which prints various messages for grades 60 or higher and a default sentence for all other values.

LISTING 4 . 5

```java
//********************************************************************
//  GradeReport.java        Java Foundations
//
//  Demonstrates the use of a switch statement.
//********************************************************************

import java.util.Scanner;

public class GradeReport
{
    //-----------------------------------------------------------------
    //  Reads a grade from the user and prints comments accordingly.
    //-----------------------------------------------------------------
    public static void main (String[] args)
    {
        int grade, category;

        Scanner scan = new Scanner (System.in);

        System.out.print ("Enter a numeric grade (0 to 100): ");
        grade = scan.nextInt();

        category = grade / 10;

        System.out.print ("That grade is ");

        switch (category)
        {
            case 10:
                System.out.println ("a perfect score. Well done.");
                break;
            case 9:
                System.out.println ("well above average. Excellent.");
                break;
            case 8:
                System.out.println ("above average. Nice job.");
                break;
            case 7:
                System.out.println ("average.");
                break;
            case 6:
                System.out.print ("below average. Please see the ");
                System.out.println ("instructor for assistance.");
                break;
```

LISTING 4.5   *continued*

```
        default:
            System.out.println ("not passing.");
        }
    }
}
```

OUTPUT

```
Enter a numeric grade (0 to 100): 87
That grade is above average. Nice job.
```

Note that any `switch` statement could be implemented as a set of nested `if` statements. However, nested `if` statements quickly become difficult for a human reader to understand and are error prone to implement and debug. But because a `switch` can evaluate only equality, sometimes nested `if` statements are necessary. It depends on the situation.

4.5 The while Statement

As we discussed in the introduction of this chapter, a repetition statement (or loop) allows us to execute another statement multiple times. A *while statement* is a loop that evaluates a boolean condition just like an `if` statement does and executes a statement (called the *body* of the loop) if the condition is true. However, unlike the `if` statement, after the body is executed, the condition is evaluated again. If it is still true, the body is executed again. This repetition continues until the condition becomes false; then processing continues with the statement after the body of the `while` loop. Figure 4.7 on the next page shows this processing.

> **KEY CONCEPT**
>
> A `while` statement executes the same statement repeatedly until its condition becomes false.

The following loop prints the values from 1 to 5. Each iteration through the loop prints one value, then increments the counter.

```
int count = 1;
while (count <= 5)
{
    System.out.println (count);
    count++;
}
```

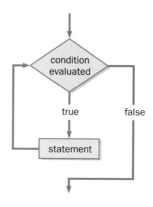

FIGURE 4.7 The logic of a `while` loop

Note that the body of the `while` loop is a block containing two statements. The entire block is repeated on each iteration of the loop.

Let's look at another program that uses a `while` loop. The `Average` program shown in Listing 4.6 reads a series of integer values from the user, sums them up, and computes their average.

We don't know how many values the user may enter, so we need to have a way to indicate that the user is done entering numbers. In this program, we designate zero to be a *sentinel value* that indicates the end of the input. The `while` loop continues to process input values until the user enters zero. This assumes that zero

---

While Statement

```
●──→( while )──→( ( )──→ Expression ──→( ) )──→ Statement ──→●
```

The `while` loop repeatedly executes the specified Statement as long as the boolean Expression is true. The Expression is evaluated first; therefore the Statement might not be executed at all. The Expression is evaluated again after each execution of Statement until the Expression becomes false.

Example:

```
while (total > max)
{
    total = total / 2;
    System.out.println ("Current total: " + total);
}
```

LISTING 4.6

```java
//********************************************************************
//  Average.java          Java Foundations
//
//  Demonstrates the use of a while loop, a sentinel value, and a
//  running sum.
//********************************************************************

import java.text.DecimalFormat;
import java.util.Scanner;

public class Average
{
   //-----------------------------------------------------------------
   //  Computes the average of a set of values entered by the user.
   //  The running sum is printed as the numbers are entered.
   //-----------------------------------------------------------------
   public static void main (String[] args)
   {
      int sum = 0, value, count = 0;
      double average;

      Scanner scan = new Scanner (System.in);

      System.out.print ("Enter an integer (0 to quit): ");
      value = scan.nextInt();

      while (value != 0)  // sentinel value of 0 to terminate loop
      {
         count++;

         sum += value;
         System.out.println ("The sum so far is " + sum);

         System.out.print ("Enter an integer (0 to quit): ");
         value = scan.nextInt();
      }
      System.out.println ();

      if (count == 0)
         System.out.println ("No values were entered.");
      else
      {
         average = (double)sum / count;
```

LISTING 4.6   *continued*

```
        DecimalFormat fmt = new DecimalFormat ("0.###");
        System.out.println ("The average is " + fmt.format(average));
    }
  }
}
```

OUTPUT

```
Enter an integer (0 to quit): 25
The sum so far is 25
Enter an integer (0 to quit): 44
The sum so far is 69
Enter an integer (0 to quit): -14
The sum so far is 55
Enter an integer (0 to quit): 83
The sum so far is 138
Enter an integer (0 to quit): 69
The sum so far is 207
Enter an integer (0 to quit): -37
The sum so far is 170
Enter an integer (0 to quit): 116
The sum so far is 286
Enter an integer (0 to quit): 0

The average is 40.857
```

is not one of the valid numbers that should contribute to the average. A sentinel value must always be outside the normal range of values entered.

Note that in the Average program, a variable called sum is used to maintain a *running sum*, which means it is the sum of the values entered thus far. The variable sum is initialized to zero, and each value read is added to and stored back into sum.

We also have to count the number of values that are entered so that after the loop concludes we can divide by the appropriate value to compute the average. Note that the sentinel value is not counted. Consider the unusual situation in which the user immediately enters the sentinel value before entering any valid values. The if statement at the end of the program avoids a divide-by-zero error.

Let's examine yet another program that uses a while loop. The WinPercentage program shown in Listing 4.7 computes the winning percentage of a sports team based on the number of games won.

LISTING 4.7

```java
//********************************************************************
//  WinPercentage.java          Java Foundations
//
//  Demonstrates the use of a while loop for input validation.
//********************************************************************

import java.text.NumberFormat;
import java.util.Scanner;

public class WinPercentage
{
   //-----------------------------------------------------------------
   //  Computes the percentage of games won by a team.
   //-----------------------------------------------------------------
   public static void main (String[] args)
   {
      final int NUM_GAMES = 12;
      int won;
      double ratio;

      Scanner scan = new Scanner (System.in);

      System.out.print ("Enter the number of games won (0 to "
                         + NUM_GAMES + "): ");
      won = scan.nextInt();

      while (won < 0 || won > NUM_GAMES)
      {
         System.out.print ("Invalid input. Please reenter: ");
         won = scan.nextInt();
      }

      ratio = (double)won / NUM_GAMES;

      NumberFormat fmt = NumberFormat.getPercentInstance();

      System.out.println ();
      System.out.println ("Winning percentage: " + fmt.format(ratio));
   }
}
```

LISTING 4.7 *continued*

OUTPUT

```
Enter the number of games won (0 to 12): -5
Invalid input. Please reenter: 13
Invalid input. Please reenter: 7

Winning percentage: 58%
```

We use a `while` loop in the `WinPercentage` program for *input validation*, meaning we guarantee that the user enters a value that we consider to be valid before continuing. In this example, that means that the value entered representing the number of games won must be greater than or equal to zero and less than or equal to the total number of games played. The `while` loop continues to execute, repeatedly prompting the user for valid input, until the entered number is indeed valid. The body of the `while` loop will not be executed at all if the user enters a valid value the first time.

We generally want our programs to be *robust*, which means that they handle potential problems as elegantly as possible. Validating input data and avoiding errors such as dividing by zero are situations that we should consciously address when designing a program. Loops and conditionals help us recognize and deal with such situations.

Infinite Loops

It is the programmer's responsibility to ensure that the condition of a loop will eventually become false. If it doesn't, the loop body will execute forever, or at least until the program is interrupted. This situation, referred to as an *infinite loop*, is a common mistake.

The following is an example of an infinite loop:

```
int count = 1;
while (count <= 25)   // Warning: this is an infinite loop!
{
    System.out.println (count);
    count = count - 1;
}
```

If you execute this loop, you should be prepared to interrupt it. On most systems, pressing the Control-C keyboard combination (hold down the Control key and press C) terminates a running program.

In this example, the initial value of count is 1 and it is decremented in the loop body. The while loop will continue as long as count is less than or equal to 25. Because count gets smaller with each iteration, the condition will always be true, or at least until the value of count gets so small that an underflow error occurs. The point is that the logic of the code is clearly wrong.

> **KEY CONCEPT**
>
> We must design our programs carefully to avoid infinite loops.

Let's look at some other examples of infinite loops:

```
int count = 1;
while (count != 50)    // infinite loop
    count += 2;
```

In this code fragment, the variable count is initialized to 1 and is moving in a positive direction. However, note that it is being incremented by 2 each time. This loop will never terminate because count will never equal 50. It begins at 1 and then changes to 3, then 5, and so on. Eventually it reaches 49, then changes to 51, then 53, and continues forever.

Now consider the following situation:

```
double num = 1.0;
while (num != 0.0)    // infinite loop
    num = num - 0.1;
```

Once again, the value of the loop control variable seems to be moving in the correct direction. And, in fact, it seems like num will eventually take on the value 0.0. However, this is an infinite loop (on most computer systems) because num will never have a value *exactly* equal to 0.0. This situation is similar to one we discussed earlier in this chapter when we explored the idea of comparing floating point values in the condition of an if statement. Because of the way the values are represented in binary, minute computational errors occur internally, making it problematic to compare two floating point values for equality.

Nested Loops

The body of a loop can contain another loop. This situation is called a *nested loop*. Keep in mind that for each iteration of the outer loop, the inner loop executes completely. Consider the following code fragment. How many times does the string "Here again" get printed?

```
int count1 = 1, count2;
while (count1 <= 10)
{
    count2 = 1;
    while (count2 <= 50)
    {
        System.out.println ("Here again");
        count2++;
    }
    count1++;
}
```

The println statement is inside the inner loop. The outer loop executes 10 times, as count1 iterates between 1 and 10. The inner loop executes 50 times, as count2 iterates between 1 and 50. For each iteration of the outer loop, the inner loop executes completely. Therefore the println statement is executed 500 times.

As with any loop situation, we must be careful to scrutinize the conditions of the loops and the initializations of variables. Let's consider some small changes to this code. What if the condition of the outer loop were (count1 < 10) instead of (count1 <= 10)? How would that change the total number of lines printed? Well, the outer loop would execute 9 times instead of 10, so the println statement would be executed 450 times. What if the outer loop were left as it was originally defined, but count2 were initialized to 10 instead of 1 before the inner loop? The inner loop would then execute 40 times instead of 50, so the total number of lines printed would be 400.

Let's look at another example that uses a nested loop. A *palindrome* is a string of characters that reads the same forward or backward. For example, the following strings are palindromes:

- radar
- drab bard
- ab cde xxxx edc ba
- kayak
- deified
- able was I ere I saw elba

Note that some palindromes have an even number of characters, whereas others have an odd number of characters. The PalindromeTester program shown in Listing 4.8 tests to see whether a string is a palindrome. The user may test as many strings as desired.

The code for PalindromeTester contains two loops, one inside the other. The outer loop controls how many strings are tested, and the inner loop scans through each string, character by character, until it determines whether the string is a palindrome.

LISTING 4.8

```java
//********************************************************************
//  PalindromeTester.java       Java Foundations
//
//  Demonstrates the use of nested while loops.
//********************************************************************

import java.util.Scanner;

public class PalindromeTester
{
   //-----------------------------------------------------------------
   //  Tests strings to see if they are palindromes.
   //-----------------------------------------------------------------
   public static void main (String[] args)
   {
      String str, another = "y";
      int left, right;

      Scanner scan = new Scanner (System.in);

      while (another.equalsIgnoreCase("y"))  // allows y or Y
      {
         System.out.println ("Enter a potential palindrome:");
         str = scan.nextLine();

         left = 0;
         right = str.length() - 1;

         while (str.charAt(left) == str.charAt(right) && left < right)
         {
            left++;
            right--;
         }

         System.out.println();
         if (left < right)
            System.out.println ("That string is NOT a palindrome.");
         else
            System.out.println ("That string IS a palindrome.");
```

LISTING 4.8   *continued*

```
        System.out.println();
        System.out.print ("Test another palindrome (y/n)? ");
        another = scan.nextLine();
      }
    }
}
```

OUTPUT

```
Enter a potential palindrome:
radar

That string IS a palindrome.

Test another palindrome (y/n)? y
Enter a potential palindrome:
able was I ere I saw elba

That string IS a palindrome.

Test another palindrome (y/n)? y
Enter a potential palindrome:
abc6996cba

That string IS a palindrome.

Test another palindrome (y/n)? y
Enter a potential palindrome:
abracadabra

That string is NOT a palindrome.

Test another palindrome (y/n)? n
```

The variables `left` and `right` store the indexes of two characters. They initially indicate the characters on either end of the string. Each iteration of the inner loop compares the two characters indicated by `left` and `right`. We fall out of the inner loop when either the characters don't match, meaning the string is not a palindrome, or when the value of `left` becomes equal to or greater than the value of `right`, which means the entire string has been tested and it is a palindrome.

Note that the following phrases would not be considered palindromes by the current version of the program:

- A man, a plan, a canal, Panama.
- Dennis and Edna sinned.
- Rise to vote, sir.
- Doom an evil deed, liven a mood.
- Go hang a salami; I'm a lasagna hog.

These strings fail our current criteria for a palindrome because of the spaces, punctuation marks, and changes in uppercase and lowercase. However, if these characteristics were removed or ignored, these strings read the same forward and backward. Consider how the program could be changed to handle these situations. These modifications are included as a programming project at the end of this chapter.

Other Loop Controls

We've seen how the `break` statement can be used to break out of the cases of a `switch` statement. The `break` statement can also be placed in the body of any loop, even though this is usually inappropriate. Its effect on a loop is similar to its effect on a `switch` statement. The execution of the loop is stopped, and the statement following the loop is executed.

It is never necessary to use a `break` statement in a loop. An equivalent loop can always be written without it. Because the `break` statement causes program flow to jump from one place to another, using a `break` in a loop is not good practice. Its use is tolerated in a `switch` statement because an equivalent `switch` statement cannot be written without it. However, you can and should avoid it in a loop.

A *continue statement* has a similar effect on loop processing. The `continue` statement is similar to a `break`, but the loop condition is evaluated again, and the loop body is executed again if it is still true. Like the `break` statement, the `continue` statement can always be avoided in a loop, and for the same reasons, it should be.

4.6 Iterators

An *iterator* is an object that has methods that allow you to process a collection of items one at a time. That is, an iterator lets you step through each item and interact with it as needed. For example, your goal may be to compute the dues for each member of a club, or print the distinct parts of a URL, or process a group of returned library books. An iterator provides a consistent and simple mechanism for systematically processing a group of items. This processing is inherently repetitive, and therefore ties into our discussion of loops.

> **KEY CONCEPT**
> An iterator is an object that helps you process a group of related items.

Technically an iterator object in Java is defined using the `Iterator` interface, which is discussed in Chapter 9. For now it is simply helpful to know that such objects exist and that they can make the processing of a collection of items easier.

Every iterator object has a method called `hasNext` that returns a `boolean` value indicating if there is at least one more item to process. Therefore the `hasNext` method can be used as a condition of a loop to control the processing of each item. An iterator also has a method called `next` to retrieve the next item in the collection to process.

There are several classes in the Java standard class library that define iterator objects. One of these is `Scanner`, a class we've used several times in previous examples to help us read data from the user. The `hasNext` method of the `Scanner` class returns true if there is another input token to process. And, as we've seen previously, it has a `next` method that returns the next input token as a string.

The `Scanner` class also has specific variations of the `hasNext` method, such as the `hasNextInt` and `hasNextDouble` methods, which allow you to determine if the next input token is a particular type. Likewise, as we've seen, there are variations of the `next` method, such as `nextInt` and `nextDouble`, that retrieve values of specific types.

When reading input interactively from the standard input stream, the `hasNext` method of the `Scanner` class will wait until there is input available, then return true. That is, interactive input read from the keyboard is always thought to have more data to process—it just hasn't arrived yet (until the user types it in). That's why in previous examples we've used special sentinel values to determine the end of interactive input.

However, the fact that a `Scanner` object is an iterator is particularly helpful when the scanner is being used to process input from a source that has a specific end point, such as processing the lines of a data file or processing the parts of a character string. Let's examine an example of this type of processing.

Reading Text Files

Suppose we have an input file called `websites.inp` that contains a list of Web page addresses (Uniform Resource Locators, or URLs) that we want to process in some way. The following are the first few lines of `websites.inp`:

```
www.google.com
newsyllabus.com/about
java.sun.com/j2se/6.0
www.linux.org/info/gnu.html
technorati.com/search/java/
www.cs.vt.edu/undergraduates/honors_degree.html
```

The program shown in Listing 4.9 reads the URLs from this file and dissects them to show the various parts of the path. It uses a `Scanner` object to process

LISTING 4.9

```java
//********************************************************************
//  URLDissector.java        Java Foundations
//
//  Demonstrates the use of Scanner to read file input and parse it
//  using alternative delimiters.
//********************************************************************

import java.util.Scanner;
import java.io.*;

public class URLDissector
{
    //-----------------------------------------------------------------
    //  Reads urls from a file and prints their path components.
    //-----------------------------------------------------------------
    public static void main (String[] args) throws IOException
    {
        String url;
        Scanner fileScan, urlScan;

        fileScan = new Scanner (new File("websites.inp"));

        // Read and process each line of the file
        while (fileScan.hasNext())
        {
            url = fileScan.nextLine();
            System.out.println ("URL: " + url);

            urlScan = new Scanner (url);
            urlScan.useDelimiter("/");

            //  Print each part of the url
            while (urlScan.hasNext())
                System.out.println ("   " + urlScan.next());

            System.out.println();
        }
    }
}
```

LISTING 4.9   *continued*

OUTPUT

```
URL: www.google.com
   www.google.com

URL: newsyllabus.com/about
   newsyllabus.com
   about

URL: java.sun.com/j2se/6.0
   java.sun.com
   j2se
   6.0

URL: www.linux.org/info/gnu.html
   www.linux.org
   info
   gnu.html

URL: technorati.com/search/java/
   technorati.com
   search
   java

URL: www.cs.vt.edu/undergraduates/honors_degree.html
   www.cs.vt.edu
   undergraduates
   honors_degree.html
```

the input. In fact, the program uses multiple `Scanner` objects—one to read the lines of the data file, and another to process each URL string.

There are two `while` loops in this program, one nested within the other. The outer loop processes each line in the file, and the inner loop processes each token in the current line.

The variable `fileScan` is created as a scanner that operates on the input file named `urls.inp`. Instead of passing `System.in` into the `Scanner` constructor, we instantiate a `File` object that represents the input file and pass it into the `Scanner` constructor. At that point, the `fileScan` object is ready to read and process input from the input file.

If for some reason there is a problem finding or opening the input file, the attempt to create a `File` object will throw an `IOException`, which is why we've added the `throws IOException` clause to the `main` method header. Processing exceptions is discussed further in Chapter 10.

The body of the outer `while` loop will be executed as long as the `hasNext` method of the input file scanner returns true—that is, as long as there is more input in the data file to process. Each iteration through the loop reads one line (one URL) from the input file and prints it out.

For each URL, a new `Scanner` object is set up to parse the pieces of the URL string, which is passed into the `Scanner` constructor when instantiating the `urlScan` object. The inner `while` loop prints each token of the URL on a separate line.

Recall that, by default, a `Scanner` object assumes that white space (spaces, tabs, and new lines) is used as the delimiters separating the input tokens. Using whitespace delimiters works in this example for the scanner that is reading each line of the input file. However, if the default delimiters do not suffice, as in the processing of a URL in this example, they can be changed.

> **KEY CONCEPT**
>
> The delimiters used to separate tokens in a `Scanner` object can be explicitly set as needed.

In this case, we are interested in each part of the path separated by the slash (/) character. A call to the `useDelimiter` method of the scanner sets the delimiter to a slash prior to processing the URL string.

If you want to use more than one alternate delimiter character, or if you want to parse the input in more complex ways, the `Scanner` class can process patterns called *regular expressions*, which are discussed in Appendix H.

4.7 The do Statement

The *do statement* is similar to the `while` statement in that it executes the loop body until a condition becomes false. However, unlike the `while` loop, whose condition is evaluated *before* the body is executed, the condition of a `do` loop is evaluated *after* the loop body executes. Syntactically, the condition in a `do` loop is written after the loop body to reflect this processing. The body of a `do` loop is always executed at least once, whereas with a `while` loop the body might not be executed at all (if the condition is initially false). Figure 4.8 shows the processing of a `do` loop.

> **KEY CONCEPT**
>
> A do statement executes its loop body at least once.

The following code prints the numbers from 1 to 5 using a `do` loop. Compare this code with the similar example earlier in this chapter that uses a `while` loop to accomplish the same task.

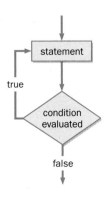

FIGURE 4.8 The logic of a do loop

```
int count = 0;
do
{
    count++;
    System.out.println (count);
}
while (count < 5);
```

A do loop begins simply with the reserved word do. The body of the do loop continues until the *while clause* that contains the boolean condition that determines whether the loop body will be executed again. Sometimes it is difficult to determine whether a line of code that begins with the reserved word while is the beginning of a while loop or the end of a do loop.

Do Statement

●—▶(do)—▶| Statement |—▶(while)—▶(( )—▶| Expression |—▶( ))—▶(;)—▶●

The do loop repeatedly executes the specified Statement as long as the boolean Expression is true. The Statement is executed at least once, then the Expression is evaluated to determine whether the Statement should be executed again.

Example:

```
do
{
    System.out.print ("Enter a word:");
    word = scan.next();
    System.out.println (word);
}
while (!word.equals("quit"));
```

Let's look at another example of the do loop. The program called ReverseNumber, shown in Listing 4.10, reads an integer from the user and reverses its digits mathematically.

LISTING 4.10

```java
//********************************************************************
//  ReverseNumber.java        Java Foundations
//
//  Demonstrates the use of a do loop.
//********************************************************************

import java.util.Scanner;

public class ReverseNumber
{
    //-----------------------------------------------------------------
    //  Reverses the digits of an integer mathematically.
    //-----------------------------------------------------------------
    public static void main (String[] args)
    {
        int number, lastDigit, reverse = 0;

        Scanner scan = new Scanner (System.in);

        System.out.print ("Enter a positive integer: ");
        number = scan.nextInt();

        do
        {
            lastDigit = number % 10;
            reverse = (reverse * 10) + lastDigit;
            number = number / 10;
        }
        while (number > 0);

        System.out.println ("That number reversed is " + reverse);
    }
}
```

OUTPUT

```
Enter a positive integer: 2896
That number reversed is 6982
```

The do loop in the ReverseNumber program uses the remainder operation to determine the digit in the 1's position, adds it into the reversed number, and then truncates that digit from the original number using integer division. The do loop terminates when we run out of digits to process, which corresponds to the point when the variable number reaches the value zero. Carefully trace the logic of this program with a few examples to see how it works.

If you know you want to perform the body of a loop at least once, then you probably want to use a do statement. A do loop has many of the same properties as a while statement, so it must also be checked for termination conditions to avoid infinite loops.

4.8 The for Statement

The while and the do statements are good to use when you don't initially know how many times you want to execute the loop body. The *for statement* is another repetition statement that is particularly well suited for executing the body of a loop a specific number of times that can be determined before the loop is executed.

> **KEY CONCEPT**
>
> A for statement is usually used when a loop will be executed a set number of times.

The following code prints the numbers 1 through 5 using a for loop, just as we did using a while loop and a do loop in previous examples:

```
for (int count=1; count <= 5; count++)
    System.out.println (count);
```

The header of a for loop contains three parts separated by semicolons. Before the loop begins, the first part of the header, called the *initialization*, is executed. The second part of the header is the boolean condition, which is evaluated before the loop body (like the while loop). If true, the body of the loop is executed, followed by the execution of the third part of the header, which is called the *increment*. Note that the initialization part is executed only once, but the increment part is executed after each iteration of the loop. Figure 4.9 shows this processing.

A for loop can be a bit tricky to read until you get used to it. The execution of the code doesn't follow a top-to-bottom, left-to-right reading. The increment code executes after the body of the loop even though it is in the header.

In this example, the initialization portion of the for loop header is used to declare the variable count as well as to give it an initial value. We are not required to declare a variable there, but it is a common practice in situations where the variable is not needed outside of the loop. Because count is declared in the for loop header, it exists only inside the loop and cannot be referenced elsewhere.

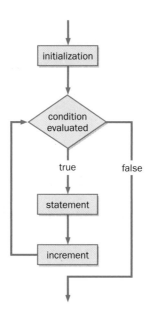

FIGURE 4.9 The logic of a for loop

For Statement

For Init

For Update

The for statement repeatedly executes the specified Statement as long as the boolean Expression is true. The For Init portion of the header is executed only once, before the loop begins. The For Update portion executes after each execution of Statement.

Examples:

```
for (int value=1; value < 25; value++)
   System.out.println (value + " squared is " + value*value);

for (int num=40; num > 0; num-=3)
   sum = sum + num;
```

The loop control variable is set up, checked, and modified by the actions in the for loop header. It can be referenced inside the loop body, but it should not be modified except by the actions defined in the loop header.

Despite its name, the increment portion of the for loop header could actually decrement a value rather than increment it. For example, the following loop prints the integer values from 100 down to 1:

```java
for (int num = 100; num > 0; num--)
    System.out.println (num);
```

In fact, the increment portion of the for loop could perform any calculation, not just a simple increment or decrement. Consider the program shown in Listing 4.11, which prints multiples of a particular value up to a particular limit.

LISTING 4.11

```java
//********************************************************************
//  Multiples.java       Java Foundations
//
//  Demonstrates the use of a for loop.
//********************************************************************

import java.util.Scanner;

public class Multiples
{
    //-----------------------------------------------------------------
    //  Prints multiples of a user-specified number up to a user-
    //  specified limit.
    //-----------------------------------------------------------------
    public static void main (String[] args)
    {
        final int PER_LINE = 5;
        int value, limit, mult, count = 0;

        Scanner scan = new Scanner (System.in);

        System.out.print ("Enter a positive value: ");
        value = scan.nextInt();

        System.out.print ("Enter an upper limit: ");
        limit = scan.nextInt();
```

```
LISTING  4 . 1 1        continued

        System.out.println ();
        System.out.println ("The multiples of " + value + " between " +
                            value + " and " + limit + " (inclusive) are:");

        for (mult = value; mult <= limit; mult += value)
        {
            System.out.print (mult + "\t");

            // Print a specific number of values per line of output
            count++;
            if (count % PER_LINE == 0)
                System.out.println();
        }
    }
}
```

O U T P U T

```
Enter a positive value: 7
Enter an upper limit: 400

The multiples of 7 between 7 and 400 (inclusive) are:
7       14      21      28      35
42      49      56      63      70
77      84      91      98      105
112     119     126     133     140
147     154     161     168     175
182     189     196     203     210
217     224     231     238     245
252     259     266     273     280
287     294     301     308     315
322     329     336     343     350
357     364     371     378     385
392     399
```

The increment portion of the for loop in the Multiples program adds the value entered by the user after each iteration. The number of values printed per line is controlled by counting the values printed and then moving to the next line whenever count is evenly divisible by the PER_LINE constant.

The Stars program in Listing 4.12 shows the use of nested for loops. The output is a triangle shape made of asterisk characters. The outer loop executes

LISTING 4.12

```java
//********************************************************************
//  Stars.java        Java Foundations
//
//  Demonstrates the use of nested for loops.
//********************************************************************

public class Stars
{
   //-----------------------------------------------------------------
   //  Prints a triangle shape using asterisk (star) characters.
   //-----------------------------------------------------------------
   public static void main (String[] args)
   {
      final int MAX_ROWS = 10;

      for (int row = 1; row <= MAX_ROWS; row++)
      {
         for (int star = 1; star <= row; star++)
            System.out.print ("*");

         System.out.println();
      }
   }
}
```

OUTPUT

```
*
**
***
****
*****
******
*******
********
*********
**********
```

exactly 10 times. Each iteration of the outer loop prints one line of the output. The inner loop performs a different number of iterations depending on the line value controlled by the outer loop. Each iteration of the inner loop prints one star on the current line. Writing programs that print variations on this triangle config-uration are included in the programming projects at the end of the chapter.

Iterators and `for` Loops

In section 4.6 we discussed that some objects are considered to be iterators, which have `hasNext` and `next` methods to process each item from a group. If an object has implemented the `Iterable` interface, then we can use a variation of the `for` loop to process items using a simplified syntax. For example, if `bookList` is an `Iterable` object that contains `Book` objects, we can use a `for` loop to process each `Book` object as follows:

```
for (Book myBook : bookList)
    System.out.println (myBook);
```

This version of the `for` loop is referred to as a *for–each statement*. It processes each object in the iterator in turn. It is equivalent to the following:

```
Book myBook;
while (bookList.hasNext())
{
    myBook = bookList.next();
    System.out.println (myBook);
}
```

The `Scanner` class is an `Iterator`, but is not `Iterable`. Therefore it has the `hasNext` and `next` methods, but cannot be used with this version of the `for` loop. On the other hand, arrays, which are discussed in Chapter 7, are `Iterable`. We use the for–each loop as appropriate in various situations throughout the rest of the book.

Comparing Loops

The three loop statements (`while`, `do`, and `for`) are functionally equivalent. Any particular loop written using one type of loop can be written using either of the other two loop types. Which type of loop we use depends on the situation.

As we mentioned earlier, the primary difference between a `while` loop and a `do` loop is when the condition is evaluated. If you know you want to execute the loop body at least once, a `do` loop is usually the better choice. The body of a `while` loop, on the other hand, might not be executed at all if the condition is initially false. Therefore we say that the body of a `while` loop is executed zero or more times, but the body of a `do` loop is executed one or more times.

A `for` loop is like a `while` loop in that the condition is evaluated before the loop body is executed. We generally use a `for` loop when the number of times we want to iterate through a loop is fixed or can be easily calculated. In many situations, it is simply more convenient to separate the code that sets up and controls the loop iterations inside the `for` loop header from the body of the loop.

Summary of Key Concepts

- Conditionals and loops allow us to control the flow of execution through a method.

- An `if` statement allows a program to choose whether to execute a particular statement.

- A loop allows a program to execute a statement multiple times.

- Logical operators are often used to construct sophisticated conditions.

- Proper indentation is important for human readability; it shows the relationship between one statement and another.

- An `if-else` statement allows a program to do one thing if a condition is true and another thing if the condition is false.

- In a nested `if` statement, an `else` clause is matched to the closest unmatched `if`.

- The relative order of characters in Java is defined by the Unicode character set.

- The `compareTo` method can be used to determine the relative order of strings.

- A `break` statement is usually used at the end of each case alternative of a `switch` statement.

- A `while` statement executes the same statement repeatedly until its condition becomes false.

- We must design our programs carefully to avoid infinite loops.

- An iterator is an object that helps you process a group of related items.

- The delimiters used to separate tokens in a `Scanner` object can be explicitly set as needed.

- A `do` statement executes its loop body at least once.

- A `for` statement is usually used when a loop will be executed a set number of times.

Self-Review Questions

SR 4.1   What is meant by the flow of control through a program?

SR 4.2   What type of conditions are conditionals and loops based on?

SR 4.3   What are the equality operators? The relational operators?

SR 4.4   What is a truth table?

SR 4.5   Why must we be careful when comparing floating point values for equality?

SR 4.6   How do we compare strings for equality?

SR 4.7   What is a nested `if` statement? A nested loop?

SR 4.8   How do block statements help us in the construction of conditionals and loops?

SR 4.9   What happens if a case in a `switch` does not end with a `break` statement?

SR 4.10   What is an infinite loop? Specifically, what causes it?

SR 4.11   Compare and contrast a `while` loop and a `do` loop.

SR 4.12   When would we use a `for` loop instead of a `while` loop?

Exercises

EX 4.1   What happens in the `MinOfThree` program if two or more of the values are equal? If exactly two of the values are equal, does it matter whether the equal values are lower or higher than the third?

EX 4.2   What is wrong with the following code fragment? Rewrite it so that it produces correct output.

```
if (total == MAX)
    if (total < sum)
        System.out.println ("total == MAX and < sum");
else
    System.out.println ("total is not equal to MAX");
```

EX 4.3   What is wrong with the following code fragment? Will this code compile if it is part of an otherwise valid program? Explain.

```
if (length = MIN_LENGTH)
    System.out.println ("The length is minimal.");
```

EX 4.4   What output is produced by the following code fragment?

```
int num = 87, max = 25;
if (num >= max*2)
    System.out.println ("apple");
    System.out.println ("orange");
System.out.println ("pear");
```

EX 4.5   What output is produced by the following code fragment?

```
int limit = 100, num1 = 15, num2 = 40;
if (limit <= limit)
{
    if (num1 == num2)
        System.out.println ("lemon");
    System.out.println ("lime");
}
System.out.println ("grape");
```

EX 4.6   Put the following list of strings in lexicographic order as if deter-
          mined by the compareTo method of the String class. Consult the
          Unicode chart in Appendix C.

```
"fred"
"Ethel"
"?-?-?-?"
"{([])}"
"Lucy"
"ricky"
"book"
"******"
"12345"
"      "
"HEPHALUMP"
"bookkeeper"
"6789"
";+<?"
"^^^^^^^^^^"
"hephalump"
```

EX 4.7   What output is produced by the following code fragment?

```
int num = 0, max = 20;
while (num < max)
{
    System.out.println (num);
    num += 4;
}
```

EX 4.8   What output is produced by the following code fragment?

```
int num = 1, max = 20;
while (num < max)
{
    if (num%2 == 0)
        System.out.println (num);
    num++;
}
```

EX 4.9   What output is produced by the following code fragment?

```
for (int num = 0; num <= 200; num += 2)
    System.out.println (num);
```

EX 4.10   What output is produced by the following code fragment?

```
for (int val = 200; val >= 0; val -= 1)
    if (val % 4 != 0)
        System.out.println (val);
```

EX 4.11   Transform the following while loop into an equivalent do loop (make sure it produces the same output).

```
int num = 1;
while (num < 20)
{
    num++;
    System.out.println (num);
}
```

EX 4.12   Transform the while loop from Exercise 4.11 into an equivalent for loop. (Make sure it produces the same output.)

EX 4.13   What is wrong with the following code fragment? What are three distinct ways it could be changed to remove the flaw?

```
count = 50;
while (count >= 0)
{
    System.out.println (count);
    count = count + 1;
}
```

EX 4.14   Write a while loop that verifies that the user enters a positive integer value.

EX 4.15   Write a do loop that verifies that the user enters an even integer value.

EX 4.16   Write a code fragment that reads and prints integer values entered by a user until a particular sentinel value (stored in SENTINEL) is entered. Do not print the sentinel value.

EX 4.17   Write a for loop to print the odd numbers from 1 to 99 (inclusive).

EX 4.18   Write a for loop to print the multiples of 3 from 300 down to 3.

EX 4.19   Write a code fragment that reads 10 integer values from the user and prints the highest value entered.

EX 4.20 Write a code fragment that computes the sum of the integers from 20 to 70, inclusive, then prints the result.

EX 4.21 Write a code fragment that determines and prints the number of times the character 'z' appears in a String object called name.

EX 4.22 Write a code fragment that prints the characters stored in a String object called str backward.

EX 4.23 Write a code fragment that prints every other character in a String object called word starting with the first character.

Programming Projects

PP 4.1 Design and implement an application that reads an integer value representing a year from the user. The purpose of the program is to determine if the year is a leap year (and therefore has 29 days in February) in the Gregorian calendar. A year is a leap year if it is divisible by 4, unless it is also divisible by 100 but not 400. For example, the year 2003 is not a leap year, but 2004 is. The year 1900 is not a leap year because it is divisible by 100, but the year 2000 is a leap year because even though it is divisible by 100, it is also divisible by 400. Produce an error message for any input value less than 1582 (the year the Gregorian calendar was adopted).

PP 4.2 Modify the solution to programming project 4.1 so that the user can evaluate multiple years. Allow the user to terminate the program using an appropriate sentinel value. Validate each input value to ensure it is greater than or equal to 1582.

PP 4.3 Design and implement an application that reads an integer value and prints the sum of all even integers between 2 and the input value, inclusive. Print an error message if the input value is less than 2. Prompt accordingly.

PP 4.4 Design and implement an application that reads a string from the user and prints it one character per line.

PP 4.5 Design and implement an application that determines and prints the number of odd, even, and zero digits in an integer value read from the keyboard.

PP 4.6   Design and implement an application that produces a multiplication table, showing the results of multiplying the integers 1 through 12 by themselves.

PP 4.7   Design and implement an application that prints the first few verses of the traveling song "One Hundred Bottles of Beer." Use a loop such that each iteration prints one verse. Read the number of verses to print from the user. Validate the input. The following are the first two verses of the song:

100 bottles of beer on the wall

100 bottles of beer

If one of those bottles should happen to fall

99 bottles of beer on the wall

99 bottles of beer on the wall

99 bottles of beer

If one of those bottles should happen to fall

98 bottles of beer on the wall

PP 4.8   Design and implement an application that plays the Hi-Lo guessing game with numbers. The program should pick a random number between 1 and 100 (inclusive), then repeatedly prompt the user to guess the number. On each guess, report to the user that he or she is correct or that the guess is high or low. Continue accepting guesses until the user guesses correctly or chooses to quit. Use a sentinel value to determine whether the user wants to quit. Count the number of guesses and report that value when the user guesses correctly. At the end of each game (by quitting or a correct guess), prompt to determine whether the user wants to play again. Continue playing games until the user chooses to stop.

PP 4.9   Create a modified version of the `PalindromeTester` program so that the spaces, punctuation, and changes in uppercase and lowercase are not considered when determining whether a string is a palindrome. *Hint:* These issues can be handled in several ways. Think carefully about your design.

PP 4.10   Create modified versions of the `Stars` program to print the following patterns. Create a separate program to produce each pattern. *Hint:* Parts b, c, and d require several loops, some of which print a specific number of spaces.

a. `* * * * * * * * * *`   b.   `*`   c. `* * * * * * * * * *`   d.   `*`
    `* * * * * * * *`   `* *`   `* * * * * * * *`   `* * *`
    `* * * * * * *`   `* * *`   `* * * * * * *`   `* * * * *`
    `* * * * * *`   `* * * *`   `* * * * * *`   `* * * * * * *`
    `* * * * *`   `* * * * *`   `* * * * *`   `* * * * * * * * *`
    `* * * *`   `* * * * * *`   `* * * *`   `* * * * * * * * * *`
    `* * *`   `* * * * * * *`   `* * *`   `* * * * * * *`
    `* *`   `* * * * * * * *`   `* *`   `* * * * *`
    `*`   `* * * * * * * * *`   `*`   `* * *`
                  `* * * * * * * * * *`   `*`

PP 4.11   Design and implement an application that prints a table showing a subset of the Unicode characters and their numeric values. Print five number/character pairs per line, separated by tab characters. Print the table for numeric values from 32 (the space character) to 126 (the ~ character), which corresponds to the printable ASCII subset of the Unicode character set. Compare your output to the table in Appendix C. Unlike the table in Appendix C, the values in your table can increase as they go across a row.

PP 4.12   Design and implement an application that reads a string from the user, then determines and prints how many of each lowercase vowel (a, e, i, o, and u) appear in the entire string. Have a separate counter for each vowel. Also count and print the number of nonvowel characters.

PP 4.13   Design and implement an application that plays the Rock-Paper-Scissors game against the computer. When played between two people, each person picks one of three options (usually shown by a hand gesture) at the same time, and a winner is determined. In the game, Rock beats Scissors, Scissors beats Paper, and Paper beats Rock. The program should randomly choose one of the three options (without revealing it), then prompt for the user's selection. At that point, the program reveals both choices and prints a statement indicating whether the user won, the computer won, or it was a tie. Continue playing until the user chooses to stop, then print the number of user wins, losses, and ties.

PP 4.14   Design and implement an application that prints the verses of the song "The Twelve Days of Christmas," in which each verse adds one line. The first two verses of the song are:

On the 1st day of Christmas my true love gave to me

A partridge in a pear tree.

On the 2nd day of Christmas my true love gave to me

Two turtle doves, and

A partridge in a pear tree.

Use a `switch` statement in a loop to control which lines get printed. *Hint:* Order the cases carefully and avoid the `break` statement. Use a separate `switch` statement to put the appropriate suffix on the day number (1st, 2nd, 3rd, etc.). The final verse of the song involves all 12 days, as follows:

On the 12th day of Christmas, my true love gave to me

Twelve drummers drumming,

Eleven pipers piping,

Ten lords a leaping,

Nine ladies dancing,

Eight maids a milking,

Seven swans a swimming,

Six geese a laying,

Five golden rings,

Four calling birds,

Three French hens,

Two turtle doves, and

A partridge in a pear tree.

PP 4.15   Design and implement an application that simulates a simple slot machine in which three numbers between 0 and 9 are randomly selected and printed side by side. Print an appropriate statement if all three of the numbers are the same, or if any two of the numbers are the same. Continue playing until the user chooses to stop.

PP 4.16   Design and implement a program that counts the number of integer values in a text input file. Produce a table listing the values you identify as integers from the input file.

PP 4.17   Design and implement a program to process golf scores. The scores of four golfers are stored in a text file. Each line represents one hole, and the file contains 18 lines. Each line contains five values: par for the hole followed by the number of strokes each golfer used on that hole. Determine the winner and produce a table showing how well each golfer did (compared to par).

PP 4.18   Design and implement a program that compares two text input files, line by line, for equality. Print any lines that are not equivalent.

PP 4.19   Design and implement a program that counts the number of punctuation marks in a text input file. Produce a table that shows how many times each symbol occurred.

Answers to Self-Review Questions

SR 4.1   The flow of control through a program determines the program statements that will be executed on a given run of the program.

SR 4.2   Each conditional and loop is based on a boolean condition that evaluates to either true or false.

SR 4.3   The equality operators are equal (==) and not equal (!=). The relational operators are less than (<), less than or equal to (<=), greater than (>), and greater than or equal to (>=).

SR 4.4   A truth table is a table that shows all possible results of a boolean expression, given all possible combinations of variable values and conditions.

SR 4.5   Because they are stored internally as binary numbers, comparing floating point values for exact equality will be true only if they are the same bit-by-bit. Therefore it's better to use a reasonable tolerance value and consider the difference between the two values.

SR 4.6   We compare strings for equality using the `equals` method of the `String` class, which returns a boolean result. The `compareTo` method of the `String` class can also be used to compare strings. It returns a positive, 0, or negative integer result depending on the relationship between the two strings.

SR 4.7   A nested `if` occurs when the statement inside an `if` or `else` clause is itself an `if` statement. A nested `if` lets the programmer make a series of decisions. Similarly, a nested loop is a loop within a loop.

SR 4.8   A block statement groups several statements together. We use block statements to define the body of an `if` statement or loop when we want to do multiple things based on the boolean condition.

SR 4.9   If a case does not end with a `break` statement, processing continues into the statements of the next case. We usually want to use `break` statements in order to jump to the end of the `switch`.

SR 4.10   An infinite loop is a repetition statement that will not terminate because of the basic logic of the condition. Specifically, the body of the loop never causes the condition to become false.

SR 4.11   A `while` loop evaluates the condition first. If it is true, it executes the loop body. The `do` loop executes the body first and then evaluates the condition. Therefore the body of a `while` loop is executed zero or more times, and the body of a `do` loop is executed one or more times.

SR 4.12   A `for` loop is usually used when we know, or can calculate, how many times we want to iterate through the loop body. A `while` loop handles a more generic situation.

Writing Classes

5

CHAPTER OBJECTIVES

- Explore techniques for identifying the classes and objects needed in a program.

- Discuss the structure and content of a class definition.

- Establish the concept of object state using instance data.

- Describe the effect of visibility modifiers on methods and data.

- Explore the structure of a method definition, including parameters and return values.

- Discuss the structure and purpose of a constructor.

- Discuss the relationships among classes.

- Describe the effect of the `static` modifier on methods and data.

- Discuss issues related to the design of methods, including method decomposition and method overloading.

In previous chapters we used classes and objects for the various services they provide. We also explored several fundamental programming statements. With that experience as a foundation, we are now ready to design more complex software by creating our own classes, which is the heart of object-oriented programming. This chapter explores the basics of class definitions, including the structure of methods and the scope and encapsulation of data. It also examines the creation of static class members and overloaded methods.

5.1 Classes and Objects Revisited

In Chapter 1 we introduced basic object-oriented concepts, including a brief overview of objects and classes. In Chapters 2 and 3 we used several predefined classes from the Java standard class library to create objects and use them for the particular functionality they provide.

In this chapter we turn our attention to writing our own classes. Although existing class libraries provide many useful classes, the essence of object-oriented program development is the process of designing and implementing our own classes to suit our specific needs.

Recall the basic relationship between an object and a class: a class is a blueprint of an object. The class represents the concept of an object, and any object created from that class is a realization of that concept.

For example, from Chapter 3 we know that the `String` class represents a concept of a character string, and that each `String` object represents a particular string that contains specific characters.

Let's consider another example. Suppose a class called `Student` represents a student at a university. An object created from the `Student` class would represent a particular student. The `Student` class represents the general concept of a student, and every object created from that class represents an actual student attending the school. In a system that helps manage the business of a university, we would have one `Student` class and thousands of `Student` objects.

Recall that an object has a *state*, which is defined by the values of the *attributes* associated with that object. For example, the attributes of a student might include the student's name, address, major, and grade point average. The `Student` class establishes that each student has these attributes and each `Student` object stores the values of these attributes for a particular student. In Java, an object's attributes are defined by variables declared within a class.

An object also has *behaviors*, which are defined by the *operations* associated with that object. The operations of a student might include the ability to update that student's address and compute that student's current grade point average. The `Student` class defines the operations, such as the details of how a grade point average is computed. These operations can then be executed on (or by) a particular `Student` object. Note that the behaviors of an object may modify the state of that object. In Java, an object's operations are defined by methods declared within a class.

Figure 5.1 lists some examples of classes, with some attributes and operations that might be defined for objects of those classes. It's up to the program designer to determine what attributes and operations are needed, which depends on the purpose of the program and the role a particular object plays in

Class	Attributes	Operations
Student	Name Address Major Grade point average	Set address Set major Compute grade point average
Rectangle	Length Width Color	Set length Set width Set color
Aquarium	Material Length Width Height	Set material Set length Set width Set height Compute volume Compute filled weight
Flight	Airline Flight number Origin city Destination city Current status	Set airline Set flight number Determine status
Employee	Name Department Title Salary	Set department Set title Set salary Compute wages Compute bonus Compute taxes

FIGURE 5.1 Examples of classes with some possible attributes and operations

that purpose. Consider other attributes and operations you might include for these examples.

Identifying Classes and Objects

A fundamental part of object-oriented software design is determining which classes should be created to define the program. We have to carefully consider how we want to represent the various elements that make up the overall solution. These classes determine the objects that we will manage in the system.

One way to identify potential classes is to identify the objects discussed in the program requirements. Objects are generally nouns. You literally may want to scrutinize a problem description, or a functional specification if available, to identify the nouns found in it. For example, Figure 5.2 on the next page shows part of a problem description with the nouns circled.

The user must be allowed to specify each product by its primary characteristics, including its name and product number. If the bar code does not match the product, then an error should be generated to the message window and entered into the error log. The summary report of all transactions must be structured as specified in section 7.A.

FIGURE 5.2 Finding potential objects by identifying the nouns in a problem description

Of course, not every noun in the problem specification will correspond to a class in a program. Some nouns may be represented as attributes of other objects, and the designer may decide not to represent other nouns explicitly in the program at all. This activity is just a starting point that allows a developer to think about the types of objects a program will manage.

Remember that a class represents a group of objects with similar behavior. A plural noun in the specification, such as products, may indicate the need for a class that represents one of those items, such as `Product`. Even if there is only one of a particular kind of object needed in your system, it may best be represented as a class.

Classes that represent objects should generally be given names that are singular nouns, such as `Coin`, `Student`, and `Message`. A class represents a single item from which we are free to create as many instances as we choose.

Another key decision is whether to represent something as an object or as a primitive attribute of another object. For example, we may initially think that an employee's salary should be represented as an integer, and that may work for much of the system's processing. But upon further reflection we might realize that the salary is based on the person's rank, which has upper and lower salary bounds that must be managed with care. Therefore the final conclusion may be that we'd be better off representing all of that data and the associated behavior as a separate class.

Given the needs of a particular program, we want to strike a good balance between classes that are too general and those that are too specific. For example, it may complicate our design unnecessarily to create a separate class for each type of appliance that exists in a house. It may be sufficient to have a single `Appliance` class, with perhaps a piece of instance data that indicates what type of appliance it is. Then again, this may not be an adequate solution. It all depends on what the software is going to accomplish.

In addition to classes that represent objects from the problem domain, we likely will need classes that support the work necessary to get the job done. For example, in addition to `Member` objects, we may want a separate class to help us manage all of the members of a club.

Keep in mind that when producing a real system, some of the classes we identify during design may already exist. Even if nothing matches exactly, there may be an old class that's similar enough to serve as the basis for our new class. The existing class may be part of the Java standard class library, part of a solution to a problem we've solved previously, or part of a library that can be bought from a third party. These are all examples of software reuse.

Assigning Responsibilities

Part of the process of identifying the classes needed in a program is the process of assigning responsibilities to each class. Each class represents an object with certain behaviors that are defined by the methods of the class. Any activity that the program must accomplish must be represented somewhere in the behaviors of the classes. That is, each class is responsible for carrying out certain activities, and those responsibilities must be assigned as part of designing a program.

The behaviors of a class perform actions that make up the functionality of a program. Thus we generally use verbs for the names of behaviors and the methods that accomplish them.

Sometimes it is challenging to determine which is the best class to carry out a particular responsibility. A good designer considers multiple possibilities. Sometimes such analysis makes you realize that you could benefit from defining another class to shoulder the responsibility.

It's not necessary in the early stages of a design to identify all the methods that a class will contain. It is often sufficient to assign primary responsibilities, and consider how those responsibilities translate to particular methods.

5.2 Anatomy of a Class

Now that we've reviewed some important conceptual ideas underlying the development of classes and objects, let's dive into the programming details. In all of our previous examples, we've written a single class containing a single `main` method. Each of these classes represents a small but complete program. These programs often instantiate objects using predefined classes from the Java class library and then use those objects for the services they provide. The library classes are part of the program too, but we generally don't have to concern ourselves with their internal details. We really just need to know how to interact with them, and simply trust them to provide the services they promise.

We will continue to rely on library classes, but now we will also design and implement other classes as needed. Let's look at an example. The SnakeEyes class shown in Listing 5.1 contains a main method that instantiates two Die objects (as in the singular of dice). The purpose of the program is to roll the dice and count the number of times both die show a 1 on the same throw (snake eyes).

The primary difference between this example and examples we've seen in previous chapters is that the Die class is not a predefined part of the Java class library. For this program to compile and run, we have to write the Die class ourselves, defining the services we want Die objects to perform.

A class can contain data declarations and method declarations, as depicted in Figure 5.3 on page 168. The data declarations represent the data that will be stored in each object of the class. The method declarations define the services that those objects will provide. Collectively, the data and methods of a class are called the *members* of a class.

The classes we've written in previous examples follow this model as well, but contain no data at the class level and contain only one method (the main method). We'll continue to define classes like this, such as the SnakeEyes class, to define the starting point of a program.

> **KEY CONCEPT**
> The heart of object-oriented programming is defining classes that represent objects with well-defined state and behavior.

True object-oriented programming, however, comes from defining classes that represent objects with well-defined state and behavior. For example, at any given moment a Die object is showing a particular face value, which we could refer to as the state of the die. A Die object also has various methods we can invoke on it, such as the ability to roll the die or get its face value. These methods represent the behavior of a die.

The Die class is shown in Listing 5.2 on page 168. It contains two data values: an integer constant (MAX) that represents the maximum face value of the die, and an integer variable (faceValue) that represents the current face value of the die. It also contains a constructor called Die and four regular methods: roll, setFaceValue, getFaceValue, and toString.

You will recall from Chapters 2 and 3 that constructors are special methods that have the same name as the class. The Die constructor gets called when the new operator is used to create a new instance of the Die class, as we do twice in the main method of the SnakeEyes class. The rest of the methods in the Die class define the various services provided by Die objects.

We use a header block of documentation to explain the purpose of each method in the class. This practice is not only crucial for anyone trying to understand the software, it also separates the code visually so that it's easy for the eye to jump from one method to the next while reading the code.

LISTING 5.1

```java
//********************************************************************
//  SnakeEyes.java        Java Foundations
//
//  Demonstrates the use of a programmer-defined class.
//********************************************************************

public class SnakeEyes
{
   //-----------------------------------------------------------------
   //  Creates two Die objects and rolls them several times, counting
   //  the number of snake eyes that occur.
   //-----------------------------------------------------------------
   public static void main (String[] args)
   {
      final int ROLLS = 500;
      int num1, num2, count = 0;

      Die die1 = new Die();
      Die die2 = new Die();

      for (int roll=1; roll <= ROLLS; roll++)
      {
         num1 = die1.roll();
         num2 = die2.roll();

         if (num1 == 1 && num2 == 1)      // check for snake eyes
            count++;
      }

      System.out.println ("Number of rolls: " + ROLLS);
      System.out.println ("Number of snake eyes: " + count);
      System.out.println ("Ratio: " + (float)count / ROLLS);
   }
}
```

OUTPUT

```
Number of rolls: 500
Number of snake eyes: 12
Ratio: 0.024
```

FIGURE 5.3 The members of a class: data and method declarations

---

LISTING 5.2

```java
//********************************************************************
//  Die.java          Java Foundations
//
//  Represents one die (singular of dice) with faces showing values
//  between 1 and 6.
//********************************************************************

public class Die
{
   private final int MAX = 6; // maximum face value

   private int faceValue; // current value showing on the die

   //-----------------------------------------------------------------
   //  Constructor: Sets the initial face value of this die.
   //-----------------------------------------------------------------
   public Die()
   {
      faceValue = 1;
   }

   //-----------------------------------------------------------------
   //  Computes a new face value for this die and returns the result.
   //-----------------------------------------------------------------
```

LISTING 5.2   *continued*

```java
    public int roll()
    {
        faceValue = (int)(Math.random() * MAX) + 1;

        return faceValue;
    }

    //-------------------------------------------------------------
    //  Face value mutator. The face value is not modified if the
    //  specified value is not valid.
    //-------------------------------------------------------------
    public void setFaceValue (int value)
    {
        if (value > 0 && value <= MAX)
            faceValue = value;
    }

    //-------------------------------------------------------------
    //  Face value accessor.
    //-------------------------------------------------------------
    public int getFaceValue()
    {
        return faceValue;
    }

    //-------------------------------------------------------------
    //  Returns a string representation of this die.
    //-------------------------------------------------------------
    public String toString()
    {
        String result = Integer.toString(faceValue);

        return result;
    }
}
```

Figure 5.4 on the next page lists the methods of the Die class. From this point of view, it looks no different from any other class that we've used in previous examples. The only important difference is that the Die class was not provided for us by the Java standard class library. We wrote it ourselves.

```
Die()
        Constructor: Sets the initial face value of the die to 1.

int roll()
        Rolls the die by setting the face value to a random number in the appropriate range.

void setFaceValue (int value)
        Sets the face value of the die to the specified value.

int getFaceValue()
        Returns the current face value of the die.

String toString()
        Returns a string representation of the die indicating its current face value.
```

FIGURE 5.4 Some methods of the Die class

The methods of the Die class include the ability to roll the die, producing a new random face value. The roll method returns the new face value to the calling method, but you can also get the current face value at any time using the getFaceValue method. The setFaceValue method sets the face value explicitly, as if you had reached over and turned the die to whatever face you wanted. The toString method returns a representation of the die as a character string—in this case it returns the numeric value of the die face as a string. The definitions of these methods have various parts, and we'll dissect them as we proceed through this chapter.

Let's mention the importance of the toString method at this point. The toString method of any object gets called automatically whenever you pass the object to a print or println method and when you concatenate an object to a character string. There is a default version of toString defined for every object, but the results are not generally useful. Therefore it's usually a good idea to define a toString method for the classes that you create. The default version of toString is available because of inheritance, which we discuss in detail in Chapter 8.

For the examples in this book, we usually store each class in its own file. Java allows multiple classes to be stored in one file. But if a file contains multiple classes, only one of those classes can be declared using the reserved word public. Furthermore, the name of the public class must correspond to the name of the file. For instance, class Die is stored in a file called Die.java.

Instance Data

Note that in the Die class, the constant MAX and the variable faceValue are declared inside the class, but not inside any method. The location at which a variable is declared defines its *scope*, which is the area within a program in which that variable can be referenced. By being declared at the class level (not within a method), these variables and constants can be referenced in any method of the class.

Attributes such as the variable `faceValue` are called *instance data* because new memory space is reserved for that variable every time an instance of the class is created. Each `Die` object has its own `faceValue` variable with its own data space. That's how each `Die` object can have its own state. That is, one die could be showing a 5 at the same time the other die is showing a 2. That's possible only because separate memory space for the `faceValue` variable is created for each `Die` object.

We can depict this situation as follows:

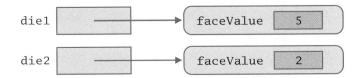

The `die1` and `die2` reference variables point to (that is, contain the address of) their respective `Die` objects. Each object contains a `faceValue` variable with its own memory space. Thus each object can store different values for its instance data.

Java automatically initializes any variables declared at the class level. For example, all variables of numeric types such as `int` and `double` are initialized to zero. However, despite the fact that the language performs this automatic initialization, it is good practice to initialize variables explicitly (usually in a constructor) so that anyone reading the code will clearly understand the intent.

UML Class Diagrams

As our programs become more complex, containing multiple classes, it's helpful to make use of a graphical notation to capture, visualize, and communicate the program design. Throughout the remainder of this book we use *UML diagrams* for this purpose. UML stands for the *Unified Modeling Language*, which has become the most popular notation for representing the design of an object-oriented program.

Several types of UML diagrams exist, each designed to show specific aspects of object-oriented programs. We focus primarily on UML *class diagrams* in this book to show the contents of classes and the relationships among them.

In a UML diagram, each class is represented as a rectangle, possibly containing three sections to show the class name, its attributes (data), and its operations

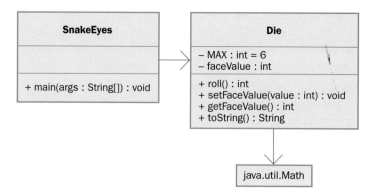

FIGURE 5.5 A UML class diagram showing the classes involved in the `SnakeEyes` program

(methods). Figure 5.5 shows a class diagram containing the classes of the `SnakeEyes` program.

UML is not designed specifically for Java programmers. It is intended to be language independent. Therefore the syntax used in a UML diagram is not necessarily the same as Java. For example, a variable's type is shown after the variable name, separated by a colon. Return types of methods are shown the same way. The initial value of an attribute can be shown in the class diagram if desired, as we do with the MAX constant in Figure 5.5. The + and – notations in front of variables and methods indicate their *visibility*, which is discussed in the next section.

A solid line connecting two classes in a UML diagram indicates that a relationship of one kind or another exists between the two classes. These lines are called *associations*, and indicate that one class "knows about" and uses the other in some way. For example, an association might indicate that an object of one class creates an object of the other, and/or that one class invokes a method of the other. Associations can be labeled to indicate the details of the association.

A directed association uses an arrowhead to indicate that the association is particularly one-way. For example, the arrow connecting the `SnakeEyes` and `Die` classes in Figure 5.5 indicates that the `SnakeEyes` class "knows about" and uses the `Die` class, but not vice versa.

An association can show *multiplicity* by annotating the ends of the connection with numeric values. In this case, the diagram indicates that `SnakeEyes` is associated with exactly two `Die` objects. Both ends of an association can show multiplicity values, if desired. Multiplicity also can be expressed in terms of a range of values and by using wildcards for unknown values, as we'll see in later examples.

Other types of object-oriented relationships between classes are shown with different types of connecting lines and arrows. We will explore additional aspects of UML diagrams as we discuss the corresponding object-oriented programming concepts throughout the book.

UML diagrams are versatile. We can include whatever appropriate information is desired, depending on what we are trying to convey in a particular diagram. We might leave out the data and method sections of a class, for instance, if those details aren't relevant for a particular diagram. For example, the fact that the Die class makes use of the Math class from the Java API is indicated in Figure 5.5, but the details of the Math class are not identified. We also could have explicitly indicated the use of the String class, but that is rarely done because of its ubiquity.

5.3 Encapsulation

We mentioned in our overview of object-oriented concepts in Chapter 1 that an object should be *self-governing*. That is, the instance data of an object should be modified only by that object. For example, the methods of the Die class should be solely responsible for changing the value of the faceValue variable. We should make it difficult, if not impossible, for code outside of a class to "reach in" and change the value of a variable that is declared inside that class. This characteristic is called *encapsulation*.

> **KEY CONCEPT**
> An object should be encapsulated, guarding its data from inappropriate access.

An object should be encapsulated from the rest of the system. It should interact with other parts of a program only through the specific set of methods that define the services that that object provides. These methods define the *interface* between that object and other objects that use it.

The nature of encapsulation is depicted graphically in Figure 5.6 on the next page. The code that uses an object, sometimes called the *client* of an object, should not be allowed to access variables directly. The client should call an object's methods, and those methods then interact with the data encapsulated within the object. For example, the main method in the SnakeEyes program calls the roll method of the die objects. The main method should not (and in fact cannot) access the faceValue variable directly.

In Java, we accomplish object encapsulation using *modifiers*. A modifier is a Java reserved word that is used to specify particular characteristics of a programming language construct. In Chapter 2 we discussed the final modifier, which is used to declare a constant. Java has several modifiers that can be used in various ways. Some modifiers can be used together, but some combinations are invalid. We discuss various Java modifiers at appropriate points throughout this book, and all of them are summarized in Appendix E.

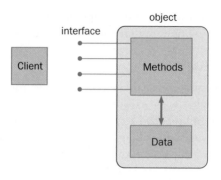

FIGURE 5.6   A client interacting with another object

Visibility Modifiers

Some of the Java modifiers are called *visibility modifiers* because they control access to the members of a class. The reserved words `public` and `private` are visibility modifiers that can be applied to the variables and methods of a class. If a member of a class has *public visibility*, it can be directly referenced from outside of the object. If a member of a class has *private visibility*, it can be used anywhere inside the class definition but cannot be referenced externally. A third visibility modifier, `protected`, is relevant only in the context of inheritance. We discuss it in Chapter 8.

> **KEY CONCEPT**
>
> Instance variables should be declared with private visibility to promote encapsulation.

Public variables violate encapsulation. They allow code external to the class in which the data is defined to reach in and access or modify the value of the data. Therefore instance data should be defined with private visibility. Data that is declared as private can be accessed only by the methods of the class.

The visibility we apply to a method depends on the purpose of that method. Methods that provide services to the client must be declared with public visibility so that they can be invoked by the client. These methods are sometimes referred to as *service methods*. A private method cannot be invoked from outside the class. The only purpose of a private method is to help the other methods of the class do their job. Therefore they are sometimes referred to as *support methods*.

The table in Figure 5.7 summarizes the effects of public and private visibility on both variables and methods.

Giving constants public visibility is generally considered acceptable because, although their values can be accessed directly, their values cannot be changed because they were declared using the `final` modifier. Keep in mind that encapsulation

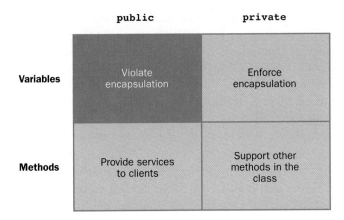

	public	**private**
Variables	Violate encapsulation	Enforce encapsulation
Methods	Provide services to clients	Support other methods in the class

FIGURE 5.7 The effects of public and private visibility

means that data values should not be able to be *modified* directly by another part of the code. Because constants, by definition, cannot be changed, the encapsulation issue is largely moot.

UML class diagrams can show the visibility of a class member by preceding it with a particular character. A member with public visibility is preceded by a plus sign (+), and a member with private visibility is preceded by a minus sign (-). Review Figure 5.5 to see this notation used.

Accessors and Mutators

Because instance data is generally declared with private visibility, a class usually provides services to access and modify data values. A method such as getFaceValue in the Die class is called an *accessor method* because it provides read-only access to a particular value. Likewise, a method such as setFaceValue is called a *mutator method* because it changes a particular value.

> **KEY CONCEPT**
>
> Most objects contain accessor and mutator methods to allow the client to manage data in a controlled manner.

Generally, accessor method names have the form getX, where X is the value to which it provides access. Likewise, mutator method names have the form setX, where X is the value they are setting. Therefore these types of methods are sometimes referred to as "getters" and "setters."

For example, if a class contains the instance variable height, it should also probably contain the methods getHeight and setHeight. Note that this naming convention capitalizes the first letter of the variable when used in the method names, which is consistent with how method names are written in general.

Some methods may provide accessor and/or mutator capabilities as a side effect of their primary purpose. For example, the `roll` method of the `Die` class changes the value of the variable `faceValue`, and returns that new value as well. Note that the code of the `roll` method is guaranteed to keep the face value of the die in the valid range (1 to `MAX`). Similarly, the `setFaceValue` method checks to see if the specified value is in the valid range, and ignores it if it is not. Service methods must be carefully designed to permit only appropriate access and valid changes. By encapsulating the data, the object can maintain this type of control.

Let's look at anther example. The program in Listing 5.3 instantiates a `Coin` object, then flips the coin multiple times, counting the number of times heads and tails come up. Notice that it uses a call to the method `isHeads` in the condition of an `if` statement to determine which result occurred.

The `Coin` class is shown in Listing 5.4 on page 178. It stores an integer constant called `HEADS` that represents the face value when the coin is showing heads. An instance variable called `face` represents the current state of the coin (which side is up) and has either the value 0 or 1. The `Coin` constructor initially flips the coin by calling the `flip` method, which determines the new state of the coin by randomly choosing a number (either 0 or 1). The `isHeads` method returns a `boolean` value based on the current face value of the coin. The `toString` method returns a character string indicating the current face showing on the coin.

A `Coin` object can be in one of two states: showing heads or showing tails. We represented this state in the `Coin` class as an integer value, 0 for tails and 1 for heads, stored in the `face` variable. Of course, this representation is arbitrary—we could have used 1 to represent tails. For that matter, we could have represented the coin's state using a `boolean` value, or a character string, or an enumerated type. We chose to use an integer because the methods for choosing a random result (`Math.random` in this case) return a numeric value, and therefore eliminated extraneous conversions.

> **KEY CONCEPT**
> The way a class represents an object's state should be independent of how that object is used.

The way the `Coin` object represents its state internally is, and should be, irrelevant to the client using the object. That is, from the perspective of the `CountFlips` program, the way the `Coin` class represents its state doesn't matter.

We could have made the constant `HEADS` public so that the client could access it. But as an integer variable, its value is meaningless to the client. Providing the `isHeads` method is a cleaner object-oriented solution. The internal details of the `Coin` class could be rewritten and, as long as the `isHeads` method is written appropriately, the client would not have to change.

Although many classes will have classic getter and setter methods, we chose to design the `Coin` class without them. The only way the coin's state can be changed is to flip it randomly. Unlike a `Die` object, the user cannot explicitly set the state of a coin. This is a design decision, which could be made differently if circumstances dictate.

LISTING 5.3

```java
//********************************************************************
//  CountFlips.java        Java Foundations
//
//  Demonstrates the use of programmer-defined class.
//********************************************************************

public class CountFlips
{
   //-----------------------------------------------------------------
   //  Flips a coin multiple times and counts the number of heads
   //  and tails that result.
   //-----------------------------------------------------------------
   public static void main (String[] args)
   {
      final int FLIPS = 1000;
      int heads = 0, tails = 0;

      Coin myCoin = new Coin();

      for (int count=1; count <= FLIPS; count++)
      {
         myCoin.flip();

         if (myCoin.isHeads())
            heads++;
         else
            tails++;
      }

      System.out.println ("Number of flips: " + FLIPS);
      System.out.println ("Number of heads: " + heads);
      System.out.println ("Number of tails: " + tails);
   }
}
```

OUTPUT

```
Number of flips: 1000
Number of heads: 486
Number of tails: 514
```

LISTING 5.4

```java
//*****************************************************************
//  Coin.java        Java Foundations
//
//  Represents a coin with two sides that can be flipped.
//*****************************************************************

public class Coin
{
   private final int HEADS = 0; // tails is 1

   private int face; // current side showing

   //----------------------------------------------------------------
   //  Sets up this coin by flipping it initially.
   //----------------------------------------------------------------
   public Coin ()
   {
      flip();
   }

   //----------------------------------------------------------------
   //  Flips this coin by randomly choosing a face value.
   //----------------------------------------------------------------
   public void flip ()
   {
      face = (int) (Math.random() * 2);
   }

   //----------------------------------------------------------------
   //  Returns true if the current face of this coin is heads.
   //----------------------------------------------------------------
   public boolean isHeads ()
   {
      return (face == HEADS);
   }

   //----------------------------------------------------------------
   //  Returns the current face of this coin as a string.
   //----------------------------------------------------------------
   public String toString()
   {
      return (face == HEADS) ? "Heads" : "Tails";
   }
}
```

Let's use the `Coin` class in another program. The `FlipRace` class is shown in Listing 5.5. The `main` method of `FlipRace` instantiates two `Coin` objects and flips them in tandem repeatedly until one of the coins comes up heads three times in a row.

The output of the `FlipRace` program shows the results of each coin flip. Note that the `coin1` and `coin2` objects are concatenated to character strings in the `println` statement. As we mentioned earlier, this situation causes the `toString` method of the object to be called, which returns a string to be printed. No explicit call to the `toString` method is needed.

The conditional operator is used in assignment statements to set the counters for the coins after they are flipped. For each coin, if the result is heads, the count

LISTING 5.5

```java
//********************************************************************
//  FlipRace.java        Java Foundations
//
//  Demonstrates the reuse of programmer-defined class.
//********************************************************************

public class FlipRace
{
    //----------------------------------------------------------------
    //  Flips two coins until one of them comes up heads three times
    //  in a row.
    //----------------------------------------------------------------
    public static void main (String[] args)
    {
        final int GOAL = 3;
        int count1 = 0, count2 = 0;
        Coin coin1 = new Coin(), coin2 = new Coin();

        while (count1 < GOAL && count2 < GOAL)
        {
            coin1.flip();
            coin2.flip();

            System.out.println ("Coin 1: " + coin1 + "\tCoin 2: " + coin2);

            // Increment or reset the counters
            count1 = (coin1.isHeads()) ? count1+1 : 0;
            count2 = (coin2.isHeads()) ? count2+1 : 0;
        }
```

LISTING 5.5   *continued*

```
    if (count1 < GOAL)
        System.out.println ("Coin 2 Wins!");
    else
        if (count2 < GOAL)
            System.out.println ("Coin 1 Wins!");
        else
            System.out.println ("It's a TIE!");
    }
}
```

OUTPUT

```
Coin 1: Tails   Coin 2: Heads
Coin 1: Heads   Coin 2: Heads
Coin 1: Tails   Coin 2: Tails
Coin 1: Tails   Coin 2: Tails
Coin 1: Tails   Coin 2: Heads
Coin 1: Heads   Coin 2: Tails
Coin 1: Heads   Coin 2: Tails
Coin 1: Heads   Coin 2: Heads
Coin 1 Wins!
```

is incremented. If not, the count is reset to zero. The `while` loop terminates when either or both counters reach the goal of three heads in a row.

`FlipRace` uses the `Coin` class as part of its program, just as `CountFlips` did earlier. A well-designed class often can be reused in multiple programs, just as we've gotten used to reusing the classes from the Java API over and over.

5.4 Anatomy of a Method

We've seen that a class is composed of data declarations and method declarations. Let's examine method declarations in more detail.

As we stated in Chapter 1, a method is a group of programming language statements that is given a name. A *method declaration* specifies the code that is executed when the method is invoked. Every method in a Java program is part of a particular class.

The header of a method declaration includes the type of the return value, the method name, and a list of parameters that the method accepts. The statements that make up the body of the method are defined in a block delimited by braces. We've defined the `main` method of a program many times in previous examples. Its definition follows the same syntax as any other method.

When a method is called, the flow of control transfers to that method. One by one, the statements of that method are executed. When that method is done, control returns to the location where the call was made and execution continues.

The *called method* (the one that is invoked) might be part of the same class as the *calling method* that invoked it. If the called method is part of the same class, only the method name is needed to invoke it. If it is part of a different class, it is invoked through a reference to an object of that other class, as we've seen many times. Figure 5.8 shows the flow of execution as methods are called.

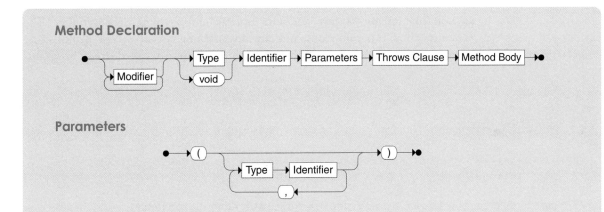

Method Declaration

Parameters

A method is defined by optional modifiers, followed by a return Type, followed by an Identifier that determines the method name, followed by a list of Parameters, followed by the Method Body. The return Type indicates the type of value that will be returned by the method, which may be void. The Method Body is a block of statements that executes when the method is invoked. The Throws Clause is optional and indicates the exceptions that may be thrown by this method.

Example:

```
public int computeArea (int length, int width)
{
    int area = length * width;
    return area;
}
```

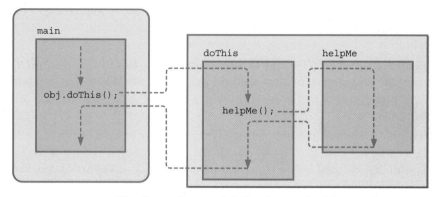

FIGURE 5.8 The flow of control following method invocations

Let's look at another example as we continue to explore the details of method declarations. The `Transactions` class shown in Listing 5.6 contains a `main` method that creates a few `Account` objects and invokes their services. The `Transactions` program doesn't really do anything useful except demonstrate how to interact with `Account` objects. Such programs are called *driver programs*

LISTING 5.6

```java
//********************************************************************
//  Transactions.java        Java Foundations
//
//  Demonstrates the creation and use of multiple Account objects.
//********************************************************************

public class Transactions
{
   //-----------------------------------------------------------------
   //  Creates some bank accounts and requests various services.
   //-----------------------------------------------------------------
   public static void main (String[] args)
   {
      Account acct1 = new Account ("Ted Murphy", 72354, 25.59);
      Account acct2 = new Account ("Angelica Adams", 69713, 500.00);
      Account acct3 = new Account ("Edward Demsey", 93757, 769.32);

      acct1.deposit (44.10);  // return value ignored
```

LISTING 5.6   *continued*

```
        double adamsBalance = acct2.deposit (75.25);
        System.out.println ("Adams balance after deposit: " +
                            adamsBalance);

        System.out.println ("Adams balance after withdrawal: " +
                            acct2.withdraw (480, 1.50));

        acct3.withdraw (-100.00, 1.50);  // invalid transaction

        acct1.addInterest();
        acct2.addInterest();
        acct3.addInterest();

        System.out.println ();
        System.out.println (acct1);
        System.out.println (acct2);
        System.out.println (acct3);
    }
}
```

OUTPUT

```
Adams balance after deposit: 575.25
Adams balance after withdrawal: 93.75

72354   Ted Murphy        $72.13
69713   Angelica Adams    $97.03
93757   Edward Demsey     $796.25
```

because all they do is drive the use of other, more interesting parts of our program. They are often used for testing purposes.

The Account class, shown in Listing 5.7 on the next page, represents a basic bank account. It contains instance data representing the name of the account's owner, the account number, and the account's current balance. The interest rate for the account is stored as a constant.

The constructor of the Account class accepts three parameters that are used to initialize the instance data when an Account object is instantiated. The other methods of the Account class perform various services on the account, such as making deposits and withdrawals. These methods examine the data passed into them to make sure the requested transaction is valid. For example, the withdraw method prevents the withdrawal of a negative amount (which essentially would

LISTING 5.7

```java
//********************************************************************
//  Account.java       Java Foundations
//
//  Represents a bank account with basic services such as deposit
//  and withdraw.
//********************************************************************

import java.text.NumberFormat;

public class Account
{
   private final double RATE = 0.035; // interest rate of 3.5%

   private String name;
   private long acctNumber;
   private double balance;

   //-----------------------------------------------------------------
   //  Sets up this account with the specified owner, account number,
   //  and initial balance.
   //-----------------------------------------------------------------
   public Account (String owner, long account, double initial)
   {
      name = owner;
      acctNumber = account;
      balance = initial;
   }

   //-----------------------------------------------------------------
   //  Deposits the specified amount into this account and returns
   //  the new balance. The balance is not modified if the deposit
   //  amount is invalid.
   //-----------------------------------------------------------------
   public double deposit (double amount)
   {
      if (amount > 0)
         balance = balance + amount;

      return balance;
   }

   //-----------------------------------------------------------------
   //  Withdraws the specified amount and fee from this account and
   //  returns the new balance. The balance is not modified if the
```

LISTING 5.7   *continued*

```java
// withdraw amount is invalid or the balance is insufficient.
//-----------------------------------------------------------------
public double withdraw (double amount, double fee)
{
    if (amount+fee > 0 && amount+fee < balance)
        balance = balance - amount - fee;

    return balance;
}


//-----------------------------------------------------------------
// Adds interest to this account and returns the new balance.
//-----------------------------------------------------------------
public double addInterest ()
{
    balance += (balance * RATE);
    return balance;
}


//-----------------------------------------------------------------
// Returns the current balance of this account.
//-----------------------------------------------------------------
public double getBalance ()
{
    return balance;
}


//-----------------------------------------------------------------
// Returns a one-line description of this account as a string.
//-----------------------------------------------------------------
public String toString ()
{
    NumberFormat fmt = NumberFormat.getCurrencyInstance();

    return (acctNumber + "\t" + name + "\t" + fmt.format(balance));
}
}
```

be a deposit). There is also an `addInterest` method that updates the balance by adding in the interest earned. These methods represent the valid ways to modify the balance, so a generic mutator such as `setBalance` is not provided.

The status of the three `Account` objects just after they were created in the `Transactions` program could be depicted as follows:

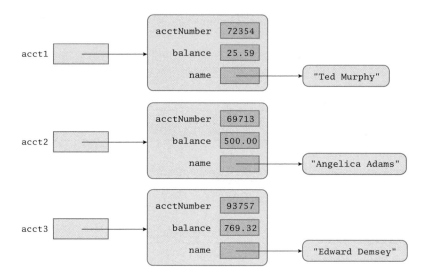

The rest of this section discusses issues related to method declarations in more detail.

The return Statement

The return type specified in the method header can be a primitive type, class name, or the reserved word `void`. When a method does not return any value, `void` is used as the return type, as is always done with the `main` method of a program. The `setFaceValue` of the `Die` class and the `flip` method of the `Coin` class also have return types of `void`.

The `getFaceValue` and `roll` methods of the `Die` class return an `int` value that represents the value shown on the die. The `isHeads` method of the `Coin` class returns a `boolean` value that represents whether the coin is currently showing heads. Several of the methods of the `Account` class return a `double` representing the updated balance. The `toString` method in all of these classes returns a `String` object.

A method that returns a value must have a *return statement*. When a return statement is executed, control is immediately returned to the statement in the

Return Statement

A `return` statement consists of the `return` reserved word followed by an optional Expression. When executed, control is immediately returned to the calling method, returning the value defined by Expression.
Examples:

```
return;
```

```
return distance * 4;
```

calling method, and processing continues there. A `return` statement consists of the reserved word `return` followed by an expression that dictates the value to be returned. The expression must be consistent with the return type specified in the method header.

A method that does not return a value does not usually contain a `return` statement. The method automatically returns to the calling method when the end of the method is reached. Such methods may contain a `return` statement without an expression.

It is usually not good practice to use more than one `return` statement in a method, even though it is possible to do so. In general, a method should have one `return` statement as the last line of the method body, unless that makes the method overly complex.

The value that is returned from a method can be ignored in the calling method. Consider the following method invocation from the `Transactions` program:

```
acct1.deposit(44.10);
```

In this situation, the `deposit` method executes normally, updating the account balance accordingly, but the calling method simply makes no use of the returned value.

Constructors do not have a return type (not even `void`) and therefore cannot return a value. We discuss constructors in more detail later in this chapter.

> **KEY CONCEPT**
>
> The value returned from a method must be consistent with the return type specified in the method header.

Parameters

We introduced the concept of a parameter in Chapter 2, defining it as a value that is passed into a method when the method is invoked. Parameters provide data to a method that allows the method to do its job. Let's explore this issue in more detail.

The method declaration specifies the number and type of parameters that a method will accept. More precisely, the *parameter list* in the header of a method declaration specifies the type of each value that is passed into the method, and the name by which the called method will refer to each value. The corresponding parameter list in the invocation specifies the values that are passed in for that particular invocation.

The names of the parameters in the header of the method declaration are called *formal parameters*. The values passed into a method when it is invoked are called *actual parameters*, or *arguments*. The parameter list in both the declaration and the invocation is enclosed in parentheses after the method name. If there are no parameters, an empty set of parentheses is used.

None of the methods in the `Coin` and `Die` classes accept parameters except for the `setFaceValue` method of the `Die` class, which accepts a single integer parameter that specifies the new value for the die. The `Account` constructor accepts several parameters of various types to provide initial values for the object's instance data (this is common for constructors). The `withdraw` method in `Account` accepts two parameters of type `double`; note that the type of each formal parameter is listed separately even if the types are the same.

> **KEY CONCEPT**
>
> When a method is called, the actual parameters are copied into the formal parameters.

The formal parameters are identifiers that serve as variables inside the method and whose initial values come from the actual parameters in the invocation. When a method is called, the value in each actual parameter is copied and stored in the corresponding formal parameter. Actual parameters can be literals, variables, or full expressions. If an expression is used as an actual parameter, it is fully evaluated before the method call and the result is passed to the method.

The parameter lists in the invocation and the method declaration must match up. That is, the value of the first actual parameter is copied into the first formal parameter, the second actual parameter into the second formal parameter, and so on, as shown in Figure 5.9. The types of the actual parameters must be consistent with the specified types of the formal parameters.

In the `Transactions` program, the following call is made:

```
acct2.withdraw (480, 1.50)
```

This call passes an integer value as the first parameter of the `withdraw` method, which is defined to accept a `double`. This is valid because the actual and formal parameters must be consistent, but not necessarily match exactly. A `double`

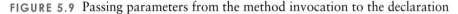

FIGURE 5.9 Passing parameters from the method invocation to the declaration

variable can be assigned an integer value because this is a widening conversion. Thus it is also allowed when passing parameters.

We explore some of the details regarding parameter passing later in this chapter.

Local Data

As we described earlier in this chapter, the scope of a variable or constant is the part of a program in which a valid reference to that variable can be made. A variable can be declared inside a method, making it *local data* as opposed to instance data. Recall that instance data is declared in a class but not inside any particular method.

Local data has scope limited to only the method in which it is declared. The variable `result` declared in the `toString` method of the `Die` class is local data. Any reference to `result` in any other method of the `Die` class would have caused the compiler to issue an error message. A local variable simply does not exist outside of the method in which it is declared. On the other hand, instance data, declared at the class level, has a scope of the entire class; any method of the class can refer to it.

> **KEY CONCEPT**
> A variable declared in a method is local to that method and cannot be used outside of it.

Because local data and instance data operate at different levels of scope, it's possible to declare a local variable inside a method with the same name as an instance variable declared at the class level. Referring to that name in the method will reference the local version of the variable. This naming practice obviously has the potential to confuse anyone reading the code, so it should be avoided.

The formal parameter names in a method header serve as local data for that method. They don't exist until the method is called, and they cease to exist when the method is exited. For example, the formal parameter `owner` in the `Account` constructor comes into existence when the constructor is called and goes out of existence when it finishes executing. To store these values in the object, the values of the parameters are copied into the instance variables of the newly created `Account` object.

Constructors Revisited

Let's discuss constructors a bit more. When we define a class, we usually define a constructor to help us set up the class. In particular, we often use a constructor to initialize the variables associated with each object.

A constructor differs from a regular method in two ways. First, the name of a constructor is the same name as the class. Therefore the name of the constructor in the `Die` class is `Die`, and the name of the constructor in the `Account` class is `Account`. Second, a constructor cannot return a value and does not have a return type specified in the method header.

> **KEY CONCEPT**
>
> A constructor cannot have any return type, even `void`.

A common mistake made by programmers is to put a `void` return type on a constructor. As far as the compiler is concerned, putting any return type on a constructor, even `void`, turns it into a regular method that happens to have the same name as the class. As such, it cannot be invoked as a constructor. This leads to error messages that are sometimes difficult to decipher.

Generally, a constructor is used to initialize the newly instantiated object. For instance, the constructor of the `Die` class sets the face value of the die to 1 initially. The constructor of the `Coin` class calls the `flip` method to put the coin in an initial, random state. The constructor of the `Account` class sets the values of the instance variables to the values passed in as parameters to the constructor. The way you use a constructor to set up an object initially is another important design decision.

If we don't provide a constructor for a class, a *default constructor* that takes no parameters is automatically created and used. The default constructor generally has no effect on the newly created object. If the programmer provides a constructor, with or without parameters, the default constructor is not defined.

5.5 Static Class Members

We've used static methods in various situations in previous examples in the book. For example, all the methods of the `Math` class are static. Recall that a static method is one that is invoked through its class name, instead of through an object of that class.

Not only can methods be static, but variables can be static as well. We declare static class members using the `static` modifier.

Deciding whether to declare a method or variable as static is a key step in class design. Let's examine the implications of static variables and methods more closely.

Static Variables

So far, we've seen two categories of variables: local variables that are declared inside a method, and instance variables that are declared in a class but not inside a method. The term *instance variable* is used because each instance of the class has its own version of the variable. That is, each object has distinct memory space for each variable so that each object can have a distinct value for that variable.

A *static variable*, which is sometimes called a *class variable*, is shared among all instances of a class. There is only one copy of a static variable for all objects of the class. Therefore, changing the value of a static variable in one object changes it for all of the others. The reserved word `static` is used as a modifier to declare a static variable as follows:

> **KEY CONCEPT**
> A static variable is shared among all instances of a class.

```
private static int count = 0;
```

Memory space for a static variable is established when the class that contains it is referenced for the first time in a program. A local variable declared within a method cannot be static.

Constants, which are declared using the `final` modifier, are often declared using the `static` modifier. Because the value of constants cannot be changed, there might as well be only one copy of the value across all objects of the class.

Static Methods

In Chapter 3 we briefly introduced the concept of a *static method* (also called a *class method*). Static methods can be invoked through the class name. We don't have to instantiate an object of the class in order to invoke the method. In Chapter 3 we noted that all the methods of the `Math` class are static methods. For example, in the following line of code the `sqrt` method is invoked through the `Math` class name:

```
System.out.println ("Square root of 27:" + Math.sqrt(27));
```

The methods in the `Math` class perform basic computations based on values passed as parameters. There is no object state to maintain in these situations;

therefore there is no good reason to force us to create an object in order to request these services.

A method is made static by using the `static` modifier in the method declaration. As we've seen many times, the `main` method of a Java program is declared with the `static` modifier; this is done so that `main` can be executed by the interpreter without instantiating an object from the class that contains `main`.

Because static methods do not operate in the context of a particular object, they cannot reference instance variables, which exist only in an instance of a class. The compiler will issue an error if a static method attempts to use a nonstatic variable. A static method can, however, reference static variables because static variables exist independent of specific objects. Therefore, all static methods, including the `main` method, can access only static or local variables.

The program in Listing 5.8 instantiates several objects of the `Slogan` class, printing each one out in turn. Then it invokes a method called `getCount` through the class name, which returns the number of `Slogan` objects that were instantiated in the program.

Listing 5.9 on page 194 shows the `Slogan` class. The constructor of `Slogan` increments a static variable called `count`, which is initialized to zero when it is declared. Therefore, `count` serves to keep track of the number of instances of `Slogan` that are created.

The `getCount` method of `Slogan` is also declared as static, which allows it to be invoked through the class name in the `main` method. Note that the only data referenced in the `getCount` method is the integer variable `count`, which is static. As a static method, `getCount` cannot reference any nonstatic data.

The `getCount` method could have been declared without the `static` modifier, but then its invocation in the `main` method would have to have been done through an instance of the `Slogan` class instead of the class itself.

5.6 Class Relationships

The classes in a software system have various types of relationships to each other. Three of the more common relationships are dependency, aggregation, and inheritance.

We've seen dependency relationships in many examples in which one class "uses" another. This section revisits the dependency relationship and explores the situation where a class depends on itself. We then explore aggregation, in which the objects of one class contain objects of another, creating a "has-a" relationship. Inheritance, which we introduced in Chapter 1, creates an "is-a"

LISTING 5.8

```
//********************************************************************
//   SloganCounter.java          Java Foundations
//
//   Demonstrates the use of the static modifier.
//********************************************************************

public class SloganCounter
{
   //-----------------------------------------------------------------
   //   Creates several Slogan objects and prints the number of
   //   objects that were created.
   //-----------------------------------------------------------------
   public static void main (String[] args)
   {
      Slogan obj;

      obj = new Slogan ("Remember the Alamo.");
      System.out.println (obj);

      obj = new Slogan ("Don't Worry. Be Happy.");
      System.out.println (obj);

      obj = new Slogan ("Live Free or Die.");
      System.out.println (obj);

      obj = new Slogan ("Talk is Cheap.");
      System.out.println (obj);

      obj = new Slogan ("Write Once, Run Anywhere.");
      System.out.println (obj);

      System.out.println();
      System.out.println ("Slogans created: " + Slogan.getCount());
   }
}
```

OUTPUT

```
Remember the Alamo.
Don't Worry. Be Happy.
Live Free or Die.
Talk is Cheap.
Write Once, Run Anywhere.

Slogans created: 5
```

LISTING 5.9

```java
//********************************************************************
//  Slogan.java        Java Foundations
//
//  Represents a single slogan or motto.
//********************************************************************

public class Slogan
{
   private String phrase;
   private static int count = 0;

   //-----------------------------------------------------------------
   //  Constructor: Sets up the slogan and increments the number of
   //  instances created.
   //-----------------------------------------------------------------
   public Slogan (String str)
   {
      phrase = str;
      count++;
   }

   //-----------------------------------------------------------------
   //  Returns this slogan as a string.
   //-----------------------------------------------------------------
   public String toString()
   {
      return phrase;
   }

   //-----------------------------------------------------------------
   //  Returns the number of instances of this class that have been
   //  created.
   //-----------------------------------------------------------------
   public static int getCount ()
   {
      return count;
   }
}
```

relationship between classes. We defer our detailed examination of inheritance until Chapter 8.

Dependency

In many previous examples, we've seen the idea of one class being dependent on another. This means that one class relies on another in some sense. Often the methods of one class will invoke the methods of the other class. This establishes a "uses" relationship.

Generally, if class A uses class B, then one or more methods of class A invoke one or more methods of class B. If an invoked method is static, then A merely references B by name. If the invoked method is not static, then A must have access to a specific instance of class B in order to invoke the method. That is, A must have a reference to an object of class B.

The way in which one object gains access to an object of another class is an important design decision. It occurs when one class instantiates the objects of another, but the access can also be accomplished by passing one object to another as a method parameter.

In general, we want to minimize the number of dependencies among classes. The less dependent our classes are on each other, the less impact changes and errors will have on the system.

Dependencies Among Objects of the Same Class

In some cases, a class depends on itself. That is, an object of one class interacts with another object of the same class. To accomplish this, a method of the class may accept as a parameter an object of the same class.

The concat method of the String class is an example of this situation. The method is executed through one String object and is passed another String object as a parameter. For example:

```
str3 = str1.concat(str2);
```

The String object executing the method (str1) appends its characters to those of the String passed as a parameter (str2). A new String object is returned as a result and stored as str3.

The RationalTester program shown in Listing 5.10 on the next page demonstrates a similar situation. A rational number is a value that can be represented as a ratio of two integers (a fraction). The RationalTester program creates two objects representing rational numbers and then performs various operations on them to produce new rational numbers.

LISTING 5.10

```java
//********************************************************************
//  RationalTester.java        Java Foundations
//
//  Driver to exercise the use of multiple Rational objects.
//********************************************************************

public class RationalTester
{
   //-----------------------------------------------------------------
   //  Creates some rational number objects and performs various
   //  operations on them.
   //-----------------------------------------------------------------
   public static void main (String[] args)
   {
      RationalNumber r1 = new RationalNumber (6, 8);
      RationalNumber r2 = new RationalNumber (1, 3);
      RationalNumber r3, r4, r5, r6, r7;

      System.out.println ("First rational number: " + r1);
      System.out.println ("Second rational number: " + r2);

      if (r1.isLike(r2))
         System.out.println ("r1 and r2 are equal.");
      else
         System.out.println ("r1 and r2 are NOT equal.");

      r3 = r1.reciprocal();
      System.out.println ("The reciprocal of r1 is: " + r3);

      r4 = r1.add(r2);
      r5 = r1.subtract(r2);
      r6 = r1.multiply(r2);
      r7 = r1.divide(r2);

      System.out.println ("r1 + r2: " + r4);
      System.out.println ("r1 - r2: " + r5);
      System.out.println ("r1 * r2: " + r6);
      System.out.println ("r1 / r2: " + r7);
   }
}
```

LISTING 5.10   *continued*

OUTPUT

```
First rational number: 3/4
Second rational number: 1/3
r1 and r2 are NOT equal.
The reciprocal of r1 is: 4/3
r1 + r2: 13/12
r1 - r2: 5/12
r1 * r2: 1/4
r1 / r2: 9/4
```

The `RationalNumber` class is shown in Listing 5.11 on the next page. Keep in mind as you examine this class that each object created from the `RationalNumber` class represents a single rational number. The `RationalNumber` class contains various operations on rational numbers, such as addition and subtraction.

The methods of the `RationalNumber` class, such as `add`, `subtract`, `multiply`, and `divide`, use the `RationalNumber` object that is executing the method as the first (left) operand and the `RationalNumber` object passed as a parameter as the second (right) operand.

The `isLike` method of the `RationalNumber` class is used to determine if two rational numbers are essentially equal. It's tempting, therefore, to call that method `equals`, similar to the method used to compare `String` objects (discussed in Chapter 4). However, in Chapter 8 we will discuss how the `equals` method is somewhat special due to inheritance, and that it should be implemented in a particular way. So to avoid confusion we call this method `isLike` for now.

Note that some of the methods in the `RationalNumber` class, including `reduce` and `gcd`, are declared with private visibility. These methods are private because we don't want them executed directly from outside a `RationalNumber` object. They exist only to support the other services of the object.

Aggregation

Some objects are made up of other objects. A car, for instance, is made up of its engine, its chassis, its wheels, and several other parts. Each of these other parts could be considered a separate object. Therefore we can say that a car is an *aggregation*—it is composed, at

> **KEY CONCEPT**
> An aggregate object is composed of other objects, forming a has-a relationship.

LISTING 5.11

```java
//*****************************************************************
//  RationalNumber.java        Java Foundations
//
//  Represents one rational number with a numerator and denominator.
//*****************************************************************

public class RationalNumber
{
   private int numerator, denominator;

   //----------------------------------------------------------------
   //  Constructor: Sets up the rational number by ensuring a nonzero
   //  denominator and making only the numerator signed.
   //----------------------------------------------------------------
   public RationalNumber (int numer, int denom)
   {
      if (denom == 0)
         denom = 1;

      // Make the numerator "store" the sign
      if (denom < 0)
      {
         numer = numer * -1;
         denom = denom * -1;
      }

      numerator = numer;
      denominator = denom;

      reduce();
   }

   //----------------------------------------------------------------
   //  Returns the numerator of this rational number.
   //----------------------------------------------------------------
   public int getNumerator ()
   {
      return numerator;
   }

   //----------------------------------------------------------------
   //  Returns the denominator of this rational number.
   //----------------------------------------------------------------
```

LISTING 5.11   *continued*

```
public int getDenominator ()
{
   return denominator;
}

//----------------------------------------------------------------
//  Returns the reciprocal of this rational number.
//----------------------------------------------------------------
public RationalNumber reciprocal ()
{
   return new RationalNumber (denominator, numerator);
}

//----------------------------------------------------------------
//  Adds this rational number to the one passed as a parameter.
//  A common denominator is found by multiplying the individual
//  denominators.
//----------------------------------------------------------------
public RationalNumber add (RationalNumber op2)
{
   int commonDenominator = denominator * op2.getDenominator();
   int numerator1 = numerator * op2.getDenominator();
   int numerator2 = op2.getNumerator() * denominator;
   int sum = numerator1 + numerator2;

   return new RationalNumber (sum, commonDenominator);
}

//----------------------------------------------------------------
//  Subtracts the rational number passed as a parameter from this
//  rational number.
//----------------------------------------------------------------
public RationalNumber subtract (RationalNumber op2)
{
   int commonDenominator = denominator * op2.getDenominator();
   int numerator1 = numerator * op2.getDenominator();
   int numerator2 = op2.getNumerator() * denominator;
   int difference = numerator1 - numerator2;

   return new RationalNumber (difference, commonDenominator);
}
```

LISTING 5.11   *continued*

```java
//----------------------------------------------------------------
//  Multiplies this rational number by the one passed as a
//  parameter.
//----------------------------------------------------------------
public RationalNumber multiply (RationalNumber op2)
{
   int numer = numerator * op2.getNumerator();
   int denom = denominator * op2.getDenominator();

   return new RationalNumber (numer, denom);
}


//----------------------------------------------------------------
//  Divides this rational number by the one passed as a parameter
//  by multiplying by the reciprocal of the second rational.
//----------------------------------------------------------------
public RationalNumber divide (RationalNumber op2)
{
   return multiply (op2.reciprocal());
}


//----------------------------------------------------------------
//  Determines if this rational number is equal to the one passed
//  as a parameter. Assumes they are both reduced.
//----------------------------------------------------------------
public boolean isLike (RationalNumber op2)
{
   return ( numerator == op2.getNumerator() &&
            denominator == op2.getDenominator());
}


//----------------------------------------------------------------
//  Returns this rational number as a string.
//----------------------------------------------------------------
public String toString ()
{
   String result;

   if (numerator == 0)
      result = "0";
   else
      if (denominator == 1)
```

LISTING 5.11   *continued*

```
            result = numerator + "";
        else
            result = numerator + "/" + denominator;

    return result;
}

//-----------------------------------------------------------------
//  Reduces this rational number by dividing both the numerator
//  and the denominator by their greatest common divisor.
//-----------------------------------------------------------------
private void reduce ()
{
    if (numerator != 0)
    {
        int common = gcd (Math.abs(numerator), denominator);

        numerator = numerator / common;
        denominator = denominator / common;
    }
}

//-----------------------------------------------------------------
//  Computes and returns the greatest common divisor of the two
//  positive parameters. Uses Euclid's algorithm.
//-----------------------------------------------------------------
private int gcd (int num1, int num2)
{
    while (num1 != num2)
        if (num1 > num2)
            num1 = num1 - num2;
    else
        num2 = num2 - num1;

    return num1;
}
}
```

least in part, of other objects. Aggregation is sometimes described as a *has-a relationship*. For instance, a car has a chassis.

In the software world, we define an *aggregate object* as any object that contains references to other objects as instance data. For example, an `Account` object contains, among other things, a `String` object that represents the name of the account owner. We sometimes forget that strings are objects, but technically that makes each `Account` object an aggregate object.

Aggregation is a special type of dependency. That is, a class that is defined in part by another class is dependent on that class. The methods of the aggregate object generally invoke the methods of the objects from which it is composed.

The more complex an object, the more likely it will need to be represented as an aggregate object. In UML, aggregation is represented by a connection between two classes, with an open diamond at the end near the class that is the aggregate. Figure 5.10 shows a UML class diagram that contains an aggregation relationship.

Note that in previous UML diagram examples, strings are not represented as separate classes with aggregation relationships, though technically they could be. Strings are so fundamental to programming that often they are represented as if they are a primitive type in a UML diagram.

The this Reference

Before we leave the topic of relationships among classes, we should examine another special reference used in Java programs called the `this` reference. The word `this` is a reserved word in Java. It allows an object to refer to itself. As we have discussed, a nonstatic method is invoked through (or by) a particular object or class. Inside that method, the `this` reference can be used to refer to the currently executing object.

For example, in a class called `ChessPiece` there could be a method called `move`, which could contain the following line:

```
if (this.position == piece2.position)
    result =false;
```

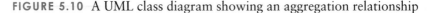

FIGURE 5.10 A UML class diagram showing an aggregation relationship

In this situation, the `this` reference is being used to clarify which position is being referenced. The `this` reference refers to the object through which the method was invoked. So when the following line is used to invoke the method, the `this` reference refers to `bishop1`:

```
bishop1.move();
```

However, when another object is used to invoke the method, the `this` reference refers to it. Therefore, when the following invocation is used, the `this` reference in the `move` method refers to `bishop2`:

```
bishop2.move();
```

Often, the `this` reference is used to distinguish the parameters of a constructor from their corresponding instance variables with the same names. For example, the constructor of the `Account` class was presented in Listing 5.7 as follows:

```
public Account (String owner, long account, double initial)
{
   name = owner;
   acctNumber = account;
   balance = initial;
}
```

When writing this constructor, we deliberately came up with different names for the parameters to distinguish them from the instance variables `name`, `acctNumber`, and `balance`. This distinction is arbitrary. The constructor could have been written as follows using the `this` reference:

```
public Account (String name, long acctNumber, double balance)
{
    this.name = name;
    this.acctNumber = acctNumber;
    this.balance = balance;
}
```

In this version of the constructor, the `this` reference specifically refers to the instance variables of the object. The variables on the right-hand side of the assignment statements refer to the formal parameters. This approach eliminates the need to come up with different yet equivalent names. This situation sometimes occurs in other methods but comes up often in constructors.

5.7 Method Design

Once you have identified classes and assigned basic responsibilities, the design of each method will determine how exactly the class will define its behaviors. Some methods are straightforward and require little thought. Others are more interesting and require careful planning.

An *algorithm* is a step-by-step process for solving a problem. A recipe is an example of an algorithm. Travel directions are another example of an algorithm. Every method implements an algorithm that determines how that method accomplishes its goals.

An algorithm is often described using *pseudocode*, which is a mixture of code statements and English phrases. Pseudocode provides enough structure to show how the code will operate, without getting bogged down in the syntactic details of a particular programming language or becoming prematurely constrained by the characteristics of particular programming constructs.

This section discusses two important aspects of program design at the method level: method decomposition and the implications of passing objects as parameters.

Method Decomposition

Occasionally, a service that an object provides is so complex that it cannot reasonably be implemented using one method. Therefore we sometimes need to decompose a method into multiple methods to create a more understandable design. As an example, let's examine a program that translates English sentences into Pig Latin.

Pig Latin is a made-up language in which each word of a sentence is modified, in general, by moving the initial sound of the word to the end and adding an "ay" sound. For example, the word *happy* would be written and pronounced *appyhay* and the word *birthday* would become *irthdaybay*. Words that begin with vowels simply have a "yay" sound added on the end, turning the word *enough* into *enoughyay*. Consonant blends such as "ch" and "st" at the beginning of a word are moved to the end together before adding the "ay" sound. Therefore the word *grapefruit* becomes *apefruitgray*.

The `PigLatin` program shown in Listing 5.12 reads one or more sentences, translating each into Pig Latin.

The workhorse behind the `PigLatin` program is the `PigLatinTranslator` class, shown in Listing 5.13 on page 207. The `PigLatinTranslator` class provides one fundamental service, a static method called `translate`, which accepts a string and translates it into Pig Latin. Note that the `PigLatinTranslator` class does not contain a constructor because none is needed.

The act of translating an entire sentence into Pig Latin is not trivial. If written in one big method, it would be very long and difficult to follow. A better solution, as implemented in the `PigLatinTranslator` class, is to decompose the `translate` method and use several other support methods to help with the task.

The `translate` method uses a `Scanner` object to separate the string into words. Recall that one role of the `Scanner` class (discussed in Chapter 3) is to separate a string into smaller elements called tokens. In this case, the tokens are separated by space characters so we can use the default whitespace delimiters. The `PigLatin` program assumes that no punctuation is included in the input.

LISTING 5.12

```java
//***********************************************************************
//  PigLatin.java            Java Foundations
//
//  Demonstrates the concept of method decomposition.
//***********************************************************************

import java.util.Scanner;

public class PigLatin
{
   //---------------------------------------------------------------
   //  Reads sentences and translates them into Pig Latin.
   //---------------------------------------------------------------
   public static void main (String[] args)
   {
      String sentence, result, another;

      Scanner scan = new Scanner (System.in);

      do
      {
         System.out.println ();
         System.out.println ("Enter a sentence (no punctuation):");
         sentence = scan.nextLine();

         System.out.println ();
         result = PigLatinTranslator.translate (sentence);
         System.out.println ("That sentence in Pig Latin is:");
         System.out.println (result);

         System.out.println ();
         System.out.print ("Translate another sentence (y/n)? ");
         another = scan.nextLine();
      }
      while (another.equalsIgnoreCase("y"));
   }
}
```

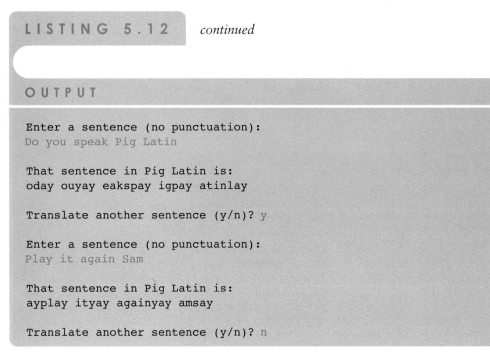

LISTING 5.12   *continued*

OUTPUT

```
Enter a sentence (no punctuation):
Do you speak Pig Latin

That sentence in Pig Latin is:
oday ouyay eakspay igpay atinlay

Translate another sentence (y/n)? y

Enter a sentence (no punctuation):
Play it again Sam

That sentence in Pig Latin is:
ayplay ityay againyay amsay

Translate another sentence (y/n)? n
```

The `translate` method passes each word to the private support method `translateWord`. Even the job of translating one word is somewhat involved, so the `translateWord` method makes use of two other private methods, `beginsWithVowel` and `beginsWithBlend`.

The `beginsWithVowel` method returns a `boolean` value that indicates whether the word passed as a parameter begins with a vowel. Note that instead of checking each vowel separately, the code for this method declares a string that contains all the vowels, and then invokes the `String` method `indexOf` to determine whether the first character of the word is in the vowel string. If the specified character cannot be found, the `indexOf` method returns a value of –1.

The `beginsWithBlend` method also returns a `boolean` value. The body of the method contains only a `return` statement with one large expression that makes several calls to the `startsWith` method of the `String` class. If any of these calls returns true, then the `beginsWithBlend` method returns true as well.

Note that the `translateWord`, `beginsWithVowel`, and `beginsWithBlend` methods are all declared with private visibility. They are not intended to provide services directly to clients outside the class. Instead, they exist to help the `translate` method, which is the only true service method in this class, to do its job. By declaring them with private visibility, they cannot be invoked from

LISTING 5.13

```java
//********************************************************************
//  PigLatinTranslator.java        Java Foundations
//
//  Represents a translator from English to Pig Latin. Demonstrates
//  method decomposition.
//********************************************************************

import java.util.Scanner;

public class PigLatinTranslator
{
   //-----------------------------------------------------------------
   //  Translates a sentence of words into Pig Latin.
   //-----------------------------------------------------------------
   public static String translate (String sentence)
   {
      String result = "";

      sentence = sentence.toLowerCase();

      Scanner scan = new Scanner (sentence);

      while (scan.hasNext())
      {
         result += translateWord (scan.next());
         result += " ";
      }

      return result;
   }

   //-----------------------------------------------------------------
   //  Translates one word into Pig Latin. If the word begins with a
   //  vowel, the suffix "yay" is appended to the word. Otherwise,
   //  the first letter or two are moved to the end of the word,
   //  and "ay" is appended.
   //-----------------------------------------------------------------
   private static String translateWord (String word)
   {
      String result = "";

      if (beginsWithVowel(word))
         result = word + "yay";
```

LISTING 5.13 *continued*

```java
    else
       if (beginsWithBlend(word))
          result = word.substring(2) + word.substring(0,2) + "ay";
       else
          result = word.substring(1) + word.charAt(0) + "ay";

    return result;
   }

   //-----------------------------------------------------------------
   //  Determines if the specified word begins with a vowel.
   //-----------------------------------------------------------------
   private static boolean beginsWithVowel (String word)
   {
      String vowels = "aeiou";

      char letter = word.charAt(0);

      return (vowels.indexOf(letter) != -1);
   }

   //-----------------------------------------------------------------
   //  Determines if the specified word begins with a particular
   //  two-character consonant blend.
   //-----------------------------------------------------------------
   private static boolean beginsWithBlend (String word)
   {
      return ( word.startsWith ("bl") || word.startsWith ("sc") ||
               word.startsWith ("br") || word.startsWith ("sh") ||
               word.startsWith ("ch") || word.startsWith ("sk") ||
               word.startsWith ("cl") || word.startsWith ("sl") ||
               word.startsWith ("cr") || word.startsWith ("sn") ||
               word.startsWith ("dr") || word.startsWith ("sm") ||
               word.startsWith ("dw") || word.startsWith ("sp") ||
               word.startsWith ("fl") || word.startsWith ("sq") ||
               word.startsWith ("fr") || word.startsWith ("st") ||
               word.startsWith ("gl") || word.startsWith ("sw") ||
               word.startsWith ("gr") || word.startsWith ("th") ||
               word.startsWith ("kl") || word.startsWith ("tr") ||
               word.startsWith ("ph") || word.startsWith ("tw") ||
               word.startsWith ("pl") || word.startsWith ("wh") ||
               word.startsWith ("pr") || word.startsWith ("wr") );
   }
}
```

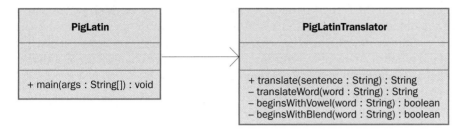

FIGURE 5.11 A UML class diagram for the `PigLatin` program

outside this class. For instance, if the `main` method of the `PigLatin` class attempted to invoke the `translateWord` method, the compiler would issue an error message.

Figure 5.11 shows a UML class diagram for the `PigLatin` program. Note the notation showing the visibility of various methods.

Whenever a method becomes large or complex, we should consider decomposing it into multiple methods to create a more understandable class design. First, however, we must consider how other classes and objects can be defined to create better overall system design. In an object-oriented design, method decomposition must be subordinate to object decomposition.

Method Parameters Revisited

Another important issue related to method design involves the way parameters are passed into a method. In Java, all parameters are passed *by value*. That is, the current value of the actual parameter (in the invocation) is copied into the formal parameter in the method header. We mentioned this issue previously in this chapter; let's examine it now in more detail.

Essentially, parameter passing is like an assignment statement, assigning to the formal parameter a copy of the value stored in the actual parameter. This issue must be considered when making changes to a formal parameter inside a method. The formal parameter is a separate copy of the value that is passed in, so any changes made to it have no effect on the actual parameter. After control returns to the calling method, the actual parameter will have the same value as it did before the method was called.

However, when we pass an object to a method, we are actually passing a reference to that object. The value that gets copied is the address of the object. Therefore the formal parameter and the actual parameter become aliases of each other. If we change the state of the

> **KEY CONCEPT**
> When an object is passed to a method, the actual and formal parameters become aliases.

object through the formal parameter reference inside the method, we are changing the object referenced by the actual parameter, because they refer to the same
object. On the other hand, if we change the formal parameter reference itself (to
make it point to a new object, for instance), we have not changed the fact that the
actual parameter still refers to the original object.

The program in Listing 5.14 illustrates the nuances of parameter passing.
Carefully trace the processing of this program and note the values that are output.
The `ParameterTester` class contains a `main` method that calls the `changeValues`
method in a `ParameterModifier` object. Two of the parameters to `changeValues`
are `Num` objects, each of which simply stores an integer value. The other parameter is a primitive integer value.

Listing 5.15 on page 212 shows the `ParameterModifier` class, and Listing 5.16
on page 213 shows the `Num` class. Inside the `changeValues` method, a modification is made to each of the three formal parameters: the integer parameter is set to
a different value, the value stored in the first `Num` parameter is changed using its
`setValue` method, and a new `Num` object is created and assigned to the second
`Num` parameter. These changes are reflected in the output printed at the end of the
`changeValues` method.

However, note the final values that are printed after returning from the
method. The primitive integer was not changed from its original value because
the change was made to a copy inside the method. Likewise, the last parameter
still refers to its original object with its original value. This is because the new `Num`
object created in the method was referred to only by the formal parameter. When
the method returned, that formal parameter was destroyed and the `Num` object it
referred to was marked for garbage collection. The only change that is "permanent" is the change made to the state of the second parameter. Figure 5.12 on
page 214 shows the step-by-step processing of this program.

5.8 Method Overloading

As we've discussed, when a method is invoked, the flow of control transfers to the
code that defines the method. After the method has been executed, control returns
to the location of the call, and processing continues.

Often the method name is sufficient to indicate which method is being called
by a specific invocation. But in Java, as in other object-oriented languages, you
can use the same method name with different parameter lists for multiple methods. This technique is called *method overloading*. It is useful when you need to
perform similar methods on different types of data.

The compiler must still be able to associate each invocation to a specific method
declaration. If the method name for two or more methods is the same, additional

LISTING 5.14

```
//********************************************************************
//  ParameterTester.java        Java Foundations
//
//  Demonstrates the effects of passing various types of parameters.
//********************************************************************

public class ParameterTester
{

   //-----------------------------------------------------------------
   //  Sets up three variables (one primitive and two objects) to
   //  serve as actual parameters to the changeValues method. Prints
   //  their values before and after calling the method.
   //-----------------------------------------------------------------
   public static void main (String[] args)
   {
      ParameterModifier modifier = new ParameterModifier();

      int a1 = 111;
      Num a2 = new Num (222);
      Num a3 = new Num (333);

      System.out.println ("Before calling changeValues:");
      System.out.println ("a1\ta2\ta3");
      System.out.println (a1 + "\t" + a2 + "\t" + a3 + "\n");

      modifier.changeValues (a1, a2, a3);

      System.out.println ("After calling changeValues:");
      System.out.println ("a1\ta2\ta3");
      System.out.println (a1 + "\t" + a2 + "\t" + a3 + "\n");
   }
}
```

OUTPUT

```
Before calling changeValues:
a1      a2      a3
111     222     333

Before changing the values:
f1      f2      f3
111     222     333
```

LISTING 5.14   *continued*

```
After changing the values:
f1      f2      f3
999     888     777

After calling changeValues:
a1      a2      a3
111     888     333
```

LISTING 5.15

```java
//********************************************************************
//  ParameterModifier.java        Java Foundations
//
//  Demonstrates the effects of changing parameter values.
//********************************************************************

public class ParameterModifier
{
   //-----------------------------------------------------------------
   //  Modifies the parameters, printing their values before and
   //  after making the changes.
   //-----------------------------------------------------------------
   public void changeValues (int f1, Num f2, Num f3)
   {
      System.out.println ("Before changing the values:");
      System.out.println ("f1\tf2\tf3");
      System.out.println (f1 + "\t" + f2 + "\t" + f3 + "\n");

      f1 = 999;
      f2.setValue(888);
      f3 = new Num (777);

      System.out.println ("After changing the values:");
      System.out.println ("f1\tf2\tf3");
      System.out.println (f1 + "\t" + f2 + "\t" + f3 + "\n");
   }
}
```

LISTING 5.16

```java
//********************************************************************
//  Num.java        Java Foundations
//
//  Represents a single integer as an object.
//********************************************************************

public class Num
{
    private int value;

    //-----------------------------------------------------------------
    //  Sets up the new Num object, storing an initial value.
    //-----------------------------------------------------------------
    public Num (int update)
    {
        value = update;
    }

    //-----------------------------------------------------------------
    //  Sets the stored value to the newly specified value.
    //-----------------------------------------------------------------
    public void setValue (int update)
    {
        value = update;
    }

    //-----------------------------------------------------------------
    //  Returns the stored integer value as a string.
    //-----------------------------------------------------------------
    public String toString ()
    {
        return value + "";
    }
}
```

information is used to uniquely identify the version that is being invoked. In Java, a method name can be used for multiple methods as long as the number of parameters, the types of those parameters, and/or the order of the types of parameters is distinct.

> **KEY CONCEPT**
>
> The versions of an overloaded method are distinguished by the number, type, and order of their parameters.

STEP 1

Before invoking changeValues

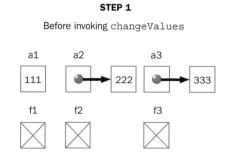

STEP 2

tester.changeValues (a1, a2, a3);

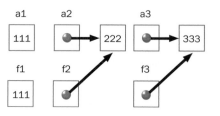

STEP 3

f1 = 999;

STEP 4

f2.setValue (888);

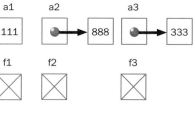

STEP 5

f3 = new Num (777);

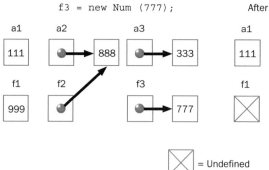

STEP 6

After returning from changeValues

= Undefined

FIGURE 5.12 Tracing the parameters in the ParameterTesting program

For example, we could declare a method called `sum` as follows:

```
public int sum (int num1, int num2)
{
    return num1 + num2;
}
```

Then we could declare another method called `sum`, within the same class, as follows:

```
public int sum (int num1, int num2, int num3)
{
    return num1 + num2 + num3;
}
```

Now, when an invocation is made, the compiler looks at the number of parameters to determine which version of the `sum` method to call. For instance, the following invocation will call the second version of the `sum` method:

```
sum (25, 69, 13);
```

A method's name, along with the number, type, and order of its parameters, is called the method's *signature*. The compiler uses the complete method signature to *bind* a method invocation to the appropriate definition.

The compiler must be able to examine a method invocation to determine which specific method is being invoked. If you attempt to specify two method names with the same signature, the compiler will issue an appropriate error message and will not create an executable program. There can be no ambiguity.

Note that the return type of a method is not part of the method signature. That is, two overloaded methods cannot differ only by their return type. This is because the value returned by a method can be ignored by the invocation. The compiler would not be able to distinguish which version of an overloaded method is being referenced in such situations.

The `println` method is an example of a method that is overloaded several times, each accepting a single type. The following is a partial list of its various signatures:

- `println (String s)`
- `println (int i)`
- `println (double d)`
- `println (char c)`
- `println (boolean b)`

The following two lines of code actually invoke different methods that have the same name:

```
System.out.println ("Number of students: ");
System.out.println (count);
```

The first line invokes the version of `println` that accepts a string. The second line, assuming `count` is an integer variable, invokes the version of `println` that accepts an integer.

We often use a `println` statement that prints several distinct types, such as:

```
System.out.println ("Number of students: " + count);
```

Remember, in this case the plus sign is the string concatenation operator. First, the value in the variable `count` is converted to a string representation, then the two strings are concatenated into one longer string, and finally the definition of `println` that accepts a single string is invoked.

Constructors can be overloaded, and often are. By providing multiple versions of a constructor, we provide multiple ways to set up an object.

5.9 Testing

As our programs become larger and more complex, it becomes more difficult to ensure their accuracy and reliability. So, before we continue with further programming details, let's explore the processes involved in testing a program.

The term *testing* can be applied in many ways to software development. Testing certainly includes its traditional definition: the act of running a completed program with various inputs to discover problems. But it also includes any evaluation that is performed by human or machine to assess the quality of the evolving system. These evaluations should occur long before a single line of code is written.

The goal of testing is to find errors. By finding errors and fixing them, we improve the quality of our program. It's likely that later on someone else will find any errors that remain hidden during development. The earlier the errors are found, the easier and cheaper they are to fix. Taking the time to uncover problems as early as possible is almost always worth the effort.

Running a program with specific input and producing the correct results establishes only that the program works for that particular input. As more and more test cases execute without revealing errors, our confidence in the program rises, but we can never really be sure that all errors have been eliminated. There could always be another error still undiscovered. Because of that, it is important to thoroughly test a program in as many ways as possible and with well-designed test cases.

> **KEY CONCEPT**
>
> Testing a program can never guarantee the absence of errors.

It is possible to prove that a program is correct, but that technique is enormously complex for large systems, and errors can be made in the proof itself. Therefore, we generally rely on testing to determine the quality of a program.

After determining that an error exists, we determine the cause of the error and fix it. After a problem is fixed, we should run previous tests again to make sure that while fixing the problem we didn't create another. This technique is called *regression testing*.

Reviews

One technique used to evaluate design or code is called a *review*, which is a meeting in which several people carefully examine a design document or section of code. Presenting our design or code to others causes us to think more carefully about it and permits others to share their suggestions with us. The participants discuss its merits and problems, and create a list of issues that must be addressed. The goal of a review is to identify problems, not to solve them, which usually takes much more time.

A design review should determine whether the requirements are addressed. It should also assess the way the system is decomposed into classes and objects. A code review should determine how faithfully the design satisfies the requirements and how faithfully the implementation represents the design. It should identify any specific problems that would cause the design or the implementation to fail in its responsibilities.

Sometimes a review is called a *walkthrough* because its goal is to step carefully through a document and evaluate each section.

Defect Testing

Since the goal of testing is to find errors, it is often referred to as *defect testing*. With that goal in mind, a good test is one that uncovers any deficiencies in a program. This might seem strange, because we ultimately don't want to have problems in our system. But keep in mind that errors almost certainly exist. Our testing efforts should make every attempt to find them. We want to increase the reliability of our program by finding and fixing the errors that exist, rather than letting users discover them.

> **KEY CONCEPT**
> A good test is one that uncovers an error.

A *test case* is a set of inputs, user actions, or other initial conditions, and the expected output. A test case should be appropriately documented so that it can be repeated later as needed. Developers often create a complete *test suite*, which is a set of test cases that covers various aspects of the system.

Because programs operate on a large number of possible inputs, it is not feasible to create test cases for all possible input or user actions. Nor is it usually necessary to test every single situation. Two specific test cases may be so similar that they actually do not test unique aspects of the program. To do both would be a wasted effort. We'd rather execute a test case that stresses the program in some new way.

> **KEY CONCEPT**
> It is not feasible to exhaustively test a program for all possible input and user actions.

Therefore we want to choose our test cases carefully. To that end, let's examine two approaches to defect testing: black-box testing and white-box testing.

As the name implies, *black-box testing* treats the thing being tested as a black box. In black-box testing, test cases are developed without regard to the internal workings. Black-box tests are based on inputs and outputs. An entire program can be tested using a black-box technique, in which case the inputs are the user-provided information and user actions such as button pushes. A test case is successful only if the input produces the expected output. A single class can also be tested using a black-box technique, which focuses on the system interface (its public methods) of the class. Certain parameters are passed in, producing certain results. Black-box test cases are often derived directly from the requirements of the system or from the stated purpose of a method.

The input data for a black-box test case is often selected by defining *equivalence categories*. An equivalence category is a collection of inputs that are expected to produce similar outputs. Generally, if a method will work for one value in the equivalence category, we have every reason to believe it will work for the others. For example, the input to a method that computes the square root of an integer can be divided into two equivalence categories: nonnegative integers and negative integers. If it works appropriately for one nonnegative value, it will likely work for all nonnegative values. Likewise, if it works appropriately for one negative value, it will likely work for all negative values.

Equivalence categories have defined boundaries. Because all values of an equivalence category essentially test the same features of a program, only one test case inside the equivalence boundary is needed. However, because programming often produces "off by one" errors, the values on and around the boundary should be tested exhaustively. For an integer boundary, a good test suite would include at least the exact value of the boundary, the boundary minus 1, and the boundary plus 1. Test cases that use these cases, plus at least one from within the general field of the category, should be defined.

Let's look at an example. Consider a method whose purpose is to validate that a particular integer value is in the range 0 to 99, inclusive. There are three equivalence categories in this case: values below 0, values in the range of 0 to 99, and values above 99. Black-box testing dictates that we use test values that surround and fall on the boundaries, as well as some general values from the equivalence categories. Therefore, a set of black-box test cases for this situation might be:–500,–1, 0, 1, 50, 98, 99, 100, and 500.

White-box testing, also known as *glass-box testing*, exercises the internal structure and implementation of a method. A white-box test case is based on the logic of the code. The goal is to ensure that every path through a program is executed at least once. A white-box test maps the possible paths through the code and ensures that the test cases cause every path to be executed. This type of testing is often called *statement coverage*.

Paths through code are controlled by various control flow statements that use conditional expressions, such as `if` statements. In order to have every path through the program executed at least once, the input data values for the test cases need to control the values for the conditional expressions. The input data of one or more test cases should cause the condition of an `if` statement to evaluate to `true` in at least one case and to `false` in at least one case. Covering both true and false values in an `if` statement guarantees that both the paths through the `if` statement will be executed. Similar situations can be created for loops and other constructs.

In both black-box and white-box testing, the expected output for each test should be established prior to running the test. It's too easy to be persuaded that the results of a test are appropriate if you haven't first carefully determined what the results should be.

Unit Testing

Another type of testing is known as *unit testing*. This approach creates a test case for each module of code (method) that has been authored. The goal of unit testing is to ensure correctness of the methods (units), one method at a time. Generally, we collect our unit tests together and execute each test and observe all of the results. We can also use these tests repeatedly as the source code changes, to observe the effect of our code changes on the results of the test (regression testing, discussed above).

Integration Testing

During *integration testing*, modules that were individually tested during unit testing are now tested as a collection. This form of testing looks at the larger picture and determines if there are bugs present when modules are brought together and integrated to work together. As with unit testing, we can use regression testing as the software changes to determine how our results may have changed as integration occurred and problems in the modules or integration approaches were modified. Typically, the goal of integration testing is to examine the correctness of large components of a system.

System Testing

System testing seeks to test the entire software system and how its implementation adheres to its requirements. You may be familiar with public alpha or beta testing of applications or operating systems. Alpha and beta tests are system tests occurring prior to the formal release and availability of a software product. Software development companies will partake in these types of public tests to increase the number of users testing a product, or to expand the hardware base that the product is tested on.

Test-Driven Development

Ideally, developers should be writing test cases at the same time as the development of the source code that our applications use. In fact, many developers have adopted a style in which they write their test cases first, and then implement only enough source code such that the test case will pass. This notion is known professionally as *test-driven development.*

The test-driven approach requires that the developer periodically (during development and implementation) test their code using the implemented test cases. If you were to look at the test-driven approach as a sequence of steps, you would generally find the following activities:

1. Create a test case that tests a specific method that has yet to be completed.
2. Execute all of the test cases present and verify that all test cases pass except for the most recently implemented test case.
3. Develop the method that the test case targets so that the test case will pass without errors.
4. Re-execute all of the test cases and verify that every test case passes, including the most recently implemented test case.
5. Clean up the code to eliminate any redundant portions introduced by the development of the most recent method. This step is known as *refactoring* the code.
6. Repeat the process starting with Step 1.

The test-driven approach is becoming increasingly popular in professional settings. Without a doubt, it requires an adjustment for many developers to stop and write test cases prior to writing methods that provide functionality to systems under development.

5.10 Debugging

Finally, we come to one of the most important concepts that you will likely come to master as a programmer—the art of *debugging* your programs. Debugging is the act of locating and correcting run-time and logic errors in your programs. We can locate errors in our programs through a number of different ways. You may notice a run-time error (the program terminating abnormally) when you execute your program and certain situations arise that you did not consider or design for. Also, you may notice a logic error in your program as it executes when your anticipated results do not match the actual results you obtain.

Ideally, through rigorous testing, we hope to discover all possible errors in our programs. However, typically a few errors slip through into the final program. Once you recognize that your program contains an error, you will want to locate the portion of code where the error is arising from. For example, if you determine that your program is terminating abnormally due to a divide-by-zero problem, you'll likely want to locate the exact line that it is happening at. You may also wish to observe the values of the variables involved in the division. The same may be true if you have a logic error (rather than a divide-by-zero problem) in that division operation.

Regardless of your motivation, often times it is very helpful to obtain detailed information about the values of variables, states of objects, and other inner workings of your program. This is where a debugger comes in. A *debugger* is a software application that allows us to observe these inner workings as the program executes. However, before we jump into discussing the debugger, we should first talk about simple debugging.

> **KEY CONCEPT**
>
> A debugger is a software program that permits developers to observe the execution of a program.

Simple Debugging with print Statements

One of the most simplistic approaches to debugging involves the use of printing. That is, scattered throughout out program can be `print` and `println` statements that output various information to either the screen or to an output file. Generally, this type of approach will serve to provide information on the value or state of a specific variable or object. Periodic printing of an object's string representation is considered to be a useful approach to observing the state of an object over time.

Other types of useful information can be printed as well. For example, sometimes we wish to know "how far our program got before it died." Programmers facing this challenge often print a series of "It got here." type of statements to output to monitor the exact path of execution of the program.

Consider the case of calling a method. It may be useful for us to print the value of each parameter after the method starts to observe how the method was called. This is particularly helpful when debugging recursive methods, discussed in the next chapter. We can also print the value of a variable prior to its being returned as the method ends.

Debugging Concepts

Debugging through printing can only take us so far. Most of the time this style of debugging can be effectively used to identify what is happening during execution or the value of a variable at a certain point in the program. However, a more powerful approach is to use a debugger in which our program will execute.

The debugger can be used to control our program's execution and provide additional functionality to the developer that we simply can't get with simple debugging through `print` statements.

A debugger allows us to do the following:

- Set one or more *breakpoints* in our program. In the debugger, we can examine the source code and set special flags or triggers on one or more lines of code. When execution of the program comes across a statement that has been flagged, execution stops.

- Print the value of a variable or object. Once we have reached a breakpoint and execution has stopped, the debugger allows us to display the value of a variable or examine the state of an object. Generally these types of displays are to the screen and only within the confines of the debugger application.

- Step into or over a method. If we set a breakpoint at a statement that is a call to a method, when execution reaches this breakpoint and the program stops, the developer can choose to enter into the method and continue debugging or to step over the method, bypassing the display of the execution of the statements contained in the method. In stepping over the method, we should note that the method is still executed, but we have chosen not to delve into the method. Consider the call to the printing of a string of output to the screen. We likely don't need to step into the `println` method of the `System.out` object. It's likely already been fully debugged (and we can't change its behavior anyway).

- Execute the next single statement. After reaching a breakpoint, the developer can choose to execute the next single statement (also known as a *step*). By executing a single step, we can literally control the execution of our program one statement at a time. Developers often perform stepping to be sure they understand the flow of execution and to provide themselves the opportunity to display the value of a variable following each step, if desired.

- Continue execution. Once a program has stopped due to a breakpoint, or is waiting for the developer to decide if they will step into, step over, or single step, the developer can also continue execution. Continuing execution will result in the program running each statement without pausing until the program ends, it encounters another breakpoint, or a run-time error occurs.

Debuggers also offer a pile of additional features to assist in the debugging task. However, for the purposes of this discussion, we can limit ourselves to the set of activities listed above. Any debugger that is worth using has at a minimum these operations.

Summary of Key Concepts

- The nouns in a problem description may indicate some of the classes and objects needed in a program.

- The heart of object-oriented programming is defining classes that represent objects with well-defined state and behavior.

- The scope of a variable, which determines where it can be referenced, depends on where it is declared.

- A UML class diagram helps us visualize the contents of and relationships among the classes of a program.

- An object should be encapsulated, guarding its data from inappropriate access.

- Instance variables should be declared with private visibility to promote encapsulation.

- Most objects contain accessor and mutator methods to allow the client to manage data in a controlled manner.

- The way a class represents an object's state should be independent of how that object is used.

- The value returned from a method must be consistent with the return type specified in the method header.

- When a method is called, the actual parameters are copied into the formal parameters.

- A variable declared in a method is local to that method and cannot be used outside of it.

- A constructor cannot have any return type, even `void`.

- A static variable is shared among all instances of a class.

- An aggregate object is composed of other objects, forming a has-a relationship.

- A complex service provided by an object can be decomposed to make use of private support methods.

- When an object is passed to a method, the actual and formal parameters become aliases.

- The versions of an overloaded method are distinguished by the number, type, and order of their parameters.

- Testing a program can never guarantee the absence of errors.

- A good test is one that uncovers an error.

- It is not feasible to exhaustively test a program for all possible input and user actions.

- In test-driven development, test cases are developed for code before the code is written.

- Debugging is the act of locating and correcting run-time and logic errors from your programs.

- A debugger is a software program that permits developers to observe the execution of a program.

Self-Review Questions

SR 5.1   What is an attribute?

SR 5.2   What is an operation?

SR 5.3   What is the difference between an object and a class?

SR 5.4   What is the scope of a variable?

SR 5.5   What are UML diagrams designed to do?

SR 5.6   Objects should be self-governing. Explain.

SR 5.7   What is a modifier?

SR 5.8   Why might a constant be given public visibility?

SR 5.9   Describe each of the following:

a. public method

b. private method

c. public variable

d. private variable

SR 5.10   What is the interface to an object?

SR 5.11   Why is a method invoked through (or on) a particular object? What is the exception to that rule?

SR 5.12   What does it mean for a method to return a value?

SR 5.13   What does the `return` statement do?

SR 5.14   Is a `return` statement required?

SR 5.15   Explain the difference between an actual parameter and a formal parameter.

SR 5.16   What are constructors used for? How are they defined?

SR 5.17   What is the difference between a static variable and an instance variable?

SR 5.18   What kinds of variables can the `main` method of any program reference? Why?

SR 5.19   Describe a dependency relationship between two classes.

SR 5.20   How are overloaded methods distinguished from each other?

SR 5.21   What is method decomposition?

SR 5.22   Explain how a class can have an association with itself.

SR 5.23   What is an aggregate object?

SR 5.24   What does the `this` reference refer to?

SR 5.25   How are objects passed as parameters?

SR 5.26   What is a defect test?

SR 5.27   What is a debugger?

Exercises

EX 5.1   For each of the following pairs, which represents a class and which represents an object of that class?

    a. Superhero, Superman

    b. Justin, Person

    c. Rover, Pet

    d. Magazine, Time

    e. Christmas, Holiday

EX 5.2   List some attributes and operations that might be defined for a class called `PictureFrame` that represents a picture frame.

EX 5.3   List some attributes and operations that might be defined for a class called `Meeting` that represents a business meeting.

EX 5.4   List some attributes and operations that might be defined for a class called `Course` that represents a college course (not a particular offering of a course, just the course in general).

EX 5.5   Rewrite the `for` loop body from the `SnakeEyes` program so that the variables num1 and num2 are not used.

EX 5.6   Write a method called `lyrics` that prints the lyrics of a song when invoked. The method should accept no parameters and return no value.

EX 5.7   Write a method called `cube` that accepts one integer parameter and returns that value raised to the third power.

EX 5.8   Write a method called `random100` that returns a random integer in the range of 1 to 100 (inclusive).

EX 5.9   Write a method called `randomInRange` that accepts two integer parameters representing a range. The method should return a random integer in the specified range (inclusive). Assume that the first parameter is greater than the second.

EX 5.10   Write a method called `powersOfTwo` that prints the first 10 powers of 2 (starting with 2). The method takes no parameters and doesn't return anything.

EX 5.11   Write a method called `alarm` that prints the string `"Alarm!"` multiple times on separate lines. The method should accept an integer parameter that specifies how many times the string is printed. Print an error message if the parameter is less than 1.

EX 5.12   Write a method called `sum100` that returns the sum of the integers from 1 to 100, inclusive.

EX 5.13   Write a method called `maxOfTwo` that accepts two integer parameters and returns the larger of the two.

EX 5.14   Write a method called `sumRange` that accepts two integer parameters that represent a range. Issue an error message and return zero if the second parameter is less than the first. Otherwise, the method should return the sum of the integers in that range (inclusive).

EX 5.15   Write a method called `larger` that accepts two floating point parameters (of type `double`) and returns true if the first parameter is greater than the second, and false otherwise.

EX 5.16   Write a method called `countA` that accepts a `String` parameter and returns the number of times the character `'A'` is found in the string.

EX 5.17   Write a method called `evenlyDivisible` that accepts two integer parameters and returns true if the first parameter is evenly divisible by the second, or vice versa, and false otherwise. Return false if either parameter is zero.

EX 5.18   Write a method called `isAlpha` that accepts a character parameter and returns true if that character is either an uppercase or lowercase alphabetic letter.

EX 5.19   Write a method called `floatEquals` that accepts three floating point values as parameters. The method should return true if the first two parameters are equal within the tolerance of the third parameter.

EX 5.20   Write a method called `reverse` that accepts a `String` parameter and returns a string that contains the characters of the parameter in reverse order. Note: there is a method in the `String` class that performs this operation, but for the sake of this exercise, you are expected to write your own.

EX 5.21   Write a method called `isIsosceles` that accepts three integer parameters that represent the lengths of the sides of a triangle. The method returns true if the triangle is isosceles but not equilateral (meaning that exactly two of the sides have an equal length), and false otherwise.

EX 5.22   Write a method called `average` that accepts two integer parameters and returns their average as a floating point value.

EX 5.23   Overload the `average` method of Exercise 5.22 such that if three integers are provided as parameters, the method returns the average of all three.

EX 5.24   Overload the `average` method of Exercise 5.22 to accept four integer parameters and return their average.

EX 5.25   Write a method called `multiConcat` that takes a `String` and an integer as parameters. Return a `String` that consists of the string parameter concatenated with itself `count` times, where `count` is the integer parameter. For example, if the parameter values are `"hi"` and 4, the return value is `"hihihihi"`. Return the original string if the integer parameter is less than 2.

EX 5.26   Overload the `multiConcat` method from Exercise 5.25 such that if the integer parameter is not provided, the method returns the string concatenated with itself. For example, if the parameter is `"test"`, the return value is `"testtest"`.

EX 5.27   Discuss the manner in which Java passes parameters to a method. Is this technique consistent between primitive types and objects? Explain.

EX 5.28   Explain why a static method cannot refer to an instance variable.

EX 5.29   Can a class implement two interfaces that each contains the same method signature? Explain.

EX 5.30   Draw a UML class diagram for the `CountFlips` program.

EX 5.31   Draw a UML class diagram for the `FlipRace` program.

EX 5.32   Draw a UML class diagram for the `Transactions` program.

Programming Projects

PP 5.1   Revise the Coin class such that its state is represented internally using a boolean variable. Test the new versions of the class as part of the CountFlips and FlipRace programs.

PP 5.2   Repeat programming project 5.1, representing the state of the coin using a character string.

PP 5.3   Repeat programming project 5.1, representing the state of the coin using an enumerated type.

PP 5.4   Design and implement a class called Sphere that contains instance data that represents the sphere's diameter. Define the Sphere constructor to accept and initialize the diameter, and include getter and setter methods for the diameter. Include methods that calculate and return the volume and surface area of the sphere (see programming project 3.5 for the formulas). Include a toString method that returns a one-line description of the sphere. Create a driver class called MultiSphere, whose main method instantiates and updates several Sphere objects.

PP 5.5   Design and implement a class called Dog that contains instance data that represents the dog's name and age. Define the Dog constructor to accept and initialize instance data. Include getter and setter methods for the name and age. Include a method to compute and return the age of the dog in "person years" (seven times the dog's age). Include a toString method that returns a one-line description of the dog. Create a driver class called Kennel, whose main method instantiates and updates several Dog objects.

PP 5.6   Design and implement a class called Box that contains instance data that represents the height, width, and depth of the box. Also include a boolean variable called full as instance data that represents if the box is full or not. Define the Box constructor to accept and initialize the height, width, and depth of the box. Each newly created Box is empty (the constructor should initialize full to false). Include getter and setter methods for all instance data. Include a toString method that returns a one-line description of the box. Create a driver class called BoxTest, whose main method instantiates and updates several Box objects.

PP 5.7   Design and implement a class called Book that contains instance data for the title, author, publisher, and copyright date. Define the Book constructor to accept and initialize this data. Include setter and getter methods for all instance data. Include a toString method that returns a nicely formatted, multiline description of the book. Create a driver class called `Bookshelf`, whose `main` method instantiates and updates several `Book` objects.

PP 5.8   Design and implement a class called `Flight` that represents an airline flight. It should contain instance data that represents the airline name, flight number, and the flight's origin and destination cities. Define the `Flight` constructor to accept and initialize all instance data. Include getter and setter methods for all instance data. Include a `toString` method that returns a one-line description of the flight. Create a driver class called `FlightTest`, whose `main` method instantiates and updates several `Flight` objects.

PP 5.9   Design and implement a class called `Bulb` that represents a light bulb that can be turned on and off. Create a driver class called `Lights`, whose `main` method instantiates and turns on some `Bulb` objects.

PP 5.10   Using the `Die` class defined in this chapter, design and implement a class called `PairOfDice`, composed of two `Die` objects. Include methods to set and get the individual die values, a method to roll the dice, and a method that returns the current sum of the two die values. Rewrite the `SnakeEyes` program using a `PairOfDice` object.

PP 5.11   Using the `PairOfDice` class from programming project 5.10, design and implement a class to play a game called Pig. In this game, the user competes against the computer. On each turn, the current player rolls a pair of dice and accumulates points. The goal is to reach 100 points before your opponent does. If, on any turn, the player rolls a 1, all points accumulated for that round are forfeited and control of the dice moves to the other player. If the player rolls two 1's in one turn, the player loses all points accumulated thus far in the game and loses control of the dice. The player may voluntarily turn over the dice after each roll. Therefore the player must decide to either roll again (be a pig) and risk losing points or relinquish control of the dice, possibly allowing the other player to win. Implement the computer player such that it always relinquishes the dice after accumulating 20 or more points in any given round.

PP 5.12   Modify the `Account` class from this chapter so that it also permits an account to be opened with just a name and an account number, assuming an initial balance of zero. Modify the `main` method of the `Transactions` class to demonstrate this new capability.

PP 5.13   Design and implement a class called `Card` that represents a standard playing card. Each card has a suit and a face value. Create a program that deals five random cards.

Answers to Self-Review Questions

SR 5.1   An attribute is a data value stored in an object and defines a particular characteristic of that object. For example, one attribute of a Student object might be that student's current grade point average. Collectively, the values of an object's attributes determine that object's current state.

SR 5.2   An operation is a function that can be done to or done by an object. For example, one operation of a Student object might be to compute that student's current grade point average. Collectively, an object's operations are referred to as the object's behaviors.

SR 5.3   A class is the blueprint of an object. It defines the variables and methods that will be a part of every object that is instantiated from it. But a class reserves no memory space for variables. Each object has its own data space and therefore its own state.

SR 5.4   The scope of a variable is the area within a program in which the variable can be referenced. An instance variable, declared at the class level, can be referenced in any method of the class. Local variables, including the formal parameters, declared within a particular method, can be referenced only in that method.

SR 5.5   A UML diagram helps us visualize the classes used in a program as well as the relationships among them. UML diagrams are tools that help us capture the design of a program prior to writing it.

SR 5.6   A self-governing object is one that controls the values of its own data. An encapsulated object, which doesn't allow an external client to reach in and change its data, is self-governing.

SR 5.7   A modifier is a Java reserved word that can be used in the definition of a variable or method and that specifically defines certain characteristics of its use. For example, if a variable is declared with the modifier private, the variable cannot be directly accessed outside of the object in which it is defined.

SR 5.8   A constant might be declared with public visibility because that would not violate encapsulation. Because the value of a constant cannot be changed, it is not generally a problem for another object to access it directly.

SR 5.9   The modifiers affect the methods and variables in the following ways:

    a. A public method is called a service method for an object because it defines a service that the object provides.

b. A private method is called a support method because it cannot be invoked from outside the object and is used to support the activities of other methods in the class.

c. A public variable is a variable that can be directly accessed and modified by a client. This explicitly violates the principle of encapsulation and therefore should be avoided.

d. A private variable is a variable that can be accessed and modified only from within the class. Variables almost always are declared with private visibility.

SR 5.10 An object's interface is the set of public operations (methods) defined on it. That is, the interface establishes the set of services the object will perform for the rest of the system.

SR 5.11 Although a method is defined in a class, it is invoked through a particular object to indicate which object of that class is being affected. For example, the Student class may define the operation that computes the grade point average of a student, but the operation is invoked through a particular Student object to compute the GPA for that student. The exception to this rule is the invocation of a static method, which is executed through the class name and does not affect any particular object.

SR 5.12 An invoked method may return a value, which means it computes a value and provides that value to the calling method. The calling method usually uses the invocation, and thus its return value, as part of a larger expression.

SR 5.13 An explicit return statement is used to specify the value that is returned from a method. The type of the return value must match the return type specified in the method definition.

SR 5.14 A return statement is required in methods that have a return type other than void. A method that does not return a value could use a return statement without an expression, but it is not necessary. Only one return statement should be used in a method.

SR 5.15 An actual parameter is a value sent to a method when it is invoked. A formal parameter is the corresponding variable in the header of the method declaration; it takes on the value of the actual parameter so that it can be used inside the method.

SR 5.16 Constructors are special methods in an object that are used to initialize the object when it is instantiated. A constructor has the same name as its class, and it does not return a value.

SR 5.17   Memory space for an instance variable is created for each object that is instantiated from a class. A static variable is shared among all objects of a class.

SR 5.18   The `main` method of any program is static, and can refer only to static or local variables. Therefore, a `main` method could not refer to instance variables declared at the class level.

SR 5.19   A dependency relationship between two classes occurs when one class relies on the functionality of the other. It is often referred to as a "uses" relationship.

SR 5.20   Overloaded methods are distinguished by having a unique signature, which includes the number, order, and type of the parameters. The return type is not part of the signature.

SR 5.21   Method decomposition is the process of dividing a complex method into several support methods to get the job done. This simplifies and facilitates the design of the program.

SR 5.22   A method executed through an object might take as a parameter another object created from the same class. For example, the `concat` method of the `String` class is executed through one `String` object and takes another `String` object as a parameter.

SR 5.23   An aggregate object is an object that has other objects as instance data. That is, an aggregate object is one that is made up of other objects.

SR 5.24   The `this` reference always refers to the currently executing object. A nonstatic method of a class is written generically for all objects of the class, but it is invoked through a particular object. The `this` reference, therefore, refers to the object through which that method is currently being executed.

SR 5.25   Objects are passed to methods by copying the reference to the object (its address). Therefore the actual and formal parameters of a method become aliases of each other.

SR 5.26   Defect testing is the act of testing to locate errors in a program.

SR 5.27   A debugger is a software application that allows us to observe and manipulate the inner workings of a program as it executes.

Graphical User Interfaces

6

CHAPTER OBJECTIVES

- Discuss the core elements needed in any Java GUI: components, events, and listeners.

- Explore the use of containers to organize components.

- Explore various types of components, including buttons, text fields, sliders, and combo boxes.

- Discuss the various types of events that components generate, and under what conditions.

- Discuss the concept of a layout manager and explore several specific ones.

- Explore various types of mouse and keyboard events.

- Discuss dialog boxes, including specialized dialog boxes for choosing files and colors.

- Explore the use of borders, tool tips, and mnemonics.

Many programs provide a graphical user interface (GUI) through which a user interacts with the program. As the name implies, a GUI makes use of graphical screen components such as windows, buttons, check boxes, menus, and text fields. GUIs often provide a more natural and rich experience for the user compared to a simple text-based, command-line environment. This chapter explores the various issues related to developing a GUI in Java.

6.1 GUI Elements

The text-based programs we've seen in previous examples are *command-line applications*, which interact with the user through simple prompts and feedback. This type of interface is straightforward to understand, but it lacks the rich user experience possible when a true *graphical user interface* (GUI) is used. With a GUI, the user is not limited to responding to prompts in a particular order and receiving feedback in one place. Instead, the user can interact as needed with various components such as buttons and text fields. This chapter explores the many issues involved in developing a GUI in Java.

Let's start with an overview of the concepts that underlie every GUI-based program. At least three kinds of objects are needed to create a GUI in Java:

- components
- events
- listeners

A GUI *component* is an object that defines a screen element used to display information or allow the user to interact with a program in a certain way. Examples of GUI components include push buttons, text fields, labels, scroll bars, and menus. A *container* is a special type of component that is used to hold and organize other components.

An *event* is an object that represents some occurrence in which we may be interested. Often, events correspond to user actions, such as pressing a mouse button or typing a key on the keyboard. Most GUI components generate events to indicate a user action related to that component. For example, a button component will generate an event to indicate that the button has been pushed. A program that is oriented around a GUI, responding to events from the user, is called *event-driven*.

A *listener* is an object that "waits" for an event to occur and responds in some way when it does. A big part of designing a GUI-based program is establishing the relationships among the listener, the event it listens for, and the component that will generate the event.

> **KEY CONCEPT**
>
> A GUI is made up of components, events that represent user actions, and listeners that respond to those events.

For the most part, we will use components and events that are predefined by classes in the Java class library. We will tailor the behavior of the components, but their basic roles have been established already. We will, however, write our own listener classes to perform whatever actions we desire when events occur.

So, to create a Java program that uses a GUI, we must:

- instantiate and set up the necessary components,
- implement listener classes that define what happens when particular events occur, and

■ establish the relationship between the listeners and the components that generate the events of interest.

Java components and other GUI-related classes are defined primarily in two packages: java.awt and javax.swing. (Note the x in javax.swing.) The *Abstract Windowing Toolkit* (AWT) was the original Java GUI package. It still contains many important classes that we will use. The *Swing* package was added later and provides components that are more versatile than those of the AWT package. Both packages are needed for GUI development, but we will use Swing components whenever there is an option.

In some respects, once you have a basic understanding of event-driven programming, the rest is just detail. There are many types of components you can use that produce many types of events that you may want to acknowledge. But they all work in the same basic way. They all have the same core relationships to one another.

Let's look at a simple example that contains all of the basic GUI elements. The PushCounter class shown in Listing 6.1 on the next page contains the driver of a program that presents the user with a single push button (labeled "Push Me!"). Each time the button is pushed, a counter is updated and displayed.

The components used in this program include a button, a label to display the count, a panel to hold the button and label, and a frame to display the panel. The panel is defined by the PushCounterPanel class, shown in Listing 6.2. Let's look at each of these pieces in more detail.

Frames and Panels

A *frame* is a container that is used to display GUI-based Java applications. A frame is displayed as a separate window with its own title bar. It can be repositioned on the screen and resized as needed by dragging it with the mouse. It contains small buttons in the corner of the frame that allow the frame to be minimized, maximized, and closed. A frame is defined by the JFrame class.

A *panel* is also a container. However, unlike a frame, it cannot be displayed on its own. A panel must be added to another container for it to be displayed. Generally a panel doesn't move unless you move the container that it's in. Its primary role is to help organize the other components in a GUI. A panel is defined by the JPanel class.

> **KEY CONCEPT**
>
> A frame is displayed as a separate window, but a panel can only be displayed as part of another container.

We can classify containers as either heavyweight or lightweight. A *heavyweight container* is one that is managed by the underlying operating system on which the program is run, whereas a *lightweight container* is managed by the Java program itself. A frame is a heavyweight component, and a panel is a lightweight component. Another heavyweight container is an *applet*, which is used to display and

LISTING 6.1

```java
//********************************************************************
//  PushCounter.java         Java Foundations
//
//  Demonstrates a graphical user interface and an event listener.
//********************************************************************

import javax.swing.JFrame;

public class PushCounter
{
   //-----------------------------------------------------------------
   //  Creates and displays the main program frame.
   //-----------------------------------------------------------------
   public static void main (String[] args)
   {
      JFrame frame = new JFrame ("Push Counter");
      frame.setDefaultCloseOperation (JFrame.EXIT_ON_CLOSE);

      PushCounterPanel panel = new PushCounterPanel();
      frame.getContentPane().add(panel);

      frame.pack();
      frame.setVisible(true);
   }
}
```

DISPLAY

Push Counter

Push Me!   Pushes: 12

Go to the end of the book for a full color version of this figure.

execute a Java program through a Web browser. Applets are discussed in Appendix G.

Heavyweight components are more complex than lightweight components in general. A frame, for example, has multiple *panes*, which are responsible for various characteristics of the frame window. All visible elements of a Java interface are displayed in a frame's *content pane*.

LISTING 6.2

```java
//********************************************************************
//   PushCounterPanel.java         Java Foundations
//
//   Demonstrates a graphical user interface and an event listener.
//********************************************************************

import java.awt.*;
import java.awt.event.*;
import javax.swing.*;

public class PushCounterPanel extends JPanel
{
    private int count;
    private JButton push;
    private JLabel label;

    //-----------------------------------------------------------------
    //   Constructor: Sets up the GUI.
    //-----------------------------------------------------------------
    public PushCounterPanel ()
    {
        count = 0;

        push = new JButton ("Push Me!");
        push.addActionListener (new ButtonListener());

        label = new JLabel ("Pushes: " + count);

        add (push);
        add (label);

        setBackground (Color.cyan);
        setPreferredSize (new Dimension(300, 40));
    }

    //********************************************************************
    //   Represents a listener for button push (action) events.
    //********************************************************************
    private class ButtonListener implements ActionListener
    {
        //-----------------------------------------------------------------
        //   Updates the counter and label when the button is pushed.
        //-----------------------------------------------------------------
```

LISTING 6.2 *continued*

```
    public void actionPerformed (ActionEvent event)
    {
       count++;
       label.setText("Pushes: " + count);
    }
  }
}
```

Generally, we can create a Java GUI-based application by creating a frame in which the program interface is displayed. The interface is often organized onto a primary panel, which is added to the frame's content pane. The components in the primary panel are sometimes organized using other panels as needed.

In the main method of the PushCounter class, the frame for the program is constructed, set up, and displayed. The JFrame constructor takes a string as a parameter, which it displays in the title bar of the frame. The call to the setDefaultCloseOperation method determines what will happen when the close button in the corner of the frame is clicked. In most cases we'll simply let that button terminate the program, as indicated by the EXIT_ON_CLOSE constant.

The content pane of the frame is obtained using the getContentPane method, immediately after which the add method of the content pane is called to add the panel. The pack method of the frame sets its size appropriately based on its contents—in this case the frame is sized to accommodate the size of the panel it contains. This is a better approach than trying to set the size of the frame explicitly, which should change as the components within the frame change. The call to the setVisible method causes the frame to be displayed on the monitor screen.

You can interact with the frame itself in various ways. You can move the entire frame to another point on the desktop by grabbing the title bar of the frame and dragging it with the mouse. You can also resize the frame by dragging the bottom-right corner of the frame.

A panel is created by instantiating the JPanel class. In the case of the PushCounter program, the panel is represented by the PushCounterPanel class, which is derived from JPanel. So a PushCounterPanel is a JPanel, inheriting all of its methods and attributes. This is a common technique for creating panels.

The constructor of the PushCounterPanel class makes calls to several methods inherited from JPanel. For example, the background color of the panel is set using the `setBackground` method (the `Color` class is described in Appendix F). The `setPreferredSize` method accepts a `Dimension` object as a parameter, which is used to indicate the width and height of the component in pixels. The size of many components can be set this way, and most also have methods called `setMinimumSize` and `setMaximumSize` to help control the look of the interface.

A panel's `add` method allows a component to be added to the panel. In the `PushCounterPanel` constructor, a newly created button and label are added to the panel, and are from that point on considered part of that panel. The order in which components are added to a container often matters. In this case, it determines that the button appears before the label.

A container is governed by a *layout manager*, which determines exactly how the components added to the panel will be displayed. The default layout manager for a panel simply displays components in the order they are added, with as many components on one line as possible. Layout managers are discussed in detail later in this chapter.

Buttons and Action Events

The `PushCounter` program displays a button and a label. A *label*, created from the `JLabel` class, is a component that displays a line of text in a GUI. A label can also be used to display an image, as shown in later examples. In the `PushCounter` program, the label displays the number of times the button has been pushed.

Labels can be found in most GUI-based programs. They are very useful for displaying information or for labeling other components in the GUI. However, labels are not interactive. That is, the user does not interact with a label directly. The component that makes the `PushCounter` program interactive is the button that the user pushes with the mouse.

A *push button* is a component that allows the user to initiate an action with a press of the mouse. There are other types of button components that we explore in later chapters. A push button is defined by the `JButton` class. A call to the `JButton` constructor takes a `String` parameter that specifies the text shown on the button.

A `JButton` generates an *action event* when it is pushed. There are several types of events defined in the Java standard class library, and we explore many of them throughout this chapter. Different components generate different types of events.

The only event of interest in this program occurs when the button is pushed. To respond to the event, we must create a listener object for that event, so we must write a class that represents the listener. In this case, we need an action event listener.

In the `PushButton` program, the `ButtonListener` class represents the action listener. We could write the `ButtonListener` class in its own file, or even in the same file but outside of the `PushCounterPanel` class. However, then we would have to set up a way to communicate between the listener and the components of the GUI that the listener updates. Instead, we define the `ButtonListener` class as

an *inner class*, which is a class defined within another class. As such, it automatically has access to the members of the class that contains it. You should only create inner classes in situations in which there is an intimate relationship between the two classes and the inner class is not accessed by any other class. The relationship between a listener and its GUI is one of the few situations in which an inner class is appropriate.

Listener classes are written by implementing an *interface*, which is a list of methods that the implementing class must define. The Java standard class library contains interfaces for many types of events. An action listener is created by implementing the `ActionListener` interface; therefore, we include the `implements` clause in the `ButtonListener` class. Interfaces are discussed in more detail in Chapter 9.

The only method listed in the `ActionListener` interface is the `actionPerformed` method, so that's the only method that the `ButtonListener` class must implement. The component that generates the action event (in this case the button) will call the `actionPerformed` method when the event occurs, passing in an `ActionEvent` object that represents the event. Sometimes we will use this event object, and other times it is simply sufficient to know that the event occurred. In this case, we have no need to interact with the event object. When the event occurs, the listener increments the count and resets the text of the label by using the `setText` method.

Remember, we not only have to create a listener for an event, we must also set up the relationship between the listener and the component that will generate the event. To do so, we add the listener to the component by calling the appropriate method. In the `PushCounterPanel` constructor, we call the `addActionListener` method, passing in a newly instantiated `ButtonListener` object.

Review this example carefully, noting how it accomplishes the three key steps to creating an interactive GUI-based program. It creates and sets up the GUI components, creates the appropriate listener for the event of interest, and sets up the relationship between the listener and the component that will generate the event.

Determining Event Sources

Let's look at an example in which one listener object is used to listen to two different components. The program represented by the `LeftRight` class, shown in Listing 6.3, displays a label and two buttons. When the Left button is pressed, the label displays the word Left and when the Right button is pressed the label displays the word Right.

LISTING 6.3

```java
//********************************************************************
//  LeftRight.java        Java Foundations
//
//  Demonstrates the use of one listener for multiple buttons.
//********************************************************************

import javax.swing.JFrame;

public class LeftRight
{
   //-----------------------------------------------------------------
   //  Creates and displays the main program frame.
   //-----------------------------------------------------------------
   public static void main (String[] args)
   {
      JFrame frame = new JFrame ("Left Right");
      frame.setDefaultCloseOperation (JFrame.EXIT_ON_CLOSE);

      frame.getContentPane().add(new LeftRightPanel());

      frame.pack();
      frame.setVisible(true);
   }
}
```

DISPLAY

Go to the end of the book for a full color version of this figure.

The LeftRightPanel class, shown in Listing 6.4 on the next page, creates one instance of the ButtonListener class, and then adds that listener to both buttons. Therefore, when either button is pressed, the actionPerformed method of the ButtonListener class is invoked.

```
LISTING  6.4
```

```java
//***********************************************************************
//  LeftRightPanel.java        Java Foundations
//
//  Demonstrates the use of one listener for multiple buttons.
//***********************************************************************

import java.awt.*;
import java.awt.event.*;
import javax.swing.*;

public class LeftRightPanel extends JPanel
{
   private JButton left, right;
   private JLabel label;
   private JPanel buttonPanel;

   //------------------------------------------------------------------
   //  Constructor: Sets up the GUI.
   //------------------------------------------------------------------
   public LeftRightPanel ()
   {
      left = new JButton ("Left");
      right = new JButton ("Right");

      ButtonListener listener = new ButtonListener();
      left.addActionListener (listener);
      right.addActionListener (listener);

      label = new JLabel ("Push a button");

      buttonPanel = new JPanel();
      buttonPanel.setPreferredSize (new Dimension(200, 40));
      buttonPanel.setBackground (Color.blue);
      buttonPanel.add (left);
      buttonPanel.add (right);

      setPreferredSize (new Dimension(200, 80));
      setBackground (Color.cyan);
      add (label);
      add (buttonPanel);
   }

   //***********************************************************************
   //  Represents a listener for both buttons.
   //***********************************************************************
```

LISTING 6.4 *continued*

```java
private class ButtonListener implements ActionListener
{
   //-----------------------------------------------------------
   //  Determines which button was pressed and sets the label
   //  text accordingly.
   //-----------------------------------------------------------
   public void actionPerformed (ActionEvent event)
   {
      if (event.getSource() == left)
         label.setText("Left");
      else
         label.setText("Right");
   }
}
}
```

On each invocation, the `actionPerformed` method uses an `if-else` statement to determine which button generated the event. The `getSource` method is called on the `ActionEvent` object that the button passes into the `actionPerformed` method. The `getSource` method returns a reference to the component that generated the event. The condition of the `if` statement compares the event source to the reference to the left button. If they don't match, then the event must have been generated by the right button.

We could have created two separate listener classes, one to listen to the left button and another to listen to the right. In that case the `actionPerformed` method would not have to determine the source of the event. Whether to have multiple listeners or determine the event source when it occurs is a design decision that should be made depending on the situation.

Note that the two buttons are put on the same panel called `buttonPanel`, which is separate from the panel represented by the `LeftRightPanel` class. By putting both buttons on one panel, we can guarantee their visual relationship to each other even when the frame is resized in various ways. For buttons labeled Left and Right, that is certainly important.

6.2 More Components

In addition to push buttons, there are a variety of other interactive components that can be used in a GUI, each with a particular role to play. Let's examine a few more.

Text Fields

A *text field* allows the user to enter typed input from the keyboard. The `Fahrenheit` program shown in Listing 6.5 presents a GUI that includes a text field into which the user can type a Fahrenheit temperature. When the user presses the Enter (or Return) key, the equivalent Celsius temperature is displayed.

The interface for the `Fahrenheit` program is set up in the `FahrenheitPanel` class, shown in Listing 6.6. The text field is an object of the `JTextField` class. The `JTextField` constructor takes an integer parameter that specifies the size of the field in number of characters based on the current default font.

The text field and various labels are added to the panel to be displayed. Remember that the default layout manager for a panel puts as many components on a line as it can fit. So if you resize the frame, the orientation of the labels and text field may change.

LISTING 6.5

```java
//********************************************************************
//  Fahrenheit.java        Java Foundations
//
//  Demonstrates the use of text fields.
//********************************************************************

import javax.swing.JFrame;

public class Fahrenheit
{
    //-----------------------------------------------------------------
    //  Creates and displays the temperature converter GUI.
    //-----------------------------------------------------------------
    public static void main (String[] args)
    {
        JFrame frame = new JFrame ("Fahrenheit");
        frame.setDefaultCloseOperation (JFrame.EXIT_ON_CLOSE);

        FahrenheitPanel panel = new FahrenheitPanel();
        frame.getContentPane().add(panel);

        frame.pack();
        frame.setVisible(true);
    }
}
```

LISTING 6.5 *continued*

DISPLAY

Go to the end of the book for a full color version of this figure.

LISTING 6.6

```java
//********************************************************************
//  FahrenheitPanel.java        Java Foundations
//
//  Demonstrates the use of text fields.
//********************************************************************

import java.awt.*;
import java.awt.event.*;
import javax.swing.*;

public class FahrenheitPanel extends JPanel
{
   private JLabel inputLabel, outputLabel, resultLabel;
   private JTextField fahrenheit;

   //-----------------------------------------------------------------
   //  Constructor: Sets up the main GUI components.
   //-----------------------------------------------------------------
   public FahrenheitPanel()
   {
      inputLabel = new JLabel ("Enter Fahrenheit temperature:");
      outputLabel = new JLabel ("Temperature in Celsius: ");
      resultLabel = new JLabel ("---");
```

LISTING 6.6   *continued*

```java
      fahrenheit = new JTextField (5);
      fahrenheit.addActionListener (new TempListener());

      add (inputLabel);
      add (fahrenheit);
      add (outputLabel);
      add (resultLabel);

      setPreferredSize (new Dimension(300, 75));
      setBackground (Color.yellow);
   }

   //*****************************************************************
   //  Represents an action listener for the temperature input field.
   //*****************************************************************
   private class TempListener implements ActionListener
   {
      //--------------------------------------------------------------
      //  Performs the conversion when the enter key is pressed in
      //  the text field.
      //--------------------------------------------------------------
      public void actionPerformed (ActionEvent event)
      {
         int fahrenheitTemp, celsiusTemp;

         String text = fahrenheit.getText();

         fahrenheitTemp = Integer.parseInt (text);
         celsiusTemp = (fahrenheitTemp-32) * 5/9;

         resultLabel.setText (Integer.toString (celsiusTemp));
      }
   }
}
```

A text field generates an action event when the Enter or Return key is pressed (and the cursor is in the text field). Therefore we need to set up a listener object to respond to action events, similar to previous examples.

The text field component calls the `actionPerformed` method when the user presses the Enter key. The method first retrieves the text from the text field by calling its `getText` method, which returns a character string. The text is converted to an integer using the `parseInt` method of the `Integer` wrapper class. Then the method performs the calculation to determine the equivalent Celsius temperature and sets the text of the appropriate label with the result.

Note that a push button and a text field generate the same kind of event: an action event. So an alternative to the Fahrenheit program design is to add to the GUI a `JButton` object that causes the conversion to occur when the user uses the mouse to press the button. For that matter, the same listener object can be used to listen to multiple components at the same time. So the listener could be added to both the text field and the button, giving the user the option. Pressing either the button or the Enter key will cause the conversion to be performed. These variations are left as programming projects.

Check Boxes

A *check box* is a button that can be toggled on or off using the mouse, indicating that a particular boolean condition is set or unset. Although you might have a group of check boxes indicating a set of options, each check box operates independently. That is, each can be set to on or off and the status of one does not influence the others.

The program in Listing 6.7 on the next page displays two check boxes and a label. The check boxes determine whether the text of the label is displayed in bold, italic, both, or neither. Any combination of bold and italic is valid. For example, both check boxes could be checked (on), in which case the text is displayed in both bold and italic. If neither is checked, the text of the label is displayed in a plain style.

The GUI for the `StyleOptions` program is embodied in the `StyleOptionsPanel` class shown in Listing 6.8 on page 259. A check box is represented by the `JCheckBox` class. When a check box changes state from selected (checked) to deselected (unchecked), or vice versa, it generates an *item event*. The `ItemListener` interface contains a single method called `itemStateChanged`. In this example, we use the same listener object to handle both check boxes.

This program also uses the `Font` class, which represents a particular character font. A `Font` object is defined by the font name, the font style, and the font size. The font name establishes the general visual characteristics of the characters. We are using the Helvetica font in this program. The style of a Java font can be plain, bold, italic, or bold and italic combined. The listener is set up to change the characteristics of our font style.

The style of a font is represented as an integer, and integer constants defined in the `Font` class are used to represent the various aspects of the style. The constant `PLAIN` is used to represent a plain style. The constants `BOLD` and `ITALIC` are used to represent bold and italic, respectively. The sum of the `BOLD` and `ITALIC` constants indicates a style that is both bold and italic.

LISTING 6.7

```java
//********************************************************************
//  StyleOptions.java        Java Foundations
//
//  Demonstrates the use of check boxes.
//********************************************************************

import javax.swing.JFrame;

public class StyleOptions
{
   //-----------------------------------------------------------------
   //  Creates and displays the style options frame.
   //-----------------------------------------------------------------
   public static void main (String[] args)
   {
      JFrame frame = new JFrame ("Style Options");
      frame.setDefaultCloseOperation (JFrame.EXIT_ON_CLOSE);

      frame.getContentPane().add (new StyleOptionsPanel());

      frame.pack();
      frame.setVisible(true);
   }
}
```

DISPLAY

Go to the end of the book for a full color version of this figure.

LISTING 6.8

```java
//********************************************************************
//   StyleOptionsPanel.java        Java Foundations
//
//   Demonstrates the use of check boxes.
//********************************************************************

import javax.swing.*;
import java.awt.*;
import java.awt.event.*;

public class StyleOptionsPanel extends JPanel
{
    private JLabel saying;
    private JCheckBox bold, italic;

    //-----------------------------------------------------------------
    //  Sets up a panel with a label and some check boxes that
    //  control the style of the label's font.
    //-----------------------------------------------------------------
    public StyleOptionsPanel()
    {
        saying = new JLabel ("Say it with style!");
        saying.setFont (new Font ("Helvetica", Font.PLAIN, 36));

        bold = new JCheckBox ("Bold");
        bold.setBackground (Color.cyan);
        italic = new JCheckBox ("Italic");
        italic.setBackground (Color.cyan);

        StyleListener listener = new StyleListener();
        bold.addItemListener (listener);
        italic.addItemListener (listener);

        add (saying);
        add (bold);
        add (italic);

        setBackground (Color.cyan);
        setPreferredSize (new Dimension(300, 100));
    }

    //********************************************************************
    //   Represents the listener for both check boxes.
    //********************************************************************
    private class StyleListener implements ItemListener
```

LISTING 6.8   *continued*

```
    {
        //---------------------------------------------------------------
        //  Updates the style of the label font style.
        //---------------------------------------------------------------
        public void itemStateChanged (ItemEvent event)
        {
            int style = Font.PLAIN;

            if (bold.isSelected())
                style = Font.BOLD;

            if (italic.isSelected())
                style += Font.ITALIC;

            saying.setFont (new Font ("Helvetica", style, 36));
        }
    }
}
```

The `itemStateChanged` method of the listener determines what the revised style should be now that one of the check boxes has changed state. It initially sets the style to be plain. Then each check box is consulted in turn using the `isSelected` method, which returns a boolean value. First, if the Bold check box is selected (checked), then the style is set to bold. Then, if the Italic check box is selected, the `ITALIC` constant is added to the style variable. Finally, the font of the label is set to a new font with its revised style.

Note that, given the way the listener is written in this program, it doesn't matter which check box was clicked to generate the event. The same listener processes both check boxes. It also doesn't matter whether the changed check box was toggled from selected to unselected or vice versa. The state of both check boxes is examined if either is changed.

Radio Buttons

A *radio button* is used with other radio buttons to provide a set of mutually exclusive options. Unlike a check box, a radio button is not particularly useful by itself. It has meaning only when it is used with one or more other radio buttons. Only one option out of the group is valid. At any point in time, one and only one button of the group of radio buttons is selected (on). When a radio button from the group is pushed, the other button in the group that is currently on is automatically toggled off.

> **KEY CONCEPT**
> Radio buttons operate as a group, providing a set of mutually exclusive options.

The term "radio buttons" comes from the way the buttons worked on an old-fashioned car radio. At any point, one button was pushed to specify the current choice of station; when another was pushed, the button that was in automatically popped out.

The QuoteOptions program, shown in Listing 6.9, displays a label and a group of radio buttons. The radio buttons determine which quote is displayed in the label.

LISTING 6.9

```java
//********************************************************************
//  QuoteOptions.java       Java Foundations
//
//  Demonstrates the use of radio buttons.
//********************************************************************

import javax.swing.JFrame;

public class QuoteOptions
{
    //-----------------------------------------------------------------
    //  Creates and presents the program frame.
    //-----------------------------------------------------------------
    public static void main (String[] args)
    {
        JFrame frame = new JFrame ("Quote Options");
        frame.setDefaultCloseOperation (JFrame.EXIT_ON_CLOSE);

        frame.getContentPane().add (new QuoteOptionsPanel());

        frame.pack();
        frame.setVisible(true);
    }
}
```

DISPLAY

Go to the end of the book for a full color version of this figure.

Because only one of the quotes can be displayed at a time, the use of radio buttons is appropriate. For example, if the Comedy radio button is selected, the comedy quote is displayed in the label. If the Philosophy button is then pressed, the Comedy radio button is automatically toggled off and the comedy quote is replaced by a philosophical one.

The `QuoteOptionsPanel` class, shown in Listing 6.10, sets up and displays the GUI components. A radio button is represented by the `JRadioButton` class. Because the radio buttons in a set work together, the `ButtonGroup` class is used to define a set of related radio buttons.

LISTING 6.10

```java
//************************************************************
//  QuoteOptionsPanel.java          Java Foundations
//
//  Demonstrates the use of radio buttons.
//************************************************************

import javax.swing.*;
import java.awt.*;
import java.awt.event.*;

public class QuoteOptionsPanel extends JPanel
{
    private JLabel quote;
    private JRadioButton comedy, philosophy, carpentry;
    private String comedyQuote, philosophyQuote, carpentryQuote;

    //-----------------------------------------------------------
    //  Sets up a panel with a label and a set of radio buttons
    //  that control its text.
    //-----------------------------------------------------------
    public QuoteOptionsPanel()
    {
        comedyQuote = "Take my wife, please.";
        philosophyQuote = "I think, therefore I am.";
        carpentryQuote = "Measure twice. Cut once.";

        quote = new JLabel (comedyQuote);
        quote.setFont (new Font ("Helvetica", Font.BOLD, 24));
```

LISTING 6.10 *continued*

```
      comedy = new JRadioButton ("Comedy", true);
      comedy.setBackground (Color.green);
      philosophy = new JRadioButton ("Philosophy");
      philosophy.setBackground (Color.green);
      carpentry = new JRadioButton ("Carpentry");
      carpentry.setBackground (Color.green);

      ButtonGroup group = new ButtonGroup();
      group.add (comedy);
      group.add (philosophy);
      group.add (carpentry);

      QuoteListener listener = new QuoteListener();
      comedy.addActionListener (listener);
      philosophy.addActionListener (listener);
      carpentry.addActionListener (listener);

      add (quote);
      add (comedy);
      add (philosophy);
      add (carpentry);

      setBackground (Color.green);
      setPreferredSize (new Dimension(300, 100));
   }

   //*****************************************************************
   //  Represents the listener for all radio buttons
   //*****************************************************************
   private class QuoteListener implements ActionListener
   {
      //--------------------------------------------------------------
      //  Sets the text of the label depending on which radio
      //  button was pressed.
      //--------------------------------------------------------------
      public void actionPerformed (ActionEvent event)
      {
         Object source = event.getSource();

         if (source == comedy)
            quote.setText (comedyQuote);
         else
```

LISTING 6.10   *continued*

```
            if (source == philosophy)
                quote.setText (philosophyQuote);
            else
                quote.setText (carpentryQuote);
        }
    }
}
```

Note that each button is added to the button group, and also that each button is added individually to the panel. A `ButtonGroup` object is not a container to organize and display components; it is simply a way to define the group of radio buttons that work together to form a set of dependent options. The `ButtonGroup` object ensures that the currently selected radio button is turned off when another in the group is selected.

A radio button produces an action event when it is selected. The `actionPerformed` method of the listener first retrieves the source of the event using the `getSource` method, and then compares it to each of the three radio buttons in turn. Depending on which button was selected, the text of the label is set to the appropriate quote.

Note that unlike push buttons, both check boxes and radio buttons are *toggle buttons*, meaning that at any time they are either on or off. Independent options (choose any combination) are controlled with check boxes. Dependent options (choose one of a set) are controlled with radio buttons. If there is only one option to be managed, a check box can be used by itself. As we mentioned earlier, a radio button, on the other hand, makes sense only in conjunction with one or more other radio buttons.

Also note that check boxes and radio buttons produce different types of events. A check box produces an item event and a radio button produces an action event. The use of different event types is related to the differences in button functionality. A check box produces an event when it is selected or deselected, and the listener could make the distinction if desired. A radio button, on the other hand, produces an event only when it is selected (the currently selected button from the group is deselected automatically).

Sliders

A *slider* is a GUI component that allows the user to specify a numeric value within a bounded range. A slider can be presented either vertically or horizontally and can have optional tick marks and labels indicating the range of values.

A program called `SlideColor` is shown in Listing 6.11. This program presents three sliders that control the RGB components of a color. The color specified by the values of the sliders is shown in a square that is displayed to the right of the sliders. Using RGB values to represent color is discussed in Appendix F.

LISTING 6.11

```java
//********************************************************************
//  SlideColor.java         Java Foundations
//
//  Demonstrates the use slider components.
//********************************************************************

import java.awt.*;
import javax.swing.*;

public class SlideColor
{
    //----------------------------------------------------------------
    //  Presents a frame with a control panel and a panel that
    //  changes color as the sliders are adjusted.
    //----------------------------------------------------------------
    public static void main (String[] args)
    {
        JFrame frame = new JFrame ("Slide Colors");
        frame.setDefaultCloseOperation (JFrame.EXIT_ON_CLOSE);

        frame.getContentPane().add(new SlideColorPanel());

        frame.pack();
        frame.setVisible(true);
    }
}
```

LISTING 6.11 *continued*

DISPLAY

Go to the end of the book for a full color version of this figure.

The `SlideColorPanel` class shown in Listing 6.12 is a panel used to display the three sliders and the color panel. Each slider is created from the `JSlider` class, which accepts four parameters. The first determines the orientation of the slider using one of two `JSlider` constants (`HORIZONTAL` or `VERTICAL`). The second and third parameters specify the maximum and minimum values of the slider, which are set to 0 and 255 for each of the sliders in the example. The last parameter of the `JSlider` constructor specifies the slider's initial value. In our example, the initial value of each slider is 0, which puts the slider knob to the far left when the program initially executes.

The `JSlider` class has several methods that allow the programmer to tailor the look of a slider. Major tick marks can be set at specific intervals using the `setMajorTickSpacing` method. Intermediate minor tick marks can be set using the `setMinorTickSpacing` method. Neither is displayed, however, unless the `setPaintTicks` method, with a parameter of `true`, is invoked as well.

LISTING 6.12

```java
//********************************************************************
//  SlideColorPanel.java        Java Foundations
//
//  Represents the slider control panel for the SlideColor program.
//********************************************************************

import java.awt.*;
import javax.swing.*;
import javax.swing.event.*;

public class SlideColorPanel extends JPanel
{
   private JPanel controls, colorPanel;
   private JSlider rSlider, gSlider, bSlider;
   private JLabel rLabel, gLabel, bLabel;

   //-----------------------------------------------------------------
   //  Sets up the sliders and their labels, aligning them along
   //  their left edge using a box layout.
   //-----------------------------------------------------------------
   public SlideColorPanel()
   {
      rSlider = new JSlider (JSlider.HORIZONTAL, 0, 255, 0);
      rSlider.setMajorTickSpacing (50);
      rSlider.setMinorTickSpacing (10);
      rSlider.setPaintTicks (true);
      rSlider.setPaintLabels (true);
      rSlider.setAlignmentX (Component.LEFT_ALIGNMENT);

      gSlider = new JSlider (JSlider.HORIZONTAL, 0, 255, 0);
      gSlider.setMajorTickSpacing (50);
      gSlider.setMinorTickSpacing (10);
      gSlider.setPaintTicks (true);
      gSlider.setPaintLabels (true);
      gSlider.setAlignmentX (Component.LEFT_ALIGNMENT);

      bSlider = new JSlider (JSlider.HORIZONTAL, 0, 255, 0);
      bSlider.setMajorTickSpacing (50);
      bSlider.setMinorTickSpacing (10);
      bSlider.setPaintTicks (true);
      bSlider.setPaintLabels (true);
      bSlider.setAlignmentX (Component.LEFT_ALIGNMENT);
```

LISTING 6.12   *continued*

```
    SliderListener listener = new SliderListener();
    rSlider.addChangeListener (listener);
    gSlider.addChangeListener (listener);
    bSlider.addChangeListener (listener);

    rLabel = new JLabel ("Red: 0");
    rLabel.setAlignmentX (Component.LEFT_ALIGNMENT);
    gLabel = new JLabel ("Green: 0");
    gLabel.setAlignmentX (Component.LEFT_ALIGNMENT);
    bLabel = new JLabel ("Blue: 0");
    bLabel.setAlignmentX (Component.LEFT_ALIGNMENT);

    controls = new JPanel();
    BoxLayout layout = new BoxLayout (controls, BoxLayout.Y_AXIS);
    controls.setLayout (layout);
    controls.add (rLabel);
    controls.add (rSlider);
    controls.add (Box.createRigidArea (new Dimension (0, 20)));
    controls.add (gLabel);
    controls.add (gSlider);
    controls.add (Box.createRigidArea (new Dimension (0, 20)));
    controls.add (bLabel);
    controls.add (bSlider);

    colorPanel = new JPanel();
    colorPanel.setPreferredSize (new Dimension (100, 100));
    colorPanel.setBackground (new Color (0, 0, 0));

    add (controls);
    add (colorPanel);
}

//****************************************************************
//  Represents the listener for all three sliders.
//****************************************************************
private class SliderListener implements ChangeListener
{
    private int red, green, blue;

    //-----------------------------------------------------------
    //  Gets the value of each slider, then updates the labels and
    //  the color panel.
    //-----------------------------------------------------------
```

LISTING 6.12   *continued*

```
    public void stateChanged (ChangeEvent event)
    {
        red = rSlider.getValue();
        green = gSlider.getValue();
        blue = bSlider.getValue();

        rLabel.setText ("Red: " + red);
        gLabel.setText ("Green: " + green);
        bLabel.setText ("Blue: " + blue);

        colorPanel.setBackground (new Color (red, green, blue));
    }
  }
}
```

Labels indicating the value of the major tick marks are displayed if indicated by a call to the setPaintLabels method.

Note that in this example, the major tick spacing is set to 50. Starting at 0, each increment of 50 is labeled. The last label is therefore 250, even though the slider value can reach 255.

A slider produces a *change event*, indicating that the position of the slider and the value it represents has changed. The ChangeListener interface contains a single method called stateChanged. In the SlideColor program, the same listener object is used for all three sliders. In the stateChanged method, which is called whenever any of the sliders are adjusted, the value of each slider is obtained, the labels of all three are updated, and the background color of the color panel is revised. It is actually only necessary to update one of the labels (the one whose corresponding slider changed). However, the effort to determine which slider was adjusted is not warranted. It's easier—and probably more efficient—to update all three labels each time. Another alternative is to have a unique listener for each slider, though that extra coding effort is not needed either.

A slider is often a good choice when a large range of values is possible but strictly bounded on both ends. Compared to alternatives such as a text field, sliders convey more information to the user and eliminate input errors.

Combo Boxes

> **KEY CONCEPT**
>
> A combo box provides a drop down menu of options.

A *combo box* allows the user to select one of several options from a "drop down" menu. When the user presses a combo box using the mouse, a list of options is displayed from which the user can choose. The current choice is displayed in the combo box. A combo box is defined by the JComboBox class.

A combo box can be either editable or uneditable. By default, a combo box is uneditable. Changing the value of an uneditable combo box can be accomplished only by selecting an item from the list. If the combo box is editable, however, the user can change the value by either selecting an item from the list or typing a particular value into the combo box area.

The options in a combo box list can be established in one of two ways. We can create an array of strings and pass it into the constructor of the JComboBox class. Alternatively, we can use the addItem method to add an item to the combo box after it has been created. An item in a JComboBox can also display an ImageIcon object, in addition to text or by itself.

The JukeBox program shown in Listing 6.13 demonstrates the use of a combo box. The user chooses a song to play using the combo box, and then presses the Play button to begin playing the song. The Stop button can be pressed at any time to stop the song. Selecting a new song while one is playing also stops the current song.

LISTING 6.13

```
//********************************************************************
//  JukeBox.java          Java Foundations
//
//  Demonstrates the use of a combo box.
//********************************************************************

import javax.swing.*;

public class JukeBox
{
   //-----------------------------------------------------------------
   //  Creates and displays the controls for a juke box.
   //-----------------------------------------------------------------
   public static void main (String[] args)
   {
      JFrame frame = new JFrame ("Java Juke Box");
      frame.setDefaultCloseOperation (JFrame.EXIT_ON_CLOSE);
```

LISTING 6.13   *continued*

```
        frame.getContentPane().add(new JukeBoxControls());

        frame.pack();
        frame.setVisible(true);
    }
}
```

DISPLAY

Go to the end of the book for a full color version of this figure.

The JukeBoxControls class shown in Listing 6.14 on the next page is a panel that contains the components that make up the jukebox GUI. The constructor of the class also loads the audio clips that will be played. An audio clip is obtained first by creating a URL object that corresponds to the wav or au file that defines the clip. The first two parameters to the URL constructor should be "file" and "localhost", respectively, if the audio clip is stored on the same machine on which the program is executing. Creating URL objects can potentially throw a checked exception; therefore they are created in a try block. However, this program assumes the audio clips will be loaded successfully and therefore does nothing if an exception is thrown.

Once created, the URL objects are used to create AudioClip objects using the static newAudioClip method of the JApplet class. The audio clips are stored in an array. The first entry in the array, at index 0, is set to null. This entry corresponds to the initial combo box option, which simply encourages the user to make a selection.

LISTING 6.14

```
//***********************************************************************
//  JukeBoxControls.java          Java Foundations
//
//  Represents the control panel for the juke box.
//***********************************************************************

import java.awt.*;
import java.awt.event.*;
import javax.swing.*;
import java.applet.AudioClip;
import java.net.URL;

public class JukeBoxControls extends JPanel
{
   private JComboBox musicCombo;
   private JButton stopButton, playButton;
   private AudioClip[] music;
   private AudioClip current;

   //-------------------------------------------------------------------
   //  Sets up the GUI for the juke box.
   //-------------------------------------------------------------------
   public JukeBoxControls()
   {
      URL url1, url2, url3, url4, url5, url6;
      url1 = url2 = url3 = url4 = url5 = url6 = null;

      // Obtain and store the audio clips to play
      try
      {
         url1 = new URL ("file", "localhost", "westernBeat.wav");
         url2 = new URL ("file", "localhost", "classical.wav");
         url3 = new URL ("file", "localhost", "jeopardy.au");
         url4 = new URL ("file", "localhost", "newAgeRythm.wav");
         url5 = new URL ("file", "localhost", "eightiesJam.wav");
         url6 = new URL ("file", "localhost", "hitchcock.wav");
      }
      catch (Exception exception) {}

      music = new AudioClip[7];
      music[0] = null;  // Corresponds to "Make a Selection..."
      music[1] = JApplet.newAudioClip (url1);
      music[2] = JApplet.newAudioClip (url2);
      music[3] = JApplet.newAudioClip (url3);
      music[4] = JApplet.newAudioClip (url4);
```

```java
      music[5] = JApplet.newAudioClip (url5);
      music[6] = JApplet.newAudioClip (url6);

      // Create the list of strings for the combo box options
      String[] musicNames = {"Make A Selection...", "Western Beat",
              "Classical Melody", "Jeopardy Theme", "New Age Rythm",
              "Eighties Jam", "Alfred Hitchcock's Theme"};

      musicCombo = new JComboBox (musicNames);
      musicCombo.setBackground (Color.cyan);

      //  Set up the buttons
      playButton = new JButton ("Play", new ImageIcon ("play.gif"));
      playButton.setBackground (Color.cyan);
      stopButton = new JButton ("Stop", new ImageIcon ("stop.gif"));
      stopButton.setBackground (Color.cyan);

      //  Set up this panel
      setPreferredSize (new Dimension (250, 100));
      setBackground (Color.cyan);
      add (musicCombo);
      add (playButton);
      add (stopButton);

      musicCombo.addActionListener (new ComboListener());
      stopButton.addActionListener (new ButtonListener());
      playButton.addActionListener (new ButtonListener());

      current = null;
   }

   //*****************************************************************
   //  Represents the action listener for the combo box.
   //*****************************************************************
   private class ComboListener implements ActionListener
   {
      //-------------------------------------------------------------
      //  Stops playing the current selection (if any) and resets
      //  the current selection to the one chosen.
      //-------------------------------------------------------------
      public void actionPerformed (ActionEvent event)
      {
         if (current != null)
            current.stop();
```

LISTING 6.14 *continued*

```
         current = music[musicCombo.getSelectedIndex()];
      }
   }

   //****************************************************************
   //   Represents the action listener for both control buttons.
   //****************************************************************
   private class ButtonListener implements ActionListener
   {
      //-------------------------------------------------------------
      //   Stops the current selection (if any) in either case. If
      //   the play button was pressed, start playing it again.
      //-------------------------------------------------------------
      public void actionPerformed (ActionEvent event)
      {
         if (current != null)
            current.stop();

         if (event.getSource() == playButton)
            if (current != null)
               current.play();
      }
   }
}
```

The list of songs that is displayed in the combo box is defined in an array of strings. The first entry of the array will appear in the combo box by default and is often used to direct the user. We must take care that the rest of the program does not try to use that option as a valid song.

This program also shows the ability for a push button to display an image. In this example, the Play and Stop buttons are displayed with both a text label and an image icon.

A combo box generates an action event whenever the user makes a selection from it. The JukeBox program uses one action listener class for the combo box and another for both of the push buttons. They could have been combined, using code to distinguish which component fired the event.

The actionPerformed method of the ComboListener class is executed when a selection is made from the combo box. The current audio selection that is playing, if any, is stopped. The current clip is then updated to reflect the new selection.

Note that the audio clip is not immediately played at that point. The way this program is designed, the user must press the Play button to hear the new selection.

The `actionPerformed` method of the `ButtonListener` class is executed when either of the buttons is pushed. The current audio selection that is playing, if any, is stopped. If the Stop button was pressed, the task is complete. If the Play button was pressed, the current audio selection is played again from the beginning.

Timers

A *timer*, created from the `Timer` class of the `javax.swing` package, can be thought of as a GUI component. However, unlike other components, it does not have a visual representation that appears on the screen. Instead, as the name implies, it helps us manage an activity over time.

A timer object generates an action event at regular intervals. To perform an animation, we can set up a timer to generate an action event periodically, and then update the animation graphics in the action listener. The methods of the `Timer` class are shown in Figure 6.1.

> **KEY CONCEPT**
>
> A timer generates action events at regular intervals and can be used to control an animation.

The program shown in Listing 6.15 on the next page displays the image of a smiling face that seems to glide across the program window at an angle, bouncing off of the window edges (though that's hard to appreciate from a screen shot).

```
Timer (int delay, ActionListener listener)
    Constructor: Creates a timer that generates an action event at
    regular intervals, specified by the delay. The event will be handled
    by the specified listener.

void addActionListener (ActionListener listener)
    Adds an action listener to the timer.

boolean isRunning ()
    Returns true if the timer is running.

void setDelay (int delay)
    Sets the delay of the timer.

void start ()
    Starts the timer, causing it to generate action events.

void stop ()
    Stops the timer, causing it to stop generating action events.
```

FIGURE 6.1 Some methods of the `Timer` class

LISTING 6.15

```java
//********************************************************************
//  Rebound.java         Java Foundations
//
//  Demonstrates an animation and the use of the Timer class.
//********************************************************************

import java.awt.*;
import java.awt.event.*;
import javax.swing.*;

public class Rebound
{
   //-----------------------------------------------------------------
   //  Displays the main frame of the program.
   //-----------------------------------------------------------------
   public static void main (String[] args)
   {
      JFrame frame = new JFrame ("Rebound");
      frame.setDefaultCloseOperation (JFrame.EXIT_ON_CLOSE);

      frame.getContentPane().add(new ReboundPanel());

      frame.pack();
      frame.setVisible(true);
   }
}
```

DISPLAY

Go to the end of the book for a full color version of this figure.

The constructor of the `ReboundPanel` class, shown in Listing 6.16, creates a `Timer` object. The first parameter to the `Timer` constructor is the delay in milliseconds. The second parameter to the constructor is the listener that handles the action events of the timer. The `ReboundPanel` constructor also sets up the initial position for the image and the number of pixels it will move, in both the vertical and horizontal directions, each time the image is redrawn.

LISTING 6.16

```java
//********************************************************************
//  ReboundPanel.java       Java Foundations
//
//  Represents the primary panel for the Rebound program.
//********************************************************************

import java.awt.*;
import java.awt.event.*;
import javax.swing.*;

public class ReboundPanel extends JPanel
{
    private final int WIDTH = 300, HEIGHT = 100;
    private final int DELAY = 20, IMAGE_SIZE = 35;

    private ImageIcon image;
    private Timer timer;
    private int x, y, moveX, moveY;

    //-----------------------------------------------------------------
    //  Sets up the panel, including the timer for the animation.
    //-----------------------------------------------------------------
    public ReboundPanel()
    {
        timer = new Timer(DELAY, new ReboundListener());

        image = new ImageIcon ("happyFace.gif");

        x = 0;
        y = 40;
        moveX = moveY = 3;

        setPreferredSize (new Dimension(WIDTH, HEIGHT));
        setBackground (Color.black);
        timer.start();
    }
```

LISTING 6.16   *continued*

```java
//-----------------------------------------------------------------
//  Draws the image in the current location.
//-----------------------------------------------------------------
public void paintComponent (Graphics page)
{
   super.paintComponent (page);
   image.paintIcon (this, page, x, y);
}

//*****************************************************************
//  Represents the action listener for the timer.
//*****************************************************************
private class ReboundListener implements ActionListener
{
   //-----------------------------------------------------------------
   //  Updates the position of the image and possibly the direction
   //  of movement whenever the timer fires an action event.
   //-----------------------------------------------------------------
   public void actionPerformed (ActionEvent event)
   {
      x += moveX;
      y += moveY;

      if (x <= 0 || x >= WIDTH-IMAGE_SIZE)
         moveX = moveX * -1;

      if (y <= 0 || y >= HEIGHT-IMAGE_SIZE)
         moveY = moveY * -1;
      repaint();
   }
}
}
```

The `actionPerformed` method of the listener updates the current x and y co-ordinate values, then checks to see if those values cause the image to "run into" the edge of the panel. If so, the movement is adjusted so that the image will make future moves in the opposite direction horizontally, vertically, or both. Note that this calculation takes the image size into account.

After updating the coordinate values, the `actionPerformed` method calls `repaint` to force the component (in this case, the panel) to repaint itself. The call to `repaint` eventually causes the `paintComponent` method to be called, which repaints the image in the new location.

The speed of the animation in this program is a function of two factors: the pause between the action events and the distance the image is shifted each time. In this example, the timer is set to generate an action event every 20 milliseconds, and the image is shifted 3 pixels each time it is updated. You can experiment with these values to change the speed of the animation. The goal should be to create the illusion of movement that is pleasing to the eye.

6.3 Layout Managers

As we mentioned earlier in this chapter, every container is managed by an object called a *layout manager* that determines how the components in the container are arranged visually. The layout manager is consulted when needed, such as when the container is resized or when a component is added to the container.

A layout manager determines the size and position of each component and may take many factors into account to do so. Every container has a default layout manager, although we can replace it if we prefer another one.

The table in Figure 6.2 describes several of the predefined layout managers provided by the Java standard class library.

> **KEY CONCEPT**
>
> Every container is managed by a layout manager, which determines how components are visually presented.

> **KEY CONCEPT**
>
> When changes occur, the components in a container reorganize themselves according to the layout manager's policy.

Layout Manager	Description
Border Layout	Organizes components into five areas (North, South, East, West, and Center).
Box Layout	Organizes components into a single row or column.
Card Layout	Organizes components into one area such that only one is visible at any time.
Flow Layout	Organizes components from left to right, starting new rows as necessary.
Grid Layout	Organizes components into a grid of rows and columns.
GridBag Layout	Organizes components into a grid of cells, allowing components to span more than one cell.

FIGURE 6.2 Some predefined Java layout managers

Every layout manager has its own particular properties and rules governing the layout of components. For some layout managers, the order in which you add the components affects their positioning, whereas others provide more specific control. Some layout managers take a component's preferred size or alignment into account, whereas others don't. To develop good GUIs in Java, it is important to become familiar with features and characteristics of various layout managers.

> **KEY CONCEPT**
>
> The layout manager for each container can be explicitly set.

We can use the setLayout method of a container to change its layout manager. For example, the following code sets the layout manager of a JPanel, which has a flow layout by default, so that it uses a border layout instead:

```
JPanel panel = new JPanel();
panel.setLayout (new BorderLayout());
```

Let's explore some of these layout managers in more detail. We'll focus on the most popular layout managers at this point: flow, border, box, and grid. The class presented in Listing 6.17 contains the main method of an application that demonstrates the use and effects of these layout managers.

LISTING 6.17

```
//********************************************************************
//   LayoutDemo.java          Java Foundations
//
//   Demonstrates the use of flow, border, grid, and box layouts.
//********************************************************************

import javax.swing.*;

public class LayoutDemo
{
    //----------------------------------------------------------------
    //   Sets up a frame containing a tabbed pane. The panel on each
    //   tab demonstrates a different layout manager.
    //----------------------------------------------------------------
    public static void main (String[] args)
    {
        JFrame frame = new JFrame ("Layout Manager Demo");
        frame.setDefaultCloseOperation (JFrame.EXIT_ON_CLOSE);

        JTabbedPane tp = new JTabbedPane();
        tp.addTab ("Intro", new IntroPanel());
        tp.addTab ("Flow", new FlowPanel());
```

```
LISTING  6.17    continued

    tp.addTab ("Border", new BorderPanel());
    tp.addTab ("Grid", new GridPanel());
    tp.addTab ("Box", new BoxPanel());

    frame.getContentPane().add(tp);

    frame.pack();
    frame.setVisible(true);
  }
}
```

The `LayoutDemo` program introduces the use of a *tabbed pane*, a container that allows the user to select (by clicking on a tab) which of several panes is currently visible. A tabbed pane is defined by the `JTabbedPane` class. The `addTab` method creates a tab, specifying the name that appears on the tab and the component to be displayed on that pane when it achieves focus by being "brought to the front" and made visible to the user.

Interestingly, there is an overlap in the functionality provided by tabbed panes and the card layout manager. Similar to the tabbed pane, a card layout allows several layers to be defined, and only one of those layers is displayed at any given point. However, a container managed by a card layout can be adjusted only under program control, whereas tabbed panes allow the user to indicate directly which tab should be displayed.

In this example, each tab of the tabbed pane contains a panel that is controlled by a different layout manager. The first tab simply contains a panel with an introductory message, as shown in Listing 6.18. As we explore each layout manager in more detail, we examine the class that defines the corresponding panel of this program and discuss its visual effect.

Flow Layout

Flow layout is one of the easiest layout managers to use. As we've mentioned, the `JPanel` class uses flow layout by default. Flow layout puts as many components as possible on a row, at their preferred size. When a component cannot fit on a row, it is put on the next row. As many rows as needed are added to fit all components that have been added to the container. Figure 6.3 depicts a container governed by a flow layout manager.

LISTING 6.18

```java
//********************************************************************
//  IntroPanel.java         Java Foundations
//
//  Represents the introduction panel for the LayoutDemo program.
//********************************************************************

import java.awt.*;
import javax.swing.*;

public class IntroPanel extends JPanel
{
   //----------------------------------------------------------------
   //  Sets up this panel with two labels.
   //----------------------------------------------------------------
   public IntroPanel()
   {
      setBackground (Color.green);

      JLabel l1 = new JLabel ("Layout Manager Demonstration");
      JLabel l2 = new JLabel ("Choose a tab to see an example of " +
                             "a layout manager.");
      add (l1);
      add (l2);
   }
}
```

DISPLAY

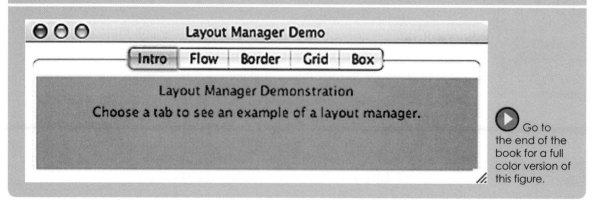

Go to
the end of the
book for a full
color version of
this figure.

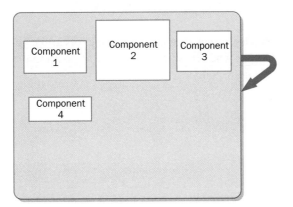

FIGURE 6.3 Flow layout puts as many components as possible on a row

The class in Listing 6.19 on the next page represents the panel that demonstrates a flow layout in the `LayoutDemo` program. It explicitly sets the layout to be a flow layout (though in this case that is unnecessary because `JPanel` defaults to flow layout). The buttons are then created and added to the panel.

The size of each button is made large enough to accommodate the size of the label that is put on it. Flow layout puts as many of these buttons as possible on one row within the panel, and then starts putting components on another row. When the size of the frame is widened (by dragging the lower-right corner with the mouse, for example), the panel grows as well, and more buttons can fit on a row. When the frame is resized, the layout manager is consulted and the components are reorganized automatically. The display in Listing 6.19 shows two screen shots of the window with different sizes.

The constructor of the `FlowLayout` class is overloaded to allow the programmer to tailor the characteristics of the layout manager. Within each row, components are either centered, left aligned, or right aligned. The alignment defaults to centered. The horizontal and vertical gap size between components also can be specified when the layout manager is created. The `FlowLayout` class also has methods to set the alignment and gap sizes after the layout manager is created.

Border Layout

A *border layout* has five areas to which components can be added: North, South, East, West, and Center. The areas have a particular positional relationship to each other, as shown in Figure 6.4.

LISTING 6.19

```java
//********************************************************************
//  FlowPanel.java        Java Foundations
//
//  Represents the panel in the LayoutDemo program that demonstrates
//  the flow layout manager.
//********************************************************************

import java.awt.*;
import javax.swing.*;

public class FlowPanel extends JPanel
{
   //-----------------------------------------------------------------
   //  Sets up this panel with some buttons to show how flow layout
   //  affects their position.
   //-----------------------------------------------------------------
   public FlowPanel ()
   {
      setLayout (new FlowLayout());

      setBackground (Color.green);

      JButton b1 = new JButton ("BUTTON 1");
      JButton b2 = new JButton ("BUTTON 2");
      JButton b3 = new JButton ("BUTTON 3");
      JButton b4 = new JButton ("BUTTON 4");
      JButton b5 = new JButton ("BUTTON 5");

      add (b1);
      add (b2);
      add (b3);
      add (b4);
      add (b5);
   }
}
```

LISTING 6.19 *continued*

DISPLAY

Go to the end of the book for full color versions of these figures.

FIGURE 6.4 Border layout organizes components in five areas

The four outer areas become as big as needed in order to accommodate the component they contain. If no components are added to the North, South, East, or West areas, these areas do not take up any room in the overall layout. The Center area expands to fill any available space.

A particular container might use only a few areas, depending on the functionality of the system. For example, a program might use only the Center, South, and West areas. This versatility makes border layout a very useful layout manager.

The add method for a container governed by a border layout takes as its first parameter the component to be added. The second parameter indicates the area to which it is added. The area is specified using constants defined in the BorderLayout class. Listing 6.20 shows the panel used by the LayoutDemo program to demonstrate the border layout.

LISTING 6.20

```java
//********************************************************************
//   BorderPanel.java         Java Foundations
//
//   Represents the panel in the LayoutDemo program that demonstrates
//   the border layout manager.
//********************************************************************

import java.awt.*;
import javax.swing.*;

public class BorderPanel extends JPanel
{
    //----------------------------------------------------------------
    //   Sets up this panel with a button in each area of a border
    //   layout to show how it affects their position, shape, and size.
    //----------------------------------------------------------------
    public BorderPanel()
    {
        setLayout (new BorderLayout());

        setBackground (Color.green);

        JButton b1 = new JButton ("BUTTON 1");
        JButton b2 = new JButton ("BUTTON 2");
        JButton b3 = new JButton ("BUTTON 3");
        JButton b4 = new JButton ("BUTTON 4");
        JButton b5 = new JButton ("BUTTON 5");
```

LISTING 6.20 *continued*

```
        add (b1, BorderLayout.CENTER);
        add (b2, BorderLayout.NORTH);
        add (b3, BorderLayout.SOUTH);
        add (b4, BorderLayout.EAST);
        add (b5, BorderLayout.WEST);
    }
}
```

DISPLAY

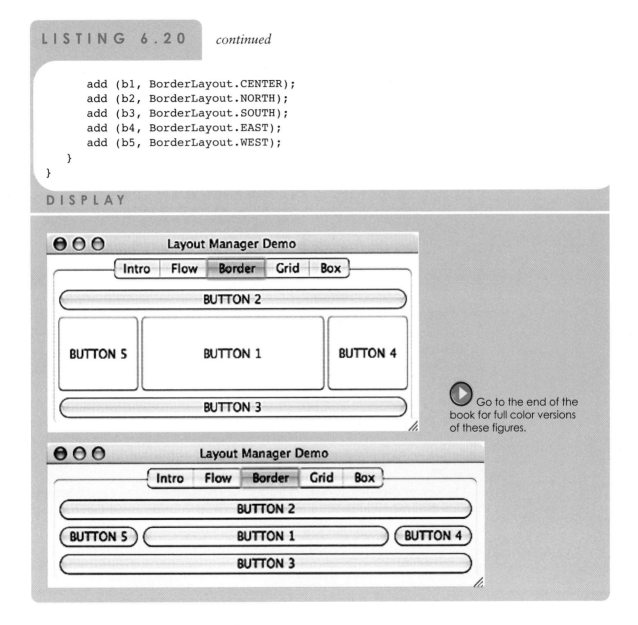

Go to the end of the book for full color versions of these figures.

In the BorderPanel class constructor, the layout manager of the panel is explicitly set to be border layout. The buttons are then created and added to specific panel areas. By default, each button is made wide enough to accommodate its label and tall enough to fill the area to which it has been assigned. As the frame (and the panel) is resized, the size of each button adjusts as needed, with the button in the Center area filling any unused space.

Each area in a border layout displays only one component. That is, only one component is added to each area of a given border layout. A common error is to add two components to a particular area of a border layout, in which case the first component added is replaced by the second, and only the second is seen when the container is displayed. To add multiple components to an area within a border layout, you must first add the components to another container, such as a JPanel, then add the panel to the area.

Note that although the panel used to display the buttons has a green background, no green is visible in the display for Listing 6.20. By default there are no horizontal or vertical gaps between the areas of a border layout. These gaps can be set with an overloaded constructor or with explicit methods of the BorderLayout class. If the gaps are increased, the underlying panel will show through.

Grid Layout

A *grid layout* presents a container's components in a rectangular grid of rows and columns. One component is placed in each grid cell, and all cells are the same size. Figure 6.5 shows the general organization of a grid layout.

The number of rows and columns in a grid layout is established using parameters to the constructor when the layout manager is created. The class in Listing 6.21 shows the panel used by the LayoutDemo program to demonstrate a grid layout. It specifies that the panel should be managed using a grid of two rows and three columns.

As buttons are added to the container, they fill the grid (by default) from left to right and top to bottom. There is no way to explicitly assign a component to a particular location in the grid other than the order in which they are added to the container.

The size of each cell is determined by the container's overall size. When the container is resized, all of the cells change size proportionally to fill the container.

FIGURE 6.5 Grid layout creates a rectangular grid of equal-size cells

LISTING 6.21

```java
//********************************************************************
//  GridPanel.java       Java Foundations
//
//  Represents the panel in the LayoutDemo program that demonstrates
//  the grid layout manager.
//********************************************************************

import java.awt.*;
import javax.swing.*;

public class GridPanel extends JPanel
{
   //-----------------------------------------------------------------
   //  Sets up this panel with some buttons to show how grid
   //  layout affects their position, shape, and size.
   //-----------------------------------------------------------------
   public GridPanel()
   {
      setLayout (new GridLayout (2, 3));

      setBackground (Color.green);

      JButton b1 = new JButton ("BUTTON 1");
      JButton b2 = new JButton ("BUTTON 2");
      JButton b3 = new JButton ("BUTTON 3");
      JButton b4 = new JButton ("BUTTON 4");
      JButton b5 = new JButton ("BUTTON 5");

      add (b1);
      add (b2);
      add (b3);
      add (b4);
      add (b5);
   }
}
```

LISTING 6.21 *continued*

DISPLAY

Go to the end of the book for full color versions of these figures.

If the value used to specify either the number of rows or the number of columns is zero, the grid expands as needed in that dimension to accommodate the number of components added to the container. The values for the number of rows and columns cannot both be zero.

By default, there are no horizontal and vertical gaps between the grid cells. The gap sizes can be specified using an overloaded constructor or with the appropriate GridLayout methods.

Box Layout

A *box layout* organizes components either vertically or horizontally, in one row or one column, as shown in Figure 6.6. It is easy to use, yet when combined with other

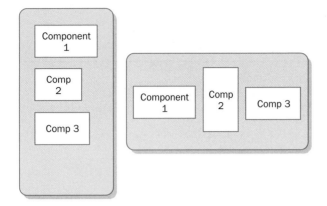

FIGURE 6.6 Box layout organizes components either vertically or horizontally

box layouts, it can produce complex GUI designs similar to those that can be accomplished with a *grid bag layout*, which in general is far more difficult to master.

When a BoxLayout object is created, we specify that it will follow either the X axis (horizontal) or the Y axis (vertical), using constants defined in the BoxLayout class. Unlike other layout managers, the constructor of the BoxLayout class takes as its first parameter the component that it will govern. Therefore a new BoxLayout object must be created for each component. Listing 6.22 on the next page shows the panel used by the LayoutDemo program to demonstrate the box layout.

Components in containers governed by a box layout are organized (top to bottom or left to right) in the order in which they are added to the container.

There are no gaps between the components in a box layout. Unlike previous layout managers we've explored, a box layout does not have a specific vertical or horizontal gap that can be specified for the entire container. Instead, we can add invisible components to the container that take up space between other components. The Box class, which is also part of the Java standard class library, contains static methods that can be used to create these invisible components.

The two types of invisible components used in the BoxPanel class are *rigid areas*, which have a fixed size, and *glue*, which specifies where excess space in a container should go. A rigid area is created using the createRigidArea method of the Box class, and takes a Dimension object as a parameter to define the size of the invisible area. Glue is created using the createHorizontalGlue method or createVerticalGlue method, as appropriate.

Note that in our example, the space between buttons separated by a rigid area remains constant even when the container is resized. Glue, on the other hand, expands or contracts as needed to fill the space.

LISTING 6.22

```java
//********************************************************************
//  BoxPanel.java          Java Foundations
//
//  Represents the panel in the LayoutDemo program that demonstrates
//  the box layout manager.
//********************************************************************

import java.awt.*;
import javax.swing.*;

public class BoxPanel extends JPanel
{
    //-----------------------------------------------------------------
    //  Sets up this panel with some buttons to show how a vertical
    //  box layout (and invisible components) affects their position.
    //-----------------------------------------------------------------
    public BoxPanel()
    {
        setLayout (new BoxLayout (this, BoxLayout.Y_AXIS));

        setBackground (Color.green);

        JButton b1 = new JButton ("BUTTON 1");
        JButton b2 = new JButton ("BUTTON 2");
        JButton b3 = new JButton ("BUTTON 3");
        JButton b4 = new JButton ("BUTTON 4");
        JButton b5 = new JButton ("BUTTON 5");

        add (b1);
        add (Box.createRigidArea (new Dimension (0, 10)));
        add (b2);
        add (Box.createVerticalGlue());
        add (b3);
        add (b4);
        add (Box.createRigidArea (new Dimension (0, 20)));
        add (b5);
    }
}
```

LISTING 6.22 *continued*

DISPLAY

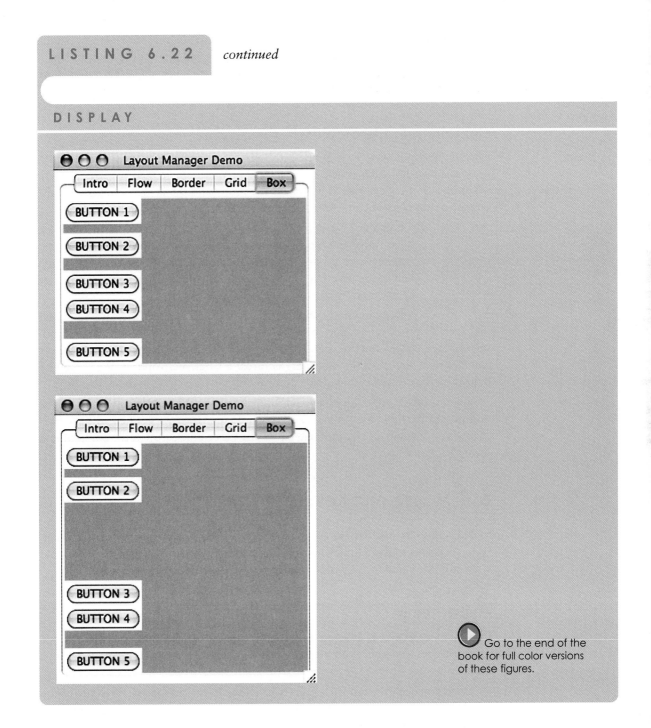

Go to the end of the book for full color versions of these figures.

A box layout—more than most of the other layout managers—respects the alignments and the minimum, maximum, and preferred sizes of the components it governs. Therefore, setting the characteristics of the components that go into the container is another way to tailor the visual effect.

Containment Hierarchies

The way components are grouped into containers, and the way those containers are nested within each other, establishes the *containment hierarchy* for a GUI. The interplay between the containment hierarchy and the layout managers of the containers involved dictates the overall visual effect of the GUI.

> **KEY CONCEPT**
>
> A GUI's appearance is a function of the containment hierarchy and the layout managers of each container.

For any Java program, there is generally one primary container, called a top-level container, such as a frame or applet. The top-level container of a program often contains one or more other containers, such as panels. These panels may contain other panels to organize the other components as desired.

Keep in mind that each container can have its own tailored layout manager. The final appearance of a GUI is a function of the layout managers chosen for each of the containers and the design of the containment hierarchy. Many combinations are possible, and there is rarely a single best option. We should be guided by the desired system goals and general GUI design guidelines.

When changes are made that might affect the visual layout of the components in a program, the layout managers of each container are consulted in turn. The changes in one may affect another. These changes ripple through the containment hierarchy as needed.

6.4 Mouse and Key Events

In addition to events that are generated when the user interacts with a component, there are events that are fired when the user interacts with the computer's mouse and keyboard. We can design a program to capture and respond to these as well.

Mouse Events

Java divides the events generated by the user interacting with the mouse into two categories: *mouse events* and *mouse motion events*. The tables in Figure 6.7 define these events.

When you click the mouse button over a Java GUI component, three events are generated: one when the mouse button is pushed down (*mouse pressed*) and two when it is let up (*mouse released* and *mouse clicked*). A mouse click is defined as

Mouse Event	Description
mouse pressed	The mouse button is pressed down.
mouse released	The mouse button is released.
mouse clicked	The mouse button is pressed down and released without moving the mouse in between.
mouse entered	The mouse pointer is moved onto (over) a component.
mouse exited	The mouse pointer is moved off of a component.

Mouse Motion Event	Description
mouse moved	The mouse is moved.
mouse dragged	The mouse is moved while the mouse button is pressed down.

FIGURE 6.7 Mouse events and mouse motion events

pressing and releasing the mouse button in the same location. If you press the mouse button down, move the mouse, and then release the mouse button, a mouse clicked event is not generated.

A component will generate a *mouse entered* event when the mouse pointer passes into its graphical space. Likewise, it generates a *mouse exited* event when the mouse pointer leaves.

Mouse motion events, as the name implies, occur while the mouse is in motion. The *mouse moved* event indicates simply that the mouse is in motion. The *mouse dragged* event is generated when the user has pressed the mouse button down and moved the mouse without releasing the button. Mouse motion events are generated many times, very quickly, while the mouse is in motion.

> **KEY CONCEPT**
>
> Moving the mouse and clicking the mouse button generate events to which a program can respond.

In a specific situation, we may care about only one or two mouse events. What we listen for depends on what we are trying to accomplish.

The `Coordinates` program shown in Listing 6.23 on the next page responds to one mouse event. Specifically, it draws a green dot at the location of the mouse pointer whenever the mouse button is pressed, and displays those coordinates. Keep in mind (as discussed in Appendix F) that the coordinate system in Java has the origin in the upper-left corner of a component (such as a panel), with x coordinates increasing to the right and y coordinates increasing downward.

The `CoordinatesPanel` class, shown in Listing 6.24 on page 297, keeps track of the (x,y) coordinates at which the user has pressed the mouse button most recently. The `getX` and `getY` methods of the `MouseEvent` object return the x and y coordinates of the location where the mouse event occurred.

LISTING 6.23

```java
//********************************************************************
//  Coordinates.java        Java Foundations
//
//  Demonstrates mouse events.
//********************************************************************

import javax.swing.JFrame;

public class Coordinates
{
    //-----------------------------------------------------------------
    //  Creates and displays the application frame.
    //-----------------------------------------------------------------
    public static void main (String[] args)
    {
        JFrame frame = new JFrame ("Coordinates");
        frame.setDefaultCloseOperation (JFrame.EXIT_ON_CLOSE);

        frame.getContentPane().add (new CoordinatesPanel());

        frame.pack();
        frame.setVisible(true);
    }
}
```

DISPLAY

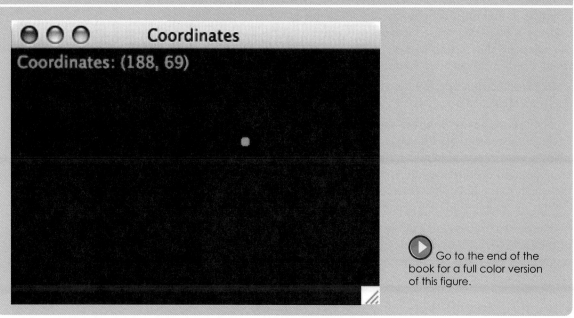

Go to the end of the book for a full color version of this figure.

LISTING 6.24

```java
//********************************************************************
//  CoordinatesPanel.java        Java Foundations
//
//  Represents the primary panel for the Coordinates program.
//********************************************************************

import javax.swing.JPanel;
import java.awt.*;
import java.awt.event.*;

public class CoordinatesPanel extends JPanel
{
    private final int SIZE = 6;  // diameter of dot

    private int x = 50, y = 50;  // coordinates of mouse press

    //----------------------------------------------------------------
    //  Constructor: Sets up this panel to listen for mouse events.
    //----------------------------------------------------------------
    public CoordinatesPanel()
    {
        addMouseListener (new CoordinatesListener());

        setBackground (Color.black);
        setPreferredSize (new Dimension(300, 200));
    }

    //----------------------------------------------------------------
    //  Draws all of the dots stored in the list.
    //----------------------------------------------------------------
    public void paintComponent (Graphics page)
    {
        super.paintComponent(page);

        page.setColor (Color.green);

        page.fillOval (x, y, SIZE, SIZE);

        page.drawString ("Coordinates: (" + x + ", " + y + ")", 5, 15);
    }

    //********************************************************************
    //  Represents the listener for mouse events.
    //********************************************************************
    private class CoordinatesListener implements MouseListener
```

LISTING 6.24   *continued*

```
{
    //-----------------------------------------------------------------
    //  Adds the current point to the list of points and redraws
    //  the panel whenever the mouse button is pressed.
    //-----------------------------------------------------------------
    public void mousePressed (MouseEvent event)
    {
        x = event.getX();
        y = event.getY();
        repaint();
    }

    //-----------------------------------------------------------------
    //  Provide empty definitions for unused event methods.
    //-----------------------------------------------------------------
    public void mouseClicked (MouseEvent event) {}
    public void mouseReleased (MouseEvent event) {}
    public void mouseEntered (MouseEvent event) {}
    public void mouseExited (MouseEvent event) {}
    }
}
```

The listener for the mouse pressed event implements the `MouseListener` interface. The panel invokes the `mousePressed` method each time the user presses down on the mouse button while it is over the panel.

Note that, unlike the listener interfaces that we've used in previous examples that contain one method each, the `MouseListener` interface contains five methods. For this program, the only event in which we are interested is the mouse pressed event. Therefore, the only method in which we have any interest is the `mousePressed` method. However, implementing an interface means we must provide definitions for all methods in the interface. Therefore, we provide empty methods corresponding to the other events. When those events are generated, the empty methods are called, but no code is executed. At the end of this section we discuss a technique for creating listeners that lets us avoid creating such empty methods.

> **KEY CONCEPT**
>
> A listener may have to provide empty method definitions for unheeded events to satisfy the interface.

Let's look at an example that responds to two mouse-oriented events. The `RubberLines` program shown in Listing 6.25 draws a line between two points.

LISTING 6.25

```java
//********************************************************************
//  RubberLines.java        Java Foundations
//
//  Demonstrates mouse events and rubberbanding.
//********************************************************************

import javax.swing.JFrame;

public class RubberLines
{
   //-----------------------------------------------------------------
   //  Creates and displays the application frame.
   //-----------------------------------------------------------------
   public static void main (String[] args)
   {
      JFrame frame = new JFrame ("Rubber Lines");
      frame.setDefaultCloseOperation (JFrame.EXIT_ON_CLOSE);

      frame.getContentPane().add (new RubberLinesPanel());

      frame.pack();
      frame.setVisible(true);
   }
}
```

DISPLAY

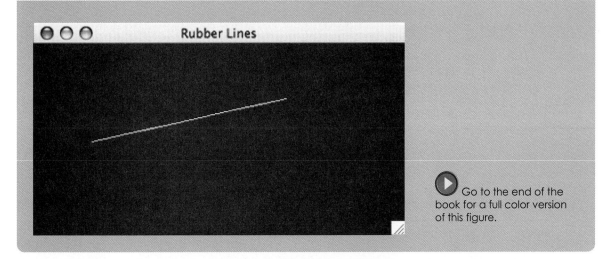

Go to the end of the book for a full color version of this figure.

The first point is determined by the location at which the mouse is first pressed down. The second point changes as the mouse is dragged while the mouse button is held down. When the button is released, the line remains fixed between the first and second points. When the mouse button is pressed again, a new line is started.

The `RubberLinesPanel` class is shown in Listing 6.26. Because we need to listen for both a mouse pressed event and a mouse dragged event, we need a listener that responds to both mouse events and mouse motion events.

LISTING 6.26

```
//***********************************************************************
//  RubberLinesPanel.java         Java Foundations
//
//  Represents the primary drawing panel for the RubberLines program.
//***********************************************************************

import javax.swing.JPanel;
import java.awt.*;
import java.awt.event.*;

public class RubberLinesPanel extends JPanel
{
    private Point point1 = null, point2 = null;

    //-------------------------------------------------------------------
    //  Constructor: Sets up this panel to listen for mouse events.
    //-------------------------------------------------------------------
    public RubberLinesPanel()
    {
        LineListener listener = new LineListener();
        addMouseListener (listener);
        addMouseMotionListener (listener);

        setBackground (Color.black);
        setPreferredSize (new Dimension(400, 200));
    }

    //-------------------------------------------------------------------
    //  Draws the current line from the intial mouse-pressed point to
    //  the current position of the mouse.
    //-------------------------------------------------------------------
    public void paintComponent (Graphics page)
```

LISTING 6.26 *continued*

```java
   {
      super.paintComponent (page);

      page.setColor (Color.yellow);
      if (point1 != null && point2 != null)
         page.drawLine (point1.x, point1.y, point2.x, point2.y);
   }

   //*****************************************************************
   //  Represents the listener for all mouse events.
   //*****************************************************************
   private class LineListener implements MouseListener,
                                         MouseMotionListener
   {
      //----------------------------------------------------------------
      //  Captures the initial position at which the mouse button is
      //  pressed.
      //----------------------------------------------------------------
      public void mousePressed (MouseEvent event)
      {
         point1 = event.getPoint();
      }

      //----------------------------------------------------------------
      //  Gets the current position of the mouse as it is dragged and
      //  redraws the line to create the rubberband effect.
      //----------------------------------------------------------------
      public void mouseDragged (MouseEvent event)
      {
         point2 = event.getPoint();
         repaint();
      }

      //----------------------------------------------------------------
      //  Provide empty definitions for unused event methods.
      //----------------------------------------------------------------
      public void mouseClicked (MouseEvent event) {}
      public void mouseReleased (MouseEvent event) {}
      public void mouseEntered (MouseEvent event) {}
      public void mouseExited (MouseEvent event) {}
      public void mouseMoved (MouseEvent event) {}
   }
}
```

Note that the listener class in this example implements both the `MouseListener` and `MouseMotionListener` interfaces. It must therefore implement all methods of both interfaces. The two methods of interest, `mousePressed` and `mouseDragged`, are implemented to accomplish our goals, and the other methods are given empty definitions to satisfy the interface contract.

> **KEY CONCEPT**
>
> Rubberbanding is the graphical effect caused when a shape seems to expand as the mouse is dragged.

When the `mousePressed` method is called, the variable `point1` is set. Then, as the mouse is dragged, the variable `point2` is continually reset and the panel repainted. Therefore the line is constantly being redrawn as the mouse is dragged, giving the appearance that one line is being stretched between a fixed point and a moving point. This effect is called *rubberbanding* and is common in graphical programs.

The starting and ending points of the line are stored as `Point` objects. The `Point` class is defined in the `java.awt` package, and encapsulates the x and y values of a two-dimensional coordinate.

Note that, in the `RubberLinesPanel` constructor, the listener object is added to the panel twice: once as a mouse listener and once as a mouse motion listener. The method called to add the listener must correspond to the object passed as the parameter. In this case, we had one object that served as a listener for both categories of events. We could have had two listener classes if desired: one listening for mouse events and one listening for mouse motion events. A component can have multiple listeners for various event categories.

Key Events

A *key event* is generated when a keyboard key is pressed. Key events allow a program to respond immediately to the user while he or she is typing or pressing other keyboard keys such as the arrow keys. If key events are being processed, the program can respond as soon as the key is pressed; there is no need to wait for the Enter key to be pressed or for some other component (like a button) to be activated.

> **KEY CONCEPT**
>
> Key events allow a program to respond immediately to the user pressing keyboard keys.

The `Direction` program shown in Listing 6.27 responds to key events. An image of an arrow is displayed and the image moves across the screen as the arrow keys are pressed. Actually, four different images are used, one for the arrow pointing in each of the primary directions (up, down, right, and left).

The `DirectionPanel` class, shown in Listing 6.28 on page 304, represents the panel on which the arrow image is displayed. The constructor loads the four arrow images, one of which is always considered to be the current image (the one displayed). The current image is set based on the arrow key that was most recently

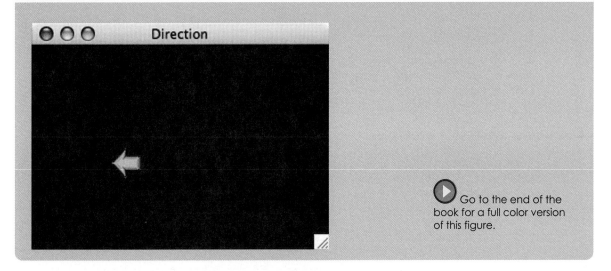

LISTING 6.27

```java
//********************************************************************
//  Direction.java        Java Foundations
//
//  Demonstrates key events.
//********************************************************************

import javax.swing.JFrame;

public class Direction
{
   //-----------------------------------------------------------------
   //  Creates and displays the application frame.
   //-----------------------------------------------------------------
   public static void main (String[] args)
   {
      JFrame frame = new JFrame ("Direction");
      frame.setDefaultCloseOperation (JFrame.EXIT_ON_CLOSE);

      frame.getContentPane().add (new DirectionPanel());

      frame.pack();
      frame.setVisible(true);
   }
}
```

DISPLAY

Go to the end of the book for a full color version of this figure.

LISTING 6.28

```java
//********************************************************************
//  DirectionPanel.java        Java Foundations
//
//  Represents the primary display panel for the Direction program.
//********************************************************************

import javax.swing.*;
import java.awt.*;
import java.awt.event.*;

public class DirectionPanel extends JPanel
{
   private final int WIDTH = 300, HEIGHT = 200;
   private final int JUMP = 10;   //  increment for image movement

   private final int IMAGE_SIZE = 31;

   private ImageIcon up, down, right, left, currentImage;
   private int x, y;

   //---------------------------------------------------------------
   //  Constructor: Sets up this panel and loads the images.
   //---------------------------------------------------------------
   public DirectionPanel()
   {
      addKeyListener (new DirectionListener());

      x = WIDTH / 2;
      y = HEIGHT / 2;

      up = new ImageIcon ("arrowUp.gif");
      down = new ImageIcon ("arrowDown.gif");
      left = new ImageIcon ("arrowLeft.gif");
      right = new ImageIcon ("arrowRight.gif");

      currentImage = right;

      setBackground (Color.black);
      setPreferredSize (new Dimension(WIDTH, HEIGHT));
      setFocusable(true);
   }
```

LISTING 6.28   *continued*

```java
//------------------------------------------------------------------
//  Draws the image in the current location.
//------------------------------------------------------------------
public void paintComponent (Graphics page)
{
    super.paintComponent (page);
    currentImage.paintIcon (this, page, x, y);
}

//******************************************************************
//  Represents the listener for keyboard activity.
//******************************************************************
private class DirectionListener implements KeyListener
{
    //--------------------------------------------------------------
    //  Responds to the user pressing arrow keys by adjusting the
    //  image and image location accordingly.
    //--------------------------------------------------------------
    public void keyPressed (KeyEvent event)
    {
        switch (event.getKeyCode())
        {
            case KeyEvent.VK_UP:
                currentImage = up;
                y -= JUMP;
                break;
            case KeyEvent.VK_DOWN:
                currentImage = down;
                y += JUMP;
                break;
            case KeyEvent.VK_LEFT:
                currentImage = left;
                x -= JUMP;
                break;
            case KeyEvent.VK_RIGHT:
                currentImage = right;
                x += JUMP;
                break;
        }

        repaint();
    }
```

LISTING 6.28 *continued*

```
    //------------------------------------------------------------
    //  Provide empty definitions for unused event methods.
    //------------------------------------------------------------
    public void keyTyped (KeyEvent event) {}
    public void keyReleased (KeyEvent event) {}
  }
}
```

pressed. For example, if the up arrow is pressed, the image with the arrow pointing up is displayed. If an arrow key is continually pressed, the appropriate image "moves" in the appropriate direction.

The arrow images are managed as `ImageIcon` objects. In this example, the image is drawn using the `paintIcon` method each time the panel is repainted. The `paintIcon` method takes four parameters: a component to serve as an image observer, the graphics context on which the image will be drawn, and the (x,y) coordinates where the image is drawn. An *image observer* is a component that serves to manage image loading; in this case we use the panel as the image observer.

The private inner class called `DirectionListener` is set up to respond to key events. It implements the `KeyListener` interface, which defines three methods that we can use to respond to keyboard activity. Figure 6.8 lists these methods.

Specifically, the `Direction` program responds to key pressed events. Because the listener class must implement all methods defined in the interface, we provide empty methods for the other events.

```
void keyPressed (KeyEvent event)
    Called when a key is pressed.

void keyReleased (KeyEvent event)
    Called when a key is released.

void keyTyped (KeyEvent event)
    Called when a pressed key or key combination produces
    a key character.
```

FIGURE 6.8 The methods of the `KeyListener` interface

The `KeyEvent` object passed to the `keyPressed` method of the listener can be used to determine which key was pressed. In the example, we call the `getKeyCode` method of the `event` object to get a numeric code that represents the key that was pressed. We use a `switch` statement to determine which key was pressed and to respond accordingly. The `KeyEvent` class contains constants that correspond to the numeric code that is returned from the `getKeyCode` method. If any key other than an arrow key is pressed it is ignored.

Key events fire whenever a key is pressed, but most systems enable the concept of *key repetition*. That is, when a key is pressed and held down, it's as if that key is being pressed repeatedly and quickly. Key events are generated in the same way. In the `Direction` program, the user can hold down an arrow key and watch the image move across the screen quickly.

The component that generates key events is the one that currently has the keyboard focus. Usually the keyboard focus is held by the primary "active" component. A component usually gets the keyboard focus when the user clicks on it with the mouse. The call to the `setFocusable` method in the panel constructor sets the keyboard focus to the panel.

The `Direction` program sets no boundaries for the arrow image, so it can be moved out of the visible window, then moved back in if desired. You could add code to the listener to stop the image when it reaches one of the window boundaries. This modification is left as a programming project.

Extending Adapter Classes

In previous event-based examples, we've created the listener classes by implementing a particular listener interface. For instance, to create a class that listens for mouse events, we created a listener class that implements the `MouseListener` interface. As we saw in the previous examples in this section, a listener interface often contains event methods that are not important to a particular program, in which case we provided empty definitions to satisfy the interface requirement.

An alternative technique for creating a listener class is to use inheritance and extend an *event adapter class*. Each listener interface that contains more than one method has a corresponding adapter class that already contains empty definitions for all of the methods in the interface. To create a listener, we can derive a new listener class from the appropriate adapter class and override any event methods in which we are interested. Using this technique, we no longer need to provide empty definitions for unused methods.

> **KEY CONCEPT**
>
> A listener class can be created by deriving it from an event adapter class.

The `MouseAdapter` class, for instance, implements the `MouseListener` interface and provides empty method definitions for the five mouse event methods (`mousePressed`, `mouseClicked`, etc.). Therefore, you can create a mouse listener class by extending the `MouseAdaptor` class instead of implementing the `MouseListener` interface directly. The new listener class inherits the empty definitions, and therefore doesn't need to define them.

Because of inheritance, we now have a choice when it comes to creating event listeners. We can implement an event listener interface, or we can extend an event adapter class. This is a design decision that should be considered carefully. The best technique depends on the situation. Inheritance is discussed further in Chapter 8.

6.5 Dialog Boxes

A component called a *dialog box* can be helpful to assist in GUI processing. A dialog box is a graphical window that pops up on top of any currently active window so that the user can interact with it. A dialog box can serve a variety of purposes, such as conveying some information, confirming an action, or allowing the user to enter some information. Usually a dialog box has a solitary purpose, and the user's interaction with it is brief.

The Swing package of the Java class library contains a class called `JOptionPane` that simplifies the creation and use of basic dialog boxes. Figure 6.9 lists some of the methods of `JOptionPane`.

The basic formats for a `JOptionPane` dialog box fall into three categories. A *message dialog box* simply displays an output string. An *input dialog box* presents

```
static String showInputDialog (Object msg)
    Displays a dialog box containing the specified message and an input text field.
    The contents of the text field are returned.

static int showConfirmDialog (Component parent, Object msg)
    Displays a dialog box containing the specified message and Yes/No button
    options. If the parent component is null, the box is centered on the screen.

static void showMessageDialog (Component parent, Object msg)
    Displays a dialog box containing the specified message. If the parent
    component is null, the box is centered on the screen.
```

FIGURE 6.9 Some methods of the `JOptionPane` class

a prompt and a single input text field into which the user can enter one string of data. A *confirm dialog box* presents the user with a simple yes-or-no question.

Let's look at a program that uses each of these types of dialog boxes. Listing 6.29 shows a program that first presents the user with an input dialog box that requests the user to enter an integer. After the user presses the OK button on the input dialog

LISTING 6.29

```java
//********************************************************************
//  EvenOdd.java        Java Foundations
//
//  Demonstrates the use of the JOptionPane class.
//********************************************************************

import javax.swing.JOptionPane;

public class EvenOdd
{
    //----------------------------------------------------------------
    //  Determines if the value input by the user is even or odd.
    //  Uses multiple dialog boxes for user interaction.
    //----------------------------------------------------------------
    public static void main (String[] args)
    {
        String numStr, result;
        int num, again;

        do
        {
            numStr = JOptionPane.showInputDialog ("Enter an integer: ");

            num = Integer.parseInt(numStr);

            result = "That number is " + ((num%2 == 0) ? "even" : "odd");

            JOptionPane.showMessageDialog (null, result);

            again = JOptionPane.showConfirmDialog (null, "Do Another?");
        }
        while (again == JOptionPane.YES_OPTION);
    }
}
```

LISTING 6.29   *continued*

DISPLAY

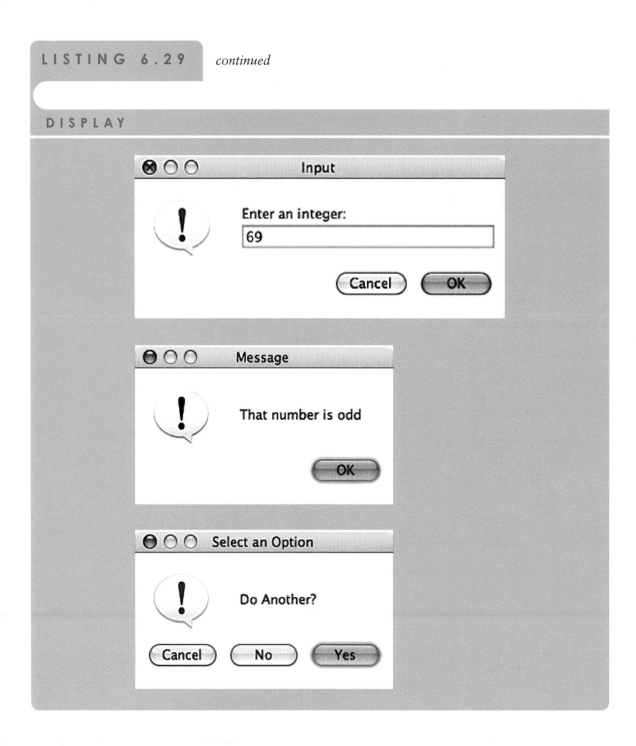

box, a second dialog box (this time a message dialog box) appears, informing the user whether the number entered was even or odd. After the user dismisses that box, a third dialog box appears, to determine whether the user would like to test another number. If the user presses the button labeled Yes, the series of dialog boxes repeats. Otherwise the program terminates.

The first parameter to the `showMessageDialog` and the `showConfirmDialog` methods specifies the governing parent component for the dialog box. Using a null reference as this parameter causes the dialog box to appear centered on the screen.

Many of the `JOptionPane` methods allow the programmer to tailor the contents of the dialog box. Furthermore, the `showOptionDialog` method can be used to create dialog boxes that combine characteristics of the three basic formats for more elaborate interactions.

Dialog boxes should only be used when the immediate attention of the user is necessary. A program that constantly has new windows popping up for different interactions is annoying to the user.

File Choosers

A *file chooser* is a specialized dialog box that allows the user to select a file from a disk or other storage medium. You have probably run many programs that allow you to open a file, such as when you are specifying which file to open in a word processing program. The need to specify a file occurs so often, the `JFileChooser` class was made part of the Java standard class library for just that purpose.

> **KEY CONCEPT**
>
> A file chooser allows the user to browse a disk and select a file to be processed.

The program shown in Listing 6.30 on the next page uses a `JFileChooser` dialog box to select a file. This program also demonstrates the use of another GUI component, a *text area*, which is similar to a text field but can display multiple lines of text at one time. In this example, after the user selects a file using the file chooser dialog box, the text contained in that file is displayed in a text area.

The file chooser dialog box is displayed when the `showOpenDialog` method is invoked. It automatically presents the list of files contained in a particular directory. The user can use the controls on the dialog box to navigate to other directories, change the way the files are viewed, and specify which types of files are displayed.

The `showOpenDialog` method returns an integer representing the status of the operation, which can be checked against constants defined in the `JFileChooser` class. In this program, if a file was not selected (perhaps by pressing the Cancel button), a default message is displayed in the text area. If the user chose a file, it is opened and its contents are read using the `Scanner` class. Note that this program assumes the selected file contains text. It does not catch any exceptions, so if the user selects an inappropriate file, the program will terminate when the exception is thrown.

LISTING 6.30

```java
//********************************************************************
//  DisplayFile.java          Java Foundations
//
//  Demonstrates the use of a file chooser and a text area.
//********************************************************************

import java.util.Scanner;
import java.io.*;
import javax.swing.*;

public class DisplayFile
{
    //-----------------------------------------------------------------
    //  Opens a file chooser dialog, reads the selected file and
    //  loads it into a text area.
    //-----------------------------------------------------------------
    public static void main (String[] args) throws IOException
    {
        JFrame frame = new JFrame ("Display File");
        frame.setDefaultCloseOperation (JFrame.EXIT_ON_CLOSE);

        JTextArea ta = new JTextArea (20, 30);
        JFileChooser chooser = new JFileChooser();

        int status = chooser.showOpenDialog (null);

        if (status != JFileChooser.APPROVE_OPTION)
            ta.setText ("No File Chosen");
        else
        {
            File file = chooser.getSelectedFile();
            Scanner scan = new Scanner (file);

            String info = "";
            while (scan.hasNext())
                info += scan.nextLine() + "\n";

            ta.setText (info);
        }

        frame.getContentPane().add (ta);
        frame.pack();
        frame.setVisible(true);
    }
}
```

LISTING 6.30   *continued*

DISPLAY

A text area component is defined by the `JTextArea` class. In this program, we pass two parameters to its constructor, specifying the size of the text area in terms of the number of characters (rows and columns) it should display. The text to display is set using the `setText` method.

A text area component, like a text field, can be set so that it is either editable or noneditable. The user can change the contents of an editable text area by clicking on the text area and typing with the mouse. If the text area is noneditable, it is used to display text only. By default, a `JTextArea` component is editable.

A `JFileChooser` component makes it easy to allow users to specify a specific file to use. Another specialized dialog box—one that allows the user to choose a color—is discussed in the next section.

Color Choosers

In many situations we may want to give the user of a program the ability to choose a color. We could accomplish this in various ways. For instance, we could provide a list of colors using a set of radio buttons. However, with the wide variety of colors available, it's nice to have an easier and more flexible technique to accomplish this common task. A specialized dialog box, often referred to as a *color chooser*, is a graphical component that serves this purpose.

The JColorChooser class represents a color chooser. It can be used to display a dialog box that lets the user click on a color of choice from a palette presented for that purpose. The user could also specify a color using RGB values or other color representation techniques. Invoking the static showDialog method of the JColorChooser class causes the color chooser dialog box to appear. The parameters to that method specify the parent component for the dialog box, the title that appears in the dialog box frame, and the initial color showing in the color chooser.

Figure 6.10 shows a color chooser dialog box.

FIGURE 6.10 A color chooser dialog box

▶ Go to the end of the book for a full color version of this figure.

6.6 Some Important Details

There are a variety of small but important details that can add considerable value to the interface of a program. Some enhance the visual effect, while others provide shortcuts to make the user more productive. Let's examine some of them now.

Borders

Java provides the ability to put a border around any Swing component. A border is not a component itself but rather defines how the edge of any component should be drawn and has an important effect on the design of a GUI. A border provides visual cues as to how GUI components are organized, and can be used to give titles to components. Figure 6.11 lists the predefined borders in the Java standard class library.

The `BorderFactory` class is useful for creating borders for components. It has many methods for creating specific types of borders. A border is applied to a component by using the component's `setBorder` method.

The program in Listing 6.31 on the next page demonstrates several types of borders. It simply creates several panels, sets a different border for each, and then displays them in a larger panel using a grid layout.

Border	Description
Empty Border	Puts buffering space around the edge of a component, but otherwise has no visual effect.
Line Border	A simple line surrounding the component.
Etched Border	Creates the effect of an etched groove around a component.
Bevel Border	Creates the effect of a component raised above the surface or sunken below it.
Titled Border	Includes a text title on or around the border.
Matte Border	Allows the size of each edge to be specified. Uses either a soild color or an image.
Compound Border	A combination of two borders.

FIGURE 6.11 Component borders

```
LISTING   6.31
```

```
//********************************************************************
//   BorderDemo.java          Java Foundations
//
//   Demonstrates the use of various types of borders.
//********************************************************************

import java.awt.*;
import javax.swing.*;
import javax.swing.border.*;

public class BorderDemo
{
   //-----------------------------------------------------------------
   //   Creates several bordered panels and displays them.
   //-----------------------------------------------------------------
   public static void main (String[] args)
   {
      JFrame frame = new JFrame ("Border Demo");
      frame.setDefaultCloseOperation (JFrame.EXIT_ON_CLOSE);

      JPanel panel = new JPanel();
      panel.setLayout (new GridLayout (0, 2, 5, 10));
      panel.setBorder (BorderFactory.createEmptyBorder (8, 8, 8, 8));

      JPanel p1 = new JPanel();
      p1.setBorder (BorderFactory.createLineBorder (Color.red, 3));
      p1.add (new JLabel ("Line Border"));
      panel.add (p1);

      JPanel p2 = new JPanel();
      p2.setBorder (BorderFactory.createEtchedBorder ());
      p2.add (new JLabel ("Etched Border"));
      panel.add (p2);

      JPanel p3 = new JPanel();
      p3.setBorder (BorderFactory.createRaisedBevelBorder ());
      p3.add (new JLabel ("Raised Bevel Border"));
      panel.add (p3);
```

LISTING 6.31 *continued*

```
    JPanel p4 = new JPanel();
    p4.setBorder (BorderFactory.createLoweredBevelBorder ());
    p4.add (new JLabel ("Lowered Bevel Border"));
    panel.add (p4);

    JPanel p5 = new JPanel();
    p5.setBorder (BorderFactory.createTitledBorder ("Title"));
    p5.add (new JLabel ("Titled Border"));
    panel.add (p5);

    JPanel p6 = new JPanel();
    TitledBorder tb = BorderFactory.createTitledBorder ("Title");
    tb.setTitleJustification (TitledBorder.RIGHT);
    p6.setBorder (tb);
    p6.add (new JLabel ("Titled Border (right)"));
    panel.add (p6);

    JPanel p7 = new JPanel();
    Border b1 = BorderFactory.createLineBorder (Color.blue, 2);
    Border b2 = BorderFactory.createEtchedBorder ();
    p7.setBorder (BorderFactory.createCompoundBorder (b1, b2));
    p7.add (new JLabel ("Compound Border"));
    panel.add (p7);

    JPanel p8 = new JPanel();
    Border mb = BorderFactory.createMatteBorder (1, 5, 1, 1,
                                                 Color.red);
    p8.setBorder (mb);
    p8.add (new JLabel ("Matte Border"));
    panel.add (p8);

    frame.getContentPane().add (panel);
    frame.pack();
    frame.setVisible(true);
    }
}
```

LISTING 6.31   *continued*

DISPLAY

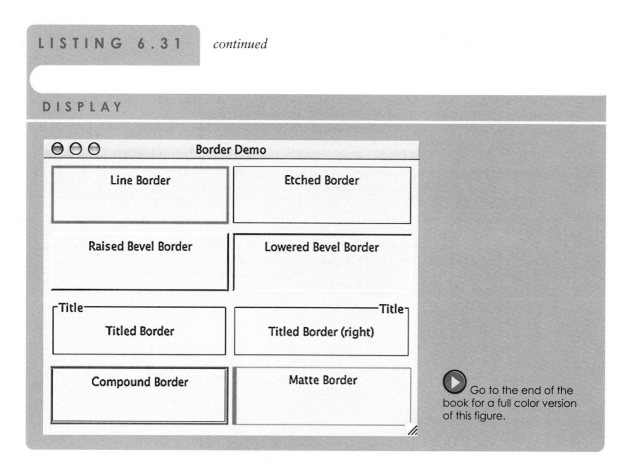

Go to the end of the book for a full color version of this figure.

Let's look at each type of border created in this program. An *empty border* is applied to the larger panel that holds all the others, to create a buffer of space around the outer edge of the frame. The sizes of the top, left, bottom, and right edges of the empty border are specified in pixels. The *line border* is created using a particular color and specifies the line thickness in pixels (3 in this case). The line thickness defaults to 1 pixel if left unspecified. The *etched border* created in this program uses default colors for the highlight and shadow of the etching, but both could be explicitly set if desired.

A *bevel border* can be either raised or lowered. The default coloring is used in this program, although the coloring of each aspect of the bevel can be tailored as desired, including the outer highlight, inner highlight, outer shadow, and inner shadow. Each of these aspects could be a different color if desired.

A *titled border* places a title on or around the border. The default position for the title is on the border at the top-left edge. Using the setTitleJustification method of the `TitledBorder` class, this position can be set to many other places above, below, on, or to the left, right, or center of the border.

A *compound border* is a combination of two or more borders. The example in this program creates a compound border using a line border and an etched border. The `createCompoundBorder` method accepts two borders as parameters and makes the first parameter the outer border and the second parameter the inner border. Combinations of three or more borders are created by first creating a compound border using two borders, then making another compound border using it and yet another one.

A *matte border* specifies the sizes, in pixels, of the top, left, bottom, and right edges of the border. Those edges can be composed of a single color, as they are in this example, or an image icon can be used.

Borders should be used carefully. They can be helpful in drawing attention to appropriate parts of your GUI and can conceptually group related items together. However, if used inappropriately, they can also detract from the elegance of the presentation. Borders should enhance the interface, not complicate or compete with it.

Tool Tips and Mnemonics

Any Swing component can be assigned a *tool tip*, which is a short line of text that will appear when the cursor is rested momentarily on top of the component. Tool tips are usually used to inform the user about the component, such as the purpose of a button.

A tool tip can be assigned using the `setToolTipText` method of a component. For example:

```
JButton button = new JButton ("Compute");
button.setToolTipText ("Calculates the area under the curve.");
```

When the button is added to a container and displayed, it appears normally. When the user rolls the mouse pointer over the button, hovering there momentarily, the tool tip text pops up. When the user moves the mouse pointer off of the button, the tool tip text disappears.

A *mnemonic* is a character that allows the user to push a button or make a menu choice using the keyboard in addition to the mouse. For example, when a mnemonic has been defined for a button, the user can hold down the Alt key and press the mnemonic character to activate the button. Using a mnemonic to activate the button causes the system to behave just as it would if the user had used the mouse to press the button.

A mnemonic character should be chosen from the label on a button or menu item. Once the mnemonic has been established using the `setMnemonic` method, the character in the label will be underlined to indicate that it can be used as a shortcut. If a letter is chosen that is not in the label, nothing will be underlined and the user won't know how to use the shortcut. You can set a mnemonic as follows:

```
JButton button = new JButton ("Calculate");
button.setMnemonic ('C');
```

When the button is displayed, the letter C in Calculate is underlined on the button label. When the user presses Alt-C, the button is activated as if the user had pressed it with the mouse.

Some components can be *disabled* if they should not be used. A disabled component will appear "grayed out," and nothing will happen if the user attempts to interact with it. To disable and enable components, we invoke the `setEnabled` method of the component, passing it a boolean value to indicate whether the component should be disabled (`false`) or enabled (`true`). For example:

```
JButton button = new JButton ("Do It");
button.setEnabled (false);
```

Disabling components is a good idea when users should not be allowed to use the functionality of a component. The grayed appearance of the disabled component is an indication that using the component is inappropriate (and, in fact, impossible) at the current time. Disabled components not only convey to the user which actions are appropriate and which aren't, they also prevent erroneous situations from occurring.

> **KEY CONCEPT**
>
> Components should be disabled when their use is inappropriate.

Let's look at an example that uses tool tips, mnemonics, and disabled components. The program in Listing 6.32 presents the image of a light bulb and provides a button to turn the light bulb on and a button to turn the light bulb off.

There are actually two images of the light bulb: one showing it turned on and one showing it turned off. These images are brought in as `ImageIcon` objects. The `setIcon` method of the label that displays the image is used to set the appropriate image, depending on the current status. This processing is controlled in the `LightBulbPanel` class shown in Listing 6.33 on page 322.

The `LightBulbControls` class shown in Listing 6.34 on page 324 is a panel that contains the On and Off buttons. Both of these buttons have tool tips assigned to them, and both use mnemonics. Also, when one of the buttons is enabled, the other is disabled, and vice versa. When the light bulb is on, there is no

LISTING 6.32

```java
//********************************************************************
//  LightBulb.java        Java Foundations
//
//  Demonstrates mnemonics and tool tips.
//********************************************************************

import javax.swing.*;
import java.awt.*;

public class LightBulb
{
   //-----------------------------------------------------------------
   //  Sets up a frame that displays a light bulb image that can be
   //  turned on and off.
   //-----------------------------------------------------------------
   public static void main (String[] args)
   {
      JFrame frame = new JFrame ("Light Bulb");
      frame.setDefaultCloseOperation (JFrame.EXIT_ON_CLOSE);

      LightBulbPanel bulb = new LightBulbPanel();
      LightBulbControls controls = new LightBulbControls (bulb);

      JPanel panel = new JPanel();
      panel.setBackground (Color.black);
      panel.setLayout (new BoxLayout(panel, BoxLayout.Y_AXIS));
      panel.add (Box.createRigidArea (new Dimension (0, 20)));
      panel.add (bulb);
      panel.add (Box.createRigidArea (new Dimension (0, 10)));
      panel.add (controls);
      panel.add (Box.createRigidArea (new Dimension (0, 10)));

      frame.getContentPane().add(panel);

      frame.pack();
      frame.setVisible(true);
   }
}
```

LISTING 6.32   *continued*

DISPLAY

Go to the end of the book for a full color version of this figure.

LISTING 6.33

```
//********************************************************************
//  LightBulbPanel.java          Java Foundations
//
//  Represents the image for the LightBulb program.
//********************************************************************

import javax.swing.*;
import java.awt.*;

public class LightBulbPanel extends JPanel
{
   private boolean on;
   private ImageIcon lightOn, lightOff;
   private JLabel imageLabel;

   //-----------------------------------------------------------------
   //  Constructor: Sets up the images and the initial state.
   //-----------------------------------------------------------------
```

LISTING 6.33   *continued*

```java
    public LightBulbPanel()
    {
        lightOn = new ImageIcon ("lightBulbOn.gif");
        lightOff = new ImageIcon ("lightBulbOff.gif");

        setBackground (Color.black);

        on = true;
        imageLabel = new JLabel (lightOff);
        add (imageLabel);
    }

    //-----------------------------------------------------------------
    //  Paints the panel using the appropriate image.
    //-----------------------------------------------------------------
    public void paintComponent (Graphics page)
    {
        super.paintComponent(page);

        if (on)
            imageLabel.setIcon (lightOn);
        else
            imageLabel.setIcon (lightOff);
    }

    //-----------------------------------------------------------------
    //  Sets the status of the light bulb.
    //-----------------------------------------------------------------
    public void setOn (boolean lightBulbOn)
    {
        on = lightBulbOn;
    }
}
```

reason for the On button to be enabled. Likewise, when the light bulb is off, there is no reason for the Off button to be enabled.

Each button has its own listener class. The `actionPerformed` method of each sets the bulb's status, toggles the enabled state of both buttons, and causes the panel with the image to repaint itself.

LISTING 6.34

```java
//********************************************************************
//  LightBulbControls.java        Java Foundations
//
//  Represents the control panel for the LightBulb program.
//********************************************************************

import javax.swing.*;
import java.awt.*;
import java.awt.event.*;

public class LightBulbControls extends JPanel
{
    private LightBulbPanel bulb;
    private JButton onButton, offButton;

    //----------------------------------------------------------------
    //  Sets up the lightbulb control panel.
    //----------------------------------------------------------------
    public LightBulbControls (LightBulbPanel bulbPanel)
    {
        bulb = bulbPanel;

        onButton = new JButton ("On");
        onButton.setEnabled (false);
        onButton.setMnemonic ('n');
        onButton.setToolTipText ("Turn it on!");
        onButton.addActionListener (new OnListener());

        offButton = new JButton ("Off");
        offButton.setEnabled (true);
        offButton.setMnemonic ('f');
        offButton.setToolTipText ("Turn it off!");
        offButton.addActionListener (new OffListener());

        setBackground (Color.black);
        add (onButton);
        add (offButton);
    }

    //********************************************************************
    //  Represents the listener for the On button.
    //********************************************************************
    private class OnListener implements ActionListener
    {
```

LISTING 6.34   *continued*

```java
        //-----------------------------------------------------------------
        //  Turns the bulb on and repaints the bulb panel.
        //-----------------------------------------------------------------
        public void actionPerformed (ActionEvent event)
        {
            bulb.setOn (true);
            onButton.setEnabled (false);
            offButton.setEnabled (true);
            bulb.repaint();
        }
    }

    //*****************************************************************
    //  Represents the listener for the Off button.
    //*****************************************************************
    private class OffListener implements ActionListener
    {
        //-----------------------------------------------------------------
        //  Turns the bulb off and repaints the bulb panel.
        //-----------------------------------------------------------------
        public void actionPerformed (ActionEvent event)
        {
            bulb.setOn (false);
            onButton.setEnabled (true);
            offButton.setEnabled (false);
            bulb.repaint();
        }
    }
}
```

Note that the mnemonic characters used for each button are underlined in the display. When you run the program, you'll see that the tool tips automatically include an indication of the mnemonic that can be used for the button.

6.7 GUI Design

As we focus on the details that allow us to create GUIs, we may sometimes lose sight of the big picture. We should always keep in mind that our goal is to solve a problem—to create software that is truly useful. Knowing the details of components, events, and other language elements gives us the tools to put GUIs together, but we must guide that knowledge with the following fundamental ideas of good GUI design:

- Know the user.
- Prevent user errors.
- Optimize user abilities.
- Be consistent.

KEY CONCEPT

The design of any GUI should adhere to basic guidelines regarding consistency and usability.

The software designer must understand the user's needs and potential activities in order to develop an interface that will serve that user well. Keep in mind that, to the user, the interface is the software. It is the only way the user interacts with the system. As such, the interface must satisfy the user's needs.

Whenever possible, we should design interfaces so that the user can make as few mistakes as possible. In many situations, we have the flexibility to choose one of several components to accomplish a specific task. We should always try to choose components that will prevent inappropriate actions and avoid invalid input. For example, if an input value must be one of a set of particular values, we should use components that allow the user to make only a valid choice. That is, constraining the user to a few valid choices with, for instance, a set of radio buttons is better than allowing the user to type arbitrary and possibly invalid data into a text field. We covered additional components appropriate for specific situations in this chapter.

Not all users are alike. Some are more adept than others at using a particular GUI or GUI components in general. We shouldn't design with only the lowest common denominator in mind. For example, we should provide shortcuts whenever reasonable. That is, in addition to a normal series of actions that will allow a user to accomplish a task, we should also provide redundant ways to accomplish the same task. Using keyboard shortcuts (mnemonics) is a good example. Sometimes these additional mechanisms are less intuitive, but they may be faster for the experienced user.

Finally, consistency is important when dealing with large systems or multiple systems in a common environment. Users become familiar with a particular organization or color scheme; these should not be changed arbitrarily.

Summary of Key Concepts

- A GUI is made up of components, events that represent user actions, and listeners that respond to those events.
- A frame is displayed as a separate window, but a panel can only be displayed as part of another container.
- Listeners are often defined as inner classes because of the intimate relationship between the listener and the GUI components.
- Radio buttons operate as a group, providing a set of mutually exclusive options.
- A slider lets the user specify a numeric value within a bounded range.
- A combo box provides a drop down menu of options.
- A timer generates action events at regular intervals and can be used to control an animation.
- Every container is managed by a layout manager, which determines how components are visually presented.
- When changes occur, the components in a container reorganize themselves according to the layout manager's policy.
- The layout manager for each container can be explicitly set.
- A GUI's appearance is a function of the containment hierarchy and the layout managers of each container.
- Moving the mouse and clicking the mouse button generate events to which a program can respond.
- A listener may have to provide empty method definitions for unheeded events to satisfy the interface.
- Rubberbanding is the graphical effect caused when a shape seems to expand as the mouse is dragged.
- Key events allow a program to respond immediately to the user pressing keyboard keys.
- A listener class can be created by deriving it from an event adapter class.
- A file chooser allows the user to browse a disk and select a file to be processed.
- A color chooser allows the user to select a color from a palette or using RGB values.
- Borders can be applied to components to group objects and focus attention.

- Components should be disabled when their use is inappropriate.
- The design of any GUI should adhere to basic guidelines regarding consistency and usability.

Self-Review Questions

SR 6.1   What three elements are needed in any Java GUI?

SR 6.2   What is the difference between a frame and a panel?

SR 6.3   What is the relationship between an event and a listener?

SR 6.4   Can we add any kind of listener to any component? Explain.

SR 6.5   What type of event does a push button generate? A text field? A check box?

SR 6.6   Compare and contrast check boxes and radio buttons.

SR 6.7   When would you use a slider?

SR 6.8   What does a `Timer` object do?

SR 6.9   When is a layout manager consulted?

SR 6.10   How does the flow layout manager behave?

SR 6.11   Describe the areas of a border layout.

SR 6.12   What effect does a glue component in a box layout have?

SR 6.13   What is the containment hierarchy for a GUI?

SR 6.14   What is a mouse event?

SR 6.15   What is a key event?

SR 6.16   What is an event adapter class?

SR 6.17   What is a dialog box?

SR 6.18   What is a file chooser? A color chooser?

SR 6.19   What is the role of the `BorderFactory` class?

SR 6.20   What is tool tip?

SR 6.21   When should a component be disabled?

Exercises

EX 6.1   Explain how two components can be set up to share the same listener. How can the listener tell which component generated the event?

EX 6.2   Explain how one component can use two separate listeners at the same time. Give an example.

EX 6.3   Explain what would happen if the radio buttons used in the QuoteOptions program were not organized into a ButtonGroup object. Modify the program to test your answer.

EX 6.4   Why, in the SlideColor program, is the value of a slider able to reach 255 but the largest labeled tick mark is 250?

EX 6.5   What are the two main factors that affect how smooth the animation is in the Rebound program? Explain how changing either would affect it.

EX 6.6   What visual effect would result by changing the horizontal and vertical gaps on the border layout used in the LayoutDemo program? Make the change to test your answer.

EX 6.7   What would happen if, in the Coordinates program, we did not provide empty definitions for one or more of the unused mouse events?

EX 6.8   The Coordinates program listens for a mouse pressed event to draw a dot. How would the program behave differently if it listened for a mouse released event instead? A mouse clicked event?

EX 6.9   What would happen if the call to super.paintComponent were removed from the paintComponent method of the CoordinatesPanel class? Remove it and run the program to test your answer.

EX 6.10   What would happen if the call to super.paintComponent were removed from the paintComponent method of the RubberLinesPanel class? Remove it and run the program to test your answer. In what ways is the answer different from the answer to exercise 6.9.

EX 6.11   Write the lines of code that will define a compound border using three borders. Use a line border on the inner edge, an etched border on the outer edge, and a raised bevel border in between.

EX 6.12   Draw a UML class diagram that shows the relationships among the classes used in the PushCounter program.

EX 6.13   Draw a UML class diagram that shows the relationships among the classes used in the Fahrenheit program.

EX 6.14   Draw a UML class diagram that shows the relationships among the classes used in the LayoutDemo program.

EX 6.15   Create a UML class diagram for the Direction program.

Programming Projects

PP 6.1   Design and implement an application that displays a button and a label. Every time the button is pushed, the label should display a random number between 1 and 100, inclusive.

PP 6.2   Design and implement an application that presents two buttons and a label to the user. Label the buttons Increment and Decrement, respectively. Display a numeric value (initially 50) using the label. Each time the Increment button is pushed, increment the value displayed. Likewise, each time the Decrement button is pressed, decrement the value displayed. Create two separate listener classes for the two buttons.

PP 6.3   Modify your solution to programming project 6.2 so that it uses only one listener for both buttons.

PP 6.4   Modify the `Fahrenheit` program so that it displays a button that, when pressed, causes the conversion calculation to take place. That is, your modification will give the user the option of pressing Enter in the text field or pressing the button. Have the listener that is already defined for the text field also listen for the button push.

PP 6.5   Modify the `Direction` program so that the image is not allowed to move out of the visible area of the panel. Ignore any key event that would cause that to happen.

PP 6.6   Modify the `Direction` program so that, in addition to responding to the arrow keys, it also responds to four other keys that cause the image to move in diagonal directions. When the T key is pressed, move the image up and to the left. Likewise, use U to move up and right, G to move down and left, and J to move down and right. Do not move the image if it has reached a window boundary.

PP 6.7   Design and implement an application that draws a traffic light and uses a push button to change the state of the light. Derive the drawing surface from the `JPanel` class and use another panel to organize the drawing surface and the button.

myCodeMate   PP 6.8   Develop an application that implements a prototype user interface for composing an email message. The application should have text fields for the To, CC, and Bcc address lists and subject line, and one for the message body. Include a button labeled Send. When the Send button is pushed, the program should print the contents of all fields to standard output using `println` statements.

PP 6.9   Design and implement an application that uses dialog boxes to obtain two integer values (one dialog box for each value) and display the sum and product of the values. Use another dialog box to see whether the user wants to process another pair of values.

PP 6.10   Design and implement a program whose background changes color depending on where the mouse pointer is located. If the mouse pointer is on the left half of the program window, display red; if it is on the right half, display green.

PP 6.11   Design and implement an application that serves as a mouse odometer, continually displaying how far, in pixels, the mouse has moved (while over the program window). Display the current odometer value using a label. *Hint:* Compare the current position of the mouse to the last position and use the distance formula to determine how far the mouse has traveled.

PP 6.12   Design and implement an application that draws a circle using a rubberbanding technique. The circle size is determined by a mouse drag. Use the original mouse click location as a fixed center point. *Hint:* Compute the distance between the mouse pointer and the center point to determine the current radius of the circle.

PP 6.13   Modify the `StyleOptions` program to allow the user to specify the size of the font. Use a text field to obtain the size.

PP 6.14   Modify your solution to programming project 6.13 such that it uses a slider to obtain the font size.

PP 6.15   Develop a simple tool for calculating basic statistics for a segment of text. The application should have a single window with a scrolling text box (a `JTextArea`) and a stats box. The stats box should be a panel with a titled border, containing labeled fields that display the number of words in the text box and the average word length, as well as any other statistics that you would like to add. The stats box should also contain a button that, when pressed, re-computes the statistics for the current contents of the text field.

PP 6.16   Modify the `Rebound` program from this chapter such that when the mouse button is clicked on the program window the animation stops, and when it is clicked again the animation resumes.

PP 6.17   Design and implement a program that uses a `JColorChooser` object to obtain a color from the user and display that color as the background of the primary program window. Use a dialog box to determine if the user wants to display another color, and if so, redisplay the color chooser.

PP 6.18   Modify the JukeBox program so that the Play and Stop button functionality can also be controlled using keyboard mnemonics.

PP 6.19   Modify the Coordinates program so that it creates its listener by extending an adapter class instead of implementing an interface.

PP 6.20   Design and implement an application that displays an animation of a car (side view) moving across the screen from left to right. Create a Car class that represents the car.

PP 6.21   Design and implement an application that plays a game called Catch-the-Creature. Use an image to represent the creature. Have the creature appear at a random location for a random duration, then disappear and reappear somewhere else. The goal is to "catch" the creature by pressing the mouse button while the mouse pointer is on the creature image. Create a separate class to represent the creature, and include in it a method that determines if the location of the mouse click corresponds to the current location of the creature. Display a count of the number of times the creature is caught.

PP 6.22   Design and implement an application that works as a stopwatch. Include a display that shows the time (in seconds) as it increments. Include buttons that allow the user to start and stop the time, and reset the display to zero. Arrange the components to present a nice interface.

Answers to Self-Review Questions

SR 6.1   A GUI in a Java program is made up of on-screen components, events that those components generate, and listeners that respond to events when they occur.

SR 6.2   Both a frame and a panel are containers that can hold GUI elements. However, a frame is displayed as a separate window with a title bar, whereas a panel cannot be displayed on its own. A panel is often displayed inside a frame.

SR 6.3   Events usually represent user actions. A listener object is set up to listen for a certain event to be generated from a particular component. The relationship between a particular component that generates an event and the listener that responds to that event is set up explicitly.

SR 6.4   No, we cannot add any listener to any component. Each component generates a certain set of events, and only listeners of those types can be added to the component.

SR 6.5   Both push buttons and text fields generate action events. A check box generates an item state changed event.

SR 6.6   Both check boxes and radio buttons show a toggled state: either on or off. However, radio buttons work as a group in which only one can be toggled on at any point in time. Check boxes, on the other hand, represent independent options. They can be used alone or in a set in which any combination of toggled states is valid.

SR 6.7   A slider is useful when the user needs to specify a numeric value within specific bounds. Using a slider to get this input, as opposed to a text field or some other component, minimizes user error.

SR 6.8   An object created from the `Timer` class produces an action event at regular intervals. It can be used to control the speed of an animation.

SR 6.9   A layout manager is consulted whenever the visual appearance of its components might be affected, such as when the container is resized or when a new component is added to the container.

SR 6.10   Flow layout attempts to put as many components on a row as possible. Multiple rows are created as needed.

SR 6.11   Border layout is divided into five areas: North, South, East, West, and Center. The North and South areas are at the top and bottom of the container, respectively, and span the entire width of the container. Sandwiched between them, from left to right, are the West, Center, and East areas. Any unused area takes up no space, and the others fill in as needed.

SR 6.12   A glue component in a box layout dictates where any extra space in the layout should go. It expands as necessary, but takes up no space if there is no extra space to distribute.

SR 6.13   The containment hierarchy of a GUI is created by nested containers. The way the containers are nested, and the layout managers that those containers employ, dictate the details of the visual presentation of the GUI.

SR 6.14   A mouse event is an event generated when the user manipulates the mouse in various ways. There are several types of mouse events that may be of interest in a particular situation, including the mouse being moved, a mouse button being pressed, the mouse entering a particular component, and the mouse being dragged.

SR 6.15   A key event is generated when a keyboard key is pressed, which allows a listening program to respond immediately to the user input. The object representing the event holds a code that specifies which key was pressed.

SR 6.16   An event adapter class is a class that implements a listener interface, providing empty definitions for all of its methods. A listener class can be created by extending the appropriate adapter class and only defining the methods of interest.

SR 6.17   A dialog box is a small window that appears for the purpose of conveying information, confirming an action, or accepting input. Generally, dialog boxes are used in specific situations for brief user interactions.

SR 6.18   A file chooser and a color chooser are specialized dialog boxes that allow the user to select a file from disk or a color, respectively.

SR 6.19   The `BorderFactory` class contains several methods used to create borders that can be applied to components.

SR 6.20   A tool tip is a small amount of text that appears when the mouse cursor is allowed to rest over a specific component. Tool tips are used to explain, briefly, the purpose of a component.

SR 6.21   GUI components should be disabled when their use is inappropriate. This helps guide the user to proper actions and minimizes error handling and special cases.

Arrays

7

CHAPTER OBJECTIVES

- Define and use arrays for basic data organization.
- Discuss bounds checking and techniques for managing capacity.
- Discuss the issues related to arrays as objects and arrays of objects.
- Explore the use of command-line arguments.
- Describe the syntax and use of variable-length parameter lists.
- Discuss the creation and use of multidimensional arrays.

When designing programs, we often want to organize objects or primitive data in a form that is easy to access and modify. This chapter introduces arrays, which are programming constructs that group data into lists. Arrays are a fundamental component of most high-level languages, and a useful tool in creating problem solutions.

7.1 Array Elements

An *array* is a simple but powerful programming language construct used to group and organize data. When writing a program that manages a large amount of information, such as a list of 100 names, it is not practical to declare separate variables for each piece of data. Arrays solve this problem by letting us declare one variable that can hold multiple, individually accessible values.

An array is a list of values. Each value is stored at a specific, numbered position in the array. The number corresponding to each position is called an *index* or a *subscript*. Figure 7.1 shows an array of integers and the indexes that correspond to each position. The array is called `height`; it contains integers that represent several peoples' heights in inches.

In Java, array indexes always begin at zero. Therefore the value stored at index 5 is actually the sixth value in the array. The array shown in Figure 7.1 has 11 values, indexed from 0 to 10.

> **KEY CONCEPT**
>
> An array of size *N* is indexed from 0 to *N*-1.

To access a value in an array, we use the name of the array followed by the index in square brackets. For example, the following expression refers to the ninth value in the array `height`:

```
height[8]
```

According to Figure 7.1, `height[8]` (pronounced height-sub-eight) contains the value 79. Don't confuse the value of the index, in this case 8, with the value stored in the array at that index, in this case 79.

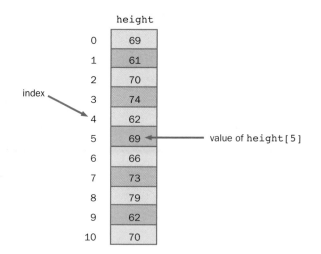

FIGURE 7.1 An array called `height` containing integer values

The expression `height[8]` refers to a single integer stored at a particular memory location. It can be used wherever an integer variable can be used. Therefore you can assign a value to it, use it in calculations, print its value, and so on. Furthermore, because array indexes are integers, you can use integer expressions to specify the index used to access an array. These concepts are demonstrated in the following lines of code:

```
height[2] = 72;
height[count] = feet * 12;
average = (height[0] + height[1] + height[2]) / 3;
System.out.println ("The middle value is " + height[MAX/2]);
pick = height[rand.nextInt(11)];
```

7.2 Declaring and Using Arrays

In Java, arrays are objects. To create an array, the reference to the array must be declared. The array can then be instantiated using the new operator, which allocates memory space to store values. The following code represents the declaration for the array shown in Figure 7.1:

> **KEY CONCEPT**
> In Java, an array is an object that must be instantiated.

```
int[] height = new int[11];
```

The variable `height` is declared to be an array of integers whose type is written as `int[]`. All values stored in an array have the same type (or are at least compatible). For example, we can create an array that can hold integers or an array that can hold strings, but not an array that can hold both integers and strings. An array can be set up to hold any primitive type or any object (class) type. A value stored in an array is sometimes called an *array element*, and the type of values that an array holds is called the *element type* of the array.

Note that the type of the array variable (`int[]`) does not include the size of the array. The instantiation of `height`, using the new operator, reserves the memory space to store 11 integers indexed from 0 to 10. Once an array object is instantiated to be a certain size, the number of values it can hold cannot be changed. A reference variable such as `height`, declared to hold an array of integers, can refer to an array of any size. And like any other reference variable, the object (that is, the array) that `height` refers to can change over time.

The example shown in Listing 7.1 creates an array called `list` that can hold 15 integers, which it loads with successive increments of 10. It then changes the value of the sixth element in the array (at index 5). Finally, it prints all values stored in the array.

Figure 7.2 on page 339 shows the array as it changes during the execution of the `BasicArray` program. It is often convenient to use for loops when handling

---

LISTING   7 . 1

```java
//********************************************************************
//  BasicArray.java         Java Foundations
//
//  Demonstrates basic array declaration and use.
//********************************************************************

public class BasicArray
{
   //-----------------------------------------------------------------
   //  Creates an array, fills it with various integer values,
   //  modifies one value, then prints them out.
   //-----------------------------------------------------------------
   public static void main (String[] args)
   {
      final int LIMIT = 15, MULTIPLE = 10;

      int[] list = new int[LIMIT];

      //  Initialize the array values
      for (int index = 0; index < LIMIT; index++)
         list[index] = index * MULTIPLE;

      list[5] = 999;  // change one array value

      //  Print the array values
      for (int value : list)
         System.out.print (value + "   ");
   }
}
```

O U T P U T

```
0   10   20   30   40   999   60   70   80   90   100   110   120   130   140
```

arrays because the number of positions in the array is constant. Note that a constant called LIMIT is used in several places in the BasicArray program. This constant is used to declare the size of the array and to control the for loop that initializes the array values.

The iterator version of the for loop is used to print the values in the array. Recall from Chapter 4 that this version of the for loop extracts each value in the

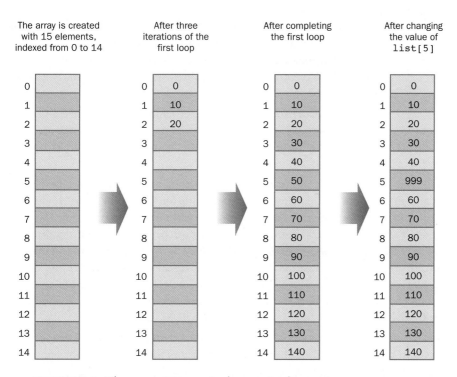

The array is created with 15 elements, indexed from 0 to 14

After three iterations of the first loop

After completing the first loop

After changing the value of `list[5]`

FIGURE 7.2 The array `list` as it changes in the `BasicArray` program

specified iterator. Every Java array is an iterator, so this type of loop can be used whenever we want to process every element stored in an array.

The square brackets used to indicate the index of an array are treated as an operator in Java. Therefore, just like the + operator or the <= operator, the *index operator* ([ ]) has a precedence relative to the other Java operators that determines when it is executed. It has the highest precedence of all Java operators.

Bounds Checking

The index operator performs automatic *bounds checking*, which ensures that the index is in range for the array being referenced. Whenever a reference to an array element is made, the index must be greater than or equal to zero and less than the size of the array. For example, suppose an array called `prices` is created with 25 elements. The valid indexes for the array are from 0 to 24. Whenever a reference is made to a particular element in the array (such as `prices[count]`), the value of the index is checked. If it is in the valid range of indexes for the array (0 to 24), the reference is carried out. If the index is not valid, an exception called `ArrayIndexOutOfBoundsException` is thrown.

In most cases, we'll want to perform our own bounds checking. That is, we'll want to be careful to remain within the bounds of the array when making references. (The alternative is to be prepared to handle the exception when it is thrown; exception handling is discussed in Chapter 10).

Because array indexes begin at zero and go up to one less than the size of the array, it is easy to create *off-by-one errors* in a program, which are problems created by processing all but one element or by attempting to index one element too many.

One way to check for the bounds of an array is to use the `length` constant, which is an attribute of the array object and holds the size of the array. It is a public constant and therefore can be referenced directly. For example, after the array `prices` is created with 25 elements, the constant `prices.length` contains the value 25. Its value is set once when the array is first created and cannot be changed. The `length` constant, which is an integral part of each array, can be used when the array size is needed without having to create a separate constant. Remember that the length of the array is the number of elements it can hold, and thus the maximum index of an array is `length-1`.

Let's look at another example. The program shown in Listing 7.2 reads 10 integers into an array called `numbers`, and then prints them in reverse order.

Note that in the `ReverseOrder` program, the array `numbers` is declared to have 10 elements and therefore is indexed from 0 to 9. The index range is controlled in

LISTING 7.2

```
//********************************************************************
//   ReverseOrder.java          Java Foundations
//
//   Demonstrates array index processing.
//********************************************************************

import java.util.Scanner;

public class ReverseOrder

{
    //----------------------------------------------------------------
    //  Reads a list of numbers from the user, storing them in an
    //  array, then prints them in the opposite order.
    //----------------------------------------------------------------
```

LISTING 7.2 *continued*

```java
public static void main (String[] args)
{
    Scanner scan = new Scanner (System.in);

    double[] numbers = new double[10];

    System.out.println ("The size of the array: " + numbers.length);

    for (int index = 0; index < numbers.length; index++)
    {
        System.out.print ("Enter number " + (index+1) + ": ");
        numbers[index] = scan.nextDouble();
    }

    System.out.println ("The numbers in reverse order:");

    for (int index = numbers.length-1; index >= 0; index--)
        System.out.print (numbers[index] + "  ");
}
}
```

OUTPUT

```
The size of the array: 10
Enter number 1: 18.51
Enter number 2: 69.9
Enter number 3: 41.28
Enter number 4: 72.003
Enter number 5: 34.35
Enter number 6: 140.71
Enter number 7: 9.60
Enter number 8: 24.45
Enter number 9: 99.30
Enter number 10: 61.08
The numbers in reverse order:
61.08   99.3   24.45   9.6   140.71   34.35   72.003   41.28   69.9   18.51
```

the for loops by using the length field of the array object. You should carefully set the initial value of loop control variables and the conditions that terminate loops to guarantee that all intended elements are processed and only valid indexes are used to reference an array element.

The `LetterCount` example, shown in Listing 7.3, uses two arrays and a `String` object. The array called upper is used to store the number of times each uppercase alphabetic letter is found in the string. The array called `lower` serves the same purpose for lowercase letters.

Because there are 26 letters in the English alphabet, both the upper and `lower` arrays are declared with 26 elements. Each element contains an integer that is

LISTING 7.3

```java
//********************************************************************
//  LetterCount.java          Java Foundations
//
//  Demonstrates the relationship between arrays and strings.
//********************************************************************

import java.util.Scanner;

public class LetterCount
{
    //-----------------------------------------------------------------
    //  Reads a sentence from the user and counts the number of
    //  uppercase and lowercase letters contained in it.
    //-----------------------------------------------------------------
    public static void main (String[] args)
    {
        final int NUMCHARS = 26;

        Scanner scan = new Scanner (System.in);

        int[] upper = new int[NUMCHARS];
        int[] lower = new int[NUMCHARS];

        char current;   // the current character being processed
        int other = 0;  // counter for non-alphabetics

        System.out.println ("Enter a sentence:");
        String line = scan.nextLine();

        //  Count the number of each letter occurrence
        for (int ch = 0; ch < line.length(); ch++)
        {
            current = line.charAt(ch);
            if (current >= 'A' && current <= 'Z')
                upper[current-'A']++;
```

LISTING 7.3   *continued*

```java
        else
            if (current >= 'a' && current <= 'z')
                lower[current-'a']++;
            else
                other++;
    }

    //  Print the results
    System.out.println ();
    for (int letter=0; letter < upper.length; letter++)
    {
        System.out.print ( (char) (letter + 'A') );
        System.out.print (": " + upper[letter]);
        System.out.print ("\t\t" + (char) (letter + 'a') );
        System.out.println (": " + lower[letter]);
    }

    System.out.println ();
    System.out.println ("Non-alphabetic characters: " + other);
  }
}
```

OUTPUT

```
Enter a sentence:
In Casablanca, Humphrey Bogart never says "Play it again, Sam."

A: 0              a: 10
B: 1              b: 1
C: 1              c: 1
D: 0              d: 0
E: 0              e: 3
F: 0              f: 0
G: 0              g: 2
H: 1              h: 1
I: 1              i: 2
J: 0              j: 0
K: 0              k: 0
L: 0              l: 2
M: 0              m: 2
N: 0              n: 4
O: 0              o: 1
P: 1              p: 1
```

LISTING 7.3   *continued*

```
Q: 0          q: 0
R: 0          r: 3
S: 1          s: 3
T: 0          t: 2
U: 0          u: 1
V: 0          v: 1
W: 0          w: 0
X: 0          x: 0
Y: 0          y: 3
Z: 0          z: 0

Non-alphabetic characters: 14
```

initially zero by default. These values serve as counters for each alphabetic character encountered in the input. The `for` loop scans through the string one character at a time. The appropriate counter in the appropriate array is incremented for each character found in the string.

Both of the counter arrays are indexed from 0 to 25. So we have to map each character to a counter. A logical way to do this is to use `upper[0]` to count the number of `'A'` characters found, `upper[1]` to count the number of `'B'` characters found, and so on. Likewise, `lower[0]` is used to count `'a'` characters, `lower[1]` is used to count `'b'` characters, and so on. A separate variable called `other` is used to count any nonalphabetic characters that are encountered.

Note that to determine if a character is an uppercase letter, we used the boolean expression (`current >= 'A' && current <= 'Z'`). A similar expression is used for determining the lowercase letters. We could have used the static methods `isUpperCase` and `isLowerCase` in the `Character` class to make these determinations, but we didn't in this example to drive home the point that each character has a specific numeric value and order that we can use in our programming, based on the Unicode character set.

We use the `current` character to calculate which index in the array to reference. We have to be careful when calculating an index to ensure that it remains within the bounds of the array and matches to the correct element. Remember that in the Unicode character set the uppercase and lowercase alphabetic letters are continuous and in order (see Appendix C). Therefore, taking the numeric value of an uppercase letter such as `'E'` (which is 69) and subtracting the numeric value of the character `'A'` (which is 65) yields 4, which is the correct index for the counter of the character `'E'`. Note that nowhere in the program do we actually need to know the specific numeric values for each letter.

Alternate Array Syntax

Syntactically, there are two ways to declare an array reference in Java. The first technique, which is used in the previous examples and throughout this text, is to associate the brackets with the type of values stored in the array. The second technique is to associate the brackets with the name of the array. Therefore the following two declarations are equivalent:

```
int[] grades;
int grades[];
```

Although there is no difference between these declaration techniques as far as the compiler is concerned, the first is consistent with other types of declarations. The declared type is explicit if the array brackets are associated with the element type, especially if there are multiple variables declared on the same line. Therefore we associate the brackets with the element type throughout this text.

Initializer Lists

You can use an *initializer list* to instantiate an array and provide the initial values for the elements of the array. This is essentially the same idea as initializing a variable of a primitive data type in its declaration, except that the initial value for an array contains multiple values.

The items in an initializer list are separated by commas and delimited by braces (`{}`). When an initializer list is used, the `new` operator is not used. The size of the array is determined by the number of items in the initializer list. For example, the following declaration instantiates the array `scores` as an array of eight integers, indexed from 0 to 7 with the specified initial values:

```
int[] scores = {87, 98, 69, 87, 65, 76, 99, 83};
```

An initializer list can be used only when an array is first declared.

The type of each value in an initializer list must match the type of the array elements. Let's look at another example:

```
char[] vowels = {'A', 'E', 'I', 'O', 'U'};
```

> **KEY CONCEPT**
>
> An initializer list can be used to instantiate an array object instead of using the new operator.

In this case, the variable `vowels` is declared to be an array of five characters, and the initializer list contains character literals.

The program shown in Listing 7.4 demonstrates the use of an initializer list to instantiate an array.

LISTING 7.4

```java
//********************************************************************
//  Primes.java        Java Foundations
//
//  Demonstrates the use of an initializer list for an array.
//********************************************************************

public class Primes
{
    //-----------------------------------------------------------------
    //  Stores some prime numbers in an array and prints them.
    //-----------------------------------------------------------------
    public static void main (String[] args)
    {
        int[] primeNums = {2, 3, 5, 7, 11, 13, 17, 19};

        System.out.println ("Array length: " + primeNums.length);

        System.out.println ("The first few prime numbers are:");

        for (int prime : primeNums)
            System.out.print (prime + "   ");
    }
}
```

OUTPUT

```
Array length: 8
The first few prime numbers are:
2   3   5   7   11   13   17   19
```

Arrays as Parameters

An entire array can be passed as a parameter to a method. Because an array is an object, when an entire array is passed as a parameter, a copy of the reference to the original array is passed. We discussed this issue as it applies to all objects in Chapter 5.

A method that receives an array as a parameter can permanently change an element of the array because it is referring to the original element value. However, the method cannot permanently change the reference to the array itself because a copy of the original reference is sent to the method. These rules are consistent with the rules that govern any object type.

> **KEY CONCEPT**
>
> An entire array can be passed as a parameter, making the formal parameter an alias of the original.

An element of an array can be passed to a method as well. If the element type is a primitive type, a copy of the value is passed. If that element is a reference to an object, a copy of the object reference is passed. As always, the impact of changes made to a parameter inside the method depends on the type of the parameter. We discuss arrays of objects further in the next section.

7.3 Arrays of Objects

In the previous examples in this chapter, we used arrays to store primitive types such as integers and characters. Arrays can also store references to objects as elements. Fairly complex information management structures can be created using only arrays and other objects. For example, an array could contain objects, and each of those objects could consist of several variables and the methods that use them. Those variables could themselves be arrays, and so on. The design of a program should capitalize on the ability to combine these constructs to create the most appropriate representation for the information.

Keep in mind that an array is an object. So if we have an array of int values called `weight`, we are actually dealing with an object reference variable that holds the address of the array, which can be depicted as follows:

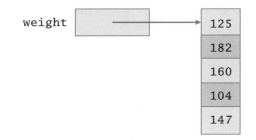

Furthermore, when we store objects in an array, each element is a separate object. That is, an array of objects is really an array of object references. Consider the following declaration:

```
String[] words = new String[5];
```

The array `words` holds references to `String` objects. The `new` operator in the declaration instantiates the array object and reserves space for five `String` references. But this declaration does not create any `String` objects; it merely creates an array that holds references to `String` objects. Initially, the array looks like this:

> **KEY CONCEPT**
>
> Instantiating an array of objects reserves room to store references only. The objects that are stored in each element must be instantiated separately.

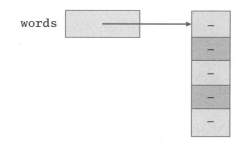

After a few `String` objects are created and put in the array, it might look like this:

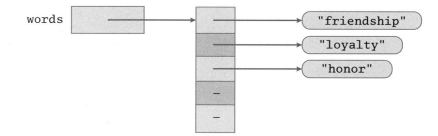

The `words` array is an object, and each character string it holds is its own object. Each object contained in an array has to be instantiated separately.

Keep in mind that `String` objects can be represented as string literals. So the following declaration creates an array called `verbs` and uses an initializer list to populate it with several `String` objects, each instantiated using a string literal:

```
String[] verbs = {"play", "work", "eat", "sleep"};
```

The program called `GradeRange` shown in Listing 7.5 creates an array of `Grade` objects, and then prints them. The `Grade` objects are created using several new operators in the initialization list of the array.

The `Grade` class is shown in Listing 7.6 on page 350. Each `Grade` object represents a letter grade for a school course and includes a numerical lower bound. The values for the grade name and lower bound can be set using the `Grade` constructor, or using appropriate mutator methods. Accessor methods are also defined, as is a `toString` method to return a string representation of the grade. The `toString` method is automatically invoked when the grades are printed in the `main` method.

Let's look at another example. Listing 7.7 on page 351 shows the `Tunes` class, which contains a `main` method that creates, modifies, and examines a compact disc (CD) collection. Each CD added to the collection is specified by its title, artist, purchase price, and number of tracks.

Listing 7.8 on page 353 shows the `CDCollection` class. It contains an array of `CD` objects representing the collection. It maintains a count of the CDs in the collection

LISTING 7.5

```java
//********************************************************************
//  GradeRange.java        Java Foundations
//
//  Demonstrates the use of an array of objects.
//********************************************************************

public class GradeRange
{
   //-----------------------------------------------------------------
   //  Creates an array of Grade objects and prints them.
   //-----------------------------------------------------------------
   public static void main (String[] args)
   {
      Grade[] grades =
      {
         new Grade("A", 95), new Grade("A-", 90),
         new Grade("B+", 87), new Grade("B", 85), new Grade("B-", 80),
         new Grade("C+", 77), new Grade("C", 75), new Grade("C-", 70),
         new Grade("D+", 67), new Grade("D", 65), new Grade("D-", 60),
         new Grade("F", 0)
      };

      for (Grade letterGrade : grades)
         System.out.println (letterGrade);
   }
}
```

OUTPUT

```
A      95
A-     90
B+     87
B      85
B-     80
C+     77
C      75
C-     70
D+     67
D      65
D-     60
F      0
```

LISTING 7.6

```java
//********************************************************************
//  Grade.java        Java Foundations
//
//  Represents a school grade.
//********************************************************************

public class Grade
{
   private String name;
   private int lowerBound;

   //------------------------------------------------------------------
   //  Constructor: Sets up this Grade object with the specified
   //  grade name and numeric lower bound.
   //------------------------------------------------------------------
   public Grade (String grade, int cutoff)
   {
      name = grade;
      lowerBound = cutoff;
   }

   //------------------------------------------------------------------
   //  Returns a string representation of this grade.
   //------------------------------------------------------------------
   public String toString()
   {
      return name + "\t" + lowerBound;
   }

   //------------------------------------------------------------------
   //  Name mutator.
   //------------------------------------------------------------------
   public void setName (String grade)
   {
      name = grade;
   }

   //------------------------------------------------------------------
   //  Lower bound mutator.
   //------------------------------------------------------------------
   public void setLowerBound (int cutoff)
   {
      lowerBound = cutoff;
   }
```

```
LISTING 7.6        continued

   //-----------------------------------------------------------------
   //  Name accessor.
   //-----------------------------------------------------------------
   public String getName()
   {
      return name;
   }

   //-----------------------------------------------------------------
   //  Lower bound accessor.
   //-----------------------------------------------------------------
   public int getLowerBound()
   {
      return lowerBound;
   }
}
```

```
LISTING 7.7

//******************************************************************
//  Tunes.java        Java Foundations
//
//  Demonstrates the use of an array of objects.
//******************************************************************

public class Tunes
{
   //-----------------------------------------------------------------
   //  Creates a CDCollection object and adds some CDs to it. Prints
   //  reports on the status of the collection.
   //-----------------------------------------------------------------
   public static void main (String[] args)
   {
      CDCollection music = new CDCollection ();

      music.addCD ("Storm Front", "Billy Joel", 14.95, 10);
      music.addCD ("Come On Over", "Shania Twain", 14.95, 16);
```

LISTING 7.7   *continued*

```
      music.addCD ("Soundtrack", "Les Miserables", 17.95, 33);
      music.addCD ("Graceland", "Paul Simon", 13.90, 11);

      System.out.println (music);

      music.addCD ("Double Live", "Garth Brooks", 19.99, 26);
      music.addCD ("Greatest Hits", "Jimmy Buffet", 15.95, 13);

      System.out.println (music);
   }
}
```

OUTPUT

```
~~~~~~~~~~~~~~~~~~~~~~~~~~~~~~~~~~~~~~~~~~~~~~~~
My CD Collection

Number of CDs: 4
Total cost: $61.75
Average cost: $15.44

CD List:

$14.95   10        Storm Front     Billy Joel
$14.95   16        Come On Over    Shania Twain
$17.95   33        Soundtrack      Les Miserables
$13.90   11        Graceland       Paul Simon


~~~~~~~~~~~~~~~~~~~~~~~~~~~~~~~~~~~~~~~~~~~~~~~~
My CD Collection

Number of CDs: 6
Total cost: $97.69
Average cost: $16.28

CD List:

$14.95   10        Storm Front     Billy Joel
$14.95   16        Come On Over    Shania Twain
$17.95   33        Soundtrack      Les Miserables
$13.90   11        Graceland       Paul Simon
$19.99   26        Double Live     Garth Brooks
$15.95   13        Greatest Hits   Jimmy Buffet
```

LISTING 7.8

```java
//********************************************************************
//   CDCollection.java        Java Foundations
//
//   Represents a collection of compact discs.
//********************************************************************

import java.text.NumberFormat;

public class CDCollection
{
   private CD[] collection;
   private int count;
   private double totalCost;

   //-----------------------------------------------------------------
   //   Constructor: Creates an initially empty collection.
   //-----------------------------------------------------------------
   public CDCollection ()
   {
      collection = new CD[100];
      count = 0;
      totalCost = 0.0;
   }

   //-----------------------------------------------------------------
   //   Adds a CD to the collection, increasing the size of the
   //   collection if necessary.
   //-----------------------------------------------------------------
   public void addCD (String title, String artist, double cost,
                      int tracks)
   {
      if (count == collection.length)
         increaseSize();

      collection[count] = new CD (title, artist, cost, tracks);
      totalCost += cost;
      count++;
   }

   //-----------------------------------------------------------------
   //   Returns a report describing the CD collection.
   //-----------------------------------------------------------------
   public String toString()
   {
```

LISTING 7.8   *continued*

```
    NumberFormat fmt = NumberFormat.getCurrencyInstance();

    String report = "~~~~~~~~~~~~~~~~~~~~~~~~~~~~~~~~~~~~~~~~~~~~~~~~\n";
    report += "My CD Collection\n\n";

    report += "Number of CDs: " + count + "\n";
    report += "Total cost: " + fmt.format(totalCost) + "\n";
    report += "Average cost: " + fmt.format(totalCost/count);

    report += "\n\nCD List:\n\n";

    for (int cd = 0; cd < count; cd++)
       report += collection[cd].toString() + "\n";

    return report;
    }

    //-------------------------------------------------------------
    //  Increases the capacity of the collection by creating a
    //  larger array and copying the existing collection into it.
    //-------------------------------------------------------------
    private void increaseSize ()
    {
       CD[] temp = new CD[collection.length * 2];

       for (int cd = 0; cd < collection.length; cd++)
          temp[cd] = collection[cd];

       collection = temp;
    }
}
```

and their combined value. It also keeps track of the current size of the collection array so that a larger array can be created if too many CDs are added to the collection. The CD class is shown in Listing 7.9.

The collection array is instantiated in the CDCollection constructor. Every time a CD is added to the collection (using the addCD method), a new CD object is created and a reference to it is stored in the collection array.

Each time a CD is added to the collection, we check to see whether we have reached the current capacity of the collection array. If we didn't perform this

LISTING 7.9

```java
//********************************************************************
//  CD.java          Java Foundations
//
//  Represents a compact disc.
//********************************************************************

import java.text.NumberFormat;

public class CD
{
   private String title, artist;
   private double cost;
   private int tracks;

   //-----------------------------------------------------------------
   //  Creates a new CD with the specified information.
   //-----------------------------------------------------------------
   public CD (String name, String singer, double price, int numTracks)
   {
      title = name;
      artist = singer;
      cost = price;
      tracks = numTracks;
   }

   //-----------------------------------------------------------------
   //  Returns a string description of this CD.
   //-----------------------------------------------------------------
   public String toString()
   {
      NumberFormat fmt = NumberFormat.getCurrencyInstance();

      String description;

      description = fmt.format(cost) + "\t" + tracks + "\t";
      description += title + "\t" + artist;

      return description;
   }
}
```

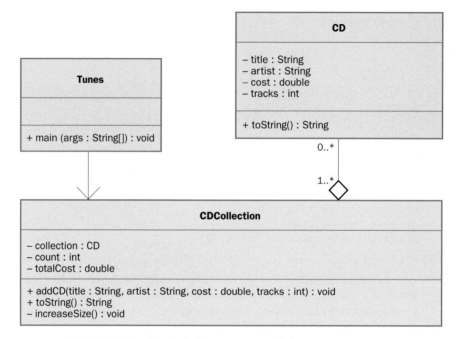

FIGURE 7.3   A UML class diagram of the `Tunes` program

check, an exception would eventually be thrown when we try to store a new CD object at an invalid index. If the current capacity has been reached, the private `increaseSize` method is invoked, which first creates an array that is twice as big as the current `collection` array. Each CD in the existing collection is then copied into the new array (that is, the references to the CD objects are copied). Finally, the `collection` reference is set to the larger array. Using this technique, we theoretically never run out of room in our CD collection. The user of the `CDCollection` object (the `main` method) never has to worry about running out of space because it's all handled internally.

Figure 7.3 shows a UML class diagram of the `Tunes` program. Recall that the open diamond indicates aggregation. The cardinality of the relationship is also noted: a `CDCollection` object contains zero or more CD objects.

The `toString` method of the `CDCollection` class returns an entire report summarizing the collection. The report is created, in part, using implicit calls to the `toString` method of each CD object stored in the collection.

7.4 Command-Line Arguments

The formal parameter to the `main` method of a Java application is always an array of `String` objects. We've ignored that parameter in previous examples, but now we can discuss how it might occasionally be useful.

The Java run-time environment invokes the `main` method when an application is submitted to the interpreter. The `String[]` parameter, which we typically call `args`, represents *command-line arguments* that are provided when the interpreter is invoked. Any extra information on the command line when the interpreter is invoked is stored in the `args` array for use by the program. This technique is another way to provide input to a program.

> **KEY CONCEPT**
>
> Command-line arguments are stored in an array of `String` objects and are passed to the `main` method.

The program shown in Listing 7.10 simply prints all of the command-line arguments provided when the program is submitted to the interpreter. Note that quotes can be used on the command line to delimit a multiword argument.

Remember that the parameter to the `main` method is always an array of `String` objects. If you want numeric information to be input as a command-line argument, the program has to convert it from its string representation.

LISTING 7.10

```java
//********************************************************************
//  CommandLine.java        Java Foundations
//
//  Demonstrates the use of command line arguments.
//********************************************************************

public class CommandLine
{
   //-----------------------------------------------------------------
   //  Prints all of the command line arguments provided by the
   //  user.
   //-----------------------------------------------------------------
   public static void main (String[] args)
   {
      for (String arg : args)
         System.out.println (arg);
   }
}
```

OUTPUT

```
> java CommandLine one two "two and a half" three
one
two
two and a half
three
```

When used, command-line arguments are typically reserved for information that tailors the way a program behaves. For example, you may provide the name of an input file as a command-line argument. Or perhaps you use an optional command-line argument that permits the user to specify a verbose or brief output format.

In program development environments that use a graphical user interface, a command line may not be the standard way to submit a program to the interpreter (that is, run the program). In such situations, command-line information can be specified in some other way. Consult the documentation for these specifics if necessary.

7.5 Variable-Length Parameter Lists

Suppose we wanted to design a method that processed a different amount of data from one invocation to the next. For example, let's design a method called average that accepts a few integer values and returns their average. In one invocation of the method we might pass in three integers to average:

```
mean1 = average(42, 69, 37);
```

In another invocation of the same method we might pass in seven integers to average:

```
mean2 = average(35, 43, 93, 23, 40, 21, 75);
```

To accomplish this we could define overloaded versions of the average method (as we did in the exercises at the end of Chapter 5). But that solution doesn't scale to an arbitrary set of input values. It would require that we know the maximum number of parameters there might be and create a separate version of the method for each possibility.

> **KEY CONCEPT**
>
> A Java method can be defined to accept a varying number of parameters.

Alternatively, we could define the method to accept an array of integers, which could be of different sizes for each call. But that would require the calling method to package the integers into an array.

Java provides a way to define methods that accept variable-length parameter lists. By using some special syntax in the formal parameter list of the method, we can define the method to accept any number of parameters. The parameters are automatically put into an array for easy processing in the method. For example, the average method could be written as follows:

```
public double average (int ... list)
{
    double result = 0.0;
```

```
    if (list.length != 0)
    {
        int sum = 0;
        for (int num : list)
            sum += num;
        result = (double)sum / list.length;
    }

    return result;
}
```

Note the way the formal parameters are defined. The ellipsis (three periods in a row) indicates that the method accepts a variable number of parameters. In this case, the method accepts any number of `int` parameters, which it automatically puts into an array called `list`. In the method, we process the array normally.

We can now pass any number of `int` parameters to the `average` method, including none at all. That's why we check to see if the length of the array is zero before we compute the average.

The type of the multiple parameters can be any primitive or object type. For example, the following method accepts and prints multiple `Grade` objects (we defined the `Grade` class earlier in this chapter):

```
public void printGrades (Grade ... grades)
{
    for (Grade letterGrade : grades)
        System.out.println (letterGrade);
}
```

A method that accepts a variable number of parameters can also accept other parameters. For example, the following method accepts an `int`, a `String` object, and then a variable number of `double` values that will be stored in an array called `nums`:

```
public void test (int count, String name, double ... nums)
{
    // whatever
}
```

The varying parameters must come last in the formal arguments. A single method cannot accept two sets of varying parameters.

Constructors can also be set up to accept a varying number of parameters. The program shown in Listing 7.11 on the next page creates two `Family` objects, passing a varying number of strings (representing the family member names) into the `Family` constructor.

The `Family` class is shown in Listing 7.12 on page 361. The constructor simply stores a reference to the array parameter until it is needed. By using a variable-length parameter list for the constructor, we make it easy to create a family of any size.

LISTING 7.11

```java
//********************************************************************
//  VariableParameters.java        Java Foundations
//
//  Demonstrates the use of a variable length parameter list.
//********************************************************************

public class VariableParameters
{
    //----------------------------------------------------------------
    //  Creates two Family objects using a constructor that accepts
    //  a variable number of String objects as parameters.
    //----------------------------------------------------------------
    public static void main (String[] args)
    {
        Family lewis = new Family ("John", "Sharon", "Justin", "Kayla",
            "Nathan", "Samantha");

        Family camden = new Family ("Stephen", "Annie", "Matt", "Mary",
            "Simon", "Lucy", "Ruthie", "Sam", "David");

        System.out.println(lewis);
        System.out.println();
        System.out.println(camden);
    }
}
```

OUTPUT

```
John
Sharon
Justin
Kayla
Nathan
Samantha

Stephen
Annie
Matt
Mary
Simon
Lucy
Ruthie
Sam
David
```

LISTING 7.12

```
//********************************************************************
//  Family.java        Java Foundations
//
//  Demonstrates the use of variable length parameter lists.
//********************************************************************

public class Family
{
   private String[] members;

   //-----------------------------------------------------------------
   //  Constructor: Sets up this family by storing the (possibly
   //  multiple) names that are passed in as parameters.
   //-----------------------------------------------------------------
   public Family (String ... names)
   {
      members = names;
   }

   //-----------------------------------------------------------------
   //  Returns a string representation of this family.
   //-----------------------------------------------------------------
   public String toString()
   {
      String result = "";

      for (String name : members)
         result += name + "\n";

      return result;
   }
}
```

7.6 Two-Dimensional Arrays

The arrays we've examined so far have all been *one-dimensional arrays* in the sense that they represent a simple list of values. As the name implies, a *two-dimensional array* has values in two dimensions, which are often thought of as the rows and columns of a table. Figure 7.4 graphically compares a one-dimensional

FIGURE 7.4   A one-dimensional array and a two-dimensional array

array with a two-dimensional array. We use two indexes to refer to a value in a two-dimensional array, one specifying the row and another the column.

Brackets are used to represent each dimension in the array. Therefore the type of a two-dimensional array that stores integers is `int[ ][ ]`. Technically, Java represents a two-dimensional array as an array of arrays. So a two-dimensional integer array is really a one-dimensional array of references to one-dimensional integer arrays. In most cases it's easier to think about a two-dimensional array as a table with rows and columns.

The `TwoDArray` program shown in Listing 7.13 instantiates a two-dimensional array of integers. As with one-dimensional arrays, the size of the dimensions is specified when the array is created. The size of the dimensions can be different.

Nested `for` loops are used in the `TwoDArray` program to load the array with values and also to print those values in a table format. Carefully trace the processing of this program to see how the nested loops eventually visit each element in the two-dimensional array. Note that the outer loops are governed by `table.length`, which represents the number of rows, and the inner loops are governed by `table[row].length`, which represents the number of columns in that row.

As with one-dimensional arrays, an initializer list can be used to instantiate a two-dimensional array, where each element is itself an array initializer list. This technique is used in the `SodaSurvey` program, which is shown in Listing 7.14.

Suppose a soda manufacturer held a taste test for four new flavors to determine if people liked them. The manufacturer got 10 people to try each new flavor and give it a score from 1 to 5, where 1 equals poor and 5 equals excellent. The two-dimensional array called `scores` in the `SodaSurvey` program stores the results of that survey. Each row corresponds to a soda and each column in that row corresponds to the person who tasted it. More generally, each row holds the responses that all testers gave for one particular soda flavor, and each column holds the responses of one person for all sodas.

LISTING 7.13

```java
//********************************************************************
//  TwoDArray.java         Java Foundations
//
//  Demonstrates the use of a two-dimensional array.
//********************************************************************

public class TwoDArray
{
   //-----------------------------------------------------------------
   //  Creates a 2D array of integers, fills it with increasing
   //  integer values, then prints them out.
   //-----------------------------------------------------------------
   public static void main (String[] args)
   {
      int[][] table = new int[5][10];

      // Load the table with values
      for (int row=0; row < table.length; row++)
         for (int col=0; col < table[row].length; col++)
            table[row][col] = row * 10 + col;

      // Print the table
      for (int row=0; row < table.length; row++)
      {
         for (int col=0; col < table[row].length; col++)
            System.out.print (table[row][col] + "\t");
         System.out.println();
      }
   }
}
```

OUTPUT

0	1	2	3	4	5	6	7	8	9
10	11	12	13	14	15	16	17	18	19
20	21	22	23	24	25	26	27	28	29
30	31	32	33	34	35	36	37	38	39
40	41	42	43	44	45	46	47	48	49

LISTING   7.14

```java
//********************************************************************
//   SodaSurvey.java        Java Foundations
//
//   Demonstrates the use of a two-dimensional array.
//********************************************************************

import java.text.DecimalFormat;

public class SodaSurvey
{
   //-----------------------------------------------------------------
   //   Determines and prints the average of each row (soda) and each
   //   column (respondent) of the survey scores.
   //-----------------------------------------------------------------
   public static void main (String[] args)
   {
      int[][] scores = { {3, 4, 5, 2, 1, 4, 3, 2, 4, 4},
                         {2, 4, 3, 4, 3, 3, 2, 1, 2, 2},
                         {3, 5, 4, 5, 5, 3, 2, 5, 5, 5},
                         {1, 1, 1, 3, 1, 2, 1, 3, 2, 4} };

      final int SODAS = scores.length;
      final int PEOPLE = scores[0].length;

      int[] sodaSum = new int[SODAS];
      int[] personSum = new int[PEOPLE];

      for (int soda=0; soda < SODAS; soda++)
         for (int person=0; person < PEOPLE; person++)
         {
            sodaSum[soda] += scores[soda][person];
            personSum[person] += scores[soda][person];
         }

      DecimalFormat fmt = new DecimalFormat ("0.#");
      System.out.println ("Averages:\n");

      for (int soda=0; soda < SODAS; soda++)
         System.out.println ("Soda #" + (soda+1) + ": " +
                     fmt.format ((float)sodaSum[soda]/PEOPLE));

      System.out.println ();
      for (int person=0; person < PEOPLE; person++)
```

LISTING 7.14   *continued*

```
        System.out.println ("Person #" + (person+1) + ": " +
                fmt.format ((float)personSum[person]/SODAS));
    }
}
```

OUTPUT

```
Averages:

Soda #1: 3.2
Soda #2: 2.6
Soda #3: 4.2
Soda #4: 1.9

Person #1: 2.2
Person #2: 3.5
Person #3: 3.2
Person #4: 3.5
Person #5: 2.5
Person #6: 3
Person #7: 2
Person #8: 2.8
Person #9: 3.2
Person #10: 3.8
```

The SodaSurvey program computes and prints the average responses for each soda and for each respondent. The sums of each soda and person are first stored in one-dimensional arrays of integers. Then the averages are computed and printed.

Multidimensional Arrays

An array can have one, two, three, or even more dimensions. Any array with more than one dimension is called a *multidimensional array*.

It's fairly easy to picture a two-dimensional array as a table. A three-dimensional array could be drawn as a cube. However, once you are past three dimensions, multi-dimensional arrays might seem hard to visualize. But consider that each subsequent dimension is simply a subdivision of the previous one. It is often best to think of larger multidimensional arrays in this way.

For example, suppose we wanted to store the number of students attending universities across the United States, broken down in a meaningful way. We might represent it as a four-dimensional array of integers. The first dimension represents the state. The second dimension represents the universities in each state. The third dimension represents the colleges in each university. Finally, the fourth dimension represents departments in each college. The value stored at each location is the number of students in one particular department. Figure 7.5 shows these subdivisions.

Two-dimensional arrays are fairly common and useful. However, care should be taken when deciding to create multidimensional arrays in a program. When dealing with large amounts of data that are managed at multiple levels, additional information and the methods needed to manage that information will probably be required. It is far more likely, for instance, that in the student example each state would be represented by an object, which may contain, among other things, an array to store information about each university, and so on.

> **KEY CONCEPT**
>
> Using an array with more than two dimensions is rare in an object-oriented system.

There is one other important characteristic of Java arrays to consider. As we established previously, Java does not directly support multidimensional arrays. Instead, they are represented as arrays of references to array objects. Those arrays could themselves contain references to other arrays. This layering continues for as many dimensions as required. Because of this technique for representing each dimension, the arrays in any one dimension could be of different lengths. These are sometimes called *ragged arrays*. For example, the number of elements in each row of a two-dimensional array may not be the same. In such situations, care must be taken to make sure the arrays are managed appropriately.

FIGURE 7.5   Visualization of a four-dimensional array

Summary of Key Concepts

- An array of size N is indexed from 0 to $N-1$.

- In Java, an array is an object that must be instantiated.

- Bounds checking ensures that an index used to refer to an array element is in range.

- An initializer list can be used to instantiate an array object instead of using the new operator.

- An entire array can be passed as a parameter, making the formal parameter an alias of the original.

- Instantiating an array of objects reserves room to store references only. The objects that are stored in each element must be instantiated separately.

- Command-line arguments are stored in an array of String objects and are passed to the main method.

- A Java method can be defined to accept a varying number of parameters.

- Using an array with more than two dimensions is rare in an object-oriented system.

Self-Review Questions

SR 7.1   What is an array?

SR 7.2   How is each element of an array referenced?

SR 7.3   What is an array's element type?

SR 7.4   Explain the concept of array bounds checking. What happens when a Java array is indexed with an invalid value?

SR 7.5   Describe the process of creating an array. When is memory allocated for the array?

SR 7.6   What is an off-by-one error? How does it relate to arrays?

SR 7.7   What does an array initializer list accomplish?

SR 7.8   Can an entire array be passed as a parameter? How is this accomplished?

SR 7.9   How is an array of objects created?

SR 7.10   What is a command-line argument?

SR 7.11   How can Java methods have variable-length parameter lists?

SR 7.12   How are multidimensional arrays implemented in Java?

Exercises

EX 7.1   Which of the following are valid declarations? Which instantiate an array object? Explain your answers.

```
int primes = {2, 3, 4, 5, 7, 11};
float elapsedTimes[] = {11.47, 12.04, 11.72, 13.88};
int[] scores = int[30];
int[] primes = new {2, 3, 5, 7, 11};
int[] scores = new int[30];
char grades[] = {'a', 'b', 'c', 'd', 'f'};
char[] grades = new char[];
```

EX 7.2   Describe five programs that would be difficult to implement without using arrays.

EX 7.3   Describe what problem occurs in the following code. What modifications should be made to it to eliminate the problem?

```
int[] numbers = {3, 2, 3, 6, 9, 10, 12, 32, 3, 12, 6};
for (int count = 1; count <= numbers.length; count++)
    System.out.println (numbers[count]);
```

EX 7.4   Write an array declaration and any necessary supporting classes to represent the following statements:

a. students' names for a class of 25 students

b. students' test grades for a class of 40 students

c. credit-card transactions that contain a transaction number, a merchant name, and a charge

d. students' names for a class and homework grades for each student

e. for each employee of the L&L International Corporation: the employee number, hire date, and the amount of the last five raises

EX 7.5   Write code that sets each element of an array called nums to the value of the constant INITIAL.

EX 7.6   Write code that prints the values stored in an array called names backwards.

EX 7.7   Write code that sets each element of a boolean array called flags to alternating values (true at index 0, false at index 1, etc.).

EX 7.8   Write a method called `sumArray` that accepts an array of floating
point values and returns the sum of the values stored in the array.

EX 7.9   Write a method called `switchThem` that accepts two integer arrays as parameters and switches the contents of the arrays. Take
into account that the arrays may be of different sizes.

Programming Projects

PP 7.1   Design and implement an application that reads an arbitrary
number of integers that are in the range 0 to 50 inclusive and
counts how many occurrences of each are entered. After all input
has been processed, print all of the values (with the number of
occurrences) that were entered one or more times.

PP 7.2   Modify the program from programming project 7.1 so that it
works for numbers in the range between –25 and 25.

PP 7.3   Design and implement an application that creates a histogram
that allows you to visually inspect the frequency distribution of a
set of values. The program should read in an arbitrary number of
integers that are in the range 1 to 100 inclusive; then produce a
chart similar to the one below that indicates how many input values fell in the range 1 to 10, 11 to 20, and so on. Print one asterisk for each value entered.

```
 1  -  10  | *****
11  -  20  | **
21  -  30  | ******************
31  -  40  |
41  -  50  | ***
51  -  60  | ********
61  -  70  | **
71  -  80  | *****
81  -  90  | *******
91  -  100 | *********
```

PP 7.4   The lines in the histogram in programming project 7.3 will be too
long if a large number of values is entered. Modify the program
so that it prints an asterisk for every five values in each category.
Ignore leftovers. For example, if a category had 17 values, print
three asterisks in that row. If a category had 4 values, do not
print any asterisks in that row.

PP 7.5 Design and implement an application that computes and prints the mean and standard deviation of a list of integers x_1 through x_n. Assume that there will be no more than 50 input values. Compute both the mean and standard deviation as floating point values, using the following formulas.

$$mean = \frac{\sum\limits_{i=1}^{n} x_i}{n}$$

$$sd = \sqrt{\frac{\sum\limits_{i=1}^{n} (x_i - mean)^2}{n - 1}}$$

PP 7.6 The L&L Bank can handle up to 30 customers who have savings accounts. Design and implement a program that manages the accounts. Keep track of key information and allow each customer to make deposits and withdrawals. Produce appropriate error messages for invalid transactions. *Hint:* You may want to base your accounts on the Account class from Chapter 5. Also provide a method to add 3 percent interest to all accounts whenever the method is invoked.

PP 7.7 The programming projects of Chapter 5 discussed a Card class that represents a standard playing card. Create a class called DeckOfCards that stores 52 objects of the Card class. Include methods to shuffle the deck, deal a card, and report the number of cards left in the deck. The shuffle method should assume a full deck. Create a driver class with a main method that deals each card from a shuffled deck, printing each card as it is dealt.

PP 7.8 Design and implement an application that reads a sequence of up to 25 pairs of names and postal (ZIP) codes for individuals. Store the data in an object designed to store a first name (string), last name (string), and postal code (integer). Assume each line of input will contain two strings followed by an integer value, each separated by a tab character. Then, after the input has been read in, print the list in an appropriate format to the screen.

PP 7.9   Modify the program you created in programming project 7.8 to support the storing of additional user information: street address (string), city (string), state (string), and 10-digit phone number (long integer, contains area code and does not include special characters such as (,), or -).

PP 7.10   Define a class called `Quiz` that manages a set of up to 25 `Question` objects. Define the `add` method of the `Quiz` class to add a question to a quiz. Define the `giveQuiz` method of the `Quiz` class to present each question in turn to the user, accept an answer for each one, and keep track of the results. Define a class called `QuizTime` with a `main` method that populates a quiz, presents it, and prints the final results.

PP 7.11   Modify your answer to programming project 7.10 so that the complexity level of the questions given in the quiz is taken into account. Overload the `giveQuiz` method so that it accepts two integer parameters that specify the minimum and maximum complexity levels for the quiz questions and only presents questions in that complexity range. Modify the `main` method to demonstrate this feature.

Answers to Self-Review Questions

SR 7.1   An array is an object that stores a list of values. The entire list can be referenced by its name, and each element in the list can be referenced individually based on its position in the array.

SR 7.2   Each element in an array can be referenced by its numeric position, called an index, in the array. In Java, all array indexes begin at zero. Square brackets are used to specify the index. For example, `nums[5]` refers to the sixth element in the array called `nums`.

SR 7.3   An array's element type is the type of values that the array can hold. All values in a particular array have the same type, or are at least of compatible types. So we might have an array of integers, or an array of `boolean` values, or an array of `Dog` objects, etc.

SR 7.4   Whenever a reference is made to a particular array element, the index operator (the brackets that enclose the subscript) ensures that the value of the index is greater than or equal to zero and less than the size of the array. If it is not within the valid range, an `ArrayIndexOutOfBoundsException` is thrown.

SR 7.5   Arrays are objects. Therefore, as with all objects, to create an array we first create a reference to the array (its name). We then instantiate the array itself, which reserves memory space to store the array elements. The only difference between a regular object instantiation and an array instantiation is the bracket syntax.

SR 7.6   An off-by-one error occurs when a program's logic exceeds the boundary of an array (or similar structure) by one. These errors include forgetting to process a boundary element as well as attempting to process a nonexistent element. Array processing is susceptible to off-by-one errors because their indexes begin at zero and run to one less than the size of the array.

SR 7.7   An array initializer list is used in the declaration of an array to set up the initial values of its elements. An initializer list instantiates the array object, so the new operator is not needed.

SR 7.8   An entire array can be passed as a parameter. Specifically, because an array is an object, a reference to the array is passed to the method. Any changes made to the array elements will be reflected outside of the method.

SR 7.9   An array of objects is really an array of object references. The array itself must be instantiated, and the objects that are stored in the array must be created separately.

SR 7.10   A command-line argument is data that is included on the command line when the interpreter is invoked to execute the program. Command-line arguments are another way to provide input to a program. They are accessed using the array of strings that is passed into the main method as a parameter.

SR 7.11   A Java method can be defined to accept a variable number of parameters by using an ellipsis (. . .) in the formal parameter list. When several values are passed to the method, they are automatically converted into an array. This allows the method to be written in terms of array processing without forcing the calling method to create the array.

SR 7.12   A multidimensional array is implemented in Java as an array of array objects. The arrays that are elements of the outer array could also contain arrays as elements. This nesting process could continue for as many levels as needed.

Inheritance

8

CHAPTER OBJECTIVES

- Explore the derivation of new classes from existing ones.
- Define the concept and purpose of method overriding.
- Discuss the design of class hierarchies.
- Examine the purpose and use of abstract classes.
- Discuss the issue of visibility as it relates to inheritance.
- Discuss object-oriented design in the context of inheritance.

This chapter explains inheritance, a fundamental technique for organizing and creating classes. It is a simple but powerful idea that influences the way we design object-oriented software and enhances our ability to reuse classes in other situations and programs. In this chapter we explore the technique for creating subclasses and class hierarchies, and we discuss a technique for overriding the definition of an inherited method. We examine the `protected` modifier and discuss the effect all visibility modifiers have on inherited attributes and methods.

8.1 Creating Subclasses

In our introduction to object-oriented concepts in Chapter 1 we presented the analogy that a class is to an object what a blueprint is to a house. In subsequent chapters we've reinforced that idea, writing classes that define a set of similar objects. A class establishes the characteristics and behaviors of an object but reserves no memory space for variables (unless those variables are declared as `static`). Classes are the plan, and objects are the embodiment of that plan.

Many houses can be created from the same blueprint. They are essentially the same house in different locations with different people living in them. Now suppose you want a house that is similar to another but with some different or additional features. You want to start with the same basic blueprint but modify it to suit new, slightly different, needs. Many housing developments are created this way. The houses in the development have the same core layout, but they have unique features. For instance, they might all be split-level homes with the same basic room configuration, but some have a fireplace or full basement while others do not, or an upgraded gourmet kitchen instead of the standard version.

It's likely that the housing developer commissioned a master architect to create a single blueprint to establish the basic design of all houses in the development, then a series of new blueprints that include variations designed to appeal to different buyers. The act of creating the series of blueprints was simplified since they all begin with the same underlying structure, while the variations give them unique characteristics that may be important to the prospective owners.

> **KEY CONCEPT**
> Inheritance is the process of deriving a new class from an existing one.

Creating a new blueprint that is based on an existing blueprint is analogous to the object-oriented concept of *inheritance*, which is the process in which a new class is derived from an existing one. Inheritance is a powerful software development technique and a defining characteristic of object-oriented programming.

Via inheritance, the new class automatically contains the variables and methods in the original class. Then, to tailor the class as needed, the programmer can add new variables and methods to the derived class or modify the inherited ones.

> **KEY CONCEPT**
> One purpose of inheritance is to reuse existing software.

In general, new classes can be created via inheritance faster, easier, and cheaper than by writing them from scratch. Inheritance is one way to support the idea of *software reuse*. By using existing software components to create new ones, we capitalize on the effort that went into the design, implementation, and testing of the existing software.

Keep in mind that the word *class* comes from the idea of classifying groups of objects with similar characteristics. Classification schemes often use levels of classes that relate to each other. For example, all mammals share certain characteristics, such as being warm-blooded. Now consider a subset of mammals, such as horses. All horses are mammals and have all of the characteristics of mammals, but they also have unique features that make them different from other mammals, such as dogs.

If we translate this idea into software terms, an existing class called `Mammal` would have certain variables and methods that describe the state and behavior of mammals. A `Horse` class could be derived from the existing `Mammal` class, automatically inheriting the variables and methods contained in `Mammal`. The `Horse` class can refer to the inherited variables and methods as if they had been declared locally in that class. New variables and methods can then be added to the derived class to distinguish a horse from other mammals.

The original class that is used to derive a new one is called the *parent class*, *superclass*, or *base class*. The derived class is called a *child class*, or *subclass*. In UML, inheritance is represented by an arrow with an open arrowhead pointing from the child class to the parent, as shown in Figure 8.1.

The process of inheritance should establish an *is-a relationship* between two classes. That is, the child class should be a more specific version of the parent. For example, a horse is a mammal. Not all mammals are horses, but all horses are mammals. For any class X that is derived from class Y, you should be able to say that "X is a Y." If such a statement doesn't make sense, then that relationship is probably not an appropriate use of inheritance.

> **KEY CONCEPT**
> Inheritance creates an is-a relationship between the parent and child classes.

Let's look at an example. The `Words` program shown in Listing 8.1 instantiates an object of class `Dictionary`, which is derived from a class called `Book`. In the `main` method, three methods are invoked through the `Dictionary` object: two that were declared locally in the `Dictionary` class and one that was inherited from the `Book` class.

FIGURE 8.1 Inheritance relationships in UML

LISTING 8.1

```java
//********************************************************************
//  Words.java          Java Foundations
//
//  Demonstrates the use of an inherited method.
//********************************************************************

public class Words
{
    //-----------------------------------------------------------------
    //  Instantiates a derived class and invokes its inherited and
    //  local methods.
    //-----------------------------------------------------------------
    public static void main (String[] args)
    {
        Dictionary webster = new Dictionary();

        System.out.println ("Number of pages: " + webster.getPages());

        System.out.println ("Number of definitions: " +
                            webster.getDefinitions());

        System.out.println ("Definitions per page: " +
                            webster.computeRatio());
    }
}
```

OUTPUT

```
Number of pages: 1500
Number of definitions: 52500
Definitions per page: 35.0
```

Java uses the reserved word extends to indicate that a new class is being derived from an existing class. The Book class (shown in Listing 8.2) is used to derive the Dictionary class (shown in Listing 8.3 on page 378) simply by using the extends clause in the header of Dictionary. The Dictionary class automatically inherits the definition of the setPages and getPages methods, as well as the pages variable. It is as if those methods and the pages variable were declared inside the Dictionary class. Note that, in the Dictionary class, the computeRatio method explicitly references the pages variable, even though that variable is declared in the Book class.

LISTING 8.2

```java
//***************************************************************
//  Book.java          Java Foundations
//
//  Represents a book. Used as the parent of a derived class to
//  demonstrate inheritance.
//***************************************************************

public class Book
{
   protected int pages = 1500;

   //---------------------------------------------------------
   //  Pages mutator.
   //---------------------------------------------------------
   public void setPages (int numPages)
   {
      pages = numPages;
   }

   //---------------------------------------------------------
   //  Pages accessor.
   //---------------------------------------------------------
   public int getPages ()
   {
      return pages;
   }
}
```

Also note that although the Book class is needed to create the definition of Dictionary, no Book object is ever instantiated in the program. An instance of a child class does not rely on an instance of the parent class.

Inheritance is a one-way street. The Book class cannot use variables or methods that are declared explicitly in the Dictionary class. For instance, if we created an object from the Book class, it could not be used to invoke the setDefinitions method. This restriction makes sense because a child class is a more specific version of the parent class. A dictionary has pages because all books have pages; but although a dictionary has definitions, not all books do.

Figure 8.2 shows the inheritance relationship between the Book and Dictionary classes.

LISTING 8.3

```java
//********************************************************************
//  Dictionary.java        Java Foundations
//
//  Represents a dictionary, which is a book. Used to demonstrate
//  inheritance.
//********************************************************************

public class Dictionary extends Book
{
   private int definitions = 52500;

   //----------------------------------------------------------------
   //  Prints a message using both local and inherited values.
   //----------------------------------------------------------------
   public double computeRatio ()
   {
      return definitions/pages;
   }

   //----------------------------------------------------------------
   //  Definitions mutator.
   //----------------------------------------------------------------
   public void setDefinitions (int numDefinitions)
   {
      definitions = numDefinitions;
   }

   //----------------------------------------------------------------
   //  Definitions accessor.
   //----------------------------------------------------------------
   public int getDefinitions ()
   {
      return definitions;
   }
}
```

The protected Modifier

As we've seen, visibility modifiers are used to control access to the members of a class. Visibility plays an important role in the process of inheritance as well. Any public method or variable in a parent class can be explicitly referenced by name in

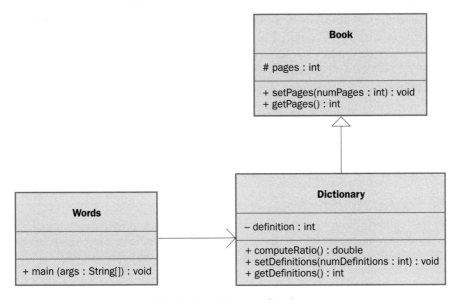

FIGURE 8.2 A UML class diagram for the Words program

the child class, and through objects of that child class. On the other hand, private methods and variables of the parent class cannot be referenced in the child class or through an object of the child class.

This situation causes a dilemma. If we declare a variable with public visibility so that a derived class can reference it, we violate the principle of encapsulation. Therefore, Java provides a third visibility modifier: protected. Note that in the Words example the variable pages is declared with protected visibility in the Book class. When a variable or method is declared with protected visibility, a derived class can reference it. And protected visibility allows the class to re-

> **KEY CONCEPT**
> Protected visibility provides the best possible encapsulation that permits inheritance.

tain some encapsulation properties. The encapsulation with protected visibility is not as tight as it would be if the variable or method were declared private, but it is better than if it were declared public. Specifically, a variable or method declared with protected visibility may be accessed by any class in the same package. The relationships among all Java modifiers are explained completely in Appendix E.

In a UML diagram, protected visibility can be indicated by preceding the protected member with a hash mark (#). The pages variable of the Book class has this annotation in Figure 8.2.

Each variable or method retains the effect of its original visibility modifier. For example, the setPages method is still considered to be public in its inherited form in the Dictionary class.

Let's be clear about our terms. All methods and variables, even those declared with private visibility, are inherited by the child class. That is, their definitions exist and memory space is reserved for the variables. It's just that they can't be referenced by name. This issue is explored in more detail in section 8.4.

Constructors are not inherited. Constructors are special methods that are used to set up a particular type of object, so it doesn't make sense for a class called Dictionary to have a constructor called Book. But you can imagine that a child class may want to refer to the constructor of the parent class, which is one of the reasons for the super reference, described next.

The super Reference

The reserved word super can be used in a class to refer to its parent class. Using the super reference, we can access a parent's members. Like the this reference, what the word super refers to depends on the class in which it is used.

A common use of the super reference is to invoke a parent's constructor. Let's look at an example. Listing 8.4 shows a modified version of the Words program, in which we use a class called Book2 (shown in Listing 8.5 on page 382) as the parent of the derived class Dictionary2 (shown in Listing 8.6 on page 383). However, unlike earlier versions of these classes, Book2 and Dictionary2 have explicit constructors used to initialize their instance variables. The output of the Words2 program is the same as it is for the original Words program.

The Dictionary2 constructor takes two integer values as parameters, representing the number of pages and definitions in the book. Because the Book2 class already has a constructor that performs the work to set up the parts of the dictionary that were inherited, we rely on that constructor to do that work. However, since the constructor is not inherited, we cannot invoke it directly, and so we use the super reference to invoke it in the parent class. The Dictionary2 constructor then proceeds to initialize its definitions variable.

In this example, it would have been just as easy to set the pages variable explicitly in the Dictionary2 constructor instead of using super to call the Book2 constructor. However, it is good practice to let each class "take care of itself." If we choose to change the way that the Book2 constructor sets up its pages variable, we would also have to remember to make that change in Dictionary2. By using the super reference, a change made in Book2 is automatically reflected in Dictionary2.

A child's constructor is responsible for calling its parent's constructor. Generally, the first line of a constructor should use the super reference call to a constructor of the parent class. If no such call exists, Java will automatically make a call to super with no parameters at the beginning of the constructor. This rule ensures that a parent class initializes its variables before the child class constructor begins to

LISTING 8.4

```
//********************************************************************
//  Words2.java        Java Foundations
//
//  Demonstrates the use of the super reference.
//********************************************************************

public class Words2
{
    //-----------------------------------------------------------------
    //  Instantiates a derived class and invokes its inherited and
    //  local methods.
    //-----------------------------------------------------------------
    public static void main (String[] args)
    {
        Dictionary2 webster = new Dictionary2 (1500, 52500);

        System.out.println ("Number of pages: " + webster.getPages());

        System.out.println ("Number of definitions: " +
                            webster.getDefinitions());

        System.out.println ("Definitions per page: " +
                            webster.computeRatio());
    }
}
```

OUTPUT

```
Number of pages: 1500
Number of definitions: 52500
Definitions per page: 35.0
```

execute. Using the super reference to invoke a parent's constructor can be done only in the child's constructor, and if included it must be the first line of the constructor.

The super reference can also be used to reference other variables and methods defined in the parent's class. We use this technique in later sections of this chapter.

Multiple Inheritance

Java's approach to inheritance is called *single inheritance*. This term means that a derived class can have only one parent. Some object-oriented languages allow a

```
LISTING  8.5
```

```
//********************************************************************
//  Book2.java        Java Foundations
//
//  Represents a book. Used as the parent of a derived class to
//  demonstrate inheritance and the use of the super reference.
//********************************************************************

public class Book2
{
   protected int pages;

   //---------------------------------------------------------------
   //  Constructor: Sets up the book with the specified number of
   //  pages.
   //---------------------------------------------------------------
   public Book2 (int numPages)
   {
      pages = numPages;
   }

   //---------------------------------------------------------------
   //  Pages mutator.
   //---------------------------------------------------------------
   public void setPages (int numPages)
   {
      pages = numPages;
   }

   //---------------------------------------------------------------
   //  Pages accessor.
   //---------------------------------------------------------------
   public int getPages ()
   {
      return pages;
   }
}
```

child class to have multiple parents. This approach is called *multiple inheritance* and is occasionally useful for describing objects that could share characteristics of more than one class. For example, suppose we had a class Car and a class Truck and we wanted to create a new class called PickupTruck. A pickup truck is

LISTING 8.6

```java
//********************************************************************
//  Dictionary2.java        Java Foundations
//
//  Represents a dictionary, which is a book. Used to demonstrate
//  the use of the super reference.
//********************************************************************

public class Dictionary2 extends Book2
{
   private int definitions;

   //-----------------------------------------------------------------
   //  Constructor: Sets up the dictionary with the specified number
   //  of pages and definitions.
   //-----------------------------------------------------------------
   public Dictionary2 (int numPages, int numDefinitions)
   {
      super(numPages);

      definitions = numDefinitions;
   }

   //-----------------------------------------------------------------
   //  Prints a message using both local and inherited values.
   //-----------------------------------------------------------------
   public double computeRatio ()
   {
      return definitions/pages;
   }

   //-----------------------------------------------------------------
   //  Definitions mutator.
   //-----------------------------------------------------------------
   public void setDefinitions (int numDefinitions)
   {
      definitions = numDefinitions;
   }

   //-----------------------------------------------------------------
   //  Definitions accessor.
   //-----------------------------------------------------------------
   public int getDefinitions ()
   {
      return definitions;
   }
}
```

FIGURE 8.3 Multiple inheritance

somewhat like a car and somewhat like a truck. With single inheritance, we must decide whether it is better to derive the new class from Car or Truck. With multiple inheritance, it can be derived from both, as shown in Figure 8.3.

Multiple inheritance works well in some situations, but it comes with a price. What if both Truck and Car have methods with the same name? Which method would PickupTruck inherit? The answer to this question is complex, and it depends on the rules of the language that supports multiple inheritance.

The designers of the Java language explicitly decided not to support multiple inheritance. Java *interfaces*, described in Chapter 9, provide the best features of multiple inheritance, without the added complexity.

8.2 Overriding Methods

> **KEY CONCEPT**
>
> A child class can override (redefine) the parent's definition of an inherited method.

When a child class defines a method with the same name and signature as a method in the parent class, we say that the child's version *overrides* the parent's version in favor of its own. The need for overriding occurs often in inheritance situations.

The program in Listing 8.7 provides a simple demonstration of method overriding in Java. The Messages class contains a main method that instantiates two objects: one from class Thought and one from class Advice. The Thought class is the parent of the Advice class.

Both the Thought class (shown in Listing 8.8 on page 386) and the Advice class (shown in Listing 8.9 on page 387) contain a definition for a method called message. The version of message defined in the Thought class is inherited by Advice, but Advice overrides it with an alternative version. The new version of the method prints out an entirely different message and then invokes the parent's version of the message method using the super reference.

The object that is used to invoke a method determines which version of the method is actually executed. When message is invoked using the parked object in the main method, the Thought version of message is executed. When message is invoked using the dates object, the Advice version of message is executed.

LISTING 8.7

```java
//********************************************************************
//  Messages.java        Java Foundations
//
//  Demonstrates the use of an overridden method.
//********************************************************************

public class Messages
{
   //----------------------------------------------------------------
   //  Creates two objects and invokes the message method in each.
   //----------------------------------------------------------------
   public static void main (String[] args)
   {
      Thought parked = new Thought();
      Advice dates = new Advice();

      parked.message();

      dates.message();    // overridden
   }
}
```

OUTPUT

```
I feel like I'm diagonally parked in a parallel universe.

Warning: Dates in calendar are closer than they appear.

I feel like I'm diagonally parked in a parallel universe.
```

A method can be defined with the `final` modifier. A child class cannot override a final method. This technique is used to ensure that a derived class uses a particular definition of a method.

Method overriding is a key element in object-oriented design. It allows two objects that are related by inheritance to use the same naming conventions for methods that accomplish the same general task in different ways. Overriding becomes even more important when it comes to polymorphism, which is discussed in Chapter 9.

Shadowing Variables

It is possible, although not recommended, for a child class to declare a variable with the same name as one that is inherited from the parent. Note the distinction

LISTING 8.8

```
//************************************************************
//  Thought.java          Java Foundations
//
//  Represents a stray thought. Used as the parent of a derived
//  class to demonstrate the use of an overridden method.
//************************************************************

public class Thought
{
    //-------------------------------------------------------------
    //  Prints a message.
    //-------------------------------------------------------------
    public void message()
    {
        System.out.println ("I feel like I'm diagonally parked in a " +
                            "parallel universe.");

        System.out.println();
    }
}
```

between redeclaring a variable and simply giving an inherited variable a particular value. If a variable of the same name is declared in a child class, it is called a *shadow variable*. It is similar in concept to the process of overriding methods but creates confusing subtleties.

Because an inherited variable is already available to the child class, there is usually no good reason to redeclare it. Someone reading code with a shadowed variable will find two different declarations that seem to apply to a variable used in the child class. This confusion causes problems and serves no useful purpose. A redeclaration of a particular variable name could change its type, but that is usually unnecessary. In general, shadowing variables should be avoided.

8.3 Class Hierarchies

A child class derived from one parent can be the parent of its own child class. Furthermore, multiple classes can be derived from a single parent. Therefore, inheritance relationships often develop into *class hierarchies*. The diagram in Figure 8.4

LISTING   8.9

```
//********************************************************************
//  Advice.java        Java Foundations
//
//  Represents some thoughtful advice. Used to demonstrate the use
//  of an overridden method.
//********************************************************************

public class Advice extends Thought
{
   //----------------------------------------------------------------
   //  Prints a message. This method overrides the parent's version.
   //----------------------------------------------------------------
   public void message()
   {
      System.out.println ("Warning: Dates in calendar are closer " +
                              "than they appear.");

      System.out.println();

      super.message();   //  explicitly invokes the parent's version
   }
}
```

shows a class hierarchy that includes the inheritance relationship between the
Mammal and Horse classes, discussed earlier.

There is no limit to the number of children a class can have or to the number of
levels to which a class hierarchy can extend. Two children of the same parent are

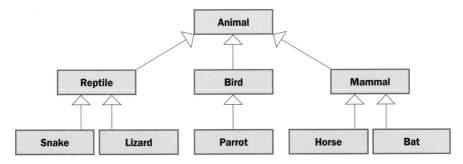

FIGURE 8.4 A class hierarchy

called *siblings*. Although siblings share the characteristics passed on by their common parent, they are not related by inheritance because one is not used to derive the other.

In class hierarchies, common features should be kept as high in the hierarchy as reasonably possible. That way, the only characteristics explicitly established in a child class are those that make the class distinct from its parent and from its siblings. This approach maximizes the potential to reuse classes. It also facilitates maintenance activities because when changes are made to the parent, they are automatically reflected in the descendants. Always remember to maintain the is-a relationship when building class hierarchies.

The inheritance mechanism is transitive. That is, a parent passes along a trait to a child class, and that child class passes it along to its children, and so on. An inherited feature might have originated in the immediate parent or possibly several levels higher in a more distant ancestor class.

There is no single best hierarchy organization for all situations. The decisions you make when you are designing a class hierarchy restrict and guide more detailed design decisions and implementation options, so you must make them carefully.

The class hierarchy shown in Figure 8.4 organizes animals by their major biological classifications, such as Mammal, Bird, and Reptile. In a different situation, however, it may be better to organize the same animals in a different way. For example, as shown in Figure 8.5, the class hierarchy might be organized around a function of the animals, such as their ability to fly. In this case, a Parrot class and a Bat class would be siblings derived from a general FlyingAnimal class. This class hierarchy is as valid and reasonable as the original one. The goals of the programs that use the classes are the determining factor, guiding the programmer to a hierarchy design that is best for the situation.

The Object Class

In Java, all classes are derived ultimately from the Object class. If a class definition doesn't use the extends clause to derive itself explicitly from another class,

FIGURE 8.5 An alternative hierarchy for organizing animals

then that class is automatically derived from the Object class by default. Therefore, this class definition:

```
class Thing
{
    // whatever
}
```

is equivalent to this one:

```
class Thing extends Object
{
    // whatever
}
```

Because all classes are derived from Object, all public methods of Object are inherited by every Java class. They can be invoked through any object created in any Java program. The Object class is defined in the java.lang package of the Java standard class library. Figure 8.6 lists some of the methods of the Object class.

As it turns out, we've been using Object methods quite often in our examples. The toString method, for instance, is defined in the Object class, so the toString method can be called on any object. As we've seen several times, when a println method is called with an object parameter, toString is called to determine what to print.

So when we define a toString method in a class, we are actually overriding an inherited definition. The definition for toString that is provided by the Object class returns a string containing the object's class name followed by a numeric value that is unique for that object. Usually, we override the Object version of toString to fit our own needs. The String class has overridden the toString method so that it returns its stored string value.

```
boolean equals (Object obj)
    Returns true if this object is an alias of the specified object.

String toString ()
    Returns a string representation of this object.

Object clone ()
    Creates and returns a copy of this object.
```

FIGURE 8.6 Some methods of the Object class

We are also overriding an inherited method when we define an `equals` method for a class. As we discussed in Chapter 4, the purpose of the `equals` method is to determine whether two objects are equal. The definition of the `equals` method provided by the `Object` class returns true if the two object references actually refer to the same object (that is, if they are aliases). Classes often override the inherited definition of the `equals` method in favor of a more appropriate definition. For instance, the `String` class overrides `equals` so that it returns true only if both strings contain the same characters in the same order.

Abstract Classes

An *abstract class* represents a generic concept in a class hierarchy. As the name implies, an abstract class represents an abstract entity that is usually insufficiently defined to be useful by itself. Instead, an abstract class may contain a partial description that is inherited by all of its descendants in the class hierarchy. An abstract class is just like any other class, except that it may have some methods that have not been defined yet. Its children, which are more specific, fill in the gaps.

> **KEY CONCEPT**
>
> An abstract class cannot be instantiated. It represents a concept on which other classes can build their definitions.

An abstract class cannot be instantiated and usually contains one or more *abstract methods*, which have no definition. That is, there is no body of code defined for an abstract method, and therefore it cannot be invoked. An abstract class might also contain methods that are not abstract, meaning that the method definition is provided as usual. And an abstract class can contain data declarations as usual.

A class is declared as abstract by including the `abstract` modifier in the class header. Any class that contains one or more abstract methods must be declared as abstract. In abstract classes, the `abstract` modifier must be applied to each abstract method. A class declared as abstract does not have to contain abstract methods, however.

Consider the class hierarchy shown in Figure 8.7. The `Vehicle` class at the top of the hierarchy may be too generic for a particular application. Therefore we may choose to implement it as an abstract class. In UML diagrams, the names of abstract classes and abstract methods are shown in italics.

Concepts that apply to all vehicles can be represented in the `Vehicle` class and are inherited by its descendants. That way, each of its descendants doesn't have to define the same concept redundantly (and perhaps inconsistently). For example, in Figure 8.7 we declare a variable called `speed` in the `Vehicle` class, and all specific vehicles below it in the hierarchy automatically have that variable because of inheritance. Any change we make to the representation of the speed of a vehicle is automatically reflected in all descendant classes. Similarly, in `Vehicle` we declare

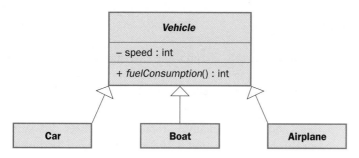

FIGURE 8.7 A vehicle class hierarchy

an abstract method called `fuelConsumption`, whose purpose is to calculate how quickly fuel is being consumed by a particular vehicle. The `Vehicle` class establishes that all vehicles consume fuel and provides a consistent method interface for computing that value. But the implementation of the `fuelConsumption` method is left up to each subclass of `Vehicle` which can tailor its method accordingly.

Some concepts don't apply to all vehicles, so we wouldn't represent those concepts at the `Vehicle` level. For instance, we wouldn't include a variable called `numberOfWheels` in the `Vehicle` class, because not all vehicles have wheels. The child classes for which wheels are appropriate can add that concept at the appropriate level in the hierarchy.

> **KEY CONCEPT**
>
> A class derived from an abstract parent must override all of its parent's abstract methods, or the derived class will also be considered abstract.

There are no restrictions as to where in a class hierarchy an abstract class can be defined. Usually they are located at the upper levels of a class hierarchy. However, it is possible to derive an abstract class from a nonabstract parent.

Usually, a child of an abstract class will provide a specific definition for an abstract method inherited from its parent. Note that this is just a specific case of overriding a method, giving a different definition than the one the parent provides. If a child of an abstract class does not give a definition for every abstract method that it inherits from its parent, then the child class is also considered abstract.

It would be a contradiction for an abstract method to be modified as `final` or `static`. Because a final method cannot be overridden in subclasses, an abstract final method would have no way of being given a definition in subclasses. A static method can be invoked using the class name without declaring an object of the class. Because abstract methods have no implementation, an abstract static method would make no sense.

Choosing which classes and methods to make abstract is an important part of the design process. You should make such choices only after careful consideration. By using abstract classes wisely, you can create flexible, extensible software designs.

8.4 Visibility

As we mentioned earlier in this chapter, all variables and methods in a parent class, even those declared as private, are inherited by child classes. Private members exist for an object of a derived class, even though they can't be referenced directly. They can, however, be referenced indirectly.

> **KEY CONCEPT**
>
> Private members are inherited by the child class, but cannot be referenced directly by name. They may be used indirectly, however.

Let's look at an example that demonstrates this situation. The program shown in Listing 8.10 contains a main method that instantiates a Pizza object and invokes a method to determine how many calories the pizza has per serving due to its fat content.

The FoodItem class shown in Listing 8.11 represents a generic type of food. The constructor of FoodItem accepts the number of grams of fat and the number of servings of that food.

LISTING 8.10

```java
//********************************************************************
//  FoodAnalyzer.java       Java Foundations
//
//  Demonstrates indirect access to inherited private members.
//********************************************************************

public class FoodAnalyzer
{
   //-----------------------------------------------------------------
   //  Instantiates a Pizza object and prints its calories per
   //  serving.
   //-----------------------------------------------------------------
   public static void main (String[] args)
   {
      Pizza special = new Pizza (275);

      System.out.println ("Calories per serving: " +
                          special.caloriesPerServing());
   }
}
```

OUTPUT

```
Calories per serving: 309
```

LISTING 8.11

```java
//********************************************************************
//  FoodItem.java        Java Foundations
//
//  Represents an item of food. Used as the parent of a derived class
//  to demonstrate indirect referencing.
//********************************************************************

public class FoodItem
{
   final private int CALORIES_PER_GRAM = 9;
   private int fatGrams;
   protected int servings;

   //-----------------------------------------------------------------
   //  Sets up this food item with the specified number of fat grams
   //  and number of servings.
   //-----------------------------------------------------------------
   public FoodItem (int numFatGrams, int numServings)
   {
      fatGrams = numFatGrams;
      servings = numServings;
   }

   //-----------------------------------------------------------------
   //  Computes and returns the number of calories in this food item
   //  due to fat.
   //-----------------------------------------------------------------
   private int calories()
   {
      return fatGrams * CALORIES_PER_GRAM;
   }

   //-----------------------------------------------------------------
   //  Computes and returns the number of fat calories per serving.
   //-----------------------------------------------------------------
   public int caloriesPerServing()
   {
      return (calories() / servings);
   }
}
```

```
LISTING 8.12

//****************************************************************
//   Pizza.java          Java Foundations
//
//   Represents a pizza, which is a food item. Used to demonstrate
//   indirect referencing through inheritance.
//****************************************************************

public class Pizza extends FoodItem
{
    //-----------------------------------------------------------
    //  Sets up a pizza with the specified amount of fat (assumes
    //  eight servings).
    //-----------------------------------------------------------
    public Pizza (int fatGrams)
    {
        super (fatGrams, 8);
    }
}
```

The calories method returns the number of calories due to fat, which the caloriesPerServing method invokes to help compute the number of fat calories per serving.

The Pizza class, shown in Listing 8.12, is derived from the FoodItem class, but it adds no special functionality or data. Its constructor calls the constructor of FoodItem using the super reference, asserting that there are eight servings per pizza.

The Pizza object called special in the main method is used to invoke the method caloriesPerServing, which is defined as a public method of FoodItem. Note that caloriesPerServing calls calories, which is declared with private visibility. Furthermore, calories references the variable fatGrams and the constant CALORIES_PER_GRAM, which are also declared with private visibility.

Even though the Pizza class cannot explicitly reference calories, fatGrams, or CALORIES_PER_GRAM, they are available for use indirectly when the Pizza object needs them. A Pizza object cannot be used to invoke the calories method, but it can call a method that can. Note that a FoodItem object was never created or needed.

8.5 Designing for Inheritance

As a major characteristic of object-oriented software, inheritance must be carefully and specifically addressed during software design. A little thought about inheritance relationships can lead to a far more elegant design, which pays huge dividends in the long term.

> **KEY CONCEPT**
> Software design must carefully and specifically address inheritance.

Throughout this chapter, several design issues have been addressed in the discussion of the nuts and bolts of inheritance in Java. The following list summarizes some of the inheritance issues that you should keep in mind during the program design stage:

- Every derivation should be an is-a relationship. The child should be a more specific version of the parent.
- Design a class hierarchy to capitalize on reuse, and potential reuse in the future.
- As classes and objects are identified in the problem domain, find their commonality. Push common features as high in the class hierarchy as appropriate for consistency and ease of maintenance.
- Override methods as appropriate to tailor or change the functionality of a child.
- Add new variables to the child class as needed, but don't shadow (redefine) any inherited variables.
- Allow each class to manage its own data. Therefore, use the `super` reference to invoke a parent's constructor and to call overridden versions of methods if appropriate.
- Design a class hierarchy to fit the needs of the application, with attention to how it may be useful in the future.
- Even if there are no current uses for them, override general methods such as `toString` and `equals` appropriately in child classes so that the inherited versions don't cause unintentional problems later.
- Use abstract classes to specify a common class interface for the concrete classes lower in the hierarchy.
- Use visibility modifiers carefully to provide the needed access in derived classes without violating encapsulation.

Restricting Inheritance

We've seen the `final` modifier used in declarations to create constants many times. The other uses of the `final` modifier involve inheritance and can have a significant influence on software design. Specifically, the `final` modifier can be used to curtail the abilities related to inheritance.

Earlier in this chapter we mentioned that a method can be declared as `final`, which means it cannot be overridden in any classes that extend the one it is in. A final method is often used to insist that particular functionality be used in all child classes.

The `final` modifier can also be applied to an entire class. A final class cannot be extended at all. Consider the following declaration:

```
public final class Standards
{
    // whatever
}
```

Given this declaration, the `Standards` class cannot be used in the `extends` clause of another class. The compiler will generate an error message in such a case. The `Standards` class can be used normally, but it cannot be the parent of another class.

Using the `final` modifier to restrict inheritance abilities is a key design decision. It should be done in situations in which a child class could possibly be used to change functionality that you, as the designer, specifically want to be handled a certain way. This issue comes up again in the discussion of polymorphism in Chapter 9.

Summary of Key Concepts

- Inheritance is the process of deriving a new class from an existing one.
- One purpose of inheritance is to reuse existing software.
- Inheritance creates an is-a relationship between the parent and child classes.
- Protected visibility provides the best possible encapsulation that permits inheritance.
- A parent's constructor can be invoked using the super reference.
- A child class can override (redefine) the parent's definition of an inherited method.
- The child of one class can be the parent of one or more other classes, creating a class hierarchy.
- Common features should be located as high in a class hierarchy as is reasonably possible.
- All Java classes are derived, directly or indirectly, from the Object class.
- The toString and equals methods are inherited by every class in every Java program.
- An abstract class cannot be instantiated. It represents a concept on which other classes can build their definitions.
- A class derived from an abstract parent must override all of its parent's abstract methods, or the derived class will also be considered abstract.
- Private members are inherited by the child class, but cannot be referenced directly by name. They may be used indirectly, however.
- Software design must carefully and specifically address inheritance.
- The final modifier can be used to restrict inheritance.

Self-Review Questions

SR 8.1   Describe the relationship between a parent class and a child class.

SR 8.2   How does inheritance support software reuse?

SR 8.3   What relationship should every class derivation represent?

SR 8.4   What does the protected modifier accomplish?

SR 8.5   Why is the super reference important to a child class?

SR 8.6   What is the difference between single inheritance and multiple inheritance?

SR 8.7   Why would a child class override one or more of the methods of its parent class?

SR 8.8   What is the significance of the `Object` class?

SR 8.9   What is the role of an abstract class?

SR 8.10   Are all members of a parent class inherited by the child? Explain.

SR 8.11   How can the `final` modifier be used to restrict inheritance?

Exercises

EX 8.1   Draw a UML class diagram showing an inheritance hierarchy containing classes that represent different types of clocks. Show the variables and method names for two of these classes.

EX 8.2   Show an alternative diagram for the hierarchy in Exercise 8.1. Explain why it may be a better or worse approach than the original.

EX 8.3   Draw a UML class diagram showing an inheritance hierarchy containing classes that represent different types of cars, organized first by manufacturer. Show some appropriate variables and method names for at least two of these classes.

EX 8.4   Show an alternative diagram for the hierarchy in Exercise 8.3 in which the cars are organized first by type (sports car, sedan, SUV, etc.). Show some appropriate variables and method names for at least two of these classes. Compare and contrast the two approaches.

EX 8.5   Draw a UML class diagram showing an inheritance hierarchy containing classes that represent different types of airplanes. Show some appropriate variables and method names for at least two of these classes.

EX 8.6   Draw a UML class diagram showing an inheritance hierarchy containing classes that represent different types of trees (oak, elm, etc.). Show some appropriate variables and method names for at least two of these classes.

EX 8.7   Draw a UML class diagram showing an inheritance hierarchy containing classes that represent different types of payment transactions at a store (cash, credit card, etc.). Show some appropriate variables and method names for at least two of these classes.

EX 8.8   Experiment with a simple derivation relationship between two
classes. Put `println` statements in constructors of both the parent
and child classes. Do not explicitly call the constructor of the parent
in the child. What happens? Why? Change the child's constructor to
explicitly call the constructor of the parent. Now what happens?

Programming Projects

PP 8.1   Design and implement a class called `MonetaryCoin` that is derived from the `Coin` class presented in Chapter 5. Store a value
in the monetary coin that represents its value and add a method
that returns its value. Create a driver class to instantiate and
compute the sum of several `MonetaryCoin` objects. Demonstrate
that a monetary coin inherits its parent's ability to be flipped.

PP 8.2   Design and implement a set of classes that define the employees
of a hospital: doctor, nurse, administrator, surgeon, receptionist,
janitor, and so on. Include methods in each class that are named
according to the services provided by that person and that print
an appropriate message. Create a driver class to instantiate and
exercise several of the classes.

PP 8.3   Design and implement a set of classes that define various types of
reading material: books, novels, magazines, technical journals,
textbooks, and so on. Include data values that describe various
attributes of the material, such as the number of pages and the
names of the primary characters. Include methods that are named
appropriately for each class and that print an appropriate message. Create a driver class to instantiate and exercise several of
the classes.

PP 8.4   Design and implement a set of classes that keep track of various
sports statistics. Have each low-level class represent a specific
sport. Tailor the services of the classes to the sport in question,
and move common attributes to the higher-level classes as appropriate. Create a driver class to instantiate and exercise several of
the classes.

PP 8.5   Design and implement a set of classes that keep track of demo-
graphic information about a set of people, such as age, national-
ity, occupation, income, and so on. Design each class to focus on
a particular aspect of data collection. Create a driver class to instantiate and exercise several of the classes.

myCodeMate　PP 8.6　Design and implement a set of classes that define a series of three-dimensional geometric shapes. For each shape, store fundamental data about its size and provide methods to access and modify this data. In addition, provide appropriate methods to compute each shape's circumference, area, and volume. In your design, consider how shapes are related and thus where inheritance can be implemented. Create a driver class to instantiate several shapes of differing types and exercise the behavior you provided.

myCodeMate　PP 8.7　Design and implement a set of classes that define various types of electronics equipment (computers, cell phones, pagers, digital cameras, etc.). Include data values that describe various attributes of the electronics, such as the weight, cost, power usage, and name of the manufacturer. Include methods that are named appropriately for each class and that print an appropriate message. Create a driver class to instantiate and exercise several of the classes.

myCodeMate　PP 8.8　Design and implement a set of classes that define various courses in your curriculum. Include information about each course such as the title, number, description, and department which teaches the course. Consider the categories of classes that comprise your curriculum when designing your inheritance structure. Create a driver class to instantiate and exercise several of the classes.

Answers to Self-Review Questions

SR 8.1　A child class is derived from a parent class using inheritance. The methods and variables of the parent class automatically become a part of the child class, subject to the rules of the visibility modifiers used to declare them.

SR 8.2　Because a new class can be derived from an existing class, the characteristics of the parent class can be reused without the error-prone process of copying and modifying code.

SR 8.3　Each inheritance derivation should represent an is-a relationship: the child *is-a* more specific version of the parent. If this relationship does not hold, then inheritance is being used improperly.

SR 8.4　The `protected` modifier establishes a visibility level (like `public` and `private`) that takes inheritance into account. A variable or method declared with protected visibility can be referenced by name in the derived class, while retaining some level of encapsulation. Protected visibility allows access from any class in the same package.

SR 8.5   The `super` reference can be used to call the parent's constructor, which cannot be invoked directly by name. It can also be used to invoke the parent's version of an overridden method.

SR 8.6   With single inheritance, a class is derived from only one parent, whereas with multiple inheritance, a class can be derived from multiple parents, inheriting the properties of each. The problem with multiple inheritance is that collisions must be resolved in the cases when two or more parents contribute an attribute or method with the same name. Java only supports single inheritance.

SR 8.7   A child class may prefer its own definition of a method in favor of the definition provided for it by its parent. In this case, the child overrides (redefines) the parent's definition with its own.

SR 8.8   All classes in Java are derived, directly or indirectly, from the `Object` class. Therefore all public methods of the `Object` class, such as `equals` and `toString`, are available to every object.

SR 8.9   An abstract class is a representation of a general concept. Common characteristics and method signatures can be defined in an abstract class so that they are inherited by child classes derived from it.

SR 8.10   A class member is not inherited if it has private visibility, meaning that it cannot be referenced by name in the child class. However, such members do exist for the child and can be referenced indirectly.

SR 8.11   The `final` modifier can be applied to a particular method, which keeps that method from being overridden in a child class. It can also be applied to an entire class, which keeps that class from being extended at all.

Polymorphism

CHAPTER OBJECTIVES

- Define polymorphism and explore its benefits.
- Discuss the concept of dynamic binding.
- Use inheritance to create polymorphic references.
- Explore the purpose and syntax of Java interfaces.
- Use interfaces to create polymorphic references.
- Discuss object-oriented design in the context of polymorphism.

This chapter discusses polymorphism, another fundamental principle of object-oriented software. We first explore the concept of binding and discuss how it relates to polymorphism. Then we look at two distinct ways to implement a polymorphic reference in Java: inheritance and interfaces. Java interfaces are explored in general, establishing the similarities between them and abstract classes, and bringing the polymorphism discussion full circle. The chapter concludes with a discussion of the design issues related to polymorphism.

9.1 Late Binding

Often, the type of a reference variable exactly matches the class of the object to which it refers. For example, consider the following reference:

```
ChessPiece bishop;
```

The `bishop` variable may be used to point to an object that is created by instantiating the `ChessPiece` class. However, it doesn't have to. The variable type and the object it refers to must be compatible, but their types need not be exactly the same. The relationship between a reference variable and the object it refers to is more flexible than that.

The term *polymorphism* can be defined as "having many forms." A *polymorphic reference* is a reference variable that can refer to different types of objects at different points in time. The specific method invoked through a polymorphic reference (the actual code executed) can change from one invocation to the next.

Consider the following line of code:

```
obj.doIt();
```

If the reference `obj` is polymorphic, it can refer to different types of objects at different times. So if that line of code is in a loop, or if it's in a method that is called more than once, that line of code could call a different version of the `doIt` method each time it is invoked.

At some point, the commitment is made to execute certain code to carry out a method invocation. This commitment is referred to as *binding* a method invocation to a method definition. In many situations, the binding of a method invocation to a method definition can occur at compile time. For polymorphic references, however, the decision cannot be made until run time. The method definition that is used is determined by the type of the object being referenced at the moment of invocation. This deferred commitment is called *late binding* or *dynamic binding*. It is slightly less efficient than binding at compile time because the decision is made during the execution of the program. This overhead is generally acceptable in light of the flexibility that a polymorphic reference provides.

We can create a polymorphic reference in Java in two ways: using inheritance and using interfaces. Let's look at each in turn.

9.2 Polymorphism via Inheritance

When we declare a reference variable using a particular class name, it can be used to refer to any object of that class. In addition, it can also refer to any object of any class that is related to its declared type by inheritance. For example, if the class `Mammal` is the parent of the class `Horse`, then a `Mammal` reference can be used to refer to an object of class `Horse`. This ability is shown in the following code segment:

```
Mammal pet;
Horse secretariat = new Horse();
pet = secretariat;  // a valid assignment
```

The ability to assign an object of one class to a reference of another class may seem like a deviation from the concept of strong typing discussed in Chapter 2, but it's not. Strong typing asserts that a variable can only be assigned a value consistent with its declared type. Well, that's what's happening here. Remember, inheritance establishes an is-a relationship. A horse *is-a* mammal. Therefore, assigning a `Horse` object to a `Mammal` reference is perfectly reasonable.

The reverse operation, assigning the `Mammal` object to a `Horse` reference, can also be done but it requires an explicit cast. Assigning a reference in this direction is generally less useful and more likely to cause problems because although a horse has all the functionality of a mammal, the reverse is not necessarily true.

> **KEY CONCEPT**
>
> A reference variable can refer to any object created from any class related to it by inheritance.

This relationship works throughout a class hierarchy. If the `Mammal` class were derived from a class called `Animal`, the following assignment would also be valid:

```
Animal creature = new Horse();
```

Carrying this idea to the limit, an `Object` reference can be used to refer to any object because ultimately all classes are descendants of the `Object` class.

The reference variable `creature` can be used polymorphically because at any point in time it can refer to an `Animal` object, a `Mammal` object, or a `Horse` object. Suppose that all three of these classes have a method called `move` that is implemented in different ways (because the child class overrode the definition it inherited). The following invocation calls the `move` method, but the particular version of the method it calls is determined at run time:

```
creature.move();
```

When this line is executed, if `creature` currently refers to an `Animal` object, the `move` method of the `Animal` class is invoked. Likewise, if `creature` currently refers to a `Mammal` object, the `Mammal` version of `move` is invoked. Similarly, if it currently refers to a `Horse` object, the `Horse` version of `move` is invoked.

Of course, since `Animal` and `Mammal` represent general concepts, they may be defined as abstract classes. This situation does not eliminate the ability to have

KEY CONCEPT

The type of the object, not the type of the reference, determines which version of a method is invoked.

polymorphic references. Suppose the move method in the Mammal class is abstract, and is given unique definitions in the Horse, Dog, and Whale classes (all derived from Mammal). A Mammal reference variable can be used to refer to any objects created from any of the Horse, Dog, and Whale classes, and can be used to execute the move method on any of them, even though Mammal itself is abstract.

Let's look at another situation. Consider the class hierarchy shown in Figure 9.1. The classes in it represent various types of employees that might be employed at a particular company. Let's explore an example that uses this hierarchy to pay a set of employees of various types.

The Firm class shown in Listing 9.1 on page 408 contains a main driver that creates a Staff of employees and invokes the payday method to pay them all. The program output includes information about each employee and how much each is paid (if anything).

The Staff class shown in Listing 9.2 on page 409 maintains an array of objects that represent individual employees of various kinds. Note that the array is declared to hold StaffMember references, but it is actually filled with objects created from several other classes, such as Executive and Employee. These classes are all descendants of the StaffMember class, so the assignments are valid. The staffList array is filled with polymorphic references.

The payday method of the Staff class scans through the list of employees, printing their information and invoking their pay methods to determine how much each employee should be paid. The invocation of the pay method is polymorphic because each class has its own version of the pay method.

The StaffMember class shown in Listing 9.3 on page 411 is abstract. It does not represent a particular type of employee and is not intended to be instantiated. Rather, it serves as the ancestor of all employee classes and contains information that applies to all employees. Each employee has a name, address, and phone number, so variables to store these values are declared in the StaffMember class and are inherited by all descendants.

The StaffMember class contains a toString method to return the information managed by the StaffMember class. It also contains an abstract method called pay, which takes no parameters and returns a value of type double. At the generic StaffMember level, it would be inappropriate to give a definition for this method. However, the descendants of StaffMember each provide their own specific definition for pay.

This example shows the essence of polymorphism. Each class knows best how it should handle a specific behavior, in this case paying an employee. Yet in one sense it's all the same behavior—the employee is getting paid. Polymorphism lets us treat similar objects in consistent but unique ways.

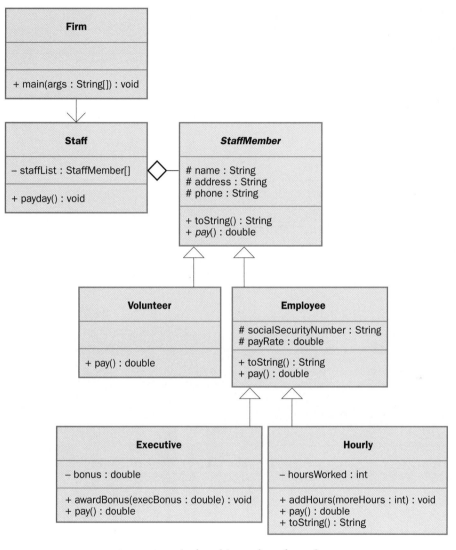

FIGURE 9.1 A class hierarchy of employees

By defining pay abstractly in StaffMember, the payday method of Staff can pay each employee polymorphically. If the pay method had not been established in StaffMember, the compiler would complain when pay was invoked through an element of the staffList array. The abstract method guarantees the compiler that any object referenced through the staffList array has a pay method defined for it.

LISTING 9.1

```java
//********************************************************************
//  Firm.java        Java Foundations
//
//  Demonstrates polymorphism via inheritance.
//********************************************************************

public class Firm
{
   //----------------------------------------------------------------
   //  Creates a staff of employees for a firm and pays them.
   //----------------------------------------------------------------
   public static void main (String[] args)
   {
      Staff personnel = new Staff();

      personnel.payday();
   }
}
```

OUTPUT

```
Name: Tony
Address: 123 Main Line
Phone: 555-0469
Social Security Number: 123-45-6789
Paid: 2923.07
-----------------------------------
Name: Paulie
Address: 456 Off Line
Phone: 555-0101
Social Security Number: 987-65-4321
Paid: 1246.15
-----------------------------------
Name: Vito
Address: 789 Off Rocker
Phone: 555-0000
Social Security Number: 010-20-3040
Paid: 1169.23
-----------------------------------
```

LISTING 9.1 *continued*

```
Name: Michael
Address: 678 Fifth Ave.
Phone: 555-0690
Social Security Number: 958-47-3625
Current hours: 40
Paid: 422.0
------------------------------------
Name: Adrianna
Address: 987 Babe Blvd.
Phone: 555-8374
Thanks!
------------------------------------
Name: Benny
Address: 321 Dud Lane
Phone: 555-7282
Thanks!
------------------------------------
```

LISTING 9.2

```java
//********************************************************************
//  Staff.java        Java Foundations
//
//  Represents the personnel staff of a particular business.
//********************************************************************

public class Staff
{
   private StaffMember[] staffList;

   //-----------------------------------------------------------------
   //  Constructor: Sets up the list of staff members.
   //-----------------------------------------------------------------
   public Staff ()
   {
      staffList = new StaffMember[6];

      staffList[0] = new Executive ("Tony", "123 Main Line",
         "555-0469", "123-45-6789", 2423.07);
```

LISTING 9.2   *continued*

```
      staffList[1] = new Employee ("Paulie", "456 Off Line",
         "555-0101", "987-65-4321", 1246.15);
      staffList[2] = new Employee ("Vito", "789 Off Rocker",
         "555-0000", "010-20-3040", 1169.23);

      staffList[3] = new Hourly ("Michael", "678 Fifth Ave.",
         "555-0690", "958-47-3625", 10.55);

      staffList[4] = new Volunteer ("Adrianna", "987 Babe Blvd.",
         "555-8374");
      staffList[5] = new Volunteer ("Benny", "321 Dud Lane",
         "555-7282");

      ((Executive)staffList[0]).awardBonus (500.00);

      ((Hourly)staffList[3]).addHours (40);
   }

   //-----------------------------------------------------------------
   //   Pays all staff members.
   //-----------------------------------------------------------------
   public void payday ()
   {
      double amount;

      for (int count=0; count < staffList.length; count++)
      {
         System.out.println (staffList[count]);

         amount = staffList[count].pay();   // polymorphic

         if (amount == 0.0)
            System.out.println ("Thanks!");
         else
            System.out.println ("Paid: " + amount);

         System.out.println ("-----------------------------------");
      }
   }
}
```

LISTING 9.3

```java
//********************************************************************
//  StaffMember.java        Java Foundations
//
//  Represents a generic staff member.
//********************************************************************

abstract public class StaffMember
{
   protected String name;
   protected String address;
   protected String phone;

   //-----------------------------------------------------------------
   //  Constructor: Sets up this staff member using the specified
   //  information.
   //-----------------------------------------------------------------
   public StaffMember (String eName, String eAddress, String ePhone)
   {
      name = eName;
      address = eAddress;
      phone = ePhone;
   }

   //-----------------------------------------------------------------
   //  Returns a string including the basic employee information.
   //-----------------------------------------------------------------
   public String toString()
   {
      String result = "Name: " + name + "\n";

      result += "Address: " + address + "\n";
      result += "Phone: " + phone;

      return result;
   }

   //-----------------------------------------------------------------
   //  Derived classes must define the pay method for each type of
   //  employee.
   //-----------------------------------------------------------------
   public abstract double pay();
}
```

LISTING 9.4

```java
//********************************************************************
//  Volunteer.java         Java Foundations
//
//  Represents a staff member that works as a volunteer.
//********************************************************************

public class Volunteer extends StaffMember
{
   //-----------------------------------------------------------------
   //  Constructor: Sets up this volunteer using the specified
   //  information.
   //-----------------------------------------------------------------
   public Volunteer (String eName, String eAddress, String ePhone)
   {
      super (eName, eAddress, ePhone);
   }

   //-----------------------------------------------------------------
   //  Returns a zero pay value for this volunteer.
   /-----------------------------------------------------------------
   public double pay()
   {
      return 0.0;
   }
}
```

The `Volunteer` class shown in Listing 9.4 represents a person that is not compensated monetarily for his or her work. We keep track only of a volunteer's basic information, which is passed into the constructor of `Volunteer`, which in turn passes it to the `StaffMember` constructor using the `super` reference. The `pay` method of `Volunteer` simply returns a zero pay value. If `pay` had not been overridden, the `Volunteer` class would have been considered abstract and could not have been instantiated.

Note that when a volunteer gets "paid" in the `payday` method of `Staff`, a simple expression of thanks is printed. In all other situations, where the pay value is greater than zero, the payment itself is printed.

The `Employee` class shown in Listing 9.5 represents an employee that gets paid at a particular rate each pay period. The pay rate, as well as the employee's social security number, is passed along with the other basic information to the Employee constructor. The basic information is passed to the constructor of StaffMember using the super reference.

The toString method of Employee is overridden to concatenate the additional information that Employee manages to the information returned by the

LISTING 9.5

```java
//********************************************************************
//  Employee.java       Java Foundations
//
//  Represents a general paid employee.
//********************************************************************

public class Employee extends StaffMember
{
    protected String socialSecurityNumber;
    protected double payRate;

    //----------------------------------------------------------------
    //  Constructor: Sets up this employee with the specified
    //  information.
    //----------------------------------------------------------------
    public Employee (String eName, String eAddress, String ePhone,
                     String socSecNumber, double rate)
    {
        super (eName, eAddress, ePhone);

        socialSecurityNumber = socSecNumber;
        payRate = rate;
    }

    //----------------------------------------------------------------
    //  Returns information about an employee as a string.
    //----------------------------------------------------------------
    public String toString()
    {
        String result = super.toString();

        result += "\nSocial Security Number: " + socialSecurityNumber;

        return result;
    }
```

LISTING 9.5 *continued*

```
//-----------------------------------------------------------------
//  Returns the pay rate for this employee.
//-----------------------------------------------------------------
public double pay()
{
    return payRate;
}
}
```

parent's version of toString, which is called using the super reference. The pay method of an Employee simply returns the pay rate for that employee.

The Executive class shown in Listing 9.6 represents an employee that may earn a bonus in addition to his or her normal pay rate. The Executive class is derived from Employee and therefore inherits from both StaffMember and Employee. The constructor of Executive passes along its information to the Employee constructor and sets the executive bonus to zero.

A bonus is awarded to an executive using the awardBonus method. This method is called in the payday method in Staff for the only executive that is part of the staffList array. Note that the generic StaffMember reference must be cast into an Executive reference to invoke the awardBonus method (because it doesn't exist for a StaffMember).

The Executive class overrides the pay method so that it first determines the payment as it would for any employee, then adds the bonus. The pay method of the Employee class is invoked using super to obtain the normal payment amount. This technique is better than using just the payRate variable because if we choose to change how Employee objects get paid, the change will automatically be reflected in Executive. After the bonus is awarded, it is reset to zero.

The Hourly class shown in Listing 9.7 on page 416 represents an employee whose pay rate is applied on an hourly basis. It keeps track of the number of hours worked in the current pay period, which can be modified by calls to the addHours method. This method is called from the payday method of Staff. The pay method of Hourly determines the payment based on the number of hours worked, and then resets the hours to zero.

LISTING 9.6

```java
//********************************************************************
//  Executive.java        Java Foundations
//
//  Represents an executive staff member, who can earn a bonus.
//********************************************************************

public class Executive extends Employee
{
   private double bonus;

   //-----------------------------------------------------------------
   //  Constructor: Sets up this executive with the specified
   //  information.
   //-----------------------------------------------------------------
   public Executive (String eName, String eAddress, String ePhone,
                     String socSecNumber, double rate)
   {
      super (eName, eAddress, ePhone, socSecNumber, rate);

      bonus = 0;  // bonus has yet to be awarded
   }

   //-----------------------------------------------------------------
   //  Awards the specified bonus to this executive.
   //-----------------------------------------------------------------
   public void awardBonus (double execBonus)
   {
      bonus = execBonus;
   }

   //-----------------------------------------------------------------
   //  Computes and returns the pay for an executive, which is the
   //  regular employee payment plus a one-time bonus.
   //-----------------------------------------------------------------
   public double pay()
   {
      double payment = super.pay() + bonus;

      bonus = 0;

      return payment;
   }
}
```

LISTING 9.7

```java
//********************************************************************
//  Hourly.java        Java Foundations
//
//  Represents an employee that gets paid by the hour.
//********************************************************************

public class Hourly extends Employee
{
    private int hoursWorked;

    //-----------------------------------------------------------------
    //  Constructor: Sets up this hourly employee using the specified
    //  information.
    //-----------------------------------------------------------------
    public Hourly (String eName, String eAddress, String ePhone,
                   String socSecNumber, double rate)
    {
        super (eName, eAddress, ePhone, socSecNumber, rate);

        hoursWorked = 0;
    }

    //-----------------------------------------------------------------
    //  Adds the specified number of hours to this employee's
    //  accumulated hours.
    //-----------------------------------------------------------------
    public void addHours (int moreHours)
    {
        hoursWorked += moreHours;
    }

    //-----------------------------------------------------------------
    //  Computes and returns the pay for this hourly employee.
    //-----------------------------------------------------------------
    public double pay()
    {
        double payment = payRate * hoursWorked;

        hoursWorked = 0;

        return payment;
    }
```

```
LISTING 9.7    continued

//---------------------------------------------------------------
//  Returns information about this hourly employee as a string.
//---------------------------------------------------------------
public String toString()
{
    String result = super.toString();

    result += "\nCurrent hours: " + hoursWorked;
    count--;

    return result;
}
}
```

9.3 Interfaces

In Chapter 5 we used the term interface to refer to the set of public methods through which we can interact with an object. That definition is consistent with our use of it in this section, but now we are going to formalize this concept using a Java language construct. Interfaces provide another way to create polymorphic references.

A Java *interface* is a collection of constants and abstract methods. As discussed in Chapter 8, an abstract method is a method that does not have an implementation. That is, there is no body of code defined for an abstract method. The header of the method, including its parameter list, is simply followed by a semicolon. An interface cannot be instantiated.

> **KEY CONCEPT**
>
> An interface is a collection of abstract methods and therefore cannot be instantiated.

Listing 9.8 on page 418 shows an interface called `Encryptable`. It contains two abstract methods: `encrypt` and `decrypt`.

An abstract method can be preceded by the reserved word `abstract`, though in interfaces it usually is not. Methods in interfaces have public visibility by default.

A class *implements* an interface by providing method implementations for each of the abstract methods defined in the interface. The `Secret` class, shown in Listing 9.9 on page 418, implements the `Encryptable` interface.

LISTING 9.8

```
//********************************************************************
//   Encryptable.java        Java Foundations
//
//   Represents the interface for an object that can be encrypted
//   and decrypted.
//********************************************************************

public interface Encryptable
{
   public void encrypt();
   public String decrypt();
}
```

LISTING 9.9

```
//********************************************************************
//   Secret.java        Java Foundations
//
//   Represents a secret message that can be encrypted and decrypted.
//********************************************************************

import java.util.Random;

public class Secret implements Encryptable
{
   private String message;
   private boolean encrypted;
   private int shift;
   private Random generator;

   //------------------------------------------------------------------
   //   Constructor: Stores the original message and establishes
   //   a value for the encryption shift.
   //------------------------------------------------------------------
   public Secret (String msg)
   {
      message = msg;
      encrypted = false;
```

LISTING 9.9 *continued*

```java
      generator = new Random();
      shift = generator.nextInt(10) + 5;
   }

   //-----------------------------------------------------------------
   //  Encrypts this secret using a Caesar cipher. Has no effect if
   //  this secret is already encrypted.
   //-----------------------------------------------------------------
   public void encrypt ()
   {
      if (!encrypted)
      {
         String masked = "";
         for (int index=0; index < message.length(); index++)
            masked = masked + (char)(message.charAt(index)+shift);
         message = masked;
         encrypted = true;
      }
   }

   //-----------------------------------------------------------------
   //  Decrypts and returns this secret. Has no effect if this
   //  secret is not currently encrypted.
   //-----------------------------------------------------------------
   public String decrypt()
   {
      if (encrypted)
      {
         String unmasked = "";
         for (int index=0; index < message.length(); index++)
            unmasked = unmasked + (char)(message.charAt(index)-shift);
         message = unmasked;
         encrypted = false;
      }

      return message;
   }
   //-----------------------------------------------------------------
   //  Returns true if this secret is currently encrypted.
   //-----------------------------------------------------------------
   public boolean isEncrypted()
   {
```

LISTING 9.9 *continued*

```
      return encrypted;
   }

   //------------------------------------------------------------
   //  Returns this secret (may be encrypted).
   //------------------------------------------------------------
   public String toString()
   {
      return message;
   }
}
```

A class that implements an interface uses the reserved word `implements` followed by the interface name in the class header. If a class asserts that it implements a particular interface, it must provide a definition for all methods in the interface. The compiler will produce errors if any of the methods in the interface are not given a definition in the class.

In the class `Secret`, both the `encrypt` and `decrypt` methods are implemented, which satisfies the contract established by the interface. These methods must be declared with the same signatures as their abstract counterparts in the interface. In the `Secret` class, the encryption is implemented using a simple Caesar cipher, which shifts the characters of the message a certain number of places. Another class that implements the `Encryptable` interface may use a completely different technique for encryption.

Note that the `Secret` class also implements additional methods that are not part of the `Encryptable` interface. Specifically, it defines the methods `isEncrypted` and `toString`, which have nothing to do with the interface. The interface guarantees that the class implements certain methods, but it does not restrict it from having others. In fact, it is common for a class that implements an interface to have other methods.

Listing 9.10 shows a program called `SecretTest`, which creates some `Secret` objects.

An interface and its relationship to a class can be shown in a UML class diagram. An interface is represented similarly to a class node except that the designation <<interface>> is inserted above the interface name. A dotted arrow with a triangular arrowhead is drawn from the class to the interface that it implements. Figure 9.2 on page 422 shows a UML class diagram for the `SecretTest` program.

LISTING 9.10

```
//********************************************************************
//  SecretTest.java        Java Foundations
//
//  Demonstrates the use of a formal interface.
//********************************************************************

public class SecretTest
{
    //----------------------------------------------------------------
    //  Creates a Secret object and exercises its encryption.
    //----------------------------------------------------------------
    public static void main (String[] args)
    {
        Secret hush = new Secret ("Wil Wheaton is my hero!");
        System.out.println (hush);

        hush.encrypt();
        System.out.println (hush);

        hush.decrypt();
        System.out.println (hush);
    }
}
```

OUTPUT

```
Wil Wheaton is my hero!
asv*arok~yx*s}*w?*ro|y+
Wil Wheaton is my hero!
```

Multiple classes can implement the same interface, providing their own definitions for the methods. For example, we could implement a class called `Password` that also implements the `Encryptable` interface. And, as mentioned earlier, each class that implements an interface may do so in different ways. The interface specifies which methods are implemented, not how they are implemented.

A class can implement more than one interface. In these cases, the class must provide an implementation for all methods in all interfaces listed. To show that a class implements multiple interfaces, they are listed in the `implements` clause, separated by commas. For example:

FIGURE 9.2 A UML class diagram for the `SecretTest` program

```
class ManyThings implements Interface1, Interface2, Interface3
{
    // implements all methods of all interfaces
}
```

In addition to, or instead of, abstract methods, an interface can contain constants, defined using the `final` modifier. When a class implements an interface, it gains access to all the constants defined in it.

Interface Hierarchies

The concept of inheritance can be applied to interfaces as well as to classes. That is, one interface can be derived from another interface. These relationships can form an *interface hierarchy*, which is similar to a class hierarchy. Inheritance relationships between interfaces are shown in UML diagrams using the same connection (an arrow with an open arrowhead) as they are with classes.

When a parent interface is used to derive a child interface, the child inherits all abstract methods and constants of the parent. Any class that implements the child interface must implement all of the methods. There are no visibility issues when dealing with inheritance between interfaces (as there are with protected and private members of a class) because all members of an interface are public.

Class hierarchies and interface hierarchies do not overlap. That is, an interface cannot be used to derive a class, and a class cannot be used to derive an interface.

A class and an interface interact only when a class is designed to implement a particular interface.

Before we see how interfaces support polymorphism, let's take a look at a couple of useful interfaces that are defined in the Java standard class library: `Comparable` and `Iterator`.

The Comparable Interface

The Java standard class library contains interfaces as well as classes. The `Comparable` interface, for example, is defined in the `java.lang` package. The `Comparable` interface contains only one method, `compareTo`, which takes an object as a parameter and returns an integer.

The purpose of this interface is to provide a common mechanism for comparing one object to another. One object calls the method and passes another as a parameter as follows:

```
if (obj1.compareTo(obj2) < 0)
    System.out.println ("obj1 is less than obj2");
```

As specified by the documentation for the interface, the integer that is returned from the `compareTo` method should be negative if `obj1` is less than `obj2`, 0 if they are equal, and positive if `obj1` is greater than `obj2`. It is up to the designer of each class to decide what it means for one object of that class to be less than, equal to, or greater than another.

In Chapter 4, we mentioned that the `String` class contains a `compareTo` method that operates in this manner. Now we can clarify that the `String` class has this method because it implements the `Comparable` interface. The `String` class implementation of this method bases the comparison of strings on the lexicographic ordering defined by the Unicode character set.

The Iterator Interface

The `Iterator` interface is another interface defined in the Java standard class library. It is used by a class that represents a collection of objects, providing a means to move through the collection one object at a time.

In Chapter 4, we defined the concept of an iterator, using a loop to process all elements in the collection. Most iterators, including objects of the `Scanner` class, are defined using the `Iterator` interface.

The two primary methods in the `Iterator` interface are `hasNext`, which returns a boolean result, and `next`, which returns an object. Neither of these methods takes any parameters. The `hasNext` method returns true if there are items left to process, and `next` returns the next object. It is up to the designer of the class that implements the `Iterator` interface to decide the order in which objects will be delivered by the `next` method.

We should note that, according to the spirit of the interface, the `next` method does not remove the object from the underlying collection; it simply returns a reference to it. The `Iterator` interface also has a method called `remove`, which takes no parameters and has a `void` return type. A call to the `remove` method removes the object that was most recently returned by the `next` method from the underlying collection.

We've seen how we can use iterators to process information from the `Scanner` class (in Chapter 4) and from arrays (in Chapter 7). Recall that the foreach version of the `for` loop simplifies this processing in many cases. We will continue to use iterators as appropriate. They are an important part of the development of collection classes, which we discuss in detail in the later chapters of this book (Chapters 14 and beyond).

9.4 Polymorphism via Interfaces

> **KEY CONCEPT**
> An interface name can be used to declare an object reference variable.

Now let's examine how we can create polymorphic references using interfaces. As we've seen many times, a class name can be used to declare the type of an object reference variable. Similarly, an interface name can be used as the type of a reference variable as well. An interface reference variable can be used to refer to any object of any class that implements that interface.

Suppose we declare an interface called `Speaker` as follows:

```
public interface Speaker
{
    public void speak();
    public void announce (String str);
}
```

The interface name, `Speaker`, can now be used to declare an object reference variable:

```
Speaker current;
```

The reference variable `current` can be used to refer to any object of any class that implements the `Speaker` interface. For example, if we define a class called `Philosopher` such that it implements the `Speaker` interface, we can then assign a `Philosopher` object to a `Speaker` reference as follows:

```
current = new Philosopher();
```

This assignment is valid because a `Philosopher` is a `Speaker`. In this sense the relationship between a class and its interface is the same as the relationship between a child class and its parent. It is an is-a relationship, similar to the relationship created via inheritance. And that relationship forms the basis of the polymorphism.

The flexibility of an interface reference allows us to create polymorphic references. As we saw earlier in this chapter, using inheritance, we can create a polymorphic reference that can refer to any one of a set of objects as long as they are related by inheritance. Using interfaces, we can create similar polymorphic references among objects that implement the same interface.

For example, if we create a class called `Dog` that also implements the `Speaker` interface, it can be assigned to a `Speaker` reference variable as well. The same reference variable, in fact, can at one point refer to a `Philosopher` object and then later refer to a `Dog` object. The following lines of code illustrate this:

```
Speaker guest;
guest = new Philosopher();
guest.speak();
guest = new Dog();
guest.speak();
```

In this code, the first time the `speak` method is called, it invokes the `speak` method defined in the `Philosopher` class. The second time it is called, it invokes the `speak` method of the `Dog` class. As with polymorphic references via inheritance, it is not the type of the reference that determines which method gets invoked; it is based on the type of the object that the reference points to at the moment of invocation.

Note that when we are using an interface reference variable, we can invoke only the methods defined in the interface, even if the object it refers to has other methods to which it can respond. For example, suppose the `Philosopher` class also defined a public method called `pontificate`. The second line of the following code segment would generate a compiler error, even though the object can in fact contain the `pontificate` method:

```
Speaker special = new Philosopher();
special.pontificate();   // generates a compiler error
```

The problem is that the compiler can determine only that the object is a `Speaker`, and therefore can guarantee only that the object can respond to the `speak` and `announce` methods. Because the reference variable `special` could refer to a `Dog` object (which cannot pontificate), it does not allow the invocation. If we know in a particular situation that such an invocation is valid, we can cast the object into the appropriate reference so that the compiler will accept it, as follows:

```
((Philosopher)special).pontificate();
```

As we can with polymorphic references based in inheritance, an interface name can be used as the type of a method parameter. In such situations, any object of any class that implements the interface can be passed into the method. For example, the following method takes a `Speaker` object as a parameter. Therefore both a `Dog` object and a `Philosopher` object can be passed into it in separate invocations:

```
public void sayIt (Speaker current)
{
    current.speak();
}
```

Using a polymorphic reference as the formal parameter to a method is a powerful technique. It allows the method to control the types of parameters passed into it, yet gives it the flexibility to accept arguments of various types.

Let's now examine a particular use of polymorphism via interfaces.

Event Processing

In Chapter 6 we examined the processing of events in a Java GUI. Recall that, in order to respond to an event, we must establish a relationship between an event listener object and a particular component that may fire the event. We establish the relationship between the listener and the component it listens to by making a method call that adds the listener to the component. This situation is actually an example of polymorphism.

Suppose a class called `MyButtonListener` represents an action listener. To set up a listener to respond to a `JButton` object, we might do the following:

```
JButton button = new JButton();
button.addActionListener (new MyButtonListener());
```

Once this relationship is established, the listener will respond whenever the button fires an action event (because the user pressed it). Now think about the `addActionListener` method carefully. It is a method of the `JButton` class, which was written by someone at Sun Microsystems years ago. On the other hand, we might have written the `MyButtonListener` class today. So how can a method written years ago take a parameter whose class was just written?

The answer is polymorphism. If you examine the source code for the `addActionListener` method, you'll discover that it accepts a parameter of type `ActionListener`, the interface. Therefore, instead of accepting a parameter of only one object type, the `addActionListener` method can accept any object of any class that implements the `ActionListener` interface. All other methods that add listeners work in similar ways.

The `JButton` object doesn't know anything particular about the object that is passed to the `addActionListener` method, except for the fact that it implements the `ActionListener` interface (otherwise the code wouldn't compile). The `JButton` object simply stores the listener object and invokes its `performAction` method when the event occurs.

In Chapter 6 we mentioned that we can also create a listener by extending an adaptor class. This is another example of polymorphism via interfaces, even though the listener class is created via inheritance. Each adaptor class is written to implement the appropriate listener interface, providing empty methods for all event handlers. So by extending an adaptor class, the new listener class automatically implements the corresponding listener interface. And that is what really makes it a listener such that it can be passed to an appropriate add listener method.

Thus, no matter how a listener object is created, we are using polymorphism via interfaces to set up the relationship between a listener and the component it listens to. GUI events are a wonderful example of the power and versatility provided by polymorphism.

Polymorphism, whether implemented via inheritance or interfaces, is a fundamental object-oriented technique that we will use as appropriate throughout the remainder of this book.

Summary of Key Concepts

- A polymorphic reference can refer to different types of objects over time.

- The binding of a method invocation to its definition is performed at run time for a polymorphic reference.

- A reference variable can refer to any object created from any class related to it by inheritance.

- The type of the object, not the type of the reference, determines which version of a method is invoked.

- An interface is a collection of abstract methods and therefore cannot be instantiated.

- Inheritance can be applied to interfaces so that one interface can be derived from another.

- An interface name can be used to declare an object reference variable.

- An interface reference can refer to any object of any class that implements that interface.

- A parameter to a method can be polymorphic, giving the method flexible control of its arguments.

- Establishing the relationship between a listener and the component it listens to is accomplished using polymorphism.

Self-Review Questions

SR 9.1 What is polymorphism?

SR 9.2 How does inheritance support polymorphism?

SR 9.3 How is overriding related to polymorphism?

SR 9.4 Why is the `StaffMember` class in the `Firm` example declared as abstract?

SR 9.5 Why is the `pay` method declared in the `StaffMember` class, given that it is abstract and has no body at that level?

SR 9.6 What is the difference between a class and an interface?

SR 9.7 How do class hierarchies and interface hierarchies intersect?

SR 9.8 Describe the `Comparable` interface.

SR 9.9 How can polymorphism be accomplished using interfaces?

Exercises

EX 9.1   Draw and annotate a class hierarchy that represents various types of faculty at a university. Show what characteristics would be represented in the various classes of the hierarchy. Explain how polymorphism could play a role in the process of assigning courses to each faculty member.

EX 9.2   Draw and annotate a class hierarchy that represents various types of animals in a zoo. Show what characteristics would be represented in the various classes of the hierarchy. Explain how polymorphism could play a role in guiding the feeding of the animals.

EX 9.3   Draw and annotate a class hierarchy that represents various types of sales transactions in a store (cash, credit, etc.). Show what characteristics would be represented in the various classes of the hierarchy. Explain how polymorphism could play a role in the payment process.

EX 9.4   What would happen if the `pay` method were not defined as an abstract method in the `StaffMember` class of the `Firm` program?

EX 9.5   Create an interface called `Visible` that includes two methods: `makeVisible` and `makeInvisible`. Both methods should take no parameters and should return a boolean result. Describe how a class might implement this interface.

EX 9.6   Draw a UML class diagram that shows the relationships among the elements of Exercise 9.5.

EX 9.7   Create an interface called `VCR` that has methods that represent the standard operations on a video cassette recorder (play, stop, etc.). Define the method signatures any way you desire. Describe how a class might implement this interface.

EX 9.8   Draw a UML class diagram that shows the relationships among the elements of Exercise 9.7.

EX 9.9   Explain how a call to the `addMouseListener` method in a GUI-based program represents a polymorphic situation.

Programming Projects

PP 9.1   Modify the `Firm` example from this chapter such that it accomplishes its polymorphism using an interface called `Payable`.

PP 9.2   Modify the `Firm` example from this chapter such that all employees can be given different vacation options depending on their classification. Modify the driver program to demonstrate this new functionality.

PP 9.3   Modify the `RationalNumber` class from Chapter 5 so that it implements the `Comparable` interface. To perform the comparison, compute an equivalent floating point value from the numerator and denominator for both `RationalNumber` objects, then compare them using a tolerance value of 0.0001. Write a `main` driver to test your modifications.

PP 9.4   Create a class called `Password` that implements the `Encryptable` interface from this chapter. Then create a `main` driver that instantiates a `Secret` object and a `Password` object, using the same reference variable, and exercises their methods. Use any type of encryption desired for `Password`, other than the Caesar cipher used by `Secret`.

PP 9.5   Implement the `Speaker` interface defined in this chapter. Create three classes that implement `Speaker` in various ways. Create a driver class whose `main` method instantiates some of these objects and tests their abilities.

PP 9.6   Design a Java interface called `Priority` that includes two methods: `setPriority` and `getPriority`. The interface should define a way to establish numeric priority among a set of objects. Design and implement a class called `Task` that represents a task (such as on a to-do list) that implements the `Priority` interface. Create a driver class to exercise some `Task` objects.

PP 9.7   Modify the `Task` class from Programming Project 9.6 so that it also implements the `Comparable` interface from the Java standard class library. Implement the interface such that the tasks are ranked by priority. Create a driver class whose `main` method shows these new features of `Task` objects.

PP 9.8   Design a Java interface called `Lockable` that includes the following methods: `setKey`, `lock`, `unlock`, and `locked`. The `setKey`, `lock`, and `unlock` methods take an integer parameter that represents the key. The `setKey` method establishes the key. The `lock` and `unlock` methods lock and unlock the object, but only if the key passed in is correct. The `locked` method returns a boolean that indicates whether or not the object is locked. A `Lockable` object represents an object whose regular methods are protected: if the object is locked, the methods cannot be invoked; if it is unlocked, they can be invoked. Redesign and implement a version of the `Coin` class from Chapter 5 so that it is `Lockable`.

PP 9.9   Redesign and implement a version of the `Account` class from Chapter 5 so that it is `Lockable` as defined by Programming Project 9.8.

Answers to Self-Review Questions

SR 9.1   Polymorphism is the ability of a reference variable to refer to objects of various types at different times. A method invoked through such a reference is bound to different method definitions at different times, depending on the type of the object referenced.

SR 9.2   In Java, a reference variable declared using a parent class can be used to refer to an object of the child class. If both classes contain a method with the same signature, the parent reference can be polymorphic.

SR 9.3   When a child class overrides the definition of a parent's method, two versions of that method exist. If a polymorphic reference is used to invoke the method, the version of the method that is invoked is determined by the type of the object being referred to, not by the type of the reference variable.

SR 9.4   The `StaffMember` class is abstract because it is not intended to be instantiated. It serves as a placeholder in the inheritance hierarchy to help organize and manage the objects polymorphically.

SR 9.5   The `pay` method has no meaning at the `StaffMember` level, so it is declared as abstract. But by declaring it there we guarantee that every object of its children will have a `pay` method. This allows us to create an array of `StaffMember` objects, which is actually filled with various types of staff members, and pay each one. The details of being paid are determined by each class as appropriate.

SR 9.6   A class can be instantiated; an interface cannot. An interface can contain only abstract methods and constants. A class provides the implementation for an interface.

SR 9.7   Class hierarchies and interface hierarchies do not intersect. A class can be used to derive a new class, and an interface can be used to derive a new interface, but these two types of hierarchies do not overlap.

SR 9.8   The `Comparable` interface contains a single method called `compareTo`, which should return an integer that is less than zero, equal to zero, or greater than zero if the executing object is less than, equal to, or greater than the object to which it is being compared, respectively.

SR 9.9   An interface name can be used as the type of a reference. Such a reference variable can refer to any object of any class that implements that interface. Because all classes implement the same interface, they have methods with common signatures, which can be dynamically bound.

Exceptions

CHAPTER OBJECTIVES

- Discuss the purpose of exceptions.
- Examine exception messages and the call stack trace.
- Examine the `try-catch` statement for handling exceptions.
- Explore the concept of exception propagation.
- Describe the exception class hierarchy in the Java standard class library.
- Explore I/O exceptions and the ability to write text files.

Exception handling is an important part of an object-oriented software system. Exceptions represent problems or unusual situations that may occur in a program. Java provides various ways to handle exceptions when they occur. We explore the class hierarchy from the Java standard library used to define exceptions, as well as the ability to define our own exception objects. This chapter also discusses the use of exceptions when dealing with input and output, and presents an example that writes a text file.

10.1 Exception Handling

As we've discussed briefly in other parts of the text, problems that arise in a Java program may generate exceptions or errors. An *exception* is an object that defines an unusual or erroneous situation. An exception is thrown by a program or the run-time environment and can be caught and handled appropriately if desired. An *error* is similar to an exception except that an error generally represents an unrecoverable situation and should not be caught.

Java has a predefined set of exceptions and errors that may occur during the execution of a program. If the predefined exceptions don't suffice, a programmer may choose to design a new class that represents an exception that is specific to a particular situation.

Problem situations represented by exceptions and errors can have various kinds of root causes. Here are some examples of situations that cause exceptions to be thrown:

- attempting to divide by zero
- an array index that is out of bounds
- a specified file that could not be found
- a requested I/O operation that could not be completed normally
- attempting to follow a null reference
- attempting to execute an operation that violates some kind of security measure

These are just a few examples. There are dozens of others that address very specific situations.

As many of these examples show, an exception can represent a truly erroneous situation. But, as the name implies, they may simply represent an exceptional situation. That is, an exception may represent a situation that won't occur under usual conditions. Exception handling is set up to be an efficient way to deal with such situations, especially given that they don't happen too often.

We have several options when it comes to dealing with exceptions. A program can be designed to process an exception in one of three ways. It can:

- not handle the exception at all,
- handle the exception where it occurs, or
- handle the exception at another point in the program.

We explore each of these approaches in the following sections.

10.2 Uncaught Exceptions

If a program does not handle the exception at all, it will terminate abnormally and produce a message that describes what exception occurred and where in the code it was produced. The information in an exception message is often helpful in tracking down the cause of a problem.

Let's look at the output of an exception. The program shown in Listing 10.1 on the next page throws an `ArithmeticException` when an invalid arithmetic operation is attempted. In this case, the program attempts to divide by zero.

Because there is no code in this program to handle the exception explicitly, it terminates when the exception occurs, printing specific information about the exception. Note that the last `println` statement in the program never executes because the exception occurs first.

The first line of the exception output indicates which exception was thrown and provides some information about why it was thrown. The remaining lines are the *call stack trace*; they indicate where the exception occurred. In this case, there is only one line in the call stack trace, but there may be several depending on where the exception originated. The first trace line indicates the method, file, and line number where the exception occurred. The other trace lines, if present, indicate the methods that were called to get to the method that produced the exception. In this program, there is only one method, and it produced the exception; therefore there is only one line in the trace.

> **KEY CONCEPT**
> The messages printed when an exception is thrown provide a method call stack trace.

The call stack trace information is also available by calling methods of the exception class that is being thrown. The method `getMessage` returns a string explaining the reason the exception was thrown. The method `printStackTrace` prints the call stack trace.

10.3 The try-catch Statement

Let's now examine how we catch and handle an exception when it is thrown. The *try-catch* statement identifies a block of statements that may throw an exception. A *catch clause*, which follows a `try` block, defines how a particular kind of exception is handled. A `try` block can have several `catch` clauses associated with it. Each `catch` clause is called an *exception handler*.

When a `try` statement is executed, the statements in the `try` block are executed. If no exception is thrown during the execution of the `try` block, processing continues with the statement following the `try` statement (after all of the `catch`

LISTING 10.1

```java
//********************************************************************
//  Zero.java          Java Foundations
//
//  Demonstrates an uncaught exception.
//********************************************************************

public class Zero
{
    //-----------------------------------------------------------------
    //  Deliberately divides by zero to produce an exception.
    //-----------------------------------------------------------------
    public static void main (String[] args)
    {
        int numerator = 10;
        int denominator = 0;

        System.out.println ("Before the attempt to divide by zero.");

        System.out.println (numerator / denominator);

        System.out.println ("This text will not be printed.");
    }
}
```

OUTPUT

```
Before the attempt to divide by zero.
Exception in thread "main" java.lang.ArithmeticException: / by zero
        at Zero.main(Zero.java:19)
```

> **KEY CONCEPT**
>
> Each `catch` clause handles a particular kind of exception that may be thrown within the `try` block.

clauses). This situation is the normal execution flow and should occur most of the time.

If an exception is thrown at any point during the execution of the `try` block, control is immediately transferred to the appropriate catch handler if it is present. That is, control transfers to the first `catch` clause whose exception class corresponds to the class of the exception that was thrown. After executing the statements in the `catch` clause, control transfers to the statement after the entire `try-catch` statement.

Let's look at an example. Suppose a hypothetical company uses codes to represent its various products. A product code includes, among other information, a

A `try` statement contains a block of code followed by one or more `catch` clauses. If an exception occurs in the `try` block, the code of the corresponding `catch` clause is executed. The `finally` clause, if present, is executed no matter how the `try` block is exited.

Example:

```
try
{
    System.out.println (Integer.parseInt(numString));
}
catch (NumberFormatException exception)
{
    System.out.println ("Caught an exception.");
}
finally
{
    System.out.println ("Done.");
}
```

character in the tenth position that represents the zone from which that product was made, and a four-digit integer in positions 4 through 7 that represents the district in which it will be sold. Due to some reorganization, products from zone R are banned from being sold in districts with a designation of 2000 or higher. The program shown in Listing 10.2 on the next page reads product codes from the user and counts the number of banned codes entered.

The programming statements in the `try` block attempt to pull out the zone and district information, and then determine whether it represents a banned product code. If there is any problem extracting the zone and district information, the product code is considered to be invalid and is not processed further. For example, a `StringIndexOutOfBoundsException` could be thrown by either the `charAt` or `substring` method. Furthermore, a `NumberFormatException` will be thrown by the `parseInt` method if the `substring` method does not contain a valid integer. A particular message is printed depending on which exception is thrown. In either case, since the exception is caught and handled, processing continues normally.

LISTING 10.2

```java
//********************************************************************
//  ProductCodes.java        Java Foundations
//
//  Demonstrates the use of a try-catch block.
//********************************************************************

import java.util.Scanner;

public class ProductCodes
{
    //-----------------------------------------------------------------
    //  Counts the number of product codes that are entered with a
    //  zone of R and district greater than 2000.
    //-----------------------------------------------------------------
    public static void main (String[] args)
    {
        String code;
        char zone;
        int district, valid = 0, banned = 0;

        Scanner scan = new Scanner (System.in);

        System.out.print ("Enter product code (STOP to quit): ");
        code = scan.nextLine();

        while (!code.equals ("STOP"))
        {
            try
            {
                zone = code.charAt(9);
                district = Integer.parseInt(code.substring(3, 7));
                valid++;
                if (zone == 'R' && district > 2000)
                    banned++;
            }
            catch (StringIndexOutOfBoundsException exception)
            {
                System.out.println ("Improper code length: " + code);
            }
            catch (NumberFormatException exception)
            {
                System.out.println ("District is not numeric: " + code);
            }
```

```
LISTING  10.2      continued

        System.out.print ("Enter product code (STOP to quit): ");
        code = scan.nextLine();
    }

    System.out.println ("# of valid codes entered: " + valid);
    System.out.println ("# of banned codes entered: " + banned);
  }
}
```

OUTPUT

```
Enter product code (STOP to quit): TRV2475A5R-14
Enter product code (STOP to quit): TRD1704A7R-12
Enter product code (STOP to quit): TRL2k74A5R-11
District is not numeric: TRL2k74A5R-11
Enter product code (STOP to quit): TRQ2949A6M-04
Enter product code (STOP to quit): TRV2105A2
Improper code length: TRV2105A2
Enter product code (STOP to quit): TRQ2778A7R-19
Enter product code (STOP to quit): STOP
# of valid codes entered: 4
# of banned codes entered: 2
```

Note that, for each code examined, the integer variable `valid` is incremented only if no exception is thrown. If an exception is thrown, control transfers immediately to the appropriate `catch` clause. Likewise, the zone and district are tested by the `if` statement only if no exception is thrown.

The `finally` Clause

A try-catch statement can have an optional *finally clause*. The `finally` clause defines a section of code that is executed no matter how the `try` block is exited. Most often, a `finally` clause is used to manage resources or to guarantee that particular parts of an algorithm are executed.

If no exception is generated, the statements in the `finally` clause are executed after the `try` block is complete. If an exception is generated in the `try` block, control first transfers to the appropriate `catch` clause. After executing the exception-handling code, control transfers to the `finally` clause and its

> **KEY CONCEPT**
>
> The `finally` clause is executed whether the `try` block is exited normally or because of a thrown exception.

statements are executed. A `finally` clause, if present, must be listed after the `catch` clauses.

Note that a `try` block does not need to have a `catch` clause at all. If there are no `catch` clauses, a `finally` clause may be used by itself if that is appropriate for the situation.

10.4 Exception Propagation

We can design our software so that an exception is caught and handled at an outer level in the method calling hierarchy. If an exception is not caught and handled in the method where it occurs, control is immediately returned to the method that invoked the method that produced the exception. If it isn't caught there, control returns to the method that called it, and so on. This process is called *exception propagation*.

> **KEY CONCEPT**
>
> If an exception is not caught and handled where it occurs, it is propagated to the calling method.

An exception will be propagated until it is caught and handled or until it is passed out of the `main` method, which causes the program to terminate and produces an exception message. To catch an exception at any level, the method that produces the exception must be invoked inside a `try` block that has `catch` clauses to handle it.

The `Propagation` program shown in Listing 10.3 succinctly demonstrates the process of exception propagation. The `main` method invokes method `level1` in the `ExceptionScope` class (see Listing 10.4 on page 442), which invokes `level2`, which invokes `level3`, which produces an exception. Method `level3` does not catch and handle the exception, so control is transferred back to `level2`. The `level2` method does not catch and handle the exception either, so control is transferred back to `level1`. Because the invocation of `level2` is made inside a `try` block (in method `level1`), the exception is caught and handled at that point.

Note that the program output does not include the messages indicating that the methods `level3` and `level2` are ending. These `println` statements are never executed because an exception occurred and had not yet been caught. However, after method `level1` handles the exception, processing continues normally from that point, printing the messages indicating that method `level1` and the program are ending.

> **KEY CONCEPT**
>
> A programmer must carefully consider how and where exceptions should be handled, if at all.

Note also that the `catch` clause that handles the exception uses the `getMessage` and `printStackTrace` methods to output that information. The stack trace shows the methods that were called when the exception occurred.

A programmer must pick the most appropriate level at which to catch and handle an exception. There is no single best answer as

LISTING 10.3

```java
//********************************************************************
//  Propagation.java       Java Foundations
//
//  Demonstrates exception propagation.
//********************************************************************

public class Propagation
{
   //-----------------------------------------------------------------
   //  Invokes the level1 method to begin the exception demonstration.
   //-----------------------------------------------------------------
   static public void main (String[] args)
   {
      ExceptionScope demo = new ExceptionScope();

      System.out.println("Program beginning.");
      demo.level1();
      System.out.println("Program ending.");
   }
}
```

OUTPUT

```
Program beginning.
Level 1 beginning.
Level 2 beginning.
Level 3 beginning.

The exception message is: / by zero

The call stack trace:
java.lang.ArithmeticException: / by zero
        at ExceptionScope.level3(ExceptionScope.java:54)
        at ExceptionScope.level2(ExceptionScope.java:41)
        at ExceptionScope.level1(ExceptionScope.java:18)
        at Propagation.main(Propagation.java:17)

Level 1 ending.
Program ending.
```

LISTING 10.4

```java
//********************************************************************
//  ExceptionScope.java        Java Foundations
//
//  Demonstrates exception propagation.
//********************************************************************

public class ExceptionScope
{
   //-----------------------------------------------------------------
   //  Catches and handles the exception that is thrown in level3.
   //-----------------------------------------------------------------
   public void level1()
   {
      System.out.println("Level 1 beginning.");

      try
      {
         level2();
      }
      catch (ArithmeticException problem)
      {
         System.out.println ();
         System.out.println ("The exception message is: " +
                             problem.getMessage());
         System.out.println ();
         System.out.println ("The call stack trace:");
         problem.printStackTrace();
         System.out.println ();
      }

      System.out.println("Level 1 ending.");
   }

   //-----------------------------------------------------------------
   //  Serves as an intermediate level. The exception propagates
   //  through this method back to level1.
   //-----------------------------------------------------------------
   public void level2()
   {
      System.out.println("Level 2 beginning.");
      level3 ();
      System.out.println("Level 2 ending.");
   }
```

LISTING 10.4   *continued*

```
//----------------------------------------------------------------
//  Performs a calculation to produce an exception.  It is not
//  caught and handled at this level.
//----------------------------------------------------------------
public void level3 ()
{
   int numerator = 10, denominator = 0;

   System.out.println("Level 3 beginning.");
   int result = numerator / denominator;
   System.out.println("Level 3 ending.");
}
}
```

to how to do this. It depends on the situation and the design of the system. Sometimes the right approach will be not to catch an exception at all and let the program terminate.

10.5 The Exception Class Hierarchy

The classes that define various exceptions are related by inheritance, creating a class hierarchy that is shown in part in Figure 10.1 on the next page.

The Throwable class is the parent of both the Error class and the Exception class. Many types of exceptions are derived from the Exception class, and these classes also have many children. Though these high-level classes are defined in the java.lang package, many child classes that define specific exceptions are part of other packages. Inheritance relationships can span package boundaries.

We can define our own exceptions by deriving a new class from Exception or one of its descendants. The class we choose as the parent depends on what situation or condition the new exception represents.

The program in Listing 10.5 on page 445 instantiates an exception object and throws it. The exception is created from the OutOfRangeException class, which is shown in Listing 10.6 on page 446. This exception is not part of the Java standard class library. It was created to represent the situation in which a value is outside a particular valid range.

> **KEY CONCEPT**
> A new exception is defined by deriving a new class from the Exception class or one of its descendants.

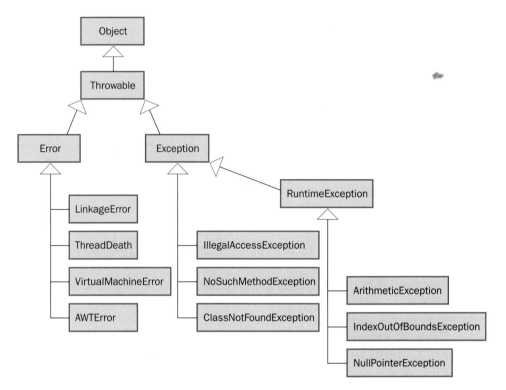

FIGURE 10.1 Part of the `Error` and `Exception` class hierarchy

After reading in an input value, the `main` method evaluates it to see whether it is in the valid range. If not, the *throw statement* is executed. A `throw` statement is used to begin exception propagation. Because the `main` method does not catch and handle the exception, the program will terminate if the exception is thrown, printing the message associated with the exception.

We created the `OutOfRangeException` class by extending the Exception class. Often, a new exception is nothing more than what you see in this example: an extension of some existing exception class that stores a particular message describing the situation it represents. The important point is that the class is ultimately a descendant of the `Exception` class and the `Throwable` class, which gives it the ability to be thrown using a `throw` statement.

LISTING 10.5

```java
//********************************************************************
//  CreatingExceptions.java        Java Foundations
//
//  Demonstrates the ability to define an exception via inheritance.
//********************************************************************

import java.util.Scanner;

public class CreatingExceptions
{
    //----------------------------------------------------------------
    //  Creates an exception object and possibly throws it.
    //----------------------------------------------------------------
    public static void main (String[] args) throws OutOfRangeException
    {
        final int MIN = 25, MAX = 40;

        Scanner scan = new Scanner (System.in);

        OutOfRangeException problem =
            new OutOfRangeException ("Input value is out of range.");

        System.out.print ("Enter an integer value between " + MIN +
                          " and " + MAX + ", inclusive: ");
        int value = scan.nextInt();

        //  Determine if the exception should be thrown
        if (value < MIN || value > MAX)
            throw problem;

        System.out.println ("End of main method.");  // may never reach
    }
}
```

OUTPUT

```
Enter an integer value between 25 and 40, inclusive: 69
Exception in thread "main" OutOfRangeException:
        Input value is out of range.
        at CreatingExceptions.main(CreatingExceptions.java:20)
```

LISTING 10.6

```java
//********************************************************************
//  OutOfRangeException.java       Java Foundations
//
//  Represents an exceptional condition in which a value is out of
//  some particular range.
//********************************************************************

public class OutOfRangeException extends Exception
{
   //-----------------------------------------------------------------
   //  Sets up the exception object with a particular message.
   //-----------------------------------------------------------------
   OutOfRangeException (String message)
   {
      super (message);
   }
}
```

The type of situation handled by this program, in which a value is out of range, does not need to be represented as an exception. We've previously handled such situations using conditionals or loops alone. Whether you handle a situation using an exception or take care of it in the normal flow of your program is an important design decision.

Checked and Unchecked Exceptions

Some exceptions are checked, whereas others are unchecked. A *checked exception* must either be caught by a method or be listed in the *throws clause* of any method that may throw or propagate it. A throws clause is appended to the header of a method definition to formally acknowledge that the method will throw or propagate a particular exception if it occurs. An *unchecked* exception requires no throws clause.

The only unchecked exceptions in Java are objects of type RuntimeException or any of its descendants. All other exceptions are considered checked exceptions. The main method of the CreatingExceptions program has a throws clause, indicating that it may throw an OutOfRangeException. This throws clause is required because the `OutOfRangeException` was derived from the `Exception` class, making it a checked exception.

10.6 I/O Exceptions

Processing input and output is a task that often produces tenuous situations, given that it relies on external resources such as user data and files. These resources can have various problems that lead to exceptions being thrown. Let's explore some I/O issues and the problems that may arise.

A *stream* is an ordered sequence of bytes. The term stream comes from the analogy that as we read and write information, the data flows from a source to a destination (or *sink*) as water flows down a stream. The source of the information is like a spring filling the stream, and the destination is like a cave into which the stream flows.

> **KEY CONCEPT**
>
> A stream is a sequential sequence of bytes; it can be used as a source of input or a destination for output.

In a program, we treat a stream as either an *input stream*, from which we read information, or as an *output stream*, to which we write information. A program can deal with multiple input and output streams at one time. A particular store of data, such as a file, can serve either as an input stream or as an output stream to a program, but it generally cannot be both at the same time.

There are three streams that are referred to as the standard I/O streams. They are listed in Figure 10.2. The `System` class contains three object reference variables (`in`, `out`, and `err`) that represent the three standard I/O streams. These references are declared as both `public` and `static`, which allows them to be accessed directly through the System class.

> **KEY CONCEPT**
>
> Three public reference variables in the `System` class represent the standard I/O streams.

We've been using the standard output stream, with calls to `System.out. prinln` for instance, in examples throughout this book. We've also used the standard input stream to create a `Scanner` object when we want to process input read interactively from the user. The `Scanner` class manages the input read

Standard I/O Stream	Description
`System.in`	Standard input stream.
`System.out`	Standard output stream.
`System.err`	Standard error stream (output for error messages).

FIGURE 10.2 Standard I/O streams

from the standard input stream in various ways that makes our programming tasks easier. It also processes various I/O exceptions internally, producing an InputMismatchException when needed.

The standard I/O streams, by default, represent particular I/O devices. System.in typically represents keyboard input, whereas System.out and System.err typically represent a particular window on the monitor screen. The System.out and System.err streams write output to the same window by default (usually the one in which the program was executed), though they could be set up to write to different places. The System.err stream is usually where error messages are sent.

In addition to the standard input streams, the java.io package of the Java standard class library provides many classes that let us define streams with particular characteristics. Some of the classes deal with files, others with memory, and others with strings. Some classes assume that the data they handle consists of characters, whereas others assume the data consists of raw bytes of binary information. Some classes provide the means to manipulate the data in the stream in some way, such as buffering the information or numbering it. By combining classes in appropriate ways, we can create objects that represent a stream of information that has the exact characteristics we want for a particular situation.

> **KEY CONCEPT**
>
> The Java class library contains many classes for defining I/O streams with various characteristics.

The broad topic of Java I/O, and the sheer number of classes in the java.io package, prohibits us from covering it in detail in this book. Our focus for the moment is on I/O exceptions.

Many operations performed by I/O classes can potentially throw an IOException. The IOException class is the parent of several exception classes that represent problems when trying to perform I/O.

An IOException is a checked exception. As described earlier in this chapter, that means that either the exception must be caught or all methods that propagate it must list it in a throws clause of the method header.

Because I/O often deals with external resources, many problems can arise in programs that attempt to perform I/O operations. For example, a file from which we want to read might not exist; when we attempt to open the file, an exception will be thrown because that file can't be found. In general, we should try to design programs to be as robust as possible when dealing with potential problems.

We've seen in previous examples how we can use the Scanner class to read and process input read from a text file. Now let's explore an example that writes data to a text output file. Writing output to a text file requires simply that we use the appropriate classes to create the output stream, then call the appropriate methods to write the data.

Suppose we want to test a program we are writing, but don't have the real data available. We could write a program that generates a test data file that contains random values. The program shown in Listing 10.7 generates a file that contains random integer values within a particular range. It also writes one line of standard output, confirming that the data file has been written.

The FileWriter class represents a text output file, but has minimal method support for manipulating data. The PrintWriter class provides print and println methods similar to the standard I/O PrintStream class.

Although we do not need to do so for the program to work, we have added a layer in the file stream configuration to include a BufferedWriter. This addition simply gives the output stream buffering capabilities, which makes the processing more efficient. While buffering is not crucial in this situation, it is usually a good idea when writing text files.

Note that in the TestData program, we have eliminated explicit exception handling. That is, if something goes wrong, we simply allow the program to terminate instead of specifically catching and handling the problem. Because all IOExceptions are checked exceptions, we must include the throws clause on the

LISTING 10.7

```java
//********************************************************************
//  TestData.java       Java Foundations
//
//  Demonstrates I/O exceptions and the use of a character file
//  output stream.
//********************************************************************

import java.util.Random;
import java.io.*;

public class TestData
{
    //-----------------------------------------------------------------
    //  Creates a file of test data that consists of ten lines each
    //  containing ten integer values in the range 10 to 99.
    //-----------------------------------------------------------------
    public static void main (String[] args) throws IOException
    {
        final int MAX = 10;
```

LISTING 10.7 *continued*

```
        int value;
        String file = "test.dat";

        Random rand = new Random();

        FileWriter fw = new FileWriter (file);
        BufferedWriter bw = new BufferedWriter (fw);
        PrintWriter outFile = new PrintWriter (bw);

        for (int line=1; line <= MAX; line++)
        {
           for (int num=1; num <= MAX; num++)
           {
              value = rand.nextInt (90) + 10;
              outFile.print (value + "   ");
           }
           outFile.println ();
        }

        outFile.close();
        System.out.println ("Output file has been created: " + file);
   }
}
```

OUTPUT

```
Output file has been created: test.dat
```

method header to indicate that they may be thrown. For each program, we must carefully consider how best to handle the exceptions that may be thrown. This requirement is especially important when dealing with I/O, which is fraught with potential problems that cannot always be foreseen.

The `TestData` program uses nested `for` loops to compute random values and write them to the output file. After all values are printed, the file is closed. Output files must be closed explicitly to ensure that the data is retained. In general, it is good practice to close all file streams explicitly when they are no longer needed.

> **KEY CONCEPT**
>
> Output file streams should be explicitly closed or they may not correctly retain the data written to them.

The data that is contained in the file `test.dat` after the `TestData` program is run might look like this:

```
85   90   93   15   82   79   52   71   70   98
74   57   41   66   22   16   67   65   24   84
86   61   91   79   18   81   64   41   68   81
98   47   28   40   69   10   85   82   64   41
23   61   27   10   59   89   88   26   24   76
33   89   73   36   54   91   42   73   95   58
19   41   18   14   63   80   96   30   17   28
24   37   40   64   94   23   98   10   78   50
89   28   64   54   59   23   61   15   80   88
51   28   44   48   73   21   41   52   35   38
```

Summary of Key Concepts

- Errors and exceptions are objects that represent unusual or invalid processing.

- The messages printed when an exception is thrown provide a method call stack trace.

- Each `catch` clause handles a particular kind of exception that may be thrown within the `try` block.

- The `finally` clause is executed whether the `try` block is exited normally or because of a thrown exception.

- If an exception is not caught and handled where it occurs, it is propagated to the calling method.

- A programmer must carefully consider how and where exceptions should be handled, if at all.

- A new exception is defined by deriving a new class from the `Exception` class or one of its descendants.

- The `throws` clause on a method header must be included for checked exceptions that are not caught and handled in the method.

- A stream is a sequential sequence of bytes; it can be used as a source of input or a destination for output.

- Three public reference variables in the `System` class represent the standard I/O streams.

- The Java class library contains many classes for defining I/O streams with various characteristics.

- Output file streams should be explicitly closed or they may not correctly retain the data written to them.

Self-Review Questions

SR 10.1   In what ways might a thrown exception be handled?

SR 10.2   What is a `catch` phrase?

SR 10.3   What happens if an exception is not caught?

SR 10.4   What is a `finally` clause?

SR 10.5   What is a checked exception?

SR 10.6   What is a stream?

SR 10.7   What are the standard I/O streams?

Exercises

EX 10.1   Create a UML class diagram for the `ProductCodes` program.

EX 10.2   Describe the output for the `ProductCodes` program if a `finally` clause were added to the `try` statement that printed the string `"Got here!"`.

EX 10.3   What would happen if the `try` statement were removed from the `level1` method of the `ExceptionScope` class in the `Propagation` program?

EX 10.4   What would happen if the `try` statement described in the previous exercise were moved to the `level2` method?

EX 10.5   What happens when the `Exception` class is used in a `catch` clause to catch an exception?

EX 10.6   Look up the following exception classes in the online Java API documentation and describe their purpose:

a. `ArithmeticException`

b. `NullPointerException`

c. `NumberFormatException`

d. `PatternSyntaxException`

EX 10.7   Describe the output file used in the `TestData` program in terms of the classes that were used to create it.

Programming Projects

PP 10.1   Design and implement a program that reads a series of 10 integers from the user and prints their average. Read each input value as a string, and then attempt to convert it to an integer using the `Integer.parseInt` method. If this process throws a `NumberFormatException` (meaning that the input is not a valid number), print an appropriate error message and prompt for the number again. Continue reading values until 10 valid integers have been entered.

PP 10.2   Design and implement a program that creates an exception class called `StringTooLongException`, designed to be thrown when a string is discovered that has too many characters in it. In the `main` driver of the program, read strings from the user until the user enters `"DONE"`. If a string is entered that has too many characters (say 20), throw the exception. Allow the thrown exception to terminate the program.

PP 10.3   Modify the solution to programming project 10.2 such that it catches and handles the exception if it is thrown. Handle the exception by printing an appropriate message, and then continue processing more strings.

PP 10.4   Design and implement a program that creates an exception class called InvalidDocumentCodeException, designed to be thrown when an improper designation for a document is encountered during processing. Suppose in a particular business all documents are given a two-character designation starting with U, C, or P, standing for unclassified, confidential, or proprietary. If a document designation is encountered that doesn't fit that description, the exception is thrown. Create a driver program to test the exception, allowing it to terminate the program.

PP 10.5   Modify the solution to programming project 10.4 such that it catches and handles the exception if it is thrown. Handle the exception by printing an appropriate message, and then continue processing.

PP 10.6   Write a program that reads strings from the user and writes them to an output file called userStrings.dat. Terminate processing when the user enters the string "DONE". Do not write the sentinel string to the output file.

PP 10.7   Suppose a library is processing an input file containing the titles of books in order to remove duplicates. Write a program that reads all of the titles from an input file called bookTitles.inp and writes them to an output file called noDuplicates.out. When complete, the output file should contain all unique titles found in the input file.

Answers to Self-Review Questions

SR 10.1   A thrown exception can be handled in one of three ways: it can be ignored, which will cause a program to terminate, it can be handled where it occurs using a try statement, or it can be caught and handled higher in the method calling hierarchy.

SR 10.2   A catch phrase of a try statement defines the code that will handle a particular type of exception.

SR 10.3   If an exception is not caught immediately when thrown, it be-
            gins to propagate up through the methods that were called to
            get to the point where it was generated. The exception can be
            caught and handled at any point during that propagation. If it
            propagates out of the `main` method, the program terminates.

SR 10.4   The `finally` clause of a `try-catch` statement is executed no
            matter how the `try` block is exited. If no exception is thrown,
            the `finally` clause is executed after the `try` block is complete.
            If an exception is thrown, the appropriate `catch` clause is exe-
            cuted, then the `finally` clause is executed.

SR 10.5   A checked exception is an exception that must be either (1) caught
            and handled or (2) listed in the `throws` clause of any method
            that may throw or propagate it. This establishes a set of excep-
            tions that must be formally acknowledged in the program one
            way or another. Unchecked exceptions can be ignored com-
            pletely in the code if desired.

SR 10.6   A stream is a sequential series of bytes that serves as a source
            of input or a destination for output.

SR 10.7   The standard I/O streams in Java are `System.in`, the standard
            input stream; `System.out`, the standard output stream; and
            `System.err`, the standard error stream. Usually, standard input
            comes from the keyboard and standard output and errors go to
            a default window on the monitor screen.

Recursion

CHAPTER OBJECTIVES

- Explain the underlying concepts of recursion.
- Explore examples that promote recursive thinking.
- Define infinite recursion and discuss ways to avoid it.
- Explain when recursion should and should not be used.
- Examine recursive methods and unravel their processing steps.
- Demonstrate the use of recursion to solve problems.

Recursion is a powerful programming technique that provides elegant solutions to certain problems. This chapter provides an introduction to recursive processing. It contains an explanation of the basic concepts underlying recursion and then explores the use of recursion in programming.

11.1 Recursive Thinking

We know that one method can call another method to help it accomplish its goal. Similarly, a method can call itself as well. *Recursion* is a programming technique in which a method calls itself in order to fulfill its purpose.

Before we get into the details of how we use recursion in a program, we need to explore the general concept of recursion first. The ability to think recursively is essential to being able to use recursion as a programming technique.

In general, recursion is the process of defining something in terms of itself. For example, consider the following definition of the word **decoration**:

decoration: n. any ornament or adornment used to decorate something

The word *decorate* is used to define the word *decoration*. You may recall your grade school teacher telling you to avoid such recursive definitions when explaining the meaning of a word. However, in many situations, recursion is an appropriate way to express an idea or definition. For example, suppose we wanted to formally define a list of one or more numbers, separated by commas. Such a list can be defined recursively as either a number or as a number followed by a comma followed by a list. This definition can be expressed as follows:

> A LIST is a: number
>
>   or a: number   comma   LIST

This recursive definition of a list defines each of the following lists of numbers:

```
24, 88, 40, 37
96, 43
14, 64, 21, 69, 32, 93, 47, 81, 28, 45, 81, 52, 69
70
```

No matter how long a list is, the recursive definition describes it. A list of one element, such as in the last example, is defined completely by the first (non-recursive) part of the definition. For any list longer than one element, the recursive part of the definition (the part which refers to itself) is used as many times as necessary until the last element is reached. The last element in the list is always defined by the non-recursive part of the definition. Figure 11.1 shows how one particular list of numbers corresponds to the recursive definition of LIST.

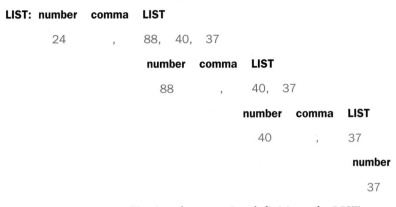

FIGURE 11.1 Tracing the recursive definition of a LIST

Infinite Recursion

Note that the definition of a list contains one option that is recursive and one option that is not. The part of the definition that is not recursive is called the *base case*. If all options had a recursive component, the recursion would never end. For example, if the definition of LIST was simply "a number followed by a comma followed by a LIST," then no list could ever end. This problem is called *infinite recursion*. It is similar to an infinite loop except that the "loop" occurs in the definition itself.

As in the infinite loop problem, a programmer must be careful to design algorithms so that they avoid infinite recursion. Any recursive definition must have a base case that does not result in a further recursion. The base case of the LIST definition is a single number that is not followed by anything. In other words, when the last number in the list is reached, the base case option terminates the recursion.

> **KEY CONCEPT**
> Any recursive definition must have a non-recursive part, called the base case, which permits the recursion to eventually end.

Recursion in Math

Let's look at an example of recursion in mathematics. The value referred to as N! (pronounced N *factorial*) is defined for any positive integer N as the product of all integers between 1 and N inclusive. Therefore, 3! is defined as:

```
3! = 3*2*1 = 6
```

and 5! is defined as:

```
5! = 5*4*3*2*1 = 120.
```

Mathematical formulas are often expressed recursively. The definition of N! can be expressed recursively as:

```
1! = 1
N! = N * (N-1)! for N > 1
```

The base case of this definition is 1!, which is defined as 1. All other values of N! (for $N > 1$) are defined recursively as N times the value (N–1)!. The recursion is that the factorial function is defined in terms of the factorial function.

Using this definition, 50! is equal to 50 * 49!. And 49! is equal to 49 * 48!. And 48! is equal to 48 * 47!. This process continues until we get to the base case of 1. Because N! is defined only for positive integers, this definition is complete and will always conclude with the base case.

The next section describes how recursion is accomplished in programs.

11.2 Recursive Programming

Let's use a simple mathematical operation to demonstrate the concept of recursive programming. Consider the process of summing the values between 1 and N inclusive, where N is any positive integer. The sum of the values from 1 to N can be expressed as N plus the sum of the values from 1 to N–1. That sum can be expressed similarly, as shown in Figure 11.2.

For example, the sum of the values between 1 and 20 is equal to 20 plus the sum of the values between 1 and 19. Continuing this approach, the sum of the values between 1 and 19 is equal to 19 plus the sum of the values between 1 and 18. This may sound like a strange way to think about this problem, but it

$$\sum_{i=1}^{N} i = N + \sum_{i=1}^{N-1} i = N + N - 1 + \sum_{i=1}^{N-2} i$$

$$= N + N - 1 + N - 2 + \sum_{i=1}^{N-3} i$$

$$\vdots$$

$$= N + N - 1 + N - 2 + \cdots + 2 + 1$$

FIGURE 11.2 The sum of the numbers 1 through N, defined recursively is a straightforward example that can be used to demonstrate how recursion is programmed.

In Java, as in many other programming languages, a method can call itself. Each call to the method creates a new environment in which to work. That is, all local variables and parameters are newly defined with their own unique data space every time the method is called. Each parameter is given an initial value based on the new call. Each time a method terminates, processing returns to the method that called it (which may be an earlier invocation of the same method). These rules are no different from those governing any "regular" method invocation.

A recursive solution to the summation problem is defined by the following recursive method called sum:

```
// This method returns the sum of 1 to num
public int sum (int num)
{
    int result;
    if (num == 1)
        result = 1;
    else
        result = num + sum (num-1);
    return result;
}
```

This method embodies our recursive definition that the sum of the numbers between 1 and N is equal to N plus the sum of the numbers between 1 and N–1. The sum method is recursive because sum calls itself. The parameter passed to sum is decremented each time sum is called until it reaches the base case of 1. Recursive methods usually contain an if-else statement, with one of the branches representing the base case.

Suppose the main method calls sum, passing it an initial value of 1, which is stored in the parameter num. Since num is equal to 1, the result of 1 is returned to main and no recursion occurs.

Now let's trace the execution of the sum method when it is passed an initial value of 2. Since num does not equal 1, sum is called again with an argument of num-1, or 1. This is a new call to the method sum, with a new parameter num and a new local variable result. Since this num is equal to 1 in this invocation, the result of 1 is returned without further recursive calls. Control returns to the first version of sum that was invoked. The return value of 1 is added to the initial value of num in that call to sum, which is 2. Therefore, result is assigned the value 3, which is returned to the main method. The method called from main correctly calculates the sum of the integers from 1 to 2 and returns the result of 3.

The base case in the summation example is when N equals 1, at which point no further recursive calls are made. The recursion begins to fold back into the earlier versions of the sum method, returning the appropriate value each time. Each return value contributes to the computation of the sum at the higher level. Without the base case, infinite recursion would result. Each call to a method requires additional memory space; therefore infinite recursion often results in a run-time error indicating that memory has been exhausted.

Trace the sum function with different initial values of num until this processing becomes familiar. Figure 11.3 illustrates the recursive calls when main invokes sum to determine the sum of the integers from 1 to 4. Each box represents a copy of the method as it is invoked, indicating the allocation of space to store the formal parameters and any local variables. Invocations are shown as solid lines, and returns as dotted lines. The return value result is shown at each step. The recursive path is followed completely until the base case is reached; the calls then begin to return their result up through the chain.

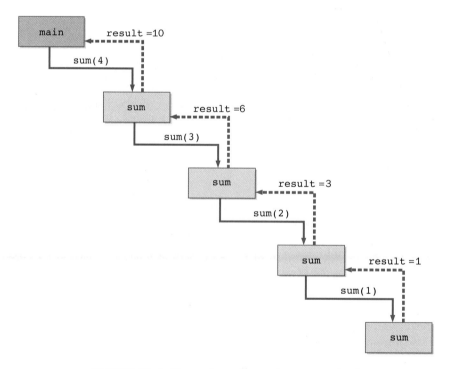

FIGURE 11.3 Recursive calls to the sum method

Recursion vs. Iteration

Of course, there is a non-recursive solution to the summation problem we just explored. One way to compute the sum of the numbers between 1 and num inclusive in an iterative manner is as follows:

```
sum = 0;
for (int number = 1; number <= num; number++)
  sum += number;
```

This solution is certainly more straightforward than the recursive version. We used the summation problem to demonstrate recursion because it is simple, not because you would use recursion to solve it under normal conditions. Recursion has the overhead of multiple method invocations and, in this case, presents a more complicated solution than its iterative counterpart.

> **KEY CONCEPT**
> Recursion is the most elegant and appropriate way to solve some problems, but for others it is less intuitive than an iterative solution.

A programmer must learn when to use recursion and when not to use it. Determining which approach is best depends on the problem being solved. All problems can be solved in an iterative manner, but in some cases the iterative version is much more complicated. Recursion, for some problems, allows us to create relatively short, elegant programs.

Direct vs. Indirect Recursion

Direct recursion occurs when a method invokes itself, such as when sum calls sum. *Indirect recursion* occurs when a method invokes another method, eventually resulting in the original method being invoked again. For example, if method m1 invokes method m2, and m2 invokes method m1, we can say that m1 is indirectly recursive. The amount of indirection could be several levels deep, as when m1 invokes m2, which invokes m3, which invokes m4, which invokes m1. Figure 11.4

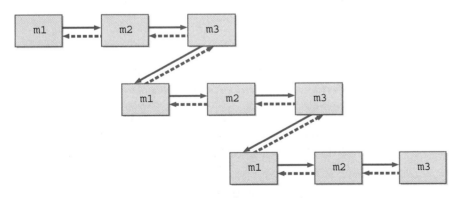

FIGURE 11.4 Indirect recursion

depicts a situation with indirect recursion. Method invocations are shown with solid lines, and returns are shown with dotted lines. The entire invocation path is followed, and then the recursion unravels following the return path.

Indirect recursion requires all of the same attention to base cases that direct recursion requires. Furthermore, indirect recursion can be more difficult to trace because of the intervening method calls. Therefore extra care is warranted when designing or evaluating indirectly recursive methods. Ensure that the indirection is truly necessary and clearly explained in the program's documentation.

11.3 Using Recursion

The following sections describe problems that we then solve using recursion. For each one, we examine exactly how recursion plays a role in the solution and how a base case is used to terminate the recursion. As you examine these examples, consider how complicated a non-recursive solution for each problem would be.

Traversing a Maze

Solving a maze involves a great deal of trial and error: following a path, backtracking when you cannot go farther, and then trying other previously untried options. Such activities often are handled nicely using recursion. The program shown in Listing 11.1 creates a Maze object and attempts to traverse it.

The Maze class shown in Listing 11.2 on page 456 uses a two-dimensional array of integers to represent the maze. The goal is to move from the top-left corner (the entry point) to the bottom-right corner (the exit point). Initially, a 1 indicates a clear path and a 0 indicates a blocked path. As the maze is solved, these array elements are changed to other values to indicate attempted paths and ultimately a successful path through the maze if one exists.

LISTING 11.1

```
//********************************************************************
//  MazeSearch.java          Java Foundations
//
//  Demonstrates recursion by solving a maze traversal.
//********************************************************************

public class MazeSearch
{
```

LISTING 11.1   *continued*

```java
//------------------------------------------------------------------
//  Creates a new maze, prints its original form, attempts to
//  solve it, and prints out its final form.
//------------------------------------------------------------------
public static void main (String[] args)
{
   Maze labyrinth = new Maze();

   System.out.println (labyrinth);

   if (labyrinth.traverse (0, 0))
      System.out.println ("The maze was successfully traversed!");
   else
      System.out.println ("There is no possible path.");

   System.out.println (labyrinth);
}
}
```

OUTPUT

```
1110110001111
1011101111001
0000101010100
1110111010111
1010000111001
1011111101111
1000000000000
1111111111111

The maze was successfully traversed!

7770110001111
3077707771001
0000707070300
7770777070333
7070000773003
7077777703333
7000000000000
777777777777
```

LISTING 11.2

```java
//********************************************************************
//  Maze.java         Java Foundations
//
//  Represents a maze of characters. The goal is to get from the
//  top left corner to the bottom right, following a path of 1's.
//********************************************************************

public class Maze
{
    private final int TRIED = 3;
    private final int PATH = 7;

    private int[][] grid = { {1,1,1,0,1,1,0,0,0,1,1,1,1},
                             {1,0,1,1,1,0,1,1,1,1,0,0,1},
                             {0,0,0,0,1,0,1,0,1,0,1,0,0},
                             {1,1,1,0,1,1,1,0,1,0,1,1,1},
                             {1,0,1,0,0,0,0,1,1,1,0,0,1},
                             {1,0,1,1,1,1,1,1,1,0,1,1,1,1},
                             {1,0,0,0,0,0,0,0,0,0,0,0,0},
                             {1,1,1,1,1,1,1,1,1,1,1,1,1} };

    //-----------------------------------------------------------------
    //  Attempts to recursively traverse the maze. Inserts special
    //  characters indicating locations that have been tried and that
    //  eventually become part of the solution.
    //-----------------------------------------------------------------
    public boolean traverse (int row, int column)
    {
        boolean done = false;

        if (valid (row, column))
        {
            grid[row][column] = TRIED;  // this cell has been tried

            if (row == grid.length-1 && column == grid[0].length-1)
                done = true;  // the maze is solved
            else
            {
                done = traverse (row+1, column);     // down
                if (!done)
                    done = traverse (row, column+1);  // right
                if (!done)
                    done = traverse (row-1, column);  // up
```

```
LISTING 11.2    continued

            if (!done)
            done = traverse (row, column-1);  // left
     }

     if (done)   // this location is part of the final path
        grid[row][column] = PATH;
     }

     return done;
}

//---------------------------------------------------------------
//  Determines if a specific location is valid.
//---------------------------------------------------------------
private boolean valid (int row, int column)
{
   boolean result = false;

   // check if cell is in the bounds of the matrix
   if (row >= 0 && row < grid.length && column >= 0 &&
      column < grid[row].length)

      // check if cell is not blocked and not previously tried
      if (grid[row][column] == 1)
         result = true;

   return result;
}

//---------------------------------------------------------------
//  Returns a string representation of the maze.
//---------------------------------------------------------------
public String toString ()
{
   String result = "\n";
   for (int row = 0; row < grid.length; row++)
   {
      for (int column=0; column < grid[row].length; column++)
         result += grid[row][column] + "";
      result += "\n";
   }

   return result;
}
}
```

The only valid moves through the maze are in the four primary directions: down, right, up, and left. No diagonal moves are allowed. In this example, the maze is 8 rows by 13 columns, although the code is designed to handle a maze of any size.

Let's think this through recursively. The maze can be traversed successfully if it can be traversed successfully from position (0, 0). Therefore, the maze can be traversed successfully if it can be traversed successfully from any positions adjacent to (0, 0), namely position (1, 0), position (0, 1), position (–1, 0), or position (0, –1). Picking a potential next step, say (1, 0), we find ourselves in the same type of situation we were in before. To successfully traverse the maze from the new current position, we must successfully traverse it from an adjacent position. At any point, some of the adjacent positions may be invalid, may be blocked, or may represent a possible successful path. We can continue this process recursively from each new position. If the base case, position (7, 12), is reached, the maze has been traversed successfully.

The recursive method in the `Maze` class is called `traverse`. It returns a boolean value that indicates whether a solution was found. First the method determines whether a move to the specified row and column is valid. A move is considered valid if it stays within the grid boundaries and if the grid contains a 1 in that location, indicating that a move in that direction is not blocked. The initial call to `traverse` passes in the upper-left location (0, 0).

If the move is valid, the grid entry is changed from a 1 to a 3, marking this location as visited so that later we don't retrace our steps. The `traverse` method then determines whether the maze has been completed by having reached the bottom-right location. Therefore, there are actually three possibilities of the base case for this problem that will terminate any particular recursive path:

- an invalid move because the move is out of bounds
- an invalid move because the move has been tried before
- a move that arrives at the final location

If the current location is not the bottom-right corner, we search for a solution in each of the primary directions, if necessary. First, we look down by recursively calling the `traverse` method and passing in the new location. The logic of the `traverse` method starts all over again using this new position. It's as if each call to `traverse` is attempting to solve a new, slightly smaller, maze.

A solution is either ultimately found by first attempting to move down from the current location, or it's not found. If a solution is not found by moving down, we try moving right. If that fails, we try up. Finally, we try left. If no direction from the current location yields a correct solution, then there is no path from this location, and `traverse` returns false. If the very first invocation of the `traverse` method returns false, then there is no possible path through the maze.

If a solution is found from the current location, the grid entry is changed to a 7. The first 7 is placed in the bottom-right corner. The next 7 is placed in the location that led to the bottom-right corner, and so on until the final 7 is placed in the upper-left corner. Therefore, when the final maze is printed, the zeros still indicate a blocked path, a 1 indicates an open path that was never tried, a 3 indicates a path that was tried but failed to yield a correct solution, and a 7 indicates a part of the final solution of the maze.

Note that there are several opportunities for recursion in each call to the `traverse` method. Any or all of them might be followed, depending on the maze configuration. Although there may be many paths through the maze, the recursion terminates when a path is found. Carefully trace the execution of this code while examining the maze array to see how the recursion solves the problem. Then consider the difficulty of producing a non-recursive solution.

The Towers of Hanoi

The *Towers of Hanoi* puzzle was invented in the 1880s by Edouard Lucas, a French mathematician. It has become a favorite among computer scientists because its solution is an excellent demonstration of recursive elegance.

The puzzle consists of three upright pegs and a set of disks with holes in the middle so that they slide onto the pegs. Each disk has a different diameter. Initially, all of the disks are stacked on one peg in order of size such that the largest disk is on the bottom, as shown in Figure 11.5.

The goal of the puzzle is to move all of the disks from their original (first) peg to the destination (third) peg. We can use the "extra" peg as a temporary place to put disks, but we must obey the following three rules:

- We can move only one disk at a time.
- We cannot place a larger disk on top of a smaller disk.
- All disks must be on some peg except for the disk in transit between pegs.

These rules imply that we must move smaller disks "out of the way" in order to move a larger disk from one peg to another. Figure 11.6 on the next page shows the step-by-step solution for the Towers of Hanoi puzzle using three disks. In order

FIGURE 11.5 The Towers of Hanoi puzzle

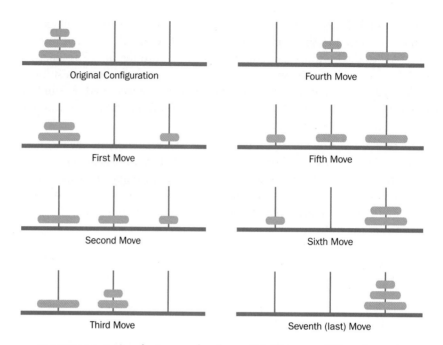

Original Configuration	Fourth Move
First Move	Fifth Move
Second Move	Sixth Move
Third Move	Seventh (last) Move

FIGURE 11.6 A solution to the three-disk Towers of Hanoi puzzle

to ultimately move all three disks from the first peg to the third peg, we first have to get to the point where the smaller two disks are out of the way on the second peg so that the largest disk can be moved from the first peg to the third peg.

The first three moves shown in Figure 11.6 can be thought of as moving the smaller disks out of the way. The fourth move puts the largest disk in its final place. The last three moves then put the smaller disks in their final place on top of the largest one.

Let's use this idea to form a general strategy. To move a stack of N disks from the original peg to the destination peg:

- Move the topmost N–1 disks from the original peg to the extra peg.
- Move the largest disk from the original peg to the destination peg.
- Move the N–1 disks from the extra peg to the destination peg.

This strategy lends itself nicely to a recursive solution. The step to move the N–1 disks out of the way is the same problem all over again: moving a stack of disks. For this subtask, though, there is one less disk, and our destination peg is what we were originally calling the extra peg. A similar situation occurs after we've moved the largest disk and we have to move the original N–1 disks again.

The base case for this problem occurs when we want to move a "stack" that consists of only one disk. That step can be accomplished directly and without recursion.

LISTING 11.3

```java
//********************************************************************
//  SolveTowers.java         Java Foundations
//
//  Demonstrates recursion by solving the classic Towers of Hanoi
//  puzzle.
//********************************************************************

public class SolveTowers
{
    //----------------------------------------------------------------
    //  Creates a TowersOfHanoi puzzle and solves it.
    //----------------------------------------------------------------
    public static void main (String[] args)
    {
        TowersOfHanoi towers = new TowersOfHanoi (4);
        towers.solve();
    }
}
```

OUTPUT

```
Move one disk from 1 to 2
Move one disk from 1 to 3
Move one disk from 2 to 3
Move one disk from 1 to 2
Move one disk from 3 to 1
Move one disk from 3 to 2
Move one disk from 1 to 2
Move one disk from 1 to 3
Move one disk from 2 to 3
Move one disk from 2 to 1
Move one disk from 3 to 1
Move one disk from 2 to 3
Move one disk from 1 to 2
Move one disk from 1 to 3
Move one disk from 2 to 3
```

The program in Listing 11.3 creates a TowersOfHanoi object and invokes its solve method. The output is a step-by-step list of instructions that describes how the disks should be moved to solve the puzzle. This example uses four disks, which is specified by a parameter to the TowersOfHanoi constructor.

The TowersOfHanoi class shown in Listing 11.4 on the next page uses the solve method to make an initial call to moveTower, the recursive method. The

LISTING 11.4

```java
//********************************************************************
//  TowersOfHanoi.java        Java Foundations
//
//  Represents the classic Towers of Hanoi puzzle.
//********************************************************************

public class TowersOfHanoi
{
   private int totalDisks;

   //-----------------------------------------------------------------
   //  Sets up the puzzle with the specified number of disks.
   //-----------------------------------------------------------------
   public TowersOfHanoi (int disks)
   {
      totalDisks = disks;
   }

   //-----------------------------------------------------------------
   //  Performs the initial call to moveTower to solve the puzzle.
   //  Moves the disks from tower 1 to tower 3 using tower 2.
   //-----------------------------------------------------------------
   public void solve ()
   {
      moveTower (totalDisks, 1, 3, 2);
   }

   //-----------------------------------------------------------------
   //  Moves the specified number of disks from one tower to another
   //  by moving a subtower of n-1 disks out of the way, moving one
   //  disk, then moving the subtower back. Base case of 1 disk.
   //-----------------------------------------------------------------
   private void moveTower (int numDisks, int start, int end, int temp)
   {
      if (numDisks == 1)
         moveOneDisk (start, end);
      else
      {
         moveTower (numDisks-1, start, temp, end);
         moveOneDisk (start, end);
         moveTower (numDisks-1, temp, end, start);
      }
   }
```

LISTING 11.4 *continued*

```
//----------------------------------------------------------
//  Prints instructions to move one disk from the specified start
//  tower to the specified end tower.
//----------------------------------------------------------
private void moveOneDisk (int start, int end)
{
    System.out.println ("Move one disk from " + start + " to " +
        end);
}
}
```

initial call indicates that all of the disks should be moved from peg 1 to peg 3, using peg 2 as the extra position.

The `moveTower` method first considers the base case (a "stack" of one disk). When that occurs, it calls the `moveOneDisk` method that prints a single line describing that particular move. If the stack contains more than one disk, we call `moveTower` again to get the N–1 disks out of the way, then move the largest disk, then move the N–1 disks to their final destination with yet another call to `moveTower`.

Note that the parameters to `moveTower` describing the pegs are switched around as needed to move the partial stacks. This code follows our general strategy and uses the `moveTower` method to move all partial stacks. Trace the code carefully for a stack of three disks to understand the processing. Compare the processing steps to Figure 11.6.

Contrary to its short and elegant implementation, the solution to the Towers of Hanoi puzzle is terribly inefficient. To solve the puzzle with a stack of N disks, we have to make 2^N-1 individual disk moves. This situation is an example of *exponential complexity*. As the number of disks increases, the number of required moves increases exponentially. Techniques for analyzing the efficiency of algorithms are discussed further in Chapter 14.

> **KEY CONCEPT**
>
> The Towers of Hanoi solution has exponential complexity, which is very inefficient. Yet the implementation of the solution is incredibly short and elegant.

Legend has it that priests of Brahma are working on this puzzle in a temple at the center of the world. They are using 64 gold disks, moving them between pegs of pure diamond. The downside is that when the priests finish the puzzle, the world will end. The upside is that even if they move one disk every second of every day, it will take them over 584 billion years to complete it. That's with a puzzle of only 64 disks! It is certainly an indication of just how intractable exponential algorithmic complexity is.

Summary of Key Concepts

- Recursion is a programming technique in which a method calls itself.

- A key to being able to program recursively is to be able to think recursively.

- Any recursive definition must have a non-recursive part, called the base case, which permits the recursion to eventually end.

- Mathematical problems and formulas are often expressed recursively.

- Each recursive call to a method creates new local variables and parameters.

- Recursion is the most elegant and appropriate way to solve some problems, but for others it is less intuitive than an iterative solution.

- The Towers of Hanoi solution has exponential complexity, which is very inefficient. Yet the implementation of the solution is incredibly short and elegant.

Self-Review Questions

SR 11.1   What is recursion?

SR 11.2   What is infinite recursion?

SR 11.3   When is a base case needed for recursive processing?

SR 11.4   Is recursion necessary?

SR 11.5   When should recursion be avoided?

SR 11.6   What is indirect recursion?

SR 11.7   Under what conditions does the recursion stop in the `MazeSearch` program?

SR 11.8   Explain the general approach to solving the Towers of Hanoi puzzle. How does it relate to recursion?

Exercises

EX 11.1   Write a recursive definition of a valid Java identifier (see Chapter 1).

EX 11.2   Write a recursive definition of x^y (x raised to the power y), where x and y are integers and $y > 0$.

EX 11.3   Write a recursive definition of $i \times j$ (integer multiplication), where $i > 0$. Define the multiplication process in terms of integer addition. For example, 4×7 is equal to 7 added to itself 4 times.

EX 11.4   Write a recursive definition of the Fibonacci numbers. The Fibonacci numbers are a sequence of integers, each of which is the sum of the previous two numbers. The first two numbers in the sequence are 0 and 1. Explain why you would not normally use recursion to solve this problem.

EX 11.5   Modify the method that calculates the sum of the integers between 1 and N shown in this chapter. Have the new version match the following recursive definition: The sum of 1 to N is the sum of 1 to (N/2) plus the sum of (N/2 + 1) to N. Trace your solution using an N of 7.

EX 11.6   Write a recursive method that returns the value of N! (N factorial) based on the definition given in this chapter. Explain why you would not normally use recursion to solve this problem.

EX 11.7   Write a recursive method to reverse a string. Explain why you would not normally use recursion to solve this problem.

EX 11.8   Design or generate a new maze for the MazeSearch program in this chapter and rerun the program. Explain the processing in terms of your new maze, giving examples of a path that was tried but failed, a path that was never tried, and the ultimate solution.

EX 11.9   Annotate the lines of output of the SolveTowers program in this chapter to show the recursive steps.

EX 11.10 Produce a chart showing the number of moves required to solve the Towers of Hanoi puzzle using the following number of disks: 2, 3, 4, 5, 6, 7, 8, 9, 10, 15, 20, and 25.

Programming Projects

PP 11.1   Design and implement a recursive version of the PalindromeTester program from Chapter 4.

PP 11.2   Design and implement a program that implements Euclid's algorithm for finding the greatest common divisor of two positive integers. The greatest common divisor is the largest integer that divides both values without producing a remainder. An iterative version of this method was part of the `RationalNumber` class presented in Chapter 5. In a class called `DivisorCalc`, define a static method called `gcd` that accepts two integers, `num1` and `num2`. Create a driver to test your implementation. The recursive algorithm is defined as follows:

> `gcd(num1, num2)` is `num2` if `num2 <= num1` and `num2` divides `num1`

> `gcd(num1, num2)` is `gcd(num2, num1)` if `num1 < num2`

> `gcd(num1, num2)` is `gcd(num2, num1%num2)` otherwise

PP 11.3   Modify the `Maze` class so that it prints out the path of the final solution as it is discovered without storing it.

PP 11.4   Design and implement a program that traverses a 3D maze.

PP 11.5   Design and implement a recursive program that solves the Non-Attacking Queens problem. That is, write a program to determine how eight queens can be positioned on an eight-by-eight chessboard so that none of them is in the same row, column, or diagonal as any other queen. There are no other chess pieces on the board.

PP 11.6   In the language of an alien race, all words take the form of Blurbs. A Blurb is a Whoozit followed by one or more Whatzits. A Whoozit is the character 'x' followed by zero or more 'y's. A Whatzit is a 'q' followed by either a 'z' or a 'd', followed by a Whoozit. Design and implement a recursive program that generates random Blurbs in this alien language.

PP 11.7   Design and implement a recursive program to determine whether a string is a valid Blurb as defined in programming project 11.6.

PP 11.8   Design and implement a recursive program to determine and print the Nth line of Pascal's Triangle, as shown on page 22. Each interior value is the sum of the two values above it. *Hint:* Use an array to store the values on each line.

PP 11.9   Design and implement a graphic version of the Towers of Hanoi puzzle. Allow the user to set the number of disks used in the puzzle. The user should be able to interact with the puzzle in two main ways. The user can move the disks from one peg to another using the mouse, in which case the program should ensure that each move is legal. The user can also watch a solution take place as an animation, with pause/resume buttons. Permit the user to control the speed of the animation.

PP 11.10   Write a program that prompts the user for a list of cities, where each city has a name and x and y coordinates. After all cities have been entered, the program should use a recursive algorithm to print the length of all possible routes that start at the first city entered, end at the last city entered, and visit every city in the list. For each route, the program should print the name of each city visited, followed by the length of the route.

Answers to Self-Review Questions

SR 11.1   Recursion is a programming technique in which a method calls itself, solving a smaller version of the problem each time, until the terminating condition is reached.

SR 11.2 Infinite recursion occurs when there is no base case that serves as a terminating condition or when the base case is improperly specified. The recursive path is followed forever. In a recursive program, infinite recursion will often result in an error that indicates that available memory has been exhausted.

SR 11.3 A base case is always required to terminate recursion and begin the process of returning through the calling hierarchy. Without the base case, infinite recursion results.

SR 11.4 Recursion is not necessary. Every recursive algorithm can be written in an iterative manner. However, some problem solutions are much more elegant and straightforward when written recursively.

SR 11.5 Avoid recursion when the iterative solution is simpler and more easily understood and programmed. Recursion has the overhead of multiple method calls, is not always intuitive, and can be very inefficient.

SR 11.6 Indirect recursion occurs when a method calls another method, which calls another method, and so on until one of the called methods invokes the original. Indirect recursion is usually more difficult to trace than direct recursion, in which a method calls itself.

SR 11.7 The MazeSearch program recursively processes each of the four positions adjacent to the "current" one unless either (1) the current position is outside of the playing grid or (2) the final destination position is reached.

SR 11.8 The Towers of Hanoi puzzle of N disks is solved by moving N–1 disks out of the way onto an extra peg, moving the largest disk to its destination, then moving the N–1 disks from the extra peg to the destination. This solution is inherently recursive because, to move the substack of N–1 disks, we can use the same process.

Analysis of Algorithms

CHAPTER OBJECTIVES

- Discuss the goals of software development with respect to efficiency.
- Introduce the concept of algorithm analysis.
- Explore the concept of asymptotic complexity.
- Compare various growth functions.

As our programs become more sophisticated, it is important to understand the concepts surrounding the efficiency of our algorithms. There are usually multiple ways a particular task can be accomplished, and a more efficient solution is generally preferred. As we explore topics such as sorting and data structures in later chapters, the ability to analyze the efficiency of our implementations becomes crucial.

12.1 Algorithm Efficiency

One of the most important resources in a computing system is CPU time. The efficiency of an algorithm we use to accomplish a particular task is a major factor that determines how fast a program executes. Although the techniques that we will discuss here may also be used to analyze an algorithm relative to the amount of memory it uses, we will focus our discussion on the efficient use of processing time.

> **KEY CONCEPT**
>
> Algorithm analysis is a fundamental computer science topic.

Algorithm analysis is a fundamental computer science topic and involves a variety of techniques and concepts. This chapter introduces the issues related to algorithm analysis and lays the groundwork for using analysis techniques.

Let's start with an everyday example: washing dishes by hand. If we assume that washing a dish takes 30 seconds and drying a dish takes an additional 30 seconds, then we can see quite easily that it would take n minutes to wash and dry n dishes. This computation could be expressed as follows:

Time (n dishes) = n * (30 seconds wash time + 30 seconds dry time)
$$= 60n \text{ seconds}$$

or, written more formally:

$$f(x) = 30x + 30x$$
$$f(x) = 60x$$

Now let's extend this example to a ridiculous extreme. Suppose each time we washed a dish, we had to dry not only that dish but also all of the dishes we had washed before that one. It would still take 30 seconds to wash each dish, but now it would take 30 seconds to dry the last dish (once), 2 * 30 or 60 seconds to dry the second-to-last dish (twice), 3 * 30 or 90 seconds to dry the third-to-last dish (three times), and so on. This computation could be expressed as follows:

Time (n dishes) = n * (30 seconds wash time) + $\sum_{i=1}^{n}(i * 30)$

Using the formula for an arithmetic series $\sum_{1}^{n} i = n(n + 1)/2$ then the function becomes

Time (n dishes) = $30n + 30n(n + 1)/2$
$$= 15n^2 + 45n \text{ seconds}$$

If there were 30 dishes to wash, the first approach would take 30 minutes, whereas the second (careless) approach would take 247.5 minutes. The more dishes we wash the worse that discrepancy becomes. For example, if there were 300 dishes to wash, the first approach would take 300 minutes or 5 hours, where as the second approach would take 908,315 minutes or roughly 15,000 hours!

12.2 Growth Functions and Big-Oh Notation

For every algorithm we want to analyze, we need to define the size of the problem. For our dishwashing example, the size of the problem is the number of dishes to be washed and dried. We also must determine the value that represents efficient use of time or space. For time considerations, we often pick an appropriate processing step that we'd like to minimize, such as our goal to minimize the number of times a dish has to be washed and dried. The overall amount of time spent at the task is directly related to how many times we have to perform that task. The algorithm's efficiency can be defined in terms of the problem size and the processing step.

Consider an algorithm that sorts a list of numbers into increasing order. One natural way to express the size of the problem would be the number of values to be sorted. The processing step we are trying to optimize could be expressed as the number of comparisons we have to make for the algorithm to put the values in order. The more comparisons we make, the more CPU time is used.

A *growth function* shows the relationship between the size of the problem (n) and the value we hope to optimize. This function represents the *time complexity* or *space complexity* of the algorithm.

> **KEY CONCEPT**
> A growth function shows time or space utilization relative to the problem size.

The growth function for our second dishwashing algorithm is

$$t(n) = 15n^2 + 45n$$

However, it is not typically necessary to know the exact growth function for an algorithm. Instead, we are mainly interested in the *asymptotic complexity* of an algorithm. That is, we want to focus on the general nature of the function as n increases. This characteristic is based on the *dominant term* of the expression—the term that increases most quickly as n increases. As n gets very large, the value of the dishwashing growth function is dominated by the n^2 term because the n^2 term grows much faster than the n term. The constants, in this case 15 and 45, and the secondary term, in this case 45n, quickly become irrelevant as n increases. That is to say, the value of n^2 dominates the growth in the value of the expression.

The table in Figure 12.1 on the next page shows how the two terms, and the value of the expression grow. As you can see from the table, as n gets larger, the $15n^2$ term dominates the value of the expression. It is important to note that the 45n term is larger for very small values of n. Saying that a term is the dominant term as n gets large does not mean that it is larger than the other terms for all values of n.

Number of dishes (n)	$15n^2$	$45n$	$15n^2 + 45n$
1	15	45	60
2	60	90	150
5	375	225	600
10	1,500	450	1,950
100	150,000	4,500	154,500
1,000	15,000,000	45,000	15,045,000
10,000	1,500,000,000	450,000	1,500,450,000
100,000	150,000,000,000	4,500,000	150,004,500,000
1,000,000	15,000,000,000,000	45,000,000	15,000,045,000,000
10,000,000	1,500,000,000,000,000	450,000,000	1,500,000,450,000,000

FIGURE 12.1 Comparison of terms in growth function

The asymptotic complexity is called the *order* of the algorithm. Thus, our second dishwashing algorithm is said to have order n^2 time complexity, written $O(n^2)$. Our first, more efficient dishwashing example, with growth function t(n) = 60(n) would have order n, written $O(n)$. Thus, the reason for the difference between our $O(n)$ original algorithm and our $O(n^2)$ sloppy algorithm is the fact each dish may to be dried multiple times.

This notation is referred to as O() or *Big-Oh notation*. A growth function that executes in constant time regardless of the size of the problem is said to have $O(1)$. In general, we are only concerned with executable statements in a program or algorithm in determining its growth function and efficiency. Keep in mind however, that some declarations may include initializations and some of these may be complex enough to factor into the efficiency of an algorithm.

As an example, assignment statements and if statements that are only executed once regardless of the size of the problem are $O(1)$. Therefore, it does not matter how many of those you string together, it is still $O(1)$. Loops and method calls may result in higher order growth functions because they may result in a statement or series of statements being executed more than once based on the size of the problem. We will discuss these separately in later sections of this chapter. Figure 12.2 on the next page shows several growth functions and their asymptotic complexity.

KEY CONCEPT

The order of an algorithm is determined by the dominant term in the algorithm's growth function.

More formally, saying that the growth function t(n) = $15n^2$ + 45n is $O(n^2)$ means that there exists a constant m and some value of

Growth Function	Order	Label
$t(n) = 17$	$O(1)$	constant
$t(n) = 3\log n$	$O(\log n)$	logarithmic
$t(n) = 20n - 4$	$O(n)$	linear
$t(n) = 12n \log n + 100n$	$O(n \log n)$	n log n
$t(n) = 3n^2 + 5n - 2$	$O(n^2)$	quadratic
$t(n) = 8n^3 + 3n^2$	$O(n^3)$	cubic
$t(n) = 2^n + 18n^2 + 3n$	$O(2^n)$	exponential

FIGURE 12.2 Some growth functions and their asymptotic complexity

n (n_0), such that $t(n) \leq m^* n^2$ for all $n > n_0$. Another way of stating this is that the order of an algorithm provides an upper bound to its growth function. It is also important to note that there are other related notations such as omega (Ω) which refers to a function that provides a lower bound and theta (Θ) which refers to a function that provides both an upper and lower bound. We will focus our discussion on Big-Oh notation.

Because the order of the function is the key factor, the other terms and constants are often not even mentioned. All algorithms within a given order are considered to be generally equivalent in terms of efficiency. For example, two algorithms accomplishing the same task may have different growth functions. If they are both $O(n^2)$, then they are considered to be roughly accomplishing equivalent with respect to efficiency.

> **KEY CONCEPT**
> The order of an algorithm provides an upper bound to the algorithm's growth function.

12.3 Comparing Growth Functions

One might assume that, with the advances in the speed of processors and the availability of large amounts of inexpensive memory, algorithm analysis would no longer be necessary. However, nothing could be farther from the truth. Processor speed and memory cannot make up for the differences in efficiency of algorithms. Keep in mind that in our previous discussion we have been eliminating constants as irrelevant when discussing the order of an algorithm. Increasing processor speed simply adds a constant to the growth function. When possible, finding a more efficient algorithm is a better solution than finding a faster processor.

The table in Figure 12.3 on the next page compares four algorithms with various time complexities and the effects of speeding up the processor by a factor of 10.

Algorithm	Time Complexity	Max Problem Size Before Speedup	Max Problem Size After Speedup
A_1	n	s_1	$10s_1$
A_2	n^2	s_2	$3.16s_2$
A_3	n^3	s_3	$2.15s_3$
A_4	n^4	s_4	$s_4 + 3.3$

FIGURE 12.3 Increase in problem size with a tenfold increase in processor speed

Algorithm A_1, with a linear time complexity of n, is indeed improved by a factor of 10. However, algorithm A_2, with a time complexity of n^2, is only improved by a factor of 3.16. Why do we not get the full tenfold increase in problem size? Because the complexity of algorithm B is n^2 our effective speedup is only the square root of 10 or 3.16.

Similarly, algorithm A_3 is only improved by a factor of 2.15 or the cube root of 10. For algorithms with *exponential complexity* like algorithm A_4, in which the size variable is in the exponent of the complexity term, the situation is far worse. The speed up is $\log_2 n$ or in this case, 3.3. Note this is not a factor of 3, but the original problem size plus 3. In the grand scheme of things, if an algorithm is inefficient, speeding up the processor will not help.

KEY CONCEPT

A faster processor cannot compensate for an inefficient algorithm as the size of the problem increases.

Figure 12.4 illustrates various growth functions graphically. Note that when n is small, there is little difference between the algorithms. That is, if you can guarantee a very small problem size (5 or less), it

FIGURE 12.4 Comparison of typical growth functions for small values of n

doesn't really matter which algorithm is used. However, as n gets larger, the differences between the growth functions become significant quickly.

```
for (int count = 0; count < n; count++)
{
    for (int count2 = count; count2 < n; count2++)
    {
        /* some sequence of O(1) steps */
    }
}
```

In this case, the inner loop index is initialized to the current value of the index for the outer loop. The outer loop executes n times. The inner loop executes n times the first time, n – 1 times the second time, etc. However, remember that we are only interested in the dominant term, not in constants or any lesser terms. If the progression is linear, regardless of whether some elements are skipped, the order is still O(n). Thus the resulting complexity for this code is O(n^2).

Method Calls

Now let's suppose that we have the following segment of code:

```
for (int count = 0; count < n; count++)
{
    printsum (count);
}
```

We know from our previous discussion that we find the order of the loop by multiplying the order of the body of the loop by the number of times the loop will execute. In this case, however, the body of the loop is a method call. Therefore, we must first determine the order of the method before we can determine the order of the code segment. Lets suppose that the purpose of the method is to print the sum of the integers from 1 to n each time it is called. We might be tempted to create a brute force method such as the following:

```
public void printsum(int count)
{
    int sum = 0;
    for (int i = 1; i < count; i++)
        sum += i;
    System.out.println (sum);
}
```

What is the time complexity of the `printsum` method? Keep in mind that only executable statements contribute to the time complexity so in this case, all of the executable statement are O(1) except for the loop. The loop on the other hand is O(n) and thus the method itself is O(n). Now to compute the time complexity of the original loop that called the method, we simply multiply the complexity of the method, which is the body of the loop, by the number of times the loop will execute. Our result, then, is O(n²) using this implementation of the `printsum` method.

However, if you recall, we know from our earlier discussion that we do not have to use a loop to calculate the sum of the numbers from 1 to n. In fact, we know that the $\sum_1^n i = n(n + 1)/2$. Now lets rewrite our `printsum` method and see what happens to the time complexity:

```
public void printsum(int count)
{
    sum = count * (count+1)/2;
    System.out.println (sum);
}
```

Now the time complexity of the `printsum` method is made up of an assignment statement which is O(1) and a print statement which is also O(1). The result of this change is that the time complexity of the `printsum` method is now O(1) meaning that loop that calls this method now goes from being O(n²) to O(n). We know from our our earlier discussion and from figure 2.3 that this is a very significant improvement. Once again, we see that there is a difference between delivering correct results and doing so efficiently.

What if the body of a method is made up of multiple method calls and loops? Consider the following code using our `printsum` method above:

```
public void sample(int n)
{
    printsum(n);                        /* this method call is O(1) */

    for (int count = 0; count < n; count++) /* this loop is O(n) */
        printsum (count);

    for (int count = 0; count < n; count++) /* this loop is O(n²)*/
    {
        for (int count2 = 0; count2 < n; count2++)
            System.out.println (count, count2);
    }
}
```

The initial call to the `printsum` method with the parameter temp is O(1) since the method is O(1). The for loop containing the call to the `printsum` method with the parameter count is O(n) since the method is O(1) and the loop executes n times. The nested loops are O(n²) since the inner loop will execute n times each time the outer loop executes and it will also execute n times. The entire method is then $O(n^2)$ since only the dominant term matters.

More formally, the growth function for the method sample is given by:

$$f(x) = 1 + n + n^2$$

Then given that we eliminate constants and all but the dominant term, the time complexity is $O(n^2)$.

Analyzing Recursive Algorithms

In Chapter 11 we explored the concept of recursive programming, in which a method calls itself to accomplish a task. Let's now discuss the efficiency of such algorithms.

When analyzing a loop, we determined the order of the body of the loop and multiplied it by the number of times the loop was executed. Analyzing a recursive algorithm uses similar thinking. Determining the order of a recursive algorithm is a matter of determining the order of the recursion (the number of times the recursive definition is followed) and multiplying that by the order of the body of the recursive method.

Consider the recursive method presented in Chapter 11 that computes the sum of the integers from 1 to some positive value. We reprint it here for convenience:

```
// This method returns the sum of 1 to num
public int sum (int num)
{
   int result;
   if (num == 1)
      result = 1;
   else
      result = num + sum (num-1);
   return result;
}
```

We realize that this is not a good example of the use of recursion, but it's a good first example to consider as we analyze the algorithm's complexity. The size of this problem is naturally expressed as the number of values to be summed. Because we are summing the integers from 1 to num, the number of values to be summed is num. The operation of interest is the act of adding two values together. The body of the recursive method performs one addition operation, and therefore is $O(1)$. Each time the recursive method is invoked, the value of num is decreased by 1. Therefore, the recursive method is called num times, so the order of the recursion is $O(n)$. Thus, since the body is $O(1)$ and the recursion is $O(n)$, the order of the entire algorithm is $O(n)$.

In some algorithms the recursive step operates on half as much data as the previous call, thus creating an order of recursion of $O(\log n)$. If the body of the method is $O(1)$, then the whole algorithm is $O(\log n)$. If the body of the method is $O(n)$, then the whole algorithm is $O(n \log n)$.

Now consider the Towers of Hanoi puzzle discussed in Chapter 11 (review it if necessary). The size of the puzzle is naturally the number of disks, and the processing operation of interest is the step of moving one disk from one peg to another. Each call to the recursive method `moveTower` results in one disk being moved. Unfortunately, except for the base case, each recursive call results in calling itself *twice more*, and each call operates on a stack of disks that is only one less than the stack that is passed in as the parameter. Thus, calling `moveTower` with 1 disk results in 1 disk being moved, calling `moveTower` with 2 disks results in 3 disks being moved, calling `moveTower` with 3 disks results in 7 disks being moved, calling `moveTower` with 4 disks results in 15 disks being moved, etc. Looking at it another way, if `f(n)` is the growth function for this problem, then:

$$f(n) = 1 \text{ when n is equal to } 1$$

for $n > 1$,

$$f(n) = 2*(f(n-1)+1)$$
$$= 2^N - 1$$

> **KEY CONCEPT**
>
> The Towers of Hanoi solution has exponential complexity, which is very inefficient. Yet the implementation of the solution is remarkably short and elegant.

Contrary to its short and elegant implementation, the solution to the Towers of Hanoi puzzle is terribly inefficient. To solve the puzzle with a stack of N disks, we have to make $2^N - 1$ individual disk moves. Therefore, the Towers of Hanoi algorithm is $O(2^n)$. As we discussed in Chapter 1, this order is an example of exponential complexity. As the number of disks increases, the number of required moves increases exponentially.

Summary of Key Concepts

- Algorithm analysis is a fundamental computer science topic.
- A growth function shows time or space utilization relative to the problem size.
- The order of an algorithm is determined by the dominant term in the algorithm's growth function.
- The order of an algorithm provides an upper bound to the algorithm's growth function.
- A faster processor cannot compensate for an inefficient algorithm as the size of the problem increases.
- Analyzing algorithm complexity often requires analyzing the execution of loops.
- The analysis of nested loops must take into account both the inner and outer loops.
- The Towers of Hanoi solution has exponential complexity, which is very inefficient. Yet the implementation of the solution is remarkably short and elegant.

Self-Review Questions

SR 12.1   What is the difference between the growth function of an algorithm and the order of that algorithm?

SR 12.2   Why does speeding up the CPU not necessarily speed up the process by the same amount?

SR 12.3   How do we use the growth function of an algorithm to determine its order?

SR 12.4   How do we determine the time complexity of a loop?

SR 12.5   How do we determine the time complexity of a method call?

Exercises

EX 12.1   What is the order of the following growth functions?

a. $10n^2 + 100n + 1000$

b. $10n^3 - 7$

c. $2n + 100n^3$

d. $n^2 \log n$

EX 12.2   Arrange the growth functions of the previous exercise in ascending order of efficiency for n=10 and again for n = 1,000,000.

EX 12.3   Write the code necessary to find the largest element in an un-sorted array of integers. What is the time complexity of this al-gorithm?

EX 12.4   Determine the growth function and order of the following code fragment:

```
for (int count=0; count < n; count++)
{
    for (int count2=0; count2 < n; count2=count2+2)
    {
        System.out.println(count, count2);
    }
}
```

EX 12.5   Determine the growth function and order of the following code fragment:

```
for (int count=0; count < n; count++)
{
    for (int count2=0; count2 < n; count2=count2*2)
    {
        System.out.println(count, count2);
    }
}
```

Answers to Self-Review Questions

SRA 12.1   The growth function of an algorithm represents the exact rela-tionship between the problem size and the time complexity of the solution. The order of the algorithm is the asymptotic time complexity. As the size of the problem grows, the complexity of the algorithm approaches the asymptotic complexity.

SRA 12.2   Linear speedup only occurs if the algorithm has a linear order, O(n). As the complexity of the algorithm grows, faster proces-sors have significantly less impact.

SRA 12.3   The order of an algorithm is found by eliminating constants and all but the dominant term from the algorithm's growth function.

SRA 12.4   The time complexity of a loop is found by multiplying the time complexity of the body of the loop times the number of times the loop will execute.

SRA 12.5   The time complexity of a method call is found by determining the time complexity of the method and then substituting that for the method call.

Searching and Sorting

CHAPTER OBJECTIVES

- Examine the linear and binary search algorithms.
- Examine the selection, insertion, bubble, quick, and merge sort algorithms.
- Discuss the complexity of the search and sort algorithms.

Two common tasks in the world of software development are searching for a particular element within a group and sorting a group of elements into a particular order. There are a variety of algorithms that can be used to accomplish these tasks, and the differences between them are worth exploring carefully.

13.1 Searching

Searching is the process of finding a designated *target element* within a group of items, or determining that the target does not exist within the group. The group of items to be searched is sometimes called the *search pool*.

> **KEY CONCEPT**
>
> Searching is the process of finding a designated target within a group of items or determining that it doesn't exist.

This section examines two common approaches to searching: a linear search and a binary search. In this chapter, we restrict ourselves to searching an array of items. In later chapters of the book we explore other search techniques that organize data in different ways.

> **KEY CONCEPT**
>
> An efficient search minimizes the number of comparisons made.

Our goal is to perform the search as efficiently as possible. In terms of algorithm analysis, we want to minimize the number of comparisons we have to make to find the target. In general, the more items there are in the search pool, the more comparisons it will take to find the target. Thus, the size of the problem is defined by the number of items in the search pool.

To be able to search for an object, we must be able to compare one object to another. Our implementations of these algorithms search an array of `Comparable` objects. Therefore, the elements involved must implement the `Comparable` interface and be comparable to each other.

Recall that the `Comparable` interface contains one method, `compareTo`, which is designed to return an integer that is less than zero, equal to zero, or greater than zero (respectively) if the object is less than, equal to, or greater than (respectively) the object to which it is being compared. Therefore, any class that implements the `Comparable` interface defines the relative order of any two objects of that class.

For our examples, we'll search an array of `Contact` objects. The `Contact` class is shown in Listing 13.1. Each `Contact` object represents a person with a last name, a first name, and a phone number.

The `Contact` class implements the `Comparable` interface and therefore provides a definition of the `compareTo` method. In this case, the contacts are sorted by last name; if two contacts have the same last name, their first names are used to determine the order.

There is a version of the `Comparable` interface that uses *generics*, a technique we explore in the next chapter. For now, we are using the basic, non-generic interface. This may cause some warnings to be issued by the compiler when this class is used, but they do not prevent an executable version of the program from being created. Don't worry about them at this point.

The program in Listing 13.2 on page 484 creates an array of `Contact` objects representing tennis players, and then searches for a particular player. It creates a

LISTING 13.1

```java
//***************************************************************
//  Contact.java       Java Foundations
//
//  Represents a phone contact that implements Comparable.
//***************************************************************

public class Contact implements Comparable
{
   private String firstName, lastName, phone;

   //----------------------------------------------------------------
   //  Sets up this contact with the specified information.
   //----------------------------------------------------------------
   public Contact (String first, String last, String telephone)
   {
      firstName = first;
      lastName = last;
      phone = telephone;
   }

   //----------------------------------------------------------------
   //  Returns a string representation of this contact.
   //----------------------------------------------------------------
   public String toString ()
   {
      return lastName + ", " + firstName + ": " + phone;
   }

   //----------------------------------------------------------------
   //  Uses both last and first names to determine lexical ordering.
   //----------------------------------------------------------------
   public int compareTo (Object other)
   {
      int result;

      if (lastName.equals(((Contact)other).lastName))
         result = firstName.compareTo(((Contact)other).firstName);
      else
         result = lastName.compareTo(((Contact)other).lastName);

      return result;
   }
}
```

LISTING 13.2

```java
//********************************************************************
//  SearchPlayerList.java        Java Foundations
//
//  Demonstrates a linear search of Comparable objects.
//********************************************************************

public class SearchPlayerList
{
   //-----------------------------------------------------------------
   //  Creates an array of Contact objects, then searches for a
   //  particular player.
   //-----------------------------------------------------------------
   public static void main (String[] args)
   {
      Contact[] players = new Contact[7];

      players[0] = new Contact ("Rodger", "Federer", "610-555-7384");
      players[1] = new Contact ("Andy", "Roddick", "215-555-3827");
      players[2] = new Contact ("Maria", "Sharapova", "733-555-2969");
      players[3] = new Contact ("Venus", "Williams", "663-555-3984");
      players[4] = new Contact ("Lleyton", "Hewitt", "464-555-3489");
      players[5] = new Contact ("Eleni", "Daniilidou", "322-555-2284");
      players[6] = new Contact ("Serena", "Williams", "243-555-2837");

      Contact target = new Contact ("Eleni", "Daniilidou", "");

      Contact found = (Contact)Searching.linearSearch(players, target);

      if (found == null)
         System.out.println ("Player was not found.");
      else
         System.out.println ("Found: " + found);
   }
}
```

OUTPUT

```
Found: Daniilidou, Eleni: 322-555-2284
```

`target` object to use in the search that contains only the values that contribute to the comparison of `Contact` objects, in this case the first and last name of the person. When the search algorithm finds that person in the list, it returns a reference to the original `Contact` object in the list. If the reference that is returned is `null`, then the target was not found in the list.

It may seem like overkill to create a target object that is so close to the one being sought, but imagine a much more complex `Contact` object that contains many more attributes and methods. In that case, creating a placeholder target object with only a first and last name is a simple way to indicate which object is being sought.

The `SearchPlayerList` program searches for a particular `Contact` object by calling the static `linearSearch` method of the `Sorting` class. Let's explore the idea of a linear search in more detail.

Linear Search

If the search pool is organized into a list of some kind, as it is with an array, one straightforward way to perform the search is to start at the beginning of the list and compare each value in turn to the target element. Eventually, we will either find the target or come to the end of the list and conclude that the target doesn't exist in the group. This approach is called a *linear search* because it begins at one end and scans the search pool in a linear manner. This process is depicted in Figure 13.1.

The `Searching` class is shown in Listing 13.3 on the next page. It contains two static methods, one that searches for an item using a linear search algorithm, and one that searches for an item using a binary search algorithm. We explore the binary search algorithm in the next section.

The `linearSearch` method accepts the array of elements to be searched and the target item sought. The method returns a reference to the item that was found, which will be `null` if the item was not found in the list.

Note that the parameters and return type of `linearSearch` refer to `Comparable` objects, not `Contact` objects. That is, the `linearSearch` method is implemented in terms of `Comparable` objects, not in terms of any particular class. Recall from Chapter 9 that this situation is an example of *polymorphism*.

FIGURE 13.1 A linear search

LISTING 13.3

```java
//********************************************************************
//   Searching.java        Java Foundations
//
//   Contains various search algorithms that operate on an array of
//   Comparable objects.
//********************************************************************

public class Searching
{
   //-----------------------------------------------------------------
   //   Searches the specified array of objects using a linear search
   //   algorithm. Returns null if the target is not found.
   //-----------------------------------------------------------------
   public static Comparable linearSearch (Comparable[] data,
                                           Comparable target)
   {
      Comparable result = null;
      int index = 0;

      while (result == null && index < data.length)
      {
         if (data[index].compareTo(target) == 0)
            result = data[index];
         index++;
      }

      return result;
   }

   //-----------------------------------------------------------------
   //   Searches the specified array of objects using a binary search
   //   algorithm. Returns null if the target is not found.
   //-----------------------------------------------------------------
   public static Comparable binarySearch (Comparable[] data,
                                           Comparable target)
   {
      Comparable result = null;
      int first = 0, last = data.length-1, mid;

      while (result == null && first <= last)
      {
         mid = (first + last) / 2; //  determine midpoint
         if (data[mid].compareTo(target) == 0)
            result = data[mid];
```

LISTING 13.3   *continued*

```
        else
            if (data[mid].compareTo(target) > 0)
                last = mid - 1;
            else
                first = mid + 1;
        }

        return result;
    }
}
```

The references to `Comparable` objects can take on any class of any object that implements the `Comparable` interface. Thus, the `linearSearch` method can be used to search any array of `Comparable` objects, and is another example that shows the versatility and beauty of polymorphism.

> **KEY CONCEPT**
> The `Comparable` interface allows an algorithm to be implemented polymorphically, without regard to a particular class.

The `while` loop in the `linearSearch` method steps through the elements of the array, terminating when either the element is found or the end of the array is reached. If the target is found, the value of `result` is set to the element in the array, the loop terminates, and the reference is returned. If the entire array is searched without finding the element, the value of `result` stays `null` and is returned, indicating that the target element was not in the list.

The linear search algorithm is fairly easy to understand, though it is not particularly efficient. Note that a linear search does not require the elements in the search pool to be in any particular order within the array. The only criterion is that we must be able to examine them, based on their implementation of `Comparable`, one at a time in turn.

The binary search algorithm, described next, improves on the efficiency of the search process, but only works if the search pool is ordered.

Binary Search

If the group of items in the search pool is sorted, then our approach to searching can be much more efficient than that of a linear search. A *binary search* algorithm eliminates large parts of the search pool with each comparison by capitalizing on the fact that the search pool is in sorted order.

> **KEY CONCEPT**
> A binary search capitalizes on the fact that the search pool is sorted.

Instead of starting the search at one end of the list, a binary search begins in the middle. If the target element is not found at that middle element, then the search continues. And because the list is sorted, we know that if the target is in the list, it will be on one side of the array or the other, depending on whether the target is less than or greater than the middle element. Thus, because the list is sorted, we eliminate half of the search pool with one carefully chosen comparison. The remaining half of the list represents the *viable candidates* in which the target element may yet be found.

The search continues in this same manner, examining the middle element of the viable candidates, eliminating half of them. Each comparison reduces the viable candidates by half until eventually the target element is found or there are no more viable candidates, which means the target element is not in the search pool. The process of a binary search is depicted in Figure 13.2.

Let's explore the idea of a binary search using a simple sorted list of integers:

```
10 12 18 22 31 34 40 46 59 67 69 72 80 84 98
```

Suppose we were trying to determine if the number 67 is in the list. Initially, the target could be anywhere in the list. That is, initially all items in the search pool are viable candidates.

The binary search approach begins by examining the middle element, in this case 46. That element is not our target, so we must continue searching. But since we know that the list is sorted, we know that if 67 is in the list, it must be in the second half of the data, because all data items to the left of the middle have values of 46 or less. This leaves the following viable candidates to search (shown in bold):

```
10 12 18 22 31 34 40 46 **59 67 69 72 80 84 98**
```

Continuing the same approach, we examine the middle value of the viable candidates (72). Again, this is not our target value, so we must continue the search. This time we can eliminate all values higher than 72, leaving:

```
10 12 18 22 31 34 40 46 **59 67 69** 72 80 84 98
```

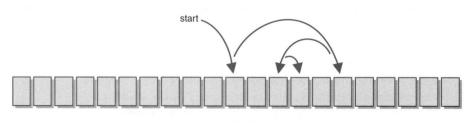

FIGURE 13.2 A binary search

Note that, in only two comparisons, we have reduced the viable candidates from 15 items down to 3 items. Employing the same approach again, we select the middle element, 67, and find the element we are seeking. If it had not been our target, we would have continued with this process until we either found the value or eliminated all possible data.

With each comparison, a binary search eliminates approximately half of the remaining data to be searched (it also eliminates the middle element as well). Therefore, a binary search eliminates half of the data with the first comparison, another quarter of the data with the second comparison, another eighth of the data with the third comparison, and so on.

> **KEY CONCEPT**
> A binary search eliminates half of the viable candidates with each comparison.

The static `binarySearch` method of the `Sorting` class in Listing 13.3 implements a binary search. Like the `linearSearch` method, it accepts an array of `Comparable` objects to be searched and the target value being sought.

The values of the integer variables `first` and `last` represent the range of indexes that make up the viable candidates at any given point during the algorithm. Initially, they are set to encompass the entire array.

Similar to the linear search, the `while` loop in the `binarySearch` method continues until the target element is found or the viable data is exhausted. If the target is found, the value of `result` is set and the loop terminates. On the other hand, if the value of `first` ever exceeds the value of `last`, then all viable candidates have been eliminated, the loop terminates, and a `null` value is returned.

In each iteration of the loop, the midpoint of the viable candidates is calculated by taking the average of the `first` and `last` indexes (using integer division). If the target value is found, the return value `result` is set to the original element from the array. Otherwise, the value of `first` or `last` is adjusted to either side of the midpoint, depending on which half of the candidates remains viable, and the search continues.

This version of the binary search algorithm is implemented iteratively. It can also be implemented recursively, which is left as a programming project.

In general, a binary search is more efficient than a linear search because it eliminates many candidates with each comparison. But a binary search requires that the list be in sorted order, whereas a linear search does not. A formal comparison of the efficiency of these search algorithms is presented in the last section of this chapter.

13.2 Sorting

Sorting is the process of arranging a group of items into a defined order, either ascending or descending, based on some criteria. For example, you may want to alphabetize a list of names or put a list of survey results into descending numeric order. Many sort algorithms have been developed and critiqued over the years. In fact, sorting is considered to be a classic area of study in computer science.

In this section we examine five different sorting algorithms: selection sort, insertion sort, bubble sort, quick sort, and merge sort. The first three are roughly equal in terms of efficiency, but approach the problem from different perspectives. The last two are much more efficient, though a bit more complicated. The last section of this chapter explores ways to examine the efficiency of algorithms, and formally compares these sorting algorithms.

As we did with our search algorithms, we currently restrict ourselves to sorting an array of objects. Other sorting techniques are examined later in the book based on alternative ways to structure our data.

The program in Listing 13.4 creates an array of `Contact` objects just like the array used in our example of search algorithms in Listing 13.2. This time, however, after populating the array, we invoke a method that sorts the elements and then prints them out in order. This example uses the same `Contact` class shown back in Listing 13.1 and relies on its implementation of the `Comparable` interface to determine the relative order of the objects. Note that when two `Contact` objects contain the same last name, the first name is used to determine the order.

The `SortPlayerList` program invokes the static `selectionSort` method of the `Sorting` class, shown in Listing 13.5 on page 492. However, any of the sorting methods in that class could be used to sort the list of `Contact` objects by changing the name of the method invoked.

Let's explore each of these algorithms in turn.

Selection Sort

The *selection sort* algorithm sorts a list of values by repetitively putting a particular value into its final, sorted position. In other words, for each position in the list, the algorithm selects the value that should go in that position and then puts it there.

The general strategy of the selection sort algorithm is as follows: Scan the entire list to find the smallest value. Exchange that value with the value in the first position of the list. Scan the rest of the list (all but the first value) to find the smallest value, and then exchange it with the value in the second position of the list. Scan the rest of the list (all but the first two values) to find the smallest value, and then exchange it with the value in the third position

LISTING 13.4

```java
//********************************************************************
//  SortPlayerList.java       Java Foundations
//
//  Demonstrates a selection sort of Comparable objects.
//********************************************************************

public class SortPlayerList
{
   //-----------------------------------------------------------------
   //  Creates an array of Contact objects, sorts them, then prints
   //  them.
   //-----------------------------------------------------------------
   public static void main (String[] args)
   {
      Contact[] players = new Contact[7];

      players[0] = new Contact ("Rodger", "Federer", "610-555-7384");
      players[1] = new Contact ("Andy", "Roddick", "215-555-3827");
      players[2] = new Contact ("Maria", "Sharapova", "733-555-2969");
      players[3] = new Contact ("Venus", "Williams", "663-555-3984");
      players[4] = new Contact ("Lleyton", "Hewitt", "464-555-3489");
      players[5] = new Contact ("Eleni", "Daniilidou", "322-555-2284");
      players[6] = new Contact ("Serena", "Williams", "243-555-2837");

      Sorting.selectionSort(players);

      for (Comparable player: players)
         System.out.println (player);
   }
}
```

OUTPUT

```
Daniilidou, Eleni: 322-555-2284
Federer, Rodger: 610-555-7384
Hewitt, Lleyton: 464-555-3489
Roddick, Andy: 215-555-3827
Sharapova, Maria: 733-555-2969
Williams, Serena: 243-555-2837
Williams, Venus: 663-555-3984
```

LISTING 13.5

```java
//********************************************************************
//  Sorting.java         Java Foundations
//
//  Contains various sort algorithms that operate on an array of
//  Comparable objects.
//********************************************************************

public class Sorting
{
   //-----------------------------------------------------------------
   //  Sorts the specified array of integers using the selection
   //  sort algorithm.
   //-----------------------------------------------------------------
   public static void selectionSort (Comparable[] data)
   {
      int min;

      for (int index = 0; index < data.length-1; index++)
      {
         min = index;
         for (int scan = index+1; scan < data.length; scan++)
            if (data[scan].compareTo(data[min]) < 0)
               min = scan;

         swap (data, min, index);
      }
   }

   //-----------------------------------------------------------------
   //  Swaps two elements in the specified array.
   //-----------------------------------------------------------------
   private static void swap (Comparable[] data, int index1, int index2)
   {
      Comparable temp = data[index1];
      data[index1] = data[index2];
      data[index2] = temp;
   }

   //-----------------------------------------------------------------
   //  Sorts the specified array of objects using an insertion
   //  sort algorithm.
   //-----------------------------------------------------------------
```

LISTING 13.5   *continued*

```java
public static void insertionSort (Comparable[] data)
{
   for (int index = 1; index < data.length; index++)
   {
      Comparable key = data[index];
      int position = index;

      //  Shift larger values to the right
      while (position > 0 && data[position-1].compareTo(key) > 0)
      {
         data[position] = data[position-1];
         position--;
      }

      data[position] = key;
   }
}

//-----------------------------------------------------------------
//  Sorts the specified array of objects using a bubble sort
//  algorithm.
//-----------------------------------------------------------------
public static void bubbleSort (Comparable[] data)
{
   int position, scan;

   for (position = data.length - 1; position >= 0; position--)
   {
      for (scan = 0; scan <= position - 1; scan++)
         if (data[scan].compareTo(data[scan+1]) > 0)
            swap (data, scan, scan+1);
   }
}

//-----------------------------------------------------------------
//  Sorts the specified array of objects using the quick sort
//  algorithm.
//-----------------------------------------------------------------
public static void quickSort (Comparable[] data, int min, int max)
{
   int pivot;

   if (min < max)
```

LISTING 13.5 *continued*

```
      {
         pivot = partition (data, min, max);  // make partitions
         quickSort(data, min, pivot-1);  // sort left partition
         quickSort(data, pivot+1, max);  // sort right partition
      }
   }

   //-----------------------------------------------------------------
   //  Creates the partitions needed for quick sort.
   //-----------------------------------------------------------------
   private static int partition (Comparable[] data, int min, int max)
   {
      // Use first element as the partition value
      Comparable partitionValue = data[min];

      int left = min;
      int right = max;

      while (left < right)
      {
         // Search for an element that is > the partition element
         while (data[left].compareTo(partitionValue) <= 0 && left < right)
            left++;

         //  Search for an element that is < the partitionelement
         while (data[right].compareTo(partitionValue) > 0)
            right--;

         if (left < right)
            swap(data, left, right);
      }

      //  Move the partition element to its final position
      swap (data, min, right);

      return right;
   }

   //-----------------------------------------------------------------
   //  Sorts the specified array of objects using the merge sort
   //  algorithm.
   //-----------------------------------------------------------------
```

LISTING 13.5   *continued*

```java
public static void mergeSort (Comparable[] data, int min, int max)
{
    if (min < max)
    {
        int mid = (min + max) / 2;
        mergeSort (data, min, mid);
        mergeSort (data, mid+1, max);
        merge (data, min, mid, max);
    }
}

//-----------------------------------------------------------------
//  Sorts the specified array of objects using the merge sort
//  algorithm.
//-----------------------------------------------------------------
public static void merge (Comparable[] data, int first, int mid,
    int last)
{
    Comparable[] temp = new Comparable[data.length];

    int first1 = first, last1 = mid;  // endpoints of first subarray
    int first2 = mid+1, last2 = last;  // endpoints of second subarray
    int index = first1;  // next index open in temp array

    //  Copy smaller item from each subarray into temp until one
    //  of the subarrays is exhausted
    while (first1 <= last1 && first2 <= last2)
    {
        if (data[first1].compareTo(data[first2]) < 0)
        {
            temp[index] = data[first1];
            first1++;
        }
        else
        {
            temp[index] = data[first2];
            first2++;
        }
        index++;
    }
```

LISTING 13.5   *continued*

```
    // Copy remaining elements from first subarray, if any
    while (first1 <= last1)
    {
        temp[index] = data[first1];
        first1++;
        index++;
    }

    // Copy remaining elements from second subarray, if any
    while (first2 <= last2)
    {
        temp[index] = data[first2];
        first2++;
        index++;
    }

    // Copy merged data into original array
    for (index = first; index <= last; index++)
        data[index] = temp[index];
    }
}
```

of the list. Continue this process for each position in the list. When complete, the list is sorted. The selection sort process is illustrated in Figure 13.3.

The selectionSort method accepts an array of Comparable objects as a parameter. When control returns to the calling method, the elements within the array are sorted. The method uses two loops to sort an array. The outer loop controls the position in the array where the next smallest value will be stored. The inner loop finds the smallest value in the rest of the list by scanning all positions greater than or equal to the index specified by the outer loop. When the smallest value is determined, it is exchanged with the value stored at index.

The exchange of two elements in the array, called *swapping*, is accomplished with a call to a support method called swap. Many of the sort algorithms we examine in this chapter swap elements and make use of this method. The swap method uses three assignment statements to make the exchange.

Note that because this algorithm finds the smallest value during each iteration, the result is an array sorted in ascending order (i.e., smallest to largest). The algorithm

	3	9	6	1	2

Scan right starting with 3.
1 is the smallest. Exchange 1 and 3.

	1	9	6	3	2

Scan right starting with 9.
2 is the smallest. Exchange 9 and 2.

	1	2	6	3	9

Scan right starting with 6.
3 is the smallest. Exchange 6 and 3.

	1	2	3	6	9

Scan right starting with 6.
6 is the smallest. Exchange 6 and 6.

	1	2	3	6	9

FIGURE 13.3 An example of section sort processing

can easily be changed to put values in descending order by finding the largest value each time through the loop.

Insertion Sort

The *insertion sort* algorithm sorts a list of values by repetitively inserting a particular value into a subset of the list that has already been sorted. One at a time, each unsorted element is inserted at the appropriate position in that sorted subset until the entire list is in order.

> **KEY CONCEPT**
>
> The insertion sort algorithm sorts a list of values by repetitively inserting a particular value into a subset of the list that has already been sorted.

The general strategy of the insertion sort algorithm is as follows: Sort the first two values in the list relative to each other by exchanging them if necessary. Insert the list's third value into the appropriate position relative to the first two (sorted) values. Then, insert the fourth value into its proper position relative to the first three values in the list. Each time an insertion is made, the number of values in the sorted subset increases by one. Continue this process until all values in the list are completely sorted. The insertion process requires that the other values in the array shift to make room for the inserted element. Figure 13.4 on the next page illustrates the insertion sort process.

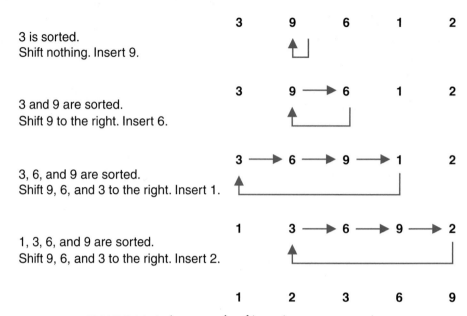

FIGURE 13.4 An example of insertion sort processing

Similar to the selection sort implementation, the insertionSort method uses two loops to sort an array of objects. In the insertion sort, however, the outer loop controls the index in the array of the next value to be inserted. The inner loop compares the current insert value with values stored at lower indexes (which make up a sorted subset of the entire list). If the current insert value is less than the value at position, then that value is shifted to the right. Shifting continues until the proper position is "opened" to accept the insert value. Each iteration of the outer loop adds one more value to the sorted subset of the list, until the entire list is sorted.

Bubble Sort

A *bubble sort* sorts values by repeatedly comparing neighboring elements in the list and swapping their position if they are not in order relative to each other.

The general strategy of the bubble sort algorithm is as follows: Scan through the list comparing adjacent elements and swap them if they are not in relative order. This has the effect of "bubbling" the largest value to the last position in the list, which is its appropriate position in the final, sorted list. Then scan through the list again, bubbling up the second-to-last value. This process continues until all elements have been bubbled into their correct positions.

Each pass through the bubble sort algorithm moves one value to its final position. A pass may also reposition other elements as well. Let's follow this process for a small list of integers. Suppose we started with this list:

```
9  6  8  12  3  1  7
```

We would first compare 9 and 6 and, finding them not in the correct order, swap them, yielding:

```
6  9  8  12  3  1  7
```

Then, we would compare 9 to 8 and, again, finding them not in the correct order, swap them, yielding:

```
6  8  9  12  3  1  7
```

Then, we would compare 9 to 12. Since they are in the correct order, we don't swap them. Instead, we move on to the next pair of values. That is, we then compare 12 and 3. Since they are not in order, we swap them, yielding:

```
6  8  9  3  12  1  7
```

We then compare 12 to 1 and swap them, yielding:

```
6  8  9  3  1  12  7
```

We then compare 12 to 7 and swap them, yielding:

```
6  8  9  3  1  7  12
```

This completes one pass through the data to be sorted. After this first pass, the largest value in the list (12) is in its correct position. The next pass will bubble the value 9 up to its final position. Each subsequent pass through the data guarantees that one more element is put into the correct position. Thus, we make n–1 passes through the data, because if n–1 elements are in the correct, sorted positions, the *n*th item must also be in the correct location.

The `bubbleSort` method in the `Sorting` class implements this approach. The outer `for` loop represents the n–1 passes through the data. The inner `for` loop scans through the data, performing the pair-wise comparisons of the neighboring data and swapping them if necessary. The support method `swap` is used to perform the exchange of two elements, just as we used it in the `selectionSort` method.

Note that the outer loop also has the effect of decreasing the position that represents the maximum index to examine in the inner loop. That is, after the first pass, which puts the last value in its correct position, there is no need to consider that value in future passes through the data. After the second pass, we can forget about the last two, and so on. Thus the inner loop examines one less value on each pass.

Quick Sort

The sort algorithms we have discussed thus far in this chapter (selection sort, insertion sort, and bubble sort) are relatively simple, but they are generally inefficient. They each use a pair of nested loops and require roughly n^2 comparisons to sort a list of n elements. Let's now turn our attention to more efficient sorts.

> **KEY CONCEPT**
>
> The quick sort algorithm sorts a list by partitioning the list and then recursively sorting the two partitions.

The *quick sort* algorithm sorts a list by partitioning the list based on an arbitrarily chosen *partition element* and then recursively sorting the sublists on either side of the partition element.

The general strategy of the quick sort algorithm is as follows: First, choose one element of the list to act as a partition element. Next, partition the list so that all elements less than the partition element are to the left of that element and all elements greater than the partition element are to the right. Finally, apply this quick sort strategy (recursively) to both partitions.

If the items to be sorted are in random order initially, the choice of the partition element is arbitrary, and we will use the first element in the list. For efficiency reasons, it would be nice if the partition element divided the list roughly in half, but the algorithm will work no matter what element is chosen as the partition.

Let's look at an example of creating a partition. Suppose we start with the following list:

```
90 65 7 305 120 110 8
```

We choose 90 as our partition element, and then rearrange the list, putting the elements that are less than 90 to the left side and those that are greater than 90 to the right side, yielding two partitions (in bold):

```
8 65 7 90 120 110 305
```

The relative order of the elements in each partition doesn't matter at this point, as long as every value in the left partition is less than 90 and every value in the right partition is greater than 90. Note that, after creating the two partitions, the partition element (90) is in its final position in the array, and we no longer have to consider or move it again.

We then apply the quick sort algorithm separately to both partitions. This process continues until a partition contains only one element, which is inherently sorted. Thus, after the algorithm is applied recursively to either side, the entire list is sorted.

The `quickSort` method in the `Sorting` class implements the quick sort algorithm. It accepts an array of objects to sort and the minimum and maximum index values used for a particular call to the method. For the initial call to the method, the values of `min` and `max` would encompass the entire set of elements to be sorted.

The `quickSort` method calls a support method called `partition`, which partitions the elements on either side of the partition element and returns the final index of the partition element (the pivot point). The `quickSort` method then calls itself twice more recursively to sort the two partitions. The `if` statement terminates the recursion when the size of the partition is one or less.

The `partition` method works by scanning in from each end of the current partition toward the middle until it finds two elements that are on the wrong side, and then swaps them. When this scanning process meets at the partition point, the partitions have been created.

The integer variables `left` and `right` are used to track the positions in the array as we scan in from either end of the current partition. The two inner loops are used to find elements that are in the wrong partitions. The first inner loop scans from left to right looking for an element that is greater than the partition element. The second inner loop scans from right to left looking for an element that is less than the partition element. When these two elements are found, they are swapped. This process continues until the right and left indexes meet in the "middle" of the list, and the outer loop terminates. The location where they meet also indicates where the partition element should reside. At the end of the method, the partition element is moved from its initial location to its final position in the sorted array.

Merge Sort

The *merge sort* algorithm sorts a list by recursively dividing the list in half until each sublist has one element and then recombining these sublists in order.

KEY CONCEPT
The merge sort algorithm sorts a list by recursively dividing the list in half until each sublist has one element and then merging these sublists into the sorted order.

The general strategy of the merge sort algorithm is as follows: Begin by dividing the list in two roughly equal parts and then recursively calling itself with each of those lists. Continue the recursive decomposition of the list until the base case of the recursion is reached, where the list is divided into lists of length one, which are inherently sorted. Then, as control passes back up the recursive calling structure, the algorithm merges the two sorted sublists resulting from the two recursive calls into one sorted list.

Suppose we started with the following initial list (the same example we used in the previous section):

```
90 65 7 305 120 110 8
```

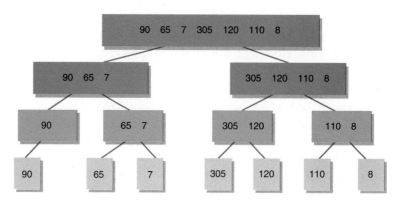

FIGURE 13.5 The decomposition of merge sort

The merge sort algorithm divides the list in half, and then divides each of those lists in half, and so on until a list of length one is reached, as shown in Figure 13.5.

The merge portion of the algorithm then recombines the lists as shown in Figure 13.6. When each sublist is merged together, their elements are kept in sorted order.

The mergeSort method in the Sorting class in Listing 13.5 implements this strategy. The midpoint of the list to be sorted is determined, and then mergeSort is called twice again recursively to sort those two halves. The recursion is terminated by the if statement when a sublist has a length of one or less. As the recursion unfolds, the two sorted sublists are merged by the merge support method.

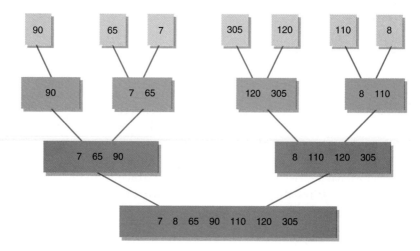

FIGURE 13.6 The merge portion of the merge sort algorithm

The merge method accepts three integers that define the two sublists within the array that have already been sorted. The values in the array from index first to index mid are in sorted order, and the values in the array from index mid+1 to index last are in sorted order. The job of the merge method is to merge these two sublists into one larger, sorted list.

As the merge occurs, values are moved from one sublist or the other into a temporary array. Then, when the merge is complete, the values are copied from the temporary array back into the original.

The first while loop in the merge method scans through the two sublists, copying the smaller values found from either list into the temp array. This process continues until all values from one sublist or the other have been copied into the temp array. Then, the remaining values are moved from the other sublist into the temp array. Since we don't know which sublist has been exhausted, both are checked (but only one or the other will be needed for any given execution of the sort).

The for loop at the end of the merge method copies all data put into the temp array, which is now sorted, back into the original array.

13.3 Analyzing Searching and Sorting Algorithms

Let's apply the concepts of algorithm analysis, discussed in Chapter 12, to the searching and sorting algorithms presented in this chapter. Keep in mind that what we're most interested in is the asymptotic complexity of an algorithm as the size of the problem grows. That is, although we could painstakingly quantify the effort represented by each line of code (assignment statements, increments, comparisons), they individually contribute some constant to the growth function, and those constants become irrelevant in the big picture. The thing that matters is the way the algorithm behaves in terms of the problem size (n).

Another issue to consider is the *best-case* and *worst-case* situations for each algorithm. For some problems, such as our dishwashing scenario or the Towers of Hanoi puzzle, there essentially is no best or worst case. Solving these problems will always require the same amount of effort for a given problem size. But in the case of searching, the effort depends on the particular value being sought. You could be "lucky" and find it quickly, or "unlucky" and not find it until late in the processing. Similarly, some sorting algorithms may be more efficient in a particular situation depending on the original configuration of the data to be sorted.

Thinking through the best-case and worse-case scenarios often helps us appreciate the *expected-case* (or *average-case*) situation for a given algorithm, which is generally the focus of algorithm analysis.

Comparing Search Algorithms

For a linear search, the best case occurs when the target element happens to be the first item we examine in the group. The worst case occurs when the target is not in the group, and we have to examine every element before we determine that it isn't present. The expected case is that we would have to search half of the list before we find the element. That is, if there are n elements in the search pool, on average we would have to examine n/2 elements before finding the one for which we were searching.

Therefore, the linear search algorithm has a linear time complexity of O(n). Because the elements are searched one at a time in turn, the complexity is linear—in direct proportion to the number of elements to be searched.

A binary search, on the other hand, is generally much faster. Because we can eliminate half of the remaining data with each comparison, we can find the element much more quickly. The best case is that we find the target in one comparison—that is, the target element happens to be at the midpoint of the array. The worst case occurs if the element is not present in the list, in which case we have to make approximately $\log_2 n$ comparisons before we eliminate all of the data. Thus, the expected case for finding an element that is in the search pool is approximately $(\log_2 n)/2$ comparisons.

> **KEY CONCEPT**
>
> A binary search has logarithmic complexity, making it very efficient for a large search pool.

Therefore, a binary search is a logarithmic algorithm and has a time complexity of O(log n). Compared to a linear search, a binary search is much faster for large values of n.

The question might be asked, if a logarithmic search is more efficient than a linear search, why would we ever use a linear search? First, a linear search is generally simpler than a binary search, and thus easier to program and debug. Second, a linear search does not require the additional overhead of sorting the search list. There is a trade-off between the effort to keep the search pool sorted and the efficiency of the search.

For small problems, there is little practical difference between the two types of algorithms. However, as n gets larger, the binary search becomes increasingly attractive. Suppose a given set of data contains one million elements. In a linear search, we'd have to examine each of the one million elements to determine that a particular target element is not in the group. In a binary search, we could make that conclusion after approximately 20 comparisons.

Comparing Sort Algorithms

Although selection sort, insertion sort, and bubble sort each solve the problem with a different technique, they all do so with approximately the same efficiency.

All three of those algorithms use two loops, one nested within the other, to arrange the elements in order, and the details all lead to an $O(n^2)$ running time.

Selection sort, for instance, has an outer loop that iterates $n - 1$ times. For each iteration of the outer loop, the inner loop iterates over a portion of the array (how much depends on which iteration of the outer loop we're doing, but it's always less than n). And there is some constant effort in each inner iteration. So the growth function of this algorithm can be expressed:

```
f(n) = (n-1) * (some constant * n + another constant)
     = an² + bn + c
```

for irrelevant constants a, b, and c. For Big-Oh analysis, only the n^2 term matters, leaving sequential sort with a complexity of $O(n^2)$.

Similar arguments can be made for the insertion sort and bubble sort algorithms. The details would vary, but the analysis would conclude that they also have quadratic complexity.

> **KEY CONCEPT**
>
> The average running time complexity for selection sort, insertion sort, and bubble sort is $O(n^2)$.

Now consider the best- and worst-case scenarios for each of these algorithms. For selection and bubble sorts, the processing is fundamentally independent of the original configuration of the elements to be sorted. There will be slight differences in the number of swaps that occur depending on the data, but the best, worst, and average cases for both selection and bubble sorts are all $O(n^2)$.

Insertion sort, on the other hand, is based on the original configuration. The worst case for insertion sort, when the original array is in reverse sorted order, will process the inner loop fully, so it is basically the same as the average case, $O(n^2)$. However, if the array is already sorted in the correct order, the inner loop of the insertion sort will make only one comparison, and thus the best case for insertion sort is $O(n)$. While starting with a fully sorted array initially is not likely, starting with a partially sorted array may be likely depending on the situation, and the insertion sort is quicker in those cases as well.

Now let's consider the quick sort algorithm. Ideally, the partition element chosen each time will divide the elements in half, so that each recursive call to `quickSort` will operate on about half of the current data, as depicted in Figure 13.7 on the next page. In this case, there will be $\log_2 n$ levels in the recursion. The act of partitioning the elements at each level requires one pass through the data, so the effort to partition an entire level of Figure 13.7 is $O(n)$. Thus, the effort to sort the entire array is $O(n \log n)$.

Figure 13.7 depicts the best case for quick sort. And if we pick a good partition element, that is the expected case as well. The worst-case scenario for quick sort is if it consistently picks a partition element that does not partition the data at all, which means each level of the recursion only handles one element. In that case the running time degrades to $O(n^2)$.

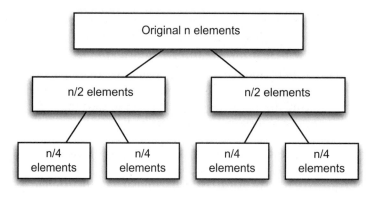

etc...

FIGURE 13.7 The ideal decomposition of quick sort

Thus the key to quick sort is picking a good partition element. In our implementation, we simply chose the first element in the partition. If the original configuration of the array is truly random, this value would be as good as any other.

This is a huge assumption—it is common for "real" data to be partially sorted in one direction or another for various reasons. If that's the case, picking the first element will lead to the worst-case scenario. A better solution would be to pick the middle element. An even better way to improve the likelihood of picking a good partition element is to pick three values (perhaps the first, middle, and last value) and use the median of those three.

The analysis of merge sort is similar to that of quick sort, except that we are guaranteed that the recursive decomposition for merge sort will always divide the data in half. Therefore, in a scenario similar to the one in Figure 13.7, the number of levels is $\log_2 n$. For the merge portion of the algorithm, one pass is needed through the data to merge two sublists. So the effort to merge an entire level is $O(n)$. Therefore, the effort of merge sort is $O(n \log n)$ in the best, worst, and average cases.

The primary downside to the merge sort algorithm is the need for temporary data space to perform the merge operation. The guaranteed savings in running time usually makes up for this expense. But that's the essence of the tradeoff between quick sort and merge sort–quick sort uses no extra memory but could degrade in efficiency if a poor partition element is chosen; merge sort is guaranteed to be efficient but uses extra memory.

Summary of Key Concepts

- Searching is the process of finding a designated target within a group of items or determining that it doesn't exist.

- An efficient search minimizes the number of comparisons made.

- A binary search capitalizes on the fact that the search pool is sorted.

- The `Comparable` interface allows an algorithm to be implemented polymorphically, without regard to a particular class.

- A binary search capitalizes on the fact that the search pool is sorted.

- A binary search eliminates half of the viable candidates with each comparison.

- Sorting is the process of arranging a list of items into a defined order based on some criteria.

- The selection sort algorithm sorts a list of values by repeatedly putting a particular value into its final, sorted position.

- The insertion sort algorithm sorts a list of values by repetitively inserting a particular value into a subset of the list that has already been sorted.

- The bubble sort algorithm sorts a list by repeatedly comparing neighboring elements and swapping them if necessary.

- The quick sort algorithm sorts a list by partitioning the list and then recursively sorting the two partitions.

- The merge sort algorithm sorts a list by recursively dividing the list in half until each sublist has one element and then merging these sublists into the sorted order.

- A binary search has logarithmic complexity, making it very efficient for a large search pool.

- The average running time complexity for selection sort, insertion sort, and bubble sort is $O(n^2)$.

- The key to quick sort is picking a good partition element.

- Merge sort has a maximum running time complexity of $O(n \log n)$.

Self-Review Questions

SR 13.1   How does the `Comparable` interface facilitate the implementation of search and sort algorithms?

SR 13.2   Which search algorithm requires that the list be sorted? Why?

SR 13.3   What are the viable candidates in a binary search?

SR 13.4   What is swapping?

SR 13.5   How does selection sort work in general?

SR 13.6   How does quick sort work in general?

SR 13.7   Which is more efficient, linear or binary search?

SR 13.8   Which is more efficient, selection sort, insertion sort, or bubble sort?

SR 13.9   Which is more efficient, quick sort or merge sort?

Exercises

EX 13.1   Which value does the `binarySearch` method use as the midpoint if the number of viable candidates is even? Explain.

EX 13.2   Trace a binary search for Eleni Daniilidou conducted on the data from the `SearchPlayerList` program. How many comparisons does it perform?

EX 13.3   Compare and contrast the linear search and binary search algorithms by searching for the numbers 45 and 54 in the following list:

        3   8   12   34   54   84   91   110

EX 13.4   Using the list from Exercise 13.3, construct a table showing the number of comparisons required to sort that list for each of the sort algorithms (selection sort, insertion sort, bubble sort, quick sort, and merge sort).

EX 13.5   Using the list from Exercise 13.3 as an example, discuss what happens to the number of comparisons for each of the sort algorithms if the list is already sorted?

EX 13.6   The `swap` method uses three assignment statements to swap two values. Can it be done with fewer assignment statements? Explain.

EX 13.7   Given the following list:

90   8   7   56   123   235   9   1   653

show a trace of execution for:

a. selection sort

b. insertion sort

c. bubble sort

d. quick sort

e. merge sort

EX 13.8   Given the resulting sorted list from Exercise 13.7, show a trace of execution for a binary search, searching for the number 235.

EX 13.9   Describe the modifications needed to make the `selectionSort` method sort in descending order.

EX 13.10   Draw a UML class diagram for the `SortPlayerList` program.

Programming Projects

PP 13.1   Modify the `SearchPlayerList` driver program to first call the `selectionSort` method of the `Sorting` class, and then call the `binarySearch` method looking for Maria Sharapova.

PP 13.2   Create a version of the `Contact` class that determines the relative ordering of contacts based on their telephone numbers instead of their names. Modify the driver program accordingly, and test both the linear and binary search algorithms.

PP 13.3   Add a recursive implementation of the binary search algorithm to the `Searching` class. Create a driver to demonstrate this implementation.

PP 13.4   The bubble sort algorithm shown in this chapter is less efficient than it could be. If a pass is made through the list without exchanging any elements, this means that the list is sorted and there is no reason to continue. Modify this algorithm so that it will stop as soon as it recognizes that the list is sorted. *Do not* use a `break` statement!

PP 13.5   There is a variation of the bubble sort algorithm called *gap sort* that, rather than comparing neighboring elements each time through the list, compares elements that are some number (i) positions apart, where i is an integer less than n. For example, the first element would be compared to the (i + 1) element, the second element would be compared to the (i + 2) element, the nth element would be compared to the (n − i) element, etc. A single iteration is completed when all of the elements that can be compared, have been compared. On the next iteration, i is reduced by some number greater than 1 and the process continues until i is less than 1. Implement a gap sort and create a driver program to exercise it.

PP 13.6   Modify the sorts listed in the chapter (selection sort, insertion sort, bubble sort, quick sort, and merge sort) by adding code to each to tally the total number of comparisons and total execution time of each algorithm. Execute the sort algorithms against the same list, recording information for the total number of comparisons and total execution time for each algorithm. Try several different lists, including at least one that is already in sorted order.

PP 13.7   Design and implement a class called TVShow that represents a particular television program. Have TVShow implement Comparable, so that it determines the relative order of the shows alphabetically by title. Create a driver program that populates an array of TVShow objects and exercises various searching and sorting algorithms.

PP 13.8   Modify the TVShow class from programming project 13.7 so that it takes the day the show is presented into account when comparing them. That is, have all shows on Sunday come before all shows on Monday, etc. Within a day, sort by title alphabetically. Create a driver program that demonstrates this new ability.

PP 13.9   The search and sort algorithms were implemented in this chapter as static methods of the classes Searching and Sorting, respectively. Sometimes such methods are incorporated into the classes of the objects upon which they operate. Create a class called ContactList that manages an array of Contact objects. In the ContactList class, implement a selectionSort method that operates without the need to pass the array as a parameter.

PP 13.10   Modify the ContactList class from programming project 13.9 so that it implements a merge sort.

Answers to Self-Review Questions

SR 13.1   The `Comparable` interface provides a specific and separate way
           to define the relative ordering of any particular class of objects.
           It is up to the class to implement the `compareTo` method appro-
           priately. The search and sort methods don't particularly "care"
           what type of objects they operate on, as long as they're
           `Comparable` objects. This is a classic application of the object-
           oriented concept of polymorphism.

SR 13.2   Binary search requires the elements to be sorted because it starts
           in the middle of the list and eliminates half of the data with one
           comparison.

SR 13.3   In a binary search, the viable candidates are the elements in the
           search pool in which the target may still be found. For a binary
           search, each comparison divides the size of the viable candidates
           in half.

SR 13.4   Swapping is the process of exchanging the position of two
           elements in an array. The need to swap two elements occurs in
           several sorting algorithms.

SR 13.5   Selection sort repeatedly puts a particular value into its final,
           sorted position. On each pass, it selects one value, such as the
           smallest value, and puts it in the correct place.

SR 13.6   Quick sort partitions a list of elements into two groups, those
           smaller than a particular partition element, and those larger
           than the partition element. Then it recursively sorts the two
           partitions.

SR 13.7   The binary search, at O(log n), is more efficient than a linear
           search, which is O(n). However, the binary search requires that
           the search pool be sorted.

SR 13.8   Selection sort, insertion sort, and bubble sort all have an aver-
           age run time of $O(n^2)$ and are generally considered to be of
           equal efficiency. Insertion sort, however, does have a better run
           time if the original data is in partially sorted order.

SR 13.9   Quick sort and merge sort are both O(n log n) algorithms, with
           basically equal efficiency. They are much better than the quad-
           ratic sorts (selection, insertion, and bubble). Merge sort has the
           added benefit of guaranteeing O(n log n) even in the worse case,
           whereas quick sort can degrade to $O(n^2)$ if bad choices are
           made for the partition element.

Stacks

CHAPTER OBJECTIVES

- Define the concepts and terminology related to collections.

- Explore the basic structure of the Java Collections API.

- Discuss the abstract design of collections.

- Explore issues surrounding collections including inheritance, polymorphism, generics, and interfaces.

- Define a stack collection.

- Use a stack collection to solve a problem.

- Examine an array implementation of a stack.

- Describe the use of references to create linked structures.

- Compare linked structures to array-based structures.

- Explore the techniques for managing a linked list.

- Discuss the need for a separate node object to form linked structures.

- Implement a stack collection using a linked list.

This chapter begins our exploration of collections and the underlying data structures used to implement them. It lays the groundwork for the study of collections by carefully defining the issues and goals related to their design. In particular, this chapter introduces a collection called a stack and uses it to exemplify the issues related to the design, implementation, and use of collections.

14.1 Introduction to Collections

A *collection* is an object that gathers and organizes other objects. It defines the specific ways in which those objects, which are called *elements* of the collection, can be accessed and managed. The user of a collection, which is usually another class or object in the software system, must interact with the collection only in the prescribed ways.

Over the past 50 years, several specific types of collections have been defined by software developers and researchers. Each type of collection lends itself to solving particular kinds of problems. The remainder of this book is devoted to exploring these classic collections.

Collections can be separated into two broad categories: linear and nonlinear. As the name implies, a *linear collection* is one in which the elements of the collection are organized in a straight line. A *nonlinear collection* is one in which the elements are organized in something other than a straight line, such as a hierarchy or a network. For that matter, a nonlinear collection may not have any organization at all.

The organization of the elements in a collection, relative to each other, is usually determined by one of two things:

- The order in which they were added to the collection.
- Some inherent relationship among the elements themselves.

For example, one linear collection may always add new elements to one end of the line, so the order of the elements is determined by the order in which they are added. Another linear collection may be kept in sorted order based on some characteristic of the elements. For example, a list of people may be kept in alphabetical order based on the characters that make up their name. The specific organization of the elements in a nonlinear collection can be determined in either of these two ways as well.

Abstract Data Types

An *abstraction* hides certain details at certain times. Dealing with an abstraction is easier than dealing with too many details at one time. In fact, we couldn't get through a day without relying on abstractions. For example, we couldn't possibly drive a car if we had to worry about all the details that make the car work: the spark plugs, the pistons, the transmission, and so on. Instead, we can focus on the *interface* to the car: the steering wheel, the pedals, and a few other controls. These

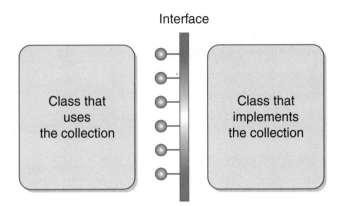

FIGURE 14.1 A well-defined interface masks the implementation
of the collection

controls are an abstraction, hiding the underlying details and allowing us to control an otherwise very complicated machine.

A collection, like any well-designed object, is an abstraction. A collection defines the interface operations through which the user can manage the objects in the collection, such as adding and removing elements. The user interacts with the collection through this interface, as depicted in Figure 14.1. However, the details of how a collection is implemented to fulfill that definition are another issue altogether. A class that implements the collection's interface must fulfill the conceptual definition of the collection, but can do so in many ways.

> **KEY CONCEPT**
>
> A collection is an abstraction where the details of the implementation are hidden.

Abstraction is an important software engineering concept. In large software systems, it is virtually impossible for any one person to grasp all of the details of the system at once. Instead, the system is divided into abstract subsystems such that the purpose of and the interactions among those subsystems can be specified. Subsystems may then be assigned to different developers or groups of developers that will develop the subsystem to meet its specification.

An object is the perfect mechanism for creating a collection because, if it is designed correctly, the internal workings of an object are *encapsulated* from the rest of the system. In almost all cases, the instance variables defined in a class should be declared with private visibility. Therefore, only the methods of that class can access and modify them. The only interaction a user has with an object should be through its public methods, which represent the services that the object provides.

As we progress through our exploration of collections, we will always stress the idea of separating the interface from the implementation. Therefore, for every collection that we examine, we should consider the following:

- How does the collection operate, conceptually?
- How do we formally define the interface to the collection?
- What kinds of problems does the collection help us solve?
- In which various ways might we implement the collection?
- What are the benefits and costs of each implementation?

Before we continue, let's carefully define some other terms related to the exploration of collections. A *data type* is a group of values and the operations defined on those values. The primitive data types defined in Java are the primary examples. For example, the integer data type defines a set of numeric values and the operations (addition, subtraction, etc.) that can be used on them.

An *abstract data type* (ADT) is a data type whose values and operations are not inherently defined within a programming language. It is abstract only in that the details of its implementation must be defined and should be hidden from the user. A collection, therefore, is an abstract data type.

> **KEY CONCEPT**
>
> A data structure is the underlying programming constructs used to implement a collection.

A *data structure* is the collection of programming constructs used to implement a collection. For example, a collection might be implemented using a fixed-size structure such as an array. One interesting artifact of these definitions and our design decision to separate the interface from the implementation (i.e., the collection from the data structure that implements it) is that we may, and often do, end up with a linear data structure, such as an array, being used to implement a nonlinear collection, such as a tree.

Historically, the terms ADT and data structure have been used in various ways. We carefully define them here to avoid any confusion, and will use them consistently. Throughout this book we will examine various data structures and how they can be used to implement various collections.

The Java Collections API

The Java programming language is accompanied by a very large library of classes that can be used to support the development of software. Parts of the library are organized into *application programming interfaces* (APIs). The *Java Collections API* is a set of classes that represent a few specific types of collections, implemented in various ways.

You might ask why we should learn how to design and implement collections if a set of collections has already been provided for us. There are several reasons.

First, the Java Collections API provides only a subset of the collections you may want to use. Second, the classes that are provided may not implement the collections in the ways you desire. Third, and perhaps most important, the study of software development requires a deep understanding of the issues involved in the design of collections and the data structures used to implement them.

As we explore various types of collections, we will also examine the appropriate classes of the Java Collections API. In each case, we analyze the various implementations that we develop and compare them to the approach used by the classes in the standard library.

14.2 A Stack Collection

Let's look at an example of a collection. A *stack* is a linear collection whose elements are added and removed from the same end. We say that a stack is processed in a *last in, first out* (LIFO) manner. That is, the last element to be put on a stack will be the first one that gets removed. Said another way, the elements of a stack are removed in the reverse order of their placement on it. In fact, one of the principle uses of a stack in computing is to reverse the order of something (e.g., an undo operation).

> **KEY CONCEPT**
>
> Stack elements are processed in a LIFO manner—the last element in is the first element out.

The processing of a stack is shown in Figure 14.2. Usually a stack is depicted vertically, and we refer to the end to which elements are added and from which they are removed as the *top* of the stack.

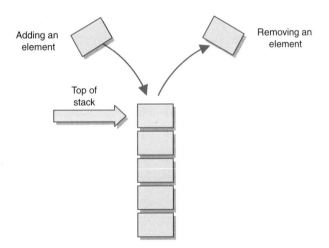

FIGURE 14.2 A conceptual view of a stack

Recall from our earlier discussions that we define an abstract data type (ADT) by identifying a specific set of operations that establishes the valid ways in which we can manage the elements stored in the data structure. We always want to use this concept to formally define the operations for a collection and work within the functionality it provides. That way, we can cleanly separate the interface to the collection from any particular implementation technique used to create it.

The operations for a stack ADT are listed in Figure 14.3. In stack terminology, we *push* an element onto a stack and we *pop* an element off a stack. We can also *peek* at the top element of a stack, examining it or using it as needed, without actually removing it from the collection. There are also the general operations that allow us to determine if the stack is empty and, if not empty, how many elements it contains.

> **KEY CONCEPT**
>
> A programmer should choose the structure that is appropriate for the type of data management needed.

Sometimes there are variations on the naming conventions for the operations on a collection. For a stack, the use of the terms push and pop are relatively standard. The `peek` operation is sometimes referred to as *top*.

Keep in mind that the definition of a collection is not universal. You will find variations in the operations defined for specific data structures from one book to another. We've been very careful in this book to define the operations on each collection so that they are consistent with its purpose.

For example, note that none of the stack operations in Figure 14.3 allow us to reach down into the stack to modify, remove, or reorganize the elements in the stack. That is the very nature of a stack—all activity occurs at one end. If we discover that, to solve a particular problem, we need to access the elements in the middle or at the bottom of the collection, then a stack is not the appropriate data structure to use.

We do provide a `toString` operation for the collection. This is not a classic operation defined for a stack, and it could be argued that this operation violates

Operation	Description
push	Adds an element to the top of the stack.
pop	Removes an element from the top of the stack.
peek	Examines the element at the top of the stack.
isEmpty	Determines if the stack is empty.
size	Determines the number of elements on the stack.

FIGURE 14.3 The operations on a stack

the prescribed behavior of a stack. However, it provides a convenient means to traverse and display the stack's contents without allowing modification of the stack and this is quite useful for debugging purposes.

14.3 Inheritance, Polymorphism, and Generics

Now lets consider what we will store in our stack. One possibility would be to simply recreate our stack data structure each time we need it and create it to store the specific object type for that application. For example, if we needed a stack of strings, we would simply copy and paste our stack code and change the object type to `String`. While copy, paste, and modify is technically a form of reuse, it is not our goal. Reuse, in its purest form, should mean that we create a collection that is written once, compiled into byte code once, and will then handle any objects we choose to store in it safely, efficiently, and effectively. To accomplish these goals, we must take *type compatibility* and *type checking* into account. Type compatibility is the concept of whether a particular assignment of an object to a reference is legal. For example, the following assignment is not legal since you cannot assign a reference declared to be of type `String` to point to an object of type `Integer`.

```
String x = new Integer(10);
```

Java provides compile-time type checking that will flag this invalid assignment. A second possibility for what to store in our collection would be to take advantage of the concepts of *inheritance* and *polymorphism* to create a collection that could store objects of any class.

> **KEY CONCEPT**
>
> A polymorphic reference uses the type of the object, not the type of the reference, to determine which version of a method to invoke.

In Chapter 9, we discussed the concept of polymorphism via inheritance, meaning that a reference of a particular type can be used to refer to any descendant of that type. Carrying this to the extreme, an `Object` reference can be used to refer to any object, because ultimately all classes are descendants of the `Object` class. An `ArrayList`, for example, uses polymorphism in that it is designed to hold `Object` references. That's why an `ArrayList` can be used to store any kind of object. In fact, a particular `ArrayList` can be used to hold several different types of objects at one time, because, in essence, they are all `Object` objects.

The result of this discussion would seem to be that we could simply store `Object` references in our stack and take advantage of polymorphism via inheritance to create a collection that can store any type of objects. However, this possible solution creates some unexpected consequences. Lets examine what can happen when dealing with polymorphic references and arrays. Consider again our classes from Chapter 9 as shown in Figure 14.4 on the next page.

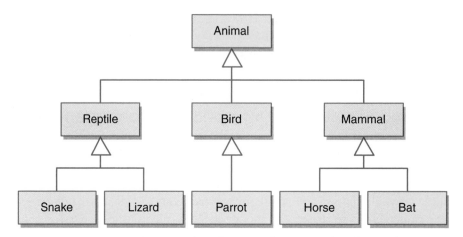

FIGURE 14.4 A UML class diagram showing a class hierarchy

Since Animal is a superclass of all of the other classes in this diagram, an assignment such as the following is allowable:

```
Animal creature = new Bird();
```

However, this also means that the following assignments will compile as well:

```
Animal[] creatures = new Mammal[];
creatures[1] = new Reptile();
```

Note that by definition, creatures[1] should be both a Mammal and an Animal, but not a Reptile. This code will compile but will generate a java.lang.ArrayStoreException at run-time. Thus, since using the Object class will not provide us with compile-time type checking, we should look for a better solution.

Generics

Beginning with Java 5.0, Java enables us to define a class based on a *generic type*. That is, we can define a class so that it stores, operates on, and manages objects whose type is not specified until the class is instantiated. Generics are an integral part of our discussions of collections and their underlying implementations throughout the rest of this book.

Let's assume we need to define a class called Box that stores and manages other objects. As we discussed, using polymorphism, we could simply define Box so that internally it stores references to the Object class. Then, any type of object could be stored inside a box. In fact, multiple types of unrelated objects could be stored in Box. We lose a lot of control with that level of flexibility in our code.

A better approach is to define the Box class to store a generic type T. (We can use any identifier we want for the generic type, though using T has become a convention.) The header of the class contains a reference to the type in angle brackets.

For example:

```
class Box<T>
{
   // declarations and code that manage objects of type T
}
```

Then, when a `Box` is needed, it is instantiated with a specific class used in place of `T`. For example, if we wanted a `Box` of `Widget` objects, we could use the following declaration:

```
Box<Widget> box1 = new Box<Widget>;
```

The type of the `box1` variable is `Box<Widget>`. In essence, for the `box1` object, the `Box` class replaces `T` with `Widget`. Now suppose we wanted a `Box` in which to store `Gadget` objects; we could make the following declaration:

```
Box<Gadget> box2 = new Box<Gadget>;
```

For `box2`, the `Box` class essentially replaces `T` with `Gadget`. So, although the `box1` and `box2` objects are both boxes, they have different types because the generic type is taken into account. This is a safer implementation, because at this point we cannot use `box1` to store gadgets (or anything else for that matter), nor could we use `box2` to store widgets. A generic type such as `T` cannot be instantiated. It is merely a placeholder to allow us to define the class that will manage a specific type of object that is established when the class is instantiated.

Given that we now have a mechanism using generic types for creating a collection that can be used to store any type of object safely and effectively, lets continue on with our discussion of the stack collection.

14.4 A Stack ADT

To facilitate the separation of the interface operations from the methods that implement them, we can define a Java interface structure for a collection. A Java interface provides a formal mechanism for defining the set of operations for any collection.

> **KEY CONCEPT**
>
> A Java interface defines a set of abstract methods and is useful in separating the concept of an abstract data type from its implementation.

Recall from Chapter 9 that a Java interface defines a set of abstract methods, specifying each method's signature but not its body. A class that implements an interface provides definitions for the methods defined in the interface. The interface name can be used as the type of a reference, which can be assigned any object of any class that implements the interface.

Listing 14.1 on the next page defines a Java interface for a stack collection. It is defined as part of the `javafoundations` package, which contains all of the collection classes and interfaces presented in this book.

Note that the stack interface is defined as `Stack<T>`, operating on a generic type `T`. In the methods of the interface, the type of various parameters and return

LISTING 14.1

```java
//********************************************************************
//  Stack.java         Java Foundations
//
//  Defines the interface to a stack collection.
//********************************************************************

package javafoundations;

public interface Stack<T>
{
    //  Adds the specified element to the top of the stack.
    public void push (T element);

    //  Removes and returns the top element from the stack.
    public T pop();

    //  Returns a reference to the top element of this stack
    //  without removing it.
    public T peek();

    //  Returns true if the stack contains no elements and false
    //  otherwise.
    public boolean isEmpty();

    //  Returns the number of elements in the stack.
    public int size();

    //  Returns a string representation of the stack.
    public String toString();
}
```

KEY CONCEPT

By using the interface name as a return type, the interface doesn't commit the method to the use of any particular class that implements a stack.

values is often expressed using the generic type T. When this interface is implemented, it will be based on a type that is substituted for T.

Later in this chapter we examine classes that implement this interface. For now, our abstract understanding of how a stack operates allows us to explore situations in which stacks help us solve particular problems.

Stacks are used quite frequently in the computing world. For example, the undo operation in a word processor is usually implemented using a stack. As we make changes to a document (add data, delete data, make format changes, etc.), the word processor keeps track of each operation by pushing some representation of it onto a stack. If we choose to undo an operation, the word processing software pops the most recently performed operation off the stack and reverses it. If we choose to undo again (undoing the second-to-last operation we performed), another element is popped from the stack. In most word processors, many operations can be reversed in this manner.

The following section explores in detail an example of using a stack to solve a problem.

14.5 Using Stacks: Evaluating Postfix Expressions

Traditionally, arithmetic expressions are written in *infix* notation, meaning that the operator is placed between its operands in the form

> *<operand> <operator> <operand>*

such as in the expression

> 4 + 5

When evaluating an infix expression, we rely on precedence rules to determine the order of operator evaluation. For example, the expression

> 4 + 5 * 2

evaluates to 14 rather than 18 because of the precedence rule that says in the absence of parentheses, multiplication evaluates before addition.

In a *postfix* expression, the operator comes after its two operands. Therefore, a postfix expression takes the form

> *<operand> <operand> <operator>*

For example, the postfix expression

> 6 9 −

is equivalent to the infix expression

> 6 − 9

A postfix expression is generally easier to evaluate than an infix expression because precedence rules and parentheses do not have to be taken into account. The order of the values and operators in the expression are sufficient to determine the result. Programming language compilers and run-time environments often use postfix expressions in their internal calculations for this reason.

The process of evaluating a postfix expression can be stated in one simple rule: Scanning from left to right, apply each operation to the two operands immediately preceding it and replace the operator with the result. At the end we are left with the final value of the expression.

Consider the infix expression we looked at earlier:

4 + 5 * 2

In postfix notation, this expression would be written

4 5 2 * +

Let's use our evaluation rule to determine the final value of this expression. We scan from the left until we encounter the multiplication (*) operator. We apply this operator to the two operands immediately preceding it (5 and 2) and replace it with the result (10), leaving us with

4 10 +

Continuing our scan from left to right, we immediately encounter the plus (+) operator. Applying this operator to the two operands immediately preceding it (4 and 10) yields 14, which is the final value of the expression.

Let's look at a slightly more complicated example. Consider the following infix expression:

(3 * 4 − (2 + 5)) * 4 / 2

The equivalent postfix expression is

3 4 * 2 5 + − 4 * 2 /

Applying our evaluation rule results in:

	12 2 5 + − 4 * 2 /
then	12 7 − 4 * 2 /
then	5 4 * 2 /
then	20 2 /
then	10

Now let's think about the design of a program that will evaluate a postfix expression. The evaluation rule relies on being able to retrieve the previous two operands whenever we encounter an operator. Furthermore, a large postfix expression will have many operators and operands to manage. It turns out that a stack is the perfect data structure to use in this case. The operations provided by a stack coincide nicely with the process of evaluating a postfix expression.

> **KEY CONCEPT**
>
> A stack is the ideal data structure to use when evaluating a postfix expression.

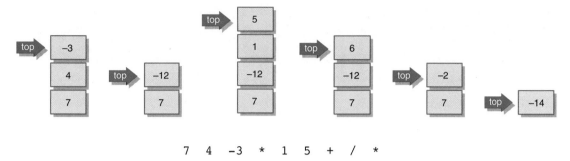

7   4   -3   *   1   5   +   /   *

FIGURE 14.5 Using a stack to evaluate a postfix expression

The algorithm for evaluating a postfix expression using a stack can be expressed as follows: Scan the expression from left to right, identifying each token (operator or operand) in turn. If it is an operand, push it onto the stack. If it is an operator, pop the top two elements off of the stack, apply the operation to them, and push the result onto the stack. When we reach the end of the expression, the element remaining on the stack is the result of the expression. If at any point we attempt to pop two elements off of the stack but there are not two elements on the stack, then our postfix expression was not properly formed. Similarly, if we reach the end of the expression and more than one element remains on the stack, then our expression was not well formed. Figure 14.5 depicts the use of a stack to evaluate a postfix expression.

The program in Listing 14.2 on the next page evaluates multiple postfix expressions entered by the user. It uses the `PostfixEvaluator` class shown in Listing 14.3 on page 527.

To keep things simple, this program assumes that the operands to the expression are integers and are literal values (not variables). When executed, the program repeatedly accepts and evaluates postfix expressions until the user chooses not to.

The `evaluate` method performs the evaluation algorithm described earlier, supported by the `isOperator` and `evalSingleOp` methods. Note that in the `evaluate` method, only operands are pushed onto the stack. Operators are used as they are encountered and are never put on the stack. This is consistent with the evaluation algorithm we discussed. An operand is put on the stack as an `Integer` object, instead of as an `int` primitive value, because the stack data structure is designed to store objects.

When an operator is encountered, the most recent two operands are popped off of the stack. Note that the first operand popped is actually the second operand in the expression, and the second operand popped is the first operand in the expression. This order doesn't matter in the cases of addition and multiplication, but it certainly matters for subtraction and division.

LISTING 14.2

```java
//********************************************************************
//  Postfix.java        Java Foundations
//
//  Demonstrates the use of a stack to evaluate postfix expressions.
//********************************************************************
import java.util.Scanner;

public class Postfix
{
   //-----------------------------------------------------------------
   //  Reads and evaluates multiple postfix expressions.
   //-----------------------------------------------------------------
   public static void main (String[] args)
   {
      String expression, again;
      int result;

      try
      {
         Scanner in = new Scanner(System.in);

         do
         {
            PostfixEvaluator evaluator = new PostfixEvaluator();
            System.out.println ("Enter a valid postfix expression: ");
            expression = in.nextLine();

            result = evaluator.evaluate (expression);
            System.out.println();
            System.out.println ("That expression equals " + result);

            System.out.print ("Evaluate another expression [Y/N]? ");
            again = in.nextLine();
            System.out.println();
         }
         while (again.equalsIgnoreCase("y"));
      }
      catch (Exception IOException)
      {
         System.out.println("Input exception reported");
      }
   }
}
```

LISTING 14.2   *continued*

OUTPUT

```
Enter a valid postfix expression:
7 4 -3 * 1 5 + / *

That expression equals -14
Evaluate another expression [Y/N]? Y

Enter a valid postfix expression:
12 4 - 3 7 * 19 - /

That expression equals 4
Evaluate another expression [Y/N]? N
```

LISTING 14.3

```java
//*********************************************************************
//  PostfixEvaluator.java        Java Foundations
//
//  Represents an integer evaluator of postfix expressions. Assumes
//  the operands are constants.
//*********************************************************************

import javafoundations.LinkedStack;
import java.util.Scanner;

public class PostfixEvaluator
{
   private final char ADD = '+', SUBTRACT = '-';
   private final char MULTIPLY = '*', DIVIDE = '/';
   private LinkedStack<Integer> stack;

   //------------------------------------------------------------------
   //  Sets up this evaluator by creating a new stack.
   //------------------------------------------------------------------
   public PostfixEvaluator()
   {
      stack = new LinkedStack<Integer>();
   }
```

LISTING 14.3 *continued*

```java
//--------------------------------------------------------------------
//  Evaluates the specified postfix expression. If an operand is
//  encountered, it is pushed onto the stack. If an operator is
//  encountered, two operands are popped, the operation is
//  evaluated, and the result is pushed onto the stack.
//--------------------------------------------------------------------
public int evaluate (String expr)
{
   int op1, op2, result = 0;
   String token;
   Scanner tokenizer = new Scanner (expr);

   while (tokenizer.hasNext())
   {
      token = tokenizer.next();

      if (isOperator(token))
      {
         op2 = (stack.pop()).intValue();
         op1 = (stack.pop()).intValue();
         result = evalSingleOp (token.charAt(0), op1, op2);
         stack.push (result);
      }
      else
         stack.push (Integer.parseInt(token));
   }

   return result;
}

//--------------------------------------------------------------------
//  Determines if the specified token is an operator.
//--------------------------------------------------------------------
private boolean isOperator (String token)
{
   return (token.equals("+") || token.equals("-") ||
      token.equals("*") || token.equals("/"));
}

//--------------------------------------------------------------------
//  Performs integer evaluation on a single expression consisting of
//  the specified operator and operands.
//--------------------------------------------------------------------
```

LISTING 14.3   *continued*

```
    private int evalSingleOp (char operation, int op1, int op2)
    {
        int result = 0;

        switch (operation)
        {
            case ADD:
                result = op1 + op2;
                break;
            case SUBTRACT:
                result = op1 - op2;
                break;
            case MULTIPLY:
                result = op1 * op2;
                break;
            case DIVIDE:
                result = op1 / op2;
        }

        return result;
    }
}
```

Note also that the postfix expression program assumes that the postfix expression entered is valid, meaning that it contains a properly organized set of operators and operands. A postfix expression is invalid if either (1) two operands are not available on the stack when an operator is encountered or (2) there is more than one value on the stack when the tokens in the expression are exhausted. Either situation indicates that there was something wrong with the format of the expression, and both can be caught by examining the state of the stack at the appropriate point in the program. We will discuss how we might deal with these situations and other exceptional cases in the next section.

Perhaps the most important aspect of this program is the use of the class that defined the stack collection. At this point, we don't know how the stack was implemented. We simply trusted the class to do its job. In this example, we used the class ArrayStack, but we could have used any class that implemented a stack as long as it performed the stack operations (defined by the StackADT interface) as expected. From the point of view of evaluating postfix expressions, the manner in which the stack is implemented is largely irrelevant. Figure 14.6 on the next page shows a UML class diagram for the postfix expression evaluation program.

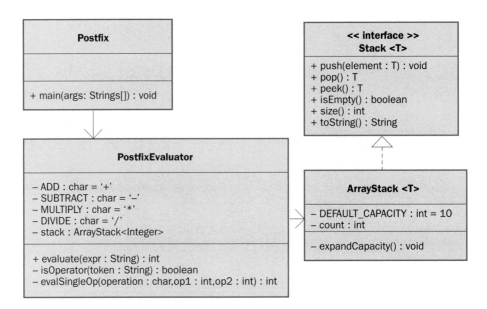

FIGURE 14.6 UML class diagram for the postfix expression evaluation program

14.6 Exceptions

As discussed in Chapter 10, one issue that we will address with each of the collections we discuss is that of exceptional behavior. What action should the collection take in the exceptional case? There are some such cases that are inherant in the collection itself. For example, in the case of a stack, what should happen if an attempt is made to pop an element from an empty stack? In this case, it does not matter what data structure is being used to implement the collection, the exception will still apply. Some such cases are artifacts of the data structure being used to implement the collection. For example, if we are using an array to implement a stack, what should happen if an attempt is made to push an element onto the stack but the array is full? Lets take a moment to explore this concept further.

In our postfix evaluation example there were several potential exceptional situations:

- If the stack were full on a push
- If the stack were empty on a pop
- If the stack held more than one value at the completion of the evaluation

Lets consider each of these separately. The possibility that the stack might be full on a push is an issue for the underlying data structure, not the collection. Conceptually speaking, there is no such thing as a full stack. Now we know that this is not reality and that all data structures will eventually reach a limit. However, the stack is not full, only the data structure that implements the stack is full. We will discuss strategies for handling this situation as we implement our stack in the next section.

What if the stack is empty on a pop? This is an exceptional case that has to do with the problem and not the underlying data structure. In our postfix evaluation example, if we attempt to pop two operands and there are not two operands available on the stack, this means that our postfix expression was not properly formed. This is a perfect case where the collection needs to report the exception and the application then must interpret that exception in context.

The third case is equally interesting. What if the stack holds more than one value at the completion of the evaluation? From the perspective of the stack collection, this is not an exception. However, from the perspective of the application, this is a problem that means once again that the postfix expression was not well formed. Since it will not generate an exception from the collection, this is a condition for which the application must test.

> **KEY CONCEPT**
> Errors and exceptions represent unusual or invalid processing.

The manner in which exceptions are used is important to the definition of a software system. Exceptions could be thrown in many situations in a collection. Usually it's best to throw exceptions whenever an invalid operation is attempted. For example, in the case of a stack, we will throw an exception whenever the user attempts to pop an element from an empty stack. The user then has the choice of checking the situation beforehand to avoid the exception:

```
if (! theStack.isEmpty())
    element = theStack.pop();
```

Or the user can use a `try-catch` statement to handle the situation when it does occur:

```
try {
   element = theStack.pop()
}
catch (EmptyCollectionException exception)
{
   System.out.println ("No elements available.");
}
```

As we explore particular implementation techniques for a collection, we will also discuss the appropriate use of exceptions.

14.7 Implementing a Stack: With Arrays

So far in our discussion of a stack collection we've described its basic conceptual nature and the operations that allow the user to interact with it. In software engineering terms, we would say that we have done the analysis for a stack collection. We've also used a stack, without knowing the details of how it was implemented, to solve a particular problem. Now let's turn our attention to the implementation details. There are various ways to implement a class that represents a stack. In this section we examine an implementation strategy that uses an array to store the objects contained in the stack. In the next chapter we examine a second technique for implementing a stack.

> **KEY CONCEPT**
>
> The implementation of the collection operations should not affect the way users interact with the collection.

To explore this implementation we must recall several key characteristics of Java arrays. The elements stored in an array are indexed from 0 to n − 1, where n is the total number of cells in the array. An array is an object, which is instantiated separately from the objects it holds. And when we talk about an array of objects, we are actually talking about an array of references to objects.

Keep in mind the separation between the collection and the underlying data structure used to implement it. Our goal is to design an efficient implementation that provides the functionality of every operation defined in the stack abstract data type. The array is just a convenient data structure in which to store the objects.

Managing Capacity

When an array object is created, it is allocated a specific number of cells into which elements can be stored. For example, the following instantiation creates an array that can store 500 elements, indexed from 0 to 499:

```
Object[] collection = Object[500];
```

The number of cells in an array is called its *capacity*. This value is stored in the `length` constant of the array. The capacity of an array cannot be changed once the array has been created.

When using an array to implement a collection, we have to deal with the situation in which all cells of the array are being used to store elements. That is, because we are using a fixed-size data structure, at some point the data structure may become "full." However, just because the data structure is full, should that mean that the collection is full?

A crucial question in the design of a collection is what to do in the case in which a new element is added to a full data structure. Three basic options exist:

- We could implement operations that add an element to the collection such that they throw an exception if the data structure is full.
- We could implement the add operations to return a status indicator that can be checked by the user to see if the add operation was successful.
- We could automatically expand the capacity of the underlying data structure whenever necessary so that, essentially, it would never become full.

In the first two cases, the user of the collection must be aware that the collection could get full and take steps to deal with it when needed. For these solutions we would also provide extra operations that allow the user to check to see if the collection is full and to expand the capacity of the data structure as desired. The advantage of these approaches is that it gives the user more control over the capacity.

> **KEY CONCEPT**
> How we handle exceptional conditions determines whether the collection or the user of the collection controls the particular behavior.

However, given our goal to separate the interface from the implementation, the third option is attractive. The capacity of the underlying data structure is an implementation detail that, in general, should be hidden from the user. Furthermore, the capacity issue is particular to this implementation. Other techniques used to implement the collection, such as the one we explore in the next chapter, are not restricted by a fixed capacity and therefore never have to deal with this issue.

In the solutions presented in this book, we opt to implement fixed data structure solutions by automatically expanding the capacity of the underlying data structure. Occasionally, other options are explored as programming projects.

14.8 The ArrayStack Class

In the Java Collections API framework, class names indicate both the underlying data structure and the collection. We follow that naming convention in this book. Thus, we define a class called ArrayStack to represent a stack with an underlying array-based implementation.

To be more precise, we define a class called ArrayStack<T> that represents an array-based implementation of a stack collection that stores objects of generic type T. When we instantiate an ArrayStack object, we specify what the generic type T represents.

> **KEY CONCEPT**
> For efficiency, an array-based stack implementation keeps the bottom of the stack at index 0.

An array implementation of a stack can be designed by making the following four assumptions: the array is an array of object references (type determined when the stack is instantiated), the bottom

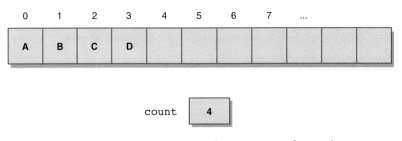

FIGURE 14.7 An array implementation of a stack

of the stack is always at index 0 of the array, the elements of the stack are stored in order and contiguously in the array, and there is an integer variable `top` that stores the index of the array immediately following the top element in the stack.

Figure 14.7 illustrates this configuration for a stack that currently contains the elements A, B, C, and D, assuming that they have been pushed on in that order. To simplify the figure, the elements are shown in the array itself rather than as objects referenced from the array. Note that the variable `top` represents both the next cell into which a pushed element should be stored as well as the count of the number of elements currently in the stack.

In this implementation, the bottom of the stack is always held at index 0 of the array, and the stack grows and shrinks at the higher indexes. This is considerably more efficient than if the stack were reversed within the array. Consider the processing that would be necessary if the top of the stack were kept at index 0.

From these assumptions, we can determine that our class will need a constant to store the default capacity, a variable to keep track of the top of the stack, and a variable for the array to store the stack. This results in the class header shown in Listing 14.4. Note that our `ArrayStack` class will be part of the `javafoundations` package and will make use of a package called `javafoundations.exceptions`.

Our class will have two constructors, one to use the default capacity and the other to use a specified capacity. Just to refresh our memory, this is an excellent example of method overloading, i.e. two methods with the same name that differ only in the parameter list. From our previous discussion of generics we recall that you cannot instantiate a generic type. This also means that you cannot instantiate an array of a generic type. This results in an interesting line of code in both of our constructors:

```
stack = (T[])(new Object[DEFAULT_CAPACITY]);
```

LISTING 14.4

```java
//***************************************************************
//  ArrayStack.java        Java Foundations
//
//  Represents an array implementation of a stack. The bottom of
//  the stack is kept at array index 0.
//***************************************************************

package javafoundations;

import javafoundations.exceptions.*;

public class ArrayStack<T> implements Stack<T>
{
   private final int DEFAULT_CAPACITY = 10;
   private int count;
   private T[] stack;

   //----------------------------------------------------------------
   //  Creates an empty stack using the default capacity.
   //----------------------------------------------------------------
   public ArrayStack()
   {
      count = 0;
      stack = (T[]) (new Object[DEFAULT_CAPACITY]);
   }

   //----------------------------------------------------------------
   //  Adds the specified element to the top of this stack, expanding
   //  the capacity of the stack array if necessary.
   //----------------------------------------------------------------
   public void push (T element)
   {
      if (count == stack.length)
         expandCapacity();

      stack[count] = element;
      count++;
   }

   //----------------------------------------------------------------
   //  Returns a string representation of this stack.
   //----------------------------------------------------------------
```

LISTING 14.4 *continued*

```java
public String toString()
{
    String result = "<top of stack>\n";

    for (int index=count-1; index >= 0; index--)
        result += stack[index] + "\n";

    return result + "<bottom of stack>";
}

//-------------------------------------------------------------------
//  Creates a new array to store the contents of this stack with
//  twice the capacity of the old one.
//-------------------------------------------------------------------
private void expandCapacity()
{
    T[] larger = (T[])(new Object[stack.length*2]);

    for (int index=0; index < stack.length; index++)
        larger[index] = stack[index];

    stack = larger;
}

//-------------------------------------------------------------------
//  The following methods are left as programming projects.
//-------------------------------------------------------------------
// public T pop () throws EmptyCollectionException { }
// public T peek () throws EmptyCollectionException { }
// public boolean isEmpty() { }
// public int size() { }
}
```

Note that in this line, we are instantiating an array of Objects and then casting it as an array of our generic type. This will create a compile-time warning for an unchecked type conversion because the Java compiler cannot guarantee the type safety of this cast. As we have seen from our earlier discussion, it is worth this warning to gain the flexibility and safety of generics.

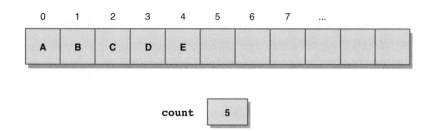

FIGURE 14.8 The stack after pushing element E

The push Operation

To push an element onto the stack, we simply insert it in the next available position in the array as specified by the variable top. Before doing so, however, we must determine if the array has reached its capacity and expand it if necessary. After storing the value, we must update the value of top so that it continues to represent the number of elements in the stack.

The expandCapacity method is implemented to double the size of the array as needed. Of course since an array cannot be resized once it is instantiated, this method simply creates a new larger array, and then copies the contents of the old array into the new one. It serves as a support method of the class and can therefore be implemented with private visibility.

Figure 14.8 illustrates the result of pushing an element E onto the stack that was depicted in Figure 14.7.

The push operation for the array implementation of a stack consists of the following steps:

- Make sure that the array is not full.
- Set the reference in position top of the array to the object being added to the stack.
- Increment the values of top and count.

Each of these steps are O(1). Thus the operation is O(1). We might wonder about the time complexity of the expandCapacity method and the impact it might have on the analysis of the push method. This method does contain a linear for loop and, intuitively, we would call that O(n). However, given how seldom the expandCapacity method is called relative to the number of times push may be called, we can amortize that complexity across all instances of push.

The pop Operation

The pop operation removes and returns the element at the top of the stack. For an array implementation, that means returning the element at index top−1. Before attempting to return an element, however, we must ensure that there is at least one element in the stack to return.

If the stack is empty when the pop method is called, an `EmptyCollectionException` is thrown. Otherwise, the value of `top` is decremented and the element stored at that location is stored into a temporary variable so that it can be returned. That cell in the array is then set to null. Note that the value of `top` ends up with the appropriate value relative to the now smaller stack.

The `pop` operation for the array implementation consists of the following steps:

- Make sure the stack is not empty.
- Decrement the `top` counter.
- Set a temporary reference equal to the element in `stack[top]`.
- Set `stack[top]` equal to null.
- Return the temporary reference.

All of these steps are also O(1). Thus, the `pop` operation for the array implementation has time complexity O(1).

The peek Operation

The `peek` operation returns a reference to the element at the top of the stack without removing it from the array. For an array implementation, that means returning a reference to the element at position top-1. This one step is O(1) and thus the `peek` operation is O(1) as well.

Other Operations

The isEmpty, size, and toString operations and their analysis are left as programming projects and exercises respectively.

14.9 References as Links

A *linked structure* is a data structure that uses object reference variables to create links between objects. Linked structures are the primary alternative to an array-based implementation of a collection. After discussing various issues involved in linked structures, we will define a new implementation of a stack collection that uses an underlying linked data structure and demonstrate its use.

> **KEY CONCEPT**
>
> Object reference variables can be used to create linked structures.

FIGURE 14.9 An object reference variable pointing to an object

Recall that an object reference variable holds the address of an object, indicating where the object is stored in memory. The following declaration creates a variable called `obj` that is only large enough to hold the numeric address of an object:

```
Object obj;
```

Usually the specific address that an object reference variable holds is irrelevant. That is, while it is important to be able to use the reference variable to access an object, the specific location in memory where it is stored is unimportant. Therefore, instead of showing addresses, we usually depict a reference variable as a name that "points to" an object, as shown in Figure 14.9. A reference variable, used in this context, is sometimes called a *pointer*.

Consider the situation in which a class defines as instance data a reference to another object of the same class. For example, suppose we have a class named `Person` that contains a person's name, address, and other relevant information. Now suppose that in addition to this data, the `Person` class also contains a reference variable to another `Person` object:

```
public class Person
{
   private String name;
   private String address;

   private Person next; // a link to another Person object

   // whatever else
}
```

Using only this one class, a linked structure can be created. One `Person` object contains a link to a second `Person` object. This second object also contains a reference to a `Person`, which contains another, and so on. This type of object is sometimes called *self-referential*.

This kind of relationship forms the basis of a *linked list*, which is a linked structure in which one object refers to the next, creating a linear ordering of the objects in the list. A linked list is depicted in Figure 14.10 on the next page. Often the objects stored in a linked list are referred to generically as the *nodes* of the list.

Note that a separate reference variable is needed to indicate the first node in the list. The list is terminated in a node whose `next` reference is `null`.

> **KEY CONCEPT**
>
> A linked list is composed of objects that each point to the next object in the list.

front

FIGURE 14.10 A linked list

A linked list is only one kind of linked structure. If a class is set up to have multiple references to objects, a more complex structure can be created, such as the one depicted in Figure 14.11. The way in which the links are managed dictates the specific organization of the structure.

> **KEY CONCEPT**
>
> A linked list dynamically grows as needed and essentially has no capacity limitations.

For now, we will focus on the details of a linked list. Many of these techniques apply to more complicated linked structures as well.

Unlike an array, which has a fixed size, a linked list has no upper bound on its capacity other than the limitations of memory in the computer. A linked list is considered to be a *dynamic* structure because its size grows and shrinks as needed to accommodate the number of elements stored. In Java, all objects are created dynamically from an area of memory called the system *heap*, or *free store*.

The next section explores some of the primary ways in which a linked list is managed.

entry

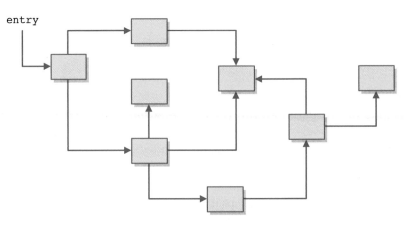

FIGURE 14.11 A complex linked structure

14.10 Managing Linked Lists

Keep in mind that our goal is to use linked lists and other linked structures to create collections. Since the principal purpose of a collection is to be able to add, remove, and access elements, we must first examine how to accomplish these fundamental operations using links.

No matter what a linked list is used to store, there are a few basic techniques involved in managing the nodes on the list. Specifically, elements in the list are accessed, elements are inserted into a list, and elements are removed from the list.

Accessing Elements

Special care must be taken when dealing with the first node in the list so that the reference to the entire list is maintained appropriately. When using linked lists, we maintain a pointer to the first element in the list. To access other elements, we must access the first one and then follow the next pointer from that one to the next one and so on. Consider our previous example of a `person` class containing the attributes `name`, `address`, and `next`. If we wanted the to find the fourth person in the list, and assuming that we had a variable `first` of type `Person` that pointed to the first person in the list, we might use the following code:

```
Person current = first;
for (int I = 0, I < 3, I++)
    current = current.next;
```

After executing this code, `current` will point to the fourth person in the list. Notice that it is very important to create a new reference variable, in this case `current`, and then start by setting that reference variable to point to the first element in the list. Consider what would happen if we used the `first` pointer in the loop instead of `current`. Once we moved the `first` pointer to point to the second element in the list, we would no longer have a pointer to or be able to access the first element. Keep in mind that with a linked list, the only way to access the elements in the list is to start with the first element and progress through the list.

Of course, a more likely scenario would be that we would need to search our list for a particular person. Assuming that the `Person` class overrides the `equals` method such that it returns true if the given `String` matches the `name` stored for that person, then the following code will search the list for Tom Jones:

```
String searchstring = "Tom Jones";
Person current = first;
while ((not(current.equals(searchstring)) && (current.next != null))
    current = current.next;
```

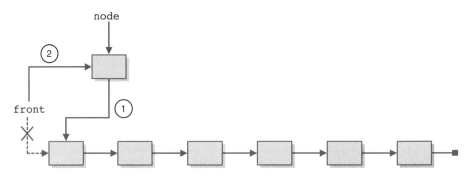

FIGURE 14.12   Inserting a node at the front of a linked list

Now that we have seen how to access elements in a linked list, lets consider how to insert elements into a list.

Inserting Nodes

> **KEY CONCEPT**
>
> The order in which references are changed is crucial to maintaining a linked list.

A node may be inserted into a linked list at any location: at the front of the list, among the interior nodes in the middle of the list, or at the end of the list. Adding a node to the front of the list requires resetting the reference to the entire list, as shown in Figure 14.12. First, the `next` reference of the added node is set to point to the current first node in the list. Second, the reference to the front of the list is reset to point to the newly added node.

Note that difficulties would arise if these steps were reversed. If we were to reset the `front` reference first, we would lose the only reference to the existing list and it could not be retrieved.

Inserting a node into the middle of a list requires some additional processing. First we have to find the node in the list that will immediately precede the new node being inserted. Unlike an array, in which we can access elements using subscripts, a linked list requires that we use a separate reference to move through the nodes of the list until we find the one we want. This type of reference is often called `current`, because it indicates the current node in the list that is being examined.

Initially, `current` is set to point to the first node in the list. Then, a loop is used to move the `current` reference along the list of nodes until the desired node is found. Once it is found, the new node can be inserted, as shown in Figure 14.13.

First, the `next` reference of the new node is set to point to the node *following* the one to which `current` refers. Then, the `next` reference of the current node is reset to point to the new node. Once again, the order of these steps is important.

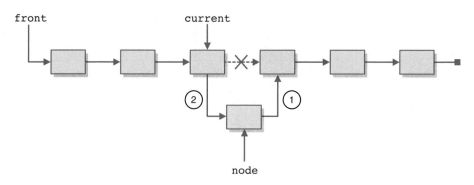

FIGURE 14.13 Inserting a node in the middle of a linked list

This process will work wherever the node is to be inserted along the list, including making it the new second node in the list or making it the last node in the list. If the new node is inserted immediately after the first node in the list, then `current` and `front` will refer to the same (first) node. If the new node is inserted at the end of the list, the `next` reference of the new node is set to `null`. The only special case occurs when the new node is inserted as the first node in the list.

Deleting Nodes

Any node in the list can be deleted. We must maintain the integrity of the list no matter which node is deleted. As with the process of inserting a node, dealing with the first node in the list represents a special case.

KEY CONCEPT

Dealing with the first node in a linked list often requires special handling.

To delete the first node in a linked list, the reference to the front of the list is reset so that it points to the current second node in the list. This process is shown in Figure 14.14 on the next page. If the deleted node is needed elsewhere, a separate reference to it must be set up before resetting the `front` reference.

FIGURE 14.14 Deleting the first node in a linked list

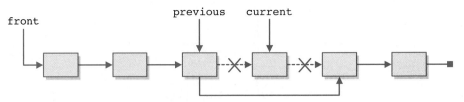

FIGURE 14.15 Deleting an interior node from a linked list

To delete a node from the interior of the list, we must first find the node *in front of* the node that is to be deleted. This processing often requires the use of two references: one to find the node to be deleted and another to keep track of the node immediately preceding that one. Thus, they are often called `current` and `previous`, as shown in Figure 14.15.

Once these nodes have been found, the `next` reference of the previous node is reset to point to the node pointed to by the `next` reference of the current node. The deleted node can then be used as needed.

Sentinel Nodes

Thus far, we have described insertion into and deletion from a list as having two cases: the case when dealing with the first node and the case when dealing with any other node. It is possible to eliminate the special case involving the first node by introducing a *sentinel node* or *dummy node* at the front of the list. A sentinel node serves as a false first node and doesn't actually represent an element in the list. By using a sentinel node, all insertions and deletions will fall under the second case and the implementations will not have as many special situations to consider.

> **KEY CONCEPT**
>
> Implementing a list with a sentinel node or dummy node as the first node eliminates the special cases dealing with the first node.

14.11 Elements Without Links

Now that we've explored some of the techniques needed to manage the nodes of a linked list, we can turn our attention to using a linked list as an alternative implementation approach for a collection. However, to do so we need to carefully examine one other key aspect of linked lists. We must separate the details of the linked list structure from the elements that the list stores.

> **KEY CONCEPT**
>
> Objects that are stored in a collection should not contain any implementation details of the underlying data structure.

Earlier in this chapter we discussed the idea of a `Person` class that contains, among its other data, a link to another `Person` object.

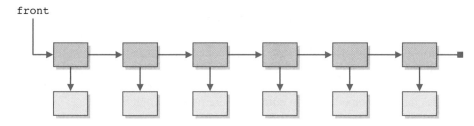

FIGURE 14.16 Using separate node objects to store an link elements

The flaw in this approach is that the self-referential `Person` class must be designed so that it "knows" it may become a node in a linked list of `Person` objects. This assumption is impractical, and it violates our goal of separating the implementation details from the parts of the system that use the collection.

The solution to this problem is to define a separate node class that serves to link the elements together. A node class is fairly simple, containing only two important references: one to the next node in the linked list and another to the element that is being stored in the list. This approach is depicted in Figure 14.16.

The linked list of nodes can still be managed using the techniques discussed in the previous section. The only additional aspect is that the actual elements stored in the list are accessed using a separate reference in the node objects.

Doubly Linked Lists

An alternative implementation for linked structures is the concept of a doubly linked list, as illustrated in Figure 14.17. In a doubly linked list, two references are maintained: one to point to the first node in the list and another to point to the last node in the list. Each node in the list stores both a reference to the next element and a reference to the previous one. If we were to use sentinel nodes with a doubly linked list, we would place sentinel nodes on both ends of the list.

FIGURE 14.17 A doubly linked list

14.12 Implementing a Stack: With Links

Let's use a linked list to implement a stack collection, defined earlier in this chapter. Note that we are not changing the way in which a stack works. Its conceptual nature remains the same, as does the set of operations defined for it. We are merely changing the underlying data structure used to implement it.

The purpose of the stack, and the solutions it helps us to create, also remains the same. The postfix expression evaluation example used the `ArrayStack<T>` class, but any valid implementation of a stack could be used instead. Once we create the `LinkedStack<T>` class to define an alternative implementation, it could be substituted into the postfix expression solution without having to change anything but the class name. That is the beauty of abstraction.

KEY CONCEPT

Any implementation of a collection can be used to solve a problem as long as it validly implements the appropriate operations.

In the following discussion, we show and discuss the methods that are important to understanding the linked list implementation of a stack. Some of the stack operations are left as programming projects.

The `LinkedStack` Class

The `LinkedStack<T>` class in Listing 14.5 implements the `StackADT<T>` interface, just as the `ArrayStack<T>` class does. Both provide the operations defined for a stack collection.

Because we are using a linked list approach, there is no array in which we store the elements of the collection. Instead, we need only a single reference to the first node in the list. We will also maintain a count of the number of elements in the list. The header and class-level data of the `LinkedStack<T>` class is therefore as shown in Listing 14.5.

The `LinearNode<T>` class serves as the node class, containing a reference to the next `LinearNode<T>` in the list and a reference to the element stored in that node. Each node stores a generic type that is determined when the node is instantiated. In our `LinkedStack<T>` implementation, we simply use the same type for the node as used to define the stack. The `LinearNode<T>` class also contains methods to set and get the element values. The `LinearNode<T>` class is shown in Listing 14.6 on page 548.

Note that the `LinearNode<T>` class is not tied to the implementation of a stack collection. It can be used in any linear linked list implementation of a collection. We will use it for other collections as needed.

LISTING 14.5

```java
//********************************************************************
//  LinkedStack.java       Java Foundations
//
//  Represents a linked implementation of a stack.
//********************************************************************

package javafoundations;

import javafoundations.exceptions.*;

public class LinkedStack<T> implements Stack<T>
{
   private int count;
   private LinearNode<T> top;

   //-------------------------------------------------------------------
   //  Creates an empty stack using the default capacity.
   //-------------------------------------------------------------------
   public LinkedStack()
   {
      count = 0;
      top = null;
   }

   //-------------------------------------------------------------------
   //  Removes the element at the top of this stack and returns a
   //  reference to it. Throws an EmptyCollectionException if the
   //  stack contains no elements.
   //-------------------------------------------------------------------
   public T pop() throws EmptyCollectionException
   {
      if (count == 0)
         throw new EmptyCollectionException ("Pop operation failed. "
            + "The stack is empty.");

      T result = top.getElement();
      top = top.getNext();
      count--;

      return result;
   }
```

LISTING 14.5   *continued*

```java
//---------------------------------------------------------------
//  Returns a string representation of this stack.
//---------------------------------------------------------------
public String toString()
{
    String result = "<top of stack>\n";
    LinearNode current = top;

    while (current != null)
    {
        result += current.getElement() + "\n";
        current = current.getNext();
    }

    return result + "<bottom of stack>";
}

//---------------------------------------------------------------
//  The following methods are left as programming projects.
//---------------------------------------------------------------
//  public void push () { }
//  public T peek () throws EmptyCollectionException { }
//  public boolean isEmpty() { }
//  public int size() { }
}
```

LISTING 14.6

```java
//************************************************************
//  LinearNode.java        Java Foundations
//
//  Represents a node in a linked list.
//************************************************************

package javafoundations;
public class LinearNode<T>
{
    private LinearNode<T> next;
    private T element;
```

LISTING 14.6 *continued*

```java
//----------------------------------------------------------------
//  Creates an empty node.
//----------------------------------------------------------------
public LinearNode()
{
   next = null;
   element = null;
}


//----------------------------------------------------------------
//  Creates a node storing the specified element.
//----------------------------------------------------------------
public LinearNode (T elem)
{
   next = null;
   element = elem;
}


//----------------------------------------------------------------
//  Returns the node that follows this one.
//----------------------------------------------------------------
public LinearNode<T> getNext()
{
   return next;
}


//----------------------------------------------------------------
//  Sets the node that follows this one.
//----------------------------------------------------------------
public void setNext (LinearNode<T> node)
{
   next = node;
}


//----------------------------------------------------------------
//  Returns the element stored in this node.
//----------------------------------------------------------------
public T getElement()
{
   return element;
}
```

LISTING 14.6 *continued*

```
//----------------------------------------------------------
//  Sets the element stored in this node.
//----------------------------------------------------------
public void setElement (T elem)
{
   element = elem;
}
}
```

Using the `LinearNode<T>` class and maintaining a count of elements in the collection creates the implementation strategy depicted in Figure 14.18.

The constructor of the `LinkedStack<T>` class sets the count of elements to zero and sets the front of the list, represented by the variable `top`, to `null`. Note that because a linked list implementation does not have to worry about capacity limitations, there is no need to create a second constructor as we did in the `ArrayStack<T>` class.

Because of the nature of a stack, only allowing elements to be added or removed from one end, we will only need to operate on one end of our linked list. We could choose to push the 1st element into the 1st position in the linked list, the second element into the second position, etc. This would mean that the top of the stack would always be at the tail end of the list. However, if we consider the efficiency of this strategy we realize that this would mean that we would have to traverse the entire list on every push and every pop operation. Instead, we can choose to operate on the front of the list making the front of the list the top of the stack. In this way we do not have to traverse the list for either the push or pop operation. Figure 14.18 illustrates this configuration for a stack containing four elements, A, B, C, and D, that have been pushed onto the stack in that order.

Let's explore the implementation of the stack operations for the `LinkedStack` class.

The push Operation

Every time a new element is pushed onto the stack, a new `LinearNode` object must be created to store it in the linked list. To position the newly created node at the top of the stack, we must set its `next` reference to the current top of the stack, and reset the `top` reference to point to the new node. We must also increment the `count` variable.

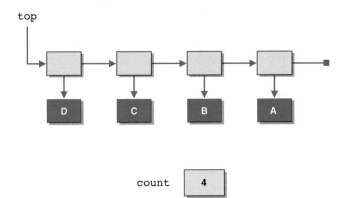

FIGURE 14.18 A linked implementation of a stack

Figure 14.19 shows the result of pushing the element E onto the stack depicted in Figure 14.18.

The push operation for the linked implementation of a stack consists of the following steps:

- Create a new node containing a reference to the object to be placed on the stack.
- Set the next reference of the new node to point to the current top of the stack (which will be null if the stack is empty).
- Set the top reference to point to the new node.
- Increment the count of elements in the stack.

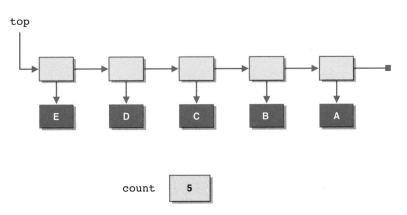

FIGURE 14.19 The stack after pushing element E

All of these steps have time complexity O(1) because they require only one processing step regardless of the number of elements already in the stack. Each of these steps would have to be accomplished once for each of the elements to be pushed. Thus, using this method, the push operation would be O(1).

The pop Operation

The pop operation is implemented by returning a reference to the element currently stored at the top of the stack and adjusting the top reference to the new top of the stack. Before attempting to return any element, however, we must first ensure that there is at least one element to return. This operation can be implemented as follows:

If the stack is empty, as determined by the isEmpty method, an EmptyCollectionException is thrown. If there is at least one element to pop, it is stored in a temporary variable so that it can be returned. Then, the reference to the top of the stack is set to the next element in the list, which is now the new top of the stack. The count of elements is decremented as well.

The pop operation for the linked implementation consists of the following steps:

- Make sure the stack is not empty.
- Set a temporary reference equal to the element on top of the stack.
- Set the top reference equal to the next reference of the node at the top of the stack.
- Decrement the count of elements in the stack.
- Return the element pointed to by the temporary reference.

As with our previous examples, each of these operations consists of a single comparison or a simple assignment and is therefore O(1). Thus, the pop operation for the linked implementation is O(1).

Other Operations

Using a linked implementation, the peek operation is implemented by returning a reference to the element pointed to by the node pointed to by the top pointer. The isEmpty operation returns true if the count of elements is 0, and false otherwise. The size operation simply returns the count of elements in the stack. The toString operation can be implemented by simply traversing the linked list. These operations are left as programming projects.

14.13 Implementing Stacks: The Java.Util.Stack Class

Class `java.util.Stack` is an implementation of a stack provided in the Java Collections API framework. This implementation provides either the same or similar operations to the ones that we have been discussing:

- The `push` operation accepts a parameter item that is a reference to an object to be placed on the stack.
- The `pop` operation removes the object on top of the stack and returns a reference to it.
- The `peek` operation returns a reference to the object on top of the stack.
- The `empty` operation behaves the same as the `isEmpty` operation that we have been discussing.
- The `size` operation returns the number of elements in the stack.

The `java.util.Stack` class is derived from the `Vector` class and uses its inherited capabilities to store the elements in the stack. Since this implementation is built upon a vector, it exhibits the characteristics of both a vector and a stack. This implementation keeps track of the top of the stack using an index similar to the array implementation and thus does not require the additional overhead of storing a `next` reference in each node. Further, like the linked implementation, the `java.util.Stack` implementation allocates additional space only as needed.

Unique Operations

The `java.util.Stack` class provides an additional operation called `search`. Given an object to search for, the `search` operation returns the distance from the top of the stack to the first occurrence of that object on the stack. If the object is found at the top of the stack, the `search` method returns the value 1. If the object is not found on the stack, `search` returns the value−1.

> **KEY CONCEPT**
>
> The `java.util.Stack` class is derived from `Vector`, which gives a stack inappropriate operations.

Unfortunately, since the `java.util.Stack` implementation is derived from the `Vector` class, quite a number of other operations are inherited from the `Vector` class that are available for use. In some cases, these additional capabilities violate the basic assumptions of a stack. Most software engineers consider this a bad use of inheritance. Since a stack is not everything a vector is (conceptually), the `Stack` class should not be derived from the `Vector` class. Well-disciplined developers can, of course, limit themselves to only those operations appropriate to a stack.

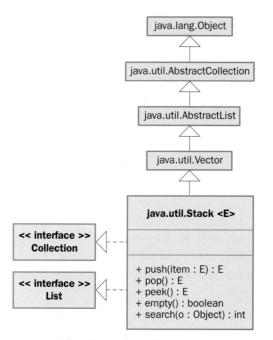

FIGURE 14.20 The derivation of the `java.util.Stack` class

Inheritance and Implementation

The class `java.util.Stack` is an extension of the class `java.util.Vector`, which is an extension of `java.util.AbstractList`, which is an extension of `java.util.AbstractCollection`, which is an extension of `java.lang.Object`. The `java.util.Stack` class implements the `cloneable`, `collection`, `list`, and `serializable` interfaces. These relationships are illustrated in the UML diagram of Figure 14.20.

14.14 Packages

You may have notice that our code for the Postfix Evaluator (Listing 14.2) imported the package `javafoundations` and that our code for `ArrayStack`, `LinkedStack`, and `StackADT` had a statement near the top of the listing that said `package javafoundations`. Up to this point book, we have used preexisting packages but we had not created our own packages until now. In Chapter 3, we briefly introduced the concept of a class library and the use of packages to organize the classes that the library contains. Software developers often organize the classes that make up a large program into packages of common functionality.

Some packages may be general enough to be used in multiple programs. The source code you develop may not be destined for only one program, but rather a class library that you create and share (or sell) to other programmers. These programmers in turn use your packaging structure to quickly locate classes of use to them, organized by functionality.

Organizing Packages

You've used classes from various packages as you have worked on projects in earlier chapters of this text. As we've seen, the `java.util` package contains a variety of classes for utility purposes, `java.lang` contains classes related to core aspects of the language, and `java.io` encompasses input and output functionality.

The javafoundations package for this chapter contains all of the classes and interfaces needed for our stack collection. If you explore the javafoundations folder, you will notice that it includes `ArrayStack`, `LinkedStack`, and `StackADT` as well a folder called exceptions. This folder actually contains a sub-package called `javafoundations.exceptions`. The contents of these packages and the associated folders will expand in future chapters. Two important points should be taken from this discussion:

- We typically organize code into packages by function, for example all collections might be together in one package with all exceptions for those collections might be in a subordinate package.
- Code for a particular package will be located in common directory/folder with subordinate packages arranged in subordinate directories/folders.

Creating directories for our packaged source code is not enough, though. We also need to modify the source code file itself. Again, notice that the first line of code in the file `ArrayStack.java` is

```
package javafoundations;
```

This statement indicates that the class contained in the file is part of the `javafoundations` package. At compile time, the compiler will check the package declaration statement and the location of the source code file in the directory tree to ensure that the source code file is in the correct location.

Since the `ArrayStack` class uses classes from the javafoundations.exceptions sub-package, it also includes an import statement to import files of that package as well.

Using CLASSPATH

An *environment variable* is a variable set up at the operating system level to establish a value needed by the overall computing system. The CLASSPATH environment variable is usually set in the command shell to indicate the list of paths (directories and other locations) where the compiler or run-time environment will look if it cannot find a class we reference in the source code. Recall that this happens automatically for classes in the Java API—such as `java.util.Scanner`, `java.lang.String`, and `java.net.URL`, for example.

The variable can be set through several mechanisms. The first is to modify it on the command line as an option to the compiler or run-time environment. For example, let's assume our `Postfix` application needed to import classes from our collections code in the `javafoundations` package. Additionally, let's assume the `javafoundations` package is located at `C:\javafoundations` on our system. At compile time, we will need to tell the compiler that there are two primary locations to search for any classes not provided by the API. To do this we add the `-cp` command-line option when invoking the compiler, as in:

```
javac -cp C:\javafoundations;. Postfix.java
```

Following the `-cp` option, we specify the two locations we instruct the compiler to search in. The first is `C:\javafoundations`, where we have placed the collections code. The second location is specified as a period (`.`), the current working directory from which the `javac` command was issued. When searching for packages that contain the classes our program is using, the compiler looks first in the Java installation area (for API classes), then the `C:\javafoundations` directory, and then the current directory.

The CLASSPATH environment variable may also be modified for temporary use in the command shell (Windows command shell, or login shell in Unix/Linux) by first setting the variable name and value prior to executing other commands, such as compiling or executing the run-time environment. Under the Windows operating system, an environment variable can be temporarily set by issuing the set command. For example,

```
set CLASSPATH=.;C:\javafoundations
```

On Unix machines the process is somewhat more complex, depending on the type of shell you are using. Check with your instructor or system administrator to determine how to set an environment variable via the command line.

Finally, the CLASSPATH variable may be permanently set in the command shell by altering the variable in the Control Panel (Windows) or the shell's login configuration file (Unix/Linux). These modifications are easy to accomplish, but beyond the scope of this book, so we encourage you to look at our tutorial about this activity on the book's Web site. By setting an environment variable through the shell, we can access it in a variety of places, such as in programs, in scripts, and in the shell itself.

Regardless of how you achieve the modification to the CLASSPATH variable, you should note that in the examples above we set our CLASSPATH to be C:\javafoundations;. (including the dot that represents the current working directory). Items in the CLASSPATH variable are separated by a semicolon (;) in Windows and a colon (:) under Unix/Linux.

Often, the same classes that we need access to during compilation will be required at run time by the interpreter. So, in a similar fashion, we can modify the CLASSPATH via the command line for the interpreter. To get the Postfix application to execute, we would issue the following:

```
java -cp C:\javafoundations;. Postfix
```

Had we set the CLASSPATH environment variable via the shell or the control panel, we could shorten our command to:

```
java Postfix
```

Here, the value of the CLASSPATH is used by the Java run-time environment automatically, so we don't need to specify it via the –cp option.

It is important to note that when we are trying to compile files that are in a package/directory structure, we must compile them from the parent directory of the package. For example, if we assume that our Postfix code is in a folder labeled Chapter14Code and that our javafoundations directory/folder is contained within this parent folder, then we should compile our stack collections code using the Chapter14Code folder as our current working directory.

Summary of Key Concepts

- A collection is an object that gathers and organizes other objects.

- Elements in a collection are typically organized by the order of their addition to the collection or by some inherent relationship among the elements.

- A collection is an abstraction where the details of the implementation are hidden.

- A data structure is the underlying programming constructs used to implement a collection.

- Stack elements are processed in a LIFO manner—the last element in is the first element out.

- A programmer should choose the structure that is appropriate for the type of data management needed.

- A polymorphic reference uses the type of the object, not the type of the reference, to determine which version of a method to invoke.

- A Java interface defines a set of abstract methods and is useful in separating the concept of an abstract data type from its implementation.

- By using the interface name as a return type, the interface doesn't commit the method to the use of any particular class that implements a stack.

- A stack is the ideal data structure to use when evaluating a postfix expression.

- Errors and exceptions represent unusual or invalid processing.

- The implementation of the collection operations should not affect the way users interact with the collection.

- How we handle exceptional conditions determines whether the collection or the user of the collection controls the particular behavior.

- For efficiency, an array-based stack implementation keeps the bottom of the stack at index 0.

- Object reference variables can be used to create linked structures.

- A linked list is composed of objects that each point to the next object in the list.

- A linked list dynamically grows as needed and essentially has no capacity limitations.

- The order in which references are changed is crucial to maintaining a linked list.

- Dealing with the first node in a linked list often requires special handling.

■ Implementing a list with a sentinel node or dummy node as the first node eliminates the special cases dealing with the first node.

■ Objects that are stored in a collection should not contain any implementation details of the underlying data structure.

■ Any implementation of a collection can be used to solve a problem as long as it validly implements the appropriate operations.

■ A linked implementation of a stack adds and removes elements from one end of the linked list.

■ The java.util.Stack class is derived from Vector, which gives a stack inappropriate operations.

Self-Review Questions

SR 14.1   What is a collection?

SR 14.2   What is a data type?

SR 14.3   What is an abstract data type?

SR 14.4   What is a data structure?

SR 14.5   What is abstraction and what advantage does it provide?

SR 14.6   Why is a class an excellent representation of an abstract data type?

SR 14.7   What is the characteristic behavior of a stack?

SR 14.8   What are the five basic operations on a stack?

SR 14.9   What are some of the other operations that might be implemented for a stack?

SR 14.10   Define inheritance?

SR 14.11   Define polymorphism?

SR 14.12   Given the example in Figure 14.4, list the subclasses of Mammal?

SR 14.13   Given the example in figure 14.4, will the following code compile?

```
Animal creature = new Parrot();
```

SR 14.14   Given the example in figure 14.4, will the following code compile?

```
Horse creature = new Mammal();
```

SR 14.15   What is the purpose of Generics in the Java language?

SR 14.16 What is the advantage of postfix notation?

SR 14.17 How do object references help us define data structures?

SR 14.18 Compare and contrast a linked list and an array.

SR 14.19 What special case exists when managing linked lists?

SR 14.20 Why should a linked list node be separate from the element stored on the list?

SR 14.21 What do the `LinkedStack<T>` and `ArrayStack<T>` classes have in common?

SR 14.22 What would be the time complexity of the push operation if we chose to push at the end of the list instead of the front?

SR 14.23 What is the difference between a doubly linked list and a singly linked list?

SR 14.24 What impact would the use of sentinel nodes or dummy nodes have upon a doubly linked list implementation?

SR 14.25 What are the advantages to using a linked implementation as opposed to an array implementation?

SR 14.26 What are the advantages to using an array implementation as opposed to a linked implementation?

SR 14.27 What are the advantages of the `java.util.Stack` implementation of a stack?

SR 14.28 What is the potential problem with the `java.util.Stack` implementation?

SR 14.29 What is the advantage of postfix notation?

Exercises

EX 14.1 Compare and contrast data types, abstract data types, and data structures.

EX 14.2 List the collections in the Java Collections API and mark the ones that are covered in this text.

EX 14.3 Define the concept of abstraction and explain why it is important in software development.

EX 14.4 Hand trace a stack X through the following operations:

```
X.push(new Integer(4));
X.push(new Integer(3));
Integer Y = X.pop();
```

```
X.push(new Integer(7));
X.push(new Integer(2));
X.push(new Integer(5));
X.push(new Integer(9));
Integer Y = X.pop();
X.push(new Integer(3));
X.push(new Integer(9));
```

EX 14.5   Given the resulting stack X from the previous exercise, what would be the result of each of the following?

```
a. Y = X.peek();
b. Y = X.pop();
   Z = X.peek();
c. Y = X.pop();
   Z = X.peek();
```

EX 14.6   What should be the time complexity of the `isEmpty()`, `size()`, and `toString()` methods?

EX 14.7   Show how the undo operation in a word processor can be supported by the use of a stack. Give specific examples and draw the contents of the stack after various actions are taken.

EX 14.8   In the postfix expression evaluation example, the two most recent operands are popped when an operator is encountered so that the subexpression can be evaluated. The first operand popped is treated as the second operand in the subexpression, and the second operand popped is the first. Give and explain an example that demonstrates the importance of this aspect of the solution.

EX 14.9   Draw an example using the five integers (12, 23, 1, 45, 9) of how a stack could be used to reverse the order (9, 45, 1, 23, 12) of these elements.

EX 14.10   Explain what would happen to the algorithms and the time complexity of an array implementation of the stack if the top of the stack were at position 0.

EX 14.12   Explain what will happen if the steps depicted in Figure 14.12 are reversed.

EX 14.13   Explain what will happen if the steps depicted in Figure 14.13 are reversed.

EX 14.14   Draw a UML diagram showing the relationships among the classes involved in the linked list implementation of a stack.

EX 14.15   Write an algorithm for the push method that will add at the end of the list instead of the beginning. What is the time complexity of this algorithm?

EX 14.16   Modify the algorithm from the previous exercise so that it makes use of a rear reference. How does this affect the time complexity of this and the other operations?

EX 14.17   Discuss the effect on all the operations if there were not a count variable in the implementation.

EX 14.18   Discuss the impact (and draw an example) of using a sentinel node or dummy node at the head of the list.

Programming Projects

PP 14.1   Complete the implementation of the `ArrayStack` class presented in this chapter. Specifically, complete the implementations of the `peek`, `isEmpty`, `size`, and `toString` methods.

PP 14.2   Design and implement an application that reads a sentence from the user and prints the sentence with the characters of each word backwards. Use a stack to reverse the characters of each word.

PP 14.3   Modify the solution to the postfix expression evaluation problem so that it checks for the validity of the expression that is entered by the user. Issue an appropriate error message when an erroneous situation is encountered.

PP 14.4   The array implementation in this chapter keeps the top variable pointing to the next array position above the actual top of the stack. Rewrite the array implementation such that stack[top] is the actual top of the stack.

PP 14.5   There is a data structure called a drop-out stack that behaves like a stack in every respect except that if the stack size is n, when the n + 1 element is pushed, the first element is lost. Implement a drop-out stack using an array. (*Hint:* a circular array implementation would make sense.)

PP 14.6   Implement an integer adder using three stacks.

PP 14.7   Implement an infix-to-postfix translator using stacks.

PP 14.8   Implement a class called reverse that uses a stack to output a set of elements input by the user in reverse order.

PP 14.9   Create a graphical application that provides a button for push and pop from a stack, a text field to accept a string as input for push, and a text area to display the contents of the stack after each operation.

PP 14.10   Complete the implementation of the `LinkedStack<T>` class by providing the definitions for the `size`, `isEmpty`, and `toString` methods.

PP 14.11   Modify the `postfix` program from this chapter so that it uses the `LinkedStack<T>` class instead of the `ArrayStack<T>` class.

PP 14.12   Create a new version of the `LinkedStack<T>` class that makes use of a dummy record at the head of the list.

PP 14.13   Create a simple graphical application that will allow a user to perform `push`, `pop`, and `peek` operations on a stack and display the resulting stack (using `toString`) in a text area.

PP 14.14   Design and implement an application that reads a sentence from the user and prints the sentence with the characters of each word backwards. Use a stack to reverse the characters of each word.

PP 14.15   Complete the solution to the iterative maze solver so that your solution marks the successful path.

PP 14.16   The linked implementation in this chapter uses a `count` variable to keep track of the number of elements in the stack. Rewrite the linked implementation without a `count` variable.

PP 14.17   There is a data structure called a drop-out stack that behaves like a stack in every respect except that if the stack size is n, when the n + 1 element is pushed, the first element is lost. Implement a drop-out stack using links.

Answers to Self-Review Questions

SRA 14.1   A collection is an object that gathers and organizes other objects.

SRA 14.2   A data type is a set of values and operations on those values defined within a programming language.

SRA 14.3   An abstract data type is a data type that is not defined within the programming language and must be defined by the programmer.

SRA 14.4   A data structure is the set of objects necessary to implement an abstract data type.

SRA 14.5   Abstraction is the concept of hiding the underlying implementation of operations and data storage in order to simplify the use of a collection.

SRA 14.6   Classes naturally provide abstraction since only those methods that provide services to other classes have public visibility.

SRA 14.7   A stack is a last in, first out (LIFO) structure.

SRA 14.8   The operations are:

push—adds an element to the end of the stack

pop—removes an element from the front of the stack

peek—returns a reference to the element at the front of the stack

isEmpty—returns true if the stack is empty, returns false otherwise

size—returns the number of elements in the stack

SRA 14.9   makeEmpty(), destroy(), full()

SRA 14.10   Inheritance is the process in which a new class is derived from an existing one. The new class automatically contains some or all of the variables and methods in the original class. Then, to tailor the class as needed, the programmer can add new variables and methods to the derived class, or modify the inherited ones.

SRA 14.11   The term *polymorphism* can be defined as "having many forms." A *polymorphic reference* is a reference variable that can refer to different types of objects at different points in time. The specific method invoked through a polymorphic reference can change from one invocation to the next.

SRA 14.12   The subclasses of Mammal are Horse and Bat.

SRA 14.13   Yes, a reference variable of a parent class or any superclass may hold a reference to one of its descendants.

SRA 14.14   No, a reference variable for a child or subclass may not hold a reference to a parent or superclass. To make this assignment, you would have to explicitly cast the parent class into the child class

(Horse creature = (Horse)(new Mammal());

SRA 14.15   Beginning with Java 5.0, Java enables us to define a class based on a *generic type*. That is, we can define a class so that it stores, operates on, and manages objects whose type is not specified until the class is instantiated. This allows for the creation of structures that can manipulate "generic" elements and still provide type checking.

SRA 14.16   Postfix notation avoids the need for precedence rules that are required to evaluate infix expressions.

SRA 14.17   An object reference can be used as a link from one object to another. A group of linked objects can form a data structure, such as a linked list, on which a collection can be based.

SRA 14.18   A linked list has no capacity limitations, while an array does. However, arrays provide direct access to elements using indexes, whereas a linked list must be traversed one element at a time to reach a particular point in the list.

SRA 14.19   The primary special case in linked list processing occurs when dealing with the first element in the list. A special reference variable is maintained that specifies the first element in the list. If that element is deleted, or a new element is added in front of it, the `front` reference must be carefully maintained.

SRA 14.20   It is unreasonable to assume that every object that we may want to put in a collection can be designed to cooperate with the collection implementation. Furthermore, the implementation details are supposed to be kept distinct from the user of the collection, including the elements the user chooses to add to the collection.

SRA 14.21   Both the `LinkedStack<T>` and `ArrayStack<T>` classes implement the `StackADT<T>` interface. This means that they both represent a stack collection, providing the necessary operations needed to use a stack. Though they both have distinct approaches to managing the collection, they are functionally interchangeable from the user's point of view.

SRA 14.22   To push at the end of the list, we would have to traverse the list to reach the last element. This traversal would cause the time complexity to be O(n). An alternative would be to modify the solution to add a `rear` reference that always pointed to the last element in the list. This would help the time complexity for `add` but would have consequences if we try to remove the last element.

SRA 14.23   A singly linked list maintains a reference to the first element in the list and then a `next` reference from each node to the following node in the list. A doubly linked list maintains two references: `front` and `rear`. Each node in the doubly linked list stores both a `next` and a `previous` reference.

SRA 14.24   It would take two dummy records in a doubly linked list, one at the front and one at the rear, to eliminate the special cases when dealing with the first and last node.

SRA 14.25   A linked implementation allocates space only as it is needed and has a theoretical limit of the size of the hardware.

SRA 14.26   An array implementation uses less space per object since it only has to store the object and not an extra pointer. However, the array implementation will allocate much more space than it needs initially.

SRA 14.27   Since the `java.util.Stack` implementation is an extension of the `Vector` class, it can keep track of the positions of elements in the stack using an index and thus does not require each node to store an additional pointer. This implementation also allocates space only as it is needed, like the linked implementation.

SRA 14.28   The `java.util.Stack` implementation is an extension of the `Vector` class and thus inherits a large number of operations that violate the basic assumptions of a stack.

SRA 14.29   Postfix notation avoids the need for precedence rules that are required to evaluate infix expressions.

Queues

CHAPTER OBJECTIVES

- Examine queue processing.
- Define a queue abstract data type.
- Demonstrate how a queue can be used to solve problems.
- Examine various queue implementations.
- Compare queue implementations.

A queue is another collection with which we are inherently familiar. A queue is a waiting line, such as the line of customers waiting in a bank for their opportunity to talk to a teller. In fact, in many countries the word queue is used habitually in this way. In such countries, a person might say "join the queue" rather than "get in line." Other examples of queues include the check-out line at the grocery store or cars waiting at a stoplight. In any queue, an item enters on one end and leaves from the other. Queues have a variety of uses in computer algorithms.

15.1 A Queue ADT

A *queue* is a linear collection whose elements are added on one end and removed from the other. Therefore, we say that queue elements are processed in a *first in, first out* (FIFO) manner. Elements are removed from a queue in the same order in which they are placed on the queue.

This is consistent with the general concept of a waiting line. When a customer arrives at a bank, he or she begins waiting at the end of the line. When a teller becomes available, the customer at the beginning of the line leaves the line to receive service. Eventually every customer that started out at the end of the line moves to the front of the line and exits. For any given set of people, the first person to get in line is the first person to leave it.

The processing of a queue is pictured in Figure 15.1. Usually a queue is depicted horizontally. One end is established as the *front* of the queue and the other as the *rear* of the queue. Elements go onto the rear of the queue and come off of the front. Sometimes the front of the queue is called the *head* and the rear of the queue the *tail*.

Compare and contrast the processing of a queue to the LIFO (last in, first out) processing of a stack, which was discussed in Chapters 3 and 4. In a stack, the processing occurs at only one end of the collection. In a queue, processing occurs at both ends.

The operations defined for a queue ADT are listed in Figure 15.2. The term *enqueue* is used to refer to the process of adding a new element to the end of a queue. Likewise, *dequeue* refers to removing the element at the front of a queue. The *first* operation allows the user to examine the element at the front of the queue without removing it from the collection.

Remember that naming conventions are not universal for collection operations. Sometimes enqueue is simply called `add` or `insert`. The `dequeue` operation is sometimes called `remove` or `serve`. The `first` operation is sometimes called `front`.

FIGURE 15.1 A conceptual view of a queue

Operation	Description
enqueue	Adds an element to the rear of the queue.
dequeue	Removes an element from the front of the queue.
first	Examines the element at the front of the queue.
isEmpty	Determines if the queue is empty.
size	Determines the number of elements on the queue.

FIGURE 15.2 The operations on a queue

Note that there is a general similarity between the operations of a queue and those of a stack. The enqueue, dequeue, and first operations correspond to the stack operations push, pop, and peek. Similar to a stack, there are no operations that allow the user to "reach into" the middle of a queue and reorganize or remove elements. If that type of processing is required, perhaps the appropriate collection to use is a list of some kind, such as those discussed in the next chapter.

As we did with stacks, we define a generic Queue interface that represents the queue operations, separating the general purpose of the operations from the variety of ways they could be implemented. A Java version of the Queue interface is shown in Listing 15.1.

LISTING 15.1

```java
//********************************************************************
//  Queue.java          Java Foundations
//
//  Defines the interface to a queue collection.
//********************************************************************

package javafoundations;

public interface Queue<T>
{
    // Adds the specified element to the rear of the queue.
    public void enqueue (T element);

    // Removes and returns the element at the front of the queue.
    public T dequeue();
```

LISTING 15.1　*continued*

```
    // Returns a reference to the element at the front of the queue
    // without removing it.
    public T first();

    // Returns true if the queue contains no elements and false
    // otherwise.
    public boolean isEmpty();

    // Returns the number of elements in the queue.
    public int size();

    // Returns a string representation of the queue.
    public String toString();
}
```

Note that in addition to the standard queue operations, we have also included a `toString` method, as we did with our stack collection. It is included for convenience and is not generally considered a classic operation on a queue.

Queues have a wide variety of application within computing. Whereas the principle purpose of a stack is to reverse order, the principle purpose of a queue is to preserve order. Before exploring various ways to implement a queue, let's examine some ways in which a queue can be used to solve problems.

15.2 Using Queues: Code Keys

A *Caesar cipher* is a simple approach to encoding messages by shifting each letter in a message along the alphabet by a constant amount k. For example, if k equals 3, then in an encoded message, each letter is shifted three characters forward: a is replaced with d, b with e, c with f, and so on. The end of the alphabet wraps back around to the beginning. Thus, w is replaced with z, x with a, y with b, and z with c.

To decode the message, each letter is shifted the same number of characters backwards. Therefore, if k equals 3, the encoded message

```
vlpsolflwb iroorzv frpsohalwb
```

would be decoded into

```
simplicity follows complexity
```

Julius Caesar actually used this type of cipher in some of his secret government correspondence (hence the name). Unfortunately, the Caesar cipher is fairly easy to break. There are only 26 possibilities for shifting the characters, and the code can be broken by trying various key values until one works.

An improvement can be made to this encoding technique if we use a *repeating key*. Instead of shifting each character by a constant amount, we can shift each character by a different amount using a list of key values. If the message is longer than the list of key values, we just start using the key over again from the beginning. For example, if the key values are

3 1 7 4 2 5

then the first character is shifted by three, the second character by one, the third character by seven, etc. After shifting the sixth character by five, we start using the key over again. The seventh character is shifted by three, the eighth by one, etc.

Figure 15.3 shows the message "knowledge is power" encoded using this repeating key. Note that this encryption approach encodes the same letter into different characters, depending on where it occurs in the message and thus which key value is used to encode it. Conversely, the same character in the encoded message is decoded into different characters.

> **KEY CONCEPT**
> A queue is a convenient collection for storing a repeating code key.

The program in Listing 15.2 on page 573 uses a repeating key to encode and decode a message. The key of integer values is stored in a queue. After a key value is used, it is put back on the end of the queue so that the key continually repeats as needed for long messages. The key in this example uses both positive and negative values. Figure 15.4 on the next page illustrates the UML description of the Codes class.

Encoded Message:	n	o	v	a	n	j	g	h	l		m	u		u	r	x	l	v
Key:	3	1	7	4	2	5	3	1	7		4	2		5	3	1	7	4
Decoded Message:	k	n	o	w	l	e	d	g	e		i	s		p	o	w	e	r

FIGURE 15.3 An encoded message using a repeating key

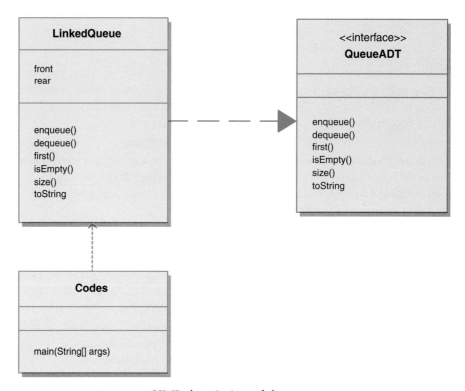

FIGURE 15.4 UML description of the `Codes` program

This program actually uses two copies of the key stored in two separate queues. The idea is that the person encoding the message has one copy of the key, and the person decoding the message has another. Two copies of the key are helpful in this program as well because the decoding process needs to match up the first character of the message with the first value in the key.

Also, note that this program doesn't bother to wrap around the end of the alphabet. It encodes any character in the Unicode character set by shifting it to some other position in the character set. Therefore, we can encode any character, including uppercase letters, lowercase letters, and punctuation. Even spaces get encoded.

Using a queue to store the key makes it easy to repeat the key by putting each key value back onto the queue as soon as it is used. The nature of a queue keeps the key values in the proper order, and we don't have to worry about reaching the end of the key and starting over.

LISTING 15.2

```java
//******************************************************************
//  Codes.java         Java Foundations
//
//  Uses a queue to encode and decode messages.
//******************************************************************

import javafoundations.CircularArrayQueue;

public class Codes
{
   //-----------------------------------------------------------------
   //  Encode and decode a message using a key of values stored in
   //  a queue.
   //-----------------------------------------------------------------
   public static void main ( String[] args)
   {
      int[] key = {5, 12, -3, 8, -9, 4, 10};
      Integer keyValue;
      String encoded = "", decoded = "";
      String message = "All programmers are playwrights and all " +
                       "computers are lousy actors.";

      CircularArrayQueue<Integer> keyQueue1 = new CircularArrayQueue<Integer>();
      CircularArrayQueue<Integer> keyQueue2 = new CircularArrayQueue<Integer>();

      // load key queue
      for (int scan=0; scan < key.length; scan++)
      {
         keyQueue1.enqueue (new Integer(key[scan]));
         keyQueue2.enqueue (new Integer(key[scan]));
      }

      // encode message
      for (int scan=0; scan < message.length(); scan++)
      {
         keyValue = keyQueue1.dequeue();
         encoded += (char) ((int)message.charAt(scan) + keyValue.intValue());
         keyQueue1.enqueue (keyValue);
      }

      System.out.println ("Encoded Message:\n" + encoded + "\n");

      // decode message
```

LISTING 15.2 *continued*

```
    for (int scan=0; scan < encoded.length(); scan++)
    {
        keyValue = keyQueue2.dequeue();
        decoded += (char) ((int)encoded.charAt(scan) - keyValue.intValue());
        keyQueue2.enqueue (keyValue);
    }

    System.out.println ("Decoded Message:\n" + decoded);
    }
}
```

15.3 Using Queues: Ticket Counter Simulation

Let's look at another example using queues. Consider the situation in which you are waiting in line to purchase tickets at a movie theatre. In general, the more cashiers there are, the faster the line moves. The theatre manager wants to keep his customers happy, but doesn't want to employ any more cashiers than necessary. Suppose the manager wants to keep the total time needed by a customer to less than seven minutes. Being able to simulate the effect of adding more cashiers during peak business hours allows the manager to plan more effectively. And, as we've discussed, a queue is the perfect collection for representing a waiting line.

> **KEY CONCEPT**
>
> Simulations are often implemented using queues to represent waiting lines.

Our simulated ticket counter will use the following assumptions:

- There is only one line and it is first come first served (a queue).
- Customers arrive on average every 15 seconds.
- If there is a cashier available, processing begins immediately upon arrival.
- Processing a customer request and getting them on their way takes on average two minutes (120 seconds) from the time they reach a cashier.

First we can create a `Customer` class, as shown in Listing 15.3. A `Customer` object keeps track of the time the customer arrives and the time the customer departs

LISTING 15.3

```java
//*******************************************************************
//   Customer.java        Java Foundations
//
//   Represents a waiting customer.
//*******************************************************************

public class Customer
{
   private int arrivalTime, departureTime;

   //-----------------------------------------------------------------
   //   Creates a new customer with the specified arrival time.
   //-----------------------------------------------------------------
   public Customer (int arrives)
   {
      arrivalTime = arrives;
      departureTime = 0;
   }

   //-----------------------------------------------------------------
   //   Returns the arrival time of this customer.
   //-----------------------------------------------------------------
   public int getArrivalTime()
   {
      return arrivalTime;
   }

   //-----------------------------------------------------------------
   //   Sets the departure time for this customer.
   //-----------------------------------------------------------------
   public void setDepartureTime (int departs)
   {
      departureTime = departs;
   }

   //-----------------------------------------------------------------
   //   Returns the departure time of this customer.
   //-----------------------------------------------------------------
   public int getDepartureTime()
   {
      return departureTime;
   }
```

LISTING 15.3   *continued*

```
//----------------------------------------------------------------
//  Computes and returns the total time spent by this customer.
//----------------------------------------------------------------
public int totalTime()
{
    return departureTime - arrivalTime;
}
}
```

after purchasing a ticket. The total time spent by the customer is therefore the departure time minus the arrival time. To keep things simple, our simulation will measure time in elapsed seconds, so a time value can be stored as a single integer. Our simulation will begin at time 0.

Our simulation will create a queue of customers, then see how long it takes to process those customers if there is only one cashier. Then we'll process the same queue of customers with two cashiers. Then we'll do it again with three cashiers. We'll continue this process for up to ten cashiers. At the end we'll compare the average time it takes to process a customer.

Because of our assumption that customers arrive every 15 seconds (on average), we can preload a queue with customers. We will process 100 customers in this simulation.

The program shown in Listing 15.4 on page 578 conducts our simulation. The outer loop determines how many cashiers are used in each pass of the simulation. For each pass, the customers are taken from the queue in turn and processed by a cashier. The total elapsed time is tracked, and at the end of each pass the average time is computed. Figure 15.5 shows the UML description of the `TicketCounter` and `Customer` classes.

The results of the simulation are shown in Figure 15.6. Note that with eight cashiers, the customers do not wait at all. The time of 120 seconds reflects only the time it takes to walk up and purchase the ticket. Increasing the number of cashiers to nine or ten or more will not improve the situation. Since the manager has decided he wants to keep the total average time to less than seven minutes (420 seconds), the simulation tells him that he should have six cashiers.

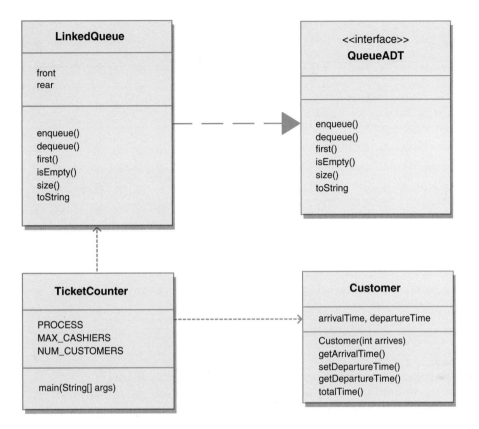

FIGURE 15.5 UML description of the TicketCounter program

Number of Cashiers:	1	2	3	4	5	6	7	8	9	10
Average Time (sec):	5317	2325	1332	840	547	355	219	120	120	120

FIGURE 15.6 The results of the ticket counter simulation

15.4 Implementing Queues: With Links

Because a queue is a linear collection, we can implement a queue as a linked list of LinearNode objects, as we did with stacks. The primary difference is that we will have to operate on both ends of the list. Therefore, in addition to a reference (called

LISTING 15.4

```java
//********************************************************************
//  DatabaseConnector.java          Java Foundations
//
//  Uses a queue to simulate a waiting line.
//********************************************************************

import javafoundations.*;

public class TicketCounter
{
   final static int PROCESS = 120;
   final static int MAX_CASHIERS = 10;
   final static int NUM_CUSTOMERS = 100;

   //-----------------------------------------------------------------
   //  Loads a queue with customers with various wait times then
   //  processes the queue.
   //-----------------------------------------------------------------
   public static void main ( String[] args)
   {
      Customer customer;
      LinkedQueue<Customer> customerQueue = new LinkedQueue<Customer>();
      int[] cashierTime = new int[MAX_CASHIERS];
      int totalTime, averageTime, departs;

      // process the simulation for various number of cashiers
      for (int cashiers=0; cashiers < MAX_CASHIERS; cashiers++)
      {
         // set each cashiers time to zero initially
         for (int count=0; count < cashiers; count++)
            cashierTime[count] = 0;

         // load customer queue
         for (int count=1; count <= NUM_CUSTOMERS; count++)
            customerQueue.enqueue(new Customer(count*15));

         totalTime = 0;

         // process all customers in the queue
         while (!(customerQueue.isEmpty()))
         {
            for (int count=0; count <= cashiers; count++)
            {
               if (!(customerQueue.isEmpty()))
               {
```

LISTING 15.4   *continued*

```
                customer = customerQueue.dequeue();
                if (customer.getArrivalTime() > cashierTime[count])
                    departs = customer.getArrivalTime() + PROCESS;
                else
                    departs = cashierTime[count] + PROCESS;
                customer.setDepartureTime (departs);
                cashierTime[count] = departs;
                totalTime += customer.totalTime();
            }
        }
    }

    // output results for this simulation
    averageTime = totalTime / NUM_CUSTOMERS;
    System.out.println ("Number of cashiers: " + (cashiers+1));
    System.out.println ("Average time: " + averageTime + "\n");
        }
    }
}
```

> **KEY CONCEPT**
>
> A linked implementation of a queue is facilitated by references to the first and last elements of the linked list.

front) pointing to the first element in the list, we will also keep track of a second reference (called rear) that points to the last element in the list. We will also use an integer variable called count to keep track of the number of elements in the queue.

Does it make a difference to which end of the list we add or enqueue elements and from which end of the list we remove or dequeue elements? If our linked list is singly linked, meaning that each node has only a pointer to the node behind it in the list, then yes, it does make a difference. In the case of the enqueue operation, it will not matter whether we add new elements to the front or the rear of the list. The processing steps will be very similar. If we add to the front of the list then we would set the next pointer of the new node to point to the front of the list and set the front variable to point to the new node. If we add to the rear of the list then we would set the next pointer of the node at the rear of the list to point to the new node and then set the rear of the list to point to the new node. In both cases, all of these processing steps are O(1) and therefore the time complexity of the enqueue operation would be O(1).

The difference between our two choices, adding to the `front` or the `rear` of the list, occurs with the `dequeue` operation. If we enqueue at the `rear` of the list and `dequeue` from the `front` of the list, then to `dequeue` we simply set a temporary variable to point to the element at the `front` of the list and then set the `front` variable to the value of the next pointer of the first node. Both processing steps are O(1) and therefore the operation would be O(1). However, if we enqueue at the `front` of the list and therefore `dequeue` at the `rear` list, our processing steps become more interesting. In order to `dequeue` from the `rear` of the list we must set a temporary variable to point to the element at the `rear` of the list and then set the `rear` pointer to point to the node before the current `rear`. Unfortunately, in a singly linked list, we cannot get to this node without traversing the list. Therefore, if we chose to enqueue at the `front` and `dequeue` at the `rear`, the `dequeue` operation would be O(n) instead of O(1) as it is with our other choice. Thus, we choose to enqueue at the `rear` and `dequeue` at the `front` of our singly linked list. Keep in mind that a doubly linked list would solve the problem of having to traverse the list and thus it would not matter which end was which in a doubly linked implementation.

Figure 15.7 depicts this strategy for implementing a queue. It shows a queue that has had the elements A, B, C, and D added to the queue or enqueued, in that order.

Remember that Figure 15.7 depicts the general case. We always have to be careful to accurately maintain our references in special cases. For an empty queue, the `front` and `rear` references are both null and the `count` is zero. If there is exactly one element in the queue, both the `front` and `rear` references point to the same object. If we were using a singly linked implementation with a sentinel node and the queue was empty, then both `front` and `rear` would point to the sentinel node.

Let's explore the implementation of the queue operations using this linked list approach as shown in Listing 15.5.

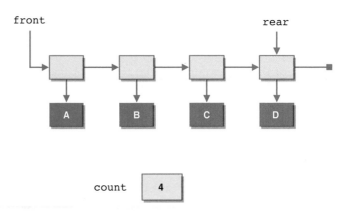

FIGURE 15.7 A linked implementation of a queue

LISTING 15.5

```java
//********************************************************************
//  LinkedQueue.java        Java Foundations
//
//  Represents a linked implementation of a queue.
//********************************************************************

package javafoundations;

import javafoundations.exceptions.*;

public class LinkedQueue<T> implements Queue<T>
{
   private int count;
   private LinearNode<T> front, rear;

   //-----------------------------------------------------------------
   //  Creates an empty queue.
   //-----------------------------------------------------------------
   public LinkedQueue()
   {
      count = 0;
      front = rear = null;
   }

   //-----------------------------------------------------------------
   //  Adds the specified element to the rear of this queue.
   //-----------------------------------------------------------------
   public void enqueue (T element)
   {
      LinearNode<T> node = new LinearNode<T>(element);

      if (count == 0)
         front = node;
      else
         rear.setNext(node);

      rear = node;
      count++;
   }

   //-----------------------------------------------------------------
   //  The following methods are left as programming projects.
   //-----------------------------------------------------------------
   //  public T dequeue () throws EmptyCollectionException { }
```

LISTING 15.5 *continued*

```
    //  public T first () throws EmptyCollectionException { }
    //  public boolean isEmpty() { }
    //  public int size() { }
    //  public String toString() { }
}
```

The enqueue Operation

The enqueue operation requires that we put the new element on the rear of the list. In the general case, that means setting the next reference of the current last element to the new one, and resetting the rear reference to the new last element. However, if the queue is currently empty, the front reference must also be set to the new (and only) element.

Note that the next reference of the new node need not be explicitly set in this method because it has already been set to null in the constructor for the LinearNode class. The rear reference is set to the new node in either case, and the count is incremented. Implementing the queue operations with sentinel nodes is left as an exercise. As we discussed earlier, this operation is O(1).

Figure 15.8 shows the linked list implementation of the queue from Figure 15.7 after element E has been added.

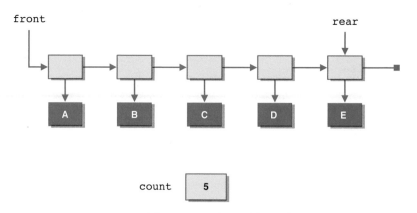

FIGURE 15.8 The queue after adding element E

The dequeue Operation

The first issue to address when implementing the `dequeue` operation is to ensure that there is at least one element to return. If not, an `EmptyCollectionException` is thrown. As we did with our stack collection in Chapters 14, it makes sense to employ a generic `EmptyCollectionException` to which we can pass a parameter specifying which collection we are dealing with. If there is at least one element in the queue, the first one in the list is returned and the `front` reference is updated.

For the `dequeue` operation, we must consider the situation in which we are returning the only element in the queue. If, after removing the front element, the queue is now empty, the `rear` reference is set to null. Note that in this case, the `front` will be null because it was set equal to the `next` reference of the last element in the list. Again, as we discussed earlier, the `dequeue` operation for our implementation is O(1).

Figure 15.9 shows the result of a `dequeue` operation on the queue from Figure 15.8. The element A at the front of the list is removed and returned to the user.

Note that, unlike the `pop` and `push` operations on a stack, the `dequeue` operation is not the inverse of `enqueue`. That is, Figure 15.9 is not identical to our original configuration shown in Figure 15.7, because the `enqueue` and `dequeue` operations are working on opposite ends of the collection.

> **KEY CONCEPT**
> The enqueue and dequeue operations work on opposite ends of the collection.

Other Operations

The remaining operations in the linked queue implementation are fairly straightforward and are similar to those in the stack collection. The `first` operation is implemented by returning a reference to the element at the front of the queue. The `isEmpty` operation returns true if the count of elements is 0, and false otherwise.

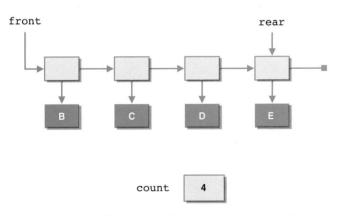

FIGURE 15.9 The queue after a `dequeue` operation

The `size` operation simply returns the count of elements in the queue. Finally, the `toString` operation returns a string made up of the `toString` results of each individual element. These operations are left as programming projects.

15.5 Implementing Queues: With Arrays

One array-based strategy for implementing a queue is to fix one end of the queue (say, the front) at index 0 of the array. The elements are stored contiguously in the array. Figure 15.10 depicts a queue stored in this manner, assuming elements A, B, C, and D have been added to the queue in that order.

The integer variable `rear` is used to indicate the next open cell in the array. Note that it also represents the number of elements in the queue.

This strategy assumes that the first element in the queue is always stored at index 0 of the array. Because queue processing affects both ends of the collection, this strategy will require that we shift the elements whenever an element is removed from the queue. This required shifting of elements would make the `dequeue` operation O(n). Like our discussion of the complexity of our singly linked list implementation above, making a poor choice in our array implementation could lead to less than optimal efficiency.

Would it make a difference if we fixed the rear of the queue at index 0 of the array instead of the front? Keep in mind that when we `enqueue` an element onto the queue, we do so at the rear of the queue. This would mean that each `enqueue` operation would result in shifting all of the elements in the queue up one position in the array making the `enqueue` operation O(n).

The key is to not fix either end. As elements are dequeued, the front of the queue will move further into the array. As elements are enqueued, the rear of the queue will also move further into the array.

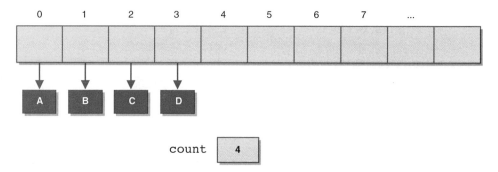

FIGURE 15.10 An array implementation of a queue

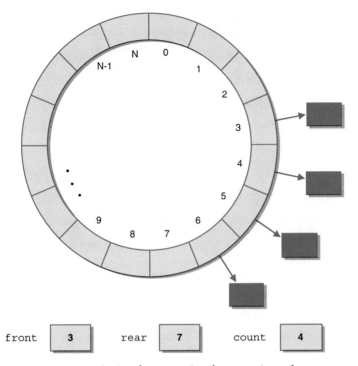

front | 3 | rear | 7 | count | 4 |

FIGURE 15.11 A circular array implementation of a queue

The challenge comes when the rear of the queue reaches the end of the array. Enlarging the array at this point is not a practical solution, and does not make use of the now empty space in the lower indexes of the array.

To make this solution work, we will use a *circular array* to implement the queue, defined in a class called `CircularArrayQueue`. A circular array is not a new construct—it is just a way to think about the array used to store the collection. Conceptually, the array is used as a circle, whose last index is followed by the first index. A circular array storing a queue is shown in Figure 15.11.

KEY CONCEPT
Treating arrays as circular eliminates the need to shift elements in an array queue implementation.

Two integer values are used to represent the front and rear of the queue. These values change as elements are added and removed. Note that the value of `front` represents the location where the first element in the queue is stored, and the value of `rear` represents the next available slot in the array (not where the last element is stored). Using `rear` in this manner is consistent with our other array implementation. Note, however, that the value of `rear` no longer represents the number of elements in the queue. We will use a separate integer value to keep a count of the elements.

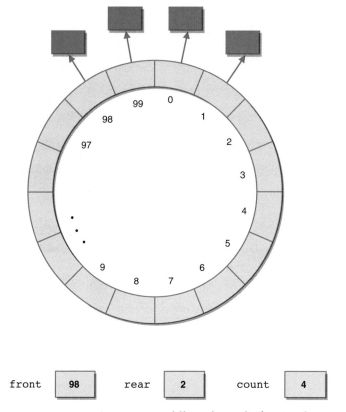

FIGURE 15.12 A queue straddling the end of a circular array

When the rear of the queue reaches the end of the list, it "wraps around" to the front of the array. The elements of the queue can therefore straddle the end of the array, as shown in Figure 15.12, which assumes the array can store 100 elements.

Using this strategy, once an element has been added to the queue, it stays in one location in the array until it is removed with a dequeue operation. No elements need to be shifted as elements are added or removed. This approach requires, however, that we carefully manage the values of front and rear.

Let's look at another example. Figure 15.13 shows a circular array (drawn linearly) with a capacity of ten elements. Initially it is shown after elements A through H have been enqueued. It is then shown after the first four elements (A through D) have been dequeued. Finally, it is shown after elements I, J, K, and L have been enqueued, which causes the queue to wrap around the end of the array.

Listing 15.6 on page 588 shows the CircularArrayQueue class.

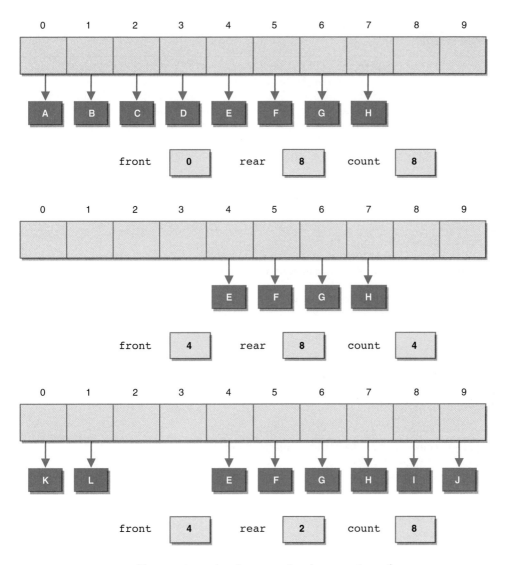

FIGURE 15.13 Changes in a circular array implementation of a queue

The enqueue Operation

In general, after an element is enqueued, the value of rear is incremented. But when an enqueue operation fills the last cell of the array (at the largest index), the value of rear must be set to 0, indicating that the next element should be stored at index 0. The appropriate update to the value of rear can be accomplished in

LISTING 15.6

```java
//********************************************************************
//  CircularArrayQueue.java        Java Foundations
//
//  Represents an array implementation of a queue in which neither
//  end of the queue is fixed in the array. The variables storing the
//  indexes of the front and rear of the queue continually increment
//  as elements are removed and added, cycling back to 0 when they
//  reach the end of the array.
//********************************************************************

package javafoundations;

import javafoundations.exceptions.*;

public class CircularArrayQueue<T> implements Queue<T>
{
    private final int DEFAULT_CAPACITY = 10;
    private int front, rear, count;
    private T[] queue;

    //-----------------------------------------------------------------
    //  Creates an empty queue using the default capacity.
    //-----------------------------------------------------------------
    public CircularArrayQueue()
    {
        front = rear = count = 0;
        queue = (T[]) (new Object[DEFAULT_CAPACITY]);
    }

    //-----------------------------------------------------------------
    //  Adds the specified element to the rear of this queue, expanding
    //  the capacity of the queue array if necessary.
    //-----------------------------------------------------------------
    public void enqueue (T element)
    {
        if (count == queue.length)
            expandCapacity();

        queue[rear] = element;
        rear = (rear+1) % queue.length;
        count++;
    }
```

LISTING 15.6   *continued*

```
//------------------------------------------------------------
//  Creates a new array to store the contents of this queue with
//  twice the capacity of the old one.
//------------------------------------------------------------
public void expandCapacity()
{
    T[] larger = (T[])(new Object[queue.length*2]);

    for (int index=0; index < count; index++)
        larger[index] = queue[(front+index) % queue.length];

    front = 0;
    rear = count;
    queue = larger;
}


//------------------------------------------------------------
//  The following methods are left as programming projects.
//------------------------------------------------------------
//  public T dequeue () throws EmptyCollectionException { }
//  public T first () throws EmptyCollectionException { }
//  public boolean isEmpty() { }
//  public int size() { }
//  public String toString() { }
}
```

one calculation by using the remainder operator (%). Recall that the remainder operator returns the remainder after dividing the first operand by the second. Therefore, if queue is the name of the array storing the queue, the following line of code will update the value of rear appropriately:

```
rear = (rear+1) % queue.length;
```

Let's try this calculation, assuming we have an array of size 10. If rear is currently 15, it will be set to 6%10, or 6. If rear is currently 9, it will be set to 10%10 or 0. Try this calculation using various situations to see that it works no matter how big the array is.

Note that this implementation strategy can still allow the array to reach capacity. As with any array-based implementation, all cells in the array may become filled. This implies that the rear of the queue has "caught up" to the front of the queue. To add another element, the array would have to be enlarged. Keep in mind, however, that the elements of the existing array must be copied into the new array in their proper order in the queue, not necessarily the order in which they appear in the current array. This makes the `expandCapacity` method slightly more complex then the one we used for stacks.

The dequeue Operation

Likewise, after an element is dequeued, the value of `front` is incremented. After enough `dequeue` operations, the value of `front` will reach the last index of the array. After removing the element at the largest index, the value of `front` must be set to 0 instead of being incremented. The same calculation we used to set the value of `rear` in the `enqueue` operation can be used to set the value of `front` in the `dequeue` operation.

Other Operations

Operations such as `toString` become a bit more complicated using this approach because the elements are not stored starting at index 0 and may wrap around the end of the array. These methods have to take the current situation into account. These operations are left as programming projects.

Summary of Key Concepts

- Queue elements are processed in a FIFO manner—the first element in is the first element out.

- A queue is a convenient collection for storing a repeating code key.

- Simulations are often implemented using queues to represent waiting lines.

- A linked implementation of a queue is facilitated by references to the first and last elements of the linked list.

- The `enqueue` and `dequeue` operations work on opposite ends of the collection.

- Because queue operations modify both ends of the collection, fixing one end at index 0 requires that elements be shifted.

- The shifting of elements in a noncircular array implementation creates an $O(n)$ complexity.

- Treating arrays as circular eliminates the need to shift elements in an array queue implementation.

Self-Review Questions

SR 15.1   What is the difference between a queue and a stack?

SR 15.2   What are the five basic operations on a queue?

SR 15.3   What are some of the other operations that might be implemented for a queue?

SR 15.4   Is it possible for the `front` and `rear` references in a linked implementation to be equal?

SR 15.5   Is it possible for the `front` and `rear` references in a circular array implementation to be equal?

SR 15.6   Which implementation has the worst time complexity?

SR 15.7   Which implementation has the worst space complexity?

Exercises

EX 15.1   Hand trace a queue X through the following operations:

```
X.enqueue(new Integer(4));
X.enqueue(new Integer(1));
Object Y = X.dequeue();
X.enqueue(new Integer(8));
X.enqueue(new Integer(2));
X.enqueue(new Integer(5));
X.enqueue(new Integer(3));
Object Y = X.dequeue();
X.enqueue(new Integer(4));
X.enqueue(new Integer(9));
```

EX 15.2   Given the resulting queue X from Exercise 15.1, what would be the result of each of the following?

a. `X.front();`
b. `Y = X.dequeue();`
   `X.front();`
c. `Y = X.dequeue();`
   `X.front();`

EX 15.3   What would be the time complexity of the `size` operation for each of the implementations if there were not a `count` variable?

EX 15.4   Under what circumstances could the `front` and `rear` references be equal for each of the implementations?

EX 15.5   Hand trace the ticket counter problem for 22 customers and 4 cashiers. Graph the total process time for each person. What can you surmise from these results?

EX 15.6   Compare and contrast the `enqueue` method of the `LinkedQueue` class to the `push` method of the `LinkedStack` class from Chapter 6.

EX 15.7   Describe two different ways the `isEmpty` method of the `LinkedQueue` class could be implemented.

EX 15.8   Name five everyday examples of a queue other than those discussed in this chapter.

EX 15.9   Explain why the array implementation of a stack does not require elements to be shifted but the noncircular array implementation of a queue does.

EX 15.10   Suppose the count variable was not used in the CircularArrayQueue class. Explain how you could use the values of front and rear to compute the number of elements in the list.

Programming Projects

PP 15.1   Complete the implementation of the LinkedQueue class presented in this chapter. Specifically, complete the implementations of the first, isEmpty, size, and toString methods.

PP 15.2   Complete the implementation of the CircularArrayQueue class described in this chapter, including all methods.

PP 15.3   Write a version of the CircularArrayQueue class that grows the list in the opposite direction from which the version described in this chapter grows the list.

PP 15.4   All of the implementations in this chapter use a count variable to keep track of the number of elements in the queue. Rewrite the linked implementation without a count variable.

PP 15.5   All of the implementations in this chapter use a count variable to keep track of the number of elements in the queue. Rewrite the circular array implementation without a count variable.

PP 15.6   A data structure called a deque (pronounced like "deck") is closely related to a queue. The name deque stands for double ended queue. The difference between the two is that with a deque, you can insert or remove from either end of the queue. Implement a deque using arrays.

PP 15.7   Implement the deque from Programming Project PP 15.6 using links. (*Hint:* each node will need a next and a previous reference.)

PP 15.8   Create a graphical application that provides buttons for enqueue and dequeue from a queue, a text field to accept a string as input for enqueue, and a text area to display the contents of the queue after each operation.

PP 15.9   Create a system using a stack and a queue to test whether a given string is a palindrome (i.e., the characters read the same forward or backward).

PP 15.10   Create a system to simulate vehicles at an intersection. Assume that there is one lane going in each of four directions, with stop-lights facing each direction. Vary the arrival average of vehicles in each direction and the frequency of the light changes to view the "behavior" of the intersection.

Answers to Self-Review Questions

SRA 15.1   A queue is a first in, first out (FIFO) collection, whereas a stack is a last in, first out (LIFO) collection.

SRA 15.2   The basic queue operations are:

enqueue—adds an element to the end of the queue.

dequeue—removes an element from the front of the queue.

first—returns a reference to the element at the front of the queue.

isEmpty—returns true if the queue is empty, returns false otherwise.

size—returns the number of elements in the queue

SRA 15.3   makeEmpty(), destroy(), full()

SRA 15.4   Yes, it happens when the queue is empty (both front and rear are null) and when there is only one element on the queue.

SRA 15.5   Yes, it can happen under two circumstances: when the queue is empty, and when the queue is full.

SRA 15.6   The noncircular array implementation with an O(n) dequeue or enqueue operation has the worst time complexity.

SRA 15.7   Both of the array implementations waste space for unfilled elements in the array. The linked implementation uses more space per element stored.

Trees

CHAPTER OBJECTIVES

- Define the terms associated with trees.
- Discuss possible strategies for implementing trees.
- Discuss the various ways trees can be traversed.
- Explore an implementation of a binary tree.
- Use binary trees to represent decision trees.

This chapter begins our exploration of nonlinear collections, and trees in particular. Trees are used in many situations in computing. In this chapter we discuss the use and implementation of trees, define the terms associated with trees, analyze possible tree implementations, and look at examples of implementing and using trees. Based on this core material, Chapter 17 continues the exploration of trees.

16.1 Tree Terminology

The collections we examined in Chapter 15 (stacks, queues, and lists) are linear data structures, meaning their elements are arranged in order one after another. A *tree* is a nonlinear structure in which elements are organized into a hierarchy. This section describes trees in general and establishes some important terminology.

A tree is composed of a set of *nodes* in which elements are stored, and *edges* that connect one node to another. Each node is at a particular *level* in the tree hierarchy. The root of the tree is the only node at the top level of the tree. There is only one root node in a tree. Figure 16.1 illustrates some tree terminology.

The nodes at lower levels of the tree are the *children* of nodes at the previous level. In Figure 16.1, the nodes labeled B, C, D, and E are the children of A. Nodes F and G are the children of B. A node can have only one parent, but a node may have multiple children. Nodes that have the same parent are called *siblings*. Thus, nodes H, I, and J are siblings because they are all children of D.

The root node is the only node in a tree that does not have a parent. A node that does not have any children is called a *leaf*. A node that is not the root and has at least one child is called an *internal node*. Note that the tree analogy is upside-down. Our trees "grow" from the root at the top of the tree to the leaves toward the bottom of the tree.

A *subtree* is a tree structure that makes up part of another tree. The tree in Figure 16.1 is made up of subtrees with roots B, C, D, and E. In turn, the subtree with root B has subtrees of its own with roots F and G.

We can follow a *path* through a tree from parent to child, starting at the root. For example, the path from node A to N in Figure 16.1 is A, D, I, N. A node is the *ancestor* of another node if it is above it on the path from the root. Thus the root is the ultimate ancestor of all nodes in a tree. Nodes that can be reached by following a path from a particular node are the *descendants* of that node.

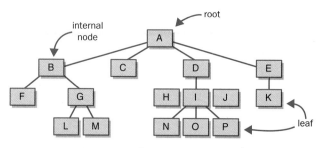

FIGURE 16.1 Some tree terminology

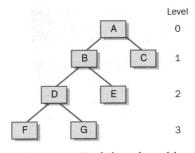

FIGURE 16.2 Path length and level

The level of a node is also the length of the path from the root to the node. This *path length* is determined by counting the number of edges that must be followed to get from the root to the node. The root is considered to be level 0, the children of the root are at level 1, the grandchildren of the root are at level 2, and so on. Path length and level are depicted in Figure 16.2.

The *height* (or *depth*) of a tree is the length of the longest path from the root to a leaf. Thus the height of the tree in Figure 16.2 is 3, because the path length from the root to leaf F (or G) is 3. The height of a particular node is defined by the level it is on. Thus the height of node B is 1.

Tree Classifications

Trees can be classified in many ways. One important criterion is the maximum number of children any node in the tree may have. This value is sometimes referred to as the *order of the tree*. A tree that has no limit to the number of children a node may have is called a *general tree*. A tree that limits each node to no more than n children is referred to as an *n-ary tree*.

> **KEY CONCEPT**
> The order of a tree specifies the maximum number of children any node in the tree may have.

A tree in which nodes may have at most two children is called a *binary tree*. This type of tree is particularly helpful in many situations. Much of our exploration of trees will focus on binary trees.

Another way to classify a tree is whether it is balanced or not. A tree is considered to be *balanced* if all of the leaves of the tree are on the same level or at least within one level of each other. Thus, the tree shown on the left in Figure 16.3 is balanced, while the one on the right is not. A balanced n-ary tree with m elements will have a height of $\log_n m$. Thus, a balanced binary tree with n nodes has a height of $\log_2 n$, a fact we used to our advantage in the analysis of certain sorting algorithms in Chapter 13.

> **KEY CONCEPT**
> A balanced n-ary tree with m elements will have height $\log_n m$.

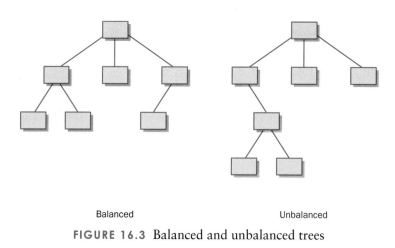

Balanced   Unbalanced

FIGURE 16.3 Balanced and unbalanced trees

An n-ary tree is *full* if all leaves of the tree are at the same level and every nonleaf node has exactly n children. A tree is *complete* if it is full, or full to the next-to-last level with all leaves at the bottom level on the left side of the tree. In Figure 16.4, the first two trees (a and b) are complete, but not full. The third tree (c) is both complete and full. As we'll see, full and complete trees can be implemented efficiently using certain techniques.

16.2 Tree Traversals

Because a tree is a nonlinear structure, the concept of traversing a tree is generally more interesting than the concept of traversing a linear structure. There are four basic ways to traverse a tree, all starting at the root node:

- *Preorder traversal* — visit the root, then traverse the subtrees from left to right
- *Inorder traversal* — traverse the left subtree, then visit the root, then traverse the remaining subtrees from left to right
- *Postorder traversal* — traverse the subtrees from left to right, then visit the root
- *Level-order traversal* — visit each node at each level of the tree from top (root) to bottom and left to right

Recall from our earlier discussions of collections that the concept of "visiting" a node during a traversal is deliberately vague. What a program does when

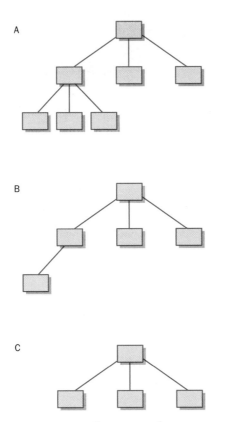

FIGURE 16.4 Some complete trees

visiting a node is up to the developer. A particular type of traversal simply dictates the order in which the elements of a collection are accessed.

The first three traversal definitions in this list are inherently recursive. For instance, when a subtree is traversed in a preorder traversal, it is traversed in a preorder fashion. The traversal techniques do not intersect. A level-order traversal is not recursive in nature because its processing is based on the tree's levels, not on subtrees.

These definitions apply to trees of any order. For example, if a particular node had four children, an inorder traversal would traverse the node's leftmost subtree, then visit the node, then traverse the second subtree completely, then the third subtree, and then the fourth. However, to simplify the following example, we focus on how each of these definitions applies to a binary tree.

Figure 16.5 on the next page shows a binary tree and its four traversals. Let's walk through the processing of each type of traversal.

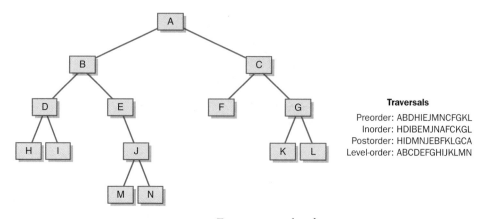

Traversals
Preorder: ABDHIEJMNCFGKL
Inorder: HDIBEMJNAFCKGL
Postorder: HIDMNJEBFKLGCA
Level-order: ABCDEFGHIJKLMN

FIGURE 16.5 Four traversals of a tree

Preorder Traversal

In a preorder traversal, the nodes are visited before any subtrees are visited. So for the binary tree in Figure 16.5, the root A is visited, then the entire subtree with root B is traversed, and then the entire subtree with root C is traversed. Note that all nodes in the left subtree are listed in the traversal before the nodes in the right subtree. This can be summarized in the following pseudocode:

```
Visit node
Traverse(left-subtree)
Traverse(right-subtree)
```

And remember, every subtree is traversed using a preorder approach. To traverse the subtree with root B, the root B is visited, then the entire subtree with root D is traversed, then the entire subtree with root E is traversed.

Let's walk through the preorder traversal from the beginning. First A is visited, followed by B, D, and H as the left subtree of each node is traversed. At this point, there is no left subtree of H, so we're ready to traverse the right subtree of H. But there is no child there either. So, having completely traversed the left subtree of D, we turn to the right subtree of D. After visiting I and finding that it has no children, the subtree with root D is finished. Next we traverse the right subtree of B, first visiting node E. Then, because there is no left subtree of E, we process its right subtree, yielding J, M, and N.

At this point, the entire left subtree with root B has been traversed, and the right subtree with root C is processed next. This yields C, F, G, K, and L.

Take a few minutes to study the tree in Figure 16.5 and its preorder traversal, tracing the route the traversal takes through the tree.

Inorder Traversal

For a binary tree, an inorder traversal visits the root in between the traversals of the left and right subtrees. This is shown in the following pseudocode:

```
Traverse(left-subtree)
Visit node
Traverse(right-subtree)
```

Compare this pseudocode to that of the preorder traversal. The recursive logic is the same, but the first two steps are reversed.

To perform an inorder traversal of the tree in Figure 16.5, we first traverse the left subtree of A completely, then visit the root A, then traverse the entire right subtree of A. Applying that logic recursively, we first follow the leftmost path down the tree to H, where there is no left subtree to process. Then the node H is visited, followed by its right subtree (which doesn't exist). Having processed the entire left subtree of D, we visit D, then process its right subtree, yielding I. Now, with the entire subtree with root D finished, we visit B, then process its right subtree. There is no left subtree of E, so we visit E, then traverse its right subtree. This yields M, J, and N.

At this point, the entire left subtree of A is finished, so we visit A, then traverse its right subtree. That yields F, C, K, G, and L.

Note that in the results of a preorder traversal, the root of the tree comes first. But in an inorder traversal, the root is visited in the "middle" of the traversal (depending on how balanced the tree is). This observation can be made for any subtree as well.

Postorder Traversal

After embracing the preorder and inorder traversals, the postorder traversal is nothing new. The only difference, once again, is the order in which the root is visited relative to the subtrees. In a postorder traversal, the root is visited last, as shown in the following pseudocode:

```
Traverse(left-subtree)
Traverse(right-subtree)
Visit node
```

To perform a postorder traversal of the tree in Figure 16.5, we first traverse the entire left subtree of A, then traverse the entire right subtree of A, then finally visit the root. Applying this approach recursively, we follow the leftmost path down to H, find no children on either side, then visit node H. Next comes the traversal of the right subtree of D, yielding I, then visiting D. With the left subtree of B finished, we traverse its right subtree, yielding M, N, J, and E. Then B is visited, finishing the left subtree of A. We then traverse the right subtree of A, yielding F, K, L, G, and C. Finally, the last node visited is the root of the entire tree, A.

Compare the results of the preorder and postorder traversals. In a preorder traversal, the root always comes first. In a postorder traversal, the root comes last. And again, this effect can be seen for all subtrees.

Level-Order Traversal

A level-order traversal is quite different from the other three because it traverses the tree across levels instead of down subtrees. Each node on each level is visited from left to right. For the tree in Figure 16.5, the level-order traversal is easy to see. We first visit the root A. Then we visit B and C on the next level. Then we visit D, E, F, and G on the next level, and so on.

But producing a level-order traversal by looking at a tree and producing it algorithmically are two different things. Recursive processing of subtrees won't work because a level-order traversal does not follow the parent/child relationships that exist inherently between the nodes of a tree. Instead, it cuts across subtrees horizontally, requiring a bit of processing to access the nodes in the proper order.

Our solution relies on the use of a queue to help manage the nodes as we encounter them. The algorithm for producing a level-order traversal can be expressed as follows:

```
Enqueue the root node of the tree
While the queue is not empty
{
    Dequeue node
    Visit node
    Enqueue left child of node
    Enqueue right child of node
}
```

> **KEY CONCEPT**
>
> A queue can be used to store the elements of a tree during a level-order traversal.

Follow the logic of this algorithm as applied to the tree in Figure 16.5. The root, A, is enqueued, and the loop begins. Node A is dequeued and visited, then B and C are enqueued in that order. Processing the loop body again, node B is dequeued and visited, and D and E are enqueued (behind C). Then C is dequeued and visited, and its children, F and G, are enqueued. This process continues for each level of the tree.

16.3 Strategies for Implementing Trees

Before getting into the details, let's discuss some general strategies for implementing trees. Because a tree is a nonlinear structure, it may not seem reasonable to attempt to implement it using an underlying linear structure such as an array.

However, sometimes array-based implementations are useful, though almost certainly a less obvious choice. We'll briefly discuss two array-based approaches. Perhaps the most obvious implementation of a tree is a linked structure, with object references pointing from each tree node to its children.

Computed Links in an Array

For certain types of trees, specifically full or complete binary trees, a computational strategy can be used for representing a tree using an array. One possible strategy is as follows: For any element stored in position n of the array, the element's left child is stored in position $(2n + 1)$ and the element's right child is stored in position $(2 * (n + 1))$. The capacity of the array can be managed in much the same way that we managed capacity for the array implementations of queues and stacks. This strategy is illustrated in Figure 16.6.

> **KEY CONCEPT**
>
> One strategy for implementing binary trees using an array places the left child of element n at position $(2n + 1)$ and the right child at position $(2*(n+1))$.

Despite the conceptual elegance of this solution, it is not without drawbacks. If the represented tree is not complete or relatively complete, this implementation strategy can waste large amounts of memory allocated in the array for positions of the tree that do not contain data.

Stored Links in an Array

Another possible array implementation of trees is modeled after the way operating systems manage memory. Instead of assigning elements of the tree to array positions based on their location in the tree, array positions are allocated contiguously on a first-come, first-served basis. Each element of the array is an object that stores a reference to the tree element and the array index of each child. This approach, illustrated in

> **KEY CONCEPT**
>
> A stored link strategy for an array-based tree implementation allows array positions to be allocated contiguously regardless of the completeness of the tree.

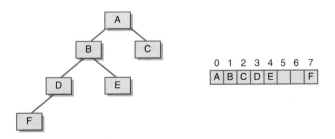

FIGURE 16.6 An array implementation of a binary tree using computed links

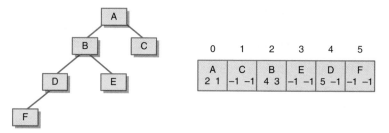

FIGURE 16.7 An array implementation of a binary tree using stored links

Figure 16.7, allows elements to be stored contiguously in the array so that space is not wasted. The order of the elements in the array is determined simply by their entry order into the tree. In this case, the entry order is assumed to have been A, C, B, E, D, F.

This approach increases the overhead for deleting elements in the tree, because it requires either that remaining elements be shifted to remain contiguous or that a list of unused locations be maintained.

This same strategy can also be used when tree structures need to be stored directly on disk. In this case, rather than using an array index as a pointer, each node stores the relative position in the file of its children so that an offset can be calculated given the base address of the file.

Linked Nodes

In a classic linked implementation, each tree node can be defined using a separate class, similar to what we did with the LinearNode class for linked lists. Each node would contain a reference to the element to be stored in that node. In addition, instead of a next reference to the next node in the list, the node will have references for each of the possible children of the node.

If the tree being represented is a binary tree, the node can simply keep track of references to the left and right child nodes. However, if the implementation is for an n-ary or general tree, with many possible children per node, more child references will be needed. And at that point it would almost certainly be best to store an array or linked list of references to the child nodes instead of using individual references.

Trees organized in this way lend themselves to recursive processing for many operations. Each node can be thought of as the root of a subtree. This concept is depicted in Figure 16.8. We explore this implementation approach for a binary tree in the following section.

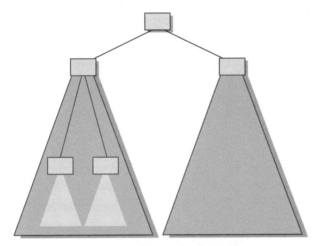

FIGURE 16.8 A tree and its subtrees

16.4 A Binary Tree Implementation

One possible set of operations for a binary tree is shown in the `BinaryTree` inter-face in Listing 16.1. Keep in mind that the definition of a collection is not universal. You will find variations in the operations defined for specific collections from one book to another.

Note that the `BinaryTree` interface has no methods to add a particular ele-ment to the tree, or to remove a particular element from the tree. In more refined versions of a binary tree, such as those described in the next chapter, the charac-teristics of those trees will dictate the semantics of adding and removing particular

LISTING 16.1

```
//*****************************************************************
//   BinaryTree.java          Java Foundations
//
//   Defines the interface to a binary tree collection.
//*****************************************************************

package javafoundations;

import java.util.Iterator;
```

LISTING 16.1 *continued*

```java
public interface BinaryTree<T> extends Iterable<T>
{
    // Returns the element stored in the root of the tree.
    public T getRootElement();

    // Returns the left subtree of the root.
    public BinaryTree<T> getLeft();

    // Returns the right subtree of the root.
    public BinaryTree<T> getRight();

    // Returns true if the binary tree contains an element that
    // matches the specified element and false otherwise.
    public boolean contains (T target);

    // Returns a reference to the element in the tree matching
    // the specified target.
    public T find (T target);

    // Returns true if the binary tree contains no elements, and
    // false otherwise.
    public boolean isEmpty();

    // Returns the number of elements in this binary tree.
    public int size();

    // Returns the string representation of the binary tree.
    public String toString();

    // Returns a preorder traversal on the binary tree.
    public Iterator<T> preorder();

    // Returns an inorder traversal on the binary tree.
    public Iterator<T> inorder();

    // Returns a postorder traversal on the binary tree.
    public Iterator<T> postorder();

    // Performs a level-order traversal on the binary tree.
    public Iterator<T> levelorder();
}
```

elements. For the general binary tree described here, the emphasis is on more basic operations. Even so, as we'll see, this type of tree is useful in certain situations.

Let's examine some of the issues related to implementing the `BinaryTree` interface. We'll focus on a linked implementation, using a recursive definition of a tree as discussed in the previous section.

The `LinkedBinaryTree` class, shown in Listing 16.2, provides an implementation of a binary tree with some operations left as programming projects. The tree stores elements of a generic type `T`, as we've done with previous collections.

LISTING 16.2

```java
//********************************************************************
//  LinkedBinaryTree.java         Java Foundations
//
//  Implements a binary tree using a linked representation.
//********************************************************************

package javafoundations;

import java.util.Iterator;
import javafoundations.*;
import javafoundations.exceptions.*;

public class LinkedBinaryTree<T> implements BinaryTree<T>
{
    protected BTNode<T> root;

    //-----------------------------------------------------------------
    //  Creates an empty binary tree.
    //-----------------------------------------------------------------
    public LinkedBinaryTree()
    {
        root = null;
    }

    //-----------------------------------------------------------------
    //  Creates a binary tree with the specified element as its root.
    //-----------------------------------------------------------------
    public LinkedBinaryTree (T element)
    {
        root = new BTNode<T>(element);
    }
```

LISTING 16.2   *continued*

```
//---------------------------------------------------------------
//  Creates a binary tree with the two specified subtrees.
//---------------------------------------------------------------
public LinkedBinaryTree (T element, LinkedBinaryTree<T> left,
   LinkedBinaryTree<T> right)
{
   root = new BTNode<T>(element);
   root.setLeft(left.root);
   root.setRight(right.root);
}


//---------------------------------------------------------------
//  Returns the element stored in the root of the tree. Throws an
//  EmptyCollectionException if the tree is empty.
//---------------------------------------------------------------
public T getRootElement()
{
   if (root == null)
      throw new EmptyCollectionException ("Get root operation "
          + "failed. The tree is empty.");

   return root.getElement();
}


//---------------------------------------------------------------
//  Returns the left subtree of the root of this tree.
//---------------------------------------------------------------
public LinkedBinaryTree<T> getLeft()
{
   if (root == null)
      throw new EmptyCollectionException ("Get left operation "
          + "failed. The tree is empty.");

   LinkedBinaryTree<T> result = new LinkedBinaryTree<T>();
   result.root = root.getLeft();

   return result;
}


//---------------------------------------------------------------
//  Returns the element in this binary tree that matches the
//  specified target. Throws a ElementNotFoundException if the
//  target is not found.
//---------------------------------------------------------------
```

LISTING 16.2   *continued*

```java
public T find (T target)
{
   BTNode<T> node = null;

   if (root != null)
      node = root.find(target);

   if (node == null)
      throw new ElementNotFoundException("Find operation failed. "
         + "No such element in tree.");

   return node.getElement();
}

//-----------------------------------------------------------------
//  Returns the number of elements in this binary tree.
//-----------------------------------------------------------------
public int size()
{
   int result = 0;

   if (root != null)
      result = root.count();

   return result;
}

//-----------------------------------------------------------------
//  Populates and returns an iterator containing the elements in
//  this binary tree using an inorder traversal.
//-----------------------------------------------------------------
public Iterator<T> inorder()
{
   ArrayIterator<T> iter = new ArrayIterator<T>();

   if (root != null)
      root.inorder (iter);

   return iter;
}

//-----------------------------------------------------------------
//  Populates and returns an iterator containing the elements in
//  this binary tree using a levelorder traversal.
//-----------------------------------------------------------------
```

LISTING 16.2   *continued*

```java
public Iterator<T> levelorder()
{
   LinkedQueue<BTNode<T>> queue = new LinkedQueue<BTNode<T>>();
   ArrayIterator<T> iter = new ArrayIterator<T>();

   if (root != null)
   {
      queue.enqueue(root);
      while (!queue.isEmpty())
      {
         BTNode<T> current = queue.dequeue();

         iter.add (current.getElement());

         if (current.getLeft() != null)
            queue.enqueue(current.getLeft());
         if (current.getRight() != null)
            queue.enqueue(current.getRight());
      }
   }

   return iter;
}

//----------------------------------------------------------------
//  Satisfies the Iterable interface using an inorder traversal.
//----------------------------------------------------------------
public Iterator<T> iterator()
{
   return inorder();
}

//----------------------------------------------------------------
//  The following methods are left as programming projects.
//----------------------------------------------------------------
// public LinkedBinaryTree<T> getRight() { }
// public boolean contains (T target) { }
// public boolean isEmpty() { }
// public String toString() { }
// public Iterator<T> preorder() { }
// public Iterator<T> postorder() { }
}
```

Like all well-designed collections, the user of the binary tree does not have to know anything about details of the underlying implementation.

The instance data of the LinkedBinaryTree class is a single link to the root node of the tree, represented by the BTNode class. The BTNode class, shown in Listing 16.3, is similar to the LinearNode class used in linked lists, but stores

LISTING 16.3

```java
//*******************************************************************
//  BTNode.java        Java Foundations
//
//  Represents a node in a binary tree with a left and right child.
//  Therefore this class also represents the root of a subtree.
//*******************************************************************

package javafoundations;

public class BTNode<T>
{
    protected T element;
    protected BTNode<T> left, right;

    //----------------------------------------------------------------
    //  Creates a new tree node with the specified data.
    //----------------------------------------------------------------
    public BTNode (T element)
    {
        this.element = element;
        left = right = null;
    }

    //----------------------------------------------------------------
    //  Returns the element stored in this node.
    //----------------------------------------------------------------
    public T getElement()
    {
        return element;
    }

    //----------------------------------------------------------------
    //  Sets the element stored in this node.
    //----------------------------------------------------------------
```

LISTING 16.3   *continued*

```java
public void setElement (T element)
{
    this.element = element;
}

//-------------------------------------------------------------------
//   Returns the left subtree of this node.
//-------------------------------------------------------------------
public BTNode<T> getLeft()
{
    return left;
}

//-------------------------------------------------------------------
//   Sets the left child of this node.
//-------------------------------------------------------------------
public void setLeft (BTNode<T> left)
{
    this.left = left;
}

//-------------------------------------------------------------------
//   Returns the right subtree of this node.
//-------------------------------------------------------------------
public BTNode<T> getRight()
{
    return right;
}

//-------------------------------------------------------------------
//   Sets the right child of this node.
//-------------------------------------------------------------------
public void setRight (BTNode<T> right)
{
    this.right = right;
}

//-------------------------------------------------------------------
//   Returns the element in this subtree that matches the
//   specified target. Returns null if the target is not found.
//-------------------------------------------------------------------
public BTNode<T> find (T target)
{
    BTNode<T> result = null;
```

LISTING 16.3 *continued*

```java
      if (element.equals(target))
         result = this;
      else
      {
         if (left != null)
            result = left.find(target);
         if (result == null && right != null)
             result = right.find(target);
      }

      return result;
   }

   //-----------------------------------------------------------------
   //  Returns the number of nodes in this subtree.
   //-----------------------------------------------------------------
   public int count()
   {
      int result = 1;

      if (left != null)
         result += left.count();

      if (right != null)
         result += right.count();

      return result;
   }

   //-----------------------------------------------------------------
   //  Performs an inorder traversal on this subtree, updating the
   //  specified iterator.
   //-----------------------------------------------------------------
   public void inorder (ArrayIterator<T> iter)
   {
      if (left != null)
         left.inorder (iter);

      iter.add (element);

      if (right != null)
         right.inorder (iter);
   }
```

LISTING 16.3 *continued*

```
   //------------------------------------------------------------
   //  The following methods are left as programming projects.
   //------------------------------------------------------------
   // public void preorder(ArrayIterator<T> iter) { }
   // public void postorder(ArrayIterator<T> iter) { }
}
```

links to the left and right children of each node. This organization is depicted in Figure 16.9. The LinkedBinaryTree class provides the formal implementation of the BinaryTree interface, but its underlying structure relies heavily on the recursive BTNode structure.

There are three overloaded constructors for the LinkedBinaryTree class: one that creates an empty binary tree, one that creates a binary tree with a single root node but no children, and one that creates a binary tree with a root node and two subtrees. In the last case, either parameter representing the subtrees could be null.

Without any methods to add elements to the tree, the tree must be created from the bottom up using the LinkedBinaryTree constructors. That is, the lowest subtrees are constructed first, and used to create larger subtrees. The last step is to create the tree that holds the root element of the entire tree.

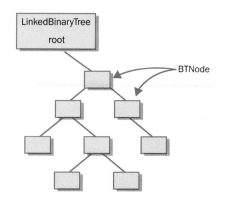

FIGURE 16.9 The implementation strategy for a linked binary tree

The `getRootElement` method provides access to the element stored in the node. The `getLeft` method returns the entire left subtree as a newly constructed `LinkedBinaryTree` object. The `getRight` method would operate similarly. Note that the `BTNode` class has its own version of `getLeft` and `getRight`, which return `BTNode` objects.

The `find` method in `LinkedBinaryTree` throws an exception if the target element is not found or the tree is empty. The actual search is performed in the find method of the `BTNode` class. It checks to see if the target element is stored in the current node, then calls `find` on the subtrees as needed. It uses the `equals` method of the stored element to determine equality. Like we've seen in other collections, this approach puts the definition of equality under the control of the class being stored in the tree. The `find` method in `BSTNode` returns `null` if the target element is not found. The `contains` method in `LinkedBinaryTree`, which is left as a programming project, could use the `find` method to determine if the target element exists in the tree.

The number of elements in the tree is equal to the number of nodes in the left subtree plus the number of nodes in the right subtree plus 1 (for the root). The `size` method in `LinkedBinaryTree` calls the `count` method in `BTNode`, which computes this value recursively. It's possible to use an integer variable to keep track of the number of elements in the collection, as we did in previous collections, but we chose to show this approach here.

The `inorder` method returns an iterator that allows the user to step through the elements of the tree in an inorder traversal. It uses an `ArrayIterator` object, as we've used in previous collections, to store the elements in the proper order. The initial call to the `inorder` method sets up an empty `ArrayIterator` object, then populates it with a call to the version of `inorder` in `BTNode` that recursively processes the subtrees. When the node is "visited," it is added to the iterator. The `preorder` and `postorder` methods will follow similar logic, visiting the nodes in the proper order for each traversal.

The `levelorder` method produces a similar iterator, with the elements in the proper order for a level-order traversal. This method follows the algorithm described earlier in this chapter, using a queue to store the nodes during processing. Unlike the other traversals, the `levelorder` method does not rely on a corresponding method in the `BTNode` class.

Finally, the `iterator` method is included to satisfy the `Iterable` interface. It simply returns the iterator produced by the `inorder` method. There is no particular reason for choosing an inorder traversal—any of the other three traversals could have been used.

The `getRight`, `contains`, `isEmpty`, `toString`, `preorder`, and `postorder` methods in `LinkedBinaryTree` are left as programming projects, which require some methods in `BTNode` as well.

16.5 Decision Trees

Let's use the binary tree implementation to solve a particular problem. A *decision tree* is a tree whose nodes represent decision points, and whose children represent the options available at that point. The leaves of a decision tree represent the possible conclusions that might be drawn based on the answers.

A simple decision tree, with yes/no questions, can be modeled by a binary tree. Figure 16.10 shows a decision tree that helps to diagnose the cause of back pain. For each question, the left child represents the answer No and the right child represents the answer Yes. To perform a diagnosis, begin with the question at the root, following the appropriate path based on the answers until a leaf is reached.

Decision trees are sometimes used as a basis for an *expert system*, which is software that attempts to represent the knowledge of an expert in a particular field. For instance, a particular expert system might be used to model the expertise of a doctor, car mechanic, or accountant. Obviously, the greatly simplified decision tree in Figure 16.10 is not fleshed out enough to do a good job diagnosing the real cause of back pain, but it should give you a feel for how such systems might work.

> **KEY CONCEPT**
>
> A decision tree can be used as the basis for an expert system.

Let's look at an example that uses the `LinkedBinaryTree` implementation discussed in the previous section to represent a decision tree. The program in Listing 16.4 uses the tree pictured in Figure 16.9 to hold a dialog with the user and draw a conclusion.

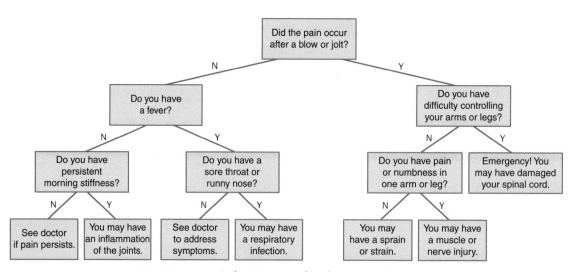

FIGURE 16.10 A decision tree for diagnosing back pain

LISTING 16.4

```
//********************************************************************
//   BackPainAnalyzer.java          Java Foundations
//
//   Demonstrates the use of a binary tree.
//********************************************************************

public class BackPainAnalyzer
{
   //----------------------------------------------------------------
   //  Asks questions of the user to diagnose a medical problem.
   //----------------------------------------------------------------
   public static void main (String[] args)
   {
      BackPainExpert expert = new BackPainExpert();
      expert.diagnose();
   }
}
```

OUTPUT

```
=======================================================
So, you're having back pain.
Did the pain occur after a blow or jolt?
Y
Do you have difficulty controlling your arms or legs?
N
Do you have pain or numbness in one arm or leg?
Y
You may have a muscle or nerve injury.
=======================================================
```

The tree is constructed and used in the BackPainExpert class, shown in Listing 16.5 on the next page. The only instance data is the variable tree that represents the entire decision tree, which is defined to store String objects as elements.

The constructor of BackPainExpert first defines the various string elements to be stored in the tree nodes. Then the nodes themselves are created, with no children for the leaves and with previously defined nodes (or subtrees) as children for internal nodes. The tree is basically created from the bottom up.

The diagnose method uses the variable current to indicate the current node in the tree being processed, beginning at the root. The while loop continues until

LISTING 16.5

```java
//********************************************************************
//  BackPainExpert.java        Java Foundations
//
//  Represents a simple expert system for back pain diagnosis.
//********************************************************************

import javafoundations.*;
import java.util.Scanner;

public class BackPainExpert
{
    private LinkedBinaryTree<String> tree;

    //-----------------------------------------------------------------
    //  Sets up the diagnosis question tree.
    //-----------------------------------------------------------------
    public BackPainExpert()
    {
        String e1 = "Did the pain occur after a blow or jolt?";
        String e2 = "Do you have a fever?";
        String e3 = "Do you have difficulty controlling your arms or legs?";
        String e4 = "Do you have persistent morning stiffness?";
        String e5 = "Do you have a sore throat or runny nose?";
        String e6 = "Do you have pain or numbness in one arm or leg?";
        String e7 = "Emergency! You may have damaged your spinal cord.";
        String e8 = "See doctor if pain persists.";
        String e9 = "You may have an inflammation of the joints.";
        String e10 = "See doctor to address symptoms.";
        String e11 = "You may have a respiratory infection.";
        String e12 = "You may have a sprain or strain.";
        String e13 = "You may have a muscle or nerve injury.";

        LinkedBinaryTree<String> n2, n3, n4, n5, n6, n7, n8, n9,
            n10, n11, n12, n13;

        n8 = new LinkedBinaryTree<String>(e8);
        n9 = new LinkedBinaryTree<String>(e9);
        n4 = new LinkedBinaryTree<String>(e4, n8, n9);

        n10 = new LinkedBinaryTree<String>(e10);
        n11 = new LinkedBinaryTree<String>(e11);
        n5 = new LinkedBinaryTree<String>(e5, n10, n11);
```

LISTING 16.5 *continued*

```java
        n12 = new LinkedBinaryTree<String>(e12);
        n13 = new LinkedBinaryTree<String>(e13);
        n6 = new LinkedBinaryTree<String>(e6, n12, n13);

        n7 = new LinkedBinaryTree<String>(e7);

        n2 = new LinkedBinaryTree<String>(e2, n4, n5);
        n3 = new LinkedBinaryTree<String>(e3, n6, n7);

        tree = new LinkedBinaryTree<String>(e1, n2, n3);
    }

    //-----------------------------------------------------------------
    //  Follows the diagnosis tree based on user responses.
    //-----------------------------------------------------------------
    public void diagnose()
    {
        Scanner scan = new Scanner(System.in);
        LinkedBinaryTree<String> current = tree;

        System.out.println ("So, you're having back pain.");
        while (current.size() > 1)
        {
            System.out.println (current.getRootElement());
            if (scan.nextLine().equalsIgnoreCase("N"))
                current = current.getLeft();
            else
                current = current.getRight();
        }

        System.out.println (current.getRootElement());
    }
}
```

a leaf is found. The current question is printed, and the answer is read from the user. If the answer is No, current is updated to point to the left child. Otherwise, it is updated to point to the right child. After falling out of the loop, the element stored in the leaf (the conclusion) is printed.

Summary of Key Concepts

- A tree is a nonlinear structure whose elements are organized into a hierarchy.
- The order of a tree specifies the maximum number of children any node in the tree may have.
- A balanced n-ary tree with m elements will have height $\log_n m$.
- There are four basic techniques for traversing a tree.
- A queue can be used to store the elements of a tree during a level-order traversal.
- One strategy for implementing binary trees using arrays places the left child of element n at position $(2n + 1)$ and the right child at position $(2*(n + 1))$.
- A stored link strategy for an array-based tree implementation allows array positions to be allocated contiguously regardless of the completeness of the tree.
- How elements are added to and removed from a general binary tree depends on the tree's purpose.
- A decision tree can be used as the basis for an expert system.

Self-Review Questions

SR 16.1   What is a tree?

SR 16.2   What is a node?

SR 16.3   What is the root of a tree?

SR 16.4   What is a leaf?

SR 16.5   What is an internal node?

SR 16.6   Define the height of a tree.

SR 16.7   Define the level of a node.

SR 16.8   What is a binary tree?

SR 16.9   Describe a balanced tree.

SR 16.10   Describe a complete tree.

SR 16.11   Describe a full tree.

SR 16.12   Compare and contrast preorder and postorder tree traversals.

SR 16.13   What are the advantages and disadvantages of implementing binary trees using computed links?

SR 16.14   What is a decision tree?

Exercises

Use the following tree to answer Exercises 16.1–16.16.

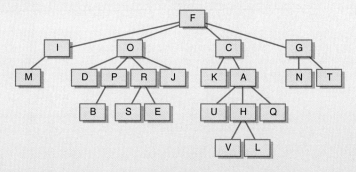

EX 16.1   Which node is the root? Explain.

EX 16.2   Which nodes are leaves?

EX 16.3   What are the siblings of node R?

EX 16.4   What are the siblings of node B?

EX 16.5   Is G an internal node? Explain.

EX 16.6   Draw the subtrees of node C.

EX 16.7   What are the descendents of node A?

EX 16.8   What are the ancestors of node S?

EX 16.9   What is the path from the root to node L?

EX 16.10   What nodes are at level 1 of the tree?

EX 16.11   What is the height of this tree?

EX 16.12   Is this tree a binary tree? Explain.

EX 16.13   What is the minimum order of this tree, based on the picture?

EX 16.14   Is this tree balanced? Explain.

EX 16.15   Is this tree complete? Explain.

EX 16.16   Is this tree full? Explain.

Use the following binary tree to answer Exercises 16.17–16.21.

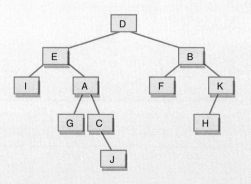

EX 16.17   Produce a preorder traversal of this tree.

EX 16.18   Produce an inorder traversal of this tree.

EX 16.19   Produce a postorder traversal of this tree.

EX 16.20   Produce a level-order traversal of this tree.

EX 16.21   Draw an array similar to the one shown in Figure 16.6 to represent this tree using the computed links implementation strategy.

EX 16.22   Is a full tree necessarily a complete tree? Explain.

EX 16.23   What do we mean when we say a traversal "visits" a tree node?

EX 16.24   Are trees of the type discussed in this chapter appropriate for modeling a family tree? Explain.

EX 16.25   What is the time complexity of the find operation in the LinkedBinaryTree class?

EX 16.26   What is the time complexity of the inorder operation in the LinkedBinaryTree class?

Programming Projects

PP 16.1   Complete the implementation of the LinkedBinaryTree class presented in this chapter. Specifically, complete the implementations of the getRight, contains, isEmpty, toString, preorder, and postorder operations. Some of these operations will require corresponding methods in the BTNode class.

PP 16.2   Implement a class called CLArrayBinaryTree that satisfies the BinaryTree interface. The class should represent the tree using the computed link implementation strategy described in this chapter.

PP 16.3   Implement a class called `SLArrayBinaryTree` that satisfies the `BinaryTree` interface. The class should represent the tree using the stored link implementation strategy described in this chapter.

PP 16.4   Modify the `BackPainAnalyzer` program so that the tree used has three additional questions (don't worry about the accuracy of the medical expertise).

PP 16.5   Design and implement a program that uses a decision tree to represent the process a car mechanic might use to determine the cause of an automotive problem.

PP 16.6   In the game called 20 Questions, one person thinks of an object, and another person tries to determine what the object is by asking yes-or-no questions. The goal is to determine the object in as few questions as possible. Design and implement a program that uses a decision tree to play a version of the 20 Questions game, based on a predetermined set of possible objects.

PP 16.7   An *ancestor tree* illustrates a person's biological heritage. Design and implement a program that uses a binary tree to represent an ancestor tree. Each node represents a person, and a node's two children represent that person's parents.

PP 16.8   Recall from Chapter 2 that an *expression tree* can be used to represent an arithmetic expression. Design and implement a program that uses a binary tree to represent an expression tree. Provide a method that evaluates the tree to determine the result of the expression.

Answers to Self-Review Questions

SR 16.1   A tree is a nonlinear collection defined by the concept that each node in the tree, other than the first node or root node, has exactly one parent.

SR 16.2   A node in a tree refers to a location in the tree where an element is stored.

SR 16.3   The root of a tree is the node at the top of the tree that does not have a parent. The root node is considered to be the "entry point" into the tree.

SR 16.4   A leaf is a tree node that does not have any children.

SR 16.5   An internal node is any non-root node that has at least one child.

SR 16.6   The height of the tree is the length of the longest path from the root to a leaf.

SR 16.7   The level of a node is measured by the number of links that must be followed to reach that node from the root.

SR 16.8   A binary tree is a tree whose nodes can have no more than two children. Binary trees are quite useful in many problem-solving situations.

SR 16.9   A balanced tree is a tree whose leaf nodes are all on one level or at most two adjacent levels.

SR 16.10   A complete tree is a balanced tree in which all leaf nodes are as far left in the tree as possible.

SR 16.11   A full tree is an n-ary tree in which all leaf nodes are at the same level and every node is either a leaf or has exactly n children.

SR 16.12   Tree traversals visit each element in the tree. The type of traversal dictates when a node is visited. A preorder traversal visits the root before visiting either subtree, and a postorder traversal visits the root after visiting both subtrees.

SR 16.13   The computed link strategy does not have to store the links between a parent to child node since that relationship is determined by its position in the array. However, this strategy may lead to substantial wasted space for trees that are not balanced and/or not complete.

SR 16.14   A decision tree is a tree used to represent the questions and responses that can be used to determine an appropriate conclusion. A decision tree can be used as the basis of an expert system, such as a medical diagnosis system.

Binary Search Trees

17

CHAPTER OBJECTIVES

- Discuss the nature of a binary search tree.
- Explore a linked implementation of a binary search tree.
- Discuss the generic version of the `Comparable` interface.
- Discuss binary search tree rotations.

Search trees, especially binary search trees, and heaps are among the most useful software structures. In this chapter, we first explore the concept of a binary search tree and its implementation. We examine algorithms for adding and removing elements from binary search trees and for maintaining balanced trees.

17.1 Binary Search Trees

A *search tree* is a tree whose elements are organized to facilitate finding a particular element when needed. That is, the elements in a search tree are stored in a particular way relative to each other so that finding an element doesn't require searching the entire tree.

KEY CONCEPT

A binary search tree is a binary tree in which, for each node, the elements in the left subtree are less than the parent, and the elements in the right subtree are greater than or equal to the parent.

A *binary search tree* is a binary tree that, for each node n, the left subtree of n contains elements less than the element stored in n, and the right subtree of n contains elements that are greater than or equal to the element stored in n.

Figure 17.1 shows a binary search tree containing integer values. Examine it carefully, noting the relationships among the nodes. Every element in the left subtree of the root is less than 45, and every element in the right subtree of the root is greater than 45. This relationship is true for every node in the tree.

Equal values are stored in the right subtree, as in the case of 42 in Figure 17.1. This decision, however, is arbitrary. Equal values could be stored to the left as long as all operations managing the tree were consistent with that decision.

To determine if a particular target element exists in the tree, we follow the appropriate path starting at the root, moving left or right from the current node depending on whether the target is less than or greater than the element in that node. We will eventually either find the element we're looking for or encounter the end of the path, which means the target is not in the tree.

This process should remind you of the binary search algorithm we discussed in Chapter 13. It is, in fact, the same logic. In Chapter 13, we searched a sorted

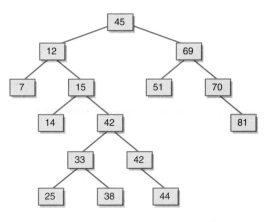

FIGURE 17.1 A binary search tree of integers

array and jumped to an appropriate index. With a binary search tree, the structure of the tree itself provides the search path.

The binary search tree in Figure 17.1 on the next page is only one of many that could be constructed using the same elements. The particular shape a binary search tree has depends on the order in which elements were added to the tree (as we explore in the next section) and on any additional processing used to reshape it. The most efficient binary search trees are balanced, so that approximately half of the viable candidates are eliminated with each comparison.

> **KEY CONCEPT**
>
> The most efficient binary search trees are balanced, so that half of the viable candidates are eliminated with each comparison.

Of course, binary search trees can hold any kind of data or object, as long as we have a way to determine their relative ordering. Objects that implement the `Comparable` interface, for instance, can be put into a binary search tree because we can determine, using the `compareTo` method, which object comes before another. For simplicity, we will use integers in the examples in this chapter.

Note that if you perform an inorder traversal (as described in Chapter 16) on a binary search tree, the elements will be visited in sorted order, ascending.

Adding an Element to a Binary Search Tree

The process of adding a new element to a binary search tree is similar to the process of searching the tree. A new element is added as a leaf node on the tree. Starting at the root, follow the path dictated by the elements in each node until there is no child node in the appropriate direction. At that point, add the new element as a leaf.

For example, let's add the following elements, in order, to a new binary search tree:

```
77  24  58  82  17  40  97
```

The first value, 77, becomes the root of our new tree. Next, because 24 is less than 77, it is added as the left child of the root. The next value, 58, is less than 77, so it goes in the left subtree of the root, but it is greater than 24, so it is added as the right child of 24. The value 82 is greater than the root value of 77, and thus is added as its right child. The value 17 is less than 77 and less than 24, so it is added as the left child of 24. This process is shown in Figure 17.2 on the next page, and continues for the remaining items in our example.

Without any additional processing to change the shape of the tree, the order in which the values are added dictates its shape. If that order is particularly skewed one way or another, the resulting

> **KEY CONCEPT**
>
> Without any additional processing, the shape of a binary search tree is dictated by the order in which elements are added to it.

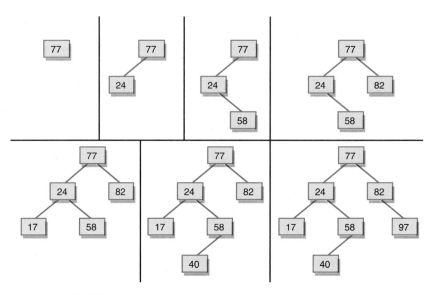

FIGURE 17.2 Adding elements to a binary search tree

tree is not particularly useful. For example, adding the following values in order creates the tree depicted in Figure 17.3:

```
20 24 37 28 44 47 69
```

The tree in Figure 17.3 is called a *degenerate tree* because it is highly unbalanced. If the input is completely sorted, the binary search tree essentially degenerates into a sorted linked list. The value of a binary search tree comes from being able to

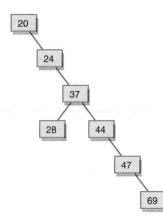

FIGURE 17.3 A degenerate binary search tree

exclude large amounts of the data with each comparison, and a degenerate tree eliminates that value.

Removing an Element from a Binary Search Tree

In linear data structures, removing a target element generally involved finding the element, then resetting a reference so that the node before the target pointed to the node after the target. For binary search trees, the process is not as simple, because there are potentially two children for each node. Keep in mind that after removing the element, the resulting tree must still be a valid binary search tree, with appropriate relationships among all the elements.

Consider the binary search tree shown in Figure 17.4. It points out the three situations that we must consider when removing an element from a binary search tree:

- Situation 1: If the node to be removed is a leaf (has no children), it can simply be deleted.
- Situation 2: If the node to be removed has one child, the deleted node is replaced by its child.
- Situation 3: If the node to be removed has two children, an appropriate node is found from lower in the tree and used to replace the node. The children of the removed node become the children of the replacement node.

> **KEY CONCEPT**
>
> There are three situations to consider when removing an element from a binary search tree, two of which are straightforward.

The first situation is trivial. If we want to remove a leaf node, such as 88 or 67, it can simply be deleted. The resulting tree remains a valid binary search tree.

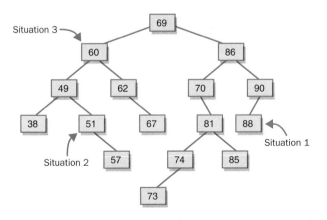

FIGURE 17.4 The three situations to consider when removing an element from a binary search tree

The second situation is pretty straightforward too. If we want to remove a node with only one child, such as 51 or 62, the child can replace the deleted parent. That is, 57 could replace 51, and 67 could replace 62. The child's relationship to the rest of the tree will remain intact. This solution works even if the child has subtrees of its own. The node containing 70, for instance, could be replaced by 81, even though 81 has its own children. The entire subtree has the appropriate relationship to the new parent (86).

The third situation is the most interesting. Suppose we want to remove a node that has two children, such as 60. Neither child can be used as a replacement without a significant reconstruction of the tree. A good choice to replace the node is its *inorder successor*, which is the element that would follow the deleted element in an inorder traversal (the next highest value). For example, in the tree in Figure 17.4, the inorder successor of 60 is 62, the inorder successor of 70 is 73, and the inorder successor of 69 is 70.

So to remove a node that has two children, we first remove its inorder successor from the tree, and then use it to replace the node that's actually being removed. The existing children of the node being removed become the children of the replacement node.

But what about the existing children of the inorder successor? Well, it's guaranteed that the inorder successor of a node will not have a left child. If it did, that child would be the inorder successor. Therefore, the inorder successor will either be a leaf or have one (right) child. So removing the inorder successor falls under one of the first two situations for removing a node.

For example, to remove element 86 from the tree in Figure 17.4, we find its inorder successor (88), remove it from the tree (which is trivial because it's a leaf), and replace 86 with it. The node containing 70 becomes the left child of 88, and the node containing 90 becomes the right child of 88.

Let's walk through another example of removing a node with two children. Starting over with the tree in Figure 17.4, let's delete the root (69). First we find its inorder successor (70) and remove it from the tree, moving the subtree with root 81 up to replace it. Then, the element 69 is replaced with the element 70. The resulting tree is shown in Figure 17.5.

17.2 Binary Search Tree Implementation

Having explored the conceptual nature of a binary search tree and discussed the techniques for some key operations, let's now discuss its implementation. Because the essence of a binary search tree is a binary tree, we can base our implementation

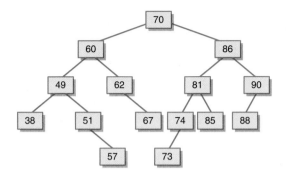

FIGURE 17.5 The resulting tree after the root is removed

on the `BinaryTree` interface and `LinkedBinaryTree` class that we discussed in Chapter 16.

Listing 17.1 shows the `BinarySearchTree` interface, which is derived from the `BinaryTree` interface. This relationship is shown in the UML diagram in

LISTING 17.1

```java
//********************************************************************
//  BinarySearchTree.java       Java Foundations
//
//  Defines the interface to a binary search tree.
//********************************************************************

package javafoundations;

public interface BinarySearchTree<T extends Comparable<T>> extends BinaryTree<T>
{
    //  Adds the specified element to the tree.
    public void add (T element);

    //  Finds and returns the element in the tree matching the
    //  specified target. Overrides the find method of BinaryTree.
    public T find (T target);

    //  Returns the minimum value in the binary search tree.
    public T findMin();
```

```
         // Returns the maximum value in the binary search tree.
         public T findMax();

         // Removes and returns the specified element from the tree.
         public T remove (T target);
      }
```

Figure 17.6. The search tree interface includes methods to add an element to the tree, to find a target element in the tree, and to remove an element from the tree. As a convenience, we also choose to include methods that find the minimum and maximum values in the tree.

The `BinarySearchTree` interface is defined to operate on a generic type `T`, which extends `Comparable`. All elements added to a binary search tree must be `Comparable` in order to determine their relative position within the tree. Generic types were introduced in Chapter 14.

Up to this point, we have been able to simply store a generic type `T` in our stack and queue collections. The generic type `T` is then replaced with a specific type at

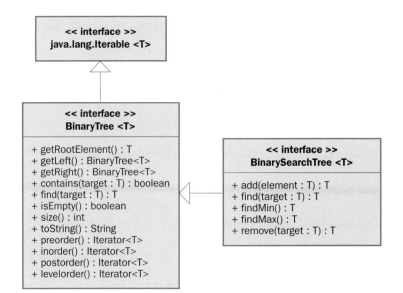

FIGURE 17.6 A UML diagram of the `BinarySearchTree` interface

the time a collection is instantiated. We have not placed any restrictions on what types could be stored in our collections. However, in dealing with a binary search tree, we must place a restriction on the type so that only classes that implement the `Comparable` interface can be stored in an ordered list. This is necessary so that we can use the classes own `compareTo` method to determine the placement of the element in the tree.

In Chapter 13, in which we discussed searching and sorting algorithms, the non-generic version of the `Comparable` interface was used. Let's now explore why that approach can lead to problems.

If the object we store in a binary search tree is simply `Comparable`, any object of any class that implements the `Comparable` interface could be stored in any node of the tree. However, just because two objects have implemented the `Comparable` interface does not mean that those objects are comparable to each other. A `Dog` might be comparable to another `Dog`, and a `Cat` might be comparable to another `Cat`, but a `Dog` might not be comparable to a `Cat`. Runtime errors could result when such inappropriate comparisons are made.

The `Comparable` interface is generic, so let's consider storing the following type of elements in our search tree:

```
<T extends Comparable<T>>
```

This still causes a problem. Suppose that both `Dog` and `Cat` are subclasses of a class `Mammal` and that the `Mammal` class implements the `Comparable<Mammal>` interface. Now if we create a binary search tree that stores `Mammal` objects, then a `Dog` and `Cat` could be added, but are not really comparable to each other. So this solution, if used in this particular way, has the same problem as using the non-generic version of `Comparable`.

A more comprehensive solution, though not as intellectually satisfying, is to write the generic type as:

```
<T extends Comparable<? super T>>
```

This declaration restricts the comparable nature of the element to any super-class of T.

However, that being said, the implementers of the Java language chose a different alternative for the types for the ordered collections in the Java Collections API. In these cases, the type is simply implemented as a generic type `T`, and the methods that add elements to the collection will throw a `ClassCastException` if the element being added cannot be compared to the elements in the collection.

We will adopt a similar philosophy, restricting our tree elements to being simply `Comparable<T>`. While this approach permits the potential problem caused by inheritance, it imposes a reasonable level of control. It's better than our non-generic version of `Comparable` used in Chapter 13, and not as unwieldy as other possibilities.

The `LinkedBinarySearchTree` class is shown in Listing 17.2, with some methods left as programming projects. It extends the `LinkedBinaryTree` class (from Chapter 16), inheriting the classic methods such as `size` and `isEmpty`, as well as the various iterator methods that provide various traversals of the tree. It also inherits the instance data, including the `left` and `right` references to the child nodes.

Similar to our approach to the implementation of a general binary tree, the `LinkedBinarySearchTree` interacts with a separate set of objects that represent

LISTING 17.2

```java
//********************************************************************
//  LinkedBinarySearchTree.java        Java Foundations
//
//  Implements the binary tree using a linked representation.
//********************************************************************

package javafoundations;

import javafoundations.*;
import javafoundations.exceptions.*;

public class LinkedBinarySearchTree<T extends Comparable<T>>
    extends LinkedBinaryTree<T> implements BinarySearchTree<T>
{
    //-----------------------------------------------------------------
    //  Creates an empty binary search tree.
    //-----------------------------------------------------------------
    public LinkedBinarySearchTree()
    {
        super();
    }

    //-----------------------------------------------------------------
    //  Creates a binary search tree with the specified element at its
    //  root.
    //-----------------------------------------------------------------
    public LinkedBinarySearchTree (T element)
    {
        root = new BSTNode<T>(element);
    }
```

LISTING 17.2   *continued*

```java
//--------------------------------------------------------------------
//  Adds the specified element to this binary search tree.
//--------------------------------------------------------------------
public void add (T item)
{
   if (root == null)
      root = new BSTNode<T>(item);
   else
      ((BSTNode)root).add(item);
}

//--------------------------------------------------------------------
//  Removes and returns the element matching the specified target
//  from this binary search tree. Throws an ElementNotFoundException
//  if the target is not found.
//--------------------------------------------------------------------
public T remove (T target)
{
   BSTNode<T> node = null;

   if (root != null)
      node = ((BSTNode)root).find(target);

   if (node == null)
      throw new ElementNotFoundException ("Remove operation failed. "
         + "No such element in tree.");

   root = ((BSTNode)root).remove(target);

   return node.getElement();
}

//--------------------------------------------------------------------
//  The following methods are left as programming projects.
//--------------------------------------------------------------------
//  public T findMin() { }
//  public T findMax() { }
}
```

the nodes of the tree. The BSTNode class, shown in Listing 17.3, is derived from the BTNode class from Chapter 16. Like LinkedBinarySearchTree, the BSTNode class manages Comparable elements.

The LinkedBinarySearchTree class inherits the reference to the root node from LinkedBinaryTree. Similarly, the BSTNode class inherits the left and

LISTING 17.3

```java
//********************************************************************
//  BSTNode.java        Java Foundations
//
//  Represents a node in a binary search tree, storing Comparable
//  elements.
//********************************************************************

package javafoundations;

public class BSTNode<T extends Comparable<T>> extends BTNode<T>
{
    //------------------------------------------------------------------
    //  Creates a new tree node with the specified data.
    //------------------------------------------------------------------
    public BSTNode (T element)
    {
        super(element);
    }


    //------------------------------------------------------------------
    //  Adds a new node containing the specified element at the
    //  appropriate place in this tree.
    //------------------------------------------------------------------
    public void add (T item)
    {
        if (item.compareTo(element) < 0)
            if (left == null)
                left = new BSTNode (item);
            else
                ((BSTNode)left).add (item);
        else
            if (right == null)
                right = new BSTNode (item);
            else
                ((BSTNode)right).add (item);
    }
```

LISTING 17.3 *continued*

```java
//-----------------------------------------------------------------
//  Returns the node in this subtree whose element matches the
//  specified target. Returns null if the target is not found.
//  Overrides the find method of BTNode to capitalize on the
//  binary search tree characteristics.
//-----------------------------------------------------------------
public BSTNode<T> find (T target)
{
   BSTNode<T> result = null;

   if (target.compareTo(element) == 0)
      result = this;
   else
   {
      if (target.compareTo(element) < 0)
      {
         if (left != null)
            result = ((BSTNode)left).find (target);
      }
      else
         if (right != null)
            result = ((BSTNode)right).find (target);
   }

   return result;
}

//-----------------------------------------------------------------
//  Removes the specified target from this subtree. Returns a
//  reference to the revised tree. The tree will be unchanged if
//  the target is not found.
//-----------------------------------------------------------------
public BSTNode<T> remove(T target)
{
   BSTNode<T> result = this;

   if (target.compareTo(element) == 0)
   {
      if (left == null && right == null)
         result = null;
      else if (left != null && right == null)
         result = (BSTNode)left;
      else if (left == null && right != null)
         result = (BSTNode)right;
```

LISTING 17.3   *continued*

```
          else
          {
              result = getSuccessor();
              result.left = left;
              result.right = right;
          }
      }
      else
          if (target.compareTo(element) < 0)
              if (left != null)
                  left = ((BSTNode)left).remove(target);
          else
              if (right != null)
                  right = ((BSTNode)right).remove(target);

          return result;
    }


    //------------------------------------------------------------------
    //  Finds and returns the node containing the inorder successor of
    //  this node, and then removes the successor from its original
    //  location in the tree.
    //------------------------------------------------------------------
    protected BSTNode<T> getSuccessor()
    {
        BSTNode<T> successor = (BSTNode)right;

        while (successor.getLeft() != null)
            successor = (BSTNode) successor.getLeft();

        ((BSTNode)right).remove (successor.getElement());

        return successor;
    }
}
```

right references to child nodes from the BTNode class. Because of their original declarations, these references will need to be cast into their true class to be able to carry out certain operations.

The first constructor of the LinkedBinarySearchTree class simply invokes the parent's constructor using the super reference. The parent constructor sets the element and child references to null. The second constructor creates a new BSTNode object, storing the element.

The add method of LinkedBinarySearchTree creates a new root node if the tree is currently empty. Otherwise, it invokes the add method of BSTNode, which searches for the location to add the new element as a leaf. It does so by first checking to see if the new element is less than the current root element. If so, it checks if a left child exists. If there is no left child, it creates a new node containing the new element, and adds it as the new left child. If the left subtree exists, the add method is invoked again to add the child to the left subtree. Similar logic is used to add the new element to the right subtree if appropriate. Note that this code ensures that if the new element and root element are equal, the new node is added to the right subtree.

The LinkedBinarySearchTree class relies on the find method inherited from the LinkedBinaryTree class to satisfy that operation in the interface. However, it invokes the find method in BSTNode, which overrides version inherited from its parent. This version of the find method first checks if the current element is a match, and if so returns that node. If not, it determines if the target would lie in the left or right subtree, and calls find again on the subtree. If the appropriate child does not exist, then the element does not exist in the tree, and a null value is returned.

It's important to understand why the find method in BSTNode overrides the version of the find method provided by the BTNode class. Because the elements in a general binary tree are not ordered, the find method of the BTNode class examines every element in the tree if necessary. The find method of BSTNode is much more efficient, narrowing down the search considerably with each comparison. This distinction is the essence of a binary search tree.

The remove method in LinkedBinarySearchTree obtains the target element using the find method so that it can return the removed value. If the tree is empty, or the target element is not found, an exception is thrown. If the element is found, the remove method of BSTNode is called to delete the specified element and return a reference to the revised tree. This return value is key to the processing of this method. As the recursive calls to the remove method unfold, the tree is essentially "rebuilt" with potentially revised subtrees. Keep in mind it may be the root node that is removed. The returned tree will be unchanged if the target element is not found in the tree.

The outer if statement in the remove method in BSTNode determines if the element to be removed matches the root element. If not, the else portion determines if the target will be found in the left or right subtree, and calls the remove method again appropriately. This logic is similar to the processing in the find method.

If the target matches the root element, the remove method deletes the node. To do so, it determines which of the three situations described in the previous section applies. If neither child exists, the return value is set to `null`. When the method returns, the appropriate parent's child reference is set to `null`, effectively deleting the node. If either the left or right subtree exists (but not both), the return value is set to that subtree. Thus, when the method returns, the subtree is "moved up" to replace the deleted node.

If none of those situations applies, then both child nodes must exist, which is the interesting third situation. When that happens, the `getSuccessor` support method is called, which returns a reference to the node containing the inorder successor of the element to be removed. The `left` and `right` child references of the replacement node are set to the corresponding subtrees of the node being deleted. The successor node, with its new subtrees, is returned from the `remove` method to replace the parent node's reference to the now deleted child.

In casual terms, the inorder successor of a node can be found by "going right" once, then "going left" as far as possible. Therefore, the `getSuccessor` method first sets the reference `successor` to the right child of the node. (This node is guaranteed to exist or we wouldn't be processing this situation.) Then, the `getSuccessor` method uses a `while` loop to traverse a straight path down the left child nodes until there is no left child. Note that this step is not recursive. Before returning a reference to this node, the successor node is removed from the tree using another call to the `remove` method. As discussed in the previous section, deleting this node is guaranteed to be one of the two straightforward situations (zero or one child).

Spend some time looking at situations that occur in Figure 17.4 and trace the logic of the `remove` method carefully.

The `findMin` and `findMax` methods are left as programming projects.

17.3 Balanced Binary Search Trees

We've mentioned that a balanced binary search tree is more efficient than searching a degenerate tree. The search and add operations on a balanced tree of n nodes have an efficiency of $O(\log_2 n)$ comparisons (the length of the longest path). The more degenerate the tree becomes, the search and add operations approach $O(n)$, which eliminates the benefits of using a search tree.

The implementation of a binary search tree that we explored in the previous section does not guarantee a balanced tree. The shape of the tree is determined solely on the order in which the elements are added to the tree.

There are more sophisticated implementations of binary search trees that ensure the trees stay balanced. AVL trees and red/black trees are two such approaches, though we do not explore them in this book. Instead, we will simply explore the

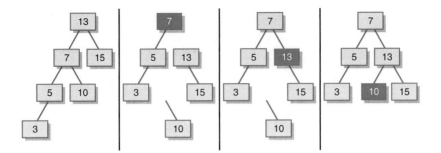

FIGURE 17.7 A right rotation on a binary search tree

general concept of performing *rotations* on a binary search tree, which are operations that assist in the process of keeping a tree balanced. These rotations do not solve all problems created by unbalanced trees, but they show the basic algorithmic processes that are used to manipulate trees in this way.

Right Rotation

Figure 17.7 shows a binary search tree that is not balanced and the processing steps necessary to rebalance it. To get this tree into balance, we need to

- Make the left child element of the root the new root element.
- Make the former root element the right child element of the new root.
- Make the right child of what was the left child of the former root the new left child of the former root.

This process is referred to as a *right rotation*. This kind of rotation can be done at any level of a tree, around the root of any subtree. This rotation corrects an imbalance caused by a long path in the left subtree of the left child of the root.

Left Rotation

Figure 17.8 on the next page shows another binary search tree that is not balanced, and the steps to correct it. However, this time the long path is in the right subtree of the right child of the root. To get this tree into balance, we need to

- Make the right child element of the root the new root element.
- Make the former root element the left child element of the new root.

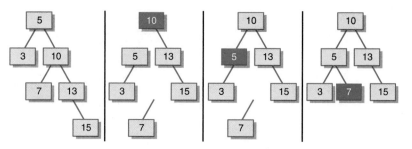

FIGURE 17.8 A left rotation on a binary search tree

- Make the left child of what was the right child of the former root the new right child of the former root.

This is referred to as a *left rotation*. It is essentially the mirror of a right rotation. As with a right rotation, a left rotation can be done at any level of the tree.

Right-Left Rotation

Unfortunately, not all imbalances can be solved by a single rotation. If the imbalance is caused by a long path in the left subtree of the right child of the root, we must first perform a right rotation around the offending subtree, and then perform a left rotation around the root. This is called a *right-left rotation*. Figure 17.9 illustrates this process.

First, a right rotation is performed around the subtree with root 13, yielding the second tree in the figure. Then, a left rotation is performed around the root of the tree (5), yielding the final tree.

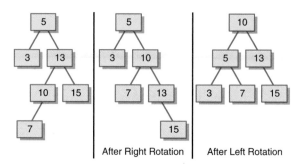

FIGURE 17.9 A right-left rotation on a binary search tree

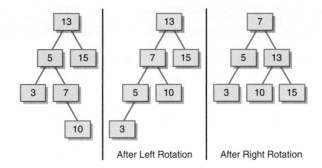

After Left Rotation | After Right Rotation

FIGURE 17.10 A left-right rotation on a binary search tree

Left-Right Rotation

Similarly, if the imbalance is caused by a long path in the right subtree of the left child of the root, we can perform a *left-right rotation*. First perform a left rotation of the offending subtree, and then perform a right rotation around the root. Figure 17.10 illustrates this process.

Summary of Key Concepts

- A binary search tree is a binary tree in which, for each node, the elements in the left subtree are less than the parent, and the elements in the right subtree are greater than or equal to the parent.

- The most efficient binary search trees are balanced, so that half of the viable candidates are eliminated with each comparison.

- Without any additional processing, the shape of a binary search tree is dictated by the order in which elements are added to it.

- There are three situations to consider when removing an element from a binary search tree, two of which are straightforward.

- When removing a node with two children from a binary search tree, the inorder successor is a good choice to replace it.

- Rotations can be performed on a binary search tree to help rebalance them.

Self-Review Questions

SR 17.1   What is the difference between a binary tree and a binary search tree?

SR 17.2   Compare a binary search tree to the binary search algorithm discussed in Chapter 13.

SR 17.3   Which method of traversing a binary search tree would result in a sorted list?

SR 17.4   What is the process of adding an element to a binary search tree?

SR 17.5   What is a degenerate tree?

SR 17.6   Why is it important for a binary search tree to be balanced (or close to balanced)?

SR 17.7   What is the most interesting situation when removing an element from a binary search tree? Explain.

SR 17.8   What is a binary search tree rotation?

Exercises

EX 17.1   Draw a binary search tree containing the same elements as those stored in Figure 17.1, but with a different structure.

EX 17.2   Will two equal elements in a binary search tree always be in a direct parent/child relationship to each other (as the two 42 values are in Figure 17.1)? Explain.

EX 17.3   Show the binary search tree that results when the following values are added, in order, to the tree shown in Figure 17.1.

57 90 42 11 31 66

EX 17.4   Show the binary search tree that results when the following values are added, in order, to a new tree.

24 61 28 17 72 4 23 49 24 80 10 36 16

EX 17.5   Show the binary search tree that results after deleting the following elements, in order, from the tree that is produced in EX 17.4.

23 4 61

EX 17.6   Show the binary search tree that results when the following values are added, in order, to a new tree.

14 45 28 49 69 12 84 76 31 69 88 79

EX 17.7   Show the binary search tree that results after deleting the following elements, in order, from the tree that is produced in EX 17.6.

49 14 31 84

EX 17.8   When deleting a node with two children from a binary search tree, we chose to replace it with its inorder successor. What other value would be an equally reasonable choice? Explain.

EX 17.9   Given that a `find` method is defined in the `BinaryTree` interface, did the `find` method need to be declared in the `BinarySearchTree` interface? Explain.

EX 17.10   Show the binary search tree that results after balancing the following tree using the rotation technique(s) described in this chapter.

EX 17.11   Show the binary search tree that results after balancing the following tree using the rotation technique(s) described in this chapter.

EX 17.12   Show the binary search tree that results after balancing the following tree using the rotation technique(s) described in this chapter.

Programming Projects

PP 17.1   Complete the implementation of the `LinkedBinarySearchTree` class presented in this chapter. Specifically, complete the implementations of the `findMin` and `findMax` operations.

PP 17.2   Implement a class called `CLArrayBinarySearchTree` that satisfies the `BinarySearchTree` interface. The class should represent the tree using the computed link implementation strategy and be derived from the `CLArrayBinaryTree` class from Programming Project 16.2 in Chapter 16.

PP 17.3   Implement a class called `SLArrayBinarySearchTree` that satisfies the `BinarySearchTree` interface. The class should represent the tree using the stored link implementation strategy and be derived from the `SLArrayBinaryTree` class from Programming Project 16.3 in Chapter 16.

PP 17.4   Design a `ClubMember` class that represents a member of a social club. Use a binary search tree to store a set of club members based on their membership id number.

PP 17.5   Modify the `ClubMember` class created in Programming Project 17.4 so that ClubMembers are ordered by their last name. Demonstrate that the same binary search tree collection can manage them without modification.

Answers to Self-Review Questions

SR 17.1   A binary search tree is a binary tree, with the added ordering property that each node is less than its left child and greater than or equal to its right child. A general binary tree has no constraints on the relationships among its elements.

SR 17.2   A binary search tree and the binary search algorithm from Chapter 13 have the same intent: to organize and process data so that approximately half of the data is removed from consideration with each comparison. The binary search algorithm works on a sorted array, while the binary search tree uses its structure to organize the data.

SR 17.3   An inorder traversal of a binary search tree produces the elements in sorted, ascending order.

SR 17.4   Adding an element to a binary search tree involves navigating the tree based on the relationship between the new element and the node elements until a location is found to add the new element as a leaf.

SR 17.5   A degenerate tree is a binary search tree that is significantly skewed one way or another, defeating the value of the tree structure.

SR 17.6   If a binary search tree is balanced, approximately half of the elements are eliminated from consideration with each comparison. The more unbalanced the tree, the closer it gets to a linear structure, which is much less efficient.

SR 17.7   The most interesting situation when removing an element from a binary search tree occurs when the element has two children, because there is no simple option to replace the element (as there are if it has one child or no children).

SR 17.8   A binary search tree rotation is an operation that helps put a binary search tree back into a balanced state.

Heaps and Priority Queues

CHAPTER OBJECTIVES

- Define a heap and discuss its particular usefulness.
- Discuss a linked implementation of a heap.
- Discuss a heap sort.
- Define a priority queue and its relationship to heaps.

We've evolved our discussion of trees throughout the last several chapters. Chapter 16 explored general concepts related to trees, and binary trees in particular. Chapter 17 extended the use of binary trees to create binary search trees, which added a relationship characteristic among the element stored in the tree. In this chapter we explore heaps, another extension of binary trees, and their implementation. Heaps are classic data structures, and are often used to implement priority queues.

18.1 Heaps

Chapter 17 focused on binary search trees, which are based on the concept of a general binary tree. Let's now turn our attention to another structure that is also fundamentally an extension of a binary tree. A *heap* is a complete binary tree in which each element is greater than or equal to both of its children.

Note that there are two interesting extensions to a general binary tree in the heap definition. The first is that it is a complete tree (recall that a complete tree is balanced with all leaves as far left in the tree as possible). The second is the constraint on the relationship among elements. The element at the root of the tree is always the largest element in the tree, and every path from the root encounters successively decreasing values. Figure 18.1 shows a heap, using integer elements for simplicity.

> **KEY CONCEPT**
>
> A heap is a complete binary tree in which each element is greater than or equal to both of its children.

As with binary search trees, there are many possible heap configurations for a given set of elements. The elements in the heap in Figure 18.1 could be organized into a different heap, as long as the properties of a heap are maintained.

To be more precise, our definition describes a *maxheap*. A heap can also be a *minheap*, in which each element is greater than or equal to its children. We will focus our discussion in this chapter on maxheaps. All of the same operations work for minheaps by reversing the comparisons.

A heap keeps the largest value of a set of elements readily available, and is useful in any situation in which that value is the dominant criteria. A heap has three primary operations: add a new element to the heap, find the maximum value, and remove the maximum value. The find operation is trivial, since the maximum value is always held in the root of the tree. Let's discuss the add and remove operations.

Adding an Element to a Heap

The strategy for adding a new element to a heap is to add the element as a new leaf, keeping the tree complete, and then moving the element up toward the root,

FIGURE 18.1 A heap

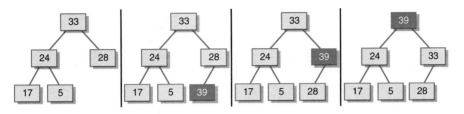

FIGURE 18.2 Adding an element to a heap

exchanging positions with its parent, until the relationship among the elements is appropriate. This approach guarantees that the resulting tree will conform to the heap criteria.

An example of this process is shown in Figure 18.2. The original heap is complete with appropriate relationships among the elements. The new element, 39, is added to the tree as a new leaf, as far left as possible. The tree is no longer a heap at this point—it is complete, but the relationship among the elements is not right. Because 39 is greater than its parent, 28, we switch them. Then, because 39 is greater than 33, those elements are switched. This results in the tree becoming a valid heap once again, with the new element incorporated.

> **KEY CONCEPT**
> Adding an element to a heap can be accomplished by adding the element as a leaf, then moving it upward as appropriate.

The relationship among the elements determines how much movement is needed after the new element is added as a leaf. It may not move at all if its parent is already greater than it. It may move part way up the tree, or perhaps all the way up to become the new root of the tree, as it did in Figure 18.2.

Removing the Largest Element from a Heap

Because of the characteristics of a heap, we know that the largest element is in the root of the tree. So removing that element requires deleting the root node, then reconstructing a heap from the two disjoint subtrees that remain.

The strategy for reconstructing the heap is to move the "last leaf" of the tree (the rightmost leaf on the last level) to the root position, then move it down through the tree as needed until the relationships among the elements are appropriate. This is somewhat the reverse of the process used to add a new element to the tree.

> **KEY CONCEPT**
> Removing the maximum element from the heap can be accomplished by replacing the root with the last leaf, then moving it downward as appropriate.

To determine if the new root element should move down, we compare it to its children. If the root element is smaller than the larger of its children, they are exchanged. This process continues until both children are less than or equal to the element being moved.

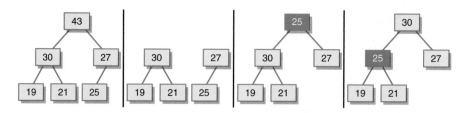

FIGURE 18.3 Removing the largest element from a heap

Figure 18.3 shows an example of removing the largest element from a heap. The current root element, 43, is guaranteed to be the largest value in the tree. It is deleted, leaving two disjoint subtrees. (Note that these subtrees are heaps themselves.) The last leaf of the tree, 25, is then moved up to become the new root of the tree. At this point the tree is no longer a heap. The new root element is switched with the larger of its children, in this case 30. At this point, because 25 is greater than both of its children (19 and 21), the tree is now a heap once again.

As with the add operation, how many times the new root value moves down through the tree depends on the relationship among the elements. In our example, the new root value only moved one level down, but it will often take more steps.

18.2 Heap Implementation

Listing 18.1 shows the MaxHeap interface. For heaps, we commit at the interface level whether the heap is a max heap or a min heap. The interface contains methods for adding a new element to the heap, getting the highest value, and removing the highest value.

Because a heap is a binary tree, its implementation can be based on the LinkedBinaryTree class defined in Chapter 16 (as we did with the implementation of a binary search tree). That's the version we'll explore now. However, because a heap is a complete tree, it also lends itself to an array-based implementation.

The LinkedMaxHeap class is shown in Listing 18.2, with one operation left as a programming project. Like our binary search tree implementation, LinkedMaxHeap extends LinkedBinaryTree and operates on a generic type T, which extends the Comparable interface.

The LinkedMaxHeap class inherits the root reference from LinkedBinaryTree. It also keeps track of the "last node" in the heap–that is, the last leaf in the complete tree. Since there is only one last node in the tree, this reference is maintained in the LinkedMaxHeap class, and not duplicated for every node.

LISTING 18.1

```
//********************************************************************
//  MaxHeap.java          Java Foundations
//
//  Defines the interface to a max heap.
//********************************************************************

package javafoundations;

public interface MaxHeap<T extends Comparable<T>> extends BinaryTree<T>
{
    //  Adds the specified object to the heap.
    public void add (T obj);

    //  Returns a reference to the element with the highest value in
    //  the heap.
    public T getMax ();

    //  Removes and returns the element with the highest value in the
    //  heap.
    public T removeMax ();
}
```

LISTING 18.2

```
//********************************************************************
//  LinkedMaxHeap.java          Java Foundations
//
//  Implements a max heap using a linked representation.
//********************************************************************

package javafoundations;

import javafoundations.exceptions.*;

public class LinkedMaxHeap<T extends Comparable<T>>
    extends LinkedBinaryTree<T> implements MaxHeap<T>
{
    private HeapNode<T> last;
```

LISTING 18.2 *continued*

```
//----------------------------------------------------------------
//  Creates a max heap with the specified element as its root.
//----------------------------------------------------------------
public LinkedMaxHeap ()
{
   super();
   last = null;
}


//----------------------------------------------------------------
//  Creates a max heap with the specified element as its root.
//----------------------------------------------------------------
public LinkedMaxHeap (T element)
{
   root = new HeapNode<T>(element);
   last = (HeapNode<T>)root;
}


//----------------------------------------------------------------
//  Adds the specified element to this heap by adding it as a leaf
//  then reestablishing the heap relationships.
//----------------------------------------------------------------
public void add (T element)
{
   HeapNode<T> node = new HeapNode<T>(element);
   HeapNode<T> newParent = null;

   if (root == null)
      root = node;
   else
   {
      newParent = ((HeapNode<T>)root).getParentAdd(last);

      if (newParent.left == null)
         newParent.setLeft(node);
      else
         newParent.setRight(node);
   }

   node.setParent(newParent);
   last = node;

   ((HeapNode<T>)root).heapifyAdd(last);
}
```

LISTING 18.2   *continued*

```java
//------------------------------------------------------------------
//  Remove the element with the largest value in this heap and
//  returns a reference to it.
//------------------------------------------------------------------
public T removeMax()
{
   if (root == null)
      throw new EmptyCollectionException ("Remove max operation " +
         "failed. Tree is empty.");

   T maxElement = root.getElement();

   if (root.count() == 1)
      root = last = null;
   else
   {
      HeapNode<T> newLast = ((HeapNode<T>)root).getNewLastNode(last);
      if (last.parent.left == last)
         last.parent.left = null;
      else
         last.parent.right = null;

      root.setElement(last.getElement());
      last = newLast;
      ((HeapNode<T>)root).heapifyRemove((HeapNode<T>)root);
   }

   return maxElement;
}

//------------------------------------------------------------------
//  The following method is left as a programming project.
//------------------------------------------------------------------
// public T getMax() { }
}
```

The LinkedMaxHeap class relies on the HeapNode class, shown in Listing 18.3 on the next page. In addition to the inherited references left and right, a HeapNode also keeps a reference to its parent node, which allows us to move up the tree paths. The constructors in LinkedMaxHeap set up empty or one-node heaps, as appropriate.

LISTING 18.3

```java
//********************************************************************
//  HeapNode.java        Java Foundations
//
//  Represents a node, and the root of a subtree, in a heap.
//********************************************************************

package javafoundations;

public class HeapNode<T extends Comparable<T>> extends BTNode<T>
{
   HeapNode<T> parent;

   //------------------------------------------------------------------
   //  Creates a new heap node with the specified data.
   //------------------------------------------------------------------
   public HeapNode (T element)
   {
      super(element);
      parent = null;
   }

   //------------------------------------------------------------------
   //  Returns the parent node of this node.
   //------------------------------------------------------------------
   public HeapNode<T> getParent()
   {
      return parent;
   }

   //------------------------------------------------------------------
   //  Returns the parent node of this node.
   //------------------------------------------------------------------
   public void setParent(HeapNode<T> parent)
   {
      this.parent = parent;
   }

   //------------------------------------------------------------------
   //  Returns the node that will be the parent of the new node.
   //------------------------------------------------------------------
   public HeapNode<T> getParentAdd (HeapNode<T> last)
   {
      HeapNode<T> result = last;
```

LISTING 18.3   *continued*

```java
    while ((result.parent != null) && (result.parent.left != result))
        result = result.parent;

    if (result.parent != null)
        if (result.parent.right == null)
            result = result.parent;
        else
        {
            result = (HeapNode<T>) result.parent.right;
            while (result.left != null)
                result = (HeapNode<T>) result.left;
        }
    else
        while (result.left != null)
            result = (HeapNode<T>) result.left;

    return result;
}

//-----------------------------------------------------------------
//  Moves a newly added leaf up the tree as far as appropriate to
//  reestablish the heap.
//-----------------------------------------------------------------
public void heapifyAdd (HeapNode<T> last)
{
    T temp;
    HeapNode<T> current = last;

    while ((current.parent != null) &&
        ((current.element).compareTo(current.parent.element) > 0))
    {
        temp = current.element;
        current.element = current.parent.element;
        current.parent.element = temp;
        current = current.parent;
    }
}

//-----------------------------------------------------------------
//  Returns the node that will be the new last node after a remove.
//-----------------------------------------------------------------
public HeapNode<T> getNewLastNode(HeapNode<T> last)
{
    HeapNode<T> result = last;
```

LISTING 18.3 *continued*

```
      while ((result.parent != null) && (result.parent.left == result))
         result = result.parent;

      if (result.parent != null)
         result = (HeapNode<T>) result.parent.left;

      while (result.right != null)
         result = (HeapNode<T>) result.right;

      return result;
   }

   //-----------------------------------------------------------------
   //  Reorders this heap after removing the root element.
   //-----------------------------------------------------------------
   public void heapifyRemove(HeapNode<T> root)
   {
      T temp;
      HeapNode<T> current = root;
      HeapNode<T> next = largerChild (current);

      while (next != null && next.element.compareTo(current.element) > 0)
      {
         temp = current.element;
         current.element = next.element;
         next.element = temp;

         current = next;
         next = largerChild (current);
      }
   }

   //-----------------------------------------------------------------
   //  Returns the larger of the two children of the specified node.
   //-----------------------------------------------------------------
   public HeapNode<T> largerChild (HeapNode<T> node)
   {
      HeapNode<T> larger = null;

      if (node.left == null && node.right == null)
         larger = null;
      else if (node.left == null)
         larger = (HeapNode<T>)node.right;
      else if (node.right == null)
```

LISTING 18.3 *continued*

```
        larger = (HeapNode<T>)node.left;
    else if (((HeapNode<T>)node.left).element.compareTo(
        ((HeapNode<T>)
    node.right).element) > 0)
        larger = (HeapNode<T>)node.left;
    else
        larger = (HeapNode<T>)node.right;

    return larger;
  }
}
```

Consider the process of adding a new element as the "last leaf" in the complete tree. For any given tree, there is only one possible position to add that leaf. But keep in mind that that position might be on the level of current leaves, or it could be the first position of the next level if the tree is currently full. Figure 18.4 shows two heaps and the next insertion point for a new leaf.

The `add` method of `LinkedMaxHeap` relies on two support methods in `HeapNode`. One (`getParentAdd`) gets the parent of the new node to be added and the other (`heapifyAdd`) reestablishes the heap after the leaf is added. This processing is consistent with our discussion of adding a new element to a heap presented in the previous section of this chapter.

Starting at the last node in the tree, the `getParentAdd` method considers all possibilities, looking for the node that will serve as the parent of the new node being added. First it looks up the tree until it discovers it is a left child of some node,

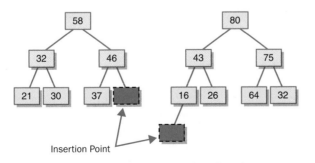

FIGURE 18.4 Insertion points in a heap

or until it hits the root. If it reaches the root, then the new parent is the leftmost descendent of the root (and the new leaf begins a new level). If not, it looks for the leftmost descendent of the right child.

Once the new leaf has been added to the tree, the `heapifyAdd` method uses the `parent` references to move up the tree, swapping elements as needed. Note that it doesn't move the nodes themselves around–it just exchanges the elements stored in them.

The `removeMax` method in `LinkedMaxHeap` removes the root of the heap, which is guaranteed to hold the largest value, and returns the element. If there is only one node in the heap, this step is straightforward. Otherwise, the `removeMax` method replaces the root with the last node in the tree, the reestablishes the heap characteristics of the tree (as described in the previous section). It relies on two support methods from `HeapNode` to accomplish this task. The `getNewLastNode` method returns the node that will be the new "last node" after the element has been removed. The `heapifyRemove` method starts at the root, swapping the element with the larger of its children, until the heap characteristic is once again established. The `getMax` operation is left as a programming project.

18.3 Heap Sort

In Chapter 13 we introduced a variety of sorting techniques, some of which were sequential sorts (bubble sort, selection sort, and insertion sort) and some of which were logarithmic sorts (merge sort and quick sort). Given the ordering property of a heap, it is natural to think of using a heap to sort a list of numbers.

> **KEY CONCEPT**
>
> A heap sort makes use of the primary characteristic of a heap to sort a set of elements.

A *heap sort* sorts a set of elements by adding each one to a heap, then removing them one at a time. Because the largest element comes off of a heap first (in a maxheap), the sequence of elements coming off the heap will be in sorted order, descending. Similarly, a minheap can be used to sort the values in ascending order. Implementing a heap sort is left as a programming project.

18.4 Priority Queues

A *priority queue* is a collection that follows two ordering rules. First, items with higher priority go first. Second, items with the same priority use a first in, first out method to determine their ordering. So note that a priority queue is not a typically FIFO queue, such as those discussed in Chapter 15. FIFO processing is only used to break ties among the same priority.

Priority queues have a variety of applications. Task scheduling in an operating system, traffic scheduling on a network, and job scheduling at your local auto mechanic are all examples of priority queues.

A priority queue could be implemented using a list of queues where each queue represents items of a given priority. A cleaner solution to this problem is to use a heap. If you think of the sort criteria in a heap as a priority value, you'll see the natural relationship between priority queues and heaps. However, note that the first in, first out ordering of items with the same priority is not addressed automatically with a heap.

One solution is to define a `PriorityQueueNode` that stores the element to be placed on the queue, the priority of the element, and the order in which elements are placed on the queue. Then, we simply define the `compareTo` method for the `PriorityQueueNode` class to compare priorities first and then compare order if there is a tie.

Listing 18.4 shows the `PriorityQueueNode` class, and Listing 18.5 on page 663 shows the `PriorityQueue` class. Note that in this solution it is completely up to the user of the priority queue to assign the priority values to the elements, and that a large priority value indicates a higher priority than a smaller value. Interpreting small values as higher priority can also be done, and may be more useful in some situations.

LISTING 18.4

```java
//********************************************************************
//  PriorityQueueNode.java       Java Foundations
//
//  Represents a node in a priority queue.
//********************************************************************

package javafoundations;

public class PriorityQueueNode<T> implements Comparable<PriorityQueueNode>
{
    private static int nextorder = 0;
    private int priority;
    private int order;
    private T element;
```

LISTING 18.4   *continued*

```java
//--------------------------------------------------------------
//  Creates a new node with the specified element.
//--------------------------------------------------------------
public PriorityQueueNode (T obj, int prio)
{
   element = obj;
   priority = prio;
   order = nextorder;
   nextorder++;
}

//--------------------------------------------------------------
//  Returns the element in this node.
//--------------------------------------------------------------
public T getElement()
{
   return element;
}

//--------------------------------------------------------------
//  Returns the priority value for the element in this node.
//--------------------------------------------------------------
public int getPriority()
{
   return priority;
}

//--------------------------------------------------------------
//  Returns the order for this node (to break priority ties).
//--------------------------------------------------------------
public int getOrder()
{
   return order;
}

//--------------------------------------------------------------
//  Returns a string representation of this node.
//--------------------------------------------------------------
public String toString()
{
   String temp = (element.toString() + priority + order);
   return temp;
}
```

LISTING 18.4   *continued*

```java
//-----------------------------------------------------------------
//  Compares this node to the parameter, based on priority. Uses
//  the order in which the elements were added to break ties.
//-----------------------------------------------------------------
public int compareTo(PriorityQueueNode obj)
{
   int result;

   if (priority < obj.getPriority())
      result = -1;
   else if (priority > obj.getPriority())
      result = 1;
   else if (order > obj.getOrder()) // break tied priorities
      result = -1;
   else
      result = 1;

   return result;
}
}
```

LISTING 18.5

```java
//******************************************************************
//  PriorityQueue.java        Java Foundations
//
//  Represents a priority queue that uses a underlying heap.
//******************************************************************

package javafoundations;

public class PriorityQueue<T> extends LinkedMaxHeap<PriorityQueueNode<T>>
{
   //-----------------------------------------------------------------
   //  Creates a new, empty priority queue.
   //-----------------------------------------------------------------
   public PriorityQueue()
   {
      super();
   }
```

LISTING 18.5   *continued*

```java
   //-------------------------------------------------------------------
   //  Adds the specified element to this priority queue.
   //-------------------------------------------------------------------
   public void addElement (T object, int priority)
   {
      PriorityQueueNode<T> node = new PriorityQueueNode<T> (object, priority);
      super.addElement(node);
   }

   //-------------------------------------------------------------------
   //  Removes the next highest priority element from this queue and
   //  returns a reference to it.
   //-------------------------------------------------------------------
   public T removeNext()
   {
      PriorityQueueNode<T> temp = (PriorityQueueNode<T>)super.removeMin();
      return temp.getElement();
   }
}
```

Summary of Key Concepts

- A heap is a complete binary tree in which each element is greater than or equal to both of its children.
- Adding an element to a heap can be accomplished by adding the element as a leaf, then moving it upward as appropriate.
- Removing the maximum element from the heap can be accomplished by replacing the root with the last leaf, then moving it downward as appropriate.
- A heap sort makes use of the primary characteristic of a heap to sort a set of elements.
- A priority queue is not a FIFO queue. It orders elements according to priority, independent of the order in which they are added to the queue.

Self-Review Questions

SR 18.1   What is the difference between a heap and a binary search tree?

SR 18.2   What is the difference between a minheap and a maxheap?

SR 18.3   How is an element added to a heap?

SR 18.4   How is the largest element removed from a heap?

SR 18.5   What is a heap sort?

SR 18.6   What is a priority queue?

Exercises

EX 18.1   Does a heap ever need rebalancing, as we discussed doing for binary search trees? Explain.

EX 18.2   Draw a heap containing the same elements as those stored in Figure 18.1, but with a different structure.

EX 18.3   In a heap, does it matter which subtree (left or right) holds equal values? Explain.

EX 18.4   Show the max heap that results when the following values are added, in order, to the heap shown in Figure 18.1.

81 25 22 86

EX 18.5   Show the max heap that results when the following values are added, in order, to a new heap.

28 19 41 35 50 37 10 39 55

EX 18.6 Show the max heap that results after deleting the three highest elements, in order, from the heap that is produced in EX 18.5.

EX 18.7 Show the max heap that results when the following values are added, in order, to a new heap.

12 31 7 38 34 81 36 29 67 77 79

EX 18.8 Show the max heap that results after deleting the three highest elements, in order, from the heap that is produced in EX 18.7.

Programming Projects

PP 18.1 Complete the implementation of the LinkedMaxHeap class presented in this chapter. Specifically, complete the implementation of the getMax operation.

PP 18.2 Design and implement a min heap collection, with an appropriate interface, implementing class, and node class. Use a linked implementation strategy.

PP 18.3 Implement a class called CLArrayMaxHeap that satisfies the MaxHeap interface. The class should represent the tree using the computed link implementation strategy and be derived from the CLArrayBinaryTree class from programming project 16.2 in Chapter 16.

PP 18.4 Implement a class called SLArrayMaxHeap that satisfies the MaxHeap interface. The class should represent the tree using the stored link implementation strategy and be derived from the SLArrayBinaryTree class from programming project 16.3 in Chapter 16.

PP 18.5 Implement a heap sort and demonstrate its functionality.

Answers to Self-Review Questions

SR 18.1 A binary search tree and a heap are both binary trees that have constraints on the relationships among their elements. The nodes in a binary search tree are less than their left child and greater than or equal to their right child, whereas the nodes in a heap (maxheap) are greater than or equal to both children.

SR 18.2 A minheap keeps the smallest value in the tree at the root, whereas a maxheap keeps the largest value at the root. Otherwise, their strategies and implementations are similar.

SR 18.3   An element is added to a heap by inserting it as a new leaf, then moving that element up the tree as appropriate to reassert the proper relationships among the elements.

SR 18.4   The maximum element is removed from a heap (maxheap) by replacing the root with the last leaf of the tree, then moving that element down the tree as appropriate to reassert the proper relationships among the elements.

SR 18.5   A heap sort is a sorting algorithm that sorts values by adding them to a heap, then removing them in sorted order.

SR 18.6   A priority queue is a queue that orders its elements according to a specified priority value, and only uses the order of arrival to break priority ties.

Graphs

CHAPTER OBJECTIVES

- Discuss directed and undirected graphs.
- Define weighted graphs and explore their use.
- Define breadth-first and depth-first traversals of a graph.
- Define a minimum spanning tree.
- Discuss strategies for implementing graphs.

We've seen that trees, as discussed in Chapters 16 and 17, are nonlinear structures with a single root node. This chapter introduces graphs, nonlinear structures in which nodes may be connected to many other nodes, with no particular parent/child relationships. The exploration of graphs and graph theory is an entire subdiscipline of both mathematics and computer science. In this chapter we introduce the basic concepts of graphs and their implementation.

19.1 Undirected Graphs

As we discussed in previous chapters, a tree is a nonlinear structure defined by the concept that each node in the tree, other than the root node, has exactly one parent. If we were to violate that premise and allow each node in the tree to be connected to a variety of other nodes with no notion of parent or child, the result would be a graph.

Like trees, a graph is made up of nodes and the connections between those nodes. In graph terminology, we refer to the nodes as *vertices* and refer to the connections among them as *edges*. Vertices are typically referenced by a name or a label. For example, we might label vertices A, B, C, and D. Edges are referenced by a pairing of the vertices that they connect. For example, we might have an edge (A, B), which means there is an edge from vertex A to vertex B.

An *undirected graph* is a graph where the pairings representing the edges are unordered. Thus, listing an edge as (A, B) means that there is a connection between A and B that can be traversed in either direction. Thus, in an undirected graph, listing an edge as (A, B) means exactly the same thing as listing the edge as (B, A). Figure 19.1 illustrates an undirected graph.

Two vertices in a graph are *adjacent* if there is an edge connecting them. For example, in the graph of Figure 19.1, vertices A and B are adjacent while vertices A and D are not. Adjacent vertices are sometimes referred to as *neighbors*. An edge of a graph that connects a vertex to itself is called a *self-loop* or a *sling*.

An undirected graph is considered *complete* if it has the maximum number of edges connecting vertices. For the first vertex, it requires (n–1) edges to connect it to the other vertices. For the second vertex, it requires only (n–2) edges since it is already connected to the first vertex. For the third vertex, it requires (n–3) edges. This sequence continues until the final vertex requires no additional edges

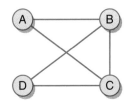

FIGURE 19.1 An undirected graph

because all the other vertices have already been connected to it. Mathematically, this is the summation:

$$\sum_{i=1}^{n-1} = \frac{n(n-1)}{2}$$

A *path* is a sequence of edges that connects two vertices in a graph. For example, in our graph from Figure 19.1, A, B, D is a path from A to D. Notice that each sequential pair, (A, B) and then (B, D), is an edge. A path in an undirected graph is bidirectional. For example, A, B, D is the path from A to D but since the edges are undirected, the inverse, D, B, A is also the path from D to A. The *length* of a path is the number of edges in the path (or the number of vertices − 1). So for our previous example, the path length is 2. Notice that this definition of path length is identical to the definition that we used in discussing trees. In fact, trees are graphs.

> **KEY CONCEPT**
> A path is a sequence of edges that connects two vertices in a graph.

An undirected graph is considered *connected* if for any two vertices in the graph there is a path between them. Our graph from Figure 19.1 is connected. The same graph with a minor modification is not connected, as illustrated in Figure 19.2.

A *cycle* is a path in which the first and last vertices are the same and none of the edges are repeated. In Figure 19.2, we would say that the path A, B, C, A is a cycle. A graph that has no cycles is called *acyclic*. Earlier we mentioned the relationship between graphs and trees. Now that we have introduced these definitions, we can formalize that relationship. An undirected tree is a connected, acyclic, undirected graph with one element designated as the root.

> **KEY CONCEPT**
> A cycle is a path in which the first and last vertices are the same and none of the edges are repeated.

19.2 Directed Graphs

A *directed graph*, sometimes referred to as a *digraph*, is a graph where the edges are ordered pairs of vertices. This means that the edges (A, B) and (B, A) are separate, directional edges in a directed

> **KEY CONCEPT**
> In a directed graph, the edges are ordered pairs of vertices.

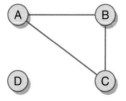

FIGURE 19.2 An example undirected graph that is not connected

graph. In our previous example we had the following description for an undirected graph:

Vertices: A, B, C, D

Edges: (A, B), (A, C), (B, C), (B, D), (C, D)

Figure 19.3 shows what happens if we interpret this earlier description as a directed graph. We represent each of the edges now with the direction of traversal specified by the ordering of the vertices. For example, the edge (A, B) allows traversal from A to B but not the other direction.

Our previous definitions change slightly for directed graphs. For example, a path in a directed graph is a sequence of directed edges that connects two vertices in a graph. In our undirected graph we listed the path A, B, D, as the path from A to D, and that is still true in our directed interpretation of the graph description. However, paths in a directed graph are not bi-directional, so the inverse is no longer true: D, B, A is not a valid path from D to A.

Our definition of a connected directed graph sounds the same as it did for undirected graphs. A directed graph is connected if for any two vertices in the graph there is a path between them. However, keep in mind that our definition of path is different. Look at the two graphs shown in Figure 19.4. The first one is connected. The second one, however, is not connected because there is no path from any other vertex to vertex 1.

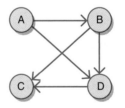

FIGURE 19.3 A directed graph

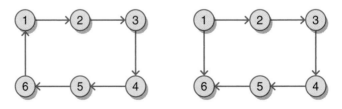

FIGURE 19.4 Directed edges determining connectivity

If a directed graph has no cycles, it is possible to arrange the vertices such that vertex A precedes vertex B if an edge exists from A to B. The order of vertices resulting from this arrangement is called *topological order* and is very useful for examples such as course prerequisites.

As we discussed earlier, trees are graphs. In fact, most of our previous work with trees actually focused on directed trees. A directed tree is a directed graph that has an element designated as the root and has the following properties:

- There are no connections from other vertices to the root.
- Every non-root element has exactly one connection to it.
- There is a path from the root to every other vertex.

19.3 Weighted Graphs

A *weighted graph*, sometimes called a *network*, is a graph with weights or costs associated with each edge. Figure 19.5 shows an undirected weighted graph of the connections and the airfares between cities. This graph could then be used to determine the cheapest path from one city to another. The weight of a path in a weighted graph is the sum of the weights of the edges in the path.

> **KEY CONCEPT**
>
> A weighted graph is a graph with costs associated with each edge.

Weighted graphs may be either undirected or directed depending upon the need. Take our airfare example from Figure 19.5. What if the airfare to fly from New York to Boston is one price but the airfare to fly from Boston to New York is a different price? This would be an excellent application of a directed weighted graph, as illustrated in Figure 19.6 on the next page.

For weighted graphs, we represent each edge with a triple including the starting vertex, ending vertex, and the weight. Keep in mind, for undirected weighted graphs, the starting and ending vertices could be swapped with no impact.

FIGURE 19.5 An undirected weighted graph

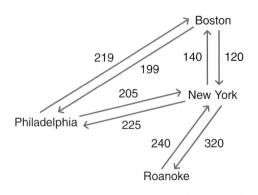

FIGURE 19.6 A directed weighted graph

However, for directed graphs, a triple must be included for every directional connection. For example, the weighted graph of Figure 19.6 would be represented as follows:

Vertices: Boston, New York, Philadelphia, Roanoke

Edges: (Boston, New York, 120), (Boston, Philadelphia, 199),
(New York, Boston, 140), (New York, Philadelphia, 225),
(New York, Roanoke, 320), (Philadelphia, Boston, 219),
(Philadelphia, New York, 205), (Roanoke, New York, 240)

19.4 Common Graph Algorithms

There are a number of common graph algorithms that may apply to undirected graphs, directed graphs, and/or weighted graphs. These include various traversal algorithms similar to those we explored with trees, as well as algorithms for finding the shortest path, algorithms for finding the least costly path in a network, and algorithms to answer simple questions about the graph such as whether or not the graph is connected or what the shortest path is between two vertices.

Traversals

In our discussion of trees in Chapter 16, we defined four types of traversals (pre-order, inorder, postorder, and level-order). There are generally two types of graph traversals: a *breadth-first traversal*, which behaves very much like the level-order traversal of a tree, and a *depth-first traversal*, which behaves very much like the preorder traversal of a tree. One difference is that there is no root node present in a graph. Thus, our traversals may start at any vertex in the graph.

We can construct a breadth-first traversal for a graph using a queue and an iterator. We will use the queue (`traversalQueue`) to manage the traversal and use the iterator (`iter`) to build our result. The first step is to enqueue the starting vertex into the queue and mark the starting vertex as visited. We then begin a loop that will continue until the queue is empty. Within this loop we will take the first vertex off of the queue and add that vertex to the iterator. Next, we will enqueue each of the vertices that are adjacent to the current one, and have not already been marked as visited, into the queue, mark each of them as visited, and then repeat the loop. We simply repeat this process for each of the visited vertices until the queue is empty, meaning we can no longer reach any new vertices. The iterator now contains the vertices in breadth-first order from the given starting point. Very similar logic can be used to construct a depth-first iterator.

The following method shows an iterative algorithm for a breadth-first traversal using an array implementation of a graph. The determination of vertices that are adjacent to the current one depends upon the implementation we choose to represent edges in a graph. We will discuss this further in section 19.4.

```
//-------------------------------------------------------------
//  Returns an iterator that performs a breadth-first search
//  traversal starting at the given index.
//-------------------------------------------------------------
public Iterator<T> iteratorBFS(int startIndex)
{
    int currentVertex;
    LinkedQueue<Integer> traversalQueue = new
        LinkedQueue<Integer>();
    ArrayIterator<T> iter = new ArrayIterator<T>();

    if (!indexIsValid(startIndex))
        return iter;

    boolean[] visited = new boolean[numVertices];
    for (int vertexIndex = 0; vertexIndex < numVertices;
        vertexIndex++)
        visited[vertexIndex] = false;

    traversalQueue.enqueue(startIndex);
    visited[startIndex] = true;

    while (!traversalQueue.isEmpty())
    {
        currentVertex = traversalQueue.dequeue();
        iter.add(vertices[currentVertex]);
```

```
            for (int vertexIndex = 0; vertexIndex < numVertices;
               vertexIndex++)
               if (adjMatrix[currentVertex][vertexIndex] &&
                  !visited[vertexIndex])
               {
                  traversalQueue.enqueue(vertexIndex);
                  visited[vertexIndex] = true;
               }
      }
      return iter;
   }
```

A depth-first traversal for a graph can be constructed using virtually the same logic by simply replacing the queue with a stack. One other difference in the algorithm, however, is that we do not want to mark a vertex as visited until it has been added to the iterator. The `iteratorDFS` method below illustrates this algorithm for an array implementation of a graph.

```
//------------------------------------------------------------
//  Returns an iterator that performs a depth-first search
//  traversal starting at the given index.
//------------------------------------------------------------
public Iterator<T> iteratorDFS(int startIndex)
{
   int currentVertex;
   LinkedStack<Integer> traversalStack =
      new LinkedStack<Integer>();
   ArrayIterator<T> iter = new ArrayIterator<T>();
   boolean[] visited = new boolean[numVertices];
   boolean found;

   if (!indexIsValid(startIndex))
      return iter;

   for (int vertexIdx = 0; vertexIdx < numVertices;
      vertexIdx++)
      visited[vertexIdx] = false;

   traversalStack.push(startIndex);
   iter.add (vertices[startIndex]);
   visited[startIndex] = true;

   while (!traversalStack.isEmpty())
   {
      currentVertex = traversalStack.peek();
      found = false;
```

```
for (int vertexIdx = 0; vertexIdx < numVertices && !found;
    vertexIdx++)
    if (adjMatrix[currentVertex][vertexIdx] && !visited [vertexIdx])
    {
        traversalStack.push(vertexIdx);
        iter.add(vertices[vertexIdx]);
        visited[vertexIdx] = true;
        found = true;
    }

    if (!found && !traversalStack.isEmpty())
        traversalStack.pop();
}
return iter;
}
```

> **KEY CONCEPT**
>
> The main difference between a depth-first traversal of a graph and a breadth-first traversal is the use of a stack instead of a queue to manage the traversal.

Let's look at an example. Figure 19.7 shows a sample undirected graph where each vertex is labeled with an integer. For a breadth-first traversal starting from vertex 9, we do the following:

1. Add 9 to the queue and mark it as visited.
2. Dequeue 9 from the queue.
3. Add 9 on the iterator.
4. Add 6, 7, and 8 to the queue, marking each of them as visited.
5. Dequeue 6 from the queue.
6. Add 6 on the iterator.

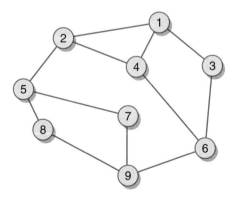

FIGURE 19.7 A traversal example

7. Add 3 and 4 to the queue, marking them both as visited.

8. Dequeue 7 from the queue and add it to the iterator.

9. Add 5 to the queue, marking it as visited.

10. Dequeue 8 from the queue and add it to the iterator. (We do not add any new vertices to the queue since there are no neighbors of 8 that have not already been visited.)

11. Dequeue 3 from the queue and add it to the iterator.

12. Add 1 to the queue, marking it as visited.

13. Dequeue 4 from the queue and add it to the iterator.

14. Add 2 to the queue, marking it as visited.

15. Dequeue 5 from the queue and add it to the iterator. (Since there are no unvisited neighbors, we continue without adding anything to the queue.)

16. Dequeue 1 from the queue and add it to the iterator. (Since there are no unvisited neighbors, we continue without adding anything to the queue.)

17. Dequeue 2 from the queue and add it to the iterator.

Thus, the iterator now contains the breadth-first order starting at vertex 9: 9, 6, 7, 8, 3, 4, 5, 1, and 2. Trace a depth-first search on the same graph from Figure 19.7.

Of course, both of these algorithms could also be expressed recursively. For example, the following algorithm recursively defines a depth-first search:

```
depthFirstSearch(node x)
{
   visit(x)
   for each node y adjacent to x
      if y not visited
         depthFirstSearch(y)
}
```

Testing for Connectivity

In our earlier discussion, we defined a graph as *connected* if for any two vertices in the graph, there is a path between them. This definition holds true for both undirected and directed graphs. Let's now put that in terms of the breadth-first traversal we just discussed: A graph is connected if and only if for each vertex v in a graph containing n vertices, the size of the result of a breadth-first traversal starting at v is n.

> **KEY CONCEPT**
>
> A graph is connected if and only if the number of vertices in the breadth-first traversal is the same as the number of vertices in the graph regardless of the starting vertex.

Let's look at the example undirected graphs in Figure 19.8. We stated earlier that the graph on the left is connected and that the graph on the right is not. Let's confirm that by following our

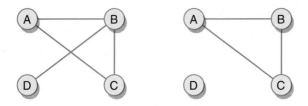

FIGURE 19.8 Connectivity in an undirected graph

Starting Vertex	Breadth-First Traversal
A	A, B, C, D
B	B, A, D, C
C	C, B, A, D
D	D, B, A, C

FIGURE 19.9 Breadth-first traversals for a connected undirected graph

algorithm. Figure 19.9 shows the breadth-first traversals for the graph on the left using each of the vertices as a starting point. As you can see, each of the traversals yield n = 4 vertices, thus the graph is connected. Figure 19.10 shows the breadth-first traversals for the graph on the right using each of the vertices as a starting point. Notice that not only do none of the traversals contain n = 4 vertices, but the one starting at vertex D has only the one vertex. Thus the graph is not connected.

Starting Vertex	Breadth-First Traversal
A	A, B, C
B	B, A, C
C	C, B, A
D	D

FIGURE 19.10 Breadth-first traversals for an unconnected undirected graph

Minimum Spanning Trees

A *spanning tree* is a tree that includes all of the vertices of a graph and some, but possibly not all, of the edges. Since trees are also graphs, for some graphs, the graph itself will be a spanning tree, and thus the only spanning tree for that graph will include all of the edges. Figure 19.11 shows a spanning tree for our graph from Figure 19.7.

One interesting application of spanning trees is to find a *minimum spanning tree* for a weighted graph. A minimum spanning tree is a spanning tree where the sum of the weights of the edges is less than or equal to the sum of the weights for any other spanning tree for the same graph.

The algorithm for developing a minimum spanning tree was developed by Prim (1957) and is quite elegant. As we discussed earlier, each edge is represented by a triple including the starting vertex, ending vertex, and the weight. We then pick an arbitrary starting vertex (it does not matter which one) and add it to our minimum spanning tree (MST). Next we add all of the edges that include our starting vertex to a minheap ordered by weight. Keep in mind that if we are dealing with a directed graph, we will only add edges that start at the given vertex.

Next we remove the minimum edge from the minheap and add the edge and the new vertex to our MST. Next we add to our minheap all of the edges that include this new vertex and whose other vertex is not already in our MST. We continue this process until either our MST includes all of the vertices in our original graph or the minheap is empty. Figure 19.12 shows a weighted network and its associated minimum spanning tree. Shown below is the `getMST` method, which illustrates this algorithm.

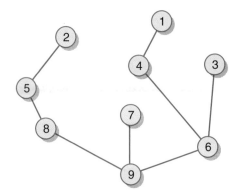

FIGURE 19.11 A spanning tree

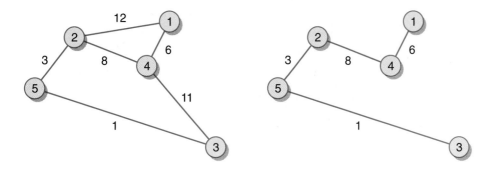

Network   Minimum Spanning Tree

FIGURE 19.12 A weighted graph and its associated minimum spanning tree

```
//-------------------------------------------------------------
//  Returns a minimum spanning tree of the graph.
//-------------------------------------------------------------
public Graph getMST()
{
    int x, y;
    int[] edge = new int[2];
    LinkedStack<int[]> vertexStack = new LinkedStack<int[]>();
    Graph<T> resultGraph = new Graph<T>();

    if (isEmpty() || !isConnected())
        return resultGraph;

    resultGraph.adjMatrix = new
        boolean[numVertices][numVertices];

    for (int i = 0; i < numVertices; i++)
        for (int j = 0; j < numVertices; j++)
            resultGraph.adjMatrix[i][j] = false;

    resultGraph.vertices = (T[])(new Object[numVertices]);
    boolean[] visited = new boolean[numVertices];

    for (int i = 0; i < numVertices; i++)
        visited[i] = false;

    edge[0] = 0;
    resultGraph.vertices[0] = this.vertices[0];
    resultGraph.numVertices++;
    visited[0] = true;
```

```
// Add all edges that are adjacent to vertex 0 to the stack.
for (int i = 0; i < numVertices; i++)
{
    if (!visited[i] && this.adjMatrix[0][i])
    {
        edge[1] = i;
        vertexStack.push(edge.clone());
        visited[i] = true;
    }
}

while ((resultGraph.size() < this.size()) &&
!vertexStack.isEmpty())
{
    // Pop an edge off the stack and add it to the
    // resultGraph.
    edge = vertexStack.pop();
    x = edge[0];
    y = edge[1];
    resultGraph.vertices[y] = this.vertices[y];
    resultGraph.numVertices++;
    resultGraph.adjMatrix[x][y] = true;
    resultGraph.adjMatrix[y][x] = true;
    visited[y] = true;

    for (int i = 0; i < numVertices; i++)
    {
        if (!visited[i] && this.adjMatrix[i][y])
        {
            edge[0] = y;
            edge[1] = i;
            vertexStack.push(edge.clone());
            visited[i] = true;
        }
    }
}
return resultGraph;
}
```

Determining the Shortest Path

There are two possibilities for determining the "shortest" path in a graph. The first, and perhaps simplest, possibility is to determine the literal shortest path between a starting vertex and a target vertex, meaning the least number of edges between the two vertices. This turns out to be a simple variation of our earlier breadth-first traversal algorithm.

To convert this algorithm to find the shortest path, we simply store two additional pieces of information for each vertex during our traversal: the path length from the starting vertex to this vertex, and the vertex that is the predecessor of this vertex in that path. Then we modify our loop to terminate when we reach our target vertex. The path length for the shortest path is simply the path length to the predecessor of the target + 1, and if we wish to output the vertices along the shortest path, we can simply backtrack along the chain of predecessors.

The second possibility for determining the shortest path is to look for the cheapest path in a weighted graph. Dijkstra (1959) developed an algorithm for this possibility that is similar to our previous algorithm. However, instead of using a queue of vertices that causes us to progress through the graph in the order we encounter vertices, we use a minheap or a priority queue storing vertex, weight pairs based upon total weight (the sum of the weights from the starting vertex to this vertex) so that we always traverse through the graph following the cheapest path first. For each vertex, we must store the label of the vertex, the weight of the cheapest path (thus far) to that vertex from our starting point, and the predecessor of that vertex along that path. On the minheap, we will store vertex, weight pairs for each possible path that we have encountered but not yet traversed. As we remove a vertex, weight pair from the minheap, if we encounter a vertex with a weight less than the one already stored with the vertex, we update the cost.

19.5 Strategies for Implementing Graphs

As we have done in the previous two chapters, we will present algorithms and strategies for the implementation of graphs but leave the implementations as programming projects. Let us begin our discussion of implementation strategies by examining what operations would need to be available for a graph. Of course, we would need to be able to add and remove vertices, and add and remove edges from the graph. There will need to be traversals (perhaps breadth first and depth first) beginning with a particular vertex, and these might be implemented as iterators, as we did for binary trees. Other operations like `size`, `isEmpty`, `toString`, and `find` will be useful as well. In addition to these, operations to determine the shortest path from a particular vertex to a particular target vertex, to determine the adjacency of two vertices, to construct a minimum spanning tree, and to test for connectivity would all likely need to be implemented.

Whatever storage mechanism we use for vertices must allow us to mark vertices as visited during traversals and other algorithms. This can be accomplished by simply adding a boolean variable to the class representing the vertices.

Adjacency Lists

Since trees are graphs, perhaps the best introduction to how we might implement graphs is to consider the discussions and examples that we have already seen concerning the implementation of trees. One might immediately think of using a set of nodes where each node contains an element and perhaps a linked list of up to n–1 links to other nodes. When we used this strategy with trees, the number of connections from any given node was limited by the order of the tree (e.g., a maximum of two directed edges starting at any particular node in a binary tree). Because of this limitation, we were able to specify, for example, that a binary-node had a left and a right child pointer. Even if the binary-node was a leaf, the pointer still existed. It was simply set to null.

In the case of a *graph-node*, since each node could have up to n–1 edges connecting it to other nodes, it would be better to use a dynamic structure such as a linked list to store the edges within each node. This list is called an *adjacency list*. In the case of a weighted graph, each edge would be stored as a triple including the weight. In the case of an undirected graph, an edge (A, B) would appear in the adjacency list of both vertex A and vertex B.

Adjacency Matrices

Keep in mind that we must somehow efficiently (both in terms of space and access time) store both vertices and edges. Since vertices are just elements, we can use any of our collections to store the vertices. In fact, we often talk about a "set of vertices," the term set implying an implementation strategy. However, another solution for storing edges is motivated by our use of array implementations of trees, but instead of using a one-dimensional array, we will use a two-dimensional array that we call an *adjacency matrix*. In an adjacency matrix, each position of the two-dimensional array represents an intersection between two vertices in the graph. Each of these intersections is represented by a boolean value indicating whether or not the two vertices are connected. Figure 19.13 shows an undirected graph and its adjacency matrix.

	A	B	C	D
A	F	T	T	F
B	T	F	T	T
C	T	T	F	F
D	F	T	F	F

FIGURE 19.13 An undirected graph and its adjacency matrix

FIGURE 19.14 A directed graph and its adjacency matrix

For any position (row, column) in the matrix, that position is true if and only if the edge (v_{row}, v_{column}) is in the graph. Since edges in an undirected graph are bi-directional, if (A, B) is an edge in the graph, then (B, A) is also in the graph.

Notice that this matrix is symmetrical—that is, each side of the diagonal is a mirror image of the other. The reason for this is that we are representing an undirected graph. For undirected graphs, it may not be necessary to represent the entire matrix but simply one side or the other of the diagonal.

However, for directed graphs, since all of the edges are directional, the result can be quite different. Figure 19.14 shows a directed graph and its adjacency matrix.

Adjacency matrices may also be used with weighted graphs by simply storing an object at each position of the matrix to represent the weight of the edge. Positions in the matrix where edges do not exist would simply be set to null.

Summary of Key Concepts

- An undirected graph is a graph where the pairings representing the edges are unordered.

- Two vertices in a graph are adjacent if there is an edge connecting them.

- An undirected graph is considered complete if it has the maximum number of edges connecting vertices.

- A path is a sequence of edges that connects two vertices in a graph.

- A cycle is a path in which the first and last vertices are the same and none of the edges are repeated.

- In a directed graph, the edges are ordered pairs of vertices.

- A path in a directed graph is a sequence of directed edges that connects two vertices in a graph.

- A weighted graph is a graph with costs associated with each edge.

- The main difference between a depth-first traversal of a graph and a breadth-first traversal is the use of a stack instead of a queue to manage the traversal.

- A graph is connected if and only if the number of vertices in the breadth-first traversal is the same as the number of vertices in the graph regardless of the starting vertex.

- A spanning tree is a tree that includes all of the vertices of a graph and some, but possibly not all, of the edges.

- A minimum spanning tree is a spanning tree where the sum of the weights of the edges is less than or equal to the sum of the weights for any other spanning tree for the same graph.

Self-Review Questions

SR 19.1   What is the difference between a graph and a tree?

SR 19.2   What is an undirected graph?

SR 19.3   What is a directed graph?

SR 19.4   What does it mean to say that a graph is complete?

SR 19.5   What is the maximum number of edges for an undirected graph? A directed graph?

SR 19.6   What is the definition of a path? A cycle?

SR 19.7   What is the difference between a weighted graph and a graph?

SR 19.8   What is a spanning tree? A minimum spanning tree?

Exercises

EX 19.1   Draw the undirected graph that is represented by the following:

vertices: 1, 2, 3, 4, 5, 6, 7

edges: (1, 2), (1, 4), (2, 3), (2, 4), (3, 7), (4, 7), (4, 6), (5, 6), (5, 7), (6, 7)

EX 19.2   Is the graph from Exercise 19.1 connected? Complete?

EX 19.3   List all of the cycles in the graph from Exercise 19.1.

EX 19.4   Draw a spanning tree for the graph of Exercise 19.1.

EX 19.5   Using the same data from Exercise 19.1, draw the resulting directed graph.

EX 19.6   Is the directed graph of Exercise 19.5 connected? Complete?

EX 19.7   List all of the cycles in the graph of Exercise 19.5.

EX 19.8   Draw a spanning tree for the graph of Exercise 19.5.

EX 19.9   Consider the weighted graph shown in Figure 19.10. List all of the possible paths from vertex 2 to vertex 3 along with the total weight of each path.

Programming Projects

PP 19.1   Implement an undirected graph using whatever underlying data structure you prefer. Keep in mind that you must store both vertices and edges. Your implementation should include methods for adding and removing vertices, adding and removing edges, `size` (which should return the number of vertices), `isEmpty`, a breadth-first iterator, and a depth-first iterator.

PP 19.2   Repeat programming project 19.1 for a directed graph.

PP 19.3   Implement a shortest path method to go along with your implementation for programming project 19.1 that will either return the length of the shortest path or return –1 if no path is found.

PP 19.4   Repeat programming project 19.3 for the directed graph implementation of programming project 19.2.

PP 19.5   Extend your implementation from programming project 19.1 to create a weighted, undirected graph and add a method to return a minimum spanning tree.

PP 19.6   Extend your implementation from programming project 19.2 to create a weighted, directed graph and add a method to return a minimum spanning tree.

PP 19.7   Create a limited airline scheduling system that will allow a user to enter city to city connections and their prices. Your system should then allow a user to enter two cities and should return the shortest path and the cheapest path between the two cities. Your system should report if there is no connection between two cities. Use an undirected weighted graph.

PP 19.8   Repeat programming project 19.7 assuming a directed weighted graph.

PP 19.9   Create a computer network routing system that, given the point-to-point connections in the network and the costs of utilizing each, will produce cheapest-path connections from each point to each point in the network, pointing out any disconnected locations.

Answers to Self-Review Questions

SR 19.1   A graph is the more general concept without the restriction that each node has one and only one parent except for the root, which does not have a parent. In the case of a graph, there is no root, and each vertex can be connected to up to n–1 other vertices.

SR 19.2   An undirected graph is a graph where the pairings representing the edges are unordered.

SR 19.3   A directed graph, sometimes referred as a digraph, is a graph where the edges are ordered pairs of vertices.

SR 19.4   A graph is considered complete if it has the maximum number of edges connecting vertices.

SR 19.5   The maximum number of edges for an undirected graph is n(n–1)/2. For a directed graph, it is n(n–1).

SR 19.6   A path is a sequence of edges that connects two vertices in a graph. A cycle is a path in which the first and last vertices are the same and none of the edges are repeated.

SR 19.7   A weighted graph is a graph, either directed or undirected, with weights or costs associated with each edge.

SR 19.8   A spanning tree is a tree that includes all of the vertices of a graph and some, but possibly not all, of the edges. A minimum spanning tree is a spanning tree where the sum of the weights of the edges is less than or equal to the sum of the weights for any other spanning tree for the same graph.

Hashing

CHAPTER OBJECTIVES

- Define hashing.
- Examine various hashing functions.
- Examine the problem of collisions in hash tables.
- Explore the Java Collections API implementations of hashing.

In Chapter 17, we discussed the idea that a binary search tree is, in effect, an efficient implementation of a set or a map. In this chapter, we examine hashing, an approach to implementing a set or map collection that can be even more efficient than binary search trees.

20.1 Hashing

In all of our discussions of the implementations of collections, we have proceeded with one of two assumptions about the order of elements in a collection:

- Order is determined by the order in which elements are added to and/or removed from our collection, as in the case of stacks, queues, unordered lists, and indexed lists.

- Order is determined by comparing the values of the elements (or some key component of the elements) to be stored in the collection, as in the case of ordered lists and binary search trees.

> **KEY CONCEPT**
>
> In hashing, elements are stored in a hash table, with their location in the table determined by a hashing function.

In this chapter we will explore the concept of *hashing*, which means that the order—and, more specifically, the location of an item within the collection—is determined by some function of the value of the element to be stored, or some function of a key value of the element to be stored. In hashing, elements are stored in a *hash table*, with their location in the table determined by a *hashing function*. Each location in the table may be referred to as a *cell* or a *bucket*. We will discuss hashing functions further in Section 20.2. We will also discuss implementation strategies and algorithms, and leave the implementations as programming projects.

Consider a simple example where we create an array that will hold 26 elements. Wishing to store names in our array, we create a hashing function that equates each name to the position in the array associated with the first letter of the name (e.g., a first letter of A would be mapped to position 0 of the array, a first letter of D would be mapped to position 3 of the array, and so on). Figure 20.1 illustrates this scenario after several names have been added.

> **KEY CONCEPT**
>
> The situation where two elements or keys map to the same location in the table is called a collision.

Notice that unlike our earlier implementations of collections, using a hashing approach results in the access time to a particular element being independent of the number of elements in the table. This means that all of the operations on an element of a hash table should be O(1). This is the result of no longer having to do comparisons to find a particular element or to locate the appropriate position for a given element. Using hashing, we simply calculate where a particular element should be.

> **KEY CONCEPT**
>
> A hashing function that maps each element to a unique position in the table is said to be a perfect hashing function.

However, this efficiency is only fully realized if each element maps to a unique position in the table. Consider our example from Figure 20.1. What will happen if we attempt to store the name "Ann" and the name "Andrew?" This situation, where two elements or keys map to the same location in the table, is called a *collision*. We will discuss how to resolve collisions in Section 20.3.

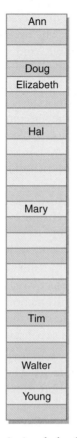

FIGURE 20.1 A simple hashing example

A hashing function that maps each element to a unique position in the table is said to be a *perfect hashing function*. While it is possible in some situations to develop a perfect hashing function, a hashing function that does a good job of distributing the elements among the table positions will still result in constant time access (O(1)) to elements in the table and an improvement over our earlier algorithms that were either O(n) in the case of our linear approaches or O(log n) in the case of search trees.

Another issue surrounding hashing is the question of how large the table should be. If the data set is of known size and a perfect hashing function can be used, then we simply make the table the same size as the data set. If a perfect hashing function is not available or practical but the size of the data set is known, a good rule of thumb is to make the table 150% the size of the data set.

The third case is very common and far more interesting. What if we do not know the size of the data set? In this case, we depend on *dynamic resizing*.

Dynamic resizing of a hash table involves creating a new hash table that is larger than, perhaps even twice as large as, the original, inserting all of the elements of the original table into the new table, and then discarding the original table. Deciding when to resize is also an interesting question. One possibility is to use the same method we used with our earlier array implementations and simply expand the table when it is full. However, it is the nature of hash tables that their performance seriously degrades as they become full. A better approach is to use a *load factor*. The load factor of a hash table is the percentage occupancy of the table at which the table will be resized. For example, if the load factor were set to 0.50, then the table would be resized each time it reached 50% capacity.

20.2 Hashing Functions

While perfect hashing functions are possible if the data set is known, we do not need the hashing function to be perfect to get good performance from the hash table. Our goal is simply to develop a function that does a reasonably good job of distributing our elements in the table such that we avoid collisions. A reasonably good hashing function will still result in constant time access (O(1)) to our data set.

There are a variety of approaches to developing a hashing function for a particular data set. The method that we used in our example in the previous section is called *extraction*. Extraction involves using only a part of the element's value or key to compute the location at which to store the element. In our previous example, we simply extracted the first letter of a string and computed its value relative to the letter A.

Other examples of extraction would be to store phone numbers according to the last four digits, or to store information about cars according to the first three characters of the license plate.

The Division Method

Creating a hashing function by *division* simply means we will use the remainder of the key divided by some positive integer p as the index for the given element. This function could be defined as follows:

```
Hashcode(key) = Math.abs(key)%p
```

This function will yield a result in the range from 0 to p−1. If we use our table size as p, we then have an index that maps directly to a location in the table.

Using a prime number p as the table size and the divisor helps provide a better distribution of keys to locations in the table.

For example, if our key value is 79 and our table size is 43, the division method would result in an index value of 36. The division method is very effective when dealing with an unknown set of key values.

The Folding Method

In the *folding method*, the key is divided into parts that are then combined or folded together to create an index into the table. This is done by first dividing the key into parts where each of the parts of the key will be the same length as the desired index, except possibly the last one. In the *shift folding method*, these parts are then added together to create the index. For example, if our key is the Social Security number 987-65-4321, we might divide this into three parts, 987, 654, and 321. Adding these together yields 1962. Assuming we are looking for a three-digit key, at this point we could use either division or extraction to get our index.

> **KEY CONCEPT**
>
> In the shift folding method, the parts of the key are added together to create the index.

A second possibility is *boundary folding*. There are a number of variations on this approach. However, generally, they involve reversing some of the parts of the key before adding. One variation on this approach is to imagine that the parts of the key are written side by side on a piece of paper and that the piece of paper is folded along the boundaries of the parts of the key. In this way, if we begin with the same key, 987-65-4321, we first divide it into parts, 987, 654, and 321. We then reverse every other part of the key, yielding 987, 456, and 321. Adding these together yields 1764 and once again we can proceed with either extraction or division to get our index. Other variations on folding use different algorithms to determine which parts of the key to reverse.

Folding may also be a useful method for building a hashing function for a key that is a string. One approach to this is to divide the string into substrings the same length (in bytes) as the desired index and then combine these strings using an exclusive-or function. This is also a useful way to convert a string to a number so that other methods, such as division, may be applied to strings.

The Mid-square Method

In the *mid-square method*, the key is multiplied by itself and then the extraction method is used to extract the appropriate number of digits from the middle of the squared result to serve as an index. The same "middle" digits must be chosen each time, to provide consistency. For example, if our key is 4321, we would multiply the key by itself, yielding 18671041. Assuming that we need a three-digit key, we might extract 671 or 710, depending upon how we construct our algorithm. It is also possible to extract bits instead of digits and then construct the index from the extracted bits.

The mid-square method may also be effectively used with strings by manipulating the binary representations of the characters in the string.

The Radix Transformation Method

In the *radix transformation method*, the key is transformed into another numeric base. For example, if our key is 23 in base 10, we might convert it to 32 in base 7. We then use the division method and divide the converted key by the table size and use the remainder as our index. Continuing our previous example, if our table size is 17, we would compute the function:

```
Hashcode(23) = Math.abs(32)%17
             = 15
```

The Digit Analysis Method

In the *digit analysis method*, the index is formed by extracting, and then manipulating, specific digits from the key. For example, if our key is 1234567, we might select the digits in positions 2 through 4, yielding 234, and then manipulate them to form our index. This manipulation can take many forms, including simply reversing the digits (yielding 432), performing a circular shift to the right (yielding 423), performing a circular shift to the left (yielding 342), swapping each pair of digits (yielding 324), or any number of other possibilities, including the methods we have already discussed. The goal is simply to provide a function that does a reasonable job of distributing keys to locations in the table.

The Length-Dependent Method

In the *length-dependent method*, the key and the length of the key are combined in some way to form either the index itself or an intermediate value that is then used

with one of our other methods to form the index. For example, if our key is 8765, we might multiply the first two digits by the length and then divide by the last digit, yielding 69. If our table size is 43, we would then use the division method, resulting in an index of 26.

The length-dependent method may also be effectively used with strings by manipulating the binary representations of the characters in the string.

Hashing Functions in the Java Language

The `java.lang.Object` class defines a method called `hashcode` that returns an integer based on the memory location of the object. This is generally not very useful. Classes that are derived from `Object` often override the inherited definition of `hashcode` to provide their own version. For example, the `String` and `Integer` classes define their own `hashcode` methods. These more specific `hashcode` functions can be very effective for hashing. By having the `hashcode` method defined in the `Object` class, all Java objects can be hashed. However, it is also possible, and often preferable, to define your own `hashcode` method for any class that you intend to store in a hash table.

> **KEY CONCEPT**
>
> Although Java provides a `hashcode` method for all objects, it is often preferable to define a specific hashing function for any particular class.

20.3 Resolving Collisions

If we are able to develop a perfect hashing function for a particular data set, then we do not need to concern ourselves with collisions, the situation where more than one element or key map to the same location in the table. However, when a perfect hashing function is not possible or practical, there are a number of ways to handle collisions. Similarly, if we are able to develop a perfect hashing function for a particular data set, then we do not need to concern ourselves with the size of the table. In this case, we will simply make the table the exact size of the data set. Otherwise, if the size of the data set is known, it is generally a good idea to set the initial size of the table to about 150 percent of the expected element count. If the size of the data set is not known, then dynamic resizing of the table becomes an issue.

Chaining

The *chaining method* for handling collisions simply treats the hash table conceptually as a table of collections rather than as a table of individual cells. Thus, each cell is a pointer to the collection associated with that location in the table. Usually this internal collection is either an unordered list or an ordered list. Figure 20.2 on the next page illustrates this conceptual approach.

> **KEY CONCEPT**
>
> The chaining method for handling collisions simply treats the hash table conceptually as a table of collections rather than as a table of individual cells.

Chaining can be implemented in a variety of ways. One approach would be to make the array holding the table larger than the number of cells in the table and use the extra space as an overflow area to store the linked lists associated with each table location. In this method, each position in the array could store both an element (or a key) and the array index of the next element in its list. The first element mapped to a particular location in the table would actually be

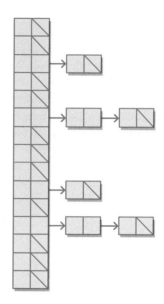

FIGURE 20.2 The chaining method of collision handling

stored in that location. The next element mapped to that location would be stored in a free location in this overflow area, and the array index of this second element would be stored with the first element in the table. If a third element is mapped to the same location, the third element would also be stored in this overflow area and the index of third element would be stored with the second element. Figure 20.3 illustrates this strategy.

Note that, using this method, the table itself can never be full. However, if the table is implemented as an array, the array can become full, requiring a decision on whether to throw an exception or simply expand capacity. In our earlier collections, we chose to expand the capacity of the array. In this case, expanding the capacity of the array but leaving the embedded table the original size would have disastrous effects on efficiency. A more complete solution is to expand the array and expand the embedded table within the array. This will, however, require that all of the elements in the table be rehashed using the new table size. We will discuss the dynamic resizing of hash tables further in Section 20.5.

Using this method, the worst case is that our hashing function will not do a good job of distributing elements to locations in the table so that we end up with one linked list of n elements, or a small number of linked lists with roughly n/k elements each, where k is some relatively small constant. In this case, hash tables become O(n) for both insertions and searches. Thus you can see how important it is to develop a good hashing function.

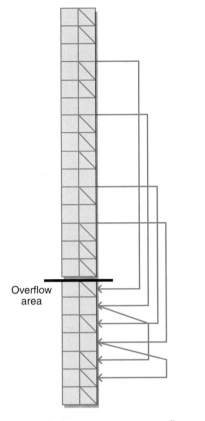

FIGURE 20.3 Chaining using an overflow area

A second method for implementing chaining is to use links. In this method, each cell or bucket in the hash table would be something like the LinearNode class used in earlier chapters to construct linked lists. In this way, as a second element is mapped to a particular bucket, we simply create a new LinearNode, set the next reference of the existing node to point to the new node, set the element reference of the new node to the element being inserted, and set the next reference of the new node to null. The result is an implementation model that looks exactly like the conceptual model shown in Figure 20.2.

A third method for implementing chaining is to literally make each position in the table a pointer to a collection. In this way, we could represent each position in the table with a list or perhaps even a more efficient collection (e.g., a balanced binary search tree) and this would improve our worst case. Keep in mind, however, that if our hashing function is doing a good job of distributing elements to locations in the table, this approach may incur a great deal of overhead while accomplishing very little improvement.

Open Addressing

KEY CONCEPT

The open addressing method for handling collisions looks for another open position in the table other than the one to which the element is originally hashed.

The *open addressing method* for handling collisions looks for another open position in the table other than the one to which the element is originally hashed. There are a variety of methods to find another available location in the table. We will examine three of these methods: linear probing, quadratic probing, and double hashing.

The simplest of these methods is *linear probing*. In linear probing, if an element hashes to position p and position p is already occupied, we simply try position (p + 1)%s, where s is the size of the table. If position (p + 1)%s is already occupied, we try position (p + 2)%s, and so on until either we find an open position or we find ourselves back at the original position. If we find an open position, we insert the new element. If we do not find an open position, we make a design decision when creating a hash table. As we have discussed previously, one possibility is to throw an exception if the table is full. A second possibility is to expand the capacity of the table and rehash the existing entries.

The problem with linear probing is that it tends to create clusters of filled positions within the table, and these clusters then affect the performance of insertions and searches. Figure 20.4 illustrates the linear probing method and the creation of a cluster using our earlier hashing function of extracting the first character of the string.

In this example, Ann was entered, followed by Andrew. Since Ann already occupied position 0 of the array, Andrew was placed in position 1. Later, Bob was entered. Since Andrew already occupied position 1, Bob was placed in the next open position, which was position 2. Doug and Elizabeth were already in the table by the time Betty arrived, thus Betty could not be placed in position 1, 2, 3, or 4 and was placed in the next open position, position 5. After Barbara, Hal, and Bill were added, we find that there is now a nine-location cluster at the front of the table, which will continue to grow as more names are added. Thus we see that linear probing may not be the best approach.

A second form of the open addressing method is *quadratic probing*. Using quadratic probing, instead of using a linear approach, once we have a collision, we follow a formula such as

```
newhashcode(x) = hashcode(x) + (-1)^(i-1)((i+1)/2)²
```

for i in the range 1 to s-1 where s is the table size.

The result of this formula is the search sequence p, p + 1, p − 1, p + 4, p − 4, p + 9, p − 9, ... Of course, this new hash code is then put through the division method to keep it within the table range. As with linear probing, the same possibility exists that we will eventually get back to the original hash code without having found an open position in which to insert. This "full" condition can be

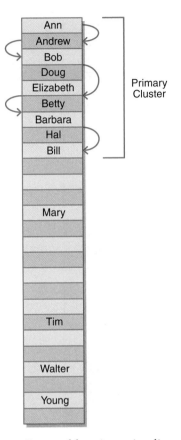

FIGURE 20.4 Open addressing using linear probing

handled in all of the same ways that we described for chaining and linear probing. The benefit of the quadratic probing method is that it does not have as strong a tendency toward clustering as does linear probing. On the next page, Figure 20.5 illustrates quadratic probing for the same key set and hashing function that we used in Figure 20.4. Notice that after the same data has been entered, we still have a cluster at the front of the table. However, this cluster occupies only six buckets instead of the nine-bucket cluster created by linear probing.

A third form of the open addressing method is *double hashing*. Using the double hashing method, we will resolve collisions by providing a secondary hashing function to be used when the primary hashing function results in a collision. For example, if a key x hashes to a position p that is already occupied, then the next position p′ that we will try will be

```
p′ = p + secondaryhashcode(x)
```

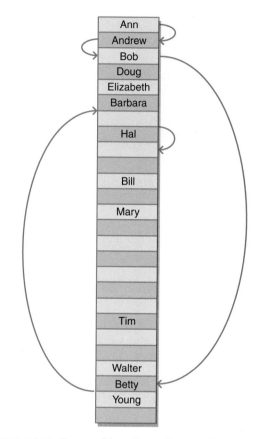

FIGURE 20.5 Open addressing using quadratic probing

If this new position is also occupied, then we look to position

```
p" = p + 2 * secondaryhashcode(x)
```

We continue searching this way, of course using the division method to maintain our index within the bounds of the table, until an open position is found. This method, while somewhat more costly because of the introduction of an additional function, tends to further reduce clustering beyond the improvement gained by quadratic probing. Figure 20.6 illustrates this approach, again using the same key set and hashing function from our previous examples. For this example, the secondary hashing function is the length of the string. Notice that with the same data, we no longer have a cluster at the front of the table. However, we have developed a six-bucket cluster from Doug through Barbara. The advantage of double hashing, however, is that even after a cluster has been created, it will tend to grow more slowly than it would if we were using linear probing or even quadratic probing.

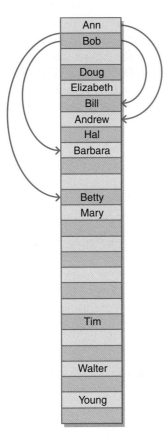

FIGURE 20.6 Open addressing using double hashing

20.4 Deleting Elements from A Hash Table

Thus far, our discussion has centered on the efficiency of insertion of and searching for elements in a hash table. What happens if we remove an element from a hash table? The answer to this question depends upon which implementation we have chosen.

Deleting from a Chained Implementation

If we have chosen to implement our hash table using a chained implementation and an array with an overflow area, then removing an element falls into one of five cases:

Case 1 The element we are attempting to remove is the only one mapped to the particular location in the table. In this case, we simply remove the element by setting the table position to null.

Case 2 The element we are attempting to remove is stored in the table (not in the overflow area) but has an index into the overflow area for the next element at the same position. In this case, we replace the element and the next index value in the table with the element and next index value of the array position pointed to by the element to be removed. We then also must set the position in the overflow area to null and add it back to whatever mechanism we are using to maintain a list of free positions.

Case 3 The element we are attempting to remove is at the end of the list of elements stored at that location in the table. In this case, we set its position in the overflow area to null, and set the next index value of the previous element in the list to null as well. We then also must set the position in the overflow area to null and add it back to whatever mechanism we are using to maintain a list of free positions.

Case 4 The element we are attempting to remove is in the middle of the list of elements stored at that location in the table. In this case, we set its position in the overflow area to null, and set the next index value of the previous element in the list to the next index value of the element being removed. We then also must add it back to whatever mechanism we are using to maintain a list of free positions.

Case 5 The element we are attempting to remove is not in the list. In this case, we throw an `ElementNotFoundException`.

If we have chosen to implement our hash table using a chained implementation where each element in the table is a collection, then we simply remove the target element from the collection.

Deleting from an Open Addressing Implementation

If we have chosen to implement our hash table using an open addressing implementation, then deletion creates more of a challenge. Consider the example in Figure 20.7. Notice that elements "Ann," "Andrew," and "Amy" all mapped to the same location in the table and the collision was resolved using linear probing. What happens if we now remove "Andrew"? If we then search for "Amy" we will not find that element because the search will find "Ann" and then follow the linear probing rule to look in the next position, find it null, and return an exception.

The solution to this problem is to mark items as deleted but not actually remove them from the table until some future point when the deleted element is overwritten by a new inserted element or the entire table is rehashed, either because it is being expanded or because we have reached some predetermined threshold for the percentage of deleted records in the table. This means that we will need to add a `boolean` flag to each node in the table and modify all of our algorithms to test and/or manipulate that flag.

FIGURE 20.7 Open addressing and deletion

20.5 Hash Tables in the Java Collections API

The Java Collections API provides seven implementations of hashing: `Hashtable`, `HashMap`, `HashSet`, `IdentityHashMap`, `LinkedHashSet`, `LinkedHashMap`, and `WeakHashMap`. To understand these different solutions we must first remind ourselves of the distinction between a *set* and a *map* in the Java Collections API as well as some of our other pertinent definitions.

> **KEY CONCEPT**
>
> The load factor is the maximum percentage occupancy allowed in the hash table before it is resized.

A *set* is a collection of objects where in order to find an object, we must have an exact copy of the object for which we are looking. A *map*, on the other hand, is a collection that stores key-value pairs so that, given the key, we can find the associated value.

Another definition that will be useful to us as we explore the Java Collections API implementations of hashing is that of a *load factor*. The load factor, as stated earlier, is the maximum percentage occupancy allowed in the hash table before it is resized. For the implementations that we are going to discuss here, the default is 0.75. Thus, using this default, when one of these implementations becomes 75% full, a new hash table is created that is twice the size of the current one, and then all of the elements from the current table are inserted into the new table. The load factor of these implementations can be altered when the table is created.

All of these implementations rely on the `hashcode` method of the object being stored to return an integer. This integer is then processed using the division method (using the table size) to produce an index within the bounds of the table. As stated earlier, the best practice is to define your own `hashcode` method for any class that you intend to store in a hash table.

Let's look at each of these implementations.

The Hashtable Class

The `Hashtable` implementation of hashing is the oldest of the implementations in the Java Collections API. In fact, it predates the Collections API and was modified in version 1.2 to implement the `Map` interface so that it would become a part of the Collections API. Unlike the newer Java Collections implementations, `Hashtable` is synchronized. Figure 20.8 shows the operations for the `Hashtable` class.

Creation of a `Hashtable` requires two parameters: initial capacity (with a default of 11) and load factor (with a default of 0.75). Capacity refers to the number of cells or locations in the initial table. Load factor is, as we described earlier, the maximum percentage occupancy allowed in the hash table before it is resized. `Hashtable` uses the chaining method for resolving collisions.

The `Hashtable` class is a legacy class that will be most useful if you are connecting to legacy code or require synchronization. Otherwise, it is preferable to use the `HashMap` class.

The HashSet Class

The `HashSet` class implements the `Set` interface using a hash table. The `HashSet` class, like most of the Java Collections API implementations of hashing, uses chaining to resolve collisions (each table position effectively being a linked list). The `HashSet` implementation does not guarantee the order of the set on iteration and does not guarantee that the order will remain constant over time. This is due to the fact that the iterator simply steps through the table in order. Since the hashing function will somewhat randomly distribute the elements to table positions, order cannot be guaranteed. Further, if the table is expanded, all of the elements are rehashed relative to the new table size, and the order may change.

Return Value	Method	Description
	`Hashtable()`	Constructs a new, empty hash table with a default initial capacity (11) and load factor, which is 0.75.
	`Hashtable(int initialCapacity)`	Constructs a new, empty hash table with the specified initial capacity and default load factor, which is 0.75.
	`Hashtable(int initialCapacity, float loadFactor)`	Constructs a new, empty hash table with the specified initial capacity and the specified load factor.
	`Hashtable (Map t)`	Constructs a new hash table with the same mappings as the given `Map`.
void	`clear()`	Clears this hash table so that it contains no keys.
Object	`clone()`	Creates a shallow copy of this hash table.
boolean	`contains(Object value)`	Tests if some key maps into the specified value in this hash table.
boolean	`containsKey(Object key)`	Tests if the specified object is a key in this hash table.
boolean	`containsValue (Object value)`	Returns true if this hash table maps one or more keys to this value.
Enumeration	`elements()`	Returns an enumeration of the values in this hash table.
Set	`entrySet()`	Returns a `Set` view of the entries contained in this hash table.
boolean	`equals(Object o)`	Compares the specified `Object` with this `Map` for equality, as per the definition in the `Map` interface.
Object	`get(Object key)`	Returns the value to which the specified key is mapped in this hash table.
int	`hashCode()`	Returns the hash code value for this `Map` as per the definition in the `Map` interface.
boolean	`isEmpty()`	Tests if this hash table maps no keys to values.
Enumeration	`keys()`	Returns an enumeration of the keys in this hash table.
Set	`keysSet()`	Returns a `Set` view of the keys contained in this hash table.
Object	`put(Object key Object value)`	Maps the specified key to the specified value in this hash table.
void	`putAll(Map t)`	Copies all of the mappings from the specified `Map` to this hash table. These mappings will replace any mappings that this hash table had for any of the keys currently in the specified `Map`.
protected void	`rehash()`	Increases the capacity of and internally reorganizes this hash table, in order to accommodate and access its entries more efficiently.
Object	`remove(Object key)`	Removes the key (and its corresponding value) from this hash table.
int	`size()`	Returns the number of keys in this hash table.
String	`toString()`	Returns a string representation of this hash table object in the form of a set of entries, enclosed in braces and separated by the ASCII characters comma and space.
Collection	`values()`	Returns a `Collection` view of the values contained in this hash table.

FIGURE 20.8 Operations on the `HashFIGURE` class

Return Value	Method	Description
	HashSet()	Constructs a new, empty set; the backing HashMap instance has the default capacity and load factor, which is 0.75.
	HashSet(Collection c)	Constructs a new set containing the elements in the specified collection.
	HashSet(int initialCapacity)	Constructs a new, empty set; the backing HashMap instance has the specified initial capacity and default load factor, which is 0.75.
	HashSet(int initial Capacity, float loadFactor)	Constructs a new, empty set; the backing HashMap instance has the specified initial capacity and the specified load factor.
boolean	add(Object o)	Adds the specified element to this set if it is not already present.
void	clear()	Removes all of the elements from this set.
Object	clone()	Returns a shallow copy of this HashSet instance: the elements themselves are not cloned.
boolean	contains(Object o)	Returns true if this set contains the specified element.
boolean	isEmpty()	Returns true if this set contains no elements.
iterator()	iterator()	Returns an iterator over the elements in this set.
boolean	remove(Object o)	Removes the given element from this set if it is present.
int	size()	Returns the number of elements in this set (its cardinality).

FIGURE 20.9 Operations on the HashSet class

Like the Hashtable class, the HashSet class also requires two parameters: initial capacity and load factor. The default for the load factor is the same as it is for Hashtable (0.75). The default for initial capacity is currently unspecified (originally it was 101). Figure 20.9 shows the operations for the HashSet class. The HashSet class is not synchronized and permits null values.

The HashMap Class

The HashMap class implements the Map interface using a hash table. The HashMap class also uses a chaining method to resolve collisions. Like the HashSet class, the HashMap class is not synchronized and allows null values. Also like the previous implementations, the default load factor is 0.75. Like the HashSet class, the current default initial capacity is unspecified though it was also originally 101.

Figure 20.10 shows the operations on the HashMap class.

Return Value	Method	Description
	`HashMap()`	Constructs a new, empty map with a default capacity and load factor, which is 0.75.
	`HashMap(int initial Capacity)`	Constructs a new, empty map with the specified initial capacity and default load factor, which is 0.75.
	`HashMap(int initial Capacity, float loadFactor)`	Constructs a new, empty map with the specified initial capacity and the specified load factor.
	`HashMap(Map t)`	Constructs a new map with the same mappings as the given map.
`void`	`clear()`	Removes all mappings from this map.
`Object`	`clone()`	Returns a shallow copy of this `HashMap` instance: the keys and values themselves are not cloned.
`boolean`	`containsKey(Object key)`	Returns true if this map contains a mapping for the specified key.
`boolean`	`containsValue (Object value)`	Returns true if this map maps one or more keys to the specified value.
`set`	`entrySet()`	Returns a collection view of the mappings contained in this map.
`Object`	`get(Object key)`	Returns the value to which this map maps the specified key.
`boolean`	`isEmpty()`	Returns true if this map contains no key-value mappings.
`Set`	`keySet()`	Returns a set view of the keys contained in this map.
`Object`	`put(Object key, Object value)`	Associates the specified value with the specified key in this map.
`void`	`putAll(Map t)`	Copies all of the mappings from the specified map to this one.
`Object`	`remove(Object key)`	Removes the mapping for this key from this map if present.
`int`	`size()`	Returns the number of key-value mappings in this map.
`Collection`	`values()`	Returns a collection view of the values contained in this map.

FIGURE 20.10 Operations on the `HashMap` class

The IdentityHashMap Class

The `IdentityHashMap` class implements the `Map` interface using a hash table. The difference between this and the `HashMap` class is that the `IdentityHashMap` class uses reference-equality instead of object-equality when comparing both keys and values. This is the difference between using `key1==key2` and using `key1.equals(key2)`.

This class has one parameter: expected maximum size. This is the maximum number of key-value pairs that the table is expected to hold. If the table exceeds this maximum, then the table size will be increased and the table entries rehashed.

Figure 20.11 shows the operations on the `IdentityHashMap` class.

Return Value	Method	Description
	`IdentityHashMap()`	Constructs a new, empty identity hash map with a default expected maximum size (21).
	`IdentityHashMap(int expectedMaxSize)`	Constructs a new, empty map with the specified expected maximum size.
	`IdentityHashMap(Map m)`	Constructs a new identity hash map containing the key-value mappings in the specified map.
void	`clear()`	Removes all mappings from this map.
Object	`clone()`	Returns a shallow copy of this identity hash map: the keys and values themselves are not cloned.
boolean	`containsKey(Object key)`	Tests whether the specified object reference is a key in this identity hash map.
boolean	`containsValue (Object value)`	Tests whether the specified object reference is a value in this identity hash map.
Set	`entrySet()`	Returns a set view of the mappings contained in this map.
boolean	`equals(Object o)`	Compares the specified object with this map for equality.
Object	`get(Object key)`	Returns the value to which the specified key is mapped in this identity hash map, or null if the map contains no mapping for this key.
int	`hashCode()`	Returns the hash code value for this map.
boolean	`isEmpty()`	Returns true if this identity hash map contains no key-value mappings.
Set	`keySet()`	Returns an identity-based set view of the keys contained in this map.
Object	`put(Object key, Object value)`	Associates the specified value with the specified key in this identity hash map.
void	`putAll(Map t)`	Copies all of the mappings from the specified map to this map. These mappings will replace any mappings that this map had for any of the keys currently in the specified map.
Object	`remove(Object key)`	Removes the mapping for this key from this map if present.
int	`size()`	Returns the number of key-value mappings in this identity hash map.
Collection	`values()`	Returns a collection view of the values contained in this map.

FIGURE 20.11 Operations on the `IdentityHashMap` class

The WeakHashMap Class

The `WeakHashMap` class implements the `Map` interface using a hash table. This class is specifically designed with weak keys so that an entry in a `WeakHashMap` will automatically be removed when its key is no longer in use. In other words, if the use of the key in a mapping in the `WeakHashMap` is the only remaining use of the key, the garbage collector will collect it anyway.

The `WeakHashMap` class allows both null values and null keys, and has the same tuning parameters as the `HashMap` class: initial capacity and load factor.

Figure 20.12 shows the operations on the `WeakHashMap` class.

Return Value	Method	Description
	`WeakHashMap()`	Constructs a new, empty `WeakHashMap` with the default initial capacity and the default load factor, which is 0.75.
	`WeakHashMap(int initialCapacity)`	Constructs a new, empty `WeakHashMap` with the given initial capacity and the default load factor, which is 0.75.
	`WeakHashMap(int initial Capacity, float loadFactor)`	Constructs a new, empty `WeakHashMap` with the given initial capacity and the given load factor.
	`WeakHashMap(Map t)`	Constructs a new `WeakHashMap` with the same mappings as the specified map.
`void`	`clear()`	Removes all mappings from this map.
`boolean`	`containsKey(Object key)`	Returns true if this map contains a mapping for the specified key.
`Set`	`entrySet()`	Returns a set view of the mappings in this map.
`Object`	`get(Object key)`	Returns the value to which this map maps the specified key.
`boolean`	`isEmpty()`	Returns true if this map contains no key-value mappings.
`Set`	`keySet()`	Returns a set view of the keys contained in this map.
`Object`	`put(Object key, Object value)`	Associates the specified value with the specified key in this map.
`void`	`putAll(Map t)`	Copies all of the mappings from the specified map to this map. These mappings will replace any mappings that this map had for any of the keys currently in the specified map.
`Object`	`remove(Object key)`	Removes the mapping for the given key from this map, if present.
`int`	`size()`	Returns the number of key-value mappings in this map.
`Collection`	`values()`	Returns a collection view of the values contained in this map.

FIGURE 20.12 Operations on the `WeakHashMap` class

LinkedHashSet and LinkedHashMap

The two remaining hashing implementations are extensions of previous classes. The LinkedHashSet class extends the HashSet class, and the LinkedHashMap class extends the HashMap class. Both of them are designed to solve the problem of iterator order. These implementations maintain a doubly linked list running through the entries to maintain the insertion order of the elements. Thus, the iterator order for these implementations is the order in which the elements were inserted.

Figure 20.13 shows the additional operations for the LinkedHashSet class. Figure 20.14 shows the additional operations for the LinkedHashMap class.

Return Value	Method	Description
	LinkedHashSet()	Constructs a new, empty linked hash set with the default initial capacity (16) and load factor (0.75).
	LinkedHashSet (Collection c)	Constructs a new linked hash set with the same elements as the specified collection.
	LinkedHashSet (int initialCapacity)	Constructs a new, empty linked hash set with the specified initial capacity and the default load factor (0.75).
	LinkedHashSet(int initialCapacity, float loadFactor)	Constructs a new, empty linked hash set with the specified initial capacity and load factor.

FIGURE 20.13 Additional operations on the LinkedHashSet class

Return Value	Method	Description
	`LinkedHashMap()`	Constructs an empty insertion-ordered `LinkedHashMap` instance with a default capacity (16) and load factor (0.75).
	`LinkedHashMap (int initialCapacity)`	Constructs an empty insertion-ordered `LinkedHashMap` instance with the specified initial capacity and a default load factor (0.75).
	`LinkedHashMap (int initialCapacity, float loadFactor)`	Constructs an empty insertion-ordered `LinkedHashMap` instance with the specified initial capacity and load factor.
	`LinkedHashMap (int initialCapacity, float loadFactor, boolean accessOrder)`	Constructs an empty `LinkedHashMap` instance with the specified initial capacity, load factor, and ordering mode.
	`LinkedHashMap(Map m)`	Constructs an insertion-ordered `LinkedHashMap` instance with the same mappings as the specified map.
`void`	`clear()`	Removes all mappings from this map.
`boolean`	`containsValue (Object value)`	Returns true if this map maps one or more keys to the specified value.
`Object`	`get(Object key)`	Returns the value to which this map maps the specified key.
`protected boolean`	`removeEldestEntry (Map.Entry eldest)`	Returns true if this map should remove its eldest entry.

FIGURE 20.14 Additional operations on the `LinkedHashMap` class

Summary of Key Concepts

- In hashing, elements are stored in a hash table, with their location in the table determined by a hashing function.

- The situation where two elements or keys map to the same location in the table is called a collision.

- A hashing function that maps each element to a unique position in the table is said to be a perfect hashing function.

- Extraction involves using only a part of the element's value or key to compute the location at which to store the element.

- The division method is very effective when dealing with an unknown set of key values.

- In the shift folding method, the parts of the key are added together to create the index.

- The length-dependent method and the mid-square method may also be effectively used with strings by manipulating the binary representations of the characters in the string.

- Although Java provides a `hashcode` method for all objects, it is often preferable to define a specific hashing function for any particular class.

- The chaining method for handling collisions simply treats the hash table conceptually as a table of collections rather than as a table of individual cells.

- The open addressing method for handling collisions looks for another open position in the table other than the one to which the element is originally hashed.

- The load factor is the maximum percentage occupancy allowed in the hash table before it is resized.

Self-Review Questions

SR 20.1   What is the difference between a hash table and the other collections we have discussed?

SR 20.2   What is a collision in a hash table?

SR 20.3   What is a perfect hashing function?

SR 20.4   What is our goal for a hashing function?

SR 20.5   What is the consequence of not having a good hashing function?

SR 20.6   What is the extraction method?

SR 20.7   What is the division method?

SR 20.8   What is the shift folding method?

SR 20.9   What is the boundary folding method?

SR 20.10   What is the mid-square method?

SR 20.11   What is the radix transformation method?

SR 20.12   What is the digit analysis method?

SR 20.13   What is the length-dependent method?

SR 20.14   What is chaining?

SR 20.15   What is open addressing?

SR 20.16   What are linear probing, quadratic probing, and double hashing?

SR 20.17   Why is deletion from an open addressing implementation a problem?

SR 20.18   What is the load factor and how does it affect table size?

Exercises

EX 20.1   Draw the hash table that results from adding the following integers (34 45 3 87 65 32 1 12 17) to a hash table of size 11 using the division method and linked chaining.

EX 20.2   Draw the hash table from Exercise 20.1 using a hash table of size 11 using array chaining with a total array size of 20.

EX 20.3   Draw the hash table from Exercise 20.1 using a table size of 17 and open addressing using linear probing.

EX 20.4   Draw the hash table from Exercise 20.1 using a table size of 17 and open addressing using quadratic probing.

EX 20.5   Draw the hash table from Exercise 20.1 using a table size of 17 and double hashing using extraction of the first digit as the secondary hashing function.

EX 20.6   Draw the hash table that results from adding the following integers (1983, 2312, 6543, 2134, 3498, 7654, 1234, 5678, 6789) to a hash table using shift folding of the first two digits with the last two digits. Use a table size of 13.

EX 20.7   Draw the hash table from Exercise 20.6 using boundary folding.

EX 20.8   Draw a UML diagram that shows how all of the various implementations of hashing within the Java Collections API are constructed.

Programming Projects

PP 20.1	Implement the hash table illustrated in Figure 20.1 using the array version of chaining.
PP 20.2	Implement the hash table illustrated in Figure 20.1 using the linked version of chaining.
PP 20.3	Implement the hash table illustrated in Figure 20.1 using open addressing with linear probing.
PP 20.4	Implement a dynamically resizable hash table to store people's names and Social Security numbers. Use the extraction method with division using the last four digits of the Social Security number. Use an initial table size of 31 and a load factor of 0.80. Use open addressing with double hashing using an extraction method on the first three digits of the Social Security number.
PP 20.5	Implement the problem from Programming Project 20.4 using linked chaining.
PP 20.6	Implement the problem from Programming Project 20.4 using the `HashMap` class of the Java Collections API.
PP 20.7	Create a new implementation of the bag collection called `HashtableBag` using a hash table.
PP 20.8	Implement the problem from Programming Project 20.4 using shift folding with the Social Security number divided into three equal three-digit parts.
PP 20.9	Create a graphical system that will allow a user to add and remove employees where each employee has an employee id (six-digit number), employee name, and years of service. Use the `hashcode` method of the `Integer` class as your hashing function and use one of the Java Collections API implementations of hashing.
PP 20.10	Complete Programming Project 20.9 using your own `hashcode` function. Use extraction of the first three digits of the employee id as the hashing function and use one of the Java Collections API implementations of hashing.
PP 20.11	Complete Programming Project 20.9 using your own `hashcode` function and your own implementation of a hash table.
PP 20.12	Create a system that will allow a user to add and remove vehicles from an inventory system. Vehicles will be represented by license number (an eight-character string), make, model, and color. Use your own array-based implementation of a hash table using chaining.

PP 20.13   Complete Programming Project 20.12 using a linked implementation with open addressing and double hashing.

Answers to Self-Review Questions

SRA 20.1   Elements are placed into a hash table at an index produced by a function of the value of the element or a key of the element. This is unique from other collections where the position/location of an element in the collection is determined either by comparison with the other values in the collection or by the order in which the elements were added or removed from the collection.

SRA 20.2   The situation where two elements or keys map to the same location in the table is called a collision.

SRA 20.3   A hashing function that maps each element to a unique position in the table is said to be a perfect hashing function.

SRA 20.4   We need a hashing function that will do a good job of distributing elements into positions in the table.

SRA 20.5   If we do not have a good hashing function, the result will be too many elements mapped to the same location in the table. This will result in poor performance.

SRA 20.6   Extraction involves using only a part of the element's value or key to compute the location at which to store the element.

SRA 20.7   The division method involves dividing the key by some positive integer p (usually the table size and usually prime) and then using the remainder as the index.

SRA 20.8   Shift folding involves dividing the key into parts (usually the same length as the desired index) and then adding the parts. Extraction or division is then used to get an index within the bounds of the table.

SRA 20.9   Like shift folding, boundary folding involves dividing the key into parts (usually the same length as the desired index). However, some of the parts are then reversed before adding. One example is to imagine that the parts are written side by side on a piece of paper, which is then folded on the boundaries between parts. In this way, every other part is reversed.

SRA 20.10   The mid-square method involves multiplying the key by itself and then extracting some number of digits or bytes from the middle of the result. Division can then be used to guarantee an index within the bounds of the table.

SRA 20.11 The radix transformation method is a variation on the division method where the key is first converted to another numeric base and then divided by the table size with the remainder used as the index.

SRA 20.12 In the digit analysis method, the index is formed by extracting, and then manipulating, specific digits from the key.

SRA 20.13 In the length-dependent method, the key and the length of the key are combined in some way to form either the index itself or an intermediate value that is then used with one of our other methods to form the index.

SRA 20.14 The chaining method for handling collisions simply treats the hash table conceptually as a table of collections rather than as a table of individual cells. Thus each cell is a pointer to the collection associated with that location in the table. Usually this internal collection is either an unordered list or an ordered list.

SRA 20.15 The open addressing method for handling collisions looks for another open position in the table other than the one to which the element is originally hashed.

SRA 20.16 Linear probing, quadratic probing, and double hashing are methods for determining the next table position to try if the original hash causes a collision.

SRA 20.17 Because of the way that a path is formed in open addressing, deleting an element from the middle of that path can cause elements beyond that on the path to be unreachable.

SRA 20.18 The load factor is the maximum percentage occupancy allowed in the hash table before it is resized. Once the load factor has been reached, a new table is created that is twice the size of the current table, and then all of the elements in the current table are inserted into the new table.

Databases

CHAPTER OBJECTIVES

- Understand the basic concept of a database as it relates to data storage.

- Explain the concepts behind of relational databases.

- Introduce how Java programs can connect to databases for the purposes of creating, reading, updating and deleting data.

- Briefly introduce the syntax of several different types of SQL statements.

This chapter provides an introduction to databases and interacting with databases using Java. A database is a large repository of data organized for efficient storage and searching. Discussing databases and the way we interact with them through a Java program is a natural extension of the concept of collections that have been a major theme throughout this book.

717

21.1 Introduction to Databases

A *database* is a potentially large repository of data, organized so that the data can be quickly stored, searched, and organized in various ways. A *database management system* is software that provides the ability to quickly search or query the data contained within the database and generally have four primary operations on the data: create, read, update, and delete (also known as CRUD). Applications such as a university's class scheduling system or an airline reservation system will use a database to organize and manage their large amounts of data.

> **KEY CONCEPT**
>
> Databases are software applications used to provide data to other programs.

There are many different types of databases that are available, each with their own strengths and weaknesses. For example, there are object-oriented databases, flat-file databases, relational databases, and so on. While a larger discussion of the various types of databases is outside the scope of this textbook, we will focus on the most commonly used type of database in existence today—a relational database. A relational database organizes its basic information into one or more *tables*. And perhaps more importantly, the relationships between various data elements are also stored in tables.

A simple example of a relational database (or a database which uses the relational model) can be expressed in the following two tables, Person and Location. Let's look at each more closely. The Person table contains a series of rows, which are called records. Each record in the table contains the information about one person in our database. Each person's record provides a number of fields, including his or her first name, last name and two integer values: `personID` and `locationID`. The `personID` is a unique integer value (that is, unique within the Person table) and is used to identify a particular record. For example, Peter's `personalID` is 1. John's `personalID` is 2. Each record also contains a `locationID`. This value is used to find (or "look up") a particular matching record in the `Location` table, hence the name `locationID` that contains the table name as part of the field name.

Person				Location		
personID	firstName	LastName	locationID	locationID	city	state
0	Matthew	Williamson	0	0	Portsmouth	RI
1	Peter	DePasquale	0	1	Blacksburg	VA
2	John	Lewis	1	2	Maple Glen	PA
3	Jason	Smithson	2	3	San Jose	CA

Thus, by using the `locationID` value in Peter's record in the Person table, and finding that value in the Location table, we can determine that Peter lives in Portsmouth, RI. Matthew Williamson lives there as well. So what do these tables really get us? There are several answers to that question. First of all, we pointed out both Matt and Peter live in the same town in the same state. If we didn't have a `Location` table in use, the city and state strings would likely be a part of the `Person` table. In doing so, we will be using more space in our database to replicate the same values over and over. By using the Location table, we can conserve space by avoiding data replication.

There's another advantage to the use of tables in this manner. We can easily query our database (ask it a question) to determine which people live in Portsmouth, RI. Each record of each person that we have stored in the `Person` table will contain the value 0 in their `locationID` field. There's actually a more complex way of *joining* the tables to determine the answer to our query, but that's really outside the scope of this text.

Our query can be quickly executed because we are using the strength of the relational database model. If we were replicating our data ("Portsmouth", "RI") over and over in several records of the Person table, searching for all residents of Portsmouth will be rather time inefficient and intensive as we'd be searching each record looking for two string values.

> **KEY CONCEPT**
> A relational database creates relationships between records in different tables by using unique identifiers.

Tables in our database are related by the use of the `locationID`. A `locationID` value helps to relate a specific person record in the `Person` table to a specific record in the Location table. Additionally, as you may have noted, each record in the Location table has its own unique identifier (`locationID`). The use of these identifiers and how we utilize them between tables is how we establish the relationships between the records in our tables.

For the purposes of this discussion, we will be using the open source database MySQL (see http://www.mysql.com to obtain a copy). There are other databases available that we could have chosen, including Oracle, SQLServer, Access, and PostgreSQL. Some of these databases are open source and freely available, while others can be purchased for a fee.

> **KEY CONCEPT**
> The JDBC API is used to establish a connection to a database.

Before we can interact with a database in a Java program, we must first establish a connection to it. To do that, we'll use the Java Database Connectivity (JDBC) API. The JDBC API provides us the classes and methods required to manage our data from within the Java program. Fortunately, the JDBC API has been a component of the Java Development Environment (JDK) since JDK 1.1, so we won't have to download any additional software to obtain the API functionality. However, to connect to our database, we will need a database-specific driver, discussed in the next section.

21.2 Establishing a Connection to a Database

In order to establish communications to our database, we'll need a specialized piece of software that communicates our database requests to the database application (known as the server, which generally resides on another machine). This software is known as a *driver*. The response from the database is communicated back to our program via the driver as well.

Obtaining A Database Driver

There are over two hundred JDBC drivers available for various databases. To find one for your system, check Java's JDBC Data Access API web page at: developers.sun.com/product/jdbc/drivers. We'll be using the MySQL connector driver (www.mysql.com/products/connector/) to provide our connection to a database hosted on another computer. We downloaded our connector in jar file form from the MySQL web site and placed in it a directed named "connector."

Once installed, we only need to refer to its location via the CLASSPATH environment variable (during compilation and execution). Depending on your configuration you can save these values in a shell configuration or just provide them on the command line. As we demonstrate the coding steps necessary to create and issue queries, and obtain and process responses from the server, we'll also show you how to include the driver into the CLASSPATH.

In Listing 21.1, we have a simple program that includes the use of several JDBC-specific classes. The code demonstrates the loading of our JDBC driver, attempting to establish a connection to our database server, and closing the connection once we have confirmed the connection was opened.

The program starts by attempting to load our JDBC driver (`com.mysql.jdbc.Driver`) from our downloaded jar file. When our driver is loaded, it will create an instance of itself and register itself with the `DriverManager` (`java.sql.DriverManager`) class.

Next, we attempt to establish a connection to our database through the `DriverManager` class. The `DriverManager` will attempt to select an appropriate driver from among the set of drivers registered with the `DriverManager`. In our case, this will be easy - we're only using one driver for this program, and it is the only possible driver that can be selected. The call to the `getConnection` method of the `DriverManager` accepts a URL that defines our database instance. It is comprised of several components that we must provide, including the hostname (the name of the machine where our database server is residing), the name of the database, and the username and password that will provide us access to the selected database.

LISTING 21.1

```java
import java.sql.*;

//*********************************************************************
//  DatabaseConnector.java        Java Foundations
//
//  Demonstrates the establishment of a JDBC connector.
//*********************************************************************

public class DatabaseConnector
{
    //------------------------------------------------------------------
    //  Establishes the connection to the database and prints an
    //  appropriate confirmation message.
    //------------------------------------------------------------------
    public static void main (String args[])
    {
        try
        {
            Connection conn = null;

            // Loads the class object for the mysql driver into the DriverManager.
            Class.forName("com.mysql.jdbc.Driver");

            // Attempt to establish a connection to the specified database via the
            // DriverManager
            conn = DriverManager.getConnection("jdbc:mysql://comtor.org/"+
                "javafoundations?user=jf2e&password=hirsch");

            if (conn != null)
            {
                System.out.println("We have connected to our database!");
                conn.close();
            }

        } catch (SQLException ex) {
            System.out.println("SQLException: " + ex.getMessage());
            ex.printStackTrace();
        } catch (Exception ex) {
            System.out.println("Exception: " + ex.getMessage());
            ex.printStackTrace();
        }
    }
}
```

If all goes well, and there are no problems (such as the database server is not running, or there is a communications issue between our machine where our Java program is executing and the host on which the database server is executing), we will be returned a Connection (java.sql.Connection) object. This object represents a single connection to our database and will be the conduit for our queries and responses to and from the database. Finally, our program checks to determine if we did in fact receive a non-null Connection object and if so, prints a success message to the user and the closes the connection to the database.

In order to execute a program called Example1, the CLASSPATH will need to reflect the location of the driver. It is not necessary to do so when we compile the Example1 program, since we only need the Driver class from the JDBC jar file at run time when the program attempts to load and register the Driver object. Working on the UNIX command line, after successful compilation, we can execute the program with the following command.

```
$ java -cp .:../connector/mysql-connector-java-5.1.7-bin.jar
Example1
```

Under Windows, the command will be:

```
java -cp .;..\connector\mysql-connector-java-5.1.7-bin.jar
Example1
```

The resulting output is shown below:

```
We have connected to our database!
```

This assumes that the download location of our JDBC jar file is the adjacent connector directory from the current directory. We could have placed our jar file in the same directory that the source code is located in, but we prefer not to mix our source code and jar files, so they are placed in the connector directory.

We'll do more with our database in the next section, including creating and altering tables in our database.

21.3 Creating and Altering Database Tables

In the previous section, we were able to show how to establish a connection to our database, check that the connection was successful, and disconnect. Let's expand on those abilities and create a new database table.

Create Table

The start of the SQL statement to create a database table is CREATE TABLE <tablename>. We will also need to specify the name of the table and any fields that will be present at creation. For example, let's create a new table of students. For now, this table will contain an ID value (known as a key), the students' first and last names. To do so, our creation command will be the following string:

```
CREATE TABLE Student (student_ID INT UNSIGNED NOT NULL
AUTO_INCREMENT, PRIMARY KEY (student_ID), firstName
varchar(255), lastName varchar(255))
```

Each field of the table is specified in the comma-separated list in the parentheses that follow the table name (Student). Our table will initially include the following fields:

- student_ID–an unsigned integer value, which can not be null, and will automatically increment each time we add a new student to the table.
- firstName–a variable length character string up to 255 characters in length.
- lastName–a variable length character string up to 255 characters in length.

You may be asking yourself about the PRIMARY KEY field which we skipped mentioning. That's not really a field, but a setting on the table itself that specifies which field(s) make the record unique among the other records. Since each student will have a unique identifier, the student_ID field will be sufficient to be our table's key. Again, this is a database topic that you really need to study in the database course, so we will leave it at that for now.

To create the table in our existing code from Listing 1, we'll add the following lines immediately after the successful connection message.

```
Statement stmt = conn.createStatement();
boolean result = stmt.execute("CREATE TABLE Student " +
  " (student_ID INT UNSIGNED NOT NULL AUTO_INCREMENT, " +
  " PRIMARY KEY (student_ID), firstName varchar(255), " +
  " lastName varchar(255))");
System.out.print("\tTable creation result: " + result + "\t");
System.out.println("(false is the expected result)");
```

The Statement class (java.sql.Statement) is an interface class, which we will use to prepare and execute our SQL statement(s). We can ask our Connection object to create our Statement object for us. Once we have our Statement object, we can call its execute method and pass it the SQL query string (our CREATE TABLE string) for execution by the database. The execute method returns a TRUE value if there is a ResultSet object (we'll talk about this shortly) returned after the call, or a false otherwise.

When we execute our code, we anticipate that we will be returned a FALSE value and the table will be created. In fact, that is what happens (see the output below). However, you should take note that if an attempt to execute the same program is again made, the program will throw an exception stating that the table already exists. That's fine for now. We'll discuss removal of tables later in this chapter.

```
We have connected to our database!
   Table creation result: false (false is the expected result)
```

Alter Table

So far, so good! Our new database has a new table called Student. Now let's add a few fields in our new table. Often the structure of a table will be established when it is created and not changed, but from time to time the need to alter an existing table will occur. We could drop (delete) the existing table and create a new one from scratch. But if we do, we'll lose the data currently stored in the table. It's usually preferred to add new fields or remove existing fields (and their data) from an existing table.

> **KEY CONCEPT**
>
> The ALTER TABLE SQL statement can be used to modify an existing database table.

Let's add age and gpa fields for our students. For the age, we can use the smallest unsigned integer field possible (conserving the most amount of space). This is an unsigned tinyint for MySQL (be sure to check the datatype listing for your database)–it will range from 0 to 255, sufficient for an age field. We'll also need an additional column for our gpa field. Here we will use an unsigned float that uses three digits total, and two digits for the fractional part.

In order to modify our table and add the missing fields, we need to create a new Statement object and use the ALTER TABLE <tablename> ADD COLUMN SQL statement. Following the ADD COLUMN portion of the string, we specify our new fields in a parenthetical list, separated by commas. Once the string is constructed, we call the execute method of the Statement object to execute the query. Again here, we expect a FALSE value to be returned–indicating that no result set is returned to us.

```
Statement stmt2 = conn.createStatement();
result = stmt2.execute("ALTER TABLE Student ADD COLUMN " +
   " (age tinyint UNSIGNED, gpa FLOAT (3,2) unsigned)");

System.out.print("\tTable modification result: " + result + "\t");
System.out.println("(false is the expected result)");
```

Our output is not surprising:

```
We have connected to our database!
    Table creation result: false (false is the expected result)
    Table modification result: false (false is the expected result)
```

Drop Column

Of course, we may also wish to alter a table by dropping a column, rather than adding one or more. To do so, we can use the ALTER TABLE Sql statement and follow the table name with the DROP COLUMN command. DROP COLUMN is followed by one or more column names, separated by commas. For example, if we wanted to drop the firstName column of our Student table, we could use the following statements.

```
Statement stmt3 = conn.createStatement();
result = stmt3.execute("ALTER TABLE Student DROP COLUMN firstName");

System.out.print("\tTable modification result: " + result + "\t");
System.out.println("(false is the expected result)");
```

Again, our output is fairly straightforward.

```
We have connected to our database!
    Table creation result: false (false is the expected result)
    Table modification result: false (false is the expected result)
    Table modification result: false (false is the expected result)
```

But how do we know this is really modifying the table? What we really want to be able to do is ask the database to tell us what the structure of our table is at any point in time. We'll discuss that in the next section.

21.4 Querying The Database

At this point, we have a single table in our database with no data. One of the activities we would like to do at this point is to query the database regarding the structure of our table. To do this, we will build another Statement and send it to the database server for processing. However, the difference here compared to our earlier examples is that we expect to be returned a ResultSet object–an object that manages a set of records that contain our result.

Obtaining a ResultSet is an important piece of the knowledge we will need to master in order to obtain information from our database. A ResultSet functions in much the same way a Scanner object does–it provides a method of accessing and traversing through a set of data (in this case, data obtained from our database). A default ResultSet object permits moving through the data from the first to last object in the set, and it cannot be updated. Other variations of the `ResultSet` object can permit bidirectional movement and the ability to be updated.

Show Columns

The simplest example we can provide of a `ResultSet` is of a query that informs us of the structure of our table. In the following sections of this chapter, we will use the `ResultSet` in more complex ways. In the code below we form our query and submit it to the server. Other than the syntax of the `SHOW COLUMNS <tablename>` statement, the remainder of the code is very straightforward and similar to our previous examples. Note that we are expecting a `ResultSet` object to be returned from our execution of the query.

```
Statement stmt5 = conn.createStatement();
ResultSet rSet = stmt5.executeQuery("SHOW COLUMNS FROM Student");
```

Once we have our results returned from the query, we can obtain some information from the `ResultSet`'s `ResultSetMetaData` object (which contains meta information about the results returned). For instance, in the next two lines of code, we use information from the `ResultSetMetaData` object to produce output for the user (including the table name and the number of columns in the result).

```
ResultSetMetaData rsmd = rSet.getMetaData();
int numColumns = rsmd.getColumnCount();
```

Our `ResultSet` is essentially a two dimensional table that contains columns (our fields) and rows of data (records in the result). By utilizing the metadata regarding the number of columns in the `ResultSet`, we can print out some basic information of the structure of our `Student` table.

```
String resultString = null;
if (numColumns > 0)
{
  resultString = "Table: Student\n" +
    "========================================================" +
    "========================================================\n\t";
  for (int colNum = 1; colNum <= numColumns; colNum++)
    resultString += rsmd.getColumnLabel(colNum) + '\t';
}
System.out.println(resultString);
System.out.println(
  "========================================================" +
  "========================================================\n\t");
```

The program will now print out a table of our column headers in the `ResultSet`, which is really a list of property names for each field in our table.

```
We have connected to our database!
  Table creation result: false (false is the expected result)
  Table modification result: false (false is the expected result)
  Table modification result: false (false is the expected result)
Table: Student
========================================================
  Field Type Null Key Default Extra
========================================================
```

Let's get the rows of data as well from the `ResultSet` so that we can see the full structure of our table. We need to add additional statements to our program that will iterate through the `ResultSet` rows and obtain the value of each column as a string.

```
We have connected to our database!
  Table creation result: false (false is the expected result)
  Table modification result: false (false is the expected result)
  Table modification result: false (false is the expected result)
Table: Student
========================================================
Field       Type       Null     Key      Default     Extra
========================================================
student_ID     int(10)   unsigned     NO     PRI     auto_increment
--------------------------------------------------------
lastName     varchar(255)       YES
--------------------------------------------------------
age     tinyint(3)   unsigned     YES
--------------------------------------------------------
gpa     float(3,2)   unsigned     YES
--------------------------------------------------------
```

It's not very pretty, but we can now see the basic configuration information for each field in our table. Each record from the `ResultSet` contains the field name, the field (data) type, if the field can hold a null value, if the field is part of a key, the default value for the field (if not provided) and any extra information.

Let's turn this printed table into something a little easier to read. With a little more work, we could have attempted to output the table structure in a format like the one shown in the following table. This is left up to you as a string formatting exercise.

Field	Type	Null	Key	Default	Extra
student_ID	int(10) unsigned	NO	PRI	auto_increment	
lastName	varchar(255)	YES			
age	tinyint(3) unsigned	YES			
gpa	float(3, 2) unsigned	YES			

We used our Statement object as the vehicle to obtain information from our database. In this case, the information we sought was the structure of the Student table. However, we can change our Statement string and query the database quite easily.

In terms of outputting the results, we'll do the same iteration through the ResultSet. However, there's one problem. Our Student table does not yet have any data in it. We'll address that problem in the next section, and then show how to query the table.

21.5 Inserting, Viewing, and Updating Data

A table without data is like a day without sunshine. It's time to put some real data into our Student table. Since the studentID field is an auto_increment field (it will automatically increment by 1 each time data is placed into the table), we really only needed to insert data for student lastnames, age and gpa. Let's add the following values into our database.

lastName	age	gpa
Campbell	19	3.79
Garcia	28	2.37
Fuller	19	3.18
Cooper	26	2.13
Walker	27	2.14
Griego	31	2.10

Insert

To insert the data, we need to create a new `Statement` and use the `INSERT <tablename>` SQL statement. The `INSERT` statement takes the following form:

```
INSERT <tablename> (column name, ...) VALUES (expression, ...)
```

Following the `tablename`, one or more columns are specified by name. Then, the value to be placed in each specified field is listed in the same order that the columns are specified. For example, to insert the Campbell row into the database, we will create a SQL statement that looks like the following.

```
INSERT Student (lastName, age, gpa) VALUES ("Campbell", 19, 3.79)
```

We can use the following two lines of source code to perform the insertion on the table.

```
Statement stmt2 = conn.createStatement(ResultSet.TYPE_FORWARD_ONLY,
  ResultSet.CONCUR_UPDATABLE);
int rowCount = stmt2.executeUpdate("INSERT Student " +
  "(lastName, age, gpa) VALUES (\"Campbell\", 19, 3.79)");
```

In order for the update on the table's data values to take place, we need to make two different method calls than we have done previously. First, when we construct the `Statement` object (via the `createStatement` method), we specify that the resulting `ResultSet`'s pointer may only move forward and that changes to the `ResultSet` are passed on to the database.

Second, we called the `executeUpdate` method, rather than the `execute` or `executeQuery` methods used earlier. The `executeUpdate` method returns the number of rows affected by the update query, in this case only 1 row was modified. Similar `executeQuery` statements can follow, permitting us to insert each row of students shown in Table 1. Alternatively, we could read our data from an input file and use a loop to process the data from the input file into the database.

It's been a while since we have seen the full body of code of our program. Along the way we have made a number of additions and changes. Listing 21.2 on the next page updates us of the source code we're using in discussing our database connections.

SELECT . . . FROM

One of the most frequent actions one performs on a database is issuing queries to view to retrieve the data. The SELECT . . . FROM SQL statement permits users to construct a request for data based

LISTING 21.2

```java
//*******************************************************************
//   DatabaseModfication.java        Java Foundations
//
//   Demonstrates interaction between a Java program and a database.
//*******************************************************************

import java.sql.*;

public class DatabaseModification
{
   //----------------------------------------------------------------
   //   Carries out various CRUD operations after establishing the
   //   database connection.
   //----------------------------------------------------------------
   public static void main (String args[])
   {
    Connection conn = null;
    try
    {
       //  Loads the class object for the mysql driver into the DriverManager.
       Class.forName("com.mysql.jdbc.Driver");

       //  Attempt to establish a connection to the specified database via the
       //  DriverManager
       conn = DriverManager.getConnection("jdbc:mysql://comtor.org/" +
         "javafoundations?user=jf2e&password=hirsch");

       //  Check the connection
       if (conn != null)
       {
         System.out.println("We have connected to our database!");

          //  Create the table and show the table structure
          Statement stmt = conn.createStatement();
          boolean result = stmt.execute("CREATE TABLE Student " +
            " (student_ID INT UNSIGNED NOT NULL AUTO_INCREMENT, " +
            " PRIMARY KEY (student_ID), lastName varchar(255), " +
            " age tinyint UNSIGNED, gpa FLOAT (3,2) unsigned)");

          System.out.println("\tTable creation result: " + result);
          DatabaseModification.showColumns(conn);

          // Insert the data into the database and show the values in the table
          Statement stmt2 = conn.createStatement(ResultSet.TYPE_FORWARD_ONLY,
            ResultSet.CONCUR_UPDATABLE);
```

LISTING 21.2   *continued*

```
      int rowCount = stmt2.executeUpdate("INSERT Student " +
        "(lastName, age, gpa) VALUES (\"Campbell\", 19, 3.79)");
      DatabaseModification.showValues(conn);

      // Close the database
      conn.close();
    }

  } catch (SQLException ex) {
    System.out.println("SQLException: " + ex.getMessage());
    ex.printStackTrace();

  } catch (Exception ex) {
    System.out.println("Exception: " + ex.getMessage());
    ex.printStackTrace();
  }
}

  //------------------------------------------------------------------
  // Obtains and displays a ResultSet from the Student table.
  //------------------------------------------------------------------
 public static void showValues(Connection conn)
 {
  try
  {
    Statement stmt = conn.createStatement();
    ResultSet rset = stmt.executeQuery("SELECT * FROM Student");
    DatabaseModification.showResults("Student", rset);
  } catch (SQLException ex) {
    System.out.println("SQLException: " + ex.getMessage());
    ex.printStackTrace();
  }
}

  //------------------------------------------------------------------
  // Displays the structure of the Student table.
  //------------------------------------------------------------------
 public static void showColumns(Connection conn)
 {
  try
  {
    Statement stmt = conn.createStatement();
    ResultSet rset = stmt.executeQuery("SHOW COLUMNS FROM Student");
    DatabaseModification.showResults("Student", rset);
  } catch (SQLException ex) {
```

LISTING 21.2   *continued*

```
      System.out.println("SQLException: " + ex.getMessage());
      ex.printStackTrace();
    }
  }

  //----------------------------------------------------------------
  // Displays the contents of the specified ResultSet.
  //----------------------------------------------------------------
  public static void showResults(String tableName, ResultSet rSet)
  {
   try
   {
     ResultSetMetaData rsmd = rSet.getMetaData();
     int numColumns = rsmd.getColumnCount();
     String resultString = null;
     if (numColumns > 0)
     {
       resultString = "\nTable: " + tableName + "\n" +
         "=====================================================\n";
       for (int colNum = 1; colNum <= numColumns; colNum++)
         resultString += rsmd.getColumnLabel(colNum) + " ";
     }
     System.out.println(resultString);
     System.out.println(
       "=====================================================");

     while (rSet.next())
     {
       resultString = "";
       for (int colNum = 1; colNum <= numColumns; colNum++)
       {
         String column = rSet.getString(colNum);
         if (column != null)
           resultString += column + " ";
       }
       System.out.println(resultString + '\n' +
         "-----------------------------------------------------------");
     }
   } catch (SQLException ex) {
     System.out.println("SQLException: " + ex.getMessage());
     ex.printStackTrace();
   }
  }
}
```

on a number of criteria. The basic syntax of the SELECT ... FROM statement is as follows:

```
SELECT <columns, ...> FROM <tablename> WHERE <condition, ...>
```

The SELECT statement has many parts (most of which are outside the scope of this text), but we will just talk about a few to get you started using the statement.

The SELECT statement allows you to ask for only certain columns to be returned following the query. For example, if we only wanted a listing of student lastNames and gpas from our Student table, we would construct our query as:

```
SELECT lastName, gpa FROM Student
```

If we wanted to make our query even more specific, and only get the lastNames and gpas of students whose age is 21 and over, our statement would look like:

```
SELECT lastName, gpa FROM Student WHERE age >= 21
```

The WHERE condition clause is optional, and if it is not provided, all rows from the specified table will be selected. A condition is an expression that must evaluate to TRUE and can contain functions and operators such as && (and), || (or), and many others. For example, we can further refine our query to limit results to those students 21 and over, and having a gpa of 3.0 or less:

```
SELECT lastName, gpa FROM Student WHERE age >= 21 && gpa <= 3.0
```

The selected items to return (lastName and gpa in our examples above) are specified by listing them with a comma between them. However, if you wish to have all of the columns from a table returned, you can substitute the column listings with an asterisk (*).

```
SELECT * FROM Student WHERE age >= 21 && gpa <= 3.0
```

As we did with our INSERT statement, the SELECT statement will be a parameter to an executeQuery method call. The output from the execution of this statement would look something like the following.

```
Table: Student
=======================================================
student_ID     lastName     age     gpa
=======================================================
2     Jones     22     2.40
-------------------------------------------------------
```

There are a number of other capabilities that the SELECT SQL statement provides, including the ability to join two or more tables, limit our output to a set number of rows, and to group our results by one or more columns. Often, the most useful additional clause is ORDER BY <columnname> <direction>.

The ORDER BY clause, appended to the statement following the where clause will direct the statement to sort our results in an ascending or descending fashion. To specify ascending, place the string ASC in the direction portion, or use DESC for descending. For example, the query

```
SELECT * FROM Student ORDER BY gpa DESC
```

produces the following results.

```
Table: Student
========================================================
lastName     age     gpa
========================================================
Hampton      31      3.88
--------------------------------------------------------
Campbell     19      3.79
--------------------------------------------------------
Smith        21      3.69
--------------------------------------------------------
Jones        22      2.40
--------------------------------------------------------
```

Update

Updating data in a database is another frequently used skill. Fortunately, it is a rather simple process. We can break the process down into three steps. First, we obtain a ResultSet and navigate to the row we wish to update. Second, we update the ResultSet's value that we wish to change. Finally, we update the database with the record from the ResultSet.

> **KEY CONCEPT**
>
> Updates to a database can be performed through changes to a ResultSet.

Let's look at these steps in more detail. We first want to obtain a ResultSet on which we will operate. Depending on the type of change you wish to make to the database (updating one row vs. updating multiple rows) will likely direct the ResultSet you obtain to operate on the data. Generally speaking, it's a good idea to limit your ResultSet to only the database rows you wish to modify. So if you are going to only change one row's values, your ResultSet should really comprise only that row.

Once we have our ResultSet, we need to navigate the ResultSet cursor (a pointer into the set). You may have noted from Listing 21.2, we iterated through the ResultSet by repeatedly calling the next method on the ResultSet object. We can actually navigate via a number of methods (first, last, next, previous, etc.). Since the cursor is placed prior to the first row in a ResultSet, we simply used the `next` method to move forward each time we attempted to read a row of data.

If we are modifying only one row of data and our `ResultSet` contains only one row, we can just jump to the first row by executing a call to our set's `first` method. Then, we can modify our data by using the `updateXXX` methods (`updateString`, `updateFloat`, etc.) on our set. We make our changes permanent in the database by calling the `updateRow` method. For example:

```
ResultSet rst = stmt2.executeQuery("SELECT * FROM Student WHERE " +
   "lastName=\"Jones\"");
rst.first();
rst.updateFloat("gpa", 3.41f);
rst.updateRow();
```

Obviously, if we are attempting to update multiple rows of records from a `ResultSet`, the navigation and updating statements will be more involved–possibly utilizing a loop. Additionally, prior to inserting, we can update any number of values in the row or rows in the `ResultSet`. The `updateRow` call simply communicates the changes back to the database once the `ResultSet` contains all of the necessary changes.

21.6 Deleting Data and Database Tables

The last piece of our JDBC knowledge is the ability delete data and tables from the database. We'll first look at the deleting of data.

Deleting Data

The SQL statement that deletes data from a table is the DELETE FROM statement. The statement has the following syntax:

> **KEY CONCEPT**
> The DELETE FROM SQL statement is used to delete data from a database table.

```
DELETE FROM <tablename> WHERE condition
```

The WHERE condition clause is optional, and if it is not provided, all rows from the specified table will be deleted. A condition is an expression that must evaluate to TRUE and can contain functions and operators such as && (and), || (or), and many others. For example, if we wished to delete all of the students whose `age` is greater than or equal to 30, we would use the following SQL statement.

```
DELETE FROM Student WHERE age >= 30
```

If we wished to delete all students whose `age` is greater than or equal to 30 and whose `gpa` is less than 3.5, we would use the following:

```
DELETE FROM Student WHERE age >=30 && gpa < 3.5
```

As with the `INSERT` statement in the previous section, we will need to use a `Statement` that produces `RecordSet` objects that are forward scrolling only (`ResultSet.TYPE_FORWARD_ONLY`), and which update the database (`ResultSet.CONCUR_UPDATABLE`).

Deleting Database Tables

Deleting tables from our database is rather simple to accomplish. We use the `executeUpdate` method of a `Statement` object and pass it the `DROP TABLE <tablename>` SQL statement.

For example, if we wanted to drop the `Student` table, we could do so using the following Java statements in our program.

```
int rowCount = stmt.executeUpdate("DROP TABLE Student");
```

Keep in mind that when the table is dropped, any data stored within the table is dropped as well.

Summary of Key Concepts

- Databases are software applications used to provide data to other programs.
- A relational database creates relationships between records in different tables by using unique identifiers.
- The JDBC API is used to establish a connection to a database.
- The CREATE TABLE SQL statement is used to create new database tables.
- The ALTER TABLE SQL statement can be used to modify an existing database table.
- The SHOW COLUMNS SQL statement can be used to obtain a list of a table's columns and configuration settings.
- The INSERT SQL statement is used to add new data to a database table.
- The SELECT SQL statement is used to retrieve data from a database table.
- The DELETE FROM SQL statement is used to delete data from a database table.
- The DROP TABLE SQL statement is used to delete an entire database table.
- Updates to a database can be performed through changes to a ResultSet.

Self-Review Questions

SR 21.1   What are the four primary operations on database data?

SR 21.2   In relational databases, where are the relationships stored, and how are they stored?

SR 21.3   Name two popular database products on the market today.

SR 21.4   Where can one obtain the JDBC?

SR 21.5   What role does a database driver fulfill?

SR 21.6   What does the java.sql.DriverManager class assist with?

SR 21.7   Which class do we use to prepare and execute SQL statements?

SR 21.8   Which JDBC class is used to manage a set of records that is usually the result of a database query?

SR 21.9   Which SQL statement is used to add new data to a database table?

SR 21.10   Which SQL statement is used to remove a database table from the database?

Exercises

EX 21.1   Design a table for storing the names and contact information (addresses, phone numbers, email addresses) of your closest friends and family. What fields would you use?

EX 21.2   Design one or more tables for managing a list of courses run by your university. How many tables do you need? What fields are in each table? Be sure to include such data as the instructor's names, number of credits, department that offers the course, and the current enrollment in the course.

EX 21.3   Research the SQL statements needed to perform the CRUD operations on an Oracle database, Access database, and PostgreSQL database. How do they differ from those presented in this chapter?

EX 21.4   Using the MySQL documentation (http://dev.mysql.com/doc), determine how to create a temporary table, and what the implications are of using a temporary table.

EX 21.5   How would you go about modifying a table and adding a new column in front of an existing one?

EX 21.6   What is the SQL statement needed to add a new column named `employeeNumber` to a table named `Employees`? Assume that the `employeeNumber` is a 7 digit integer value.

EX 21.7   What is the SQL statement needed to delete a column named `ProductCode` from a table named `Products`?

EX 21.8   Given the `Person` and `Location` tables provided at the start of the chapter, what is the SQL statement needed to return a query that lists all of the states that any person resides in?

EX 21.9   What is the SQL statement needed to insert a new field in the `Student` table that would store the total number of credits each student has accumulated? What data type should we use, and why?

EX 21.10   What is the SQL statement required to delete the age column from the `Student` table discussed earlier in the chapter?

Programming Projects

Use the MySQL world database (http://dev.mysql.com/doc/world-setup/en/world-setup.html) to populate a database and complete the following 5 projects.

PP 21.1   Write a program to query the world database to obtain a list of all of the cities of the world that contain a population that exceeds 5 million residents.

PP 21.2   Write a Java program that uses the world database that queries the database to determine the total population of all cities in New Jersey.

PP 21.3   Write a program that queries the world database to determine which country has the greatest life expectancy.

PP 21.4   Research how to accomplish a JOIN on two tables (see http://en.wikipedia.org/wiki/Join_(SQL)). Then, write a program that queries the world database to list the population of the capitol city for any country in Asia.

PP 21.5   Write a program with a graphical user interface that connects to a database, creates a CDs table (if it does not already exist) and provides the user the ability to manage a music album database. The database should include fields for the album title, artist name, number of tracks, and price. The user should be able to enter new album information, delete existing albums, and obtain a listing of albums in the database.

PP 21.6   Using the free tool at http://www.fakenamegenerator.com, create 1,000 fake identifications to a text file. Then, write a Java program that will populate a database table with the fake names from the text file. Finally, print a list of individuals in the database whose first (given) name is John and who live in Tennessee.

PP 21.7   Write a program that connects to a database, creates a Movies table (if it does not already exist) and provides the user the ability to manage a movie listing database. The database should include fields for a movie's name, run time, rating code, date of release, and two primary stars. The user should be able to enter new movie information, delete existing movies, and obtain a listing of movies in the database.

PP 21.8   Write a program with a graphical user interface that prompts the user to enter a database hostname, username, password, and database name. Once connected, the program should allow the user to browse the database by selecting a table, and then choosing to display either the structure of the table (SHOW COLUMNS), or the data contained within the selected table.

PP 21.9　　Write a program that connects to a database, creates two tables (Teams and Games, if they don't already exist) and allows the user to manage a series of games between different opponents. Games include a score value for each team, a unique identifier for each game. Teams include identifiers for each team, as well as their names and overall win/loss records. This problem can be solved with or without the knowledge of table joins in SQL statements. The user should be able enter new game results, add new teams, and navigate through each table or read the data.

PP 21.10　　Write program that connects to a database, creates and populates, the Student table, prints a display of the data contained in the Student table, and then deletes the Student table along with its data.

Answers to Self-Review Questions

SR 21.1　　The four primary database operations are create, read, update, and delete.

SR 21.2　　Relational database store their relationships in the database tables themselves in the form of unique identifiers that are used to join the database tables.

SR 21.3　　Some popular database products include MySQL, PostgreSQL, SQLServer, Oracle and Access.

SR 21.4　　As of JDK 1.1, the JDBC API is part of the JDK.

SR 21.5　　A database driver helps to establish communications from our JDBC statements to the specific database we are attempting to communicate with.

SR 21.6　　The `java.sql.DriverManager` class registers and manages each of the database drivers loaded at run time.

SR 21.7　　The `java.sql.Statement` is used to prepare and execute SQL statements.

SR 21.8　　The `ResultSet` object is a JDBC class that is used to manage a set of database query result records.

SR 21.9　　The INSERT SQL statement is used to add new data to a database table.

SR 21.10　　The DROP TABLE SQL statement is used to delete a database table and its data.

Glossary

abstract—A Java reserved word that serves as a modifier for classes, interfaces, and methods. An `abstract` class cannot be instantiated and is used to specify bodiless abstract methods that are given definitions by derived classes. Interfaces are inherently abstract.

abstract class—*See* abstract.

abstract data type (ADT)—A collection of data and the operations that are defined on that data. An abstract data type might be implemented in a variety of ways, but the interface operations are consistent.

abstract method—*See* abstract.

Abstract Windowing Toolkit (AWT)—The package in the Java API (`java.awt`) that contains classes related to graphics and GUIs. *See also* Swing.

abstraction—The concept of hiding details. If the right details are hidden at the right times, abstraction can significantly help control complexity and focus attention on appropriate issues.

access—The ability to reference a variable or invoke a method from outside the class in which it is declared. Controlled by the visibility modifier used to declare the variable or method. Also called the level of encapsulation. *See also* visibility modifier.

access modifier—*See* visibility modifier.

actual parameter—The value passed to a method as a parameter. *See also* formal parameter.

adaptor class—*See* listener adaptor class.

address—(1) A numeric value that uniquely identifies a particular memory location in a computer's main memory. (2) A designation that uniquely identifies a computer among all others on a network.

adjacency list—A list of all of the edges in a graph grouped by the vertices that each edge touches. *See also* edge, graph, vertex.

adjacency matrix—A matrix (two-dimensional array) that stores the list of edges in a graph. Each position in the array represents an intersection between two vertices in the graph. *See also* array, edge, graph, vertex.

ADT—*See* abstract data type.

aggregate object—An object that contains variables that are references to other objects. *See also* has-a relationship.

aggregation—Something that is composed, at least in part, of other things. *See also* aggregate object.

algorithm—A step-by-step process for solving a problem. A program is based on one or more algorithms.

alias—A reference to an object that is currently also referred to by another reference. Each reference is an alias of the other.

analog—A representation that is in direct proportion to the source of the information. *See also* digital.

animation—A series of images or drawings that gives the appearance of movement when displayed in order at a particular speed.

ANT—A build tool generally used with Java program development. *See also* build tool.

API—*See* application programming interface (API).

applet—A Java program that is linked into an HTML document, then retrieved and executed using a Web browser, as opposed to a stand-alone Java application.

appletviewer—A software tool that interprets and displays Java applets through links in HTML documents. Part of the Java Development Kit.

application—(1) A generic term for any program. (2) A Java program that can be run without the use of a Web browser, as opposed to a Java applet.

application programming interface (API)—A set of classes that defines services for a programmer. Not part of the language itself, but often relied on to perform even basic tasks. *See also* class library.

arc angle—When defining an arc, the radial distance that defines the arc's length. *See also* start angle.

architectural design—A high-level design that identifies the large portions of a software system and key data structures. *See also* detailed design.

architecture—*See* computer architecture.

architecture neutral—Not specific to any particular hardware platform. Java code is considered architecture neutral because it is compiled into bytecode and then interpreted on any machine with a Java interpreter. *See also* bytecode.

arithmetic operator—An operator that performs a basic arithmetic computation, such as addition or multiplication.

arithmetic promotion—The act of promoting the type of a numeric operand to be consistent with the other operand.

array—A programming language construct used to store an ordered list of primitive values or objects. Each element in the array is referenced using a numerical index from 0 to $N-1$, where N is the size of the array.

array element—A value or object that is stored in an array.

array element type—The type of the values or objects that are stored in an array.

ASCII—A popular character set used by many programming languages. ASCII stands for American Standard Code for Information Interchange. It is a subset of the Unicode character set, which is used by Java.

assembly language—A low-level language that uses mnemonics to represent program commands.

assert—A Java reserved word that is used to make an assertion that a condition is fulfilled. *See also* assertion.

assertion—A programming language construct that is used to declare a programmatic assumption (that is usually true). Assertions are used by JUnit for the purposes of unit testing. *See also* JUnit, unit testing.

assignment conversion—Some data types can be converted to another data type in an assignment statement. *See* widening conversion.

assignment operator—An operator that results in an assignment to a variable. The = operator performs basic assignment. Many other assignment operators perform additional operations prior to the assignment, such as the *= operator.

association—A relationship between two classes in which one uses the other or relates to it in some way. *See also* operator association, use relationship.

asymptotic complexity—The order, or dominant term, of a growth function. *See also* dominant term, growth function.

AWT—*See* Abstract Windowing Toolkit.

background color—(1) The color of the background of a GUI component. (2) The color of the background of an HTML page. *See also* foreground color.

bag—A collection that facilitates the selection of random elements from a group. *See also* collection.

balanced tree—A tree whose leaves are all on the same level or within one level of each other. *See also* leaf, tree.

base—The numerical value on which a particular number system is based. It determines the number of digits available in that number system and the place value of each digit in a number. *See also* binary, decimal, hexadecimal, octal, place value.

base 2—*See* binary.

base 8—*See* octal.

base 10—*See* decimal.

base 16—*See* hexadecimal.

base case—The situation that terminates recursive processing, allowing the active recursive methods to begin returning to their point of invocation.

base class—*See* superclass.

behavior—The functional characteristics of an object, defined by its methods. *See also* identity, state.

binary—The base-2 number system. Modern computer systems store information as strings of binary digits (bits).

binary operator—An operator that uses two operands.

binary search—A searching algorithm that requires that the list be sorted. It repetitively compares the "middle" element of the list to the target value, narrowing the scope of the search each time. *See also* linear search.

binary search tree—A binary tree with the added property that, for each node, the left child is less than the parent, and the right child is greater than or equal to the parent. *See also* node, tree.

binary string—A series of binary digits (bits).

binary tree—A tree data structure in which each node can have no more than two child nodes.

binding—The process of associating an identifier with the construct that it represents. For example, the process of binding a method name to the specific definition that it invokes.

bit—A binary digit, either 0 or 1.

bit shifting—The act of shifting the bits of a data value to the left or right, losing bits on one end and inserting bits on the other.

bits per second (bps)—A measurement rate for data transfer devices.

bitwise operator—An operator that manipulates individual bits of a value, either by calculation or by shifting.

black-box testing—Producing and evaluating test cases based on the input and expected output of a software component. The test cases focus on covering the equivalence categories and boundary values of the input. *See also* white-box testing.

block—A group of programming statements and declarations delimited by braces ({ }).

boolean—A Java reserved word representing a logical primitive data type that can only take the values true or false.

boolean expression—An expression that evaluates to a true or false result, primarily used as conditions in selection and repetition statements.

boolean operator—Any of the bitwise operators AND (&), OR (|), or XOR (^) when applied to boolean operands. The results are equivalent to their logical counterparts, except that boolean operators are not short-circuited.

border—A graphical edge around a GUI component to enhance its appearance or to group components visually. An empty border creates a buffer of space around a component.

boundary values—The input values corresponding to the edges of equivalence categories. Used in black-box testing.

bounding rectangle—A rectangle that delineates a region in which an oval or arc is defined.

bounds checking—The process of determining whether an array index is in bounds, given the size of the array. Java performs automatic bounds checking.

bps—*See* bits per second.

breadth-first traversal—A graph traversal that starts at a given vertex, then visits all neighboring vertices one edge from the starting vertex, then visits all vertices two edges from the starting vertex, and so on. *See also* depth-first traversal, graph, vertex.

break—A Java reserved word used to interrupt the flow of control by breaking out of the current loop or `switch` statement.

breakpoints—A special flag or tag in a debugger that pauses execution of the program being debugged when the execution reaches the breakpoint.

browser—Software that retrieves HTML documents across network connections and formats them for viewing. A browser is the primary vehicle for accessing the World Wide Web. *See also* Netscape Navigator.

bubble sort—A sorting algorithm in which values are repeatedly compared to neighboring elements in the list and their positions are swapped if they are not in order relative to each other. *See also* heap sort, insertion sort, merge sort, quick sort, radix sort, selection sort.

bug—A slang term for a defect or error in a computer program.

build-and-fix approach—An approach to software development in which a program is created without any significant planning or design, then modified until it reaches some level of acceptance. It is a prevalent, but unwise, approach.

build tool—A software application used to automate, define, and execute a consistent process for building software applications.

bus—A group of wires in the computer that carries data between components such as the CPU and main memory.

button—A GUI component that allows the user to initiate an action, set a condition, or choose an option with a mouse click. There are several kinds of GUI buttons. *See also* check box, push button, radio button.

byte—(1) A unit of binary storage equal to 8 bits. (2) A Java reserved word that represents a primitive integer type, stored using 8 bits in two's complement format.

byte stream—An I/O stream that manages 8-bit bytes of raw binary data. *See also* character stream.

bytecode—The low-level format into which the Java compiler translates Java source code. The bytecode is interpreted and executed by the Java interpreter, perhaps after transportation over the Internet.

capacity—*See* storage capacity.

case—(1) A Java reserved word that is used to identify each unique option in a switch statement. (2) The orientation of an alphabetic character (uppercase or lowercase).

case sensitive—Differentiating between the uppercase and lowercase versions of an alphabetic letter. Java is case sensitive; therefore the identifier total and the identifier Total are considered to be different identifiers.

cast—A Java operation expressed using a type or class name in parentheses to explicitly convert and return a value of one data type into another.

catch—A Java reserved word that is used to specify an exception handler, defined after a try block.

CD-Recordable (CD-R)—A compact disc on which information can be stored once using a home computer with an appropriate drive. *See also* CD-Rewritable, CD-ROM.

CD-Rewritable (CD-RW)—A compact disc on which information can be stored and rewritten multiple times using a home computer with an appropriate drive. *See also* CD-Recordable, CD-ROM.

CD-ROM—An optical secondary memory medium that stores binary information in a manner similar to a musical compact disc.

central processing unit (CPU)—The hardware component that controls the main activity of a computer, including the flow of information and the execution of commands.

char—A Java reserved word that represents the primitive character type. All Java characters are members of the Unicode character set and are stored using 16 bits.

character font—A specification that defines the distinct look of a character when it is printed or drawn.

character set—An ordered list of characters, such as the ASCII or Unicode character sets. Each character corresponds to a specific, unique numeric value within a given character set. A programming language adopts a particular character set to use for character representation and management.

character stream—An I/O stream that manages 16-bit Unicode characters. *See also* byte stream.

character string—A series of ordered characters. Represented in Java using the String class and string literals such as "hello".

check box—A GUI component that allows the user to set a boolean condition with a mouse click. A check box can be used alone or independently among other check boxes. *See also* radio button.

checked exception—A Java exception that must be either caught or explicitly thrown to the calling method. *See also* unchecked exception.

child class—*See* subclass.

circular array—Conceptually, an array whose last index is followed by the first index.

class—(1) A Java reserved word used to define a class. (2) The blueprint of an object—the model that defines the variables and methods an object will contain when instantiated.

class diagram—A diagram that shows the relationships between classes, including inheritance and use relationships. *See also* Unified Modeling Language.

class hierarchy—A tree-like structure created when classes are derived from other classes through inheritance. *See also* interface hierarchy.

class library—A set of classes that defines useful services for a programmer. *See also* application programming interface (API).

class method—A method that can be invoked using only the class name. An instantiated object is not required as it is with instance methods. Defined in a Java program by using the `static` reserved word.

class variable—A variable that is shared among all objects of a class. It can also be referenced through the class name, without instantiating any object of that class. Defined in a Java program by using the `static` reserved word.

CLASSPATH—An operating system setting that determines where the Java interpreter searches for class files.

client-server model—A manner in which to construct a software design based on objects (clients) making use of the services provided by other objects (servers).

coding guidelines—A series of conventions that describe how programs should be constructed. They make programs easier to read, exchange, and integrate. Sometimes referred to as coding standards, especially when they are enforced.

coding standard—*See* coding guidelines.

cohesion—The strength of the relationship among the parts within a software component. *See also* coupling.

collection—An object that serves as a repository for other objects.

collision—The process of two hash values producing the same hash code. *See also* hash code, hashing.

color chooser—A GUI component, often displayed as a dialog box, that allows the user to select or specify a color.

combo box—A GUI component that allows the user to select one of several options. A combo box displays the most recent selection. *See also* list.

command-line arguments—The values that follow the program name on the command line. Accessed within a Java program through the `String` array parameter to the `main` method.

command shell—A text-based user interface for issuing commands to a computer operating system.

comment—A programming language construct that allows a programmer to embed human-readable annotations into the source code. *See also* documentation.

compile-time error—Any error that occurs during the compilation process, often indicating that a program does not conform to the language syntax or that an operation was attempted on an inappropriate data type. *See also* logical error, run-time error, syntax error.

compiler—A program that translates code from one language to equivalent code in another language. The Java compiler translates Java source code into Java bytecode. *See also* interpreter.

complete tree—A tree that is balanced and all of whose leaves at the bottom level are on the left side of the tree. *See also* balanced tree, leaf.

component—Any portion of a software system that performs a specific task, transforming input to output. *See also* GUI component.

computer architecture—The structure and interaction of the hardware components of a computer.

concatenation—*See* string concatenation.

condition—A boolean expression used to determine whether the body of a selection or repetition statement should be executed.

conditional coverage—A strategy used in white-box testing in which all conditions in a program are executed, producing both `true` and `false` results. *See also* statement coverage.

conditional operator—A Java ternary operator that evaluates one of two expressions based on a condition.

conditional statement—*See* selection statement.

connected graph—A graph in which a path exists between any two vertices. *See also* graph, path, vertex.

const—A Java reserved word that is not currently used.

constant—An identifier that contains a value that cannot be modified. Used to make code more readable and to facilitate changes. Defined in Java using the `final` modifier.

constant complexity—A growth function of an algorithm that executes in a set amount of time regardless of the size of the problem. *See also* growth function.

constructor—A special method in a class that is invoked when an object is instantiated from the class. Used to initialize the object.

container—A Java GUI component that can hold other components. *See also* containment hierarchy.

containment hierarchy—The relationships among graphical components of a user interface. *See also* container.

content pane—The part of a top-level container to which components are added.

control characters—*See* nonprintable characters.

controllers—Hardware devices that control the interaction between a computer system and a particular kind of peripheral.

coupling—The strength of the relationship between two software components. *See also* cohesion.

CPU—*See* central processing unit.

cycle—A path in a graph in which the first and last vertices are the same and none of the edges are repeated. *See also* graph.

data stream—An I/O stream that represents a particular source or destination for data, such as a file. *See also* processing stream.

data structure—Any programming construct, either defined in the language or by a programmer, used to organize data into a format to facilitate access and processing. Arrays, linked lists, and stacks can all be considered data structures.

data transfer device—A hardware component that allows information to be sent between computers, such as a modem.

data type—A designation that specifies a set of values (which may be infinite). For example, each variable has a data type that specifies the kinds of values that can be stored in it.

debugger—A software tool that allows a programmer to step through an executing program and examine the value of variables at any point. *See also* jdb.

debugging—The act of locating and correcting run-time and logic errors in your programs.

decimal—The base-10 number system, which humans use in everyday life. *See also* binary.

default—A Java reserved word that is used to indicate the default case of a `switch` statement, used if no other cases match.

default visibility—The level of access designated when no explicit visibility modifier is used to declare a class, interface, method, or variable. Sometimes referred to as package visibility. Classes and interfaces declared with default visibility can be used within their package. A method or variable declared with default visibility is inherited and accessible by all subclasses in the same package.

defect testing—Testing designed to uncover errors in a program.

defined—Existing for use in a derived class, even if it can only be accessed indirectly. *See also* inheritance.

degenerate tree—A tree whose nodes are located primarily on one side. *See also* tree.

delimiter—Any symbol or word used to set the boundaries of a programming language construct, such as the braces (`{}`) used to define a Java block.

deprecated—Something, such as a particular method, that is considered old-fashioned and should not be used.

depth-first traversal—A graph traversal that starts at a given vertex, and traverses as far as possible along a sequence of edges before backtracking and traversing alternative, skipped edges. *See also* breadth-first traversal, graph, vertex.

derived class—*See* subclass.

design—(1) The plan for implementing a program, which includes a specification of the classes and objects used and an expression of the important program algorithms. (2) The process of creating a program design.

desk check—A type of review in which a developer carefully examines a design or program to find errors.

detailed design—(1) The low-level algorithmic steps of a method. (2) The development stage at which low-level algorithmic steps are determined.

development stage—The software lifecycle stage in which a software system is first created, preceding use, maintenance, and eventual retirement.

dialog box—A graphical window that pops up to allow brief, specific user interaction.

digital—A representation that breaks information down into pieces, which are in turn represented as numbers. All modern computer systems are digital.

digitize—The act of converting an analog representation into a digital one by breaking it down into pieces.

digraph—*See* directed graph.

dimension—The number of index levels of a particular array.

direct recursion—The process of a method invoking itself. *See also* indirect recursion.

directed graph—A graph data structure in which each edge has a specific direction. *See also* edge.

disable—Make a GUI component inactive so that it cannot be used. A disabled component is grayed to indicate its disabled status. *See also* enable.

DNS—*See* Domain Name System.

do—A Java reserved word that represents a repetition construct. A do statement is executed one or more times. *See also* for, while.

documentation—Supplemental information about a program, including comments in a program's source code and printed reports such as a user's guide.

domain name—The portion of an Internet address that specifies the organization to which the computer belongs.

Domain Name System (DNS)—Software that translates an Internet address into an IP address using a domain server.

domain server—A file server that maintains a list of Internet addresses and their corresponding IP addresses.

dominant term—The term in a growth function that increases the most as the problem size (n) increases. The dominant term is the basis of determining the order of an algorithm. *See also* growth function, order.

double—A Java reserved word that represents a primitive floating point numeric type, stored using 64 bits in IEEE 754 format.

doubly linked list—A linked list with two references in each node: one that refers to the next node in the list and one that refers to the previous node in the list.

dynamic binding—The process of associating an identifier with its definition during run time. *See also* binding.

dynamic structure—A set of objects that are linked using references, which can be modified as needed during program execution.

edge—A connector (in a linked structure, a reference) between two nodes in a tree or graph. *See also* graph, node, tree.

editor—A software tool that allows the user to enter and store a file of characters on a computer. Often used by programmers to enter the source code of a program.

efficiency—The characteristic of an algorithm that specifies the required number of a particular operation in order to complete its task. For example, the efficiency of a sort can be measured by the number of comparisons required to sort a list. *See also* order.

element—A value or object stored in another object such as an array.

element type—*See* array element type.

else—A Java reserved word that designates the portion of code in an `if` statement that will be executed if the condition is false.

enable—Make a GUI component active so that it can be used. *See also* disable.

encapsulation—The characteristic of an object that limits access to the variables and methods contained in it. All interaction with an object occurs through a well-defined interface that supports a modular design.

environment variable—A variable located in the system's settings or command shell that can store a value (typically the path to a file or directory). Environment variables can be used within a command shell or program for configuration purposes. *See also* command shell.

equality operator—One of two Java operators that returns a boolean result based on whether two values are equal (`==`) or not equal (`!=`).

equivalence category—A range of functionally equivalent input values as specified by the requirements of the software component. Used when developing black-box test cases.

error—(1) Any defect in a design or program. (2) An object that can be thrown and processed by special `catch` blocks, though usually errors should not be caught. *See also* compile-time error, exception, logical error, run-time error, syntax error.

escape sequence—In Java, a sequence of characters beginning with the backslash character (\), used to indicate a special situation when printing values. For example, the escape sequence `\t` specifies that a horizontal tab should be printed.

exception—(1) A situation that arises during program execution that is erroneous or out of the ordinary. (2) An object that can be thrown and processed by special `catch` blocks. *See also* error.

exception handler—The code in a `catch` clause of a `try` statement, executed when a particular type of exception is thrown.

exception propagation—The process that occurs when an exception is thrown: control returns to each calling method in the stack trace until the exception is caught and handled or until the exception is thrown from the `main` method, terminating the program.

exponent—The portion of a floating point value's internal representation that specifies how far the decimal point is shifted. *See also* mantissa.

exponential complexity—An equation that specifies the efficiency of an algorithm whose dominant term contains the problem size as an exponent (e.g., 2^n). *See also* growth function.

expression—A combination of operators and operands that produces a result.

extends—A Java reserved word used to specify the parent class in the definition of a child class.

event—(1) A user action, such as a mouse click or key press. (2) An object that represents a user action, to which the program can respond. *See also* event-driven programming.

event-driven programming—An approach to software development in which the program is designed to acknowledge that an event has occurred and to act accordingly. *See also* event.

factorial—The product of all integers between 1 and any positive integer N (written N!).

false—A Java reserved word that serves as one of the two boolean literals (`true` and `false`).

fetch-decode-execute—The cycle through which the CPU continually obtains instructions from main memory and executes them.

FIFO—*See* first-in, first-out.

file—A named collection of data stored on a secondary storage device such as a disk. *See also* text file.

file chooser—A GUI component, usually displayed as a dialog box, that allows the user to select a file from a storage device.

file server—A computer in a network, usually with a large secondary storage capacity, that is dedicated to storing software needed by many network users.

filtering stream—*See* processing stream.

final—A Java reserved word that serves as a modifier for classes, methods, and variables. A final class cannot be used to derive a new class. A final method cannot be overridden. A final variable is a constant.

finalize—A Java method defined in the `Object` class that can be overridden in any other class. It is called after the object becomes a candidate for garbage collection and before it is destroyed. It can be used to perform "clean-up" activity that is not performed automatically by the garbage collector.

finalizer method—A Java method, called `finalize`, that is called before an object is destroyed. *See also* finalize.

finally—A Java reserved word that designates a block of code to be executed when an exception is thrown, after any appropriate catch handler is processed.

first-in, first-out (FIFO)—A data management technique in which the first value that is stored in a data structure is the first value that comes out. *See also* last-in, first-out; queue.

float—A Java reserved word that represents a primitive floating point numeric type, stored using 32 bits in IEEE 754 format.

flushing—The process of forcing the contents of the output buffer to be displayed on the output device.

font—*See* character font.

for—A Java reserved word that represents a repetition construct. A for statement is executed zero or more times and is usually used when a precise number of iterations is known.

foreground color—The color in which any current drawing will be rendered. *See also* background color.

formal parameter—An identifier that serves as a parameter name in a method. It receives its initial value from the actual parameter passed to it. *See also* actual parameter.

fourth-generation language—A high-level language that provides built-in functionality such as automatic report generation or database management, beyond that of traditional high-level languages.

full tree—An n-ary tree whose leaves are all on the same level and in which every node is a leaf or has exactly *n* children. *See also* leaf, level, node, tree.

function—A named group of declarations and programming statements that can be invoked (executed) when needed. A function that is part of a class is called a method. Java has no functions because all code is part of a class.

garbage—(1) An unspecified or uninitialized value in a memory location. (2) An object that cannot be accessed anymore because all references to it have been lost.

garbage collection—The process of reclaiming unneeded, dynamically allocated memory. Java performs automatic garbage collection of objects that no longer have any valid references to them.

general tree—A tree with no limit to the number of children a node may contain or reference. *See also* node, tree.

generic type—A class designed so that it stores, operates on, and manages objects whose type is not specified until the class is instantiated.

gigabyte (GB)—A unit of binary storage, equal to 2^{30} (approximately 1 billion) bytes.

glass-box testing—*See* white-box testing.

goto—(1) A Java reserved word that is not currently used. (2) An unconditional branch.

grammar—A representation of language syntax that specifies how reserved words, symbols, and identifiers can be combined into valid programs.

graph—A nonlinear data structure made up of vertices and edges that connect the vertices. *See also* directed graph, undirected graph, vertex, edge.

graphical user interface (GUI)—Software that provides the means to interact with a program or operating system by making use of graphical images and point-and-click mechanisms such as buttons and text fields.

graphics context—The drawing surface and related coordinate system on which a drawing is rendered or GUI components are placed.

growth function—A function that shows the complexity of an algorithm relative to the size of the problem (n). A growth function can represent the time complexity or space complexity of the algorithm. *See also* order.

GUI component—A visual element, such as a button or text field, that is used to make up a GUI.

hardware—The tangible components of a computer system, such as the keyboard, monitor, and circuit boards.

has-a relationship—The relationship between two objects in which one is composed, at least in part, of one or more of the other. *See also* aggregate object, is-a relationship.

hash code—An integer value calculated from any given data value or object, used to determine where a value should be stored in a hash table. Also called a hash value. *See also* hashing.

hash method—A method that calculates a hash code from a data value or object. The same data value or object will always produce the same hash code. Also called a hash function. *See also* hashing.

hash table—A data structure in which values are stored for efficient retrieval. *See also* hashing.

hashing—A technique for storing items so that they can be found efficiently. Items are stored in a hash table at a position specified by a calculated hash code. *See also* hash method.

heap—A complete binary tree in which each element is greater than or equal to both of its children. *See also* binary tree, minheap.

heap sort—A sorting algorithm in which a set of elements is sorted by adding each one to a heap, then removing them one at a time. *See also* bubble sort, merge sort, quick sort, radix sort, selection sort.

hexadecimal—The base-16 number system, often used as an abbreviated representation of binary strings.

hierarchy—An organizational technique in which items are layered or grouped to reduce complexity.

high-level language—A programming language in which each statement represents many machine-level instructions.

HTML—*See* HyperText Markup Language.

hybrid object-oriented language—A programming language that can be used to implement a program in a procedural manner or an object-oriented manner, at the programmer's discretion. *See also* pure object-oriented language.

hypermedia—The concept of hypertext extended to include other media types such as graphics, audio, video, and programs.

hypertext—A document representation that allows a user to easily navigate through it in other than a linear fashion. Links to other parts of the document are embedded at the appropriate places to allow the user to jump from one part of the document to another. *See also* hypermedia.

HyperText Markup Language (HTML)— The notation used to define Web pages. *See also* browser, World Wide Web.

icon—A small, fixed-sized picture, often used to decorate a GUI. *See also* image.

IDE—*See* integrated development environment.

identifier—Any name that a programmer makes up to use in a program, such as a class name or variable name.

identity—The designation of an object, which, in Java, is an object's reference name. See also *state, behavior.*

IEEE 754—A standard for representing floating point values. Used by Java to represent `float` and `double` data types.

if—A Java reserved word that specifies a simple conditional construct. *See also* else.

image—A picture, often specified using a GIF or JPEG format. *See also* icon.

IMAP—*See* Internet Message Access Protocol.

immutable—The characteristic of something that does not change. For example, the contents of a Java character string are immutable once the string has been defined.

implementation—(1) The process of translating a design into source code. (2) The source code that defines a method, class, abstract data type, or other programming entity.

implements—A Java reserved word that is used in a class declaration to specify that the class implements the methods specified in a particular interface.

import—A Java reserved word that is used to specify the packages and classes that are used in a particular Java source code file.

index—The integer value used to specify a particular element in an array.

index operator—The brackets (`[ ]`) in which an array index is specified.

indirect recursion—The process of a method invoking another method, which eventually results in the original method being invoked again. *See also* direct recursion.

infinite loop—A loop that does not terminate because the condition controlling the loop never becomes false.

infinite recursion—A recursive series of invocations that does not terminate because the base case is never reached. *See also* base case.

infix expression—An expression in which the operators are positioned between the operands on which they work. *See also* postfix expression.

inheritance—The ability to derive a new class from an existing one. Inherited variables and methods of the original (parent) class are available in the new (child) class as if they were declared locally.

initialize—To give an initial value to a variable.

initializer list—A comma-separated list of values, delimited by braces ({}), used to initialize and specify the size of an array.

inline documentation—Comments that are included in the source code of a program.

inner class—A nonstatic, nested class.

inorder traversal—A tree traversal that is accomplished by visiting the left child of the node, then the node, then any remaining nodes. *See also* level-order traversal, postorder traversal, preorder traversal.

input/output buffer—A storage location for data on its way from the user to the computer (input buffer) or from the computer to the user (output buffer).

input/output devices—Hardware components that allow the human user to interact with the computer, such as a keyboard, mouse, and monitor.

input/output stream—A sequence of bytes that represents a source of data (input stream) or a destination for data (output stream).

insertion sort—A sorting algorithm in which each value, one at a time, is inserted into a sorted subset of the entire list. *See also* bubble sort, heap sort, merge sort, quick sort, radix sort, selection sort.

inspection—*See* walkthrough.

instance—An object created from a class. Multiple objects can be instantiated from a single class.

instance method—A method that must be invoked through a particular instance of a class, as opposed to a class method.

instance variable—A variable that must be referenced through a particular instance of a class, as opposed to a class variable.

instanceof—A Java reserved word that is also an operator, used to determine the class or type of a variable.

instantiation—The act of creating an object from a class.

int—A Java reserved word that represents a primitive integer type, stored using 32 bits in two's complement format.

integrated development environment (IDE)—A software application used by software developers to create and debug programs.

integration test—The process of testing software components that are made up of other interacting components. Stresses the communication between components rather than the functionality of individual components.

interface—(1) A Java reserved word that is used to define a set of abstract methods that will be implemented by particular classes. (2) The set of messages to which an object responds, defined by the methods that can be invoked from outside of the object. (3) The techniques through which a human user interacts with a program, often graphically. *See also* graphical user interface.

interface hierarchy—A tree-like structure created when interfaces are derived from other interfaces through inheritance. *See also* class hierarchy.

internal node—A tree node that is not the root node and that has at least one child. *See also* node, root, tree.

Internet—The most pervasive wide-area network in the world; it has become the primary vehicle for computer-to-computer communication. *See also* wide-area network.

Internet address—A designation that uniquely identifies a particular computer or device on the Internet.

Internet Message Access Protocol (IMAP)—Protocol that defines the communications commands required to communicate with another machine for the purposes of reading email.

Internet Naming Authority—The governing body that approves all Internet addresses.

interpreter—A program that translates and executes code on a particular machine. The Java interpreter translates and executes Java bytecode. *See also* compiler.

invisible component—A GUI component that can be added to a container to provide buffering space between other components.

invocation—*See* method invocation.

I/O devices—*See* input/output devices.

IP address—A series of several integer values, separated by periods (.), that uniquely identifies a particular computer or device on the Internet. Each Internet address has a corresponding IP address.

is-a relationship—The relationship created through properly derived classes via inheritance. The subclass *is-a* more specific version of the superclass. *See also* has-a relationship.

ISO-Latin-1—A 128-character extension to the ASCII character set defined by the International Organization for Standardization (ISO). The characters correspond to the numeric values 128 through 255 in both ASCII and Unicode.

iteration—(1) One execution of the body of a repetition statement. (2) One pass through a cyclic process, such as an iterative development process.

iteration statement—*See* repetition statement.

iterative development process—A step-by-step approach for creating software, which contains a series of stages that are performed repetitively.

jar—A file format used by Java to package and compress a group of files and directories, suitable for exchanging with another computer. The jar file format is based on the zip file format. *See also* zip.

java—The Java command-line interpreter, which translates and executes Java bytecode. Part of the Java Development Kit (JDK).

Java—The programming language used throughout this text to demonstrate software development concepts. Described by its developers as object oriented, robust, secure, architecture neutral, portable, high-performance, interpreted, threaded, and dynamic.

Java API—*See* application programming interface (API).

Java Development Kit (JDK)—A collection of software tools available free from Sun Microsystems, the creators of the Java programming language. *See also* Software Development Kit.

Java Virtual Machine (JVM)—The conceptual device, implemented in software, on which Java bytecode is executed. Bytecode, which is architecture neutral, does not run on a particular hardware platform; instead, it runs on the JVM.

javac—The Java command-line compiler, which translates Java source code into Java bytecode. Part of the Java Development Kit.

javadoc—A software tool that creates external documentation in HTML format about the contents and structure of a Java software system. Part of the Java Development Kit.

javah—A software tool that generates C header and source files, used for implementing `native` methods. Part of the Java Development Kit.

javap—A software tool that disassembles a Java class file, containing unreadable bytecode, into a human-readable version. Part of the Java Development Kit.

jdb—The Java command-line debugger. Part of the Java Development Kit.

JDK—*See* Java Development Kit.

JUnit—A unit testing framework for Java applications. *See also* unit testing.

JVM—*See* Java Virtual Machine.

kilobit (Kb)—A unit of binary storage, equal to 2^{10}, or 1024, bits.

kilobyte (K or KB)—A unit of binary storage, equal to 2^{10}, or 1024, bytes.

label—(1) A GUI component that displays text, an image, or both. (2) An identifier in Java used to specify a particular line of code. The `break` and `continue` statements can jump to a specific, labeled line in the program.

LAN—*See* local-area network.

last-in, first-out (LIFO)—A data management technique in which the last value that is stored in a data structure is the first value that comes out. *See also* first-in, first-out; stack.

layout manager—An object that specifies the presentation of GUI components. Each container is governed by a particular layout manager.

leaf—A tree node that has no children. *See also* node, tree.

level—A conceptual horizontal line in a tree on which all elements of the same distance from the root node are located.

level-order traversal—A tree traversal that is accomplished by visiting all of the nodes at each level, one level at a time. *See also* inorder traversal, level, postorder traversal, preorder traversal.

lexicographic ordering—The ordering of characters and strings based on a particular character set such as Unicode.

life cycle—The stages through which a software product is developed and used.

LIFO—*See* last-in, first-out.

linear search—A search algorithm in which each item in the list is compared to the target value until the target is found or the list is exhausted. *See also* binary search.

link—(1) A designation in a hypertext document that "jumps" to a new document (or to a new part of the same document) when clicked. (2) An object reference used to connect two items in a dynamically linked structure.

linked list—A structure in which one object refers to the next, creating a linear ordering of the objects in the list. *See also* linked structure.

linked structure—A dynamic data structure in which objects are connected using references.

Linux—A computer operating system, similar to Unix, developed by hobbyists and generally available for free. *See also* operating system, Unix.

list—(1) A GUI component that presents a list of items from which the user can choose. The current selection is highlighted in the list. *See also* combo box. (2) A collection of objects arranged in a linear manner. *See also* linked list.

listener—An object that is set up to respond to an event when it occurs.

listener adaptor class—A class defined with empty methods corresponding to the methods invoked when particular events occur. A listener object can be derived from an adaptor class. *See also* listener interface.

listener interface—A Java interface that defines the methods invoked when particular events occur. A listener object can be created by implementing a listener interface. *See also* listener adaptor class.

literal—A primitive value used explicitly in a program, such as the numeric literal 147 or the string literal "hello".

local-area network (LAN)—A computer network designed to span short distances and connect a relatively small number of computers. *See also* wide-area network.

local variable—A variable, defined within a method, that does not exist except during the execution of the method.

logarithmic complexity—An equation that specifies the efficiency of an algorithm whose dominant term contains the problem size as the base of a logarithm (e.g., $\log_2 n$). *See also* growth function.

logical error—A problem stemming from inappropriate processing in the code. It does not cause an abnormal termination of the program, but it produces incorrect results. *See also* compile-time error, run-time error, syntax error.

logical line of code—A logical programming statement in a source code program, which may extend over multiple physical lines. *See also* physical line of code.

logical operator—One of the operators that perform a logical NOT (!), AND (&&), or OR (||), returning a boolean result. The logical operators are short-circuited, meaning that if their left operand is sufficient to determine the result, the right operand is not evaluated.

long—A Java reserved word that represents a primitive integer type, stored using 64 bits in two's complement format.

loop—*See* repetition statement.

loop control variable—A variable whose value specifically determines how many times a loop body is executed.

low-level language—Either machine language or assembly language, considered "low" because they are conceptually close to the basic processing of a computer when compared to high-level languages.

machine language—The native language of a particular CPU. Any software that runs on a particular CPU must be translated into its machine language.

main memory—The volatile hardware storage device where programs and data are held when they are actively needed by the CPU. *See also* secondary memory.

maintenance—(1) The process of fixing errors in or making enhancements to a released software product. (2) The software life-cycle phase in which the software is in use and changes are made to it as needed.

make—A build tool generally used with C and C++ program development. *See also* build tool.

mantissa—The portion of a floating point value's internal representation that specifies the magnitude of the number. *See also* exponent.

max heap—A complete binary tree in which each element is greater than or equal to both of its children. *See also* binary tree, min heap.

megabyte (MB)—A unit of binary storage, equal to 2^{20} (approximately 1 million) bytes.

member—A variable or method in an object or class.

memory—Hardware devices that store programs and data. *See also* main memory, secondary memory.

memory location—An individual, addressable cell inside main memory into which data can be stored.

memory management—The process of controlling dynamically allocated portions of main memory, especially the act of returning allocated memory when it is no longer required. *See also* garbage collection.

merge sort—A sorting algorithm in which a list is recursively divided in half until each sublist has one element. Then, the sublists are recombined in order. *See also* bubble sort, heap sort, insertion sort, quick sort, radix sort, selection sort.

method—A named group of declarations and programming statements that can be invoked (executed) when needed. A method is part of a class.

method call conversion—The automatic widening conversion that can occur when a value of one type is passed to a formal parameter of another type.

method definition—The specification of the code that gets executed when the method is invoked. The definition includes declarations of local variables and formal parameters.

method invocation—A line of code that causes a method to be executed. It specifies any values that are passed to the method as parameters.

method overloading—*See* overloading.

min heap—A complete binary tree in which each element is less than or equal to both of its children. *See also* binary tree, max heap.

minimum spanning tree—A spanning tree where the sum of the weights of the edges is less than or equal to the sum of the weights for any other spanning tree for the same graph. *See also* edge, spanning tree.

mnemonic—(1) A word or identifier that specifies a command or data value in an assembly language. (2) A keyboard character used as a alternative means to activate a GUI component such as a button.

modal—Having multiple modes (such as a dialog box).

modem—A data transfer device that allows information to be sent along a telephone line.

modifier—A designation used in a Java declaration that specifies particular characteristics to the construct being declared.

monitor—The screen in the computer system that serves as an output device.

multidimensional array—An array that uses more than one index to specify a value stored in it.

multiple inheritance—Deriving a class from more than one parent, inheriting methods and variables from each. Multiple inheritance is not supported in Java.

multiplicity—The numeric relationship between two objects, often shown in class diagrams.

n-ary tree—A tree that limits to the value of n the number of children a node can contain or reference.

NaN—An abbreviation that stands for "not a number," which is the designation for an inappropriate or undefined numeric value.

narrowing conversion—A conversion between two values of different but compatible data types. Narrowing conversions could lose information because the converted type usually has an internal representation smaller than the original storage space. *See also* widening conversion.

native—A Java reserved word that serves as a modifier for methods. A native method is implemented in another programming language.

natural language—A language that humans use to communicate, such as English or French.

negative infinity—A special floating point value that represents the "lowest possible" value. *See also* positive infinity.

nested class—A class declared within another class in order to facilitate implementation and restrict access.

nested if statement—An `if` statement that has as its body another `if` statement.

Netscape Navigator—A World Wide Web browser.

network—(1) Two or more computers connected together so that they can exchange data and share resources. (2) *See* weighted graph.

network address—*See* address.

new—A Java reserved word that is also an operator, used to instantiate an object from a class.

newline character—A nonprintable character that indicates the end of a line.

nodes—Objects in a collection that generally manage the structure of the collection. Nodes can be found in linked implementations of graphs, linked structures, and trees. *See also* graph, linked structure, trees.

nonprintable characters—Any character, such as an escape or newline character, that does not have a symbolic representation that can be displayed on a monitor or printed by a printer. *See also* printable characters.

nonvolatile—The characteristic of a memory device that retains its stored information even after the power supply is turned off. Secondary memory devices are nonvolatile. *See also* volatile.

null—A Java reserved word that is a reference literal, used to indicate that a reference does not currently refer to any object.

number system—A set of values and operations defined by a particular base value that determines the number of digits available and the place value of each digit.

object—(1) The primary software construct in the object-oriented paradigm. (2) An encapsulated collection of data variables and methods. (3) An instance of a class.

object diagram—A visual representation of the objects in a program at a given point in time, often showing the status of instance data.

object-oriented programming—An approach to software design and implementation that is centered around objects and classes. *See also* procedural programming.

octal—The base-8 number system, sometimes used to abbreviate binary strings. *See also* binary, hexadecimal.

off-by-one error—An error caused by a calculation or condition being off by one, such as when a loop is set up to access one too many array elements.

operand—A value on which an operator performs its function. For example, in the expression 5 + 2, the values 5 and 2 are operands.

operating system—The collection of programs that provides the primary user interface to a computer and manages its resources, such as memory and the CPU.

operator—A symbol that represents a particular operation in a programming language, such as the addition operator (+).

operator association—The order in which operators within the same precedence level are evaluated, either right to left or left to right. *See also* operator precedence.

operator overloading—Assigning additional meaning to an operator. Operator overloading is not supported in Java, though method overloading is.

operator precedence—The order in which operators are evaluated in an expression as specified by a well-defined hierarchy.

order—The dominant term in an equation that specifies the efficiency of an algorithm. For example, selection sort is of order n^2.

order of tree—The maximum number of children a tree node may contain or reference. *See also* node, tree.

overflow—A problem that occurs when a data value grows too large for its storage size, which can result in inaccurate arithmetic processing. *See also* underflow.

overloading—Assigning additional meaning to a programming language construct, such as a method or operator. Method overloading is supported by Java but operator overloading is not.

overriding—The process of modifying the definition of an inherited method to suit the purposes of the subclass. *See also* shadowing variables.

package—A Java reserved word that is used to specify a group of related classes.

package visibility—*See* default visibility.

panel—A GUI container that holds and organizes other GUI components.

parameter—(1) A value passed from a method invocation to its definition. (2) The identifier in a method definition that accepts the value passed to it when the method is invoked. *See also* actual parameter, formal parameter.

parameter list—The list of actual or formal parameters to a method.

parameterized type—*See* generic type.

parent class—*See* superclass.

partition element—An arbitrarily chosen element in a list of values that is used by the quick sort algorithm to partition the list for recursive processing. *See also* quick sort.

pass by reference—The process of passing a reference to a value into a method as the parameter. In Java, all objects are managed using references, so an object's formal parameter is an alias to the original. *See also* pass by value.

pass by value—The process of making a copy of a value and passing the copy into a method. Therefore any change made to the value inside the method is not reflected in the original value. All Java primitive types are passed by value.

path—A sequence of edges in a tree or graph that connects two nodes. *See also* edge, graph, node, tree.

PDL—*See* Program Design Language.

peripheral—Any hardware device other than the CPU or main memory.

persistence—The ability of an object to stay in existence after the executing program that creates it terminates. *See also* serialize.

physical line of code—A line in a source code file, terminated by a newline or similar character. *See also* logical line of code.

pixel—A picture element. A digitized picture is made up of many pixels.

place value—The value of each digit position in a number, which determines the overall contribution of that digit to the value. *See also* number system.

point-to-point connection—The link between two networked devices that are connected directly by a wire.

pointer—A variable that can hold a memory address. Instead of pointers, Java uses references, which provide essentially the same functionality as pointers but without the complications.

polyline—A shape made up of a series of connected line segments. A polyline is similar to a polygon, but the shape is not closed.

polymorphism—An object-oriented technique by which a reference that is used to invoke a method can result in different methods being invoked at different times. All Java method invocations are potentially polymorphic in that they invoke the method of the object type, not the reference type.

polynomial complexity—An equation that specifies the efficiency of an algorithm whose dominant term contains the problem size raised to a power (e.g., n^2). *See also* growth function.

POP—*See* Post Office Protocol.

portability—The ability of a program to be moved from one hardware platform to another without having to change it. Because Java bytecode is not related to any particular hardware environment, Java programs are considered portable. *See also* architecture neutral.

positive infinity—A special floating point value that represents the "highest possible" value. *See also* negative infinity.

Post Office Protocol—Protocol that defines the communications commands required to communicate with another machine for the purposes of reading email.

postfix expression—An expression in which an operator is positioned after the operands on which it works. *See also* infix expression.

postfix operator—In Java, an operator that is positioned behind its single operand, whose evaluation yields the value prior to the operation being performed. Both the increment (++) and decrement (—) operators can be applied postfix. *See also* prefix operator.

postorder traversal—A tree traversal that is accomplished by visiting the children, then the node. *See also* inorder traversal, level-order traversal, preorder traversal.

precedence—*See* operator precedence.

prefix operator—In Java, an operator that is positioned in front of its single operand, whose evaluation yields the value after the operation has been performed. Both the increment (++) and decrement (—) operators can be applied prefix. *See also* postfix operator.

preorder traversal—A tree traversal which is accomplished by visiting each node, followed by its children. *See also* inorder traversal, level-order traversal, postorder traversal.

primitive data type—A data type that is predefined in a programming language.

printable characters—Any character that has a symbolic representation that can be displayed on a monitor or printed by a printer. *See also* nonprintable characters.

private—A Java reserved word that serves as a visibility modifier for methods and variables. Private methods and variables are not inherited by subclasses, and can only be accessed in the class in which they are declared.

procedural programming—An approach to software design and implementation that is centered around procedures (or functions) and their interaction. *See also* object-oriented programming.

processing stream—An I/O stream that performs some type of manipulation on the data in the stream. Sometimes called a filtering stream. *See also* data stream.

program—A series of instructions executed by hardware, one after another.

Program Design Language (PDL)—A language in which a program's design and algorithms are expressed. *See also* pseudocode.

programming language—A specification of the syntax and semantics of the statements used to create a program.

programming language statement—An individual instruction in a given programming language.

prompt—A message or symbol used to request information from the user.

propagation—*See* exception propagation.

protected—A Java reserved word that serves as a visibility modifier for methods and variables. Protected methods and variables are inherited by all subclasses and are accessible from all classes in the same package.

prototype—A program used to explore an idea or prove the feasibility of a particular approach.

pseudocode—Structured and abbreviated natural language used to express the algorithmic steps of a program. *See also* Program Design Language.

pseudo–random number—A value generated by software that performs extensive calculations based on an initial seed value. The result is not truly random because it is based on a calculation, but it is usually random enough for most purposes.

public—A Java reserved word that serves as a visibility modifier for classes, interfaces, methods, and variables. A public class or interface can be used anywhere. A public method or variable is inherited by all subclasses and is accessible anywhere.

pure object-oriented language—A programming language that enforces, to some degree, software development using an object-oriented approach. *See also* hybrid object-oriented language.

push button—A GUI component that allows the user to initiate an action with a mouse click. *See also* check box, radio button.

queue—An abstract data type that manages information in a first-in, first-out manner.

quick sort—A sorting algorithm in which the list to sort is partitioned based on an arbitrarily chosen element. Then, the sublists on either side of the partition element are recursively sorted. *See also* bubble sort, heap sort, insertion sort, merge sort, radix sort, selection sort.

radio button—A GUI component that allows the user to choose one of a set of options with a mouse click. A radio button is useful only as part of a group of other radio buttons. *See also* check box.

radix—The base, or number of possible unique digits, of a number system.

radix sort—A sorting algorithm that utilizes a series of queues. *See also* bubble sort, heap sort, insertion sort, merge sort, selection sort, quick sort.

RAM—*See* random access memory.

random access device—A memory device whose information can be directly accessed. *See also* random access memory, sequential access device.

random access memory (RAM)—A term basically interchangeable with main memory. Should probably be called read-write memory, to distinguish it from read-only memory.

random-number generator—Software that produces a pseudo-random number, generated by calculations based on a seed value.

read-only memory (ROM)—Any memory device whose stored information is stored permanently when the device is created. It can be read from, but not written to.

recursion—The process of a method invoking itself, either directly or indirectly. Recursive algorithms sometimes provide elegant, though perhaps inefficient, solutions to a problem.

refactoring—The process of modifying existing source code to clean up redundant portions introduced during the development of additional source code.

reference—A variable that holds the address of an object. In Java, a reference can be used to interact with an object, but its address cannot be accessed, set, or operated on directly.

refinement—One iteration of an evolutionary development cycle in which a particular aspect of the system, such as the user interface or a particular algorithm, is addressed.

refinement scope—The specific issues that are addressed in a particular refinement during evolutionary software development.

register—A small area of storage in the CPU of the computer.

regression testing—The process of reexecuting test cases following the addition of a new feature or the correcting of an existing bug to ensure that code modifications did not introduce any new problems.

relational operator—One of several operators that determine the ordering relationship between two values: less than (<), less than or equal to (<=), greater than (>), and greater than or equal to (>=). *See also* equality operator.

release—A version of a software product that is made available to the customer.

repetition statement—A programming construct that allows a set of statements to be executed repetitively as long as a particular condition is true. The body of the repetition statement should eventually make the condition false. Also called an iteration statement or loop. *See also* do, for, while.

requirements—(1) The specification of what a program must and must not do. (2) An early phase of the software development process in which the program requirements are established.

reserved word—A word that has special meaning in a programming language and cannot be used for any other purpose.

retirement—The phase of a program's life cycle in which the program is taken out of active use.

return—A Java reserved word that causes the flow of program execution to return from a method to the point of invocation.

return type—The type of value returned from a method, specified before the method name in the method declaration. Could be `void`, which indicates that no value is returned.

reuse—Using existing software components to create new ones.

review—The process of critically examining a design or program to discover errors. There are many types of reviews. *See also* desk check, walkthrough.

RGB value—A collection of three values that defines a color. Each value represents the contribution of the primary colors red, green, and blue.

ROM—*See* read-only memory.

rotation—An operation on a tree that seeks to relocate nodes in an attempt to assist in the balance of the tree. *See also* balanced tree, node.

run-time error—A problem that occurs during program execution that causes the program to terminate abnormally. *See also* compile-time error, logical error, syntax error.

scope—The areas within a program in which an identifier, such as a variable, can be referenced. *See also* access.

scroll pane—A GUI container that offers a limited view of a component and provides horizontal and/or vertical scroll bars to change that view.

SDK—*See* Software Development Kit.

search pool—A group of items over which a search is performed.

search tree—A tree whose elements are structured to facilitate finding a particular element when needed. *See also* tree.

searching—The process of determining the existence or location of a target value within a list of values. *See also* binary search, linear search.

secondary memory—Hardware storage devices, such as magnetic disks or tapes, that store information in a relatively permanent manner. *See also* main memory.

seed value—A value used by a random-number generator as a base for the calculations that produce a pseudo-random number.

selection sort—A sorting algorithm in which each value, one at a time, is placed in its final, sorted position. *See also* bubble sort, heap sort, insertion sort, merge sort, quick sort, radix sort.

selection statement—A programming construct that allows a set of statements to be executed if a particular condition is true. *See also* if, switch.

self-loop—An edge of a graph that connects a vertex to itself.

self-referential object—An object that contains a reference to a second object of the same type.

semantics—The interpretation of a program or programming construct.

sentinel value—A specific value used to indicate a special condition, such as the end of input.

serialize—The process of converting an object into a linear series of bytes so it can be saved to a file or sent across a network. *See also* persistence.

service methods—Methods in an object that are declared with public visibility and define a service that the object's client can invoke.

shadowing variables—The process of defining a variable in a subclass that supersedes an inherited version.

shell—*See* command shell.

short—A Java reserved word that represents a primitive integer type, stored using 16 bits in two's complement format.

siblings—Two items in a tree or hierarchy, such as a class inheritance hierarchy, that have the same parent.

sign bit—A bit in a numeric value that represents the sign (positive or negative) of that value.

signed numeric value—A value that stores a sign (positive or negative). All Java numeric values are signed. A Java character is stored as an unsigned value.

signature—The number, types, and order of the parameters of a method. Overloaded methods must each have a unique signature.

Simple Mail Transfer Protocol—Protocol that defines the communications commands required to send email.

slider—A GUI component that allows the user to specify a numeric value within a bounded range by moving a knob to the appropriate place in the range.

sling—*See* self-loop.

SMTP—See *Simple Mail Transfer Protocol*.

software—(1) Programs and data. (2) The intangible components of a computer system.

software component—*See* component.

Software Development Kit (SDK)—A collection of software tools that assists in the development of software. The Java Software Development Kit is another name for the Java Development Kit.

software engineering—The discipline within computer science that addresses the process of developing high-quality software within practical constraints.

sort key—A particular value present in each member of a collection of objects upon which a sort is based.

sorting—The process of putting a list of values into a well-defined order. *See also* bubble sort, heap sort, insertion sort, merge sort, radix sort, selection sort, quick sort.

spanning tree—A tree that includes all of the vertices of a graph and some, but possibly not all, of the edges. *See also* edge, vertex.

split pane—A GUI container that displays two components, either side by side or one on top of the other, separated by a moveable divider bar.

stack—An abstract data type that manages data in a last-in, first-out manner.

stack trace—The series of methods called to reach a certain point in a program. When an exception is thrown, the stack trace can be analyzed to assist the programmer in tracking down the problem.

standard I/O stream—One of three common I/O streams representing standard input (usually the keyboard), standard output (usually the monitor screen), and standard error (also usually the monitor). *See also* stream.

start angle—When defining an arc, the angle at which the arc begins. *See also* arc angle.

state—The state of being of an object, defined by the values of its data. *See also* behavior, identity.

statement—*See* programming language statement.

statement coverage—A strategy used in white-box testing in which all statements in a program are executed. *See also* condition coverage.

static—A Java reserved word that serves as a modifier for methods and variables. A static method is also called a class method and can be referenced without an instance of the class. A static variable is also called a class variable and is common to all instances of the class.

static data structure—A data structure that has a fixed size and cannot grow and shrink as needed. *See also* dynamic data structure.

step—The execution of a single program statement in a debugger. *See also* debugger.

storage capacity—The total number of bytes that can be stored in a particular memory device.

stream—A source of input or a destination for output.

strictfp—A Java reserved word that is used to control certain aspects of floating point arithmetic.

string—*See* character string.

string concatenation—The process of attaching the beginning of one character string to the end of another, resulting in one longer string.

strongly typed language—A programming language in which each variable is associated with a particular data type for the duration of its existence. Variables are not allowed to take on values or be used in operations that are inconsistent with their type.

structured programming—An approach to program development in which each software component has one entry and exit point and in which the flow of control does not cross unnecessarily.

stub—A method that simulates the functionality of a particular software component. Often used during unit testing. *See also* unit testing.

subclass—A class derived from another class via inheritance. Also called a derived class or child class. *See also* superclass.

subscript—*See* index.

super—A Java reserved word that is a reference to the parent class of the object making the reference. Often used to invoke a parent's constructor.

super reference—*See* super.

superclass—The class from which another class is derived via inheritance. Also called a base class or parent class. *See also* subclass.

support methods—Methods in an object that are not intended for use outside the class. They provide support functionality for service methods. As such, they are usually not declared with public visibility.

swapping—The process of exchanging the values of two variables.

Swing—The package in the Java API (`javax.swing`) that contains classes related to GUIs. Swing provides alternative components from those in the Abstract Windowing Toolkit package, but does not replace it.

switch—A Java reserved word that specifies a compound conditional construct.

synchronization—The process of ensuring that data shared among multiple threads cannot be accessed by more than one thread at a time. *See also* synchronized.

synchronized—A Java reserved word that serves as a modifier for methods. Separate threads of a process can execute concurrently in a method, unless the method is synchronized, making it a mutually exclusive resource. Methods that access shared data should be synchronized.

syntax error—An error produced by the compiler because a program did not conform to the syntax of the programming language. Syntax errors are a subset of compile-time errors. *See also* compile-time error, logical error, run-time error, syntax rules.

syntax rules—The set of specifications that govern how the elements of a programming language can be put together to form valid statements.

system test—The process of testing an entire software system. Alpha and beta tests (also known as alpha and beta releases of software applications) are system tests.

tabbed pane—A GUI container that presents a set of cards from which the user can choose. Each card contains its own GUI components.

target element—*See* target value.

target value—The value that is sought when performing a search on a collection of data.

targets—User-defined groups of actions present in an ANT build file.

TCP/IP—Software that controls the movement of messages across the Internet. The acronym stands for Transmission Control Protocol/Internet Protocol.

terabyte (TB)—A unit of binary storage, equal to 2^{40} (approximately 1 trillion) bytes.

termination—The point at which a program stops executing.

ternary operator—An operator that uses three operands.

test case—A set of input values and user actions, along with a specification of the expected output, used to find errors in a system.

test-driven development—A software development style that encourages the developer to write test cases first, and then develop just enough source code to see the test cases pass.

test fixture—A method used to instantiate objects used during a test.

test suite—A set of tests that covers various aspects of the system.

testing—(1) The process of running a program with various test cases in order to discover problems. (2) The process of critically evaluating a design or program.

text area—A GUI component that displays, or allows the user to enter, multiple lines of data.

text field—A GUI component that displays, or allows the user to enter, a single line of data.

text file—A file that contains data formatted as ASCII or Unicode characters.

this—A Java reserved word that is a reference to the object executing the code making the reference.

thread—An independent process executing within a program. A Java program can have multiple threads running in a program at one time.

throw—A Java reserved word that is used to start an exception propagation.

throws—A Java reserved word that specifies that a method may throw a particular type of exception.

timer—An object that generates an event at regular intervals.

token—A portion of a string defined by a set of delimiters.

tool tip—A short line of text that appears when the mouse pointer is allowed to rest on top of a particular component. Usually, tool tips are used to inform the user of the component's purpose.

top-level domain—The last part of a network domain name, such as edu or com.

transient—A Java reserved word that serves as a modifier for variables. A transient variable does not contribute to the object's persistent state, and therefore does not need to be saved. *See also* serialize.

tree—A nonlinear data structure that forms a hierarchy stemming from a single root node.

true—A Java reserved word that serves as one of the two boolean literals (`true` and `false`).

truth table—A complete enumeration of all permutations of values involved in a boolean expression, as well as the computed result.

try—A Java reserved word that is used to define the context in which certain exceptions will be handled if they are thrown.

two-dimensional array—An array that uses two indices to specify the location of an element. The two dimensions are often thought of as the rows and columns of a table. *See also* multidimensional array.

two's complement—A technique for representing numeric binary data. Used by all Java integer primitive types (`byte`, `short`, `int`, `long`).

type—*See* data type.

UML—*See* Unified Modeling Language.

unary operator—An operator that uses only one operand.

unchecked exception—A Java exception that does not need to be caught or dealt with if the programmer so chooses.

underflow—A problem that occurs when a floating point value becomes too small for its storage size, which can result in inaccurate arithmetic processing. *See also* overflow.

undirected graph—A graph data structure in which each edge can be traversed in either direction. *See also* edge.

Unicode—The international character set used to define valid Java characters. Each character is represented using a 16-bit unsigned numeric value.

Unified Modeling Language (UML)—A graphical notation for visualizing relationships among classes and objects. There are many types of UML diagrams. *See also* class diagrams.

uniform resource locator (URL)—A designation for a resource that can be located through a Web browser.

unit testing—The process of testing an individual software component. May require the creation of stub modules to simulate other system components.

Unix—A computer operating system developed by AT&T Bell Labs. *See also* Linux, operating system.

unsigned numeric value—A value that does not store a sign (positive or negative). The bit usually reserved to represent the sign is included in the value, doubling the magnitude of the number that can be stored. Java characters are stored as unsigned numeric values, but there are no primitive numeric types that are unsigned.

URL—*See* uniform resource locator.

use relationship—A relationship between two classes, often shown in a class diagram, that establishes that one class uses another in some way, such as relying on its services. *See also* association.

user interface—The manner in which the user interacts with a software system, which is often graphical. *See also* graphical user interface.

variable—An identifier in a program that represents a memory location in which a data value is stored.

vertex—A node in a graph. *See also* graph.

visibility modifier—A Java modifier that defines the scope in which a construct can be accessed. The Java visibility modifiers are `public`, `protected`, `private`, and default (no modifier used).

void—A Java reserved word that can be used as a return value for a method, indicating that no value is returned.

volatile—(1) A Java reserved word that serves as a modifier for variables. A volatile variable might be changed asynchronously and therefore indicates that the compiler should not attempt optimizations on it. (2) The characteristic of a memory device that loses stored information when the power supply is interrupted. Main memory is a volatile storage device. *See also* nonvolatile.

von Neumann architecture—The computer architecture named after John von Neumann in which programs and data are stored together in the same memory devices.

walkthrough—A form of review in which a group of developers, managers, and quality assurance personnel examines a design or program in order to find errors. Sometimes referred to as an inspection. *See also* desk check.

WAN—*See* wide-area network.

waterfall model—One of the earliest software development process models. It defines a basically linear interaction between the requirements, design, implementation, and testing stages.

Web—*See* World Wide Web.

weighted graph—A graph with weights or costs associated with each edge. Weighted graphs are also sometimes known as networks.

while—A Java reserved word that represents a repetition construct. A while statement is executed zero or more times. *See also* do, for.

white-box testing—Producing and evaluating test cases based on the interior logic of a software component. The test cases focus on stressing decision points and ensuring coverage. *See also* blackbox testing, condition coverage, statement coverage.

white space—Spaces, tabs, and blank lines that are used to set off sections of source code to make programs more readable.

wide-area network (WAN)—A computer network that connects two or more local-area networks, usually across long geographic distances. *See also* local-area network.

widening conversion—A conversion between two values of different but compatible data types. Widening conversions usually leave the data value intact because the converted type has an internal representation equal to or larger than the original storage space. *See also* narrowing conversion.

word—A unit of binary storage. The size of a word varies by computer, and is usually 2, 4, or 8 bytes. The word size indicates the amount of information that can be moved through the machine at one time.

World Wide Web (WWW or Web)—Software that makes the exchange of information across a network easier by providing a common GUI for multiple types of information. Web browsers are used to retrieve and format HTML documents.

wrapper class—A class designed to store a primitive type in an object. Usually used when an object reference is needed and a primitive type would not suffice.

WWW—*See* World Wide Web.

zip—A file format used to compress and store one or more files and directories into a single file suitable for exchanging to another computer.

Number Systems

Tis appendix contains a detailed introduction to number systems and their underlying characteristics. The particular focus is on the binary number system, its use with computers, and its similarities to other number systems. This introduction also covers conversions between bases.

In our everyday lives, we use the *decimal number system* to represent values, to count, and to perform arithmetic. The decimal system is also referred to as the *base-10 number system*. We use 10 digits (0 through 9) to represent values in the decimal system.

Computers use the *binary number system* to store and manage information. The binary system, also called the *base-2 number system*, has only two digits (0 and 1). Each 0 and 1 is called a *bit*, short for binary digit. A series of bits is called a *binary string*.

There is nothing particularly special about either the binary or decimal systems. Long ago, humans adopted the decimal number system probably because we have 10 fingers on our hands. If humans had 12 fingers, we would probably be using a base-12 number system regularly and find it as easy to deal with as we do the decimal system now. It all depends on what you get used to. As you explore the binary system, it will become more familiar and natural.

Binary is used for computer processing because the devices used to manage and store information are less expensive and more reliable if they have to represent only two possible values. Computers have been made that use the decimal system, but they are not as convenient.

There are an infinite number of number systems, and they all follow the same basic rules. You already know how the binary number system works, but you just might not be aware that you do. It all goes back to the basic rules of arithmetic.

Place Value

In decimal, we represent the values of 0 through 9 using only one digit. To represent any value higher than 9, we must use more than one digit. The position of each digit has a *place value* that indicates the amount it contributes to the overall value. In decimal, we refer to the one's column, the ten's column, the hundred's column, and so on forever.

Each place value is determined by the *base* of the number system, raised to increasing powers as we move from right to left. In the decimal number system, the place value of the digit furthest to the right is 10^0, or 1. The place value of the next digit is 10^1, or 10. The place value of the third digit from the right is 10^2, or 100, and so on. Figure B.1 shows how each digit in a decimal number contributes to the value.

FIGURE B.1 Place values in the decimal number system

The binary number system works the same way except that we exhaust the available digits much sooner. We can represent 0 and 1 with a single bit, but to represent any value higher than 1, we must use multiple bits.

The place values in binary are determined by increasing powers of the base as we move right to left, just as they are in the decimal system. However, in binary, the base value is 2. Therefore the place value of the bit furthest to the right is 2^0, or 1. The place value of the next bit is 2^1, or 2. The place value of the third bit from the right is 2^2, or 4, and so on. Figure B.2 shows a binary number and its place values.

The number 1101 is a valid binary number, but it is also a valid decimal number as well. Sometimes to make it clear which number system is being used, the base value is appended as a subscript to the end of a number. Therefore you can distinguish between 1101_2, which is equivalent to 13 in decimal, and 1101_{10} (one thousand one hundred and one), which in binary is represented as 10001001101_2.

A number system with base N has N digits (0 through N–1). As we have seen, the decimal system has 10 digits (0 through 9), and the binary system has two digits (0 and 1). They all work the same way. For instance, the base-5 number system has five digits (0 through 4).

Note that, in any number system, the place value of the digit furthest to the right is 1, since any base raised to the zero power is 1. Also notice that the value 10, which we refer to as "ten" in the decimal system, always represents the base value in any number system. In base 10, 10 is one 10 and zero 1's. In base 2, 10 is one 2 and zero 1's. In base 5, 10 is one 5 and zero 1's.

You may have seen the following geeky joke on a t-shirt: There are 10 types of people in the world, those who understand binary, and those who don't.

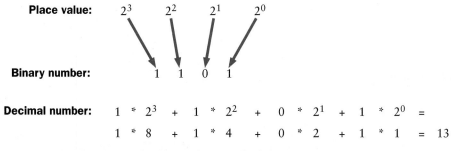

FIGURE B.2 Place values in the binary number system

Bases Higher Than 10

Since all number systems with base N have N digits, then base 16 has 16 digits. But what are they? We are used to the digits 0 through 9, but in bases higher than 10, we need a single digit, a single symbol, that represents the decimal value 10. In fact, in *base 16*, which is also called *hexadecimal,* we need digits that represent the decimal values 10 through 15.

For number systems higher than 10, we use alphabetic characters as single digits for values greater than 9. The hexadecimal digits are 0 through F, where 0 through 9 represent the first 10 digits, and A represents the decimal value 10, B represents 11, C represents 12, D represents 13, E represents 14, and F represents 15.

Therefore, the number 2A8E is a valid hexadecimal number. The place values are determined as they are for decimal and binary, using increasing powers of the base. So in hexadecimal, the place values are powers of 16. Figure B.3 shows how the place values of the hexadecimal number 2A8E contribute to the overall value.

All number systems with bases greater than 10 use letters as digits. For example, base 12 has the digits 0 through B and base 19 has the digits 0 through I. However, beyond having a different set of digits and a different base, the rules governing each number system are the same.

Keep in mind that when we change number systems, we are simply changing the way we represent values, not the values themselves. If you have 18_{10} pencils, it may be written as 10010 in binary or as 12 in hexadecimal, but it is still the same number of pencils.

Figure B.4 shows the representations of the decimal values 0 through 20 in several bases, including *base 8*, which is also called *octal.* Note that the larger the base, the higher the value that can be represented in a single digit.

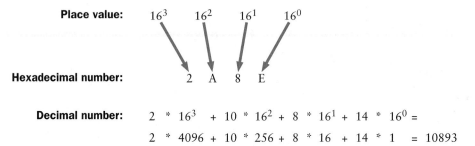

Place value:	16^3	16^2	16^1	16^0
Hexadecimal number:	2	A	8	E

Decimal number:

$$2 * 16^3 + 10 * 16^2 + 8 * 16^1 + 14 * 16^0 =$$
$$2 * 4096 + 10 * 256 + 8 * 16 + 14 * 1 = 10893$$

FIGURE B.3 Place values in the hexadecimal number system

Binary (base 2)	Octal (base 8)	Decimal (base 10)	Hexadecimal (base 16)
0	0	0	0
1	1	1	1
10	2	2	2
11	3	3	3
100	4	4	4
101	5	5	5
110	6	6	6
111	7	7	7
1000	10	8	8
1001	11	9	9
1010	12	10	A
1011	13	11	B
1100	14	12	C
1101	15	13	D
1110	16	14	E
1111	17	15	F
10000	20	16	10
10001	21	17	11
10010	22	18	12
10011	23	19	13
10100	24	20	14

FIGURE B.4 Counting in various number systems

Conversions

We've already seen how a number in another base is converted to decimal by determining the place value of each digit and computing the result. This process can be used to convert any number in any base to its equivalent value in base 10.

Now let's reverse the process, converting a base-10 value to another base. First, find the highest place value in the new number system that is less than or equal to the original value. Then, divide the original number by that place value to determine the digit that belongs in that position. The remainder is the value that must be represented in the remaining digit positions. Continue this process, position by position, until the entire value is represented.

For example, Figure B.5 shows the process of converting the decimal value 180 into binary. The highest place value in binary that is less than or equal to 180 is 128 (or 2^7), which is the eighth bit position from the right. Dividing 180 by 128 yields 1 with 52 remaining. Therefore the first bit is 1, and the decimal value 52 must be represented in the remaining seven bits. Dividing 52 by 64, which is the next place value (2^6), yields 0 with 52 remaining. So the second bit is 0. Dividing 52 by 32 yields 1 with 20 remaining. So the third bit is 1 and the remaining five bits must represent the value 20. Dividing 20 by 16 yields 1 with 4 remaining. Dividing 4 by 8 yields 0 with 4 remaining. Dividing 4 by 4 yields 0 with 0 remaining.

Since the number has been completely represented, the rest of the bits are zero. Therefore 180_{10} is equivalent to 10110100 in binary. This can be confirmed by converting the new binary number back to decimal to make sure we get the original value.

This process works to convert any decimal value to any target base. For each target base, the place values and possible digits change. If you start with the correct place value, each division operation will yield a valid digit in the new base.

In the example in Figure B.5, the only digits that could have resulted from each division operation were 1 or 0, since we were converting to binary. However, when we are converting to other bases, any valid digit in the new base could result. For example, Figure B.6 shows the process of converting the decimal value 1967 into hexadecimal.

Place value	Number	Digit
128	180	1
64	52	0
32	52	1
16	20	1
8	4	0
4	4	1
2	0	0
1	0	0

$$180_{10} = 10110100_2$$

FIGURE B.5 Converting a decimal value into binary

Place value	Number	Digit
256	1967	7
16	175	A
1	15	F

$$1967_{10} = 7AF_{16}$$

FIGURE B.6 Converting a decimal value into hexadecimal

The place value 256, which is 16^2, is the highest place value less than or equal to the original number, since the next highest place value is 16^3 or 4096. Dividing 1967 by 256 yields 7 with 175 remaining. Dividing 175 by 16 yields 10 with 15 remaining. Remember that 10 in decimal can be represented as the single digit A in hexadecimal. The 15 remaining can be represented as the digit F. Therefore 1967_{10} is equivalent to 7AF in hexadecimal.

Shortcut Conversions

We have established techniques for converting any value in any base to its equivalent representation in base 10, and from base 10 to any other base. Therefore you can now convert a number in any base to any other base by going through base 10. However, an interesting relationship exists between the bases that are powers of 2, such as binary, octal, and hexadecimal, which allows very quick conversions between them.

To convert from binary to hexadecimal, for instance, you can simply group the bits of the original value into groups of four, starting from the right, then convert each group of four into a single hexadecimal digit. The example in Figure B.7 demonstrates this process.

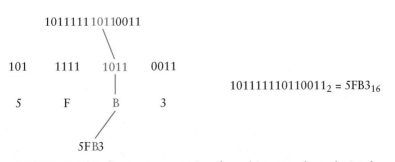

$$101111110110011_2 = 5FB3_{16}$$

FIGURE B.7 A shortcut conversion from binary to hexadecimal

FIGURE B.8 A shortcut conversion from hexadecimal to binary

To go from hexadecimal to binary, we reverse this process, expanding each hexadecimal digit into four binary digits. Note that you may have to add leading zeros to the binary version of each expanded hexadecimal digit if necessary to make four binary digits. Figure B.8 shows the conversion of the hexadecimal value 40C6 to binary.

Why do we use groups of four bits when converting between binary and hexadecimal? The answer comes from the relationship between the bases 2 and 16. We use groups of four bits because $2^4 = 16$. The shortcut conversions work between binary and any base that is a power of 2. We section the bits into groups of that power.

Therefore, converting from binary to octal is the same process except that the bits are sectioned into groups of three, since $2^3 = 8$. Likewise, when converting from octal to binary, we expand each octal digit into three bits.

To convert between, say, hexadecimal and octal is now a process of doing two shortcut conversions. First convert from hexadecimal to binary, then take that result and perform a shortcut conversion from binary to octal.

By the way, these types of shortcut conversions can be performed between any base B and any base that is a power of B. For example, conversions between base 3 and base 9 can be accomplished using the shortcut grouping technique, sectioning or expanding digits into groups of two, since $3^2 = 9$.

Exercises

EX B.1   What is the difference between the binary and decimal number systems?

EX B.2   Why do modern computers use a binary number system to represent information?

EX B.3   How many digits are used in the base-6 number system? What are they?

EX B.4   How many digits are used in the base-12 number system? What are they?

EX B.5   Convert the following binary numbers to decimal.

   a. 10

   b. 10110

   c. 11100

   d. 10101010

   e. 11001011

   f. 10000000001

EX B.6   Convert the following octal numbers to decimal.

   a. 10

   b. 125

   c. 5401

   d. 7777

   e. 46034

   f. 65520

EX B.7   Convert the following hexadecimal numbers to decimal.

   a. 10

   b. 904

   c. 6C3

   d. ABC

   e. 5D0BF

   f. FFF

EX B.8   Convert the following decimal numbers into binary.

a. 2

b. 10

c. 64

d. 80

e. 145

f. 256

EX B.9   Convert the following decimal numbers into octal.

a. 8

b. 10

c. 512

d. 406

e. 349

f. 888

EX B.10   Convert the following decimal numbers into hexadecimal.

a. 16

b. 10

c. 175

d. 256

e. 422

f. 4199

EX B.11   Convert the following binary numbers into hexadecimal.

a. 101000110110

b. 1110101111

c. 1100110000010111

d. 1000000000011011

e. 1010111100010

f. 11000111000010001111110000

EX B.12 Convert the following binary numbers into octal.

      a. 101011111011

      b. 1001101011

      c. 111111000101110

      d. 11010000110111110001

      e. 111110101100011010001

      f. 1100010001110101111011100111

EX B.13 Convert the following hexadecimal numbers into binary.

      a. 555

      b. B74

      c. 47A9

      d. FDCB

      e. 10101010

      f. 5B60F9D

EX B.14 Convert the following octal numbers into binary.

      a. 555

      b. 760

      c. 152

      d. 3032

      e. 76543

      f. 6351732

The Unicode Character Set

The Java programming language uses the Unicode character set for managing text. A *character set* is simply an ordered list of characters, each corresponding to a particular numeric value. Unicode is an international character set that contains letters, symbols, and ideograms for languages all over the world. Each character is represented as a 16-bit unsigned numeric value. Unicode, therefore, can support over 65,000 unique characters. Only about half of those values have characters assigned to them at this point. The Unicode character set continues to be refined as characters from various languages are included.

Many programming languages still use the ASCII character set. ASCII stands for the American Standard Code for Information Interchange. The 8-bit extended ASCII set is quite small, so the developers of Java opted to use Unicode in order to support international users. However, ASCII is essentially a subset of Unicode, including the corresponding numeric values, so programmers used to ASCII should have no problems with Unicode.

Figure C.1 shows a list of commonly used characters and their Unicode numeric values. These characters also happen to be ASCII characters. All of the characters in Figure C.1 are called *printable characters* because they have a symbolic representation that can be displayed on a monitor or printed by a printer. Other characters are called *nonprintable characters* because they have no such symbolic representation. Note that the space character (numeric value 32) is considered a printable character, even though no symbol is printed when it is displayed. Nonprintable characters are sometimes called *control characters* because many of them can be generated by holding down the control key on a keyboard and pressing another key.

The Unicode characters with numeric values 0 through 31 are nonprintable characters. Also, the delete character, with numeric value 127, is a nonprintable character. All of these characters are ASCII characters as well. Many of them have

Value	Char	Value	Char	Value	Char	Value	Char	Value	Char
32	*space*	51	3	70	F	89	Y	108	l
33	!	52	4	71	G	90	Z	109	m
34	"	53	5	72	H	91	[	110	n
35	#	54	6	73	I	92	\	111	o
36	$	55	7	74	J	93	]	112	p
37	%	56	8	75	K	94	^	113	q
38	&	57	9	76	L	95	–	114	r
39	'	58	:	77	M	96	`	115	s
40	(	59	;	78	N	97	a	116	t
41	)	60	<	79	O	98	b	117	u
42	*	61	=	80	P	99	c	118	v
43	+	62	>	81	Q	100	d	119	w
44	'	63	?	82	R	101	e	120	x
45	–	64	@	83	S	102	f	121	y
46	.	65	A	84	T	103	g	122	z
47	/	66	B	85	U	104	h	123	{
48	0	67	C	86	V	105	i	124		
49	1	68	D	87	W	106	j	125	}
50	2	69	E	88	X	107	k	126	~

FIGURE C.1 The printable ASCII subset of the Unicode character set fairly common and well-defined uses, while others are more general. The table in Figure C.2 lists a small sample of the nonprintable characters.

Nonprintable characters are used in many situations to represent special conditions. For example, certain nonprintable characters can be stored in a text document to indicate, among other things, the beginning of a new line. An editor will process these characters by starting the text that follows it on a new line, instead of printing a symbol to the screen. Various types of computer systems use different nonprintable characters to represent particular conditions.

Except for having no visible representation, nonprintable characters are essentially equivalent to printable characters. They can be stored in a Java character variable and be part of a character string. They are stored using 16 bits, can be converted to their numeric value, and can be compared using relational operators.

The first 128 characters of the Unicode character set correspond to the common ASCII character set. The first 256 characters correspond to the ISO-Latin-1 extended ASCII character set. Many operating systems and Web browsers will handle these characters, but they may not be able to print the other Unicode characters.

The Unicode character set contains most alphabets in use today, including Greek, Hebrew, Cyrillic, and various Asian ideographs. It also includes Braille, and several sets of symbols used in mathematics and music. Figure C.3 shows a few characters from non-Western alphabets.

Value	Character
0	*null*
7	*bell*
8	*backspace*
9	*tab*
10	*line feed*
12	*form feed*
13	*carriage return*
27	*escape*
127	*delete*

FIGURE C.2 Some nonprintable characters in the Unicode character set

Value	Character	Source
1071	Я	Russian (Cyrillic)
3593	ฌ	Thai
5098	Ꮟ	Cherokee
8478	℞	Letterlike Symbols
8652	⇌	Arrows
10287	⠇	Braille
13407	�	Chinese/Japanese/Korean (Common)

FIGURE C.3 Some non-Western characters in the Unicode character set

Appendix D

Java Operators

Java operators are evaluated according to the precedence hierarchy shown in Figure D.1. Operators at low precedence levels are evaluated before operators at higher levels. Operators within the same precedence level are evaluated according to the specified association, either right to left (R to L) or left to right (L to R). Operators in the same precedence level are not listed in any particular order.

The order of operator evaluation can always be forced by the use of parentheses. It is sometimes a good idea to use parentheses even when they are not required, to make it explicitly clear to a human reader how an expression is evaluated.

Precedence Level	Operator	Operation	Associates
1	[ ] . (*parameters*) ++ --	array indexing object member reference parameter evaluation and method invocation postfix increment postfix decrement	L to R
2	++ -- + − ~ !	prefix increment prefix decrement unary plus unary minus bitwise NOT logical NOT	R to L
3	new (*type*)	object instantiation cast	R to L
4	* / %	multiplication division remainder	L to R
5	+ + −	addition string concatenation subtraction	L to R
6	<< >> >>>	left shift right shift with sign right shift with zero	L to R
7	< <= > >= instanceof	less than less than or equal greater than greater than or equal type comparison	L to R
8	== !=	equal not equal	L to R

FIGURE D.1 Java operator precedence

For some operators, the operand types determine which operation is carried out. For instance, if the + operator is used on two strings, string concatenation is performed, but if it is applied to two numeric types, they are added in the arithmetic sense. If only one of the operands is a string, the other is converted to a string, and string concatenation is performed. Similarly, the operators &, ^, and | perform bitwise operations on numeric operands but boolean operations on boolean operands.

The boolean operators & and | differ from the logical operators && and || in a subtle way. The logical operators are "short-circuited" in that if the result of an expression can be determined by evaluating only the left operand, the right operand

Precedence Level	Operator	Operation	Associates
9	& &	bitwise AND boolean AND	L to R
10	^ ^	bitwise XOR boolean XOR	L to R
11	| |	bitwise OR boolean OR	L to R
12	&&	logical AND	L to R
13	||	logical OR	L to R
14	?:	conditional operator	R to L
15	= += += -= *= /= %= <<= >>= >>>= &= &= ^= ^= |= |=	assignment addition, then assignment string concatenation, then assignment subtraction, then assignment multiplication, then assignment division, then assignment remainder, then assignment left shift, then assignment right shift (sign), then assignment right shift (zero), then assignment bitwise AND, then assignment boolean AND, then assignment bitwise XOR, then assignment boolean XOR, then assignment bitwise OR, then assignment boolean OR, then assignment	R to L

FIGURE D.1 Java operator precedence, continued

is not evaluated. The boolean versions always evaluate both sides of the expression. There is no logical operator that performs an exclusive OR (XOR) operation.

Java Bitwise Operators

The Java *bitwise operators* operate on individual bits within a primitive value. Because they are not discussed in the chapters of this book, we explore them here further. The bitwise operators are defined only for integers and characters. They are unique among all Java operators because they let us work at the lowest level of binary storage. Figure D.2 on the next page lists the Java bitwise operators.

Three of the bitwise operators are similar to the logical operators !, &&, and ||. The bitwise NOT, AND, and OR operations work basically the same way as their

Operator	Description
~	bitwise NOT
&	bitwise AND
|	bitwise OR
^	bitwise XOR
<<	left shift
>>	right shift with sign
>>>	right shift with zero fill

FIGURE D.2 The Java bitwise operators

logical counterparts, except they work on individual bits of a value. The rules are essentially the same. Figure D.3 shows the results of bitwise operators on all combinations of two bits. Compare this chart to the truth tables for the logical operators in Chapter 4 to see the similarities.

The bitwise operators include the XOR operator, which stands for *exclusive OR*. The logical || operator is an *inclusive OR* operation, which means it returns true if both operands are true. The | bitwise operator is also inclusive and yields a 1 if both corresponding bits are 1. However, the exclusive OR operator (^) yields a 0 if both operands are 1. There is no logical exclusive OR operator in Java.

When the bitwise operators are applied to integer values, the operation is performed individually on each bit in the value. For example, suppose the integer variable number is declared to be of type byte and currently holds the value 45. Stored as an 8-bit byte, it is represented in binary as 00101101. When the bitwise complement operator (~) is applied to number, each bit in the value is inverted, yielding 11010010. Since integers are stored using two's complement representation, the value represented is now negative, specifically –46.

a	b	~ a	a & b	a | b	a ^ b
0	0	1	0	0	0
0	1	1	0	1	1
1	0	0	0	1	1
1	1	0	1	1	0

FIGURE D.3 Bitwise operations on individual bits

num1 & num2	num1 | num2	num1 ^ num2
00101101	00101101	00101101
& 00001110	| 00001110	^ 00001110
= 00001100	= 00101111	= 00100011

FIGURE D.4 Bitwise operations on bytes

Similarly, for all bitwise operators, the operations are applied bit by bit, which is where the term "bitwise" comes from. For binary operators (with two operands), the operations are applied to corresponding bits in each operand. For example, assume `num1` and `num2` are `byte` integers, `num1` holds the value 45, and `num2` holds the value 14. Figure D.4 shows the results of several bitwise operations.

The operators `&`, `|`, and `^` can also be applied to boolean values, and they have basically the same meaning as their logical counterparts. When used with boolean values, they are called *boolean operators*. However, unlike the operators `&&` and `||`, which are "short-circuited," the boolean operators are not short-circuited. Both sides of the expression are evaluated every time.

Like the other bitwise operators, the three bitwise shift operators manipulate the individual bits of an integer value. They all take two operands. The left operand is the value whose bits are shifted; the right operand specifies how many positions they should move. Prior to performing a shift, `byte` and `short` values are promoted to `int` for all shift operators. Furthermore, if either of the operands is `long`, the other operand is promoted to `long`. For readability, we use only 16 bits in the examples in this section, but the concepts are the same when carried out to 32- or 64-bit strings.

When bits are shifted, some bits are lost off one end, and others need to be filled in on the other. The *left-shift* operator (`<<`) shifts bits to the left, filling the right bits with zeros. For example, if the integer variable `number` currently has the value 13, then the statement

```
number = number << 2;
```

stores the value 52 into `number`. Initially, `number` contains the bit string 0000000000001101. When shifted to the left, the value becomes 0000000000110100, or 52. Notice that for each position shifted to the left, the original value is multiplied by 2.

The sign bit of a number is shifted along with all of the others. Therefore the sign of the value could change if enough bits are shifted to change the sign bit. For example, the value –8 is stored in binary two's complement form as

1111111111111000. When shifted left two positions, it becomes 1111111111100000, which is –32. However, if enough positions are shifted, a negative number can become positive and vice versa.

There are two forms of the right-shift operator: one that preserves the sign of the original value (>>) and one that fills the leftmost bits with zeros (>>>).

Let's examine two examples of the *right-shift-with-sign-fill* operator. If the int variable number currently has the value 39, the expression (number >> 2) results in the value 9. The original bit string stored in number is 0000000000100111, and the result of a right shift two positions is 0000000000001001. The leftmost sign bit, which in this case is a zero, is used to fill from the left.

If number has an original value of –16, or 1111111111110000, the right-shift (with sign fill) expression (number >>> 3) results in the binary string 1111111111111110, or –2. The leftmost sign bit is a 1 in this case and is used to fill in the new left bits, maintaining the sign.

If maintaining the sign is not desirable, the *right-shift-with-zero-fill* operator (>>>) can be used. It operates similarly to the >> operator but fills with zero no matter what the sign of the original value is.

Java Modifiers

This appendix summarizes the modifiers that give particular characteristics to Java classes, interfaces, methods, and variables. For discussion purposes, the set of all Java modifiers is divided into two groups: visibility modifiers and all others.

Java Visibility Modifiers

The table in Figure E.1 describes the effect of Java visibility modifiers on various constructs. Some relationships are not applicable (N/A). For instance, a class cannot be declared with protected visibility. Note that each visibility modifier operates in the same way on classes and interfaces and in the same way on methods and variables.

Default visibility means that no visibility modifier was explicitly used. Default visibility is sometimes called *package visibility,* but you cannot use the reserved word `package` as a modifier. Classes and interfaces can have default or public visibility; this visibility determines whether a class or interface can be referenced outside of its package. Only an inner class can have private visibility, in which case only the enclosing class may access it.

A Visibility Example

Consider the situation depicted in Figure E.2. Class P is the parent class that is used to derive child classes C1 and C2. Class C1 is in the same package as P, but C2 is not. Class P contains four methods, each with different visibility modifiers. One object has been instantiated from each of these classes.

The public method `a()` has been inherited by C1 and C2, and any code with access to object x can invoke x.a(). The private method `d()` is not visible to C1 or C2, so objects y and z have no such method available to them. Furthermore, d() is fully encapsulated and can only be invoked from within object x.

The protected method `b()` is visible in both C1 and C2. A method in y could invoke x.b(), but a method in z could not. Furthermore, an object of any class

Modifier	Classes and interfaces	Methods and variables
default (no modifier)	Visible in its package.	Visible to any class in the same package as its class.
`public`	Visible anywhere.	Visible anywhere.
`protected`	N/A	Visible by any class in the same package as its class.
`private`	Visible to the enclosing class only	Not visible by any other class.

FIGURE E.1 Java visibility modifiers

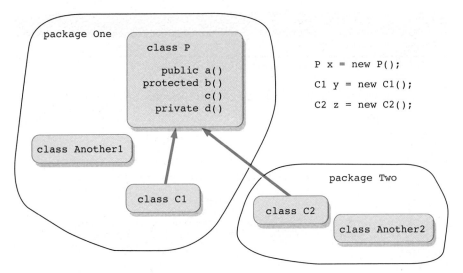

FIGURE E.2 A situation demonstrating Java visibility modifiers

in package `One` could invoke `x.b()`, even those that are not related to class `P` by inheritance, such as an object created from class `Another1`.

Method `c()` has `default` visibility, since no visibility modifier was used to declare it. Therefore, object `y` can refer to the method `c()` as if it were declared locally, but object `z` cannot. Object `y` can invoke `x.c()`, as can an object instantiated from any class in package `One`, such as `Another1`. Object `z` cannot invoke `x.c()`.

These rules generalize in the same way for variables. The visibility rules may appear complicated initially, but they can be mastered with a little effort.

Other Java Modifiers

Figure E.3 summarizes the rest of the Java modifiers, which address a variety of issues. These modifiers have different effects on classes, interfaces, methods, and variables. Some modifiers cannot be used with certain constructs and therefore are listed as not applicable (N/A).

The `transient` modifier is used to indicate data that need not be stored in a persistent (serialized) object. That is, when an object is written to a serialized stream, the object representation will include all data that is not specified as transient.

Modifier	Class	Interface	Method	Variable
abstract	The class may contain abstract methods. It cannot be instantiated.	All interfaces are inherently abstract. The modifier is optional.	No method body is defined. The method requires implementation when inherited.	N/A
final	The class cannot be used to drive new classes.	N/A	The method cannot be overridden.	The variable is a constant, whose value cannot be changed once initially set.
native	N/A	N/A	No method body is necessary since implementation is in another language.	N/A
static	N/A	N/A	Defines a class method. It does not require an instantiated object to be invoked. It cannot reference non-static methods or variables. It is implicitly final.	Defines a class variable. It does not require an instantiated object to be referenced. It is shared (common memory space) among all instances of the class.
synchronized	N/A	N/A	The execution of the method is mutually exclusive among all threads.	N/A
transient	N/A	N/A	N/A	The variable will not be serialized.
volatile	N/A	N/A	N/A	The variable is changed asynchronously. The compiler should not perform optimizations on it.

FIGURE E.3 The rest of the Java modifiers

Java Graphics

F

Chapter 6 covers the issues related to developing a graphical user interface (GUI) for a Java program but does not discuss the mechanisms for drawing shapes and managing color. This appendix is provided to introduce the concepts and techniques used to manage Java graphics.

A picture is represented on a computer by breaking it down into *pixels*, a term that is short for picture elements. A complete picture is stored by storing the color of each individual pixel. The more pixels used to represent a picture, the more realistic it looks when it is reproduced. The number of pixels used to represent a picture is called the *picture resolution*. The number of pixels that can be displayed by a monitor is called the *monitor resolution*.

Coordinate Systems

When drawn, each pixel is mapped to a pixel on the monitor screen. Each computer system and programming language defines a coordinate system so that we can refer to particular pixels.

A traditional two-dimensional Cartesian coordinate system has two axes that meet at the origin. Values on either axis can be negative or positive. The Java programming language has a relatively simple coordinate system in which all of the visible coordinates are positive. Figure F.1 compares a traditional coordinate system to the Java coordinate system.

Each point in the Java coordinate system is represented using an (x, y) pair of values. Each graphical component in a Java program, such as a panel, has its own coordinate system, with the origin in the top-left corner at coordinates (0, 0). The *x*-axis coordinates get larger as you move to the right, and the *y*-axis coordinates get larger as you move down.

Representing Color

There are various ways to represent the color of a pixel. In the Java programming language, every color is represented as a mix of three *primary colors*: red, green, and blue. A color is specified using three numbers that are collectively referred to as an *RGB value*. RGB stands for Red-Green-Blue. Each number represents the relative contribution of a primary color.

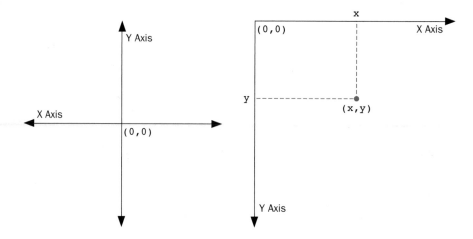

FIGURE F.1 A traditional coordinate system and the Java coordinate system

Color	Object	RGB Value
black	`Color.black`	0, 0, 0
blue	`Color.blue`	0, 0, 255
cyan	`Color.cyan`	0, 255, 255
gray	`Color.gray`	128, 128, 128
dark gray	`Color.darkGray`	64, 64, 64
light gray	`Color.lightGray`	192, 192, 192
green	`Color.green`	0, 255, 0
magenta	`Color.magenta`	255, 0, 255
orange	`Color.orange`	255, 200, 0
pink	`Color.pink`	255, 175, 175
red	`Color.red`	255, 0, 0
white	`Color.white`	255, 255, 255
yellow	`Color.yellow`	255, 255, 0

FIGURE F.2 Predefined colors in the `Color` class

Using 1 byte (8 bits) to store each of the three components of an RGB value, the numbers can range from 0 to 255. The level of each primary color determines the overall color. For example, high values of red and green combined with a low level of blue results in a shade of yellow.

In Java, a programmer uses the `Color` class, which is part of the `java.awt` package, to define and manage colors. Each object of the `Color` class represents a single color. The class contains several instances of itself to provide a basic set of predefined colors. Figure F.2 lists the predefined colors of the `Color` class. It also contains methods to define and manage many other colors.

Drawing Shapes

The Java standard class library provides many classes that let us present and manipulate graphical information. The `Graphics` class, which is defined in the `java.awt` package, is fundamental to all such processing.

The `Graphics` class contains various methods that allow us to draw shapes, including lines, rectangles, and ovals. Figure F.3 on the next page lists some of the fundamental drawing methods of the `Graphics` class. These methods also let us draw circles and squares, which are just specific types of ovals and rectangles, respectively.

```
void drawLine (int x1, int y1, int x2, int y2)
   Paints a line from point (x1, y1) to point (x2, y2).

void drawRect (int x, int y, int width, int height)
   Paints a rectangle with upper left corner (x, y) and dimensions width and
   height.

void drawOval (int x, int y, int width, int height)
   Paints an oval bounded by the rectangle with an upper left corner of (x, y) and
   dimensions width and height.

void drawString (String str, int x, int y)
   Paints the character string str at point (x, y), extending to the right.

void drawArc (int x, int y, int width, int height, int
startAngle, int arcAngle)
   Paints an arc along the oval bounded by the rectangle defined by x, y, width,
   and height.  The arc starts at startAngle and extends for a distance defined by
   arcAngle.

void fillRect (int x, int  y, int width, int height)
   Same as their draw counterparts, but filled with the current foreground color.

void fillOval (int x, int y, int width, int height)

void fillArc (int x, int y, int width, int height,
int startAngle, int arcAngle)

Color getColor ()
   Returns this graphics context's foreground color.

void setColor (Color color)
   Sets this graphics context's foreground color to the specified color.
```

FIGURE F.3 Some methods of the `Graphics` class

The methods of the `Graphics` class allow us to specify whether we want a shape filled or unfilled. An unfilled shape shows only the outline of the shape and is otherwise transparent (you can see any underlying graphics). A filled shape is solid between its boundaries and covers any underlying graphics.

Many of these methods accept parameters that specify the coordinates at which the shape should be drawn. Shapes drawn at coordinates that are outside the visible area will not be seen.

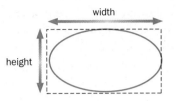

FIGURE F.4 An oval and its bounding rectangle

Many of the `Graphics` drawing methods are self-explanatory, but some require a little more discussion. Note, for instance, that an oval drawn by the `drawOval` method is defined by the coordinate of the upper-left corner and dimensions that specify the width and height of a *bounding rectangle*. Shapes with curves, such as ovals, are often defined by a rectangle that encompasses their perimeters. Figure F.4 depicts a bounding rectangle for an oval.

An arc can be thought of as a segment of an oval. To draw an arc, we specify the oval of which the arc is a part and the portion of the oval in which we're interested. The starting point of the arc is defined by the *start angle* and the ending point of the arc is defined by the *arc angle*. The arc angle does not indicate where the arc ends, but rather its range. The start angle and the arc angle are measured in degrees. The origin for the start angle is an imaginary horizontal line passing through the center of the oval and can be referred to as 0°, as shown in Figure F.5.

Every graphics context has a current *foreground color* that is used whenever shapes or strings are drawn. Every surface that can be drawn on has a

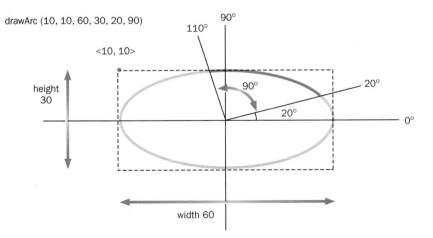

FIGURE F.5 An arc defined by an oval, a start angle, and an arc angle

background color. The foreground color is set using the `setColor` method of the `Graphics` class, and the background color is set using the `setBackground` method of the component on which we are drawing, such as the panel.

Listing F.1 shows a program that uses various drawing and color methods to draw a winter scene featuring a snowman. The drawing is done on a `JPanel`, defined by the `SnowmanPanel` class, which is shown in Listing F.2.

The `paintComponent` method of a graphical component is called automatically when the component is rendered on the screen. Note that the `paintComponent` method accepts a `Graphics` object as a parameter. A `Graphics` object defines a particular *graphics context* with which we can interact. The graphics context passed into a panel's `paintComponent` method represents the graphics context in which the panel is drawn.

LISTING F.1

```java
//********************************************************************
//  Snowman.java        Java Foundations
//
//  Demonstrates the use of basic drawing methods.
//********************************************************************

import javax.swing.JFrame;

public class Snowman
{
    //----------------------------------------------------------------
    //  Displays a winter scene featuring a snowman.
    //----------------------------------------------------------------
    public static void main (String[] args)
    {
        JFrame frame = new JFrame ("Snowman");
        frame.setDefaultCloseOperation (JFrame.EXIT_ON_CLOSE);

        frame.getContentPane().add(new SnowmanPanel());

        frame.pack();
        frame.setVisible(true);
    }
}
```

LISTING F.1 *continued*

DISPLAY

LISTING F.2

```
//********************************************************************
//  SnowmanPanel.java          Java Foundations
//
//  Represents the primary drawing panel for the Snowman application.
//********************************************************************

import java.awt.*;
import javax.swing.*;

public class SnowmanPanel extends JPanel
{
    private final int MID = 150;
    private final int TOP = 50;
```

LISTING F.2   *continued*

```java
//-----------------------------------------------------------------
//  Sets up the snowman panel.
//-----------------------------------------------------------------
public SnowmanPanel ()
{
   setPreferredSize (new Dimension(300, 225));
   setBackground (Color.cyan);
}

//-----------------------------------------------------------------
//  Draws a snowman.
//-----------------------------------------------------------------
public void paintComponent (Graphics page)
{
   super.paintComponent (page);
   page.setColor (Color.blue);
   page.fillRect (0, 175, 300, 50);  // ground

   page.setColor (Color.yellow);
   page.fillOval (-40, -40, 80, 80);  // sun

   page.setColor (Color.white);
   page.fillOval (MID-20, TOP, 40, 40);       // head
   page.fillOval (MID-35, TOP+35, 70, 50);   // upper torso
   page.fillOval (MID-50, TOP+80, 100, 60);  // lower torso

   page.setColor (Color.black);
   page.fillOval (MID-10, TOP+10, 5, 5);   // left eye
   page.fillOval (MID+5, TOP+10, 5, 5);    // right eye

   page.drawArc (MID-10, TOP+20, 20, 10, 190, 160);   // smile

   page.drawLine (MID-25, TOP+60, MID-50, TOP+40);  // left arm
   page.drawLine (MID+25, TOP+60, MID+55, TOP+60);  // right arm

   page.drawLine (MID-20, TOP+5, MID+20, TOP+5);  // brim of hat
   page.fillRect (MID-15, TOP-20, 30, 25);         // top of hat
   }
}
```

The drawing of the snowman figure is based on two constant values called MID and TOP, which define the midpoint of the snowman (left to right) and the top of the snowman's head. The entire snowman figure is drawn relative to these values. Using constants like these makes it easier to create the snowman and to make modifications later. For example, to shift the snowman to the right or left in our picture, only one constant declaration would have to change.

The call to the `super.paintComponent` method as the first line in the `paintComponent` method ensures that the background color will be painted. The version of `paintComponent` defined in the `JPanel` class handles the display of the panel's background. The examples in Chapter 6, which add graphical components such as buttons to a panel, do not need this call. If a panel contains graphical components, the parent's `paintComponent` method is automatically called. This is a key distinction between drawing on a component and adding a component to a container.

LISTING F.3

```
//********************************************************************
//  Splat.java        Java Foundations
//
//  Demonstrates the use of graphical objects.
//********************************************************************

import javax.swing.JFrame;

public class Splat
{
    //-----------------------------------------------------------------
    //  Presents a set of circles.
    //-----------------------------------------------------------------
    public static void main (String[] args)
    {
        JFrame frame = new JFrame ("Splat");
        frame.setDefaultCloseOperation (JFrame.EXIT_ON_CLOSE);

        frame.getContentPane().add(new SplatPanel());

        frame.pack();
        frame.setVisible(true);
    }
}
```

LISTING F . 3   *continued*

DISPLAY

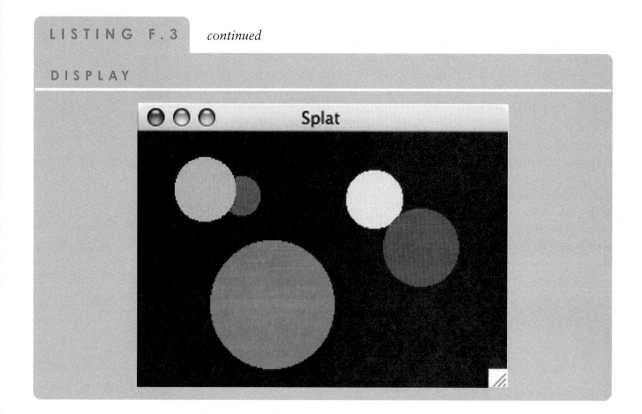

Let's look at another example. The Splat class shown in Listing F.3 simply draws a few filled circles. The interesting thing about this program is not what it does, but how it does it—each circle drawn in this program is represented by its own object.

The main method instantiates a SplatPanel object and adds it to the frame. The SplatPanel class is shown in Listing F.4. It is derived from JPanel, and holds as instance data five Circle objects, which are instantiated in the panel's constructor. The paintComponent method in the SplatPanel class draws the panel by calling the draw method of each circle.

The Circle class is shown in Listing F.5 on page 812. It defines instance data to store the size of the circle, its (x, y) location, and its color. The draw method of the Circle class simply draws the circle based on the values of its instance data.

The design of the Splat program embodies fundamental object-oriented thinking. Each circle manages itself and will draw itself in whatever graphics context you pass it. The Circle class is defined in a way that can be used in other situations and programs. There is a clean separation between the object being drawn and the component on which it is drawn.

LISTING F.4

```java
//********************************************************************
//  SplatPanel.java        Java Foundations
//
//  Demonstrates the use of graphical objects.
//********************************************************************

import javax.swing.*;
import java.awt.*;

public class SplatPanel extends JPanel
{
   private Circle circle1, circle2, circle3, circle4, circle5;

   //-----------------------------------------------------------------
   //  Creates five Circle objects.
   //-----------------------------------------------------------------
   public SplatPanel()
   {
      circle1 = new Circle (30, Color.red, 70, 35);
      circle2 = new Circle (50, Color.green, 30, 20);
      circle3 = new Circle (100, Color.cyan, 60, 85);
      circle4 = new Circle (45, Color.yellow, 170, 30);
      circle5 = new Circle (60, Color.blue, 200, 60);

      setPreferredSize (new Dimension(300, 200));
      setBackground (Color.black);
   }

   //-----------------------------------------------------------------
   //  Draws this panel by requesting that each circle draw itself.
   //-----------------------------------------------------------------
   public void paintComponent (Graphics page)
   {
      super.paintComponent(page);

      circle1.draw(page);
      circle2.draw(page);
      circle3.draw(page);
      circle4.draw(page);
      circle5.draw(page);
   }
}
```

LISTING F.5

```java
//*****************************************************************
//  Circle.java         Java Foundations
//
//  Represents a circle with a particular position, size, and color.
//*****************************************************************

import java.awt.*;

public class Circle
{
    private int diameter, x, y;
    private Color color;

    //----------------------------------------------------------------
    //  Sets up this circle with the specified values.
    //----------------------------------------------------------------
    public Circle (int size, Color shade, int upperX, int upperY)
    {
        diameter = size;
        color = shade;
        x = upperX;
        y = upperY;
    }

    //----------------------------------------------------------------
    //  Draws this circle in the specified graphics context.
    //----------------------------------------------------------------
    public void draw (Graphics page)
    {
        page.setColor (color);
        page.fillOval (x, y, diameter, diameter);
    }
}
```

Polygons and Polylines

A polygon is a multisided shape that is defined in Java using a series of (x, y) points that indicate the vertices of the polygon. Arrays are often used to store the list of coordinates.

Polygons are drawn using methods of the `Graphics` class, similar to how we draw rectangles and ovals. Like these other shapes, a polygon can be drawn filled or unfilled. The methods used to draw a polygon are called `drawPolygon` and `fillPolygon`. Both of these methods are overloaded. One version uses arrays of integers to define the polygon, and the other uses an object of the `Polygon` class to define the polygon. We discuss the `Polygon` class later in this appendix.

In the version that uses arrays, the `drawPolygon` and `fillPolygon` methods take three parameters. The first is an array of integers representing the x coordinates of the points in the polygon, the second is an array of integers representing the corresponding y coordinates of those points, and the third is an integer that indicates how many points are used from each of the two arrays. Taken together, the first two parameters represent the (x, y) coordinates of the vertices of the polygons.

A polygon is always closed. A line segment is always drawn from the last point in the list to the first point in the list.

Similar to a polygon, a *polyline* contains a series of points connected by line segments. Polylines differ from polygons in that the first and last coordinates are not automatically connected when they are drawn. Since a polyline is not closed, it cannot be filled. Therefore there is only one method, called `drawPolyline`, used to draw a polyline. The parameters of the `drawPolyline` method are similar to those of the `drawPolygon` method.

The program shown in Listing F.6 on page 814 uses polygons to draw a rocket. In the `RocketPanel` class, shown in Listing F.7 on page 815, the arrays called `xRocket` and `yRocket` define the points of the polygon that make up the main body of the rocket. The first point in the arrays is the upper tip of the rocket, and the points progress clockwise from there. The `xWindow` and `yWindow` arrays specify the points for the polygon that form the window in the rocket. Both the rocket and the window are drawn as filled polygons.

The `xFlame` and `yFlame` arrays define the points of a polyline that are used to create the image of flame shooting out of the tail of the rocket. Because it is drawn as a polyline, and not a polygon, the flame is not closed or filled.

The `Polygon` Class

A polygon can also be defined explicitly using an object of the `Polygon` class, which is defined in the `java.awt` package of the Java standard class library. Two versions of the overloaded `drawPolygon` and `fillPolygon` methods take a single `Polygon` object as a parameter.

A `Polygon` object encapsulates the coordinates of the polygon sides. The constructors of the `Polygon` class allow the creation of an initially empty polygon, or

LISTING F.6

```
//********************************************************************
//  Rocket.java          Java Foundations
//
//  Demonstrates the use of polygons and polylines.
//********************************************************************

import javax.swing.JFrame;

public class Rocket
{
   //-----------------------------------------------------------------
   //  Displays a rocket in flight.
   //-----------------------------------------------------------------
   public static void main (String[] args)
   {
      JFrame frame = new JFrame ("Rocket");
      frame.setDefaultCloseOperation (JFrame.EXIT_ON_CLOSE);

      frame.getContentPane().add(new RocketPanel());

      frame.pack();
      frame.setVisible(true);
   }
}
```

DISPLAY

LISTING F.7

```java
//********************************************************************
//  RocketPanel.java        Java Foundations
//
//  Demonstrates the use of polygons and polylines.
//********************************************************************

import javax.swing.JPanel;
import java.awt.*;

public class RocketPanel extends JPanel
{
   private int[] xRocket = {100, 120, 120, 130, 130, 70, 70, 80, 80};
   private int[] yRocket = {15, 40, 115, 125, 150, 150, 125, 115, 40};

   private int[] xWindow = {95, 105, 110, 90};
   private int[] yWindow = {45, 45, 70, 70};

   private int[] xFlame = {70, 70, 75, 80, 90, 100, 110, 115, 120,
                           130, 130};
   private int[] yFlame = {155, 170, 165, 190, 170, 175, 160, 185,
                           160, 175, 155};

   //------------------------------------------------------------------
   //  Sets up the basic characteristics of this panel.
   //------------------------------------------------------------------
   public RocketPanel()
   {
      setBackground (Color.black);
      setPreferredSize (new Dimension(200, 200));
   }

   //------------------------------------------------------------------
   //  Draws a rocket using polygons and polylines.
   //------------------------------------------------------------------
   public void paintComponent (Graphics page)
   {
      super.paintComponent (page);

      page.setColor (Color.cyan);
      page.fillPolygon (xRocket, yRocket, xRocket.length);

      page.setColor (Color.gray);
      page.fillPolygon (xWindow, yWindow, xWindow.length);
```

LISTING F.7   *continued*

```
        page.setColor (Color.red);
        page.drawPolyline (xFlame, yFlame, xFlame.length);
    }
}
```

one defined by arrays of integers representing the point coordinates. The `Polygon` class contains methods to add points to the polygon and to determine whether a given point is contained within the polygon shape. It also contains methods to get a representation of a bounding rectangle for the polygon, as well as a method to translate all of the points in the polygon to another position. Figure F.6 lists these methods.

```
Polygon ()
    Constructor: Creates an empty polygon.

Polygon (int[] xpoints, int[] ypoints, int npoints)
    Constructor: Creates a polygon using the (x, y) coordinate pairs
    in corresponding entries of xpoints and ypoints.

void addPoint (int x, int y)
    Appends the specified point to this polygon.

boolean contains (int x, int y)
    Returns true if the specified point is contained in this polygon.

boolean contains (Point p)
    Returns true if the specified point is contained in this polygon.

Rectangle getBounds ()
    Gets the bounding rectangle for this polygon.

void translate (int deltaX, int deltaY)
    Translates the vertices of this polygon by deltaX along the x axis
    and deltaY along the y axis.
```

FIGURE F.6 Some methods of the `Polygon` class

Exercises

EX F.1   Compare and contrast a traditional coordinate system and the coordinate system used by Java graphical components.

EX F.2   How many bits are needed to store a color picture that is 400 pixels wide and 250 pixels high? Assume color is represented using the RGB technique described in this appendix and that no special compression is done.

EX F.3   Assuming you have a `Graphics` object called `page`, write a statement that will draw a line from point (20, 30) to point (50, 60).

EX F.4   Assuming you have a `Graphics` object called `page`, write a statement that will draw a rectangle with height 70 and width 35, such that its upper-left corner is at point (10, 15).

EX F.5   Assuming you have a `Graphics` object called `page`, write a statement that will draw a circle centered on point (50, 50) with a radius of 20 pixels.

EX F.6   The following lines of code draw the eyes of the snowman in the `Snowman` program. The eyes seem centered on the face when drawn, but the first parameters of each call are not equally offset from the midpoint. Explain.

```
page.fillOval (MID-10, TOP+10, 5, 5);

page.fillOval (MID+5, TOP+10, 5, 5);
```

EX F.7   Write a method called `randomColor` that creates and returns a `Color` object that represents a random color.

EX F.8   Write a method called `drawCircle` that draws a circle based on the method's parameters: a `Graphics` object through which to draw the circle, two integer values representing the (x, y) coordinates of the center of the circle, another integer that represents the circle's radius, and a `Color` object that defines the circle's color. The method does not return anything.

Programming Projects

PP F.1   Create a revised version of the `Snowman` program with the following modifications:

- Add two red buttons to the upper torso.
- Make the snowman frown instead of smile.
- Move the sun to the upper-right corner of the picture.

- Display your name in the upper-left corner of the picture.

- Shift the entire snowman 20 pixels to the right.

PP F.2   Write a program that writes your name using the `drawString` method.

PP F.3   Write a program that draws the Big Dipper. Add some extra stars in the night sky.

PP F.4   Write a program that draws some balloons tied to strings. Make the balloons various colors.

PP F.5   Write a program that draws the Olympic logo. The circles in the logo should be colored, from left to right, blue, yellow, black, green, and red.

PP F.6   Write a program that displays a business card of your own design. Include both graphics and text.

PP F.7   Write a program that shows a pie chart with eight equal slices, all colored differently.

PP F.8   Write a program that draws a house with a door (and doorknob), windows, and a chimney. Add some smoke coming out of the chimney and some clouds in the sky.

PP F.9   Modify the program from programming project F.8 to include a simple fence with vertical, equally spaced slats backed by two horizontal support boards. Make sure the house is visible between the slats in the fence.

PP F.10   Write a program that draws 20 horizontal, evenly spaced parallel lines of random length.

PP F.11   Write a program that draws the side view of stair steps from the lower left to the upper right.

PP F.12   Write a program that draws 100 circles of random color and random diameter in random locations. Ensure that in each case the entire circle appears in the visible area of the applet.

PP F.13   Write a program that draws 10 concentric circles of random radius.

PP F.14   Write a program that draws a brick wall pattern in which each row of bricks is offset from the row above and below it.

PP F.15   Design and implement a program that draws a rainbow. Use tightly spaced concentric arcs to draw each part of the rainbow in a particular color.

PP F.16   Design and implement a program that draws 20,000 points in random locations within the visible area. Make the points on the left half of the panel appear in red and the points on the right half of the panel appear in green. Draw each point by drawing a line with a length of only one pixel.

PP F.17   Design and implement a program that draws 10 circles of random radius in random locations. Fill in the largest circle in red.

PP F.18   Write a program that draws a quilt in which a simple pattern is repeated in a grid of squares.

PP F.19   Modify the program from programming project F.18 such that it draws a quilt using a separate class called `Pattern` that represents a particular pattern. Allow the constructor of the `Pattern` class to vary some characteristics of the pattern, such as its color scheme. Instantiate two separate `Pattern` objects and incorporate them in a checkerboard layout in the quilt.

PP F.20   Design and implement a class called `Building` that represents a graphical depiction of a building. Allow the parameters to the constructor to specify the building's width and height. Each building should be colored black, and contain a few random windows of yellow. Create a program that draws a random skyline of buildings.

PP F.21   Write a program that displays a graphical seating chart for a dinner party. Create a class called `Diner` (as in one who dines) that stores the person's name, gender, and location at the dinner table. A diner is graphically represented as a circle, color-coded by gender, with the person's name printed in the circle.

PP F.22   Create a class called `Crayon` that represents one crayon of a particular color and length (height). Design and implement a program that draws a box of crayons.

PP F.23   Create a class called `Star` that represents a graphical depiction of a star. Let the constructor of the star accept the number of points in the star (4, 5, or 6), the radius of the star, and the center point location. Write a program that draws a sky containing various types of stars.

PP F.24   Design and implement an application that displays an animation of a horizontal line segment moving across the screen, eventually passing across a vertical line. As the vertical line is passed, the horizontal line should change color. The change of color should occur while the horizontal line crosses the vertical one; therefore, while crossing, the horizontal line will be two different colors.

PP F.25 Create a class that represents a spaceship, which can be drawn (side view) in any particular location. Use it to create a program that displays the spaceship so that it follows the movement of the mouse. When the mouse button in pressed down, have a laser beam shoot out of the front of the spaceship (one continuous beam, not a moving projectile) until the mouse button is released.

Java Applets

There are two kinds of Java programs: Java applications and Java applets. A Java *application* is a stand-alone program that can be executed using a Java interpreter. The programs presented in the main chapters of this book are Java applications. A Java *applet* is a Java program that is intended to be embedded into an HTML document, transported across a network, and executed using a Web browser. This appendix explores Java applets.

The Web enables users to send and receive various types of media, such as text, graphics, and sound, using a point-and-click interface that is extremely convenient and easy to use. Java applets are considered just another type of media that can be exchanged across the Web.

When we surf the Web, we tend to think in terms of visiting a site. Of course, the reality is that we are downloading a page to our local computer to view it. Therefore, security is an issue with applets. As you browse Web pages, you may download a page containing an applet and suddenly an unknown program is executing on your machine. Because of the dangers inherent in that process, applets are restricted in the kinds of operations they can perform. For instance, an applet cannot write data to a local drive.

Though Java applets are generally intended to be transported across a network, they don't have to be. They can be viewed locally using a Web browser. For that matter, they don't even have to be executed through a Web browser at all. A tool in Sun's Java Software Development Kit called *appletviewer* can be used to interpret and execute an applet. We use appletviewer to display applets in this appendix. However, usually the point of making a Java applet is to provide a link to it on a Web page and allow it to be retrieved and executed by Web users anywhere in the world.

Java bytecode (not Java source code) is linked to an HTML document and sent across the Web. A version of the Java interpreter embedded in a Web browser is used to execute the applet once it reaches its destination. A Java applet must be compiled into bytecode format before it can be used with the Web.

There are some important differences between the structure of a Java applet and the structure of a Java application. Because the Web browser that executes an applet is already running, applets can be thought of as a part of a larger program. As such they do not have a `main` method where execution starts. The `paint` method in an applet is automatically invoked when the applet program executes. Consider the program in Listing G.1, in which the `paint` method is used to draw a few shapes and write a quotation by Albert Einstein to the screen.

A class that defines an applet extends the `JApplet` class, as indicated in the header line of the `Einstein` class declaration. Applet classes must be declared as `public`.

LISTING G.1

```
//********************************************************************
//  Einstein.java          Java Foundations
//
//  Demonstrates a basic applet.
//********************************************************************

import javax.swing.JApplet;
import java.awt.*;

public class Einstein extends JApplet
{
    //----------------------------------------------------------------
    //  Draws a quotation by Albert Einstein among some shapes.
    //----------------------------------------------------------------
    public void paint (Graphics page)
```

LISTING G.1   *continued*

```
    {
        page.drawRect (50, 50, 40, 40);      // square
        page.drawRect (60, 80, 225, 30);     // rectangle
        page.drawOval (75, 65, 20, 20);      // circle
        page.drawLine (35, 60, 100, 120);    // line

        page.drawString ("Out of clutter, find simplicity.", 110, 70);
        page.drawString ("-- Albert Einstein", 130, 100);
    }
}
```

DISPLAY

The `paint` method is one of several applet methods that have particular significance. It is invoked automatically whenever the graphic elements of the applet need to be painted to the screen, such as when the applet is first run or when another window that was covering it is moved.

Note that the `paint` method accepts a `Graphics` object as a parameter. As discussed in Appendix F, a `Graphics` object defines the *graphics context* of a component and provides a variety of methods for drawing shapes on a component. The graphics context passed into an applet's `paint` method represents the applet window.

Embedding Applets in HTML

In order for the applet to be executed, either by the appletviewer or by being transmitted over the Web and executed by a browser, it must be referenced in a HyperText Markup Language (HTML) document. An HTML document contains *tags* that specify formatting instructions and identify the special types of media that are to be included in a document.

An HTML tag is enclosed in angle brackets. The following is an example of an applet tag:

```
<applet code="Einstein.class" width="350" height="175">
</applet>
```

This tag dictates that the bytecode stored in the file `Einstein.class` should be transported over the network and executed on the machine that wants to view this particular HTML document. The applet tag also indicates the width and height of the applet.

There are other tags that can be used to reference an applet in an HTML file, including the `<object>` tag and the `<embed>` tag. The `<object>` tag is actually the tag that should be used, according to the World Wide Web Consortium (W3C). However, browser support for the `<object>` tag is not consistent. For now, the most reliable solution is to use the `<applet>` tag.

Note that the applet tag refers to the bytecode file of the `Einstein` applet, not to the source code file. Before an applet can be transported using the Web, it must be compiled into its bytecode format. Then, as shown in Figure G.1, the document can be loaded using a Web browser, which will automatically interpret and execute the applet.

More Applet Methods

An applet has several other methods that perform specific duties. Because an applet is designed to work with Web pages, some applet methods are specifically designed with that concept in mind. Figure G.2 lists several applet methods.

The `init` method is executed once when the applet is first loaded, such as when the browser or appletviewer initially views the applet. Therefore the `init` method is the place to initialize the applet's environment and permanent data.

The `start` and `stop` methods of an applet are called when the applet becomes active or inactive, respectively. For example, after we use a browser to initially load an applet, the applet's `start` method is called. We may then leave that page to visit another one, at which point the applet becomes inactive and the `stop`

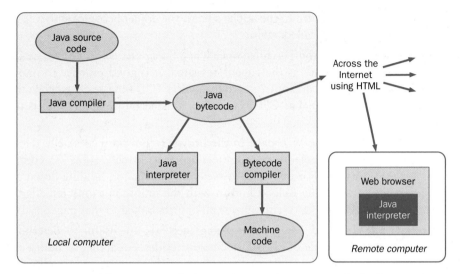

FIGURE G.1 The Java translation and execution process, including applets

```
public void init ()
    Initializes the applet. Called just after the applet is loaded.

public void start ()
    Starts the applet. Called just after the applet is made active.

public void stop ()
    Stops the applet. Called just after the applet is made inactive.

public void destroy ()
    Destroys the applet. Called when the browser is exited.

public URL getCodeBase ()
    Returns the URL at which this applet's bytecode is located.

public URL getDocumentBase ()
    Returns the URL at which the HTML document containing this applet is
    located.

public AudioClip getAudioClip (URL url, String name)
    Retrieves an audio clip from the specified URL.

public Image getImage (URL url, String name)
    Retrieves an image from the specified URL.
```

FIGURE G.2 Some methods of the JApplet class

method is called. If we return to the applet's page, the applet becomes active again and the start method is called again.

Note that the init method is called once when the applet is loaded, but start may be called several times as the page is revisited. It is good practice to implement start and stop for an applet if it actively uses CPU time, such as when it is showing an animation, so that CPU time is not wasted on an applet that is not visible.

Note that reloading the Web page in the browser does not necessarily reload the applet. To force the applet to reload, most browsers provide some key combination for that purpose. For example, in Netscape Navigator, holding down the Shift key while pressing the Reload button with the mouse not only reloads the Web page, it also reloads (and reinitializes) all applets linked to that page.

The getCodeBase and getDocumentBase methods are useful to determine where the applet's bytecode or HTML document resides. An applet could use the appropriate URL to retrieve additional resources, such as an image or audio clip, using the methods getImage or getAudioClip.

Let's look at another example of an applet. Carefully examine the display for the TiledPictures applet shown in Listing G.2. There are actually three unique images among the menagerie. The entire area is divided into four equal quadrants. A picture of the world (with a circle indicating the Himalayan mountain region) is shown in the bottom-right quadrant. The bottom-left quadrant contains a picture of Mt. Everest. In the top-right quadrant is a picture of a mountain goat.

The interesting part of the picture is the top-left quadrant. It contains a copy of the entire collage, including itself. In this smaller version you can see the three simple pictures in their three quadrants. And again, in the top-left corner, the picture is repeated (including itself). This repetition continues for several levels. It is similar to the effect you can create when looking at a mirror in the reflection of another mirror.

This visual effect is created using recursion. The applet's init method initially loads the three images. The paint method then invokes the drawPictures method, which accepts a parameter that defines the size of the area in which pictures are displayed. It draws the three images using the drawImage method, with parameters that scale the picture to the correct size and location. The drawPictures method is then called recursively to draw the upper-left quadrant.

On each invocation, if the drawing area is large enough, the drawPictures method is invoked again, using a smaller drawing area. Eventually, the drawing area becomes so small that the recursive call is not performed. Note that drawPictures assumes the origin (0, 0) coordinate as the relative location of the new images, no matter what their size is.

LISTING G.2

```java
//********************************************************************
//  TiledPictures.java        Java Foundations
//
//  Demonstrates an applet.
//********************************************************************

import java.awt.*;
import javax.swing.JApplet;

public class TiledPictures extends JApplet
{
   private final int APPLET_WIDTH = 320;
   private final int APPLET_HEIGHT = 320;
   private final int MIN = 20;   // smallest picture size

   private Image world, everest, goat;

   //-----------------------------------------------------------------
   //  Loads the images.
   //-----------------------------------------------------------------
   public void init()
   {
      world = getImage (getDocumentBase(), "world.gif");
      everest = getImage (getDocumentBase(), "everest.gif");
      goat = getImage (getDocumentBase(), "goat.gif");

      setSize (APPLET_WIDTH, APPLET_HEIGHT);
   }

   //-----------------------------------------------------------------
   //  Draws the three images, then calls itself recursively.
   //-----------------------------------------------------------------
   public void drawPictures (int size, Graphics page)
   {
      page.drawImage (everest, 0, size/2, size/2, size/2, this);
      page.drawImage (goat, size/2, 0, size/2, size/2, this);
      page.drawImage (world, size/2, size/2, size/2, size/2, this);

      if (size > MIN)
          drawPictures (size/2, page);
   }
```

LISTING G.2   *continued*

```
//-----------------------------------------------------------------
//   Performs the initial call to the drawPictures method.
//-----------------------------------------------------------------
public void paint (Graphics page)
{
    drawPictures (APPLET_WIDTH, page);
}
}
```

DISPLAY

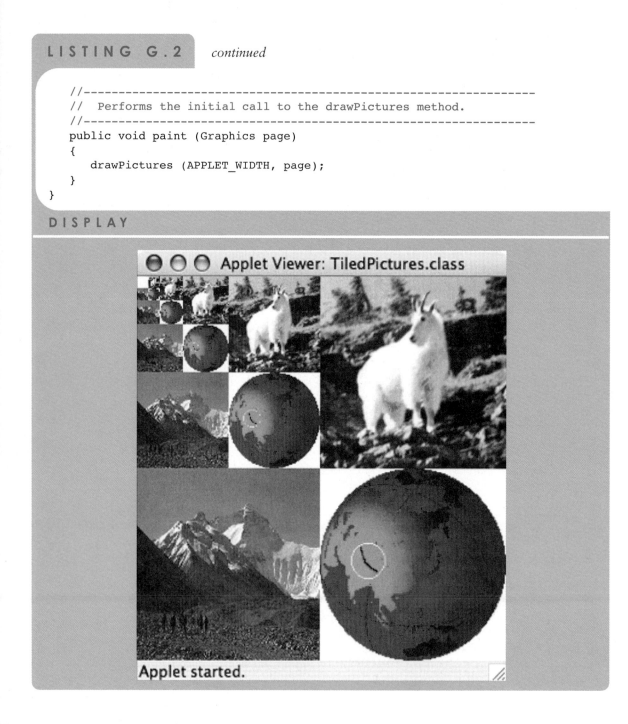

The base case of the recursion in this problem specifies a minimum size for the drawing area. Because the size is decreased each time, the base case eventually is reached and the recursion stops. This is why the upper-left corner is empty in the smallest version of the collage.

GUIs in Applets

In Chapter 6, we explored issues related to the development of programs that use graphical user interfaces (GUIs). The examples in those sections are presented as Java applications, using `JFrame` components as the primary heavyweight container. An applet can also be used to present GUI-based programs. Like a `JFrame`, a `JApplet` is a heavyweight container.

Let's look at an applet that contains interactive components. Our example will contain buttons that determine the level of a displayed fractal. A *fractal* is a geometric shape that can be made up of the same pattern repeated at different scales and orientations. The nature of a fractal lends itself to a recursive definition. Interest in fractals has grown immensely in recent years, largely due to Benoit Mandelbrot, a Polish mathematician born in 1924. He demonstrated that fractals occur in many places in mathematics and nature. Computers have made fractals much easier to generate and investigate. Over the past quarter century, the bright, interesting images that can be created with fractals have come to be considered as much an art form as a mathematical interest.

One particular example of a fractal is called the Koch snowflake, named after Helge von Koch, a Swedish mathematician. It begins with an equilateral triangle, which is considered to be the Koch fractal of order 1. Koch fractals of higher orders are constructed by repeatedly modifying all of the line segments in the shape.

To create the next higher order Koch fractal, each line segment in the shape is modified by replacing its middle third with a sharp protrusion made of two line segments, each having the same length as the replaced part. Relative to the entire shape, the protrusion on any line segment always points outward. Figure G.3

FIGURE G.3 Several orders of the Koch snowflake

shows several orders of Koch fractals. As the order increases, the shape begins to look like a snowflake.

The applet shown in Listing G.3 draws a Koch snowflake of several different orders. The buttons at the top of the applet allow the user to increase and decrease the order of the fractal. Each time a button is pressed, the fractal image is redrawn. The applet serves as the listener for the buttons.

LISTING G.3

```java
//********************************************************************
//   KochSnowflake.java        Java Foundations
//
//   Demonstrates the use of recursion in graphics.
//********************************************************************

import java.awt.*;
import java.awt.event.*;
import javax.swing.*;

public class KochSnowflake extends JApplet implements ActionListener
{
   private final int APPLET_WIDTH = 400;
   private final int APPLET_HEIGHT = 440;

   private final int MIN = 1, MAX = 9;

   private JButton increase, decrease;
   private JLabel titleLabel, orderLabel;
   private KochPanel drawing;
   private JPanel appletPanel, tools;
   //-----------------------------------------------------------------
   //   Sets up the components for the applet.
   //-----------------------------------------------------------------
   public void init()
   {
      tools = new JPanel ();
      tools.setLayout (new BoxLayout(tools, BoxLayout.X_AXIS));
      tools.setPreferredSize (new Dimension (APPLET_WIDTH, 40));
      tools.setBackground (Color.yellow);
      tools.setOpaque (true);

      titleLabel = new JLabel ("The Koch Snowflake");
      titleLabel.setForeground (Color.black);
```

LISTING G.3   *continued*

```java
      increase = new JButton (new ImageIcon ("increase.gif"));
      increase.setPressedIcon (new ImageIcon ("increasePressed.gif"));
      increase.setMargin (new Insets (0, 0, 0, 0));
      increase.addActionListener (this);

      decrease = new JButton (new ImageIcon ("decrease.gif"));
      decrease.setPressedIcon (new ImageIcon ("decreasePressed.gif"));
      decrease.setMargin (new Insets (0, 0, 0, 0));
      decrease.addActionListener (this);

      orderLabel = new JLabel ("Order: 1");
      orderLabel.setForeground (Color.black);

      tools.add (titleLabel);
      tools.add (Box.createHorizontalStrut (40));
      tools.add (decrease);
      tools.add (increase);
      tools.add (Box.createHorizontalStrut (20));
      tools.add (orderLabel);

      drawing = new KochPanel (1);

      appletPanel = new JPanel();
      appletPanel.add (tools);
      appletPanel.add (drawing);

      getContentPane().add (appletPanel);

      setSize (APPLET_WIDTH, APPLET_HEIGHT);
   }

   //-----------------------------------------------------------------
   //  Determines which button was pushed, and sets the new order
   //  if it is in range.
   //-----------------------------------------------------------------
   public void actionPerformed (ActionEvent event)
   {
      int order = drawing.getOrder();

      if (event.getSource() == increase)
         order++;
      else
         order--;
```

LISTING G.3   *continued*

```
    if (order >= MIN && order <= MAX)
    {
        orderLabel.setText ("Order: " + order);
        drawing.setOrder (order);
        repaint();
    }
  }
}
```

DISPLAY

The fractal image is drawn on a panel defined by the KochPanel class shown in Listing G.4. The paint method makes the initial calls to the recursive method drawFractal. The three calls to drawFractal in the paint method represent the original three sides of the equilateral triangle that make up a Koch fractal of order 1.

LISTING G.4

```java
//********************************************************************
//  KochPanel.java        Java Foundations
//
//  Represents a drawing surface on which to paint a Koch Snowflake.
//********************************************************************

import java.awt.*;
import javax.swing.JPanel;

public class KochPanel extends JPanel
{
    private final int PANEL_WIDTH = 400;
    private final int PANEL_HEIGHT = 400;

    private final double SQ = Math.sqrt(3.0) / 6;

    private final int TOPX = 200, TOPY = 20;
    private final int LEFTX = 60, LEFTY = 300;
    private final int RIGHTX = 340, RIGHTY = 300;

    private int current; // current order

    //-----------------------------------------------------------------
    //  Sets the initial fractal order to the value specified.
    //-----------------------------------------------------------------
    public KochPanel (int currentOrder)
    {
        current = currentOrder;
        setBackground (Color.black);
        setPreferredSize (new Dimension(PANEL_WIDTH, PANEL_HEIGHT));
    }

    //-----------------------------------------------------------------
    //  Draws the fractal recursively. The base case is order 1 for
    //  which a simple straight line is drawn. Otherwise three
    //  intermediate points are computed, and each line segment is
    //  drawn as a fractal.
    //-----------------------------------------------------------------
```

LISTING G.4 *continued*

```java
public void drawFractal (int order, int x1, int y1, int x5, int y5,
                         Graphics page)
{
   int deltaX, deltaY, x2, y2, x3, y3, x4, y4;

   if (order == 1)
      page.drawLine (x1, y1, x5, y5);
   else
   {
      deltaX = x5 - x1; // distance between end points
      deltaY = y5 - y1;

      x2 = x1 + deltaX / 3; // one third
      y2 = y1 + deltaY / 3;

      x3 = (int) ((x1+x5)/2 + SQ * (y1-y5)); // tip of projection
      y3 = (int) ((y1+y5)/2 + SQ * (x5-x1));

      x4 = x1 + deltaX * 2/3; // two thirds
      y4 = y1 + deltaY * 2/3;

      drawFractal (order-1, x1, y1, x2, y2, page);
      drawFractal (order-1, x2, y2, x3, y3, page);
      drawFractal (order-1, x3, y3, x4, y4, page);
      drawFractal (order-1, x4, y4, x5, y5, page);
   }
}

//-------------------------------------------------------------------
//  Performs the initial calls to the drawFractal method.
//-------------------------------------------------------------------
public void paintComponent (Graphics page)
{
   super.paintComponent (page);

   page.setColor (Color.green);

   drawFractal (current, TOPX, TOPY, LEFTX, LEFTY, page);
   drawFractal (current, LEFTX, LEFTY, RIGHTX, RIGHTY, page);
   drawFractal (current, RIGHTX, RIGHTY, TOPX, TOPY, page);
}
```

LISTING G.4   *continued*

```java
//-----------------------------------------------------------
//  Sets the fractal order to the value specified.
//-----------------------------------------------------------
public void setOrder (int order)
{
   current = order;
}

//-----------------------------------------------------------
//  Returns the current order.
//-----------------------------------------------------------
public int getOrder ()
{
   return current;
}
}
```

The variable `current` represents the order of the fractal to be drawn. Each recursive call to `drawFractal` decrements the order by 1. The base case of the recursion occurs when the order of the fractal is 1, which results in a simple line segment between the coordinates specified by the parameters.

If the order of the fractal is higher than 1, three additional points are computed. In conjunction with the parameters, these points form the four line segments of the modified fractal. Figure G.4 on the next page shows the transformation.

Based on the position of the two end points of the original line segment, a point one-third of the way and a point two-thirds of the way between them are computed. The calculation of <x3, y3>, the point at the tip of the protrusion, is more convoluted and uses a simplifying constant that incorporates multiple geometric relationships. The calculations to determine the three new points actually have nothing to do with the recursive technique used to draw the fractal, and so we won't discuss the details of these computations here.

An interesting mathematical feature of a Koch snowflake is that it has an infinite perimeter but a finite area. As the order of the fractal increases, the perimeter grows exponentially larger, with a mathematical limit of infinity. However, a rectangle large enough to surround the second-order fractal for the Koch snowflake is large enough to contain all higher-order fractals. The shape is restricted forever in area, but its perimeter gets infinitely longer.

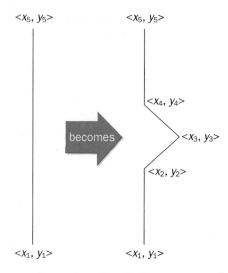

FIGURE G.4 The transformation of each line segment of a Koch snowflake

Programming Projects

PP G.1   Convert any of the applications described by the programming projects in Appendix F (Graphics) into applets.

PP G.2   Convert any of the applications described by the programming projects in Chapter 7 (GUIs) into applets, excluding those that require data written to a file.

Regular Expressions

Throughout the book we've used the Scanner class to read interactive input from the user and parse strings into individual tokens such as words. In Chapter 4 we also used it to read input from a data file. Usually we used the default whitespace delimiters for tokens in the scanner input.

The Scanner class can also be used to parse its input according to a *regular expression*, which is a character string that represents a pattern. A regular expression can be used to set the delimiters used when extracting tokens, or it can be used in methods like findInLine to match a particular string.

Some of the general rules for constructing regular expressions include:

- The dot (.) character matches any single character.
- The asterisk (*) character, which is called the Kleene star, matches zero or more characters.
- A string of characters in brackets ([ ]) matches any single character in the string.
- The \ character followed by a special character (such as the ones in this list) matches the character itself.
- The \ character followed by a character matches the pattern specified by that character (see Figure H.1) on the next page.

For example, the regular expression B.b* matches Bob, Bubba, and Baby. The regular expression T[aei]*ing matches Taking, Tickling, and Telling.

Figure H.1 shows some of the patterns that can be matched in a Java regular expression. This list is not complete—see the online documentation for the Pattern class for a complete list.

Regular Expression	Matches
x	The character x
.	Any character
[abc]	a, b, or c
[^abc]	Any character except a, b, or c (negation)
[a-z][A-Z]	a through z or A through Z, inclusive (range)
[a-o[m-p]]	a through d or m through p (union)
[a-z&&[def]]	d, e, or f (intersection)
[a-z&&[^bc]]	a through z, except for b and c (subtraction)
[a-z&&[^m-p]]	a through z but not m through p (subtraction)
\d	A digit: [0–9]
\D	A non-digit: [^0–9]
\s	A whitespace character
\S	A non-whitespace character
^	The beginning of a line
$	The end of a line

FIGURE H.1 Some patterns that can be specified in a Java regular expression

Javadoc Documentation Generator

Appendix

*J*avadoc is a tool for creating documentation about Java source code in HTML format by examining the source code itself. The utility extracts specially marked information from the comments in the source code, and then produces Web pages that summarize the software.

Documentation comments, also referred to as doc comments, specify the format for comments processed by the javadoc tool. Special labels called *tags* are also parsed by the javadoc tool. Together, doc comments and tags can be used to construct a complete Java application programming interface (API) specification, which describes how to work with a set of classes.

Javadoc can be run on packages or individual files (or both). It produces a well-structured, integrated set of HTML documents each time it is run. However, javadoc does not support incremental additions.

Javadoc comes as a standard part of the Java Software Development Kit (SDK). The tool executable, javadoc.exe, resides in the bin folder of the installation directory along with the javac compiler and java run-time tool. Therefore, if you are able to compile and execute your code using the command line, javadoc should also work.

Using javadoc is simple in its plain form; it is very much like compiling a Java source file. The javadoc command can be issued from the command line. For example:

```
> javadoc myfile.java
```

The source file name must contain the .java extension (similar to the javac compiler command). Various options can be used with the javadoc command as well.

Doc Comments

The document comments are made up of descriptions and tags. Descriptions should be written to provide an overview of the functionality of the code. Tags address the specifics of the functionality, such as code version (for classes or interfaces) or return types (for methods).

Javadoc comments begin with /** and end with */. Any comments written in this form will be examined and processed by the javadoc tool. Like regular comments that begin with /* and end with */, javadoc comments may span multiple lines. However, each intermediate line begins with a * character, which is, along with any white space before it, discarded by the tool. These comments are allowed to contain HTML tags. For example:

```
/**
 *    This is an <strong>example</strong> document comment.
 */
```

Javadoc comments should be constructed carefully. The javadoc tool automatically copies the first sentence from each comment to a summary at the top of the HTML document. The sentence begins after any white space following the * character and ends at the first period. Document comments are recognized only if they are placed immediately before a class, constructor, method, interface, or field declaration.

The use of HTML inside the description should be limited to proper comment separation and display rather than styling. Javadoc automatically structures the document based on certain HTML elements, such as heading tags. Appropriate use of paragraph or list elements should result in proper formatting.

Tags

Tags may be included in a javadoc comment. Each tag must start on a separate line, hence it must be preceded by the * character. Tags are case sensitive and begin with the @ symbol.

Certain tags are required in some situations. The @param tag must be supplied for every parameter to a method and is used to describe the purpose of the parameter. The @return tag must be supplied for every method that returns a value other than void, to describe what the method returns. The @author and the @version tags are required for classes and interfaces only.

Figure I.1 lists the various tags used in javadoc comments.

Note the two different types of tags listed in Figure I.1 on the next page. The *block tags*, which begin with the @ symbol (such as @author), must be placed in the tag section following the main description. The *inline tags*, enclosed in { and } delimiters, can be placed anywhere in the description section or in the comments for block tags. For example:

```
/**
 * This is an <strong>example</strong> document comment.
 * The {@link Glossary} provides definitions of types used.
 *
 * @author Sebastian Niezgoda
 */
```

Files Generated

The javadoc tool analyzes a Java source file or package and produces a three-part HTML document for each class. The HTML file is often referred to as a documentation file. It contains cleanly organized information about the class file derived from the javadoc comments included in the code.

The first part of the document contains an overall description of the class. The class name appears first followed by a graphical representation of the inheritance relationships. A general description is displayed next, which is extracted from the first sentence of each doc comment entity (as discussed previously).

Next, a list of constructors and methods is provided. The signatures of all the constructors and methods included in the source file are listed along with

Tag Name	Description
`@author`	Inserts an "Author" entry with the specified text.
`{ @code}`	Same as `<code>{@literal}</code>`.
`@deprecated`	Inserts a bold "Deprecated" entry with the specified text.
`{ @docRoot}`	Relative link to the root of the document.
`@exception`	See `@throws`.
`{ @inheritDoc}`	Copies documentation from the closest inherited class or implemented interface where used allowing for more general comments of hierarchically higher classes to be reused.
`{ @link}`	Inserts a hyperlink to an HTML document. Use: `{@link name url}`.
`{ @linkPlain}`	Same as `{ @link}` but is displayed as plain text. Use: `{@linkPlain link label}`.
`{ @literal}`	Text enclosed in the tag is denoted literally, as containing any HTML. For example, `{@literal <td> TouchDown}` would be displayed as `<td> TouchDown` (`<td>` not interpreted as a table cell).
`@param`	Inserts a "Parameters" section, which lists and describes parameters for a particular constructor/method.
`@return`	Inserts a "Returns" section, which lists and describes any return values for a particular constructor/method. Use: `@return description`. An error will be thrown if included in a comment of a method with the void return type.
`@see`	Included a "See Also" comment with a link pointing to a document with more information. Use: `@see link`.
`@serial`	Used for a serializable field. Use: `@serial text`.
`@serialData`	Used to document used to describe data written by the `writeObject`, `readObject`, `writeExternal`, and `readExternal` methods. Use: `@serialdata text`.
`@serialField`	Used to comment on the `ObjectStreamField`. Use: `@serialField name type description`.
`@since`	Inserts a new "Since" heading that is used to denote when particular features were first introduced. Use: `@since text`.
`@throws`	Includes a "Throws" heading. Use: `@throws name description`.
`{ @value}`	Returns the value of a code element it refers to. Use: `@value code-member label`.
`@version`	Add a "Version" heading when the `-version` command-line option is used. Use: `@version text`.

FIGURE I.1 Various tags used in javadoc comments

one-sentence descriptions. The name of the constructor/method is a hyperlink to a more detailed description in the third part of the document.

Third, a complete description of each method is provided. Again, the signature is provided first followed by an explanation of the method (this time without the one-sentence limit), which is obtained from the javadoc comments. If applicable, a list of parameters and return values, along with their descriptions, is provided in the respective sections.

The HTML document makes extensive use of hyperlinks to provide necessary additional information, using the @see tag for example, and for navigational purposes. The header and the footer of the page are navigation bars, with the following links:

- *Package* provides a list of classes included in the package along with a short purpose and description of each class.

- *Tree* presents a visual hierarchy of the classes within the package. Each class name is a link to the appropriate documentation HTML file.

- *Deprecated* lists functionality that is considered deprecated that is used in any of the class files contained in the package.

- *Index* provides an alphabetical listing of classes, constructors, and methods in the package. The class name is also associated with a short purpose and description of the class. Each appearance of the class name is a link to the appropriate HTML documentation. The signature of every constructor and method is a link to the appropriate detailed description. A one-sentence description presented next to the signature associates the constructor/method with the appropriate class.

- *Help* loads a help page with how-to instructions for using and navigating the HTML documentation.

All pages could be viewed with or without the use of HTML frames. Each class summary has links that can be used to quickly access any of the parts of the document.

The output content can be modified by command-line options used when executing the javadoc tool. By default, if no options are specified, the output returned is equivalent to using the protected option. The options include:

- private shows all classes, methods, and variables.

- public shows only public classes, methods, and variables.

- protected shows only protected and public classes, methods, and variables.

- help presents the online help.

- keywords includes HTML meta tags to the output file generated to assist with searching.

Java Syntax

This appendix contains syntax diagrams that collectively describe the way in which Java language elements can be constructed. Rectangles indicate something that is further defined in another syntax diagram, and ovals indicate a literal word or character. Though largely complete, not all Java constructs are represented in this collection of syntax diagrams.

Compilation Unit

Package Declaration

Import Declaration

Type Declaration

Class Declaration

Class Associations

Class Body

Class Member

Interface Declaration

Interface Body

Interface Member

Field Declaration

Variable Declarator

Type

Modifier

Primitive Type

Array Initializer

Name

Name List

Method Declaration

Parameters

Throws Clause

Method Body

Constructor Declaration

Constructor Body

Constructor Invocation

Block

Block Statement

Local Variable Declaration

Statement

If Statement

Switch Statement

Switch Case

While Statement

Do Statement

For Statement

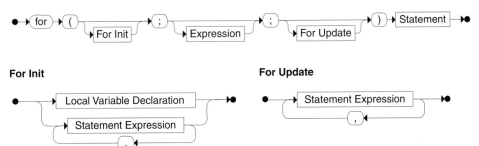

For Init   **For Update**

Basic Assignment

Return Statement

Throw Statement

Try Statement

Synchronized Statement

Empty Statement

Break Statement

Continue Statement

Labeled Statement

Expression

Primary Expression

Primary Suffix

Arguments

Allocation

Array Dimensions

Statement Expression

Assignment

Arithmetic Expression

Equality Expression

Relational Expression

Logical Expression

Bitwise Expression

Conditional Expression

Instance Expression

Cast Expression

Unary Expression

Prefix Expression

Postfix Expression

Literal

Integer Literal

Decimal Integer Literal

Octal Integer Literal

Hex Digit

Hex Integer Literal

Floating Point Literal

Exponent Part

Float Suffix

Character Literal

Boolean Literal

String Literal

Escape Sequence

Identifier

Java Letter

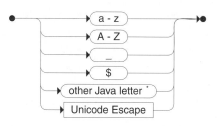

* The "other Java letter" category includes letters
from many languages other than English.

Java Digit

* The "other Java digit" category includes
additional digits defined in Unicode.

Unicode Escape*

* In some contexts, the character represented
by a Unicode Escape is restricted.

Index

LISTING 6.1: DISPLAY

LISTING 6.3: DISPLAY

LISTING 6.5: DISPLAY

LISTING 6.7: DISPLAY

LISTING 6.9: DISPLAY

FIGURE 6.10: A color chooser dialog box

LISTING 6.11: DISPLAY

LISTING 6.13: DISPLAY

LISTING 6.15: DISPLAY

LISTING 6.18: DISPLAY

LISTING 6.19: DISPLAY

LISTING 6.19: DISPLAY (continued)

LISTING 6.20: DISPLAY

LISTING 6.20: DISPLAY (continued)

LISTING 6.21: DISPLAY

LISTING 6.21: DISPLAY (continued)

LISTING 6.22: DISPLAY

LISTING 6.22: DISPLAY (continued)

LISTING 6.23: DISPLAY

LISTING 6.25: DISPLAY

LISTING 6.27: DISPLAY

LISTING 6.31: DISPLAY

LISTING 6.32: DISPLAY